College Ethics

College Ethics

A Reader on Moral Issues That Affect You

BOB FISCHER

Texas State University

New York   Oxford

OXFORD UNIVERSITY PRESS

Oxford University Press is a department of the University of Oxford.
It furthers the University's objective of excellence in research,
scholarship, and education by publishing worldwide.

Oxford is a registered trademark of Oxford University Press
in the UK and certain other countries.

Published in the United States of America by Oxford University Press
198 Madison Avenue, New York, NY 10016, United States of America.

Library of Congress Cataloging-in-Publication Data

Names: Fischer, Bob (Assistant professor of philosophy), editor.
Title: College ethics : a reader on moral issues that affect you / [edited
    by] Bob Fischer, Texas State University.
Description: New York : Oxford University Press, 2016.
Identifiers: LCCN 2016021506 (print) | LCCN 2016030662 (ebook) | ISBN
    9780190498658 (pbk.) | ISBN 9780190498719 (Ebook)
Subjects: LCSH: Ethics.
Classification: LCC BJ21 .C65 2016 (print) | LCC BJ21 (ebook) | DDC 170--dc23
LC record available at https://lccn.loc.gov/2016021506

9 8 7 6 5 4 3 2 1

Printed by LSC Communications, United States of America

TABLE OF CONTENTS

PART III Sexism, Gender, and Racism

PART IV Affirmative Action in Admissions

PART V Speech and Protest

PART VI Drugs and Drinking

PART X　Dishonesty, Enhancement, and Extra Credit

PART XI　The Aims of Education

PREFACE

I've often taught—and think it's important to teach—the "standard" problems in applied ethics: warfare, capital punishment, euthanasia, cloning, and so on. But there are other problems worth presenting to students. Some of them concern decisions they face in the here and now, like how to conduct their sexual lives, what (not) to buy, and whether to protest some injustice. Others concern decisions that others make about the institutions of which they're members—for example, whether to take race into account in admissions decisions, and whether colleges ought to invest as much as they do in athletics programs. Such are the problems in this book.

This book owes its structure to my own ethics course. I try to grab students' attention with conversations about sex, sexuality, sexism, and racism. (Abortion always comes up when we discuss sex, so it too makes an early appearance.) Then, I cover a range of topics that they tend to find engaging, such as speech on campus, consumer ethics, and the ethics of entertainment. I close with issues about plagiarism, the nature of education, and their responsibilities as students. Some people might want to begin how I conclude, and I can certainly understand why. The order I've chosen is based on a worry about sounding "preachy" were I to begin with plagiarism and the student role—I want to build a relationship with students before having those conversations. Others, of course, might think exactly that about discussing sex, sexuality, race, and racism. Makes sense.

I think you'll find, though, that it's easy to take a different path through the material I've collected. My classes meet twice per week, so depending on the semester, they have twenty-seven or twenty-eight readings. Let's suppose that's your schedule too, and you want to use the aims of education as the frame. Then, for example, you might cover the material about the university and the student role, followed by discussions of dishonesty, college sports, and material about affirmative action in admissions. The last topic naturally leads into material about racism and sexism. Given what's been happening on college campuses over the last few years, discussions of racism and sexism can lead naturally into debates about speech and protest—not a bad way to wrap up a class. If you prefaced all of that with my introduction for students (split over two days), that would be twenty-seven readings.

Alternately, you might want to begin with the "light" stuff—entertainment—and get progressively heavier. In that case, you could begin with essays about gaming, music, and humor, go on to discuss college sports, and then move into consumer ethics. At that point, you could delve into sex and relationships, concluding with essays about sex, abortion, and prejudice. With or without my introduction, it would be easy to find twenty-seven or twenty-eight readings to fill out that plan.

I'll mention just one more option. You might be someone who wants to focus squarely on the issues that have received so much attention in the last few years—trigger warnings, racism on college campuses, student protests, the nature of sex and gender. If so, then you could begin with the material about sexism, gender, and racism, use a few of the essays in the "Sex and Relationships" section on sexual violence, and then go on to cover both affirmative action in admissions and debates about speech and protest. You might end the class with readings on the aims of education (especially Nussbaum's "Education for Citizenship in an Era of Global Connection"). Whether or not you were to start with a brief discussion of theory and critical thinking, you'd have no trouble finding enough to keep you busy for a semester.

My hope is that this book will help your classes have better conversations about the moral issues that face and affect college students. If you have ideas about how I might improve it, please let me know—you can reach me at fischer@txstate.edu. And thanks for reading.

ACKNOWLEDGMENTS

I'll begin by thanking the folks at Oxford University Press. I'm grateful to Alyssa Palazzo for being positive about the idea for this book when I first mentioned it—I wouldn't have written the proposal otherwise. I appreciate Robert Miller for getting behind this project as soon as he saw it, as well as for such helpful advice along the way. And, of course, this book wouldn't exist in its current form were it not for the hard work of the production team.

Thanks too to the reviewers who helped me improve the manuscript: Jacob Affolter, Arizona State University; Emily Austin, Wake Forest University; Rochelle Green, University of Arkansas–Little Rock; Mitchell Haney, University of North Florida; Evan Kreider, University of Wisconsin–Fox Valley; Felipe Leon, El Camino College; Tracy Lupher, James Madison University; Timothy Madigan, St. John Fisher College; Scott McElreath, William Peace University; James McRae, Westminster College; Ryan Mott, Emmanuel College; Nicholas Tirone, New England College; Anand Vaidya, San Jose State University; Mathias Warnes, Sierra College.

I'm also grateful to a bunch of people who suggested topics and/or readings: Philip Antin, Shawn Bawulski, Adam Betz, Ben Bramble, Tim and Laura Brown, Jacob Busch, Drew Costanza, Eric English, Blake Hereth, Diann Insley, Jeff Johnson, David Killoren, Colin Klein, Diann McCabe, Audrey McKinney, Burkay Ozturk, Hyacinth Piel, Beau Pihlaja, Rebecca Raphael, Katherine Rompel, Rebekah Ross, Katie Ruelas, Mike Sauter, Kristen Scott, Jonathan Smalter, and Derek Torres. (To anyone I forgot: my sincere apologies.)

A number of others deserve special mention. First, those who helped me revise the introduction: Peter Hutcheson, Jonathan Surovell, Amanda Walker, and especially Sean McMains. Second, the graduate students who taught this material with me as it was coming into final form: Ashley Allcorn, Jonathan Lollar, Quique Montemayor, and Shiniece Owens. Third, Shelley Fischer and Eric Gilbertson for helping me check the proofs. Fourth, Matt Bower, who had to spend much more time thinking about this manuscript than he'd have liked.

Finally, thanks to Craig Hanks, who offered support at every turn.

INSTRUCTOR AND STUDENT RESOURCES

A variety of supplemental materials are available to accompany *College Ethics*. A free, open-access companion website for students (www.oup.com/us/fischer) contains web links to sites of interest and interactive self-quizzes that allow students to check their understanding of key points. For instructors, the book's Ancillary Resource Center (ARC) contains an Instructor's Manual with sample syllabi, a computerized test bank, and PowerPoint lecture outlines. Please visit www.oup.com/us/fischer for more information or contact your local Oxford University Press representative.

INTRODUCTION

This Book

This is a book about what's right and wrong. But it isn't a book that tries to teach you *what's* right and wrong. My goal isn't to make you believe the things I believe about all the issues we're going to explore. I didn't put this volume together to make you see the world my way.

Sometimes people *do* have that aim. At my university, the faculty and staff have to go through "ethics training." Among other things, we learn that we aren't supposed to use the university's money to buy drugs, that we aren't allowed to hit or hit on students, and that you can't hire someone to cater your luncheon just because he happens to be your husband who could really use the business. However, the takeaway isn't that we're being trained in the obvious. Instead, the thing to notice is that *the rules aren't up for debate*. You don't get to say, "But what if . . . ?" There is no "what if." You just learn the rules and follow them, whether or not they're good rules.

Not so when doing philosophy. There are two reasons for this. The first is that when we do ethics training, someone gets to say what the rules are—the members of the board, or the director of the company's HR department, or the founders of a professional organization. But in philosophy, no one gets to say. Instead, philosophy involves understanding, evaluating, and constructing *arguments*—that is, bits of reasoning that support a conclusion. So, you always get to ask, "What's the argument for that?" And if you don't find the argument convincing, then—after articulating your

1

objection—your conversation partner has to reply to what you've said, offer an entirely new argument, or abandon his position. In that sense, nothing is settled in philosophy. There's always room for discussion.

This means that there's a lot of controversy in philosophy. There's even more because philosophers like to discuss controversial *topics*, like abortion and affirmative action, where it's especially difficult to get people to see eye to eye. Additionally, we philosophers don't just care *that* something's true; we also care about *why* it's true. So even if the claim itself isn't controversial—for example, you shouldn't cheat—the explanation for its truth might be. (At bottom, should you avoid cheating because things will go better *for you* if you don't, at least in the long run? Or because it's disrespectful to others to cheat? Or because it's dishonest? Something else entirely?) Finally, you should know that philosophers tend to think that some of the "obvious" isn't. The odds are good that you don't think that there's anything wrong with buying a new outfit, even if you've got plenty of others already in your closet. However, some philosophers say that it *is* wrong to do that—instead, you should give the money to help people in the developing world who are dying of treatable diseases. (That escalated quickly!)

The upshot of all this is that, unlike ethics training, it's fine if we disagree about whether you should pursue a friends-with-benefits situation, or whether a college education should be free, or what counts as racism—all topics you'll find in the pages to follow. Instead, what's important is that you walk away with some tools for thinking more clearly and critically about moral matters. Of course, agreeing would be great, at least if we agree because we're all convinced by the same arguments. The point is just that we aren't after agreement *per se*. This book is designed to teach you how to approach moral questions, not what you should offer as answers to them.

Getting Our Bearings

Let's step back for a minute. I've been throwing around words like "ethics" and "morality" (which I'm using as synonyms). What am I talking about?

Ethics is about what's right and wrong, good and bad, worthwhile and worthless. It's about how we should live our lives, about who we ought to become. It's about whether there are lines that we should never cross. It's about what we should hope to achieve in our daily lives, on our campuses, in our country, and in the world.

That all sounds nice. However, those statements don't constitute a nice, neat definition. I wish that I had one of those to offer you, but I don't. (Frankly, I'm a bit suspicious of people who think they do.) What I can do, however, is supplement the above with some ideas about what ethics *isn't*, and we can see how far that gets us.

Ethics and the Law

First, it's a mistake to think of ethics as just another way of talking about the law. On this sort of view, what's legal is what's moral, what's illegal is what isn't.

This definitely isn't right. First, there are plenty of things that are legal and immoral. The law, for example, allows you to be a pretty terrible parent. As too many of you know, parents can abuse their kids emotionally without anyone stepping in to stop them, and this can have huge consequences for those kids down the line. Second, there are plenty of things that are illegal and perfectly moral. When riding your bicycle, you're supposed to come to a complete stop at every stop sign. No one does this, and it's hard to see why it would be morally wrong to roll through. Still, it's illegal.

Moreover, there are cases in which it isn't just *permissible*—morally OK—to break the law. Instead, something stronger is true: The law *ought* to be broken. For example: some cities, like San Antonio, TX, have banned feeding the homeless. But many people think that they've got a moral obligation to feed the hungry. If they're right—and it seems plausible that they are—then they ought to do exactly what the law prohibits. So, what's legal isn't what's moral and vice versa.

Ethics and Your Behavior

Second, ethics isn't just about *the choices you would make* in various situations. It's important to remember that while your choices might be *relevant* to what's right—in the sense of being evidence for it, at least insofar as you're a decent person—your choices might be wrong. It's easy to have overly rosy views of ourselves; we tend to think we're good people, whether or not we are. So, we're strongly inclined to think that what we'd do is what we ought to do, or at least what it's OK to do. But if we're honest with ourselves, we'll admit that we don't always do what we think is right. (Let's be more honest: sometimes the gap between our ideals and our behavior is *huge*.) So before jumping from "I'd do that" to "That's OK," we need to be very careful to consider whether we're simply trying to protect our respective self-images.

Ethics and What You've Got Good Reason to Do

Third, ethics isn't just what it makes sense for you to do, or what you've got good reason to do. After all, you've got reasons to do all sorts of things: have lunch, get a college education, watch reruns of *Law & Order* (the original is the best), and so on. Sometimes, it makes sense to do one of these things. But there are plenty of cases in which the sensible choice is just plain wrong.

It's 11 p.m. on a Sunday. You've got a paper due at midnight. You've been working hard on things for your other classes, so you haven't had time to write. Moreover, you've got two big exams during the week, so you can't afford to turn this in late; it's got to be done so that you can study for bio-chem, which is going to be a beast. What should you do?

Well, your professor has a strict no-late-papers policy, so you can't just take a hit on the grade. But she's got a lot of students, so you think that she might only skim the papers to see whether people have made a good-faith attempt. She probably wouldn't detect a little copying and pasting, especially if you switch a few words around. Moreover, everybody games the system once in a while, and it's not like you've just been sitting around playing video games for the last three weeks. Shouldn't you cheat?

Of course, it's *wrong* to steal someone else's work and then lie about it being yours—which is what plagiarism involves. But there are plenty of times when it makes a lot of sense—maybe even the *most* sense—to do what's wrong. So whatever ethics is, it isn't about making an "understandable" choice, at least if we cash out that idea in terms of what would be good (or even best) for *you*. Ethics is about other people's interests too. (In this case, for example, it requires thinking about your professor's interest in getting what she asked for—namely, your work—and other students' interest in competing on a level playing field.)

Ethics and What's Realistic

Finally, ethics isn't always about what's realistic or achievable. For example, it seems plain that slavery has always been wrong, even when it was legal. However, when it *was* legal, I'm sure there were people who said things like this:

> We're never going to be rid of slavery. The economic argument for owning slaves is just too strong: We just couldn't run our plantations

without them. Of course, we should try to make the lives of slaves better. For example, people shouldn't be allowed to whip their slaves for trivial offenses. But there's no point criticizing owning humans in and of itself.

The idea here is that *it doesn't make sense to criticize the institution of slavery*; there's no way to change such a deeply entrenched aspect of the culture. And at the time, this idea wasn't unreasonable. Surely there were periods in American history when slavery seemed like it would be with us forever. Moreover, it would have been good for someone to be opposed to whipping slaves for trivial offenses. However, even if there was a time when it would have been useless to advocate publicly for the end of slavery—even if criticizing people for owning slaves wouldn't have made any difference at all—it doesn't follow that there was no point in criticizing the idea that it's OK to own humans. Maybe people will never change (thankfully, of course, they have!), but it's still worth asking how things *ought* to be, even if it seems impossible to make them that way. In part, this is because we can be completely wrong (as our imaginary speaker was) about what sorts of changes are possible. But it's also because it's worth knowing what we should strive for, even if those goals are unattainable. Knowing what we should hope to achieve helps us think more clearly about what is, and isn't, true progress.

Some of the essays in this book argue for claims that might sound pretty idealistic. I've mentioned one of them already—namely, the claim that college should be free. Obviously, this isn't nearly as important an idea as the thought that people shouldn't be able to buy and sell other people. Still, it's a big and important claim, and if it's true (which it may not be—we'll have to inspect the arguments!), it has big implications for the way society allocates resources. And given that it has such big implications, it would be easy to dismiss it as a pie-in-the-sky fantasy. But we should be wary of that response. Again, it's worth knowing what we should strive for.

So . . . ?

I've now said a tiny bit about what ethics is, and a fair amount about what ethics isn't. The takeaway, I think, is that there really are big moral questions out there for us to examine, and we should be careful about how we try to answer them. First, the law matters, but it answers to ethics—not the other way around. Second, you might be someone who makes good choices, but you might not be. So, what you'd do isn't always the best guide to what should be done. Third, don't confuse what's *reasonable* for you to do with what you *ought* to do. Lots of reasonable things are wrong; some unreasonable things may be morally mandatory. Fourth, don't confuse what's realistic with what's right. Sometimes, a campus or a country gets things entirely wrong. When that happens, even *hoping* to make progress can seem crazy. That doesn't mean, however, that it wouldn't be progress—that change wouldn't be for the better.

Thinking, Fast and Critically

With those preliminaries behind us, let's turn to some of the resources you'll need to think more clearly about moral matters. Later on, we'll talk about some moral theories, which help you ask better questions about ethically complex situations. First, though, we're going to focus on the process of thinking itself—how to think about your own moral judgments, as well as how to make moral arguments.

Intuition

There are some real hurdles to thinking clearly. Perhaps the biggest one is that *things just seem true to us.* In other words, it's incredibly hard to get some critical distance from your own moral judgments—your own ideas about what should and shouldn't be done. Instead, we all experience our own ideas as the right ones (if we didn't, we'd have different ideas!), so it's hard to imagine being mistaken.

In lots of contexts, that's fine. I don't want my students wondering whether it's OK to cheat on a test, and I don't want my doctor wondering whether he's *really* got an obligation not to do any harm. But when we're trying to engage in serious debate about moral matters, this psychological tendency usually leads us into shouting matches rather than careful exchanges.

In part, this is because *our intuitions drive our ethical judgments.* Translation: In everyday life, we tend to trust our gut. If it feels right, we think it *is* right, and vice versa for things being wrong. But is our gut that reliable?

Well, there are plenty of non-moral cases in which our intuitions can't be *that* far off—if they were, we wouldn't survive for long. (Driving, for example, would go pretty poorly; it's kind of important that we be good at judging when to brake.) However, there are lots of other cases in which our intuitions lead us astray—consistently, systematically, and without any hint of what's happening.

That, in essence, is the lesson of Daniel Kahneman's *Thinking, Fast and Slow*. It's a great book, and I want to share just two examples from it. The first is quite famous: the "Linda Problem." In that study, Kahneman and his partner, Amos Tversky, told participants about Linda:

> Linda is thirty-one years old, single, outspoken, and very bright. She majored in philosophy. As a student, she was deeply concerned with issues of discrimination and social justice, and also participated in antinuclear demonstrations.

The participants were then asked whether it was more probable that Linda is a bank teller, or that she's a bank teller and active in the feminist movement. Overwhelmingly, participants said that the second option was more probable. But this can't be right: the probability of *p* (e.g., her being a bank teller) is always *lower* than the probability of *p* and *q* (e.g., her being a bank teller who's active in the feminist movement). Why? Because you get the probability of *p* and *q* by multiplying the two together, which is going to give you a number that's lower than whatever you started out with.[1]

You might think that people are hearing more in "Linda is a bank teller" than is actually being said. As a result, they take the options to be: (a) Linda is a bank teller *who isn't active in the feminist movement* and (b) Linda is a bank teller who *is* active in that movement. But if that's what's happening, then they're making a different mistake. The world is chock full of bank tellers, and there are a great many people who *were* socially engaged in college, but let go of their idealism right around graduation. There aren't very many people, however, who are currently active in the feminist movement (on the assumption that Facebook slacktivism doesn't count). So even given her description, it's still more likely that Linda isn't active in the feminist movement. (This error has a name. Ignoring the relative numbers of bank tellers, once-activists, and current activists is called "the base rate fallacy.")

What's going on? Plainly, people aren't assessing the probabilities of these statements in the way that statisticians do. Instead, they're using their *stereotype* about people who are active in the feminist movement, and they're matching that stereotype to the description of Linda. There are, of course, cases where a stereotype gives you the right answer. In this one, however, it leads people astray. And I'll bet you can imagine plenty of more serious cases—think, for example, of scenarios in which young black men are accused of crimes—where relying on stereotypes might lead people to assess probabilities in much more disastrous ways. Your gut might say one thing, but the evidence says another.

In other cases, intuition—our fast, effortless judgment about a case—doesn't exactly lead us to believe the wrong thing. However, even when it doesn't lead us into error *per se*, it still might not be as consistent as we think it is. Consider, for example, the "Asian Disease Problem." First, Kahneman and Tversky had people read this prompt:

> Imagine that the United States is preparing for the outbreak of an unusual Asian disease, which is expected to kill six hundred people. One possible program to combat the disease has been proposed. Assume that the exact scientific estimate of the consequences of this program is as follows:

Then, they had to choose between two options. However, not everyone was given the same options. Some people were given Options A and B:

A. If this program is adopted, two hundred people will be saved.
B. If this program is adopted, there is a one-third probability that six hundred people will be saved and a two-thirds probability that no people will be saved.

Other people were given Options C and D:

C. If this program is adopted, four hundred people will die.
D. If this program is adopted, there is a one-third probability that nobody will die and a two-thirds probability that six hundred people will die.

Take a second and do the math: Option A is equivalent to Option C, and Option B is equivalent to Option D. So, people should choose Options A and C at equal rates and Options B and D at equal rates. But they don't.

What Kahneman and Tversky found was that people tended to prefer the sure thing when faced with Options A and B, but they tended to prefer the gamble when they were faced with Options C and D. What does this mean? In short, it suggests that people are skittish about taking risks when it sounds like they might lose something they've already got, and open to taking risks when they see themselves as being in a situation where loss is unavoidable. This is a *framing effect*—the way the options are framed affects how people respond, even though the options are identical. This phenomenon can make a big difference when we're considering arguments about different military strategies, or affirmative action, or health care policies. (For example: people are much more open to "aid in dying" than they are to "physician-assisted suicide," even though the terms are synonymous. What's different is the frame, not the reality.) We have to pay attention to how information comes to us, and think about alternative ways of representing it.

These aren't the only examples of intuition being misleading or inconsistent. There are lots of others. For example, we like to infer causes when there aren't any—we can't accept that some things just happen. We tend to think that personality-based explanations of behavior— "He did it because he's a jerk!"—are much better than situational explanations— "He did it because he was under a lot of pressure at work." We're inclined to think that past events—such as a terrorist attack—were predictable, even though no one could have known that they were going to happen. And familiar ideas seem more true to us than unfamiliar ones, regardless of whether we have any evidence for or against them. We jump to the wrong conclusions all the time.

Fallacies

What's more, we often go wrong even when we aren't relying on our intuitions. We take the time to form an argument, but not one that supports its intended conclusion. It's an easy thing to do. After all, plenty of arguments *sound* good, but are really pretty poor.

When a bunch of poor arguments are poor for the same reason, we call them instances of an *informal fallacy*, and we give that sort of argument a name. If you become familiar with some informal fallacies, they become easier to spot, and so you can avoid being taken in by bad reasoning (whether yours or someone else's).

There are lots of informal fallacies, but I'll just mention a few of them here. The first to know is the *ad hominem* fallacy—that is, arguing "against the man." The idea here is that it's a mistake to criticize the *source* of the argument, rather than the argument's premises or logic. So, for example, you shouldn't reject a pro-choice person's pro-choice argument—or a pro-life person's pro-life argument—simply because a pro-choice or pro-life person made it. Instead, you should think about the merits of arguments on their own terms.

We often don't do this. Instead, we often think: "Well, of *course* she'd say that—she's pro-[fill in the blank]!" But this is really a defense mechanism. Instead of having to engage seriously with someone's ideas, we can use his or her identity to write them off. That's both intellectually lazy and unkind. We owe our conversation partners more respect than that.[2]

You can find some of the same vices behind the *straw man* fallacy. Imagine a student who comes to a professor at the end of the semester and says, "I know that I haven't earned a B in this course, but it's been a really hard semester for me, and I'll lose my scholarship if I don't maintain my GPA. Please, Professor, let me do some extra credit to bump up my grade!" The professor says, "I'd love to help you, but there isn't anything I can do for you that wouldn't be unfair to other students. If I don't give them the same opportunity, then I can't give it to you. I'm sorry." The student replies: "So you don't care if I lose my scholarship!" That reply is an example of the straw man fallacy. First, the professor didn't say that she doesn't care about the student's scholarship; she just said that she can't help the student because she has to act on a policy that's fair to all the students who are taking her course. So the student *misrepresented* the professor. Second, the student is putting a much weaker argument in the professor's mouth than the one she actually gave. If the professor were denying the student an opportunity to do extra credit based on not caring about the student's fate, she would be acting insensitively. But that wasn't the story!

A different way of going wrong is to set up a *false dilemma*. A dilemma is when you're forced to choose between two options; a *false* dilemma is when someone presents only two options, but there are really others. Let's suppose that someone says, "Look, we just have to close the borders entirely. If we don't, we're going to have drugs and guns pouring into the country." This is a false dilemma: it presents two options (closing the borders entirely / having drugs and guns pouring into the country) when there are others, such as improving border security without preventing any and all traffic.

False dilemmas are common because we like simplicity so much. It's just *easier* to think that there are only two options, whatever the issue at hand. Recognizing all the options, and then holding them all in your head, takes significant mental energy. False dilemmas are also common because they're really effective as a strategy in a debate. In the example I just gave, imagine having someone give the "close the borders or face an influx of drugs and guns" line to you in the middle of a heated exchange. It would take a minute to realize that you're being set up, to recognize and reject the assumption behind the choice that's being offered to you. And because of that, false dilemmas can be good ways of winning points—albeit by obscuring the truth. But again: We owe our conversation partners better. We're not here to win points; we're here to think clearly together. With some effort, we can hope to figure out what's true.

I'll mention just two more informal fallacies. The first is called the *red herring* fallacy. The basic idea is that a statement is a red herring when it changes the subject or otherwise dodges the issue at hand. Consider, for example, a debate about whether fraternity culture fosters sexist attitudes. In response to an argument that they do foster such attitudes, someone might say, "But they do so much good in the community! The guys of SAE participate in the Adopt-a-Highway program, and they also volunteer at the elementary school as tutors." All of this might be true, but none of it's relevant to whether fraternity culture in general—or even the culture of that particular fraternity—encourages sexist attitudes.

Of course, the good deeds of fraternity brothers might be relevant to a *different* question—namely, whether we should have fraternities on campus at all. They just aren't relevant to the issue that's actually being discussed. Unfortunately, red herrings—irrelevant statements—get in the way of careful conversations. They distract us from the very thing on which we were trying to focus.

Finally, let's talk about the *slippery slope* fallacy. This is an especially common one, and I think it's one of the most important. Suppose that someone says, "We shouldn't legalize marijuana. If we do, then we'll soon be legalizing heroin, and that would be disastrous." In other words, if we get on this slippery slope—if we legalize marijuana—we'll soon slide down to the bottom, where much harder drugs are legal.

Even though this is a fallacy, *the prediction might be true.* The problem is *not* that the prediction is necessarily mistaken. Rather, the problem is that the prediction is baseless; we aren't given any reason to think that the prediction will come true. Maybe it's the case that once you legalize some drugs, the public will think that it's arbitrary to ban others, and so marijuana legalization will lead to the end of drug prohibition generally. Alternately, maybe the public is very sensitive to the severe effects of some drugs, so they'd never support complete legalization. To make a reasonable judgment one way or the other, we'd need some evidence. And that's precisely what we didn't get in the example I just gave. In short, then, the problem with slippery slope reasoning is that it involves making a big claim about the consequences of a course of action, but without explaining why we should expect those consequences.

You see slippery slope reasoning all the time. "If we allow gay marriage, we'll have to let people marry their pets." "If we let people carry firearms in public, then we'll eventually have to let them have firearms in elementary schools." And so on. As before, I think this is partly a function of laziness. It takes a lot of work to build the case for a prediction, and we'd rather just say something that sounds reasonable and wins us points in a debate. But it's also because we often don't realize that there are other possibilities—that, for example, we might legalize marijuana *without* there being certain negative consequences. It just seems so obvious to us that two things are linked, we don't even see that we need to argue for the link. Nevertheless, we do.

I've discussed five fallacies: *ad hominem*, straw man, false dilemma, red herring, and slippery slope. I've discussed these because I think they're the ones you'll find most often in conversation.[3] Knowing about these reasoning errors isn't going to make you a perfect reasoner, nor will it help you win every argument. (Nothing will do that!) However, knowing about them can make it easier to have more focused and productive conversations. When you know what to avoid, and can call out the errors of others, you can avoid some unnecessary distractions.

Doing Better

So there are plenty of cases in which what seems true—our intuitive reaction—is just wildly wrong. Likewise, there are plenty of cases in which what feels like a good argument isn't. This doesn't sound like good news, but it is. We can learn more about how our minds work; we can become better at noticing when we're likely to go wrong; we can foster the discipline of slowing down, thinking hard, and double-checking whether the reasons in front of us support what they're supposed to support. Of course, these things take a lot of effort, and we're not going to achieve perfection. Still, we can make progress. We can do better.

In *The Righteous Mind*, Jonathan Haidt has some good advice about where to start:

> [E]ach individual reasoner is really good at one thing: finding evidence to support the position he or she already holds, usually for intuitive reasons. We should not expect individuals to produce good, open-minded, truth-seeking reasoning, particularly when self-interest

or reputational concerns are in play. But if you put individuals together in the right way, such that some individuals can use their reasoning powers to disconfirm the claims of others, and all individuals feel some common bond or shared fate that allows them to interact civilly, you can create a group that ends up producing good reasoning as an emergent property of the social system. This is why it's so important to have intellectual and ideological diversity within any group or institution whose goal is to find truth (such as an intelligence agency or a community of scientists) or to produce good public policy (such as a legislature or advisory board).

Clearly, Haidt thinks that we can make some progress as reasoners: We just need to reason *together*, in *diverse groups*, rather than working on these issues independently or in homogeneous groups. If we do, then we can go beyond the wisdom of any one particular individual or culture, finding new and better ways to think about the problems we face.

In any case, what I've said in this section barely scratches the surface of the literature on intuitions, reasoning, and how to move forward. I don't share this sketch with you because it's adequate, but because it should be the starting point for further investigation on your part. At this stage, all I'm trying to do is cultivate a healthy degree of skepticism. We need to go beyond trusting our gut, and we need to take a harder look at our reasons.

Making Arguments

With all that behind us, let's think a bit more carefully about how to make and evaluate arguments. Granted, you aren't going to operate this way all the time. Usually, we go with the flow. When we read an article on Facebook, we don't think much about the author's argument—we just skim. We certainly don't check the sources. And we absolutely don't look for *another* article that defends the opposite view, just to see what can be said for the alternative.

Sometimes, that's fine. We don't always have to have our guard up. But we should be *able* to slow down and evaluate things carefully. We should have the capacity for critical, careful thought. In practice, this means:

1. *Slowing down*, taking the time to really process what you're reading, hearing, watching, and so on.

2. *Asking the right questions*, the most important ones being:
   a. *What* am I being asked to believe? In other words, what's the *main claim* that the author (or whoever) wants me to accept?
   b. *Why* am I supposed to believe it? That is, what's the *argument* for this claim?
   c. *How good* is the argument for this claim? This breaks down into two questions. First, is this the *kind* of argument that's worth taking seriously? Second, how plausible are the premises of *this particular* argument?

I'm going to focus here on (2b) and (2c). In particular, I want to explain what philosophers mean when they talk about arguments.

From Reasons to Arguments

When philosophers try to convince one another that different things are true, they offer arguments. Arguments aren't loud disagreements. Instead, an argument is composed of some *premises* (statements) that are supposed to support a *conclusion* (another statement). The crucial thing here is to learn how to interpret ordinary reason-giving—that is, someone saying "We ought to do this *because*" or "Such and such, *so*"—as a way of making arguments. If you get a handle on that, you'll be able to see the link between what you normally do and what philosophers do.

When you ask someone why it's wrong to steal, his first response is often something like "Because it's illegal." Philosophers rewrite this claim as follows:

1. If an act is illegal, then it's always morally wrong.
2. Stealing is illegal.
3. So, stealing is always morally wrong.

Again, the last line in an argument is its *conclusion*; the other lines are its *premises*. The advantage of expressing a reason this way is that we can see its complexity. Here, what looked like one idea ("Stealing is wrong because it's an illegal act") is really two (Premise 1 and Premise 2) plus an inference (the move from Premise 1 and Premise 2 to the conclusion).

How did I get from the original claim ("Stealing is wrong because it's illegal") to the argument above? Essentially, I worked backward. In this case, someone—let's call him Bill—is trying to defend why he thinks that stealing is wrong. That's his conclusion; that's what he wants to justify. The task now is to figure out the premises that are supposed to support it.

Bill said that stealing is wrong "because it's illegal." He seems to think that stealing's being illegal is *enough* to make it wrong, since he didn't mention anything else. He could have added that stealing *violates the original owner's right to her property* or *causes financial hardship for the original owner of the property*. But he didn't say either of these things. Hence, Bill didn't give us any reason to think that he sees something special about the act of stealing; the problem is simply that it's illegal. So, I came up with Premise 1 as a way to express the idea that being illegal is sufficient—in and of itself—to make an action wrong.

Premise 1 amounts to a link between two things: an action's being illegal and an action's being wrong. But that's all it is; you can't get the conclusion from Premise 1 alone. After all, someone might believe Premise 1 while insisting that *stealing* isn't illegal—it's only stealing *in certain circumstances* that's problematic. After all, police can take your vehicle in an emergency, regardless of whether you want to give it to them. That seems to be stealing, but it isn't illegal.

Now, you might deny that this is *really* stealing, precisely because it's legal. The cops are *allowed* to commandeer your car in special situations. But unless it's totally settled that a kind of action is wrong, it's a mistake to define that act so that it includes illegality or immorality. When we do that, we can't ask whether the action *should* be illegal, or really is immoral. It's better to define the action in a neutral way—stealing, for example, we might define as *taking someone's property against his or her will*—so that we don't beg any questions in the debate.

By the way: Many people now use the phrase "begs the question" to mean something like "invites the question" or "leads us to ask the question." But this isn't how philosophers use this phrase. We use it to mean something like "assume what you set out to prove." So, for example, by defining stealing so that stealing is the *wrongful* taking of someone else's property, you beg the question against someone who thinks that stealing is sometimes permissible. And since that seems like a reasonable view— I'd think that it's permissible to steal food to feed your starving children— you shouldn't beg the question against that person. Instead, you should define it neutrally, and then *argue* that stealing is always wrong, assuming that you take that claim to be true.

In any case, if a person thinks that stealing isn't *always* illegal, then Premise 1 wouldn't give her cause to believe that it's always morally wrong. Premise 2 is there to show that Bill *does* think stealing is an illegal act. So when we unpack Bill's claim, we discover that it's got three parts:

first, there's the idea that an action's being illegal is sufficient for its
being wrong;
second, there's the idea about stealing's being illegal;
third, there's an inference from these two claims to the conclusion.

The form of this little argument is called *modus ponens*. The name
doesn't matter much, but the form itself is worth remembering:

1. If X, then Y.
2. X.
3. So, Y.

Modus ponens is a *valid* form of inference—which is to say that if the
premises are true, then the conclusion *must* be true. The nice thing about
valid inference forms is that you can be sure that the conclusion is true if
the premises are. (Not every argument form is like this.[4]) The practical
upshot is that, if an argument uses a valid (or truth-preserving) inference
form, then you can't deny the conclusion without denying at least one of
the premises. So if you can represent a line of reasoning this way, then you
won't have to worry about whether the logic is squirrely. Instead, you can
focus on deciding what you think about the premises.[5]

Granted, it takes some work to put things this way. Is the hassle
worth it? In lots of contexts, probably not. But when we're talking about
important issues (like ethics!), it can be. When you first thought about
Bill saying that stealing is wrong because it's illegal, you probably had one
of two reactions:

1. You found yourself agreeing, or
2. You felt the urge to throw out a different reason entirely.

You probably didn't think to say:

3. "Maybe you're right: stealing is illegal. So what?"

Reaction #1 is probably explicable in terms of confirmation bias: You
tend to think that stealing is wrong; someone gave a reason that doesn't
sound crazy; so, you went with it. Reaction #2 just disregards what Bill
said, and we've got to resist this temptation. Some ideas deserve to be ignored, but Bill's isn't one of them. True, it's not the most sophisticated
reply in the world, but it's a good start. And if we don't slow down and
evaluate Bill's response, then we can't learn from it.

The interesting reaction is #3, which targets Premise 1. We might not
be sure whether stealing is inherently illegal, or whether there are more

complicated conditions involved. However, we can be pretty confident that it's not always wrong to do things that are illegal. The most inspiring examples of civil disobedience—for example, Gandhi's program of non-violent resistance, which inspired the work of Martin Luther King Jr.—were certainly against the law. They were illegal, but certainly not immoral. So, we've got a *counterexample* to Premise 1—which is just to say that we have a case demonstrating that there can be illegal actions that *aren't* morally wrong. That means that Premise 1 is false. Bill's argument, while valid, isn't *sound*—that is, at least one of the premises is false. It follows that he hasn't given us a good reason to believe its conclusion.

Our gut doesn't tell us to think about Bill's first premise; we default to the second, or we jump to a new theory of the wrongness of stealing. And maybe there's some wisdom to that. But if we never formulate reasons as arguments, then we can miss pretty serious problems with those reasons—and that makes progress harder than it needs to be.[6]

Progress, Such as It Is

Here, in short, is the method I just summarized: We come up with a reason; we try to reformulate it as an argument; and then we think about whether there are any counterexamples to the premises. Let's call this the "Counterexample Method." This method primes us to look for flaws, and there are usually flaws to find.

In a sense, the progress here is *negative*. In the example above, what we discovered was that *Bill's reason wasn't a good one*. We didn't actually figure out *whether there is anything wrong with stealing*; we just figured out that we shouldn't criticize it on the basis Bill gave.

Making that sort of progress is better than making none at all. But it probably isn't the forward movement you wanted. What you'd probably like—what I'm sure I'd like—is a set of answers to the hard questions we face. Is there anything wrong with abortion? Should I be giving more of my money to the poor? Is it OK to lie to a friend if it makes everyone's life a bit easier? Should we be executing certain violent criminals? And while we're wishing, it would be nice to know *why* the correct answers are correct.

The Counterexample Method can help us get there, but only in a roundabout way. Why? Well, this method amounts to a process of elimination, throwing out all the bad reasons in hopes of being left with a good one. It's a sort of "trial by fire" approach to finding the truth. Of course, when almost any interesting argument is on the table, you can come up with cases that seem to make trouble for one or more of its premises. So, it's unlikely that, when the stakes are high—as they are in the issues just mentioned—we're going to find arguments where it's uncontroversial that each premise is true. Still, if you come across a valid argument and you can't find anything wrong with any of the premises, then that's a pretty good reason to take the argument seriously. That's progress.

Much of the hard work of critical thinking is figuring out what, exactly, you're being asked to believe, and then why, exactly, you're supposed to believe it. The rest of the work is evaluating the argument that you've uncovered. And what you'll find is that thinking critically in ethics tends to have a negative payoff: It rules things out instead of ruling things in. That said, the last argument standing might just be the one to believe.

Moral Theory

Now that you've got a better handle on how philosophers think about arguments, let's spend a little time on the premises. Where do they come from? One important source is *moral theory*. Traditionally, the goal of moral theory is to explain why some actions are morally right and others are morally wrong. In other words, we try to find the features that are shared by right actions that *make* them right, and hence the features that *aren't* had by wrong actions. Along the way, it would be nice to be able to give an account of some other moral concepts: goodness and badness, praiseworthiness and blameworthiness, and so forth. The hope is that we can find the One True Moral Theory. If we can, then we'll put it to use as a premise in moral arguments.

Or so the story goes. I'm a bit skeptical of finding the One True Moral Theory, but I won't go into my reasons for that here. Instead, I want to emphasize the practical. A concrete way to think about moral theory is in terms of the questions you ask when you consider a moral problem. After asking those questions, you can think about how best to assemble an argument.

Here's a case—let's call it the "Dave and Gabriela case"—to get us started:

> You're a senior in college. You've known Dave and Gabriela since freshman year, and you've been good friends with them both since then. Dave and Gabriela started dating shortly after you met them, and they are, by all accounts, a great couple. And if any college relationship looks like it might go the distance, theirs does.

One night, you're out with Dave at the local watering hole. He's had a few too many, and an attractive young lady—let's call her "Jezebel"—has been making googly eyes at him from across the bar. You've told him to ignore her, and for the most part, he has. But as the night wears on, you excuse yourself to go to the bathroom, leaving him unattended. On your way back, you see Dave and Jezebel slipping out the front door. The bar is crowded, so it takes you a minute to get outside. When you do, you see them climbing into a cab. And off they go.

What should you do? (And to be clear: I'm asking what you *should* do, not what you *would* do. We don't always do what we think we should!)[7]

An answer probably comes to mind. ("Text him!" *or* "Text Gabriela!" *or* "Have another drink!") But let's set that answer aside for the moment. Instead, let's ask this: What do you need to know to answer the "What should you do" question? In other words, what information is *relevant* to answering the question, "What should you do?" This is the most important point where moral theories differ.

Utilitarianism

Utilitarianism is a moral theory that says you ought to ask how *everyone* is going to be made better and worse off given different courses of action.[8] Then, it says you ought to choose the course of action that makes everyone best off overall.

So what are your options? First, you could contact him. Second, you could contact Gabriela. Third, you could do nothing.

Trying to contact him *now* probably won't do much. You've already tried to prevent him from paying attention to Jezebel, and he didn't take your advice. So that's just going to waste time. The option I have in mind is contacting Dave *tomorrow*. Of course, there are lots of things you might say to him. One idea is: "Tell Gabriela, or I will." Let's suppose you take that course of action.

Giving Dave an ultimatum might bring about the end of your friendship, and you'd both be worse off for that. It also might spell the end of his relationship with Gabriela. (At the very least, it means they've got a hard road ahead.) But you'd also be sparing yourself—and Dave—from having to live with secrets. And you could be sparing Gabriela from discovering this information much later in their relationship, when their lives are more deeply intertwined and it's harder to start over.

The same considerations apply when it comes to your second choice: contacting Gabriela right off the bat. Of course, contacting her immediately increases the odds that you won't remain friends with Dave, since you're acting without confirming that he actually cheated. After all, he *could* change his mind in the middle of the ride home. It's unlikely, but not impossible, and this might be a reason to go with the first option. At the same time, you're letting Gabriela know ASAP, which prevents another unlikely event: namely, Dave's bringing home an STI, and passing it onto Gabriela before either knows he's contracted one.

Your third option is to do nothing. For now, it doesn't matter why you find this option attractive. The issue here is what the consequences would be. And the upshot is that it isn't so easy to say. It could work out that Dave and Jezebel have a pleasant evening, and Gabriela is none the wiser. Then you and Dave will have to carry some secrets, but things will otherwise be as they would have been *without* the infidelity. Life will go on. However, there's always a chance that Gabriela will find out some other way. Then, their relationship will suffer just as it would have if you'd said something, and as a bonus, your friendship with her will suffer for your silence.

Remember: Utilitarianism says that you should do whatever makes everyone best off. Not *you* best off. Not the victim best off. *Everyone.* It involves a radically egalitarian idea: everyone's interests matter equally, no matter whose interests they are. So which of these options makes everyone best off?

Well, it's a hard call. It seems to me that the first two options have pretty similar results. In both cases, the major costs involve jeopardizing your friendship with Dave and his relationship with Gabriela. If you take the third option, the relationship is still on the line, though now it's much less likely that Gabriela will find out about Dave's activities. Of course, if she *does* find out, then your friendship with her is on the line, as is their relationship. But everything comes down to the odds. If you think that Dave will be able to hide this from Gabriela, then utilitarianism probably favors option three: Hang tight. But if you think it's more likely he won't, then you should probably say something, so that instead of having Dave's escapade ruin a relationship *and* a friendship, it only ruins the former. It all comes down to the consequences.

Kantianism

If you've been reading along slack-jawed—wondering how this could possibly be described as a *moral* theory—don't worry. There are other moral theories to discuss, and they lead us to ask very different questions of the Dave and Gabriela case.

So let's start over. *Kantianism* offers us a very different perspective.[9] According to Kantianism—which gets its name from Immanuel Kant, an eighteenth-century German philosopher—we shouldn't focus on an action's consequences. Instead, we should consider whether, in so acting, you would be *treating people as mere means, rather than as ends in themselves.*

Here, very roughly, is the idea. Let's suppose that you're thinking about not doing anything at all in the Dave and Gabriela case. Your plan is to lie low. It should be obvious that, by going with this plan, you're proposing to withhold information from Gabriela. And not just any information. It's not like you're considering whether to tell her what's new on Netflix, and you opt to take a nap instead. No: This is information that's likely to matter to her, information on which she would probably act if it were made available. So, by *not* sharing this information—or pushing Dave to share it—you're compromising Gabriela's ability to make choices that reflect her values. You're making it so that she can't act based on what's important to her, such as being in a faithful relationship. In this respect, you aren't respecting Gabriela's *autonomy*—her freedom. And that, according to Kantianism, is wrong. To treat Gabriela as an end in herself is to respect her autonomy. Silence doesn't accomplish that.

Instead, silence treats Gabriela as a mere means. We often treat people as means to our ends: I just want the clerk at the grocery store to ring up the total; I want the barista to make my coffee; I want the cab driver to take me to the airport. But I'm not treating any of these people as a *mere* means, since in each case my relationship with the person is completely transparent. Those people agree to ring up my groceries, or make my coffee, or take me to the airport, because they're getting what they want out of the exchange—namely, money. If I *weren't* going to pay—if, for example, I was planning on sprinting out the cab without settling up—then I would be using the driver as a mere means. I wouldn't be respecting his autonomy, since I wouldn't have come through on the deal that led him to drive me in the first place (a ride for cash). Instead, I'd have been using him—even manipulating him—to get what I want.

It's somewhat similar with Gabriela. What you want is a certain kind of interaction with friends—simple, drama-free, and so on. And Gabriela wants it too. But she doesn't want it at the expense of important information. By staying silent, however, you preserve what you want—the easy friendship—but you get it via a kind of manipulation. If she knew that you were the sort of person who wouldn't tell her the truth when it matters, she wouldn't be friends with you.

So the third option is out: You've got to say something. But Kantianism might not tell you which of the other options you should pursue. From a utilitarian perspective, there's always a best option (or a tie for best). From a Kantian angle, however, there isn't. Some things are definitely ruled out, and then there's freedom to select from among the remaining options. In this case, however, Kantianism does probably make a further recommendation. Recall: In the first option, you give Dave the ultimatum tomorrow; in the second, you contact Gabriela now. It seems to me that the first option does a better job of respecting *Dave's* autonomy, and is therefore preferable. After all, by contacting Gabriela immediately, you take away Dave's chance to take responsibility for what he did. In that respect, allowing him to confess his wrongdoing to her directly would be better than having someone else report what he did. (It might be better in other respects too, but it's Dave's autonomy on which we're focusing.)

The upshot? If you look at this situation as a utilitarian, everything depends on the consequences. What will happen given different courses of action? And which of those makes everyone best off? That's what you should do. Alternately, if you look at things as a Kantian, some options are just off the table, and you're free to choose between the remaining ones. In this particular case, however, Kantian considerations probably favor giving Dave the ultimatum.

Virtue Ethics

Let me offer you just one more angle on the Dave and Gabriela case. Very roughly, *virtue ethics* says that you should do whatever the virtuous person would do. So what would a virtuous person do in your shoes?

A little background. You know some virtuous people. You also know some vicious ones. Virtuous people are self-controlled, honest, wise, faithful, thoughtful, patient, merciful, loving, judicious, humble, and so on. Vicious people are cold, cruel, insensitive, thoughtless, stubborn, ill-tempered, biased, proud. From the perspective of virtue ethics, you should imitate the former, not the latter. (Bold claim, I know.) So when we come to the Dave and Gabriela case, we should think about how a virtuous person would handle it. What would she do?

Well, a virtuous person understands that our values conflict. We want good outcomes; we want to treat people with respect; we want to be honest and kind and brave. However, there are plenty of situations where we can't manage all these things at the same time. In such cases, we have to make hard calls about what to do. Virtuous people know how to navigate these conflicts. For any given situation, they're better at seeing what matters than the rest of us.

So the virtuous person would care about the consequences: She wouldn't want to ruin a good relationship unnecessarily. However, she wouldn't care about all the consequences in the same way. If honesty cost her a friendship, that might be an acceptable cost. A virtuous person would also appreciate the value of autonomy. However, she might be willing to compromise that value for something else. After a talk with Dave the next morning, she might see how devastated he is by the mistake. She might tell him that, although she won't lie for him, she won't say anything to Gabriela if Dave swears that he'll curb his drinking. The compromise isn't ideal, but no compromise is. And perhaps it's better to salvage an otherwise good relationship—which is awfully hard to come by—than it is to lay everything on the table.

Alternately, a virtuous person might make a very different call. Perhaps she knows that Dave and Gabriela are deeply private people—they wouldn't want any intrusion into their romantic lives, even over something like this. In that case, she'd respect their wishes, even if they run counter to her own judgments about what would be best. Or perhaps she knows that Dave can be an angry drunk, in which case she might be concerned for Jezebel's safety. Or perhaps she knows that Gabriela was expecting Dave to come over later, so if she doesn't let her know what's going on, Gabriela may well end up sleeping with someone who just cheated on her. Whatever the virtuous person does, it's going to be deeply informed by the details of the situation. The virtuous person is sensitive to what matters.

Finally, a virtuous person is going to *feel* certain things. (Notice that your feelings don't matter in the same way from the other perspectives. What matters is either the consequences or treating people as ends. It isn't that these perspectives deny that you've got feelings; it's just that they don't take them to be as important.) A virtuous person might be *troubled* by Dave's unfaithfulness. She might be *disappointed* in him for putting her in a difficult moral situation. She might *sympathize* with Gabriela, who doesn't yet know what's going on. She might feel *guilty* for lying by omission (if she decides not to say anything), even if she decides that—ultimately—lying by omission is the best choice. The virtuous person doesn't just have an appropriate *outward* response. She has an appropriate *inward* response too.

Another Case

Utilitarianism, Kantianism, and virtue ethics invite you to ask different questions when confronted with a moral choice. Utilitarianism suggests that you should ask about the consequences—not just for you, and not of all kinds. Instead, utilitarianism suggests that we ask about the consequences *for all* in terms of how well off it makes them. Then, we should choose the course of action that makes everyone best off. Kantianism, on the other hand, recommends that we *not* treat people as mere means—that we not use or manipulate them, that we not prevent them from making free and informed choices. So we should ask whether a particular plan would do that. Once we rule out the bad options, we can choose among those that remain. Finally, virtue ethics encourages us to imitate the virtuous person. Accordingly, we should think about what the virtuous person would do. How would a kind, patient, gracious, attentive, thoughtful, courageous person handle the situation in front of us?

These approaches sometimes lead us to the same conclusion. When they do, however, they don't lead us there for the same reasons. They invite us to understand moral situations quite differently, and they're valuable precisely because they draw our attention to the differences between the things we value—consequences, autonomy, and virtue. It might help to see them in action again, though, so let's consider another case—the "Steve case."

> Suppose you attend one of the many colleges in the United States where it's hard to get around without a car. And you don't have one. Steve, however, does. In fact, Steve has a really nice car. Unfortunately, that's all he's got, as Steve is entirely friendless. He's nice enough, but he's also hugely awkward, and spending all his time on his own is just making the problem worse. It's a shame.
>
> You have a big test coming up, so you commit to studying for the evening. However, you find that you've got a better handle on things than you thought, and you're free by a relatively early hour. As it happens, though, your pals have all made other plans. And with this free time, you would just *love* to see *Star Wars XXVII*. But as I said, you've

got no car. Of course, if you messaged Steve, he'd definitely drive you—he'd love to see *Star Wars XXVII* too. And he'd be especially glad to have someone to go with. You aren't really planning to become buds, but he doesn't need to know that, and you'll both have a nice time. Is it OK to message him?

Before we think through this case, take a few minutes and run through the three theories. What do you think they'd say about the Steve case?

As before, let's begin with utilitarianism. From this perspective, the central question concerns how Steve's going to feel if (a) you go to the movies together and (b) you don't end up being friends afterward. If he isn't going to be bothered by that, then heading to the theater is probably your best choice. You'll be happy because you got to see the movie. He'll be happy for the same reason, and also because someone messaged him. And if he isn't bothered by the fact that you didn't become BFFs, then it's a win: more happiness all around.

But suppose that Steve will be really hurt if you give him the cold shoulder after the film. Then, that lingering disappointment will probably outweigh the pleasure that each of you two got from watching it. In that case, you shouldn't message him.

How do things look from a Kantian perspective? Well, it's pretty clear that you're using Steve: You're letting Steve think you might want to be friends just to get a ride. Of course, he might agree to that deal if you made things clear to him. But you aren't giving him that choice. So, you shouldn't message him if you don't intend to disclose your intentions. (Or you should get better intentions.)

Finally, if you look at things as a virtue ethicist, the failure is in the setup. The basic issue is that you aren't sufficiently compassionate. You should never have been willing to risk letting him suffer lingering disappointment, and you should never have been open to using him. What's more, though you have no obligation to befriend someone just because he needs friends, a virtuous person might well befriend someone for just that reason. Alternately, he might try to include Steve in social events where Steve could make friends who share his interests, perhaps as a result of some thoughtful introductions.

Getting Perspective

As we wrap up this section, it's worth reflecting on the uses and abuses of these three moral theories. Perhaps the most common *abuse* of these moral theories is to use them to say whatever you already wanted to say. So, for example, if you want torture to be OK, you suddenly argue like a utilitarian; if you're critical of sex work, you're now a Kantian; if you're in favor of helping the homeless, virtue ethics becomes your thing. This is to use the theories to avoid thinking about reasons that don't fit with the beliefs we bring to the table.

A better use of these theories is to use them as I've already suggested: as ways to focus our attention. When we want to defend a moral claim, we should look at it from at least three angles. What would the consequences be? Will we have to take advantage of anyone—or otherwise be unfair—in the process? And what kind of people will we become by acting this way? These questions help us get a more complete picture of the moral situation. Once we've got that picture, we can begin thinking about how to make an argument for one proposal over another. Maybe you think that, in this case, Kantian considerations get to the heart of the moral issue. Then, you might make an argument in those terms:

1. If you get Steve to drive you to the movie under false pretenses, you'll be using him.
2. You shouldn't use Steve.
3. So, you shouldn't get Steve to drive you to the movie under false pretenses.

Of course, you'll need to explain why you think that the second premise is true—why, in other words, you think it would be wrong to use Steve. Moreover, let's acknowledge that having all this information can make defending your view harder, not easier. But that's why we have to engage in serious, informed, and humble dialogue. That's why we've got to listen to one another, thinking carefully about how to rank these considerations in different contexts. Sure, it would be nice if things were simpler. But since they aren't, let's not pretend otherwise.

Relativism

I spoke earlier about cultivating a healthy skepticism. I want to conclude this introduction by addressing a certain kind of *un*healthy skepticism.

A lot of people seem to be convinced that there are facts and there are opinions, and ethical claims are definitely in the "opinions" camp. Ethical claims might be important insofar as they help us to regulate our communities, but they aren't binding across cultures. There are just

American values and Afghani values, and there's no choosing between them.

I find this hard to swallow. Every year, thousands and thousands of girls—usually between the ages of four and twelve—have their genitals mutilated by women in their communities. Those who maintain this practice do so for a number of reasons. An important one is promoting chastity: They think that "uncut" girls are too interested in sex. Uncut girls can't be trusted to remain pure for their future husbands, nor can they be trusted to remain faithful to those husbands once they're married. Cutting solves this problem by making sex painful: You won't stray if there's no pleasure in it.

This practice seriously injures its victims. They face many medical complications as a result, as do their children. (The risk of neonatal mortality is higher among cut women.) It is, moreover, a way of maintaining a social system in which women are systematically disenfranchised. Women don't benefit from having their genitals mutilated—men do.

In cultures that practice female circumcision, the practitioners are not horrified by it. Indeed, they think that it would be wrong *not* to damage young girls in this way. What I take to be a great evil, they regard as an important good. This is a disturbing example of *cultural variation*—the thesis that people in different cultures have different beliefs about what's right and wrong.

Cultural variation is a well-established fact. *Cultural relativism* is a further thesis: It says that each culture has the *correct* moral views, even though those views conflict with the ones in other cultures. More precisely, it says that actions are right and wrong *because* of the norms of the culture. So, if my culture says that it's wrong to cut young girls, it's wrong in my culture to do so; if your culture says that it isn't, then—in yours—it isn't. Cultural relativism is *not* the claim that cultures don't see eye to eye on moral issues; rather, it's the (much stronger) claim that all their respective views are true (or, at least, true within their respective cultures).

Should we be cultural relativists? Should we think that culture determines not just what we *believe* to be right and wrong, but what's *actually* right and wrong?

It's a tempting view. However, this isn't the sort of thing you want to be mistaken about, so we'd better not jump to conclusions. If cultural relativism is true, then we might need to rethink (for example) the way we intervene to prevent human rights violations. After all, if cultural relativism is true, then the things that *our* culture regards as human rights violations *aren't* human rights violations in the cultures that tolerate those practices. However, if cultural relativism is false, then perhaps we should be more concerned to disrupt traditions like female genital mutilation. After all, if *anything* is wrong, that is. Moreover, given the huge costs to the victims, why shouldn't we stop it from happening insofar as we can?

So let's just consider one of the main factors that seems to push people toward relativism—namely, *persistent disagreement.*

The idea is as follows. If I like vanilla, and you like chocolate, it doesn't seem to matter how much we rave about our respective favorites: I'll still think that vanilla is the best, and you'll still believe that chocolate deserves that accolade. In the face of this disagreement, the natural conclusion is that there's no fact of the matter about which is better. I like vanilla more, and so it's true—for me—that it's the best. You like chocolate best, and so it's true—for you—that chocolate is the best. But there's no "absolute" truth here—just truth relative to people with preferences.

Cultural relativism approaches ethics the same way. People continue to disagree about moral matters, and there doesn't seem to be much we can say—if anything—to change people's minds. So, the natural conclusion is that there's no fact of the matter about what's right and wrong. Ethics is just the name we give to the norms of particular groups.

This argument may carry the day. But it's worth noting that we've got *another* way to explain disagreement. We are, after all, beings who rely heavily on our intuitive responses to situations; we tend not to reason deeply about moral matters. Moreover, people are often ignorant of the empirical facts that are relevant in moral disputes, though they aren't willing to admit as much. (Would policy X really have consequence Y? Well, we're not sure. But we'll certainly make up something that sounds good.) And, of course, we often have a horse in the race, which makes us unwilling to think things through in a dispassionate way. (If I'm a wealthy white male, I might want to preserve laws that benefit wealthy white males—even if I can see that they're horrendously bad for other people.)

So now we have two competing explanations of persistent disagreement: On the one hand, there's the claim that there's no fact of the matter; on the other, there's the claim that there *is* a fact of the matter, but there are a thousand hurdles to our determining what it is. With respect to the example mentioned earlier, the two options are, on the one hand, that there's no transcultural fact of the matter as to whether female genital mutilation is morally wrong, or, on the other, the claim that there *is* a fact of the matter, and it's just really hard for some people to see that.

Which should you believe? The choice isn't simple or straightforward. But let's add one more wrinkle—the one that led me to say, at the beginning of this section, that skepticism about ethics is unhealthy skepticism.

I'm inclined to say that there is a fact of the matter about whether female genital mutilation is wrong. But let's suppose you aren't. Instead, you think that everything is up to your culture. Even if that's right, *we still have to talk to people who support female genital mutilation*. Or, at the very least, we're going to have to talk to people who disagree with us about abortion, or whether there should be guns on college campuses, or whether we should eat meat that comes from factory farms. In this messy, interconnected, highly globalized world, we're going to have conversations with people who deeply disagree with us about moral matters. Sometimes, we'll have to make decisions that affect them, or we'll have to make decisions together. When that happens, we'll need to think about how to dialogue well. We'll have to figure out how to talk about our values, and theirs, and how to reason together toward conclusions that everyone can accept—or at least live with. We can't avoid moral debate.

The upshot is this. You can think that there are facts of the matter in ethics—that we can get it wrong, sometimes do, and need to discover the truth. Or you can be a pragmatist about ethics. You can think that there is no fact of the matter. Still, our values help us coordinate our lives, and as the world becomes more connected, it becomes harder and harder to avoid negotiations about how, exactly, the coordination should go. Healthy skepticism takes seriously the possibility that we're making things up as we go along, but recognizes that if that's true, we've still got to learn how to make it up together. *Unhealthy* skepticism says that, if we're making things up as we go along, then ethics doesn't matter. Don't believe it.

Going Forward

That should be enough to get you started. As you go forward, here are a few things to keep in mind:

1. Ethics isn't about the law, or about what you'd do, or what's sensible. It's about what you *should* do, even if the law isn't on your side, or you'd normally never act that way, or that course of action seems a bit radical.

2. Don't just trust your gut: it can lead you astray.
3. Think before you reason—or before you trust someone else's reasoning. Sometimes, what sounds like good reasoning, isn't.
4. You're about to spend a lot of time reading and thinking about arguments. Figure out their structure. Then figure out whether they're any good.
5. There are at least three questions to ask when confronted with a moral situation:
   a. What are the consequences going to be *for everyone*?
   b. If I did this, would I be using someone?
   c. How would a kind, patient, gracious, attentive, thoughtful, courageous person handle this situation?
6. Ethics is hard, and we might disagree about ethics for that reason. Either way, though, learn how to talk about your values and the values of others.
7. Remember: This is not ethics training. I'm not here to teach you what to think. If you ever feel like this book is pointless, ask yourself whether you've been waiting for a sound bite—for some "gotcha" line that will silence your racist uncle. If that's what you want, check out memes on Tumblr. Here, we're after arguments. And let me tell you: They're pretty fascinating.

Notes

1. I'm assuming that the probability of either p or q isn't 1.
2. Things are different when we're trying to assess whether someone's lying. If the victim's mother is on the stand, she might well say anything that increases the likelihood of a conviction. In such circumstances, we should take her testimony with a grain of salt. That's very different from having the victim's mother make an *argument* that the accused person did it, and then ignoring that argument just because the victim's mother made it.
3. For others, and for much more about critical thinking, I highly recommend Lewis Vaughn's *The Power of Critical Thinking: Effective Reasoning about Ordinary and Extraordinary Claims*, fifth edition (New York: Oxford University Press, 2015).
4. . . . which isn't to say that the others are necessarily bad. There are lots of good arguments that aren't valid, such as *strong inductive* arguments. Strong inductive arguments make their conclusions *highly probable*—which means that it's possible for the premises to be true and the conclusion false, but the conclusion is, nevertheless, very likely to be true if the premises are.

5. Modus ponens isn't the only valid form of inference; there are lots of them. See Vaughn's *The Power of Critical Thinking* for more.

6. Of course, despite all this, Bill's conclusion might still be true (albeit not for the reason he gave). The show isn't over after we tackle the first consideration we encounter. The conversation continues when Bill gives us a new reason, we bang it into the shape of an argument, and we turn to the merits of *those* premises. And on we go.

7. Moreover, it's worth considering whether your response to the "What should you do?" question is affected by your gender relative to Dave's. Would you respond the same way if Gabriela were the one (probably) cheating?

8. In particular, it says you ought to ask how everyone is going to be made better and worse off in terms of happiness—not integrity, or being respected, or knowing how things really are in the world. But let's ignore this wrinkle for the time being. Also, I should mention that utilitarianism is a particular version of consequentialism—the view that actions are right or wrong based on their consequences. Utilitarianism is the version that says that the relevant consequences are those that concern well-being.

9. Kantianism is a *deontological* moral theory. According to deontological theories, you acted rightly if you followed a particular rule, and this even if the consequences of following that rule are worse than if you hadn't followed it. There are plenty of other deontological theories, but we won't worry about them here.

PART I

Sex and Relationships

1

Why Shouldn't Tommy and Jim Have Sex?

A Defense of Homosexuality

John Corvino

Corvino defends homosexual relationships against two charges: first, that they are unnatural; second, that they violate biblical teaching. In both cases, Corvino argues that these challenges fail. It doesn't look like there is a link between naturalness and morality that condemns homosexual sex, and if we reflect on the historical contexts in which the Bible was written, we can see that even conservative readers don't need to draw an anti-gay conclusion. And since sex has obvious benefits (it can be good for you and for your relationship), Corvino concludes that there is no reason for gay couples to abstain.

Tommy and Jim are a homosexual couple I know. Tommy is an accountant; Jim is a botany professor. They are in their forties and have been together fourteen years, the last five of which they've lived in a Victorian house that they've lovingly restored. Although their

Corvino, John. 1997. "Why Shouldn't Tommy and Jim Have Sex?" In *Same Sex: Debating the Ethics, Science, and Culture of Homosexuality*, edited by John Corvino, 3–16. Lanham, MD: Rowman & Littlefield. Reprinted with permission.

relationship has had its challenges, each has made sacrifices for the sake of the other's happiness and the relationship's long-term success.

I assume that Tommy and Jim have sex with each other (although I've never bothered to ask). Furthermore, I contend that they probably should have sex with each other. For one thing, sex is pleasurable. But it is also much more than that: A sexual relationship can unite two people in a way that virtually nothing else can. It can be an avenue of growth, of communication, and of lasting interpersonal fulfillment. These are reasons why most heterosexual couples have sex even if they don't want children, don't want children yet, or don't want additional children. And if these reasons are good enough for most heterosexual couples, then they should be good enough for Tommy and Jim.

Of course, having a reason to do something does not preclude there being an even better reason for not doing it. Tommy might have a good reason for drinking orange juice (it's tasty and nutritious) but an even better reason for not doing so (he's allergic). The point is that one would need a pretty good reason for denying a sexual relationship to Tommy and Jim, given the intense benefits widely associated with such relationships. The question I shall consider in this paper is thus quite simple: Why shouldn't Tommy and Jim have sex?

Homosexual Sex Is "Unnatural"

Many contend that homosexual sex is "unnatural." But what does that mean? Many things that people value—clothing, houses, medicine, and government, for example—are unnatural in some sense. On the other hand, many things that people detest—disease, suffering, and death, for example—are "natural" in the sense that they occur "in nature." If the unnaturalness charge is to be more than empty rhetorical flourish, those who levy it must specify what they mean. Borrowing from Burton Leiser, I will examine several possible meanings of "unnatural."

What Is Unusual or Abnormal Is Unnatural

One meaning of "unnatural" refers to that which deviates from the norm, that is, from what most people do. Obviously, most people engage in heterosexual relationships. But does it follow that it is wrong to engage in homosexual relationships? Relatively few people read Sanskrit, pilot ships, play the mandolin, breed goats, or write with both hands, yet none of these activities is immoral simply because it is unusual. As the Ramsey Colloquium, a group of Jewish and Christian scholars who oppose homosexuality, writes, "The statistical frequency of an act does not determine its moral status." So while homosexuality might be unnatural in the sense of being unusual, that fact is morally irrelevant.

What Is Not Practiced by Other Animals Is Unnatural

Some people argue, "Even animals know better than to behave homosexually; homosexuality must be wrong." This argument is doubly flawed. First, it rests on a false premise. Numerous studies—including Anne Perkins's study of "gay" sheep and George and Molly Hunt's study of "lesbian" seagulls—have shown that some animals do form homosexual pair-bonds. Second, even if animals did not behave homosexually, that fact would not prove that homosexuality is immoral. After all, animals don't cook their food, brush their teeth, participate in religious worship, or attend college; human beings do all of these without moral censure. Indeed, the idea that animals could provide us with our standards— especially our sexual standards—is simply amusing.

What Does Not Proceed from Innate Desires Is Unnatural

Recent studies suggesting a biological basis for homosexuality have resulted in two popular positions. One side proposes that homosexual people are "born that way" and that it is therefore natural (and thus good) for them to form homosexual relationships. The other side maintains that homosexuality is a lifestyle choice, which is therefore unnatural (and thus wrong). Both sides assume a connection between the origin of homosexual orientation, on the one hand, and the moral value of homosexual activity, on the other. And insofar as they share that assumption, both sides are wrong.

Consider first the pro-homosexual side: "They are born that way; therefore it's natural and good." This inference assumes that all innate desires are good ones (i.e., that they should be acted upon). But that assumption is clearly false. Research suggests that some people are born with a predisposition toward violence, but such people have no more right to strangle their neighbors than anyone else. So while people like Tommy and Jim may be born with homosexual tendencies, it doesn't follow that they ought to act on them. Nor does it follow that they ought not to act on them, even if the tendencies are not innate. I probably do not have any innate tendency to write with my left hand (since I, like everyone else in my family, have always been right-handed), but it doesn't follow that it would be immoral for me to do so. So simply asserting that homosexuality is a lifestyle choice will not show that it is an immoral lifestyle choice.

Do people "choose" to be homosexual? People certainly don't seem to choose their sexual feelings, at least not in any direct or obvious way. (Do you? Think about it.) Rather, they find certain people attractive and certain activities arousing, whether they "decide" to or not. Indeed, most people at some point in their lives wish that they could control their feelings more—for example, in situations of unrequited love—and find it frustrating that they cannot. What they can control to a considerable degree is how and when they act upon those feelings. In that sense, both homosexuality and heterosexuality involve lifestyle choices. But in either case, determining the origin of the feelings will not determine whether it is moral to act on them.

What Violates an Organ's Principal Purpose Is Unnatural

Perhaps when people claim that homosexual sex is unnatural they mean that it cannot result in procreation. The idea behind the argument is that human organs have various natural purposes: eyes are for seeing, ears are for hearing, genitals are for procreating. According to this argument, it is immoral to use an organ in a way that violates its particular purpose.

Many of our organs, however, have multiple purposes. Tommy can use his mouth for talking, eating, breathing, licking stamps, chewing gum, kissing women, or kissing Jim; and it seems rather arbitrary to claim that all but the last use are "natural." (And if we say that some of the other uses are "unnatural, but not immoral," we have failed to specify a morally relevant sense of the term "natural.")

Just because people can and do use their sexual organs to procreate, it does not follow that they should not use them for other purposes. Sexual organs seem very well suited for expressing love, for giving and receiving pleasure, and for celebrating, replenishing, and enhancing a relationship— even when procreation is not a factor. Unless opponents of homosexuality are prepared to condemn heterosexual couples who use contraception or individuals who masturbate, they must abandon this version of the unnaturalness argument. Indeed, even the Roman Catholic Church, which forbids contraception and masturbation, approves of sex for sterile couples and of sex during pregnancy, neither of which can lead to procreation. The Church concedes here that intimacy and pleasure are morally legitimate purposes for sex, even in cases where procreation is impossible. But since homosexual sex can achieve these purposes as well, it is inconsistent for the Church to condemn it on the grounds that it is not procreative.

One might object that sterile heterosexual couples do not intentionally turn away from procreation, whereas homosexual couples do. But this distinction doesn't hold. It is no more possible for Tommy to procreate with a woman whose uterus has been removed than it is for him to procreate with Jim. By having sex with either one, he is intentionally engaging in a nonprocreative sexual act.

Yet one might press the objection further and insist that Tommy and the woman could produce children if the woman were fertile: whereas homosexual relationships are essentially infertile, heterosexual relationships are only incidentally so. But what does that prove? Granted, it might require less of a miracle for a woman without a uterus to become pregnant than for Jim to become pregnant, but it would require a miracle nonetheless. Thus it seems that the real difference here is not that one couple is fertile and the other not, nor that one couple "could" be fertile (with the help of a miracle) and the other not, but rather that one couple is male-female and the other male-male. In other words, sex between Tommy and Jim is wrong because it's male-male—i.e., because it's homosexual. But that, of course, is no argument at all.

What Is Disgusting or Offensive Is Unnatural

It often seems that when people call homosexuality "unnatural" they really just mean that it's disgusting. But plenty of morally neutral activities—handling snakes, eating snails, performing autopsies, cleaning toilets, and so on—disgust people. Indeed, for centuries, most people found interracial relationships disgusting, yet that feeling—which has by no means disappeared—hardly proves that such relationships are wrong. In sum, the charge that homosexuality is unnatural, at least in its most common forms, is longer on rhetorical flourish than on philosophical cogency. At best it expresses an aesthetic judgment, not a moral judgment . . .

Homosexuality Violates Biblical Teaching

At this point in the discussion, many people turn to religion. "If the secular arguments fail to prove that homosexuality is wrong," they say, "so much the worse for secular ethics. This failure only proves that we need God for morality." Since people often justify their moral beliefs by appeal to religion, I will briefly consider the biblical position.

At first glance, the Bible's condemnation of homosexual activity seems unequivocal. Consider, for example, the following two passages, one from the "Old" Testament and one from the "New":

> You shall not lie with a male as with a woman; it is an abomination. (Lev. 18:22)
>   For this reason God gave them up to degrading passions. Their women exchanged natural intercourse for unnatural, and in the same way also the men, giving up natural intercourse with women, were consumed with passion for one another. Men committed shameless acts with men and received in their own persons the due penalty for their error. (Rom. 1:26–27)

Note, however, that these passages are surrounded by other passages that relatively few people consider binding. For example, Leviticus also declares,

> The pig . . . is unclean for you. Of their flesh you shall not eat, and their carcasses you shall not touch; they are unclean for you. (11:7–8)

Taken literally, this passage not only prohibits eating pork, but also playing football, since footballs are made of pigskin. (Can you believe that the University of Notre Dame so flagrantly violates Levitical teaching?)

Similarly, St. Paul, author of the Romans passage, also writes, "Slaves, obey your earthly masters with fear and trembling, in singleness of heart, as you obey Christ" (Eph. 6:5)—morally problematic advice if there ever were any. Should we interpret this passage (as Southern plantation owners once did) as implying that it is immoral for slaves to escape? After all, God himself says in Leviticus,

> [Y]ou may acquire male and female slaves . . . from among the aliens residing with you, and from their families that are with you, who have been born in your land; and they may be your property. You may keep them as a possession for your children after you, for them to inherit as property. (25:44–46)

How can people maintain the inerrancy of the Bible in light of such passages? The answer, I think, is that they learn to interpret the passages in their historical context.

Consider the Bible's position on usury, the lending of money for interest (for any interest, not just excessive interest). The Bible condemns this practice in no uncertain terms. In Exodus God says that "if you lend money to my people, to the poor among you shall not exact interest from them" (22:25). Psalm 15 says that those who lend at interest may not abide in the Lord's tent or dwell on his holy hill (1–5). Ezekiel calls usury "abominable"; compares it to adultery, robbery, idolatry, and bribery; and states that anyone who "takes advanced or accrued interest . . . shall surely die; his blood shall be upon himself" (18:13). Should believers therefore close their savings accounts? Not necessarily. According to orthodox Christian teaching, the biblical prohibition against usury no longer applies. The reason is that economic conditions have changed substantially since biblical times, such that usury no longer has the same negative consequences it had when the prohibitions were issued. Thus, the practice that was condemned by the Bible differs from contemporary interest banking in morally relevant ways.

Yet are we not in a similar position regarding homosexuality? Virtually all scholars agree that homosexual relations during biblical times were vastly different from relationships like Tommy and Jim's. Often such relations were integral to pagan practices. In Greek society, they typically involved older men and younger boys. If those are the kinds of features that the biblical authors had in mind when they issued their condemnations, and such features are no longer typical, then the biblical condemnations no longer apply. As with usury, substantial changes in cultural context have altered the meaning and consequences—and thus the moral value—of the practice in question. Put another way, using the Bible's condemnations of homosexuality against contemporary homosexuality is like using its condemnations of usury against contemporary banking.

Let me be clear about what I am not claiming here. First, I am not claiming that the Bible has been wrong before and therefore may be wrong this time. The Bible may indeed be wrong on some matters, but for the purpose of this argument I am assuming its infallibility. Nor am I claiming that the Bible's age renders it entirely inapplicable to today's issues. Rather, I am claiming that when we do apply it, we must pay attention to morally, relevant cultural differences between biblical times and today. Such attention will help us distinguish between specific time-bound prohibitions (for example, laws against usury or homosexual relations) and the enduring moral values they represent (for example, generosity or respect for persons). And as the above argument shows, my claim is not very controversial. Indeed, to deny it is to commit oneself to some rather strange views on slavery, usury, women's roles, astronomy, evolution, and the like.

Here, one might also make an appeal to religious pluralism. Given the wide variety of religious beliefs (e.g., the Muslim belief that women should cover their faces, the Orthodox Jewish belief against working on Saturday, the Hindu belief that cows are sacred and should not be eaten), each of us inevitably violates the religious beliefs of others. But we normally don't view such violations as occasions for moral censure, since we distinguish between beliefs that depend on particular revelations and beliefs that can be justified independently (e.g., that stealing is wrong). Without an independent justification for condemning homosexuality, the best one can say is, "My religion says so." But in a society that cherishes religious freedom, that reason alone does not normally provide grounds for moral or legal sanctions. That people still fall back on that reason in discussions of homosexuality suggests that they may not have much of a case otherwise.

Conclusion

As a last resort, opponents of homosexuality typically change the subject: "But what about incest, polygamy, and bestiality? If we accept Tommy and Jim's sexual relationship, why shouldn't we accept those as well?" Opponents of interracial marriage used a similar slippery-slope argument in the 1960s when the Supreme Court struck down anti-miscegenation laws. It was a bad argument then, and it is a bad argument now.

Just because there are no good reasons to oppose interracial or homosexual relationships, it does not follow that there are no good reasons to oppose incestuous, polygamous, or bestial relationships. One might argue, for instance, that incestuous relationships threaten delicate familial bonds, or that polygamous relationships result in unhealthy jealousies (and sexism), or that bestial relationships—do I need to say it?—aren't really "relationships" at all, at least not in the sense we've been discussing. Perhaps even better arguments could be offered (given much more space than I have here). The point is that there is no logical connection between homosexuality, on the one hand, and incest, polygamy, and bestiality, on the other.

Why, then, do critics continue to push this objection? Perhaps it's because accepting homosexuality requires them to give up one of their favorite arguments: "It's wrong because we've always been taught that it's wrong." This argument—call it the argument from tradition—has an obvious appeal: people reasonably favor tried-and-true ideas over unfamiliar ones, and they recognize the foolishness of trying to invent morality from scratch. But the argument from tradition is also a dangerous argument, as any honest look at history will reveal.

I conclude that Tommy and Jim's relationship, far from being a moral abomination, is exactly what it appears to be to those who know them: a morally positive influence on their lives and on others. Accepting this conclusion takes courage, since it entails that our moral traditions are fallible. But when these traditions interfere with people's happiness for no sound reason, they defeat what is arguably the very point of morality: promoting individual and communal well-being. To put the argument simply, Tommy and Jim's relationship makes them better people. And that's not just good for Tommy and Jim: that's good for everyone.

Comprehension Questions

1. Why does Corvino think that Tommy and Jim should have sex (assuming that there aren't any good reasons for them *not* to have sex)?
2. Why does Corvino bring up "lesbian" seagulls? What is that example supposed to show?
3. Does Corvino think it matters whether gay people were "born that way"? Why or why not?
4. Would it be legitimate for a conservative reader of the Bible to complain that Corvino isn't willing to take the Bible literally?

Discussion Questions

1. People often appeal to the "naturalness" of eating animals to justify eating animals. Is that argument any better than the appeal to naturalness to criticize homosexuality? Why or why not?
2. Can you think of any other issues where people appeal to "naturalness" as a moral consideration?
3. Let's assume that Corvino is right about needing to put the biblical passages on homosexuality in their historical context. If so, then why do you think that most conservative readers of the Bible *have* done this for usury, but *haven't* done this for homosexuality?

Case

In a longer discussion of homosexuality and Christianity, Corvino writes:

> [Some people] claim that without the Bible, one can have no secure foundation for moral claims. It seems to me that quite the reverse is true: Without an independent moral sense, one can have no confidence that a given text is God's word. After all, many different and incompatible texts claim to be divinely inspired, one cannot sift the good from the bad (or, at least, the better from the worse) without invoking an independent standard. It doesn't follow that the standard is "above" God—remember, believers hold that God is the creator of everything. I recall a Christian friend of mine who once wrote me a long letter trying to "save" me from homosexuality. "We trust our own fallible minds," she lamented, "but we do not trust the infallible mind of Christ!" But whose mind do I use to do the trusting, if not my own fallible one? Again, belief in an infallible God does not make the believer infallible.[1]

What do you make of Corvino's argument here? If it's a good argument, then what (if anything) does it imply about invoking our religious traditions in moral debates?

Note

1. John Corvino, *What's Wrong with Homosexuality?* (New York: Oxford University Press, 2015): 47.

2

What's Love Got to Do with It?

Epicureanism and Friends with Benefits

William O. Stephens

Is it a good idea to have a friend . . . with benefits? Stephens argues that, from the perspective of the Epicureans, it probably isn't. As he puts it, "good friends are far more reliable, and so ultimately more desirable, than good sex. [So,] the wise Epicurean chooses to populate his tranquil, happy life not with friends with benefits, but with friends." Stephens isn't arguing that it's *wrong* to have friends with benefits, but he is contending that it isn't in your interest to have these sorts of relationships.

Epicureans and Pleasure

The ancient Greek philosopher Epicurus and his followers believed that the good, the ultimate goal of all our actions, is pleasure. By nature all animals pursue pleasure and avoid pain and behave appropriately in doing so. Since human beings are animals too, and particularly intelligent ones at that, the good life for human beings is, the Epicureans

Stephens, William O. 2010. "What's Love Got to Do with It: Epicureanism and Friends with Benefits." In *College Sex: Philosophers with Benefits*, ed. Michael Bruce and Robert M. Stuart, 77–90. Malden, MA: Blackwell. Reprinted with permission of John Wiley & Sons.

argued, the pleasant life. This conception of the good life has an obvious appeal, and not only for college students. But the best strategy for achieving this pleasant life may not be quite so obvious. It may seem safe to suppose that Epicureans would consider all kinds of gratification, including sex, to be worth pursuing, but in fact they rejected the idea that all pleasures should be sought equally. Epicurus writes: "No pleasure is a bad thing in itself. But the things which produce certain pleasures bring troubles many times greater than the pleasures."[1]

Epicurus and his followers also rejected the common opinion that the more pleasant something is, the more vigorously one should go for it. The Epicureans believed that the best kind of pleasure is the purest kind, and the purest kind of pleasure results in no pain at all. They argued that happiness consists in freedom from pain and in particular from pain caused by unfulfilled desires. Consequently, we need to understand the nature of different kinds of desires and use reason to distinguish among them in order to lead a happy life. Epicurean ethical philosophy thereby provides a conceptual framework that enables us to fulfill those desires that need to be fulfilled, to avoid pursuing those desires that are difficult to satisfy, to avoid pursuing those desires which tend to result in greater pains than pleasures, and to eliminate altogether those desires that are impossible to fulfill or that always result in more pain than pleasure.

What did the Epicureans think about sex? In this essay I will explore how Epicurean philosophy applies to sex and the idea of friends with benefits among college students. I will argue that Epicureans regard good friends to be much more reliable than good sex, and so college students ought to keep their friends by avoiding having sex with them.

Freedom from Anxiety and Types of Desires

The Epicureans distinguished between two kinds of pain that our natural powers of reason can remove: physical pain and mental distress. Physical pains afflict us only in the present. Mental distress includes present unpleasant memories, present regrets about the past, present fears, and present worries about the future. Whereas present pangs are ever transient, the scope of past and anticipated future pains is much broader. Consequently, the Epicureans believed that mental suffering threatens a pleasant life much more than physical pains do. Physical pains, they argued, tend to be either mild (and so easy to bear) if they are chronic, or relatively short if they are intense. Mental distress includes all kinds of emotional upset and perturbation, including fear, frustration, anxiety, and grief. So the Epicureans offered a set of principles from which they derived arguments designed as therapy for the mental afflictions that ruin peace of mind and painless living. To rid oneself of all those desires which disrupt mental tranquility is to attain what the Greeks called ataraxia, that is, the ideal state of freedom from anxiety. The fear of death, fear of a future harm, the Epicureans considered to be the greatest obstacle to this life free of anxiety. So the Epicureans developed strategies for eliminating false beliefs that occasion worries about the future and for dispelling false beliefs that generate painful thoughts about the past.

If pleasure results from getting what you want and displeasure results from failing to get what you want, then two strategies suggest themselves for dealing with any desire that arises. You can try to satisfy the desire or you can work to get rid of it.[2] If a certain kind of desire cannot be eliminated because it arises from the natural constitution of human beings, then that desire counts as natural for the Epicureans. Natural desires may be either natural and necessary or natural but non-necessary. Of natural and necessary desires some are necessary for life itself, some for freeing the body from troubles, and some for happiness. When one is hungry or thirsty, it is because one's body lacks food or drink necessary for its healthy operation. All animals require food and water. Consequently, desires to eat and to drink are natural and necessary for life itself. Eating eliminates the lack of food, thereby removing the pain of hunger and satisfying the desire to eat. Eating thus has a natural limit. Drinking water eliminates the lack that is dehydration, thereby removing the pain of thirst and satisfying the desire to drink. Drinking, too, has a natural limit. Similarly, wearing clothing and inhabiting shelter to protect oneself from the elements satisfy desires natural and necessary for freeing the body from troubles. But so long as one's clothing and shelter remove the troubles of being too hot, too cold, or too wet, these desires are satisfied, since they too have a natural limit.[3]

Sex, Shoes, and the Needs of College Students

Now the ordinary college undergraduate won't worry much (or at all) about suffering from lacking the clothing, shelter, food, and drink needed to survive. Yet she may still have a host of concerns about certain kinds of food, certain kinds of drink, certain kinds of clothing, and various kinds of fun possessions and entertainments. Moreover, the ordinary college student is likely to have urgent concerns about whether, when, and with whom to engage in sexual activity of one kind or another. Is having sex with a friend a good idea? Other concerns may include grades, papers, lab reports, deciding on a major, roommates, friends, drinking alcohol, and how to behave at parties. All these concerns and associated desires can easily generate many serious worries and thereby threaten her tranquility.

Are all these desires on the same footing? The Epicureans hold that vain and empty desires are not natural desires because they do not arise from any depletion of the body and so have no natural limit. Consequently, desires for political power, fame, wealth, luxuries, jewelry, toys, artworks, and the like count as "vain and empty" for the Epicureans. All too often the more of these things one gets, the more one wants. Consider an example. A person can wear only one pair of shoes at a time, so wanting to own many pairs of fashionable shoes is vain and empty, from the Epicurean perspective. A pair of feet does not hunger for more than one pair of shoes at a time for shelter, yet one can be fooled by advertisers and fashionistas in our materialistic society into falsely believing that getting more shoes will make one happier. But in fact wanting more shoes than one's feet need endangers one's ataraxia. Fancy, trendy, expensive clothing keeps one's body no more comfortable than basic, cheap, readily available clothing. Jewelry, iPods, gaming stations, stereo systems, and plasma TV sets provide neither calories nor nutrients for, and remove no pains from, the body. Therefore, desires for such things are neither natural nor, Epicureans would argue, necessary for happiness. Since inability to satisfy desires for these kinds of things frustrates and perturbs us, the Epicureans urge us to eliminate all such vain and empty desires and limit ourselves entirely to natural desires and mostly to necessary desires.

To maximize our chances of achieving ataraxia, wouldn't the Epicureans advise us to limit our desires entirely to the natural and necessary ones? Here they make modest room for natural but non-necessary desires. These include expensive, gourmet foods and beverages: truffles, caviar, filet mignon, lobster, fine wines, elegant desserts, pricey chocolates, and the like. After all, champagne, espresso, and milkshakes fail to quench thirst better than water. One can enjoy these delicacies if they happen to be available, since as food and drink they do remove the physical pains of hunger and thirst by replenishing the body.[4] But to foster a habitual desire for extravagant goodies so as to make one's happiness depend on getting them inevitably causes mental distress whenever such treats are unavailable. Consequently, harboring such a psychological dependency is wildly imprudent because it considerably and unnecessarily risks one's ataraxia. So the Epicureans recommend that we be wise and cautious about our natural and non-necessary desires. The pleasures they afford are real, but they are necessary neither for our survival nor for our peace of mind. Being ever mindful of this reality enables us to be happy in both plentiful times and lean times. We must not allow occasional indulgence in a special treat to undermine our habituated satisfaction with simple food and drink. To believe that we ever need rich foods or costly beverages is to be deluded.

The Dangers of Sex

The Epicureans considered sexual appetite to belong in the class of natural but non-necessary desires. Sexual appetite arises from the body and its hormonal activity, and so it is natural. But one can live serenely without satisfying sexual desires, the Epicureans believed, so they are not necessary. Orgasms are undeniably pleasant, but in order to preserve one's ataraxia one must be careful and selective about satisfying one's sexual desires. Epicurus writes:

> I understand from you that your natural disposition is too much inclined toward sexual passion. Follow your inclination as you will provided only that you neither violate the laws, disturb well-established customs, harm any one of your neighbors, injure your own body, nor waste your possessions. That you be not checked by some one of these provisos is impossible; for a man never gets any good from sexual passion, and he is fortunate if he does not receive harm.[5]

First, notice that Epicurus's friend's natural inclination toward sexual passion is excessive. Passions are dangerous because of their extreme intensity, and this extremity usually creates trouble. One kind of trouble would be violating the law, since excessive sexual passion could lead one to commit adultery, incest, or other illegal acts like date rape. Another kind of trouble is disturbing those well-established customs that facilitate harmonious, cooperative, and pleasant social living. The pursuit of sexual passion could also result in harm to one's neighbor, either physical harm through a minor sexually transmitted disease, or emotional damage, or both, say through a serious STD or an unwanted pregnancy. Indulging one's sexual passion could also result in injury to oneself. This could take the form of an STD, an unwanted pregnancy, or emotional anguish when one is spurned or betrayed by one's lover, or physical injury at the hands of one's lover's jealous ex-lover, or even an assault by a lover one has jilted. Finally, Epicurus warns that excessive inclination to sexual passion could result in squandering your possessions and money in wooing the person(s) you lust after. Epicurus thinks it impossible to avoid every single one of these possible harmful consequences. Sooner or later, at least one of these harms will afflict the person who gives in to his excessive erotic inclination. Though the appetite for sex in itself is natural, according to the Epicureans, sexual passion is fraught with many dangerous consequences. So not only is it not necessary to satisfy sexual passion to live a happy, untroubled, peaceful life, it is wiser still to eliminate this hazardous disposition. Epicurus concludes that a person never gets any good from sexual passion, and is lucky not to receive harm from it. In short, sexual passion is of no benefit. . . .

Romance, Beautiful Illusions, and Sound Minds

So if a college Joey O'Montague finds himself falling passionately in love with a Julie Capulet in his entomology class, what advice would Joey's Epicurean advisor give him? I suggest that Joey would be sternly cautioned against being seduced by the bewitching fairy tales of romance peddled relentlessly by Hollywood and the popular media. Joey ought to rein in his wild-running imagination from insidious fantasies about how he and Julie will crash together in ecstatic union, serenaded by a swooning soundtrack, to become the Brangelina of their campus, self-heroized in their omnipotent, triumphant love. Such is the stuff that dreams are made of,[6] by the movie, television, and music industries that so richly profit by perpetuating these delusions on celluloid and compact discs for mass consumption. Commercialized, fairy tale romance is big business and a monstrous myth. [The Epicurean] warns that images of idyllic, beatified, electrified, passionate love are ephemeral images, mirages, incapable of feeding our real, earthly, embodied human relationships but fully capable of poisoning them. Hollywood stars make horrible models for personal relationships among college students (or any other couples, for that matter). To fall prey to the delusion, the vaunted fantasy, that Julie will be for Joey O. what Angelina Jolie is (portrayed by Hollywood to be) for Brad Pitt and vice versa is to bury what could be a healthy, pleasant relationship under an avalanche of utterly unrealistic and ultimately impossible expectations. She is no Aphrodite, even if she is a homecoming queen. He is no godlike superhunk, even if he is a homecoming king. . . .

Hollywood filmmakers and Madison Avenue magazine moguls enlist armies of make-up artists and post-production wizards to erase all blemishes and tiny wrinkles from the complexions and sculpted bodies digitally perfected to bedazzle us. The media-bloated imagination of a college student can do as much for him when he finds a mortal to idolize and enshrine on his pedestal of love. The benighted, lovesick dreamer will be bitterly disappointed when his zealously constructed fantasy of a perfect goddess is dissolved by the flaws and frailties of what was all along a mere mortal. This is why [the Epicurean] thinks it is easier to avoid being ensnared by erotic love than to free oneself from its nets once entangled. . . .

Skip the Sex and Keep the Friend

For college students, who generally are less emotionally experienced and under considerable academic, social, and sometimes athletic pressures, [the miseries of frustrated and unrequited love] can include depression, drinking problems, drug abuse, eating disorders, crippling driving accidents, attempted suicide, and suicide.[7] These troubles ruin one's academic progress and worse. Therefore, the wise Epicurean advice is for Joey O. and Julie C. to cool it, to stay focused on their studies, to prepare for and attend every class, to take notes attentively and participate in class, and to complete and turn in their assignments on time. Better for them to remain study buddies, at least until the semester ends.

What if they really like each other a lot? I propose that the Epicureans would consider wanting friends to be in the class of natural desires necessary for happiness. Friendship is hugely important for achieving ataraxia. Epicurus beams about it: "Friendship dances through the world bidding us all to awaken to the recognition of happiness."[8] But friends are not just for happy times. When college students are distraught, to whom do they turn? When they need a sympathetic ear or a shoulder to lean on, on whom do they rely? When they are in conflict with their parents or siblings or bosses or co-workers, who provides emotional support? Amid romantic disasters so devastating that they may even consider suicide, who is there to help them regain perspective? Their friends, naturally. As Epicurus advises, "Of the things which wisdom provides for the blessedness of one's whole life, by far the greatest is the possession of friendship."[9]

Desires to engage in sex with others are natural but not necessary for life, for freeing the body from troubles, or for happiness. Desires to have friends are natural and necessary for happiness. So I argue that the Epicureans would advise college students to avoid having sex with their friends in order to protect their friendships. Epicurus writes: "Do not spoil what you have by desiring what you have not; but remember that what you now have was once among the things only hoped for."[10] As tempting as it may be to upgrade a friend to a friend with benefits, friendships can be counted on to last much longer than either bouts of sexual passion or the flings which they punctuate. . . . Perhaps a key insight of Epicurean philosophy is that good friends are far more reliable, and so ultimately more desirable, than good sex. If so, the wise Epicurean chooses to populate his tranquil, happy life not with friends with benefits, but with friends. Friends are the real benefits.

Comprehension Questions

1. Is Stephens saying that it would be *wrong* to have a "friends with benefits" arrangement? If so, what's his argument for that? If not, what *is* he saying?
2. Epicureans distinguish between desires that need to be fulfilled, desires that are difficult to satisfy, desires that tend to result in greater pains than pleasures, and desires that are impossible to fulfill or that always result in more pain than pleasure. Can you give examples of desires that match each description?
3. What is *ataraxia*?
4. According to Epicureans, what's the problem with "vain and empty desires"?
5. According to Epicureans, what's so valuable about friendship?

Discussion Questions

1. It's often the case that people are friends before they become romantically involved. Does the Epicurean view imply that it would always be a mistake to make that transition? If so, why? If not, why not?
2. Stephens lists many potential costs to frustrated and unrequited love: depression, drinking problems, drug abuse, eating disorders, crippling driving accidents, attempted suicide. Are the risks of such costs big enough to justify not pursuing a romantic relationship with a friend? If so, why? If not, why not?
3. Stephens says that we need to be "sternly cautioned against being seduced by the bewitching fairy tales of romance peddled

relentlessly by Hollywood and the popular media." What are some of these fairy tales? Do you know people who have been negatively affected by trying to have one of these fairy-tale relationships? How (if at all) does the Epicurean outlook help you understand what went wrong?

Case

Consider Tracy Clark-Flory's story:

> For six months, this guy and I would hang out and sleep together—euphemistically and literally—roughly once a week. In his self-deprecating style, he made no secret of his undatability. He was prone to post-coital declarations like, "You'll be done with me soon. I'm a drunken emotional mess!" Only that was kind of the point: So was I. The relationship started just a few weeks after my mom's lung cancer diagnosis. When you're in crisis, there is something oddly comforting about someone who smells of whiskey and cigarettes; misery loves company. It might have been a preemptive strike: In my most vulnerable state, the idea of someone who was emotionally available terrified me. I wanted company, warmth and no danger of attachment. The guy openly refers to himself as "a slut" and has the words "forgive me" tattooed on his arm—there was no ambiguity here.
>
> Except that in reality there was. I actually liked him, quite a bit, as a human being. We weren't dating, but then he would invite me out for an evening that sounded a whole lot like a date, and sometimes he would pay. We would talk on the phone for hours. With my head resting on his chest, he would ask me, "We like each other, we have fun, why aren't we dating?" as though it were actually something he was considering. He would ask me about my mom while running his fingers over the ridges of my ear—our naked, sweaty bodies pressed together. At some point I realized that, despite my insistence otherwise, I actually wanted those sorts of intimacies, only with an actual commitment. So, now we're "friends who do not sleep together" and he is continuing his two-year-long "friends with benefits" situation with his ex-girlfriend.[11]

This "friends with benefits" situation didn't work out for Clark-Flory, and on the face of it, it supports Stephens's view that "friends are the real benefits." However, you might argue that Clark-Flory needed this six-month affair to get through a difficult season of her life—she wasn't ready for a real relationship, she wanted the intimacy that sex involves, and it ultimately led her to a better understanding of her own desires. Was it a mistake for her to get involved with this guy?

Notes

1. Epicurus, Principal Doctrine VIII, in Brad Inwood and L. P. Gerson (eds.) *The Epicurus Reader: Selected Writings and Testimonia* (Indianapolis: Hackett, 1994), p. 32.
2. See Tim O'Keefe, "Epicurus," *The Internet Encyclopedia of Philosophy*, available online at www.iep.utm.edu/e/epicur.htm (accessed July 9, 2009).
3. Vatican Saying 33 reads: "The cry of the flesh: not to be hungry, not to be thirsty, not to be cold. For if someone has these things and is confident of having them in the future, he might contend even with [Zeus] for happiness." In Inwood and Gerson, *The Epicurus Reader*, p. 38.
4. Epicurus says "we believe that . . . if we do not have a lot we can make do with few, being genuinely convinced that those who least need extravagance enjoy it most." Letter to Menoeceus 130, in Inwood and Gerson, *The Epicurus Reader*, p. 30.
5. Epicurus, Vatican Saying LI, in R. M. Geer (ed.) *Letters, Principal Doctrines, and Vatican Sayings* (New York: Macmillan, 1985), pp. 69–70.
6. Epicurus, Vatican Saying LII, in Geer, *Letters, Principal Doctrines, and Vatican Sayings*, p. 70.
7. Epicurus, Principal Doctrine XXVII, in Inwood and Gerson, *The Epicurus Reader*, p. 34.
8. Epicurus, Vatican Saying XXXV, in Geer, *Letters, Principal Doctrines, and Vatican Sayings*, p. 68.
9. Epicurus, Principal Doctrine XXVII, in Inwood and Gerson, *The Epicurus Reader*, p. 34.
10. Epicurus, Vatican Saying XXXV, in Geer, *Letters, Principal Doctrines, and Vatican Sayings*, p. 68.
11. http://www.salon.com/2011/01/24/friends_with_benefits_2/

3

Virtue Ethics, Casual Sex, and Objectification

Raja Halwani

Is it OK to have casual sex? Halwani argues that it can be. First, he contends that casual sex is compatible with being virtuous, though we have to guard against treating sex as being more important than it is. Second, he argues that casual sex doesn't need to involve objectifying your partner. Although a casual sex partner is replaceable, he points that you have to attend to your partner's interests and desires to have a good sexual experience. So on Halwani's view, although there is a sense in which casual sex involves using one another, it isn't morally problematic.

Little has been written philosophically about casual sex. In any case, casual sex is not usually considered morally good, even if there is agreement that its practitioners tend to find it pleasurable. I shall discuss the ethics of casual sex, arguing that from the point of view of virtue whether casual sex is immoral depends on the case, but that in general it is not morally wrong in itself. I also discuss objectification,

Halwani, Raja. 2008. "Virtue Ethics, Casual Sex, and Objectification." In *Philosophy of Sex: Contemporary Readings 5E*, edited by Alan Soble and Nicholas Power, 338–346. Lanham, MD: Rowman & Littlefield. Reprinted with permission.

a phenomenon that is thought to find a natural home in casual sex, concluding that it does not deserve a sweeping negative moral judgment; it, too, requires case-sensitive judgments.

What Is Casual Sex?

It is difficult to define "casual sex" if we understand this to mean the provision of necessary and sufficient conditions (Halwani 2006). Casual sex is sexual activity that occurs outside the context of a love relationship. Usually, but not invariably, the parties who engage in it do so with the sole intention of deriving sexual pleasure from the act. Typical examples include two people picking each other up in a bar for the purpose of sex, people meeting through the Internet for sex and anonymous encounters in gay bath houses and straight swingers' clubs. Note some departures. First, the parties to a casual sexual encounter may not be motivated solely by sexual pleasure. Some do it for the money, as in sex between a prostitute and client and sex between pornography actors. Second, people sometimes engage in casual sex without intending to do so. Two people might pick each other up in a bar, proceed to have sex, yet they intended (or hoped) that it would lead to a relationship. As it happened, the sex does not lead to a relationship, so they end up having casual sex despite their intentions.

Virtue Ethics

Virtue ethics is often construed as a moral theory independent of, and perhaps rivaling, other theories, such as consequentialism and Kantian ethics. Most virtue ethicists mine the writings of the ancient Greek philosophers, especially Aristotle, to develop a plausible version.

Virtues and vices are character traits that dispose their possessor, the agent, to act according to their dictates (so to speak). On an Aristotelian view, the virtues are infused with wisdom, a form of practical intelligence that allows the agent to differentiate between what is right or proper to do, and what is wrong or improper to do. The virtues incline their agents not only to behave rightly, thereby judging rightly how to proceed in a particular situation but also to exhibit, when applicable, the proper emotions.

Consider courage. According to Aristotle, this virtue allows its agent to handle fear and dangerous situations properly. He claims that the courageous agent feels the right amount of fear when in danger; otherwise he would be either rash or cowardly (*NE* 1115b17–20). The goods for the sake of which the agent faces fear must be worthwhile.[1] Overcoming one's fear and stepping into the bathroom despite the presence of a cockroach does not count as being courageous—the good at stake is trivial. By contrast, overcoming fear of retribution and reprisals and speaking up in a crowded and hostile room in defense of an innocent victim would count as being courageous. Aristotle also requires[2] that the agent must act for the right reason or out of the right motive (this is also required by Kant). To be virtuous, the agent must speak up *because* an innocent victim must be defended and an injustice stopped, not because he is motivated by anticipated rewards for doing so.

Thus the virtuous agent is one who makes the right decision about what to do in a particular situation, makes this decision for the right reason, and feels the right kind and amount of any associated emotion.

Casual Sex and Virtue

A virtue ethics approach is neither inherently hostile to nor inherently in favor of sexual behavior. Aristotle's views on sex are found mostly in his treatment of temperance—the virtue that best expresses the proper attitudes and actions towards bodily desires. (Halwani 2003 [chap. 3], 2007a; Young 1988). Whether a sexual action or desire is permissible or worthwhile depends on the object of the actions or desire, much like whether fear is appropriate depends on its object.[3] One question, then, is: Are people's desires for casual sex permissible or worthwhile? Is there anything wrong with desiring to have casual sex?

Further, assuming that desires for casual sex are morally permissible, ought they be acted on? The *type* of desire, say, a desire for heterosexual, vanilla sex, might be morally impeccable, yet acting on it in a particular case (having sex with my best friend's spouse) might not be. There might be types of casual sex such that desiring them is wrong and indicative of a lack of virtue. For example, rape is wrong; if it is casual sex, then it is wrong casual sex, and both desiring it and acting on the desire would be wrong. Similar reasoning applies to sex with children. What seems to be wrong about rape, pedophilia, and so forth, is something other than the fact that they are casual. They involve coercion, manipulation, deception, and harm, to name a few moral faults. In these cases, desire indicates a defective character.

If we focus on the usual cases of casual sex, they seem not to include these faults. If two adults pick each other up in a bar with the intention and the knowledge that they are to have casual sex, what might be wrong? Setting objectification aside for a moment, and assuming—*contra* Kant—that sexual desire is not inherently morally suspicious, it would seem that nothing is wrong with desiring casual sex or acting on the desire as long as, from a virtue-centered perspective, two conditions are satisfied (beyond that the type of casual sex desired must avoid the standard wrong-making features).

The first condition is one which the advocates of virtues ethics must insist, given virtue theory's inclusion of character and motives under the moral umbrella: The agent's desire for casual sex should not consume his or her life. That is, desires should not be so strong or numerous that they overshadow other important aspects of life. Further, there might be something especially pernicious about letting sexual desire take control of one's life. The first condition is bound to be controversial. Why should no single activity take over one's life, if that activity is worthwhile? And if there is nothing morally wrong or vicious in general with a worthwhile activity taking control of one's life, why be suspicious of sex? Perhaps when it comes to casual sex the idea is that an agent's life being consumed by it is hard to defend, because sex is not sufficiently worthwhile to justify sacrificing other things. But casual sex is not special here, for life-consuming sex between a loving couple would perhaps not redeem such lives.

There is a tradition is philosophy and theology, which includes Plato, Augustine, and even John Stuart Mill, that doesn't view sexual pleasure as valuable. The pleasures and goods of sex, though intense, are brief and tend to vanish (as opposed to, say, the pleasures and goods of reading a book). One can fondly remember sexual encounters, and can even dwell on these memories, but this is not worthwhile, if the activities that one dwells on are not worthwhile to begin with. One can manifest excellence when it comes to sex, but this, too, amounts to little if the activity at which one excels is not worthwhile.

I think this view is largely correct. Although sex is pleasurable, it is not the sort of activity that ordinarily enriches the agent or leaves its mark on humanity. Here casual sex might be especially vulnerable, since one cannot redeem it even on the grounds that one meets interesting people and thereby enriches one's life (as it often said about taxi drivers). The meetings tend to be fleeting; they involve superficial conversations (if any) between strangers; one's partner (and oneself) may well be dull and shallow. Casual sex seems not to merit letting one's life revolve around it, let alone letting it consume one's life. However, the argument has limits: if casual sex and the desire for it are not all-consuming, they could satisfy the first condition.

The second condition is another one on which advocates of virtues ethics would insist: what motivates the parties in subject to moral assessment, and casual sex must be engaged in for the right reason. Sometimes those who are motivated by desire for sexual pleasure have other motives that actually account for their behavior. Having casual sex with X in order to spite Y, to make Y jealous, or to exact revenge on Y are morally pernicious motives.

Objectification

To objectify a person is to treat him or her only as an object. For examples, a person treats another as an object if the first uses the second as a chair while reading the paper. If objectification is always morally wrong and is an essential feature of casual sex, casual sex is always wrong. It would not avoid one of the standard wrong-making characteristics of acts. Further, it would be tainted to the extent that the desire for casual sex included the vicious motive of objectifying one's partner. Objectification poses a problem for anyone who thinks that casual sex is morally permissible.

Why assume that objectification is always morally wrong? Its moral wrongness cannot simply be read off from the definition; it is not obvious why treating an entity that is not an object (in particular, a person) only as an object constitutes conclusive grounds for moral condemnation. Something else must be added, to the effect that the person does not merit object-like treatment in virtue of some characteristic he has that morally blocks object-like treatment. So, in treating the person only as an object, one is trespassing this moral boundary. For persons, it might be their rationality, sophisticated desires and mental structures, hopes, wishes, happiness, capacity for flourishing, or their affinity to God that morally elevated them above objects. Note that any of these features—not only rationality—could be on the basis on which persons can legitimately demand nonobjectifying treatment. Objectification, then, though it has its natural home and origin in Kantian ethics, is a concept that fits well with other moral frameworks, including virtue ethics.

Why assume that objectification is an essential feature of casual sex? In typical cases of casual sex, two people engage in sex only for sexual pleasure. In doing so, we might argue, they use each other—treating each other as objects, as sophisticated dildos or plastic vaginas—for the purpose of pleasure. Even when one party has other reasons or motives (money), there is still objectification, for X uses Y to fulfill that purpose. This argument need not rely on the implausible assumption that in typical cases of casual sex the parties intend to objectify each other. Even if X does not intend to objectify Y, X still does so in and by using Y for sexual pleasure.

The defender of casual sex can argue that objectification is not an essential feature of casual sex, and that whether casual sex objectifies depends on the particular case. Casual partners do not usually think of each other as mere objects. A woman who picks up a man in a bar does so precisely because she thinks him a man, not a cleverly constructed robot or a penis with some sort of body attached to it. A gay man who sucks another's penis through a glory hole does so precisely because he thinks the penis is attached to a man, a man whom he likely saw earlier and was attracted to. Thus, the parties to casual sex usually desire interactions with other persons, not objects. On its own, this fact means little, for even as we know that our casual sexual partner is a person, we can nonetheless proceed to objectify him or her. But the fact is still important in reminding us that casual sexual interaction is close to many other types of human interaction, sexual and nonsexual. In casual sex, as elsewhere, we are aware of the humanity of others, and we usually attempt to respect their wishes, desires, and wants. Paying the grocer for the chewing gum, in a civil fashion, is a form of respect: I respect his wishes to be treated as a seller and kindly, not merely someone to be abused and robbed. This is no less true in casual sex; in typical cases, the partners attend each other's sexual needs, desires, and wishes.

Perhaps the defense of casual sex has gone through so easily because we have been employing a superficial definition of objectification. As argued by Martha Nussbaum (1995), objectification may be more complex, and treating someone as an object can take many forms and have different meanings. If so, a defense of casual sex should take this complexity into account. Of the seven senses of "objectification" Nussbaum lists, however, only two pose difficulties; the other five—denial of autonomy, inertness, violability, ownership, and denial of subjectivity—do not. On the contrary, what typically occurs during casual sex is the opposite. In taking into account my partner's sexual desires, I consider him to have autonomy, self-determination, and agency. Furthermore, I do not consider him to be violable, for I attribute to him boundaries and integrity in two ways: first, by not treating him contrary to his desires and, second, precisely by treating him in accordance with his desires. I also, for the same reason, do not treat him as an owned object. Finally in taking his sexual desires into account, I certainly do not treat him "as something whose experience and feelings . . . need not be taken into account" (257).

This leaves us with two objectifications, instrumentality and fungibility. Instrumentality is a problem only if the person is treated merely as a tool (which Nussbaum acknowledges, 265). But people frequently use each other as tools (students use teachers for educational purposes; teachers use students for career purposes). In interactions with each other, if we use each other as tools but also, in doing so, act in accordance with each other's wishes and desires, it seems that objectification disappears. Since in casual sex the partners typically do this, instrumentalization, understood as the *mere* use of another as a tool, is not a problem.

Fungibility—the treatment of something or someone "as interchangeable (a) with other objects of the same type, and/or (b) with objects of other types" (Nussbaum 1995, 257)—is an interesting type of objectification. When we objectify someone, he would make perfect sense were he to say, "I demand that I not be treated this way," given that we ought not to objectify people. However, fungibility does not license such reactions. Suppose I enter a coffee shop, do not like the selection, and go somewhere else. In doing so, I treat the owner of the store as fungible with other coffee shop owners. Yet for him to protest that I have wronged him in this treatment would be silly. Similarly, if I go to a bar in search of casual sex, no one can demand that I pick him or her up. In considering people as "interchangeable with other objects of the same type" I do nothing wrong. When objectification is wrong, others can demand of objectifiers that they, the objectified, not be objectified. This seems out of place regarding fungibility. Unless I have preexisting obligations, no one can demand of me that I purchase coffee from his shop rather than another shop or that I have sex with him instead of someone else.

The reason why fungibility seems wrong is that it is like treating people like pens or paper cups, discarding one and using another for our own purposes. But this indicates that fungibility is wrong when it occurs with actions that are otherwise wrong, in which case fungibility itself is not the problem, or when it occurs in special relationships. If I kidnap my neighbor's child and bring them a child from the local shelter, declaring "Have this one. He'll do," the wrongness is fungibility, but only because I acted, wrongly, as if no special relationship has existed between parents and child, that is, as if any child of a certain age would for them be an adequate substitute. Now, if I were in a bar cruising for a one-night stand, eyeing potential sexual partners, I would be treating them as fungible; I view them, individually, as interchangeable with other men in general or with other men of a particular sort, say, thirty-something Indian or Pakistani men ("of the same type"). But since none of them can rightly demand of me that I sleep with him, and since I cannot sexually impose myself on any one of them or demand any one of them that he sleep with me, in treating them as fungible I not only do not do them wrong, I do not objectify them. So fungibility, when it comes to casual sex, should be stricken from the list of possible ways to objectify others.

I have argued that virtue ethics morally permits casual sex in some cases but not in others. Moreover objectification in casual sex is much less frequent than thought; it requires morally nasty behavior in which casual sexual partners do not usually engage.

Comprehension Questions

1. Is every one-night stand an instance of casual sex? Why or why not?
2. How are character traits important within virtue ethics?
3. Why isn't virtue ethics inherently hostile to casual sex?
4. What are some reasons why it's wrong to objectify someone?

Discussion Questions

1. Are you inclined to be critical of people who have casual sex? Why or why not?
2. Are you convinced by Halwani's claim that casual sex needn't involve objectifying your partner? Why or why not?
3. Halwani says that casual sex is wrong if the desire for it consumes your life. What would it look like to have that desire consume your life? (Don't think about extreme cases. What's *the most ordinary way* for that desire to consume someone's life?)

Case

Consider this:

> It was Friday night. Ted was at his local bar having some drinks. He'd had just gotten out of a long relationship, and he was looking for something simple and commitment-free to shake off the last two years. Suddenly, a very pretty girl called Robin walked in to the bar with some of her friends. As it happened, Robin had just found out her boyfriend was cheating on her, and since they hadn't ended things officially, she was looking for a way to get back at him. After a short while, Robin and Ted found themselves chatting in a corner. After a few drinks, their stories came out. Neither person minded why the other was interested in sex. So, they ended up going back to Ted's place.

It's pretty clear that Ted is rebounding with Robin, which seems like a way of using her. It's also pretty clear that Robin is using Ted to get revenge on her (soon-to-be-ex-)boyfriend, which seems like a way of using Ted. Is this kind of casual sex morally OK? Why or why not?

Notes

1. *NE* 1115a10–15.
2. *NE* 1105a30–1105b1.
3. *NE* 1118b25.

References

Aristotle. 1999. [ca. 330 BCE] *Nicomachean Ethics*. Trans. Terence Irwin, 2nd ed. Indianapolis, Ind.: Hackett.

Halwani, Raja. 2003. *Virtuous Liaisons: Care, Love, Sex, and Virtue Ethics*. Chicago: Open Court.

Halwani, Raja. 2006. "Casual Sex." In Alan Soble, ed., *Sex from Plato to Paglia: A Philosophical Encyclopedia*. Westport, Conn.: Greenwood Press, 136–42.

Halwani, Raja. 2007a. "Sexual Temperance and Intemperance." In Raja Halwani, ed., *Sex and Ethics: Essays on Sexuality, Virtue, and the Good Life*. New York: Palgrave Macmillan, 122–33.

Nussbaum, Martha. 1995. "Objectification." *Philosophy and Public Affairs* 24: 249–91.

Nussbaum, Martha. 1995. "Objectification." *Philosophy and Public Affairs* 24: 257.

Nussbaum, Martha. 1995. "Objectification." *Philosophy and Public Affairs* 24: 265.

Young, Charles. 1988. "Aristotle on Temperance." *Philosophical Review* 97: 521–42.

4

Sexism in Practice
Feminist Ethics Evaluating the Hookup Culture

Conor Kelly

Everyone's hooking up (or so it might seem). But should we be OK
with the culture that casual sex has created? Conor Kelly thinks not.
He argues that hook up culture is sexist: women are made worse off
by the absence of commitment, language that creates sexual pressure,
excessive alcohol use, and social expectations to go along with the
crowd. From Kelly's feminist perspective, the hook up culture looks
like it offers freedom, but instead disempowers women.

Hooking up—the practice of pursuing sexual activity without
any expectation of a relationship—has become a fixture of the
U.S. college experience, resulting in an identifiable hookup
culture across the country that can and should benefit from a feminist
analysis. Sociological research reveals that this practice appeals to
college students by ostensibly providing greater independence than

---

An edited and modified version of: Kelly, Conor. 2012. "Sexism in Practice: Feminist Ethics
Evaluating the Hookup Culture." *Journal of Feminist Studies in Religion* 28(2): 27–48.
Reprinted with permission of Indiana University Press.

traditional relationships. An outside analysis of these claims, however, demonstrates that the heterosexual hookup culture operates in a decidedly sexist fashion. In fact, the four common features of this culture: lack of commitment, ambiguous language, alcohol use, and social pressure to conform, all undermine the freedom, equality, and safety of women on campus. An intentionally feminist perspective is in a unique position to highlight and critique these faults and the additional resources of feminist ethics have the potential to help change this sexism in practice.

On college campuses all across the country, a hookup culture appears as a unifying feature. Although an exact definition is difficult to pinpoint, scholars and students alike agree that a pursuit of some level of sexual activity without the constraints and expectations of a relationship is a common element of the U.S. college experience . . . Four common elements—a lack of commitment, an acceptance of ambiguity, a role for alcohol, and a social pressure to conform—make it possible to speak of an identifiable hookup culture across the collegiate landscape in the United States. . . .

[. . . The] primary commitment that men and women seek to avoid in the hookup culture is a long-term relationship. From a feminist perspective, this is particularly troubling because the avoidance of relationships builds implicitly upon an autonomous understanding of the self and a devaluation of relationality. [Feminist thought] has sought to correct both of these trends, suggesting that relationality is an integral piece of what it means to be human and critiquing the autonomous self as the byproduct of a predominantly male perspective.[1]

Reinforcing the claim that the hookup culture is based upon this troubling conception of the autonomous self, research shows that those who hook up identify the removal of relationships as one of the hookup culture's chief advantages because it preserves autonomy. Specifically, they view hooking up as a way to get sexual gratification without compromising their freedom.[2] This is hardly a surprising byproduct of U.S. culture, which traditionally places great emphasis on independence. High-achieving college students have been encouraged by both parents and peers to lead multitasking lives in which their success in academics and extracurricular activities is touted as their ticket to a bright future. Women in particular are placing higher burdens of perfection upon themselves, and assume that they can have a successful career or a love life, but never both. Love actually appears as a stumbling block to the independent, successful lives these students have been raised to expect, so hookups "appeal to them as useful, even necessary, in achieving what they want and what others want for them."[3] . . .

Other scholars have also noted the striking lack of dating in the traditional sense of a pair doing activities together and getting to know each other before moving to physical intimacy. Bogle has argued that the hookup culture is in essence a reversal of the once common dating "script," since it begins with sexual activity and has the potential (albeit a very small one) to lead to a relationship, whereas dating began with a relationship and had the potential to move to the physical level at a later date.[4] In the hookup framework, though, there are no clear steps to a relationship and there are few examples of what a relationship can or ought to look like in the aberrant situation when one should arise. As a result, students often imagine that a relationship is an overwhelming commitment that will completely consume their lives. They have no means to envision something between hookups and weddings.[5] So, on campuses all across America, students choose hookups now and postpone marriage for later. . . .

Beyond the avoidance of relationships and commitment, when students choose to hook up, the ambiguous nature of language in the hookup culture appears as another benefit. As mentioned before, when referring to specific practices, hooking up can mean anything from "fairly chaste making out" to sexual intercourse, depending on the situation and the person utilizing the term.[6] Researchers have found this to be the value of the phrase in the first place, with the ambiguity serving a curious double duty in female and male circles. In general, the imprecision provides women the opportunity to speak about hooking up without revealing the sorts of specifics that might damage reputations, while allowing men to suggest to their friends that they engaged in more sexual activity than they actually did.[7]

The very purpose of the ambiguity seems to be the creation of a level of privacy in what most college students assume to be a public element of their lives. Bogle suggests that this function is particularly important because her research discovered that college students believed their peers were constantly watching their sexual behavior and judging them for it.[8] In Stepp's view, college students have responded by developing "a vocabulary that gives them maximum freedom. The distance between what one says and what one means has never been greater."[9] For these students, simply to say that they "hooked up" with a classmate allows them to satisfy peer expectations without divulging too much detail and prevents others from challenging their behavior since what they say and what another person hears are not necessarily the same thing. Like the avoidance of committed relationships, the vague language allows for the preservation of one of a college student's most important assets: independence.

In addition to this linguistic open-endedness, a third common feature across the hookup culture is its connection with the party culture, specifically alcohol use. There is some disagreement over the exact role that alcohol plays in the practice of hooking up, with some students maintaining that alcohol is not a significant factor in their self-reported hookup experiences, and other research discovering the opposite. Freitas's interviews, for example, identified few instances in which her subjects had been drinking.[10] Stepp, however, wrote, "of the hundreds of young women I interviewed about hookup experiences, less than a half-dozen said they were sober at the time."[11] These discrepancies are most likely linked to the institutional differences among the subjects and varying types of research undertaken by these scholars.[12] Significantly, even at the schools where most students self-reported that their hookup habits did not involve alcohol, these same students still identified drinking as a key component of the hookup culture on their campus.[13] Regardless of what students self-report, it seems that alcohol is a central component in the social expectations of the hookup culture, even if it is not always an element in isolated practices. . . .

While alcohol, like noncommittal sex and ambiguous language, can be another element of the hookup culture that provides its participants with the independence they seem so desperately to crave, the prevalence of hooking up demands an initial sacrifice of freedom before bestowing these benefits. In fact, the social pressure to conform to the hookup culture is so great that students may feel absolute freedom when working within the script but no one has the liberty to avoid the system altogether. Certainly, abstaining from the hookup scene is possible, but this decision is rife with social consequences that all contribute to the perpetuation of the hookup culture.

The first element ensuring the hookup culture's power and prevalence is the potential for social marginalization. As mentioned in the discussion about the noncommittal nature of hookups, little space exists on campus for the development of relationships.[14] Thus students who wish to avoid the hookup culture leave themselves with few alternatives for forming intimate and romantic relationships while at college. As Bogle explains, these individuals "are on the margins of the social scene and they know it." For this reason, most of the students who choose to opt out of the hookup culture are already in committed relationships, usually with long-distance boyfriends or girlfriends.[15]

The second element arises from the fact that the hookup culture is the dominant form for relating between the sexes, with the result that every heterosexual college student seems to expect all his or her peers to follow its script. Indeed, while it may seem oxymoronic, Stepp adamantly insists that the hookup culture "is a way of thinking about relationships, period," so that in the midst of the hookup culture, young women and men assume that relationships never carry any form of commitment. Consequently, for individuals choosing to leave the hookup culture after they enter an exclusive relationship with someone else, the temptation to continue hooking up with individuals back on campus is always present and the general presumption against commitment offers no real reason to pursue strict fidelity. Underscoring this latter point, Stepp actually discovered that when college students did choose to make a commitment to an exclusive relationship, both individuals expected that their partners would likely cheat on them while they were apart. Additionally, due to the prevalence of the hookup script, men and women who remove themselves from the hookup culture run into difficulties should they attempt to have social lives on campus because other classmates presume that any interest—from dancing to talking—is a signal for a hookup. Truly, then, it is impossible to completely sever oneself from the hookup culture, no matter how distasteful one might find it.[16]

The Hookup Culture: Why Should It Be Concerning?

If certain elements of the hookup culture help students maintain their independence and if it serves their lifestyle, some might want to challenge the idea that anyone outside the culture itself should critique it.... Indeed, if any of the aforementioned arguments about independence holds true, then the case could be made that the hookup culture *itself* is not problematic. The truth of the matter, however, is that even the elements that afford participants freedom are more complex and more hazardous than the culture acknowledges. Bogle summarizes the situation quite succinctly, noting that "in many ways, the hookup system creates an illusion of choice. Although students may have many options about how they conduct themselves within the hookup culture, they cannot change the fact that hooking up is the dominant script on campus."[17] An outside perspective illustrates the sexism inherent in this arrangement, revealing that each of the four common features of the hookup culture operates in such a way as to put college students—especially women—at risk. . . .

To begin, removing commitment from the interactions between men and women produces three issues that challenge the assumption that a noncommittal existence provides the freedom that students allege they seek. First, a true expulsion of commitment requires a separation of emotions from physical activity that is challenging to accomplish. A number of students report feeling awkwardness toward their partners in the days after a hookup and both individuals appear unsure of how to proceed without any sense of obligation to each other.[18] Stepp acknowledges that this takes a substantial toll on women, whom she observed to have a more difficult time engaging in sexual activity in a way that removed attachment completely, and who readily blamed themselves "when, by what seem[ed] like accident or error, attachment [did occur]."[19] . . .

Second, researchers have found that however much young men and women value freedom, they do not actually wish to eschew all relationships. Admittedly, the extent to which this is a problem seems to vary by sex and age. Bogle observed that when men and women arrive on campus, both seem to want the same freedom to play the field, so to speak.[20] As time goes on, though, women quickly become disenchanted with the hookup culture, hoping for something more. . . .

[Scholars] have also raised concerns about the challenges an abandonment of commitment poses for future relationships. Zimmerman has argued that the skills the hookup culture encourages young men and women to develop—specifically a detachment from emotion in relationships and an aversion to commitment—are not only unhelpful for creating and sustaining relationships and marriages later in life, they are antithetical [to the skills needed for long-term commitment].[21] . . .

The reliance on ambiguous language further contests the perceived benefits of the hookup culture in much the same vein.

First, just as a lack of commitment may be a detriment to future relationships, the ambiguity in language has the potential to stifle the development of character traits that would promote healthy interactions between the sexes. As Stepp pinpoints, relationships, and the trust upon which they are built, require frank conversations. This task is hardly aided by years of employing ambiguous language. The fact that this vagueness develops around relationships and sexual activity only serves to increase the possibility for future challenges.[22]

In addition, one of the most beneficial traits of the ambiguity embedded in the term *hooking up* is its ability to leave as much as possible to the imagination of the listener.[23] Intentionally or otherwise, this has the end result of fostering some level of misperception about the sorts of practices in which college students are actually choosing to engage. This might not seem like much of a problem, but as Bogle notes, in a culture with few rules to guide students' behavior, perceptions about what one's peers are doing play a huge role in determining how far individuals are willing to go sexually with a hookup partner.[24] In general, college students believe their classmates are all engaging in more promiscuous activity than they themselves have experienced, a view that the research does not support.[25] This belief is at least facilitated, if not directly caused, by the ambiguous nature of the language surrounding hooking up and only serves to encourage individuals to pursue riskier activities than they might choose on their own.[26] . . .

Like the value of ambiguous language, the supposed assets of alcohol's role in the hookup culture are also challenged by a negative potential to facilitate risky behavior. To begin, a belief that one's drunkenness will exculpate bad decisions can, and ostensibly does, lead individuals to make more perilous choices in deciding with whom to hook up and how far to go. Of primary concern, however, is the way in which an inebriation-induced lack of control puts women at risk for rape and sexual assault. This is particularly dangerous for women who may want to hook up but not have intercourse. To achieve this goal, the hookup culture requires them to express some interest in a partner. For some men, this initial attention is the only thing they see, and they choose to interpret a woman's later resistance as inauthentic after the first expression of attraction. This view is only encouraged by the popular belief among males in the hookup culture that they are entitled to sexual gratification and that women who express interest in them will be at their beck and call. Couple this with the fact that women will often drink in order to lower their inhibitions when they begin this process, and a woman's capacity to offer resistance can be further limited. What is just as troubling as these male expectations is the notion taught to and accepted by some females that it is a woman's responsibility to look after herself and not get into a position where she is uncomfortable or loses control. . . .

Lack of control in the hookup culture is not created by alcohol alone, though. The prevalence of social pressure to hook up, and the lack of viable alternatives, are just as restrictive. Once again, for a variety of reasons, it affects women more than men. For example, women must deal with a separate set of social pressures than men do: the legacy of the feminist movement. It may seem counterintuitive, but Stepp insists that "feminism is undeniably a driving force behind the phenomenon of hooking up."[27] In particular, Bogle notes that the push for full equality between the sexes in the early years of feminism contributed to a decrease in the viability and prevalence of dating as the main process for finding a spouse.[28] The initial message of female empowerment and total equality has been interpreted to say that women should participate in the hookup culture in order to match the freedom of men, who have (as a sex, on the whole) traditionally pursued sexual activity for individual gratification without worrying about consequences. As a result, women are told, and sometimes accept, that enjoying the freedoms of the hookup culture is supposed to be an empowering experience. One female Duke student told Stepp, "A strong woman who desired a particular man should, provided he was willing, be able to take that man to bed and do whatever she damn well pleased. . . . If she couldn't do this, she wasn't really empowered."[29] . . .

Further underscoring the conclusion that the structures of the hookup culture are skewed against women, a double standard clearly exists with regard to conduct. While the pressure to conform encourages women to participate in the social scene by hooking up, Bogle notes they are repeatedly scrutinized as they do so. As Freitas observes, female students have to walk a fine line between playing the social games of the hookup culture enough to maintain status while avoiding the "slut" label for participating too much. The discriminatory quality of this tension is clearly evident in comparison with the experience of male students in Bogle's research. Unlike women, men in the hookup culture quickly learn that promiscuity on their part is either identified jokingly or for the sake of praise. As a result, men have virtually no restrictions on their hookup habits while women have to carefully navigate a set of unwritten rules in order to avoid ruining their reputations. Should their reputations be damaged, women can expect either social marginalization or a shrinking pool of viable hookup partners, since few men would be willing to hook up with a known "slut."[30] . . .

Combining all these negative implications identified by a feminist analysis, the conclusion is clearly that the four central elements of the hookup culture offer only the perception of freedom. While this is arguably true for both sexes, it is indisputably the case for women. The removal of commitment places an undue burden upon all students to separate their emotions, deny their actual desires, and inhibit their potential for future relationships. The ambiguous language encourages them to avoid frank conversations with their friends and leaves them with little guidance beyond a constant pressure to go further sexually, while the presence of alcohol as a crutch puts women at greater risk for assault. Last, the social pressures to participate in the hookup culture are magnified for women, and work more for men's interests. All of this is worsened by the fact that "alternatives" to this phenomenon are perhaps even more damaging for women and their social standing. Placed alongside the positive claims about the fostering of independence, these challenges offer a more complete picture of what the hookup culture actually entails and highlight its sexist nature.

Comprehension Questions

1. According to Kelly, what are the four features of U.S. hookup culture?
2. What does Kelly mean when he says that the hookup culture is a reversal of the dating "script"?
3. What are some consequences of the ambiguity of the phrase, "hooked up"?
4. In what sense might someone think that hookup culture promotes independence? Why, exactly, is Kelly skeptical of that idea?
5. Why does Kelly think that hookup culture makes it harder to develop committed relationships?
6. What is the double standard in hookup culture?

Discussion Questions

1. College students tend to overestimate how sexually active their peers are, and Kelly says that the ambiguities of the term "hookup" partly explain that. What do you think of that explanation? And what else might explain why students think that their peers have more sex than they do?

2. Kelly says that you can be socially marginalized if you opt not to participate in hookup culture. Is that true to your experience? If so, why do you think that happens? If not, how would you explain why some people feel marginalized for not participating?

3. Kelly says that feminism helped create hookup culture, insofar as feminism has always pressed for female empowerment. However, he's skeptical about the kind of "empowerment" that hookup culture represents. Why is he critical of that form of empowerment? What, in his view, would a better version look like? Do *you* think that hookup culture promotes true empowerment? Why or why not?

Case

Consider this:

> In the first experimental study to examine this issue, researchers found an imbalanced gender ratio affects views about casual sex for both men and women in ways that people may not consciously realize. . . . In one experiment, 129 heterosexual university students (82 women, 47 men) read one of two fake news articles stating that colleges in the local surrounding area were becoming either more female-prevalent or male-prevalent. The participants then completed a survey about their attitudes toward casual sex and their prior sexual history. . . . When the gender ratio was favorable (one's own gender was in the minority), both men and women adopted more traditional sexual roles with women less interested in casual sex than men, according to the study findings. When the gender ratio was unfavorable (one's own gender was in the majority), those roles shifted as men and women tried to appear more desirable to the opposite sex. If there were more women than men, women stated they were more willing to engage in casual sex. If there were more men than women, men tended to place less importance on casual sex and be more open to long-term commitment.[31]

There are slightly more college-aged males in the United States than there are college-aged females (roughly 51/49). However, there are significantly fewer males enrolled in college than there are females enrolled in college (45/55). This suggests that there might be additional, structural pressure on women to engage in casual sex, whether or not that's their considered preference. What do you make of this? Does it help Kelly's case, or is it irrelevant? Either way, why?

Notes

1. For a comprehensive account of this strand in feminism, see Catherine Keller, *From a Broken Web: Separation, Sexism, and Self* (Boston: Beacon Press, 1986), esp. 1–6.
2. Norval Glenn and Elizabeth Marquardt, *Hooking Up, Hanging Out, and Hoping for Mr. Right: College Women on Dating and Mating Today* (New York: Institute for American Values, 2001), 21–22; and Laura Sessions Stepp, *Unhooked: How Young Women Pursue Sex, Delay Love, and Lose at Both* (New York: Riverhead Books, 2007), 36–37, 81.
3. Stepp, *Unhooked*, 169, 172, 174–75, quotation on 38.
4. Kathleen A. Bogle, *Hooking Up: Sex, Dating, and Relationships on Campus* (New York: New York University Press, 2008), 47–48.
5. Stepp, *Unhooked*, 190.
6. See Donna Freitas, *Sex and the Soul: Juggling Sexuality, Spirituality, Romance, and Religion on America's College Campuses* (Oxford: Oxford University Press, 2008), 119.
7. Glenn and Marquardt, *Hooking Up, Hanging Out*, 22; and Bogle, *Sex, Dating, and Relationships*, 28.
8. Bogle, *Sex, Dating, and Relationships*, 72.
9. Stepp, *Unhooked*, 28.
10. Freitas, *Sex and the Soul*, 140.
11. Stepp, *Unhooked*, 115.
12. Freitas, for example, created an online survey and followed up with on-campus interviews in a structured environment. See Freitas, *Sex and the Soul*, 11–12. Stepp's "research" occurred while following her interviewees to bars, clubs, and parties. See Stepp, *Unhooked*, 13.
13. Freitas, *Sex and the Soul*, 95.
14. See Glenn and Marquardt, *Hooking Up, Hanging Out*, 25–28. See also Bogle, *Sex, Dating and Relationships*, 126.
15. Bogle, *Sex, Dating, and Relationships*, 71, quotation on 69, 65.
16. Stepp, *Unhooked*, quotation on 5, 135, 51–52.
17. Bogle, *Sex, Dating, and Relationships*, 184.
18. Bogle, *Sex, Dating, and Relationships*, 40; see also Glenn and Marquardt, *Hooking Up, Hanging Out*, 17.
19. Stepp, *Unhooked*, quotation on 121, see also 25, 226–27.
20. Bogle, *Sex, Dating, and Relationships*, 97.
21. Kari-Shane Davis Zimmerman, "In Control? The Hookup Culture and the Practice of Relationships," in *Leaving and Coming Home: New Wineskins for Catholic Sexual Ethics*, ed. David Cloutier (Eugene, OR: Wipf and Stock Publishers, 2010).
22. Stepp, *Unhooked*, 241.
23. Bogle, *Sex, Dating, and Relationships*, 28.

24. Ibid., 74, 89.
25. Ibid., 77, 82.
26. Ibid., 37; see also Stepp, *Unhooked*, 106, 124.
27. Stepp, *Unhooked*, 143.
28. Bogle, *Sex, Dating, and Relationships*, 21–22.
29. Stepp, *Unhooked*, 33, quotation on 142.
30. Bogle, *Sex, Dating, and Relationships*, 73; Freitas, *Sex and the Soul*, 95; and Bogle, *Sex, Dating, and Relationships*, 104–6, 112–14.
31. http://www.sciencedaily.com/releases/2015/12/151209105057.htm

===== ✿ =====

5

Sexual Privacy

Laurie Shrage and Robert Stewart

Privacy matters to us. However, it isn't always clear why it matters to us, or how important privacy is compared to other things we value. Shrage and Stewart introduce us to some distinctions and theories that can help on this score. Then, they turn to explore the issue of sexting and privacy. Is there anything that shouldn't be shared via Snapchat? They also raise questions about how we should punish privacy violations, as well as how technology makes privacy that much harder to protect.

Privacy can take at least three forms: (i) control over who has access to sensitive information about us (informational privacy), (ii) access to physical spaces where our activities are not visible to others (physical privacy), and (iii) control over important life decisions without undue interference from others (decisional privacy). In terms of our sexual lives, we generally want to protect all three types of privacy. For example, the decision to use birth control and engage in non-procreative sex is one that, some argue, should be encompassed under the third form of privacy. Being able to keep from public view information about our sexual interests and relationships, or images of our intimate activities, involves the first two forms of privacy. In this digital age, where images and information can travel great distances in a matter of seconds, it is becoming especially difficult to protect the first two types, so we will focus below on violations of informational and physical privacy. Moral and political philosophers are especially interested in understanding when our expectations of privacy are reasonable, and when these expectations should be respected by others and protected by our government. For example, . . . when someone takes and sends images of us to others that show us in our so-called "private moments" (e.g., in bed, getting undressed, kissing someone, etc.) is this always wrong?

Why Is Sexual Privacy Important?

Political theorists draw a distinction between the public and private spheres. Simply put, in a democratic state, there should be a domain of activity beyond the government's reach. A robust private sphere or "civil society" is necessary for a democracy, where citizens have the freedom to communicate about public matters, criticize their government, practice their faith, organize their family lives, and so on. The civil society includes private, nongovernmental organizations and associations, such as the press, houses of worship, and the family, and is a "public" sphere, in the sense that it can be a space for democratic deliberation and non-market exchanges.

There are many meanings to the term "private," including "nongovernmental" and the three senses identified [earlier]. Similarly, the term "public" has different meanings, and very often these terms overlap. For example, a news organization may be private in the sense of not being owned or sponsored by the government, but it can be publicly owned, in the sense of selling ownership shares to members of the public, and it mainly exists to serve the general public. Reporters claim the right to keep their sources private (informational privacy), and to make decisions about what to publish without undue government interference (decisional privacy). Sexual conduct can be both private and public, in these different ways. Most sexual conduct is not visible to third parties (e.g., is physically private), but it can occur in public venues, such as beaches or "adult" clubs, and, in these places, such conduct may be visible to others. Information and decisions about our sexual lives are generally beyond the reach of the government (and other third parties), except when our sexual conduct poses a nuisance to, or threatens to harm, others.

In this chapter, we shall explore why protecting the privacy of our sexual lives is important.

It will be helpful at the outset of this discussion to consider why privacy, in general, is important. The philosopher James Rachels has isolated three distinct, though connected, views about this matter: the conventional view, the core person view, and the view that privacy is necessary for maintaining a variety of personal relationships.[1]

Conventional View

On this view, privacy is important because it enables us to keep our secrets. This is significant, in turn, because revealing these secrets could be harmful or detrimental to us in some way. Revealing our sexual secrets might merely embarrass us or others, but in some cases it could damage our reputations, cause tensions among our families or friends, or make us more vulnerable to discriminatory treatment.

Core Person View

On this view, there are integral parts of myself that I show to only some of the people with whom I interact. Thomas Nagel presents a view of this sort when he explains that, if we couldn't keep private a lot about ourselves and what goes through our heads in a typical day, life would be impossible. Making ourselves transparent to others takes work, and it isn't necessary for much of our dealings with people, so we generally don't share many aspects of our core self with others—especially sexual aspects. According to Nagel,

> most of us, when sexually engaged, do not wish to be seen by anyone but our partners; full sexual expression and release leave us entirely vulnerable and without a publicly presentable "face." Sex transgresses these protective boundaries, breaks us open, and exposes the uncontrolled and unpresentable creature underneath; that is its essence. We need privacy in order not to have to integrate our sexuality in its fullest expression with the controlled surface we present to the world.[2]

Nagel here suggests that privacy is important so that the unruly or unvarnished aspects of ourselves can be detached to some degree from our public selves. Rachels points out, however, that it isn't just our beastly, "uncontrolled and unpresentable" selves that we want to keep separate from our public personas; we also want to leave out some very mundane aspects of ourselves, such as how often we do or don't have sex.[3]

The view that privacy is necessary for maintaining a variety of personal relationships

Personal relationships are defined, in part, by how much we share about ourselves. Without the ability to close off parts of ourselves to others, there would be little distinction between friends with whom we are intimate and acquaintances with whom we are not. In "Why Lovers Can't Be Friends," James Conlon[4] suggests that different types of relationships— from the most intimate to the casual—ought to be compared to different genres of literature, each with its own definitional and evaluative criteria. This isn't to claim, according to Conlon, that our relationships form a hierarchy of intimacy or shared secrets, starting with acquaintances at the bottom and lovers at the top. Such hierarchies imply that those at the top know more about us than anyone else. Yet it is possible that our long-time best friend knows things about us that our lover does not, and that even our colleagues, at least with respect to our work lives, know things about us that our lover or best friend does not know. What Conlon's (and Rachels's) view does imply is that the various relationships we have are, in part, defined by the *kinds* as well as the *amounts* of information we share. Hence, a lover typically has more information about our sex life than a friend, while a long-time friend may know more about our childhood.

Rachels prefers this third view of the value of privacy. The conventional view implies that privacy is about keeping secrets, or preventing others from knowing the truth about us in order to avoid harm. The core person view suggests that there are aspects of ourselves we need to keep hidden because they are too raw or unprocessed. By contrast, the third view suggests that privacy is less about hiding ugly truths or primitive selves, and more about differentiating relationships with others and understanding the kinds of sharing that are appropriate or inappropriate to each.

Of course, sometimes people share personal aspects of themselves indiscriminately, such as when someone writes a memoir about a past love relationship, or performs as an exotic dancer. Privacy rules are valuable not so much to restrict sharing, but rather to prevent forced sharing. We often appreciate writers and performers (and even friends) who share things that most of us keep private, as they have trusted us with their story or creativity so we might learn something or be entertained. Yet even writers and entertainers maintain different levels of intimacy with different people and audiences. In the remainder of this chapter, we will assume that Rachels's third view best explains the value of privacy.

When Does "Sexting" Violate a Person's Privacy?

"Sexting" involves using electronic messaging to send text, photos, or video that contain sexual content.[5] Most of the uproar over sexting is over the sharing of nude or sexually explicit images.[6] Although adults can engage in sexting—for example, former US congressman Anthony Weiner was caught sexting in 2011—sexting creates more concern when it occurs among minors.[7] Sexting surveys offer us some idea of the prevalence of sexting, though their figures vary. Some report that only 4 percent of cell-owning teens (12–17) have sexted, while others maintain that as many as 20 percent of teens (13–19) and 33 percent of young adults (20–26) have done so. The surveys also suggest that more teens and young adults have received a sext message than have sent one, with the numbers ranging from 15 to 31 percent.[8] Teens most frequently sext with a current boyfriend or girlfriend, but they sometimes sext with someone they are romantically pursuing, a close friend, or someone they barely know or only know online.[9]

. . . The recent case of Rehtaeh Parsons is becoming too common. Rehtaeh was a teenager from Dartmouth, Nova Scotia, who committed suicide when she was seventeen years old. In November 2011, when she was fifteen, she attended a party with a friend where she was allegedly raped by four young men. According to many reports, she was so intoxicated that she had trouble standing and walking, when one man allegedly sexually assaulted her. It was during that assault that a photo was taken, which then circulated widely within three days of the event. As a result of the electronic messaging showing her assault, Rehtaeh became, bizarrely, the victim of "cyberbullying" by other teenagers in her school, who called her a "slut." A year after the incident, the Royal Canadian Mounted Police (RCMP) stated that there was "insufficient evidence to lay charges."[10] The distribution of photos of her rape is believed to have led to Rehtaeh Parsons's suicide.

One issue is whether the police mishandled the investigation of the rape, which is controversial. What is uncontroversial, however, is that those who took photos of the rape and then distributed them widely by electronic means, without Rehtaeh's consent, acted unethically and with appalling meanness and callousness. Moreover, many recipients of the images compounded her assault by publicly attacking her, thereby escalating her humiliation and the psychological damage it caused. Fortunately, most cases of sexting do not involve rape and, generally, they do not trigger the kind of cyberbullying to which Rehtaeh was subjected. Yet sexts exchanged among teenagers frequently involve violations of privacy. Given the nature of the technology, it is exceedingly easy for a "private" interchange between two people to get communicated publicly to a great number of people at an incredibly fast rate.[11] According to some recent surveys, 14 percent of teens (13–19) said they have shared a sext message with someone other than the person it was originally meant for, and 29 percent of teens said they have had sext messages shared with them that were not meant for them to see.[12]

How Should Violations of Sexual Privacy Be Treated and Punished?

As we noted [earlier], there are different kinds of privacy that we value and want protected. One form involves controlling who has access to sensitive information about ourselves, such as our medical or school records, our sexual tastes and history, or any history of criminal charges or convictions. Another form of privacy involves the ability to make decisions about one's personal life without undue interference from others. A third form of privacy involves being able to control who can see or hear, or otherwise monitor, our ordinary, daily physical acts.[13] In many countries there are laws or constitutional provisions that aim to protect informational, decisional, and physical privacy. For example, many countries restrict access to a person's medical or school records, limit the government's authority to search our homes or our cell phones, limit the government's power to spy on its citizens, and limit the government's power to interfere with the decisions people make about their nonpublic sexual activities or their reproductive options.

In 2012, a Rutgers University student was convicted of invading the privacy of his roommate when he used a webcam to spy on his roommate's intimate activities with another man.[14] Tragically, the victim committed suicide several days after the incident. In this case, the victim's informational and physical privacy were violated. The perpetrator disclosed, without consent, his roommate's sexual orientation and dormroom activities to others, by sharing a webcam video stream from his computer with friends over the Internet. This case was probably more vigorously prosecuted than others because the violations of privacy contributed to a suicide, although the link to the suicide was difficult to prove. However, had the victim not committed suicide, the accused's actions still involved a criminal invasion of privacy, as the victim had the "reasonable expectation of privacy" (under U.S. law) regarding his actions or property in his dorm room.

Determining when and where a person should have a reasonable expectation of privacy is somewhat complicated.[15] Should we have it in a store dressing room, a public restroom, a hospital waiting room, or the office space our employer provides? Do we have a reasonable expectation of privacy with regard to our phone call records, our library borrowing records, or our bank account records? And when can this expectation or right be denied: when someone is on parole, when there are signs posted that security cameras are operating, or when we've discarded our personal materials in a public wastebin? The Rutgers case was not a difficult one in terms of privacy: We generally have a reasonable expectation of privacy in our own homes, even when our curtains are not drawn or someone is using a camera, and a dorm room is analogous to a home.

Sexual privacy involves all three forms of privacy mentioned above. We should be able to restrict access to information about our non-public sexual activities and thoughts—information that could be gleaned from medical or other institutional records, or from documents in our homes, such as photos, personal letters, or books. We should also be free from coercion or interference by others when we make decisions about our nonpublic sexual activities. Furthermore, we should have a high degree of control over who can view our nonpublic sexual acts. When these forms of privacy are violated by governmental or nongovernmental agents, we should be able to seek remedies under our criminal or civil law.

But there are many borderline cases. Consider, for example, whether people should have a legally protected expectation of privacy in the following situations. Suppose someone shares personal information on Facebook, and restricts access using various privacy settings, but the information leaks to those who were not given permission to view it. Or suppose someone takes a picture of two people kissing in a car, but viewable from a public street, and then makes the picture public. Suppose someone sees you buy gay porn in a public venue, and then casually mentions this in front of your friends. Suppose a former lover tells stories about what you were like in bed in his next novel, but does not use your name. Suppose he posts nude photos of you that you once gave him.[16] Suppose your employer announces that he disapproves of premarital sex and adultery, and will fire any employee who is found to engage in such practices. Suppose your employer disapproves of non-procreational sex and will not offer health insurance that covers contraception. Suppose you inadvertently discover that a friend of yours is transgender and you disclose this to another person, who later physically assaults your friend. Suppose your roommate thinks you're asleep and begins to have sex with her partner, but you're only pretending to be asleep so you can watch.

All of the cases above involve invasions of privacy, but the difficult issue is whether these invasions are serious enough to warrant criminal or civil action. How serious we take them to be will probably depend on how damaging they are to the victims and how reasonable we find a person's expectation of privacy in such circumstances. Another issue concerns who should be charged in any given privacy violation: a commercial website that publishes an image and that may stand to profit from it, or an individual who shares information or material received legally and who does not benefit financially from sharing it? The constant introduction of new technologies will make it increasingly difficult to protect the forms of privacy we value. Nevertheless, ethicists, legislators, legal scholars, and concerned citizens will need to devise new rules and procedures for protecting our privacy, including our sexual privacy.

Comprehension Questions

1. What's the difference between informational, physical, and decisional privacy?
2. What's the difference between the conventional, "core person," and "differentiating relationships" views of privacy?
3. What are some examples of situations in which we do, and don't, have a clear expectation of privacy?

Discussion Questions

1. Suppose your ex sent you a bunch of sexy pictures over the course of your relationship. Is it always wrong to share those pictures with someone else? If so, is that just because of privacy considerations, or is something else at stake?
2. Someone might say that if you don't want sexy pictures of you to be shared with unintended audiences, then you shouldn't share them at all. Is this good advice? Why or why not?
3. You suspect that your roommate is having sex with one of your friends in your dorm room. Is it a violation of their privacy to try to find out whether that's true? Why or why not? And if not, then what investigative methods are in and out of bounds?

Case

One of my students shared this with me:

> A few years back, my friend Alice had her first experience with a guy who was interested in sexting. She's always been rather conservative in her beliefs, her outward appearance, and even to the things she listened to. If not for the fact that we have been friends since elementary, I likely would have never gotten along with her since we're very different. However, because of this conservative lifestyle, she found herself in a dilemma when it came to sexting for the first time. Her boyfriend sent her a message, and she really liked him and wanted to make him happy. But not only did she not know how to even begin writing that kind of stuff, she didn't even know if she felt comfortable writing that kind of stuff. So, she wanted to consult me for advice. First, we talked through whether she should sext with him at all. I told her that sexting is really up to the couple; it works for some and for some it doesn't. Alice was really concerned about disappointing him, and I told her that while I understand that she wants to please him, she needs to be more concerned about herself. If she's not comfortable with it, then let him know. A reasonable boyfriend would understand and at the very least would wait until she's more comfortable being that open with him. Then, she decided that she wanted to start sexting, but she needed some tips. The problem was that she wasn't sure whether she should show me what he'd sent her, and I said that I couldn't give her real advice unless I knew what he'd sent. Do you think it would be OK for her to show me?

What do you think? Is it OK for Alice to show her friend what her boyfriend had sent?

Another student shared this story with me:

> A friend asked me if I would think about her differently if she told me she had sexted the other night with a guy she really didn't like in real life. She said he's the type of guy she isn't interest in, but he kept texting her. She said she did it just because he kept texting her, and she felt badly for him. Still, she ended up having fun and didn't feel guilty about it. I asked her if she would do it again if he texted her again. She said that she probably would, but she wouldn't do anything more with him.
>
> I had no comment because she was my friend. However, I really didn't think it was right of her: it was insensitive to the guy. I thought of how the guy might be feeling. He may be happy and think he now has some type of chance of doing more, but to her he's just a way to pass the time.

What do you think of this student's assessment of her friend's behavior?

Notes

1. James Rachels, "Sex and Personal Privacy," paper delivered in Cape Town, South Africa, August, 1999, http://www.jamesrachels.org/sex.pdf; James Rachels, "Why Privacy Is Important," *Philosophy and Public Affairs* 4, no. 4 (1975): 323–33, http://www.jstor.org/stable/pdfplus/2265077.pdf?acceptTC=true.
2. Quoted in Rachels, "Sex and Personal Privacy," 9.
3. Ibid.
4. James Conlon, "Why Lovers Can't Be Friends," in *Philosophical Perspectives on Sex and Love*, ed. Robert M. Stewart (Oxford & New York: Oxford University Press), 295–300.
5. See, e.g., Elizabeth Eraker, "Stemming Sexting: Sensible Legal Approaches to Teenager Exchange of Self-Produced Pornography," *Berkeley Technology Law Journal* 25 (2010): 555–671, http://www.btlj.org/data/articles/25_1/0555-0596%20Eraker_Web.pdf.
6. Richard Chalfen, "'It's Only a Picture': Sexting, 'Smutty' Snapshots and Felony Charges," *Visual Studies* 24, no. 3 (2009): 258–68.
7. K. Albury, K. Crawford, and P. Byron, *Young People and Sexting in Australia: Ethics, Representation and the Law*, ARTC Centre for Creative Industries and Innovation/Journalism and Media Research Centre, University of New South Wales, Australia, 2013, http://www.cci.edu.au/node/1522.
8. See Amanda Lenhart, "Teens and Sexting: Pew Internet Survey," 2009, http://www.pewinternet.org/Reports/2009/Teens-and-Sexting/Main-Report/1-The-PIP-Study.aspx; and National Campaign to Prevent Teen and Unplanned Pregnancy, *Sex and Tech: Results from a Survey of Teens and Young Adults*, 2008, http://thenationalcampaign.org/resource/sex-and-tech.
9. Luke Gilkerson,"Sexting Statistics: What Do the Surveys Say?" Covenanteyes.com, January 10, 2012, http://www.covenanteyes.com/2012/01/10/sexting-statistics-what-do-the- surveys-say/.
10. Selena Ross, "Who Failed Rehtaeh Parsons?" *The Chronicle Herald*, April 9, 2013, http:// thechronicleherald.ca/metro/1122345-who-failed-rehtaeh-parsons.
11. Chalfen, "'It's Only a Picture,'" 261.
12. See, e.g., National Campaign to Prevent Teen and Unplanned Pregnancy, *Sex and Tech*.
13. Judith De Cew, "Privacy," *The Stanford Encyclopedia of Philosophy* (2013), http://plato.stanford.edu/entries/privacy/.
14. Emily Bazelon, "Dharun Ravi Found Guilty," *Slate*, March 16, 2012, http://www.slate.com/articles/news_and_politics/crime/2012/03/rutgers_spying_verdict_dharun_ravi_found_guilty_of_invading_the_privacy_of_tyler_clementi.html
15. See Electronic Frontier Foundation, "Surveillance Self-Defense," https://ssd.eff.org/en.
16. See http://www.huffingtonpost.com/huff-wires/20131115/us-revenge-porn/.

=== 🍒 ===

6

Date Rape's Other Victim

Katie Roiphe

···

Are we facing a rape crisis? Katie Roiphe doesn't think so. Instead, she argues that some feminists define rape too broadly—so broadly that *regretted* sex counts as rape. This is bad in itself, since it creates a culture of fear. Worse, though, Roiphe claims that "rape crisis feminists" are setting back women's interests by denying their sexual autonomy. In other words, they're treating women in a way that they'd never treat men: namely, as less than fully responsible for what they do, as less than fully able to communicate and act on their sexual desires.

···

One in four college women has been the victim of rape or attempted rape. One in four. I remember standing outside the dining hall in college, looking at a purple poster with this statistic written in bold letters. It didn't seem right. If sexual assault was really so pervasive, it seemed strange that the intricate gossip networks hadn't picked up more than one or two shadowy instances of rape. If I was really standing in the middle of an "epidemic," a "crisis"—if 25 percent of my women friends were really being raped—wouldn't I know it?

Roiphe, Katie. 1993. "Date Rape's Other Victim." *New York Times* Magazine, June 13, 1993. Reprinted with permission of the author.

These posters were not presenting facts. They were advertising a mood. Preoccupied with issues like date rape and sexual harassment, campus feminists produce endless images of women as victims—women offended by a professor's dirty joke, women pressured into sex by peers, women trying to say no but not managing to get it across.

This portrait of the delicate female bears a striking resemblance to that 1950s ideal my mother and other women of her generation fought so hard to leave behind. They didn't like her passivity, her wide-eyed innocence. They didn't like the fact that she was perpetually offended by sexual innuendo. They didn't like her excessive need for protection. She represented personal, social and intellectual possibilities collapsed, and they worked and marched, shouted and wrote to make her irrelevant for their daughters. But here she is again, with her pure intentions and her wide eyes. Only this time it is the feminists themselves who are breathing new life into her.

Is there a rape crisis on campus? Measuring rape is not as straightforward as it might seem. Neil Gilbert, a professor of social welfare at the University of California at Berkeley, questions the validity of the one-in-four statistic. Gilbert points out that in a 1985 survey undertaken by *Ms. Magazine* and financed by the National Institute of Mental Health, 73 percent of the women categorized as rape victims did not initially define their experience as rape; it was Mary Koss, the psychologist conducting the study, who did.

One of the questions used to define rape was: "Have you had sexual intercourse when you didn't want to because a man gave you alcohol or drugs?" The phrasing raises the issue of agency. Why aren't college women responsible for their own intake of alcohol or drugs? A man may give her drugs, but she herself decides to take them. If we assume that women are not all helpless and naive, then they should be held responsible for their choice to drink or take drugs. If a woman's "judgment is impaired" and she has sex, it isn't necessarily always the man's fault; it isn't necessarily always rape.

As Gilbert delves further into the numbers, he does not necessarily disprove the one-in-four statistic, but he does clarify what it means—the so-called rape epidemic on campuses is more a way of interpreting, a way of seeing, than a physical phenomenon. It is more about a change in sexual politics than a change in sexual behavior. Whether or not one in four college women has been raped, then, is a matter of opinion, not a matter of mathematical fact.

That rape is a fact in some women's lives is not in question. It's hard to watch the solemn faces of young Bosnian girls, their words haltingly translated, as they tell of brutal rapes; or to read accounts of a suburban teenager raped and beaten while walking home from a shopping mall. We all agree that rape is a terrible thing, but we no longer agree on what rape is. Today's definition has stretched beyond bruises and knives, threats of death or violence to include emotional pressure and the influence of alcohol. The lines between rape and sex begin to blur. The one-in-four statistic on those purple posters is measuring something elusive. It is measuring her word against his in a realm where words barely exist. There is a gray area in which one person's rape may be another's bad night. Definitions become entangled in passionate ideological battles. There hasn't been a remarkable change in the number of women being raped; just a change in how receptive the political climate is to those numbers.

The next question, then, is who is identifying this epidemic and why. Somebody is "finding" this rape crisis, and finding it for a reason. Asserting the prevalence of rape lends urgency, authority to a broader critique of culture.

In a dramatic description of the rape crisis, Naomi Wolf writes in *The Beauty Myth* that "Cultural representation of glamorized degradation has created a situation among the young in which boys rape and girls get raped *as a normal course of events.*" The italics are hers. Whether or not Wolf really believes rape is part of the "normal course of events" these days, she is making a larger point. Wolf's rhetorical excess serves her larger polemic about sexual politics. Her dramatic prose is a call to arms. She is trying to rally the feminist troops. Wolf uses rape as a red flag, an undeniable sign that things are falling apart.

From Susan Brownmiller—who brought the politics of rape into the mainstream with her 1975 best seller, *Against Our Will: Men, Women and Rape*—to Naomi Wolf, feminist prophets of the rape crisis are talking about something more than forced penetration. They are talking about what they define as a "rape culture." Rape is a natural trump card for feminism. Arguments about rape can be used to sequester feminism in the teary province of trauma and crisis. By blocking analysis with its claims to unique pandemic suffering, the rape crisis becomes a powerful source of authority.

Dead serious, eyes wide with concern, a college senior tells me that she believes one in four is too conservative an estimate. This is not the first time I've heard this. She tells me the right statistic is closer to one in two. That means one in two women are raped. It's amazing, she says, amazing that so many of us are sexually assaulted every day.

What is amazing is that this student actually believes that 50 percent of women are raped. This is the true crisis. Some substantial number of young women are walking around with this alarming belief: a hyperbole containing within it a state of perpetual fear.

"Acquaintance Rape: Is Dating Dangerous?" is a pamphlet commonly found at counseling centers. The cover title rises from the shards of a shattered photograph of a boy and girl dancing. Inside, the pamphlet offers a sample date-rape scenario. She thinks:

> "He was really good looking and he had a great smile. . . . We talked and found we had a lot in common. I really liked him. When he asked me over to his place for a drink I thought it would be OK. He was such a good listener and I wanted him to ask me out again."

She's just looking for a sensitive boy, a good listener with a nice smile, but unfortunately his intentions are not as pure as hers. Beneath that nice smile, he thinks:

> "She looked really hot, wearing a sexy dress that showed off her great body. We started talking right away. I knew that she liked me by the way she kept smiling and touching my arm while she was speaking. She seemed pretty relaxed so I asked her back to my place for a drink. . . . When she said 'Yes' I knew that I was going to be lucky!"

These cardboard stereotypes don't just educate freshmen about rape. They also educate them about "dates" and about sexual desire. With titles like "Friends Raping Friends: Could It Happen to You?" date-rape pamphlets call into question all relationships between men and women. Beyond warning students about rape, the rape-crisis movement produces its own images of sexual behavior, in which men exert pressure and women resist. By defining the dangerous date in these terms—with this type of male and this type of female, and their different expectations— these pamphlets promote their own perspective on how men and women feel about sex: men are lascivious, women are innocent.

The sleek images of pressure and resistance projected in rape education movies, videotapes, pamphlets and speeches create a model of acceptable sexual behavior. The don'ts imply their own set of do's. The movement against rape, then, not only dictates the way sex shouldn't be but also the way it should be. Sex should be gentle, it should not be aggressive; it should be absolutely equal, it should not involve domination and submission; it should be tender, not ambivalent; it should communicate respect, it shouldn't communicate consuming desire.

In *Real Rape*, Susan Estrich, a professor of law at the University of Southern California Law Center, slips her ideas about the nature of sexual encounters into her legal analysis of the problem of rape. She writes: "Many feminists would argue that so long as women are powerless relative to men, viewing a 'yes' as a sign of true consent is misguided. . . . Many women who say yes to men they know, whether on dates or on the job, would say no if they could. . . . Women's silence sometimes is the product not of passion and desire but of pressure and fear."

Like Estrich, most rape-crisis feminists claim they are not talking about sex; they're talking about violence. But, like Estrich, they are also talking about sex. With their advice, their scenarios, their sample aggressive male, the message projects a clear comment on the nature of sexuality: women are often unwilling participants. They say yes because they feel they have to, because they are intimidated by male power.

The idea of "consent" has been redefined beyond the simple assertion that "no means no." Politically correct sex involves a yes, and a specific yes at that. According to the premise of "active consent," we can no longer afford ambiguity. We can no longer afford the dangers of unspoken consent. A former director of Columbia's date-rape education program told New York magazine, "Stone silence throughout an entire physical encounter with someone is not explicit consent."

This apparently practical, apparently clinical proscription cloaks retrograde assumptions about the way men and women experience sex. The idea that only an explicit yes means yes proposes that, like children, women have trouble communicating what they want. Beyond its dubious premise about the limits of female communication, the idea of active consent bolsters stereotypes of men just out to "get some" and women who don't really want any. . . .

By viewing rape as encompassing more than the use or threat of physical violence to coerce someone into sex, rape-crisis feminists reinforce traditional views about the fragility of the female body and will. According to common definitions of date rape, even "verbal coercion" or "manipulation" constitutes rape. Verbal coercion is defined as "a woman's consenting to unwanted sexual activity because of a man's verbal arguments not including verbal threats of force." The belief that "verbal coercion" is rape pervades workshops, counseling sessions and student opinion pieces. The suggestion lurking beneath this definition of rape is that men are not just physically but also intellectually and emotionally more powerful than women.

Imagine men sitting around in a circle talking about how she called him impotent and how she manipulated him into sex, how violated and dirty he felt afterward, how coercive she was, how she got him drunk first, how he hated his body and he couldn't eat for three weeks afterward. Imagine him calling this rape. Everyone feels the weight of emotional pressure at one time or another. The question is not whether people pressure each other but how our minds and our culture transform that pressure into full-blown assault. There would never be a rule or a law or even a pamphlet or peer counseling group for men who claimed to have been emotionally raped or verbally pressured into sex. And for the same reasons—assumption of basic competence, free will and strength of character—there should be no such rules or groups or pamphlets about women. . . .

Calling It Rape, a play by Sonya Rasminsky, a recent Harvard graduate, is based on interviews with date-rape victims. [. . . In the play, a] boy and girl are watching videos and he starts to come on to her. She does not want to have sex. As the situation progresses, she says, in an oblique effort to communicate her lack of enthusiasm, "If you're going to [expletive] me, use a condom." He interprets that as a yes, but it's really a no. And, according to this play, what happens next, condom or no condom, is rape.

This is a central idea of the rape-crisis movement: that sex has become our tower of Babel. He doesn't know what she wants (not to have sex) and she doesn't know what he wants (to have sex)—until it's too late. He speaks boyspeak and she speaks girlspeak and what comes out of all this verbal chaos is a lot of rapes. . . .

People have asked me if I have ever been date-raped. And thinking back on complicated nights, on too many glasses of wine, on strange and familiar beds, I would have to say yes. With such a sweeping definition of rape, I wonder how many people there are, male or female, who haven't been date-raped at one point or another. People pressure and manipulate and cajole each other into all sorts of things all of the time. . . . No human interactions are free from pressure, and the idea that sex is, or can be, makes it . . . vulnerable to the inconsistent expectations of double standard.

With their expansive version of rape, rape-crisis feminists are inventing a kinder, gentler sexuality. Beneath the broad definition of rape, these feminists are endorsing their own utopian vision of sexual relations: sex without struggle, sex without power, sex without persuasion, sex without pursuit. If verbal coercion constitutes rape, then the word rape itself expands to include any kind of sex a woman experiences as negative.

When Martin Amis spoke at Princeton, he included a controversial joke: "As far as I'm concerned, you can change your mind before, even during, but just not after sex." The reason this joke is funny, and the reason it's also too serious to be funny, is that in the current atmosphere you can change your mind afterward. Regret can signify rape. A night that was a blur, a night you wish hadn't happened, can be rape. Since "verbal coercion" and "manipulation" are ambiguous, it's easy to decide afterwards that he manipulated you. You can realize it weeks or even years later. This is a movement that deals in retrospective trauma.

Rape has become a catchall expression, a word used to define everything that is unpleasant and disturbing about relations between the sexes. Students say things like "I realize that sexual harassment is a kind of rape." If we refer to a whole range of behavior from emotional pressure to sexual harassment as "rape," then the idea itself gets diluted. It ceases to be powerful as either description or accusation. . . .

There are a few feminists involved in rape education who object to the current expanding definitions of sexual assault. Gillian Greensite, founder of the rape prevention education program at the University of California at Santa Cruz, writes that the seriousness of the crime "is being undermined by the growing tendency of some feminists to label all heterosexual miscommunication and insensitivity as acquaintance rape." From within the rape-crisis movement, Greensite's dissent makes an important point. If we are going to maintain an idea of rape, then we need to reserve it for instances of physical violence, or the threat of physical violence. . . .

When my fifty-five-year-old mother was young, navigating her way through dates, there was a definite social compass. There were places not to let him put his hands. There were invisible lines. The Pill wasn't available. Abortion wasn't legal. And sex was just wrong. Her mother gave her "mad money" to take out on dates in case her date got drunk and she needed to escape. She had to go far enough to hold his interest and not far enough to endanger her reputation.

Now the rape-crisis feminists are offering new rules. They are giving a new political weight to the same old no. My mother's mother told her to drink sloe gin fizzes so she wouldn't drink too much and get too drunk and go too far. Now the date rape pamphlets tell us: "Avoid excessive use of alcohol and drugs. Alcohol and drugs interfere with clear thinking and effective communication." My mother's mother told her to stay away from empty rooms and dimly lighted streets. In *I Never Called It Rape*, Robin Warshaw writes, "Especially with recent acquaintances, women should insist on going only to public places such as restaurants and movie theaters."

There is a danger in these new rules. We shouldn't need to be reminded that the rigidly conformist 1950s were not the heyday of women's power. Barbara Ehrenreich writes of "re-making love," but there is a danger in remaking love in its old image. The terms may have changed, but attitudes about sex and women's bodies have not. Rape-crisis feminists threaten the progress that's been made. They are chasing the same stereotypes our mothers spent so much energy escaping.

One day I was looking through my mother's bookshelves and I found her old battered copy of Germaine Greer's feminist classic, *The Female Eunuch*. The pages were dog-eared and whole passages marked with penciled notes. It was 1971 when Germaine Greer fanned the fires with *The Female Eunuch* and it was 1971 when my mother read it, brand new, explosive, a tough and sexy terrorism for the early stirrings of the feminist movement.

Today's rape-crisis feminists threaten to create their own version of the desexualized woman Greer complained of twenty years ago. Her comments need to be recycled for present-day feminism. "It is often falsely assumed," Greer writes, "even by feminists, that sexuality is the enemy of the female who really wants to develop these aspects of her personality. . . . It was not the insistence upon her sex that weakened the American woman student's desire to make something of her education, but the insistence upon a passive sexual role. In fact, the chief instrument in the deflection and perversion of female energy is the denial of female sexuality for the substitution of femininity or sexlessness."

It is the passive sexual role that threatens us still, and it is the denial of female sexual agency that threatens to propel us backward.

Comprehension Questions

1. Why doesn't Roiphe think that there's a rape crisis?
2. Roiphe says that most rape-crisis feminists claim they are *not* talking about sex, but about violence. However, Roiphe says that these feminists are also talking about sex. What does she mean?
3. Why is Roiphe skeptical of saying that, if someone is verbally coerced into sex, then she was raped?
4. Roiphe says that "[r]ape has become a catchall expression, a word used to define everything that is unpleasant and disturbing about relations between the sexes." Let's suppose she's right. Why would certain feminists *want* the word "rape" to have such a broad meaning? What are the *advantages* of defining "rape" this way?
5. What does Greer mean by the "passive sexual role"?

Discussion Questions

1. What statistics have you heard about rape? Roiphe published this essay more than twenty years ago. How, if at all, has the rhetoric about rape changed since then?
2. Reread Roiphe's summary of *Calling It Rape*—the play by Sonya Rasminsky. Do you think that the girl in the play was raped? Why or why not?
3. Roiphe is highly critical of the idea that, if a person regrets a sexual encounter, then she may well have been raped. Why? Can you imagine a scenario in which it *is* plausible that regret is evidence of rape?
4. In Bloomingdale's 2015 Christmas catalog, there was an ad that featured a man staring at a woman who is laughing and looking away. The text reads: "Spike your best friend's eggnog when they're not looking." Critics claimed that this is just one more manifestation of rape culture. Is it? If so, how does that affect Roiphe's argument?

Case

Consider a story that a student shared with me:

> On New Year's Eve, Javi and his friends go to a party that an acquaintance of theirs is throwing. After a few drinks, Javi sees Steph, a girl who was in his English class. They start chatting, and he quickly notices that she is pretty drunk. Soon after, she proposes that they go take a few shots, and although Javi is aware that the shots will definitely get her wasted, he agrees anyway. After taking the shots, Javi is really buzzed, but Steph is so drunk that she can't walk in a straight line. Regardless, they keep drinking and spend the rest of the party dancing together. At midnight, Steph kisses Javi, and she suggests that they sneak off to his car to continue things. On their way, Steph is stumbling and Javi has to help her along. Once in the car, one thing leads to another, and ultimately they have sex. When Steph wakes up the next morning, she can't remember last night. This scares her. When Javi wakes up, however, he remembers everything. After a while, he feels guilty when he recalls how drunk Steph was.

Should Javi feel guilty? Did he do something wrong? Why or why not? How would Roiphe think about this case?

===== ✿ =====

7

Alcohol and Rape

Nicholas Dixon

··

Imagine a woman who's had a lot to drink. She isn't blackout drunk, but her speech is slurred, she's unsteady on her feet, and her judgment isn't what it normally would be. Can she consent to sex? If not, then would it be rape if you were to have sex with her? These are the questions that Dixon explores in his essay. Ultimately, he argues that "[s]ince [a man] cannot be reasonably sure that the woman consents [in a situation like this], he should refrain from sexual intercourse."

··

Many date or acquaintance rapes, especially those that occur in a college setting, involve the use of alcohol by both rapist and victim.[1] To what extent, if any, should the fact that a woman has been drinking alcohol before she has sexual relations affect our determination of whether or not she has been raped?[2] . . .

I will take for granted that, regardless of a woman's alcoholic intake, she has been raped whenever a man forces himself on her after she says "no" or otherwise resists. I will focus instead on situations when women who have been drinking provide varying levels of acquiescence to sex.

Dixon, Nicholas. 2001. "Alcohol and Rape." *Public Affairs Quarterly* 15(4): 341–354. Reprinted with permission.

Let us begin by considering two relatively straightforward examples, which we can use as limiting cases, of sexual encounters involving alcohol.

I. Two Limiting Cases

A. Fraternity Gang Rape

In 1988 four Florida State University fraternity members allegedly had sex with an eighteen-year-old female student after she had passed out with an almost lethal blood alcohol level of .349 percent. Afterwards, she was allegedly "dumped" in a different fraternity house.[3]

If these events, which led to a five-year ban on the fraternity chapter, really happened, the woman was certainly raped. Since a woman who is unconscious after heavy drinking is unable to consent,[4] the fraternity members committed . . . rape. Moreover, any claim that they were unaware of her lack of consent . . . would ring hollow. We may extrapolate beyond this extreme case to situations where a person is so drunk that, while she is conscious, she is barely aware of where she is and who her partner is, and she has no recollection of what has happened the following day. She may acquiesce and give the physiological responses that indicate consent, and she may even say "yes" when asked whether she wants to have sex, but her mental state is so impaired by alcohol that she cannot give a sufficiently meaningful level of consent to rebut rape charges against the man with whom she has sexual relations.

B. A Regretted Sexual Encounter

A male and female college student go on a dinner date, and both drink a relatively small amount of alcohol, say a glass of wine or beer. The conversation flows freely, and she agrees to go back to his place to continue the evening. They have one more drink there, start kissing and making out, and he asks her to spend the night. She is not drunk and, impressed by his gentle and communicative manner, accepts his offer. However, she is not used to drinking, and, although she is not significantly cognitively impaired—her speech is not slurred and her conversation is lucid—her inhibitions have been markedly lowered by the alcohol. When she wakes up alongside him the following morning, she bitterly regrets their lovemaking.

No rape has occurred. While she now regrets having spent the night with her date, and would quite likely not have agreed to do so had she not drunk any alcohol, her consent at the time was sufficiently voluntary to rule out any question of rape. While their sexual encounter violated her more lasting values, this no more entails that she did not "really" consent than the fact that my overeating at dinner violates my long-term plan to diet entails that my indulgence was not an autonomous action. . . . Unwisely having sex after unwisely drinking alcohol is not necessarily rape. We do a lot of unwise things when drinking, like *continuing* to drink too long and getting a bad hangover, and staying up too late when we have to work the next day. In neither case would we question our consent to our act of continuing to drink or staying up late. Why should a person's consent to sex after moderate amounts of drinking be any more suspect?

II. Problematic Intermediate Cases: Impaired Sex

Real sexual encounters involving alcohol tend to fall in between these two limiting cases. Imagine, for instance, a college student who gets very drunk at a party. Her blood alcohol level is well above the legal limit for driving. She is slurring her words and is unsteady on her feet, but she knows where she is and with whom she is speaking or dancing. She ends up spending the night with a guy at the party—perhaps someone she has just met, perhaps an acquaintance, but no one with whom she is in an ongoing relationship. She willingly responds to his sexual advances, but, like the woman in case I.B., horribly regrets her sexual encounter the next day. Although she remembers going home with the guy from the party, she cannot recall much else from the evening and night. Let us call this intermediate case, in which the woman's judgment is significantly impaired by alcohol, "impaired sex." Has she been raped?

In the next two subsections I will examine two competing analyses of impaired sex, each one suggested by one of the limiting cases in Section I. First, though, I pause to consider how relevant the degree to which the man has helped to bring about the woman's impaired state is to the question of whether rape has occurred. Suppose that he has deliberately got her drunk, cajoling her to down drink after drink, with the intention of lowering her resistance to his planned sexual advances? The very fact that he uses such a strategy implies that he doubts that she would agree to have sex with him if she were sober. Should she bring rape charges, on the ground that her acquiescence to sex when she was drunk was invalid, his claim that he believed that she voluntarily consented would appear disingenuous . . . (Remember that in this section we are discussing women who are very drunk to the point of slurring their words and being unsteady on their feet, not those who are less inhibited after drinking a moderate amount of alcohol.)

For the remainder of this paper, I will focus instead on the more difficult variant of impaired sex in which the man does not use alcohol as a tool for seduction. Instead, he meets the woman when she is already drunk, or else he drinks with her with no designs on getting her drunk. In either case, he spontaneously takes advantage of the situation in which he finds himself. Is he guilty of rape?

A. Women's Responsibility for Their Own Actions

Few would deny that the woman in section I.B. is responsible for her own unwise decision to engage in a sexual encounter that she now regrets. Katie Roiphe . . . would extend this approach to impaired sex, involving a woman who is very drunk but not incoherent. Roiphe insists that women are autonomous adults who are responsible for the consequences of their use of alcohol and other drugs.[5] . . . Rather than complain about sexual assault, women who desire to be sexually active should take steps to minimize its danger, by being alert to warning signs, learning self-defense, and avoiding getting drunk when doing so would put them at risk for rape.[6]

[Roiphe is] vulnerable to powerful criticisms. For instance, Roiphe's blanket dismissal of the extensive date rape literature is based on her own flimsy anecdotal evidence and a superficial reading of the studies.[7] . . . Even if it does result from a woman's recklessness, rape is still rape and the rapist is primarily to blame. We would not dream of exonerating a Central Park mugger because the victim was foolish to go there at 4 a.m. Indeed, the whole point of "Take Back the Night" marches is precisely that the burden is on *aggressors* to stop their violence, not on women to change their behavior to accommodate aggressors.

However, we can isolate from their more dubious views a relatively uncontroversial underlying principle, which is surely congenial to liberal and most other types of feminists: namely, that we should respect women's status as agents, and we should not degrade them by treating them as incapable of making autonomous decisions about alcohol and sexuality. We should, instead, hold women at least partly responsible for the consequences of their voluntary decision to drink large amounts of alcohol, made in full knowledge that it may result in choices that they will later regret. This principle would count against regarding impaired sex as rape.[8] A plausible corollary of this principle is that women, as autonomous beings, have a duty to make their wishes about sex clear to their partners. When a woman drinks heavily and ends up having a sexual encounter that she later regrets she has failed to exercise this positive duty of autonomous people. Her actions have sent the wrong message to her partner, and to blame him for the sex in which she willingly engages but that she later regrets seems unfair . . . The onus is on the woman to communicate her lack of consent and, in the absence of such communication, his belief in her consent is quite reasonable. . . .

B. Communicative Sexuality: Men's Duty to Ensure That Women Consent

The "women's responsibility for sex" approach is very plausible in case I.B., where a woman later regrets sex in which she willingly engaged after moderate drinking. However, men's accountability for unwanted sex becomes unavoidable in the gang rape described in Subsection I.A. Granted, the female student may have voluntarily and very unwisely chosen to drink massive amounts of alcohol, but once she had passed out, the four fraternity members who allegedly had intercourse with her had absolutely no reason to believe that she consented to sex. Regardless of whether they deliberately got her drunk or, on the other hand, took advantage of her after finding her in this condition, they are guilty of recklessly ignoring the evident risk that she did not consent. . . .

In cases such as this, Lois Pineau's model of "communicative sexuality" becomes enormously plausible.[9] While Pineau's view does not preclude regarding women as having a duty to clearly communicate their wishes regarding sexual intimacy—indeed, such a duty may be an integral part of communicative sexuality—its central tenet is that men too are responsible for ensuring that effective communication occurs. In particular, the burden is on men to ensure that their female partners really do consent to sexual intimacy, and they should refrain from sexual activity if they are not sure of this consent. A reasonable belief that a woman consented to sex will still count as a defense against rape, but the reasonableness of this belief will itself be judged on whether it would have been reasonable, from the woman's point of view, to consent to sex. Since virtually no woman would want four men to have sex with her after she has passed into an alcoholic coma, in the absence of some miraculous evidence that the female student actually wanted sex in such unpleasant circumstances, the four fraternity members blatantly violated their duty to be sure of the woman's consent, and are indeed guilty of rape.

More generally, Pineau argues that it is never reasonable to assume that a woman consents to "aggressive noncommunicative sex." Not only does her approach regard the extreme case of sex with an unconscious person as rape, but it would put any man who fails to take reasonable precautions to ensure that a woman consents to sex at risk for a rape conviction should she later declare that she did not consent. When doubt exists about consent, the burden is on the man to *ask*. The much-discussed Antioch University "Sexual Offense Policy," which requires explicit consent to each new level of sexual intimacy every time it occurs, is a quasi-legal enactment of Pineau's model of communicative sexuality.[10]

Pineau's approach entails a very different analysis of our central case of impaired sex than the "women's responsibility for sex" model discussed in the previous section. At first blush, one might think that all that Pineau would require of a man would be to ask the woman whether she is really sure that she wants to continue with sexual intimacy. If he boldly forges ahead without even asking the woman this question, and if the woman later claims that she was too drunk for her acquiescence to sex to constitute genuine consent, he risks being found guilty of Pineau's proposed category of "nonaggravated sexual assault," which would carry a lighter penalty than "standard" rape when a woman communicates her lack of consent by saying "no" or otherwise resisting. But even explicitly asking the woman for consent may be insufficient to protect him from blame and liability under the communicative sexuality model. The issue is precisely whether the word "yes," when spoken by a woman who is very drunk, is sufficient evidence of her consent. Being very drunk means that her judgment is impaired, as is evident from her horror and regret the following morning when she realizes what she has done. Given that we are only too aware of our propensity to do things that we later regret when we are very drunk, the man in this situation has good reason to doubt whether the woman's acquiescence to his advances and her "yes" to his explicit question is a fully autonomous reflection of lasting values and desires. Since he cannot be reasonably sure that the woman consents, he should refrain from sexual intercourse. Even if he is unaware of the danger that she does not consent, he *should* be aware and is, therefore, guilty of negligence. His belief that she consents may be sincere, but it is unreasonable and does not provide a defense to charges of nonaggravated sexual assault. . . .

Pineau's claim that men have a *moral obligation* to ensure that their partners consent to sex is very plausible. Given alcohol's tendency to cloud people's judgment, men should be especially careful to ensure that a woman consents to sex when she is very drunk. In most circumstances, this requires simply refraining from sexual activity. Imposing this relatively minor restriction on men's sexual freedom seems amply justified by the goal of preventing the enormous harm of rape.

Comprehension Questions

1. What's Dixon trying to show with the "Fraternity Gang Rape" and "Regretted Sexual Encounter" stories?
2. Why does Dixon think that it would be "disingenuous" for a man to claim that the woman voluntarily consented to sex if he has been encouraging her to drink for the purpose of having sex with her?
3. What's the point of the Dixon's example about the Central Park mugger?
4. What does Dixon mean when he says that we should "respect women's status as agents"?
5. What is the "communicative sexuality" model? Under what circumstances does this model say that it's OK to have sex?

Discussion Questions

1. People used to say "No means no," which is a way of saying that if someone clearly indicates that he or she isn't interested in sex, then you should stop trying to have sex with that person. People now often say "Yes means yes," which is a way of saying you haven't consented to sex unless you've explicitly said that you want to have sex. Would Dixon be satisfied with the "Yes means yes" approach to sexual consent? Why or why not?
2. Do you think that Dixon puts too much of the blame on men? Why or why not?
3. Imagine someone saying this: "Clearly, you shouldn't let a drunk person drive a car. Similarly, you shouldn't let a drunk person have sex." How good is this analogy? If it breaks down, where, exactly, does that happen? Is the basic idea a good one, even if the analogy isn't perfect? Why or why not?
4. Are there *any* circumstances in which Dixon should say that impaired sex is morally permissible? Imagine two people who have been in a relationship for a few years. Would impaired sex be permissible for them? If not, why not? If so, then what is it about their situation that makes sex permissible?

Case

When we discuss rape, we often focus on men as perpetrators and women as victims. But consider this case:

> In December 2002, [Brad] was a Florida college student working as a bartender when, he says, he was drugged and raped by a woman. An athletic 22-year-old, Brad says he'd had only a couple of beers before two women—one a friend and the other a stranger—offered him a drink called a Surfer on Acid. Soon after, Brad says, he "went from zero to shit-faced in, like, three seconds," which he doubts alcohol alone could have accomplished. While he was falling in and out of consciousness, Brad says, he was taken to the apartment of the woman he didn't know, and she dragged him into a bedroom and undressed him. "I was pretty wasted, so I couldn't put up much of a struggle," he says. Soon, the woman fondled him into an erection and, without using a condom, climbed on top of him. "At that point, it was going to happen," Brad says matter-of-factly, "so after about five minutes, I pretended to orgasm and rolled over. If anything happened after that, I don't know."[11]

Bill O'Reilly, a conservative political commentator, talked about this sort of case on his show:

> If you're lucky enough as a guy to have some girl come on to you in that manner," he said, "but you don't want to reciprocate, you stand up and you leave, unless the woman is 240 pounds and tackles you. The man is traditionally stronger and better equipped to leave the room.[12]

In O'Reilly's view, it sounds like the woman in Brad's story can assume that Brad consented to sex—if he didn't want it, he could have rolled over earlier. So in O'Reilly's view, Brad wasn't raped. But Brad thinks he *was* raped. Who's right? Relatedly, how does O'Reilly's view about consent and permissible sex differ from Dixon's? Which view is more plausible?

Notes

1. Partly for the sake of convenience, I will refer throughout to alleged male on female rapes. Although same-sex rape is all too real and female on male rape is possible, the vast majority of rapes that come to trial are male on female. The two main competing principles to which I refer are gender-specific: the need to recognize women's status as autonomous beings who are responsible for their own sexuality, and men's obligation to ensure that their partners consent (as opposed to the traditional view that the burden is on women to demonstrate their nonconsent by physical resistance).

2. Of course, in such situations her male partner has often been drinking, too. The reason I do not discuss men's intake of alcohol is that it seems of little relevance to the issue of whether rape has occurred. The fact that a man is blind drunk when he has sex without a woman's consent shows at best that he did not *intentionally* rape her. He is still responsible for getting drunk in the first place. Because he willingly got into a state in which his judgment was severely impaired, and then engaged in sexual activity, he may be guilty of recklessness. At the very least, he may be guilty of negligence: he may not have been aware of the woman's lack of consent, but he should have been aware of it. Both recklessness and negligence are sufficient to meet the *mens rea* requirement for rape.

3. See Patricia Yancey Martin and Robert A. Hummer, "Fraternities and Rape on Campus," Steven Jay Gold (ed.), *Moral Controversies: Race, Class and Gender in Applied Ethics* (Belmont, CA: Wadsworth Publishing Co., 1993), p. 325.

4. As I will discuss below, in some cases, a person may be able to give *prior* consent to sex, which will operate even when she is unable to give or for some reason does not give fully voluntary consent at the actual time that sex occurs. We may safely assume that no such prior consent occurred in the case of the gang rape.

5. The relevant passage from Roiphe's book *The Morning After* is reprinted in Robert Trevas, Arthur Zucker, and Donald Borchert (eds.), *Philosophy of Sex and Love: A Reader* (Upper Saddle River, NJ: Prentice Hall, 1997), p. 365.

6. Camille Paglia, "Date Rape: Another Perspective," William H. Shaw (ed.), *Social and Personal Ethics,* 2nd edition (Belmont, CA: Wadsworth Publishing Co., 1996).

7. See Kate Pollit's review, "Not Just Bad Sex," *Reasonable Creatures: Essays on Women and Feminism* (New York: Alfred A. Knopf, 1994).

8. Granted, Estrich has shown that women can be coerced into sex, and hence raped, without the use or threat of physical force. See Susan Estrich, "Rape," *Yale Law Journal* 95 (1986). However, no coercion or trickery seems present in the situation we are considering.

9. Lois Pineau, "Date Rape: A Feminist Analysis," *Law and Philosophy* 8 (1989).

10. See Alan Soble, "Antioch's' Sexual Offense Policy": A Philosophical Exploration," *Journal of Social Philosophy*, vol. 28, no. 1 (Spring 1997) for an excellent analysis and critique of Antioch's policy.

11. https://www.washingtonpost.com/posteverything/wp/2014/07/01/my-own-rape-shows-how-badly-we-stereotype-perps-and-victims/

12. https://www.washingtonpost.com/posteverything/wp/2014/07/01/my-own-rape-shows-how-badly-we-stereotype-perps-and-victims/

8

===== ᚤ =====

Just Pushy Enough

Anne Barnhill

....

Sometimes we start relationships by violating people's boundaries. He hasn't said he wants you to hold his hand, but you do anyway— and he doesn't let go. She says she isn't interested, but then she replies to your texts. Normally, it isn't OK to grab people's hands or send them unwanted messages. But when it comes to romantic relationships, things are slightly more complicated. In Barnhill's essay, she discusses the ethics of "prospective" boundary violations—that is, the ones that are supposed to start relationships. In particular, she proposes four rules to guide prospective boundary violations: (1) you must not harm someone when you violate her boundaries; (2) you may treat someone as if you're in a somewhat closer relationship, but not a very much closer relationship; (3) you must genuinely want to be in the closer relationship that your boundary violation might help to establish; and (4) the closer relationship that you hope to establish by violating boundaries must be the kind of relationship the other person would plausibly want to have.

....

In one of romantic comedy's iconic moments, John Cusack (as Lloyd Dobler, in the 1989 movie *Say Anything*) serenades Ione Skye (as Diane Court) with Peter Gabriel's "In Your Eyes." Diane has broken up with

Barnill, Anne. 2010. "Just Pushy Enough." In *Dating: Flirting with Big Ideas*, ed. Kristie Miller and Marlene Clark, 90–100. Malden, MA: Blackwell. Reprinted with permission of John Wiley & Sons.

Lloyd and told him to leave her alone, but Lloyd doesn't comply. Instead, he shows up at her house at daybreak and stands there resolutely, holding his boom box above his head. Though she doesn't immediately admit it, Diane is won over by Lloyd's serenade—and so are we, as viewers. Lloyd's serenade is so charming that we don't stop to consider what he's really doing. He's violating Diane's boundaries, and in more ways than one. He's violating her expressed wish to be left alone. He's showing up uninvited at an ungodly hour—usually an intolerably rude and pushy thing to do. For all he knows, he's waking her up and making a scene (surely the loud music will wake the neighbors, too!). He might even be trespassing on her lawn.

In *The Sure Thing* (1985), John Cusack engages in another instance of charming boundary violation. Daphne Zuniga (as Alison Bradbury) has rejected John Cusack (as Walter "Gib" Gibson), but again he won't take no for an answer. While Alison is swimming laps in a pool, Gib tries to convince her to tutor him (which will lead ineluctably to falling in love with him). He paces up and down the lane as she swims, and tells a pitiful tale about what will happen to him without her help—he won't get his grades up, he'll get a bad job, and he'll lead a loserly and unsatisfying life.

He's pestering her, and he's trying to give her a guilt trip, a manipulative little tug on her heart-strings. She ignores him and briskly swims on. In a final bid for Alison's attention, Gib jumps fully clothed into the pool.

Another more recent example of a charming boundary violation is from the American television series *The Office*. Andy Bernard (played by Ed Helms) has asked his co-worker Angela Martin (played by Angela Kinsey) to go out with him, and she's turned him down. Andy is eager to change her mind, so while Angela is working at her desk, and in front of their colleagues, he nervously but energetically serenades her with the song "Take a Chance on Me."[1] Andy's serenade is a clear violation of Angela's many boundaries. Angela is uptight; she insists upon strictly proper conduct (she's the "office stickler," in the words of the boss Michael) and she's very concerned with appearances. She maintains a wide interpersonal berth with her colleagues—she's aloof and secretive about her personal life. Angela meticulously maintains all of these boundaries, and Andy violates them all when he serenades her in front of her colleagues. His serenade is also manipulative—by asking her out in such a public and crowd-pleasing way, he makes it more difficult for her to reject him. Despite all this, Andy's serenade is utterly charming.

We cheer on Andy Bernard, Lloyd Dobler, and Walter Gibson even though we generally frown upon these kinds of boundary violations.

Typically, we find it inappropriate to bother people who've told us to leave them alone, to pester and manipulate, to show up uninvited (especially in the middle of the night), to make a potentially embarrassing scene, to physically trespass on someone's property, and to violate someone's personal space (especially while she's sleeping, or swimming, or working at her desk). In some cases, these boundary violations are morally wrong (for example, breaking into a stranger's house, or stalking an ex-girlfriend). At the very least, these kinds of boundary violation are typically rude, annoying, and off-putting.

So why do we find *these* boundary violations charming and untroubling? Part of the explanation is surely the unique appeal of John Cusack and Ed Helms—how could anyone mind having their boundaries violated by such beseeching and adorably vulnerable guys? Another part of the explanation is that our responses to these scenes are influenced by regrettable gender norms and retrograde romantic notions—we find it romantic and fitting for the man to violate the woman's boundaries, despite her protests.

I think, however, that there is a further explanation as to why these particular boundary violations are unproblematic even though these kinds of boundary violations are typically inappropriate and sometimes even morally wrong. In these cases, Lloyd, Gib, and Andy are acting like boundaries don't exist, in the hope that the boundaries will cease to exist. They're acting as if they're in a closer relationship in which those boundaries don't exist (e.g., Lloyd would be welcome to show up unannounced if Diane were his girlfriend) because they hope this will forge the closer relationship. In other words, they're faking it till they make it: faking a closer relationship without boundaries in order to make this closer relationship. In my opinion, faking it till you make it is often appropriate, even when it involves violating boundaries in manipulative and pushy ways.

This opinion puts me at odds with some Kantian moral philosophers—a popular and powerful lot. According to these Kantians, we must always treat people as rational agents. If we want to get someone to date us, or to get back together with us, we must not pull stunts that are designed to manipulate or overwhelm, or to elicit an irrational response. These Kantians are wrong—and luckily so, for the career of John Cusack. Contrary to this Kantian view, many kinds of nonrational and even irrational influence are appropriate. The dividing line between appropriate and inappropriate behavior isn't whether it treats someone as a rational agent. Hence the dividing line between appropriate and inappropriate boundary violations in dating contexts isn't whether they treat someone as a rational agent. There's a more complicated story about what distinguishes appropriate boundary violations from inappropriate boundary violations in dating contexts. In the rest of this essay, I give part of that story.

The Difference Between Appropriate and Inappropriate Boundary Violations

. . . Kantian moral philosophers . . . maintain that many kinds of verbal behavior are morally wrong. These moral philosophers are followers of German philosopher Immanuel Kant, and they interpret Kant's famous injunction to *treat others as ends in themselves and never as mere means* as an injunction to treat people always as rational agents. This means that we must not manipulate people, or trick them, or try to influence them nonrationally in any other way, or try to exert control over them rather than letting them be guided by their own reason. For example, listen to philosopher Thomas Hill's interpretation of Kant: "Since the exercise of rationality is something to be cherished, in trying to influence others one should appeal to their reason rather than try to manipulate them by nonrational techniques."[2] And Kantian philosopher Christine Korsgaard seconds that interpretation of Kant:

> To treat others as ends in themselves is always to address and deal with them as rational beings. Every rational being gets to reason out, for herself, what she is to think, choose, or do. So if you need someone's contribution to your end, you must put the facts before her and ask for her contribution. If you think she is doing something wrong, you may try to convince her by argument but you may not resort to tricks or force.[3]

[However, sometimes] it's inappropriate to manipulate, to violate someone's personal space, or to touch someone without her consent; and sometimes it's perfectly all right. For example, having sexual intercourse with someone who hasn't consented is a physical boundary violation that is always morally wrong. But unexpectedly putting your hand on someone's knee is a physical boundary violation that's only *sometimes* inappropriate; in some contexts, it's a perfectly appropriate attempt to initiate a physical relationship. To give another slightly different example, some instances of manipulation are appropriate but others aren't. Imagine a variation on the "Take a Chance on Me" serenade from *The Office*: Andy Bernard isn't seeking a date with Angela, but is trying to persuade her to loan him money. If he's just seeking a loan, it seems inappropriate to serenade her publicly, given that it will embarrass her and manipulate her by putting her on the spot. Nevertheless, it seems all right for Andy to violate Angela's boundaries in those same ways to get a date.

So when exactly is it appropriate to violate boundaries? The answer to this question is complicated, as there are many varieties of boundary violations and the moral rules governing each variety are different. Here I focus on just one species of boundary violation, which I call *prospective boundary violation*. Prospective boundary violation, as I define it, is ignoring or violating an interpersonal boundary that doesn't exist in a closer relationship, in order to establish that closer relationship. Prospective boundary violation is strategic—you're strategically violating boundaries in order to destroy those boundaries, not just violating boundaries carelessly or for the fun of it.

To get a handle on the difference between prospective boundary violations and other boundary violations, consider these two cases:

> *Nosey Questions*: Kenny gets along with his neighbor Maria, but has no interest in becoming better friends with her. He has often seen her in the company of a man. One day he asks her, out of curiosity, "Is that your boyfriend?" Maria says, "Yes, it is." Kenny asks, "How long have you been together?" Maria says, "Six months." Kenny asks, "How's the sex?"

> *Becoming Friends*: Kenny is friendly with his neighbor Maria and wants to become better friends with her. He thinks that they could become close friends, once he breaks the ice. He has often seen her in the company of a man. One day, he asks her, "Is that your boyfriend?" Maria says, "Yes, it is." Kenny asks, "How long have you been together?" Maria says, "Six months." Kenny asks, "How's the sex?"

In *Nosey Questions* Kenny asks an intrusive question just to slake his own curiosity. But in *Becoming Friends* Kenny asks an intrusive question in order to establish emotional intimacy between him and Maria so that they'll become friends. Kenny treats Maria as someone already a friend, in the hope that she'll play along and become his friend. Kenny violates an interpersonal boundary—the boundary against talking about sex that exists between people who don't know each other well—in order to destroy that interpersonal boundary. People who are friends don't have that interpersonal boundary between them, so to become friends that boundary must somehow be destroyed. . . .

Lloyd, Gib, and Andy's boundary violations are all examples of prospective boundary violation—ignoring or violating an interpersonal boundary that doesn't exist in a closer relationship, in order to establish that closer relationship. What makes the boundary violation appropriate in these cases is that it's meant to establish a closer relationship. If the boundary violation were done for certain other reasons—if Kenny were just curious about Maria's sex life, or Andy were just trying to get Angela to loan him money—then it would be inappropriate.

Why Does Prospective Action Work?

When Lloyd Dobler and Andy Bernard get the girl, it makes sense to us. We intuitively understand that violating boundaries—and more generally, acting like you're in a closer relationship with someone than you actually are—can help to establish a closer relationship. But why exactly does it work? Why does acting like he's in a closer relationship with a woman work to establish that closer relationship, rather than just confuse and alienate her?

It works because she'll often play along with it. For example, Maria might play along with Kenny's intrusive questions by telling him about her sex life. In telling Kenny about her sex life, they have one of the central experiences of close friendship—sharing intimate details. By having this experience, Maria might come to feel closer to Kenny, in the way that friends feel close—to trust him, and to feel comforted by having him as her confidant. In this way, Maria's feelings catch up with her actions: her feelings of friendship catch up with her action of sharing intimate details. We have a phrase for this phenomenon: we call it *faking it till you make it.* . . .

Faking it till you make it is a common strategy and a time-tested one. Aristotle recommended that we act virtuously, even if we don't think or feel as the virtuous person does. Over time, Aristotle counseled, we will be habituated into virtuous thoughts and feelings by performing virtuous actions. It's an interesting feature of human psychology that this kind of habituation works—that our thoughts and feelings do sometimes catch up with our actions. Prospective boundary violation is a way of faking it till you make it, and it must rely upon this feelings-catch-up-with-actions feature of human psychology: by acting as if boundaries don't exist, we come to feel that they really don't exist.

In close relationships, people don't maintain the interpersonal boundaries that they maintain with strangers and acquaintances. So violating a boundary—acting like that boundary isn't there—is a way of acting like you're in a closer relationship already. When someone plays along with what you're doing—when she, too, acts like the boundary isn't there—she might come to feel that the boundary isn't there. So by acting like you're in a closer relationship, you bring it about that you're in a closer relationship.

But violating boundaries is a high-risk strategy for establishing a closer relationship. When you violate someone's boundaries—for example, you ask her intrusive questions, or you show up uninvited at her house, or you jump into the pool, or you serenade her in front of her colleagues even though she's intensely private—you are interfering with how she's chosen to control herself and to control what happens to her. What happens to her is now under your control and not her own control, to some extent. This might make her feel closer to you and receptive to your next move or, alternately, it might put her off entirely. Depending on how you handle the situation, you might build a closer relationship or forever destroy the possibility of one. If she tells you the troubling details of her sex life and you ridicule her, she's probably not going to trust you or like you anymore. But if you're sensitive and helpful, then she might come to trust you, feel closer to you, and open up to you in the future. By treating her in ways characteristic of a closer relationship, you've created a test for yourself: a test of whether or not you're worthy of a closer relationship. Depending on how you treat her, you prove yourself worthy or unworthy of being close to.

Rules on Prospective Boundary Violation

What makes Lloyd Dobler's, Walter Gibson's, Andy Bernard's, and Kenny's boundary violations appropriate is that they're meant to establish a closer relationship. If the boundary violations were done for some other reasons—if Kenny is just curious about Maria's sex life, or Andy is just trying to get Angela to loan him money—then they would be inappropriate. Does this mean that any prospective boundary violation—that is, any boundary violation that's meant to establish a closer relationship—is appropriate? No, certainly not. There are rules governing prospective boundary violation:

> *Rule 1*: You must not harm someone when you violate her boundaries.

However, making her a little embarrassed or annoyed is all right.

> *Rule 2*: You may treat someone as if you're in a somewhat closer relationship, but not a very much closer relationship.

For example, suppose you're on a first date and you want to establish a sexual relationship with your date. So far, both of you have awkwardly kept your distance. You need to break the ice. Unexpectedly putting your hand on her knee might be an appropriate boundary violation that breaks the ice and helps to establish a sexual relationship. Unexpectedly forcing her to have sex with you, however, isn't an appropriate way to establish a sexual relationship.

> *Rule 3*: You must genuinely want to be in the closer relationship that your boundary violation might help to establish.

This is the rule that we most often violate.

We sometimes unwittingly violate this rule because we're self-deceived about our desires for closer relationships. For example, it seems to you that you want a romantic relationship with someone, but you're deceiving yourself; really you just want to have sex with her. Also, there's a great temptation to pretend we want closer relationships, because acting as if you want a closer relationship with someone is an effective way to get her to do what you want. . . .

> *Rule 4*: The closer relationship that you hope to establish by violating boundaries must be the kind of relationship the other person would plausibly want to have.

Sometimes we want a closer relationship with someone that she wouldn't want. In these cases we shouldn't violate her boundaries in pursuit of a relationship we know (or should know) she wouldn't want. For example, Maggie is strapped for cash and hopes to establish a benefactor/recipient relationship with a rich acquaintance, Tina. So Maggie takes money from Tina's wallet when Tina isn't looking. Maggie has committed a prospective boundary violation that succeeds in establishing the closer relationship (the benefactor-recipient relationship), which is a closer relationship than Maggie genuinely wants to establish. But however successful, Maggie's boundary violation is clearly morally wrong because Tina wouldn't want to be in that closer relationship and Maggie should know that. A more commonplace example is trying to establish a straight (or gay) romantic relationship with someone who's only interested in gay (or straight) romantic relationships. You shouldn't violate a gay (or straight) person's boundaries in a futile bid to establish a straight (or gay) relationship—it's inappropriate, not to mention a waste of your time.

In some cases, a moment's reflection will make it clear that someone doesn't want the kind of closer relationship you want. But in other cases it's difficult to discern whether someone wants a closer relationship, both because we have limited understanding of other people and because we're apt to be self-deceived.

Conclusions

How does John Cusack always get the girl? It's not by scrupulously respecting her boundaries. It's by violating her boundaries—but in a strategic and morally permissible way. He doesn't act aggressively willynilly, he doesn't disregard her feelings, and he doesn't use her. Rather, he figures out how to push the limits in a way that doesn't harm her (Rule 1) and doesn't push the limits too much too fast (Rule 2). Also, he's genuine about wanting to have a relationship with her (Rule 3), and he's perceptive enough to realize that he has a real shot (Rule 4).

Comprehension Questions

1. What does Barnhill mean by a "boundary violation"?
2. What, exactly, is the Kantian objection to violating people's boundaries?
3. What is a "prospective boundary violation"?
4. What are the "Nosey Questions" and "Becoming Friends" cases supposed to show?
5. Why does Barnhill think that prospective boundary violations sometimes work?

Discussion Questions

1. According to Barnhill, Kantians think that all boundary violations are wrong. Given this, how would Kantians try to start relationships? What would they say is OK?

2. What are some non-romantic examples of morally OK prospective boundary violations?
3. Rule 2 says that you may treat someone as if you're in a somewhat closer relationship, but not a very much closer relationship. The phrases "somewhat closer" and "very much closer" are pretty vague. Could you offer more precise guidelines for the early stages of a dating relationship?
4. Barnhill says that Rule 3 is the one we violate most often. Does this seem right to you? Why or why not?
5. Rule 4 says that the closer relationship that you hope to establish by violating boundaries must be the kind of relationship the other person would plausibly want to have. How are you supposed to determine the sort of relationship that the other person would plausibly want to have?

Case

> Consider this story:
>
>> Alicia had asked another student, Kevin, to be her "platonic date" at a college sorority formal. The two of them went out for dinner first with friends and then to the dance. She remembers that they got drunk but not what she would call sloppy wasted.
>>
>> After the dance, they went to Kevin's room and, eventually, started making out. She told him flat out that she didn't want it to proceed to sex, and he said okay. But after another half hour of kissing, groping, and grinding, he pulled her dress up, laid her down on the couch, and positioned himself on top of her.
>>
>> "No. Stop," she thought. She tried to say something, but he kissed her. When he entered her, she tensed up and tried to go numb until it was over. He fell asleep afterward, and she left for her dorm, "having this dirty feeling of not knowing what to do or who to tell or whether it was my fault." While it felt like rape to her—she had not wanted to have sex with Kevin—she was not sure if that's what anyone else would call it.[4]
>
> Is this a prospective boundary violation gone wrong? Like the women in Barnhill's essay, Alicia says she doesn't want anything to happen. However, after a lot of foreplay, it might be reasonable to think that Alicia is open to a sexual encounter. And although Kevin agreed to go on a "platonic" date, perhaps he really was interested in Alicia. Did Kevin violate any of Barnhill's rules? If so, which one? Is this case a good argument for having a "Yes Means Yes" approach to sexual consent—where only explicit verbal consent makes sex OK? Why or why not?

Notes

1. You can watch the scene at www.hulu.com/watch/83434/the-office-andy-serenades-angela. I'm sorry that the three paradigm examples of charming boundary violation I've found all feature young, white, middle-class straight people, and that they're examples of men violating women's boundaries. But such is the stuff of mainstream film and television.

2. Thomas Hill, *Dignity and Practical Reason in Kant's Moral Theory* (Ithaca, NY: Cornell University Press, 1992), p. 50.

3. Christine Korsgaard, *Creating the Kingdom of Ends* (Cambridge: Cambridge University Press, 1996), p. 142.

4. I've adapted this story from: http://www.cosmopolitan.com/sex-love/advice/a1912/new-kind-of-date-rape/

PART II

Abortion

=== 🐌 ===

9

Is Abortion a Question
of Personal Morality?

Julie Kirsch

Is abortion one of those "to each her own" sort of issues? The kind of
thing we don't need to settle, since it's really about personal values and
not public ones? Lots of people seem to think so. However, Kirsch isn't
convinced. She considers four ways of understanding the claim that
abortion is a matter of personal morality, and she concludes that each
way of interpreting the claim makes it very hard to defend. According
to Kirsch, we probably can't say that abortion is a question of personal
morality unless we've already settled prior questions about the status
of the fetus—questions that are, of course, really difficult to answer.

. . . Nobody is tempted to think that rape, war, murder, or child abuse are
questions of personal morality. But many are attracted to the view that
abortion is a question of personal morality. A defender of this view might
express it in the following way:

> Personally, I believe that abortion is wrong (or right). But whether or
> not abortion is wrong is a question that each person must consider
> and answer for herself.

Kirsch, Julie. 2013. "Is Abortion a Question of Personal Morality?" *International Journal of
Applied Philosophy* 27(1): 91–99. DOI: 10.5840/ijap20132715

This view implies that we can distinguish between an individual's *personal* beliefs and her *public* beliefs about abortion. Typically, the defender of this view is reluctant to claim that her individual beliefs settle the issue, as it were, or translate into constraints upon the behavior others. An individual's public beliefs about abortion will often concern matters of policy and law. Someone who believes publicly that abortion is a question of personal morality would likely support the legalization and accessibility of abortion. In this view, the law should not prevent women from making up their own minds about the ethics of abortion and acting accordingly.

At first glance, and perhaps upon closer examination, the view that abortion is a question of personal morality is puzzling. Ordinarily, when one believes that something, e.g., murder, is wrong, one believes that it is wrong for everyone. The fact that you and I disagree about the ethics of murder does not show that it is a question of personal morality. Our disagreement does not imply that murder is, say, wrong for me but right for you. But if one believes that abortion is a question of personal morality, then this is what one appears to be saying. The problem with this view is especially clear if we focus upon an individual who is personally, but not publicly, opposed to abortion. For such an individual, the belief that abortion is publicly permissible seems to undermine the belief that it is personally impermissible. How can one simultaneously believe that abortion is personally wrong but publicly permissible? How can one encourage or tolerate the performance of acts within the public domain that one takes to be seriously wrong within the private domain? More needs to be said about abortion as a question of personal morality before we can answer these and other questions.

Politically Correct Cultural Relativism

Let us first dispose of the least defensible, but quite popular, interpretation of the claim that abortion is a question of personal morality. For some, the claim that abortion is a question of personal morality is the expression of tolerance in the face of religious and cultural differences. We should "live and let live," instead of imposing our own narrow and culturally-relative conception of the good upon others. It is often thought to be politically incorrect, or culturally insensitive, to announce or defend one's own moral beliefs in the presence of others. On this interpretation, abortion is a question of personal morality because it is culturally relative or contingent upon one's own religious, spiritual, or philosophical beliefs. Hereafter, I will refer to this view as "politically correct cultural relativism."

Politically correct cultural relativists often understand belief in a personal, relativistic kind of way. It is not uncommon for one person to respond to the moral views of another by claiming that "She has her beliefs, and I have mine," or by asking, "Who am I to judge?" Within such circles, belief is thought to be something that is equally justified or lacking in justification by all. Accordingly, one belief is just as good as another, and one believer is just as good as another. There is rarely talk about the evidence in support of any particular belief, or about the epistemic virtues possessed by any particular believer.

One problem with politically correct cultural relativism is that it is rarely supported by argumentation. Instead, it is put forward in the name of tolerance; it is a strategy for minimizing social turbulence and maintaining congenial relations with others. It is socially useful and polite, but often at the expense of being completely unthinking. It is largely a social policy that its adherents adopt as a way of living peacefully with others in a multicultural society. It also has nothing unique and insightful to say about why *abortion* is a question of personal morality. The best that it can do is to say that abortion is a question of personal morality because *everything* is a question of personal morality. There are no universal standards of morality because religions and cultures disagree about what is good or right.

Mill's Harm Principle

[Alternately, we] might view abortion as a question of personal, not public, morality because we value individuality and freedom of choice. Defenders of this view might find inspiration in John Stuart Mill's celebrated harm principle. The principle is:

> [T]he sole end for which mankind are warranted, individually or collectively, in interfering with the liberty of action of any of their number, is self-protection. . . .[1]

In Mill's view, the function and scope of the state has definite limits; it cannot extend its reach to questions of personal choice or morality that do not directly harm others. . . . If abortion is a choice that does not harm others, then we might have grounds for viewing it as a question of personal morality.

The problem with this view ... is that it appears to be question-begging. One of the major points of disagreement between liberals and conservatives concerns the status of abortion as a victimless act. Liberals and feminists often argue that abortion is morally permissible because it is victimless; conservatives argue that abortion is morally wrong precisely because there is a victim, i.e., the innocent human fetus. [. . . So] it does not *immediately* or *obviously* follow from Mill's harm principle that abortion is a question of personal morality. . . .

Standards of Justification

Thomas Nagel offers a promising account of what one means when one says that abortion, or any other question, is a matter of personal morality. Nagel's discussion of personal morality arises in the course of a more general discussion about toleration and political legitimacy. Nagel is interested in how a liberal can support freedom of choice about an issue within the public domain while at the same time holding strong beliefs about the issue within the personal domain. The liberal's doxastic state of mind seems to suggest that she is unsure or skeptical about her own moral beliefs. But Nagel rejects this conclusion.[2] Instead, he argues that the liberal's standards of justification within the public domain are higher than they are within the personal domain. When it comes to state intervention, or limitations upon individual freedom of choice, liberals demand that strict standards of justification be met. While it may be permissible to base beliefs within the personal domain upon instinct or faith, it is impermissible to do so within the public domain. Within the public domain, the grounds of one's beliefs must be made available to all and subjected to rational criticism.[3] The upshot of this is that a person can take her beliefs to be personally but not publicly justified. The fact that she is unable to justify her personal beliefs to the public does not show that she is irrational, skeptical, or insincere. Rather, it shows that she holds beliefs within the public domain to stricter standards of justification.

Nagel applies this distinction between personal and public justification to the issue of abortion. He states that at least some who oppose the legal prohibition of abortion "believe that it is morally wrong, but that their reasons for this belief cannot justify the use of state power against those who are convinced otherwise."[4]

[. . . However, as] we have already seen, a main point of contention between liberals and conservatives concerns the status of abortion as a victimless act. If abortion is closer to murder than it is to a haircut, then [. . . the] debate about abortion would more closely resemble debates about other issues within the public domain, issues that are far from personal. Nagel responds to this concern by claiming that issues of personal morality deal with matters of individual conduct. In his view, public debates, such as the debates surrounding nuclear deterrence and capital punishment,

> [A]re poor candidates for liberal toleration because they are not matters of individual conduct, which the state may or may not decide to regulate. So no conclusion about what the state should do can be derived from the refusal to justify the use of state power by reference to any particular position on the issue. The application of the death penalty or the possession of the military of nuclear weapons cannot be left to the private conscience of each individual citizen: the state *must* decide.[5]

Nagel is right to insist that the state must decide or develop a stance on capital punishment and nuclear deterrence. As he observes, these issues are clearly not issues of individual conduct or choice. But these considerations alone do not show that abortion is just an issue of individual conduct. Undoubtedly, decisions about abortion are decisions that individuals can and do make about their own conduct. But, depending upon one's view of the fetus, they may also be decisions that affect others. [. . . Nagel] does not adequately distinguish between abortion and other acts of conduct, such as rape, child abuse, and murder, that no one would judge to be issues of personal morality. Still wanting is an explanation of why the choice to have an abortion is *personal*.

Unique Importance

We can make some progress towards answering this question by taking a closer look at the choice to have an abortion. My suspicion is that those who take abortion to be a question of personal morality believe that reproductive choices are uniquely important and private. The decision to continue or terminate a pregnancy is one that can profoundly change the course of a woman's life. Being a parent is typically a lifetime commitment that can involve enormous sacrifices in one's education, career, relationships, finances, personal aspirations, and more. In choosing to become a parent, a woman may at the same time be choosing not to complete her degree, become a doctor, have children later in life, or end a toxic relationship. All miracles aside, decisions about whether or when to have children simultaneously open and close a variety of other possibilities for women.

Reproductive choices also involve an individual's body in a way that other choices do not. A pregnancy unfolds within a woman's body; a woman cannot take a break from her pregnancy, or lock it in her bedroom while she devotes herself to other projects. The fetus gestating within her womb becomes a semi-permanent part of her expanding, swollen, and often burdensome body. Unless she chooses adoption (and perhaps even then), the choice to continue a pregnancy will stay with her for the rest of her life. For some, the bodily aspect of pregnancy is welcomed as a source of building an intimacy with the fetus understood as the future child. It has been said that the pain and suffering of pregnancy is preparation for a future of motherhood. But when the pregnancy itself is unwanted, so also may be the experience of carrying another within oneself.

Finally, unlike murder, rape, and child abuse, the choice to have an abortion is typically not motivated by hatred or malice. The woman who contemplates an abortion is not trying to bring about suffering, or to humiliate her victim. A critic may take her choice to be misguided, or accuse her of negligence, irresponsibility, or selfishness. These accusations may or may not be appropriate in any particular case. But even those who object to abortion are reluctant to attribute to the woman who chooses an abortion the mindset of a rapist or serial killer. The context surrounding an abortion, and the motivation of the woman in question, shape our understanding of the choice to have an abortion.

Those who take abortion to be a question of personal morality seem to weigh the uncertainty about the status of the fetus against the certainty of what the choice to have an abortion means for women. Using Nagel's terminology, we might say that defenders of this view believe that high standards of justification must be met within the domain of public morality, and are not met in the case of abortion. They then weigh this failure of justification against the certain, or nearly certain, understanding of what the choice to have an abortion means for women. This interpretation of abortion as a question of personal morality avoids two serious problems associated with the others: (1) It is not an unthinking strategy for maintaining polite relations with others. Instead, it is based upon an understanding of abortion, and the epistemic situation of any moral believer; (2) it is mindful of the unique set of issues surrounding abortion, and the features of abortion decisions that make them particularly private and personal. There is, however, one problem with the interpretation that remains: It fails to establish that abortion is a victimless act, and thus purely personal.

As we have seen, there is good reason to view the choice to have an abortion as a deeply personal matter of individual conduct. But what is comparatively less clear is that the issue is *purely* personal, i.e., that it does not involve another person. If the choice to have an abortion involves a second person, and is not victimless, then we may have a difficult time justifying its position within the realm of personal morality. As we have seen, Nagel argues that abortion is a question of personal morality because one's stance on the issue cannot satisfy the strict standards of public justification. But this cannot be all that there is to matters of personal morality. After all, we often have a difficult time justifying various public stances as well. A person may not be able to formulate a knockdown argument that polygamy is wrong even though she believes both publicly and personally that it is. She may judge polygamy to be an issue of public morality because it involves the well-being of others.

It is also important to note that some conservatives wholeheartedly believe that the grounds of their beliefs fully satisfy the standards of public morality. John Finnis, for instance, denies that the abortion issue is "even a close call."[6] He claims that anyone who examines the arguments on both sides without bias will conclude that abortion is wrong. In his view, "the self-preferences of men and women" interfere with their ability to consider the arguments impartially.[7] . . . Whether or not we agree with Finnis, it should be clear that the content of the abortion question involves a possible other person. The question itself asks us to consider whether or not a certain kind of being (in this case, the human fetus) is a member of the moral community. It is a fundamental moral question that must be open to public discussion and debate, even if we ultimately accept the liberal answer. We cannot form a policy on abortion without knowing something about the moral status of the fetus. In so doing, we must ask ourselves whether the fetus more closely resembles an unwanted patch of hair, say, or a "normal" adult human being. . . .

One problem with encouraging public debate about the abortion question is that we might end up without a solution; for, no agreement on the issue seems forthcoming. If this is the case, which position should we adopt as a matter of public policy? Should we adopt the position of the majority or most powerful—whether or not their arguments are decisive? Stephen Macedo, who does take the disagreement about abortion to be a reasonable one, recommends that the two sides strike a compromise:

> On policy issues such as abortion, which seems, as things stand, to come down to a fairly close call between two well-reasoned set of arguments, the best thing for reasonable people to do might be to acknowledge the difficulty of the argument and the burdens of reason, to respect their opponents and to compromise with them, and to find some middle ground that gives something to each side while the argument goes forward. The right kind of middle ground on abortion would acknowledge both the great weight due to the judgment of the mother and the fact that this choice concerns the continuance of another life. It would, perhaps, honor a woman's choice up to a certain point in the pregnancy and also countenance a variety of measures that would not be permitted were abortion simply a matter of an individual's right to choose.[8]

Macedo's suggestion here is reasonable. But the stakes of the abortion debate are so high that the two sides might find this suggestion impossible to accept. If, like Finnis, one sincerely believes that abortion is murder, then any sort of compromise may appear unconscionable; for it would involve the willed abandonment of vulnerable children to certain death. If one is thoroughly convinced that an embryo is "just a clump of cells," then any restrictions upon a woman's right to choose may seem inappropriate or invasive. We would, again, be at a standstill with no satisfactory way out. Perhaps the only solution that both sides can live with in good conscience is a perpetual tug-of-war in which each side resolutely stands its own ground. To compromise would be to betray oneself on what I have argued is a fundamental question of moral concern.

. . . Still, the fact that we are unable to abandon our convictions or compromise does not show that the question stands beyond the scope of public morality. . . . We cannot establish that abortion is a question of personal morality without knowing something about the status of the fetus.

Comprehension Questions

1. Why does Kirsch say that, at first glance, it's surprising that someone would take abortion to be a question of personal morality?
2. What is Politically Correct Cultural Relativism? What's supposed to be wrong with it?

3. What does Mill's Harm Principle say? Why doesn't it show that abortion is a question of personal morality?

4. What is the "Different Standards of Justification" view? Why doesn't it show that abortion is a question of personal morality?

5. What is the "Unique Importance" view? Why doesn't it show that abortion is a question of personal morality?

Discussion Questions

1. Before reading this essay, would you have said that abortion is a question of personal morality? If so, why? Did your reasons match some of the ones that Kirsch discusses, or did you have different ones? If you *wouldn't* have said that abortion is a question of personal morality, why do you think that others have this view? Is it for one of the reasons that Kirsch discusses, or other ones?

2. What do you think people trying to accomplish, whether socially or politically, when they say that abortion is a question of personal morality?

3. Can you think of any negative consequences of having "private" and "public" standards for believing things? Are there any costs to not having a single standard—whatever it would be?

4. What sort of public policies might we have if we went with Stephen Macedo's call for compromise?

Case

Mark Lawrence Schrad and his wife are self-described "pro-choice liberals." Still, when they were given an in utero diagnosis of Down syndrome, they decided not to terminate the pregnancy. After telling this story, Schrad uses it to inform his criticism of some proposed legislation in Ohio:

> That abortion is not the exception, but rather the expectation in cases of Down syndrome, is not limited to medical professionals. Though precise numbers are unavailable, at least two-thirds and as many as 90 percent of fetuses found to have Down syndrome in utero are aborted . . . So it raised eyebrows when we—a couple of pro-choice liberals—informed our doctors that we had chosen not to terminate the pregnancy. There was pushback: Did we not understand the decision?
>
> We were sure that we'd love and care for our child regardless of her abilities. Today, despite complications and frustrations beyond those

of raising a typical child, Sophia is an exuberant eight-year-old, soaking up the last rays of summer fun before entering third grade.

We have never had second thoughts, even though we understand why some parents might choose otherwise. Which is why it was particularly distressing to learn that this fall Ohio is likely to become the second state (after North Dakota) to outlaw abortion after an in utero diagnosis of Down syndrome.

... [A]s my wife and I learned, when it comes to abortion and special needs, there is no easy answer—and the idea that these deeply personal ethical and social decisions could simply be legislated away is ridiculous. ...

For one thing, conventional pro-life versus pro-choice debates quickly become tinged with overtones about "slippery-slope" genocide, predicting the eventual disappearance of people with Down syndrome as a group. Such claims are often hysterical, but they're not ungrounded: As our ability to screen for "undesirable" genetic traits expands, so does the potential for abortion based upon those characteristics. ...

In a typical pregnancy, women who choose to have an abortion are often saddled with shame and social stigma, even from friends, relatives and the broader public. Meanwhile, despite recent strides, there remains significant stigma associated with being the parent of a child with special needs.

In the end, my wife and I *chose* to have Sophia. We had to fight for her in the face of widespread medical and societal pressures to terminate. And that was our choice.

The Ohio bill would do away with that choice, forcing everyone placed in that unenviable situation to carry to term a child with developmental disabilities, regardless of their willingness and ability to love and care for that child once it is born.[9]

Contra Kirsch, Schrad seems to think that abortion is a personal choice. What's his argument for that claim? And how might Kirsch reply? Why do you think that the doctors were less inclined to treat abortion as a personal choice after a Down syndrome diagnosis? Are their reasons good ones? Why or why not?

Notes

1. John Stuart Mill, *On Liberty. John Stuart Mill On Liberty and Other Essays*, ed. John Gray (Oxford: Oxford University Press, 1991), 14.
2. Thomas Nagel, "Moral Conflict and Political Legitimacy," *Philosophy and Public Affairs* 16 (1987): 228.
3. Ibid., 232.
4. Ibid., 234.

5. Ibid.

6. John Finnis, "Is Natural Law Theory Compatible with Limited Government?," in *Natural Law, Liberalism, and Morality*, ed. Robert P. George (Oxford: Clarendon Press, 1996), 1–26, 18.

7. Ibid.

8. Stephen Macedo, "In Defense of Liberal Public Reason: Are Slavery and Abortion Hard Cases?," in *Natural Law and Public Reason*, ed. Robert P. George and Christopher Wolfe (Washington, DC: Georgetown University Press, 2000), 11–49, 30.

9. http://www.nytimes.com/2015/09/04/opinion/does-down-syndrome-justify-abortion.html

===== 🐦 =====

10

Abortion

John Harris and Søren Holm

....

Is a fetus a person? If so, why? If not, then could it still be wrong to
abort it? Harris and Holm survey various answers to these questions.
First, they discuss the Lockean view, according to which you need to
have various sophisticated cognitive capacities to be a person. They
then explore the possibility that personhood begins when life begins
and the value of being a *potential* person. Finally, they consider the
ethics of abortion if fetuses *aren't* persons. Might abortion still be
wrong because it robs fetuses of "a future like ours"?

....

1. The Status of the Fetus

One of the main strategies for showing the moral respectability of abortion or at least its moral neutrality is to show that the killing of the fetus
that is part of the abortion procedure is not morally wrong. The main
class of arguments trying to show this are the so-called "personhood arguments." These build on ideas in John Locke. . .

In the following sections we will first lay out the personhood arguments and then look at arguments trying to show that killing a fetus is
actually wrong, and that the personhood analysis is misguided.

Harris, John and Søren Holm. 2003. "Abortion." In *The Oxford Handbook of Practical Ethics*,
ed. Hugh LaFollette, 112–135. New York: Oxford University Press.

2. What Is "Personhood"?

In the middle of the seventeenth century in his *Essay Concerning Human Understanding* the philosopher John Locke attempted to give an account of the sorts of features that make an individual a person:

> We must consider what person stands for; which I think is a thinking intelligent being, that has reason and reflection, and can consider itself the same thinking thing, in different times and places; which it does only by that consciousness which is inseparable from thinking and seems to me essential to it; it being impossible for anyone to perceive without perceiving that he does perceive (Locke 1690/1964: 188).

This account of personhood identifies a range of capacities as the preconditions for personhood. These capacities are interesting in that they are species, gender, race, and organic-life-form neutral. Thus persons might, in principle, be members of any species, or indeed machines, if they have the right sorts of capacities. The connection between personhood and moral value arises in two principal ways. One of these ways involves the fact that the capacity for self-consciousness coupled with a minimum intelligence, identified by Locke, is not only necessary for moral agency but is also the minimum condition for almost any deliberative behavior. More significantly, however, is the fact that it is these capacities that allow individuals to value their own existence and that of others. It allows individuals to take an interest in their own futures, and to take a view about how important it is for them to experience whatever future existence may be available (Harris 1980, 1985, 1992).

In this view, the wrong done to an individual when his existence is ended prematurely is the wrong of depriving that individual of something that he values. On the other hand, to kill or to fail to sustain the life of a non-person, in that it cannot deprive that individual of anything that he, she, or it could conceivably value, does that individual no harm. It takes from such individuals nothing that they would prefer not to have taken from them. This does not, of course, exhaust the wrongs that might be done in ending or failing to sustain the life of another sentient creature. Some of these wrongs will have to do with causing pain or suffering or apprehension to a creature, others will have to do with wrongs that may be done to those persons that take a benevolent interest in the individual concerned (Marquis 1989; Harris 1992).

This account gives one answer to the ethics of abortion and this is why theories of personhood have come to figure significantly in the abortion debate. To this extent, it does what a theory of personhood should try to do. It explains many of the judgments that we intuitively make about these issues, resolves some of the dilemmas that we have about the ethics of decision making, and gives us ways to approach new and possibly unforeseen dilemmas. In uniting and explaining some of our basic intuitions in biomedical ethics, it of course also violates some of these intuitions. In telling us how to handle existing hard cases, it creates some new hard cases.

2.1 Criteria for Personhood

This account offers criteria for personhood in that any self-conscious, minimally intelligent being will be a person. The problem is that we not only want reliable criteria for personhood, but we want *detectable evidence of personhood*. Here matters are not so simple, and we need to know whether and why we should assume that the sorts of creatures that we know to be normally capable of developing self-consciousness—namely, human creatures—are persons at some time prior to the manifestation of the "symptoms" of personhood.

Those who give prominence to theories of personhood do so because they think that accounts of personhood help with questions about the ethics of killing and letting die. Many people who have been interested in the distinctions between different sorts of creatures that personhood highlights have followed John Locke in emphasizing a particular sort of mental life as characterizing personhood. Personhood provides a species-neutral way of grouping creatures that have lives that it would be wrong to end by killing or by letting die. These may include animals, machines, extraterrestrials, gods, angels, and devils. All, if they were capable of valuing existence, would, whatever else they were, be persons.

Personhood applied to human individuals implies that the life cycle of a given individual passes through a number of stages of different moral significance. The human individual comes into being before it acquires personhood. This individual will gradually move from being a potential or a pre-person into an actual person when she develops whatever characteristics are thought to be distinctive of personhood. And if, eventually, she permanently loses these characteristics prior to death, she will have ceased to be a person.

Personhood then is an idea used to characterize individuals who have the highest moral importance or value. The term "respect for persons" encapsulates this "ultimate" moral importance and attempts to give it content—to explain just what those who accept the moral importance of persons are committed to in concrete terms. Respect for persons understood as a moral principle sets out the ways in which it is appropriate to behave towards those who matter morally in this "ultimate" sense. Non-persons may, of course, be harmed in other ways; by being caused pain, for example. Respect for persons then not only describes the outcome—treating others in morally appropriate ways—but also points to the origin of this obligation in the ultimate or supreme moral value of particular sorts of individuals. We have examined one account of personhood derived from John Locke, which attempts to connect personhood with value and which gives one account of the wrongfulness of ending the lives of persons and hence one account of the rights and wrongs of abortion. On this account of personhood, abortion is permitted so long as neither the embryo nor the fetus is an individual possessing self-consciousness and an intelligence sufficient to value its own existence.

This account of personhood has a number of disadvantages. The first is that, depending on how the criteria for personhood are interpreted, it can lead to the conclusion that infanticide is permissible, since it is difficult to show relevant differences between the capacities of the late fetus and the newborn. For those who are clear that infanticide is morally impermissible, this will tend to rule out adoption of personhood as a criterion of moral worth. Whether accounts of personhood also permit ending the lives of severely mentally retarded adults will depend on whether the degree of retardation is such as to totally rule out self-consciousness and rudimentary intelligence. There will be few such cases. However, those in a permanent vegetative state (PVS) will have lost their personhood.

Are there other accounts of when a creature is a person?

3. Persons Exist When Human Life Begins

Many people have thought that the problem of when life becomes morally important, in the ultimate sense that personhood demands, is answered by knowing when life begins. When can human life be said to begin and is it plausible to believe that the life of a person begins simultaneously with human life? Human sperm and eggs are both alive prior to conception, and the egg undergoes a process of maturation without which conception would be impossible. Both sperm and egg are alive and are human, although this does not, of course, mean that either of them individually constitutes "human life." The event most popularly taken to mark the starting point of human life is conception. But conception can result in a hydatidiform mole, a cancerous multiplication of cells that will never become a person, and, even when human life does begin at conception, it is not necessarily the life of an individual; twins may form at any point up to approximately fourteen days following conception.

Cloning also has raised problems for our understanding of when life begins. If one has a pre-implantation embryo in the early stages of development when all cells are toti-potent—that is, where any of the cells could become any part of the resulting individual, or indeed the whole individual—and one splits this early cell mass (anything up to the sixty-four-cell stage) into, say, four clumps of cells, each of the four clumps would constitute a new, viable embryo that could be implanted with every hope of successful development into adulthood. Each clump is the clone or identical "twin" of each of the others and comes into being not through conception but because of the division of the early cell mass. These four clumps of cells can be recombined into one embryo. Thus, without the destruction of a single human cell, one human can be split into four and can be recombined again into one. Did "life" in such a case begin as an individual, become four individuals, and then turn into a singleton again? All this occurred without the creation of extra matter and without the destruction of a single cell. Those who think that ensoulment, the point at which the divinely sent immortal soul is supposed to enter and animate the body, takes place at conception have an interesting problem to account for the splitting of one soul into four, and for the destruction of three souls when the four embryos are recombined into one, and to account for the destruction of three individuals without a single human cell being removed or killed.

3.1 Speciesism and Natural Kinds

It is possible simply to stipulate that membership of the human species confers moral importance and hence personhood (Warnock 1983). This stipulation of a preference for one kind of creature over another (particularly when this preference is asserted by self-interested individuals on behalf of their own kind) requires justification. Claims in which the moral priority and superiority of "our own kind" have been asserted on behalf of Greeks at the expense of barbarians, whites over blacks, Nazis over Jews, and men over women have been common and seem of doubtful logic and more doubtful morality. Assertion of the superiority of our own kind, whether defined by species membership, race, gender, nationality, or religion, seems not only unjustified but unjustifiable. What then would support assertion of moral priority for membership of a natural kind?

3.2 Potentiality

How then to distinguish, in some morally significant respect, human embryos from the embryos and indeed the adult members of any other species? One feature of human embryos that members of other species do not share is their potential, not simply to be born and to be human, but to become the sort of complex, intelligent, self-conscious, multifaceted creatures typical of the human species.

There seem to be two problems with potentiality interpreted as the idea that human embryos or fetuses are morally important beings in virtue of their potential. The first is logical: acorns are not oak trees, nor eggs omelettes. It does not follow from the fact that something has potential to become something different that we must treat it always as if it had achieved that potential. We are all potentially dead but it does not follow that we must be treated now as if we are already dead.

The second difficulty with the potentiality argument involves the scope of the potential for personhood. If the human zygote has the potential to become an adult human being and is supposedly morally important in virtue of that potential, then what of the potential to become a zygote? Something has the potential to become a zygote, and whatever has the potential to become the zygote has whatever potential the zygote has. It follows that the unfertilized egg and the sperm also have the potential to become fully functioning adult humans. In addition, it is theoretically possible to stimulate eggs, including human eggs, to divide and develop without fertilization (parthenogenesis). As yet it has not been possible to continue the development process artificially beyond early stages of embryogenesis, but if it ever does become possible, then the single unfertilized egg, without need of sperm or cloning, would itself have the potential of the zygote.

Cloning by nuclear transfer, which involves deleting the nucleus of an unfertilized egg, inserting the nucleus taken from any adult cell, and electrically stimulating the resulting newly created egg to develop, can, in theory, produce a new human. This was the method used to produce the first cloned animal, Dolly the sheep, in 1997. This means that any cell from a normal human body has the potential to become a new "twin" of that individual. All that is needed is an appropriate environment and appropriate stimulation. The techniques of parthenogenesis and cloning by nuclear substitution mean that conception is no longer the necessary precursor of human beings.

Thus, if the argument from potential is understood to afford protection and moral status to whatever has the potential to grow into a normal adult human being, then potentially every human cell deserves protection.

However, defenders of the argument from potential will claim that this view of potentiality misrepresents their position. John Finnis, for example, has argued that: "An organic capacity for developing eyesight is not 'the bare fact that something will become' sighted; it is an existing reality, a thoroughly unitary ensemble of dynamically inter-related primordia of, bases and structures for, development." He concludes that "there is no sense whatever in which the unfertilized ovum and that sperm constitute one organism, a dynamic unity, identity, whole" (1995: 50).

However, it is surely the case that A has the potential for Z if, when a certain number of things do and do not happen to A (or to A plus N), then A (or A plus N) will become Z. Even a "unitary ensemble of dynamically interrelated primordia of, bases and structures, for development" must have a certain number of things happen to it and a certain number of things that do not happen to it if its potential is to be actualized. If A is a zygote, it must implant, be nourished, and have a genetic constitution compatible with survival to term and beyond. Moreover, insistence on a "unitary ensemble," on "one organism," seems also to apply to cloning by nuclear substitution, surely an embarrassing fact. In any adult cell there is a complete single human genome, which, if treated appropriately, might be cloned. Thus this method of cloning allows for the "existing reality" of a complete genome that exhibits the "dynamic unity, identity, whole[ness]" that the Finnis analysis requires and we can therefore now ascribe potentiality in the Finnis sense to the nucleus of every cell in every body.

The moral importance of drawing attention to the potentiality of something suggests that it is actualizing a particular potential that matters. Our moral concern with what it is that has the potential to become an adult human being would be inexplicable if persons or adult humans did not matter. We are interested in the potentiality argument because we are interested in the potential to become a particular, and particularly valuable, sort of thing. If the zygote is important because it has the potential for personhood, and *that* is what makes it a matter of importance to protect and actualize its potential, then whatever has the potential to become a zygote must also be morally significant *for the same reason*. Those who value potentiality for personhood surely do so not because the potential is contained within "one organism," but because it is the potential to become something the actualization of which has moral importance.

4. The Rejection of Abortion

Traditionally rejection of abortion has been based on the idea that killing innocent human beings is ethically wrong, and that the fetus obviously falls within the class of innocent human beings. As we have argued above, personhood arguments attempt to show this traditional argument to be false by showing that the wrongness of killing is based in the possession of features that the fetus does not have.

We will now look at the positive arguments that support the traditional view that there is something seriously wrong involved in killing the fetus.

5. A Life Like Ours

Personhood arguments claim that the wrongness of killing should be dissociated from species membership and membership of any other natural class, and should instead be located in the thwarting of an interest that the individual who is killed possesses. It is, however, possible to develop arguments with a similar structure that leads to the conclusion that killing the fetus is morally wrong.

One such argument has been proposed by Marquis (1989). He suggests that what is wrong with killing adult human beings is that we deprive them of their future, and that this can be further explicated as depriving them of "a life like ours." The harm done to someone who is killed is not just that we go against their desire to keep on living (which may conceivably have many different levels of strength and importance, thereby making the magnitude of the wrongness of killing different in each case), but that we deprive them of their whole future, a future that is so multifaceted that it only makes sense to describe it in broad terms like "a life like ours." We do, for instance, deprive them not only of the future fulfilment of their present desires, but also of the future formation of new desires and preferences.

This analysis of the wrongness of killing has the great advantage that it can explain why it would be wrong to kill someone who temporarily has no preferences for going on living. It also avoids being speciesist, because it would make it wrong to kill any being or machine having a future sufficiently like the one we have.

On this analysis, the fetus that is killed is deprived of a life like ours in exactly the same way as any other human being who is killed. There may be other wrong-making factors involved in killing adults (for instance, relating to their preferences not to be killed), but the basic wrong-making factor is involved in killing both fetuses and adults. Killing a fetus is, therefore, seriously wrong and the same is *eo ipse* true for abortion. What is wrong in killing the fetus is not that we kill a being with potentiality for attaining the feature that would make it wrong to kill it, but that we kill a being that already has this feature (that is, a future like ours). The future of the fetus is no more logically uncertain or contingent than the future of any other biological individual.

This analysis faces two difficulties. One involves the apparent arbitrariness of the stipulation of a future "like mine." We can imagine the future of persons from other planets—brainy fish, for example—being very unlike "mine" but morally important in ways we could recognize. One way out is to attach importance to the content of the future that then becomes the person-making feature or to make personhood turn not on the character of the future but on the present capacity to want to experience it. A second difficulty may be to stop this argument collapsing into a form of the potentiality argument in that a given unfertilized egg and a sperm (or even the nucleus of one of my own cells) may also be said to have "a future like mine," a future that would include fertilization or cell nuclear substitution (cloning) as one of its events (see the discussion of this above).

6. Becoming a Person

A certain puzzle seems to be inherent in the idea that I at some point in my biological life become a person, and then at some later point before my death may again become a non-person. The puzzle is the following. There seems to be no doubt that I am presently both a biological being and a person, and it would be difficult to argue that only one of these is essential to who I am. In a computer it may be possible to separate hardware and software, but in human beings and all other biological beings the two aspects of me seem to be inextricably and necessarily linked. However, if any personhood view is correct, then we can trace my biological identity as an individual further back in time than we can trace my personal identity. But if "person" is part of what I essentially am, this is a peculiar result, because it would mean that the two sortals—both describing what I essentially am: that is, "Peter Jones (biological individual)" and "Peter Jones (person)"—would have a different analysis. The first would be a substance sortal, whereas the second would be a phase sortal (like "child" or "adult"). This problem can be resolved in three ways: (1) by denying that I am essentially a biological being, (2) by denying that I am essentially a person, or (3) by admitting that both sortals must be of the same type. Of these options only the third is attractive, and, since there is no doubt that "Peter Jones (biological individual)" is a substance sortal, this entails that "Peter Jones (person)" must also be a substance sortal—that is, that, if I am now essentially a person, then I must have been a person for as long as I have been a biological individual.

Against this it can be argued that I cannot have a biological identity and a personal identity. If I am essentially a person, I cannot also be essentially a living organism; if I am essentially a living organism, I cannot also be a person, unless "person" is a phase sortal. . . .

References

Finnis, J. (1995a). "A Philosophical Case against Euthanasia," in J. Keown (ed.), *Euthanasia Examined: Ethical Clinical and Legal Perspectives*. Cambridge: Cambridge University Press, 23–36.

Finnis, J. (1995b). "The Fragile Case for Euthanasia: A Reply to John Harris," in J. Keown (ed.), *Euthanasia Examined: Ethical Clinical and Legal Perspectives*. Cambridge: Cambridge University Press, 46–56.

Harris, J. (1980). *Violence and Responsibility*. London: Routledge & Kegan Paul.

Harris, J. (1985). *The Value of Life*. London: Routledge & Kegan Paul.

Harris, J. (1992). *Wonderwoman and Superman*. Oxford: Oxford University Press.

Harris, J. (1998). "Rights and Reproductive Choice," in J. Harris and S. Holm (eds.), *The Future of Human Reproduction*. Oxford: Oxford University Press.

Locke, J. (1690/1964). *Essay Concerning Human Understanding*, ed. A. S. Pringle-Pattison. Oxford: Clarendon Press.

Marquis, D. (1989). "Why Abortion is Immoral." *Journal of Philosophy* 86, 183–202.

Warnock, Mary. (1983). "In Vitro Fertilization: The Ethical Issues." *Philosophical Quarterly* 33, 241.

Comprehension Questions

1. Why is it that, in Locke's view, a fetus isn't a person?
2. Why do Harris and Holm bring up hydatidiform moles? What is that example supposed to show?
3. Why do pre-implantation embryos make trouble for the "life begins at conception" view?
4. "Acorns are not oak trees." So what?
5. Why, according to Marquis, is abortion usually wrong?
6. You're a person now. Were you ever a fetus? If the answer is "Yes," then what is that supposed to show?

Discussion Questions

1. Harris and Holm say that "we not only want reliable criteria for personhood, but we want *detectable evidence of personhood*." Why? What would be bad about *not* having detectable evidence of personhood?
2. Reread Lock's description of a person. At what point in human development do we fit that description? Does it seem plausible to you that we aren't persons until that point? Why or why not?
3. John Finnis responds to the "any sperm and egg have the potential to be a person" objection. What's his response, and how do Harris and Holm criticize that response? Do those criticisms seem right to you? Explain your answer.
4. In response to Marquis, someone might say that we don't *know* whether the fetus will have a future like ours. It might die as an infant due to some horrible illness. Is this a good objection to Marquis? Does it have any worrisome implications? If so, what are they?

Case

Consider this:

> According to Catholic moral theology, certain basic moral truths are available to all human beings through rational deliberation, and to some through divine revelation within the Church. Among these is the idea that killing innocent human beings is wrong. Within the Church the combination of these two sources of moral truth enables moral theologians to see that the killing of innocent human beings is a special case of the killing of any innocent beings in possession of a rational soul....

Within the Catholic tradition the question about the wrongness of abortion therefore centers on the question of at what time the embryo or fetus becomes ensouled. The Catholic position is often described to be one of immediate ensoulment—that is, that the soul is present from the time of fertilization, but this is actually not the case. . . .

While immediate ensoulment has been defended by some Catholic theologians, the position held by the Church is actually more complicated. Within a rich theological tradition like the Catholic one, a problem very quickly occurs with regard to what one should do in cases of uncertainty, either factual uncertainty or moral uncertainty where bona fide moral authorities disagree on what the right analysis or course of action is. In the case of the ensoulment of the fetus, we have both factual and moral uncertainty. Some authorities defend immediate ensoulment, whereas others defend delayed ensoulment, with different views among the latter on when ensoulment actually occurs. In this situation the Church has adopted the position that, because killing is such a grave moral wrong, one should act cautiously and presume that there may be ensoulment from conception. Abortion and the destruction of embryos should therefore be treated as the killing of an ensouled being.[1]

People often look to their religious traditions to resolve uncertainty. However, it looks like the Catholic tradition has embraced uncertainty in this case, and yet has still tried to offer moral guidance. What do you make of this reasoning? If, at a particular moment in its development, it's uncertain whether the fetus matters, should you err on the side of caution? Or can it be OK to gamble? (If so, when?)

Note

1. Harris, John and Soren Holm. (2003). "Abortion." In *The Oxford Handbook of Practical Ethics*, ed. Hugh LaFollette (New York: Oxford University Press): 120–21.

11

Virtue Theory and Abortion

Rosalind Hursthouse

Does virtue theory have anything to say about abortion? If so, what?
Hursthouse considers these two questions in her essay. First, she
explains that virtue theory doesn't approach abortion the way that
people often do, which is either in terms of women's rights or the
status of the fetus. On Hursthouse's view, neither approach is relevant. She argues that it can be wrong to get an abortion even if you have
the right to get one, and instead of focusing on when personhood
begins, we should focus on well-known biological and social facts.
Second, Hursthouse discusses a host of complicated issues: the seriousness of abortion, whether abortion can ever be a selfish choice,
whether seeing pregnancy as "one more medical condition" is always
an expression of a vice, and the like. She concludes by arguing that
the appropriate response to an abortion may be complex: even if it's
the right choice, it may still be fitting to regret it.

. . . As everyone knows, the morality of abortion is commonly discussed
in relation to just two considerations: first, and predominantly, the status
of the fetus and whether or not it is the sort of thing that may or may not
be innocuously or justifiably killed; and second, and less predominantly

Hursthouse, Rosalind. 1991. "Virtue Theory and Abortion." *Philosophy & Public Affairs*
20(3): 223–246. Reprinted with permission of John Wiley & Sons.

(when, that is, the discussion concerns the *morality* of abortion rather than the question of permissible legislation in a just society), women's rights. If one thinks within this familiar framework, one may well be puzzled about what virtue theory, as such, could contribute. Some people assume the discussion will be conducted solely in terms of what the virtuous agent would or would not do. . . . Others assume that only justice, or at most justice and charity, will be applied to the issue. . . .

[. . . However,] virtue theory quite transforms the discussion of abortion by dismissing the two familiar dominating considerations as, in a way, fundamentally irrelevant. In what way or ways, I hope to make both clear and plausible.

Let us first consider women's rights. Let me emphasize again that we are discussing the *morality* of abortion, not the rights and wrongs of laws prohibiting or permitting it. If we suppose that women do have a moral right to do as they choose with their own bodies, or, more particularly, to terminate their pregnancies, then it may well follow that a *law* forbidding abortion would be unjust. . . . But, putting all questions about the justice or injustice of laws to one side, and supposing only that women have such a moral right, *nothing* follows from this supposition about the morality of abortion, according to virtue theory, once it is noted (quite generally, not with particular reference to abortion) that in exercising a moral right I can do something cruel, or callous, or selfish, light-minded, self-righteous, stupid, inconsiderate, disloyal, dishonest—that is, act viciously. . . . So whether women have a moral right to terminate their pregnancies is irrelevant within virtue theory, for it is irrelevant to the question "In having an abortion in these circumstances, would the agent be acting virtuously or viciously or neither?"

What about the consideration of the status of the fetus—what can virtue theory say about that? One might say that this issue is not in the province of *any* moral theory; it is a metaphysical question, and an extremely difficult one at that. Must virtue theory then wait upon metaphysics to come up with the answer?

At first sight it might seem so. For virtue is said to involve knowledge, and part of this knowledge consists in having the *right* attitude to things. "Right" here does not just mean "morally right" or "proper" or "nice" in the modem sense; it means "accurate, true." One cannot have the right or correct attitude to something if the attitude is based on or involves false beliefs. And this suggests that if the status of the fetus is relevant to the rightness or wrongness of abortion, its status must be known, as a truth, to the fully wise and virtuous person.

But the sort of wisdom that the fully virtuous person has is not supposed to be recondite; it does not call for fancy philosophical sophistication, and it does not depend upon, let alone wait upon, the discoveries of academic philosophers. And this entails the following, rather startling, conclusion: that the status of the fetus—that issue over which so much ink has been spilt—is, according to virtue theory, simply not relevant to the rightness or wrongness of abortion (within, that is, a secular morality).

Or rather, since that is clearly too radical a conclusion, it is in a sense relevant, but only in the sense that the familiar biological facts are relevant. By "the familiar biological facts" mean the facts that most human societies are and have been familiar with—that, standardly (but not invariably), pregnancy occurs as the result of sexual intercourse, that it lasts about nine months, during which time the fetus grows and develops, that standardly it terminates in the birth of a living baby, and that this is how we all come to be.

It might be thought that this distinction—between the familiar biological facts and the status of the fetus—is a distinction without a difference. But this is not so. To attach relevance to the status of the fetus, in the sense in which virtue theory claims it is not relevant, is to be gripped by the conviction that we must go beyond the familiar biological facts, deriving some sort of conclusion from them, such as that the fetus has rights, or is not a person, or something similar. It is also to believe that this exhausts the relevance of the familiar biological facts, that all they are relevant to is the status of the fetus and whether or not it is the sort of thing that may or may not be killed. . . .

[However,] if we are using virtue theory, our first question is not "What do the familiar biological facts show—what can be derived from them about the status of the fetus?" but "How do these facts figure in the practical reasoning, actions and passions, thoughts and reactions, of the virtuous and the nonvirtuous? What is the mark of having the right attitude to these facts and what manifests having the wrong attitude to them?" This immediately makes essentially relevant not only all the facts about human reproduction I mentioned above, but a whole range of facts about our emotions in relation to them as well. I mean such facts as that human parents, both male and female, tend to care passionately about their offspring, and that family relationships are among the deepest and strongest in our lives—and, significantly, among the longest-lasting.

These facts make it obvious that pregnancy is not just one among many other physical conditions; and hence that anyone who genuinely believes that an abortion is comparable to a haircut or an appendectomy is mistaken. The fact that the premature termination of a pregnancy is, in some sense, the cutting off of a new human life, and thereby, like the procreation of a new human life, connects with all our thoughts about human life and death, parenthood, and family relationships, must make it a serious matter. To disregard this fact about it, to think of abortion as nothing but the killing of something that does not matter, or as nothing but the exercise of some right or rights one has, or as the incidental means to some desirable state of affairs, is to do something callous and light-minded, the sort of thing that no virtuous and wise person would do. It is to have the wrong attitude not only to fetuses, but more generally to human life and death, parenthood, and family relationships.

Although I say that the facts make this obvious, I know that this is one of my tendentious points. In partial support of it I note that even the most dedicated proponents of the view that deliberate abortion is just like an appendectomy or haircut rarely hold the same view of spontaneous abortion, that is, miscarriage. It is not so tendentious of me to claim that to react to people's grief over miscarriage by saying, or even thinking, "What a fuss about nothing!" would be callous and light-minded, whereas to try to laugh someone out of grief over an appendectomy scar or a botched haircut would not be. . . .

To say that the cutting off of a human life is always a matter of some seriousness, at any stage, is not to deny the relevance of gradual fetal development. Notwithstanding the well-worn point that clear boundary lines cannot be drawn, our emotions and attitudes regarding the fetus do change as it develops, and again when it is born, and indeed further as the baby grows. Abortion for shallow reasons in the later stages is much more shocking than abortion for the same reasons in the early stages in a way that matches the fact that deep grief over miscarriage in the later stages is more appropriate than it is over miscarriage in the earlier stages (when, that is, the grief is solely about the loss of *this* child, not about, as might be the case, the loss of one's only hope of having a child or of having one's husband's child). Imagine (or recall) a woman who already has children; she had not intended to have more, but finds herself unexpectedly pregnant. Though contrary to her plans, the pregnancy, once established as a fact, is welcomed—and then she loses the embryo almost immediately. If this were bemoaned as a tragedy, it would, I think, be a misapplication of the concept of what is tragic. But it may still properly be mourned as a loss. The grief is expressed in such terms as "I shall always wonder how she or he would have turned out" or "When I look at the others, I shall think, 'How different their lives would have been if this other one had been part of them.'" It would, I take it, be callous and light-minded to say, or think, "Well, she has already *got* four children; what's the problem?"; it would be neither, nor arrogantly intrusive in the case of a close friend, to try to correct prolonged mourning by saying, "I know it's sad, but it's not a tragedy; rejoice in the ones you have." The application of *tragic* becomes more appropriate as the fetus grows, for the mere fact that one has lived with it for longer, conscious of its existence, makes a difference. To shrug off an early abortion is understandable just because it is very hard to be fully conscious of the fetus's existence in the early stages and hence hard to appreciate that an early abortion is the destruction of life. It is particularly hard for the young and inexperienced to appreciate this, because appreciation of it usually comes only with experience.

I do not mean "with the experience of having an abortion" (though that may be part of it) but, quite generally, "with the experience of life." Many women who have borne children contrast their later pregnancies with their first successful one, saying that in the later ones they were conscious of a new life growing in them from very early on. And, more generally, as one reaches the age at which the next generation is coming up close behind one, the counterfactuals "If I, or she, had had an abortion, Alice, or Bob, would not have been born" acquire a significant application, which casts a new light on the conditionals "If I or Alice have an abortion then some Caroline or Bill will not be born."

The fact that pregnancy is not just one among many physical conditions does not mean that one can never regard it in that light without manifesting a vice. When women are in very poor physical health, or worn out from childbearing, or forced to do very physically demanding jobs, then they cannot be described as self-indulgent, callous, irresponsible, or light-minded if they seek abortions mainly with a view to avoiding pregnancy as the physical condition that it is. To go through with a pregnancy when one is utterly exhausted, or when one's job consists of crawling along tunnels hauling coal, as many women in the nineteenth century were obliged to do, is perhaps heroic, but people who do not achieve heroism are not necessarily vicious. That they can view the pregnancy only as eight months of misery, followed by hours if not days of agony and exhaustion, and abortion only as the blessed escape from this prospect, is entirely understandable and does not manifest any lack of serious respect for human life or a shallow attitude to motherhood. What it does show is that something is terribly amiss in the conditions of their lives, which make it so hard to recognize pregnancy and childbearing as the good that they can be. . . .

The foregoing discussion, insofar as it emphasizes the right attitude to human life and death, parallels to a certain extent those standard discussions of abortion that concentrate on it solely as an issue of killing. But it does not, as those discussions do, gloss over the fact, emphasized by those who discuss the morality of abortion in terms of women's rights, that abortion, wildly unlike any other form of killing, is the termination of a pregnancy, which is a condition of a woman's body and results in *her* having a child if it is not aborted. This fact is given due recognition not by appeal to women's rights but by emphasizing the relevance of the familiar biological and psychological facts and their connection with having the right attitude to parenthood and family relationships. But it may well be thought that failing to bring in women's rights still leaves some important aspects of the problem of abortion untouched.

Speaking in terms of women's rights, people sometimes say things like, "Well, it's her life you're talking about too, you know; she's got a right to her own life, her own happiness." And the discussion stops there. But in the context of virtue theory, given that we are particularly concerned with what constitutes a good human life, with what true happiness or *eudaimonia* is, this is no place to stop. We go on to ask, "And is this life of hers a good one? Is she living well?"

If we are to go on to talk about good human lives, in the context of abortion, we have to bring in our thoughts about the value of love and family life, and our proper emotional development through a natural life cycle. The familiar facts support the view that parenthood in general, and motherhood and childbearing in particular, are intrinsically worthwhile, are among the things that can be correctly thought to be partially constitutive of a flourishing human life. If this is right, then a woman who opts for not being a mother (at all, or again, or now) by opting for abortion may thereby be manifesting a flawed grasp of what her life should be, and be about—a grasp that is childish, or grossly materialistic, or shortsighted, or shallow.

I said "*may* thereby"; this *need* not be so. Consider, for instance, a woman who has already had several children and fears that to have another will seriously affect her capacity to be a good mother to the ones she has—she does not show a lack of appreciation of the intrinsic value of being a parent by opting for abortion. Nor does a woman who has been a good mother and is approaching the age at which she may be looking forward to being a good grandmother. Nor does a woman who discovers that her pregnancy may well kill her, and opts for abortion and adoption. Nor, necessarily, does a woman who has decided to lead a life centered around some other worthwhile activity or activities with which motherhood would compete.

People who are childless by choice are sometimes described as "irresponsible," or "selfish," or "refusing to grow up," or "not knowing what life is about." But one can hold that having children is intrinsically worthwhile without endorsing this, for we are, after all, in the happy position of there being more worthwhile things to do than can be fitted into one lifetime. Parenthood, and motherhood in particular, even if granted to be intrinsically worthwhile, undoubtedly take up a lot of one's adult life, leaving no room for some other worthwhile pursuits. But some women who choose abortion rather than have their first child, and some men who encourage their partners to choose abortion, are not avoiding parenthood for the sake of other worthwhile pursuits, but for the worthless one of "having a good time," or for the pursuit of some false vision of the ideals of freedom or self-realization. And some others who say "I am not ready for parenthood yet" are making some sort of mistake about the extent to which one can manipulate the circumstances of one's life so as to make it fulfill some dream that one has. Perhaps one's dream is to have two perfect children, a girl and a boy, within a perfect marriage, in financially secure circumstances, with an interesting job of one's own. But to care too much about that dream, to demand of life that it give it to one and act accordingly, may be both greedy and foolish, and is to run the risk of missing out on happiness entirely. Not only may fate make the dream impossible, or destroy it, but one's own attachment to it may make it impossible. Good marriages, and the most promising children, can be destroyed by just one adult's excessive demand for perfection.

Once again, this is not to deny that girls may quite properly say "I am not ready for motherhood yet," especially in our society, and, far from manifesting irresponsibility or light-mindedness, show an appropriate modesty or humility, or a fearfulness that does not amount to cowardice. However, even when the decision to have an abortion is the right decision—one that does not itself fall under a vice-related term and thereby one that the perfectly virtuous could recommend—it does not follow that there is no sense in which having the abortion is wrong, or guilt inappropriate. For, by virtue of the fact that a human life has been cut short, some evil has probably been brought about, and that circumstances make the decision to bring about some evil the right decision will be a ground for guilt if getting into those circumstances in the first place itself manifested a flaw in character.

What "gets one into those circumstances" in the case of abortion is, except in the case of rape, one's sexual activity and one's choices, or the lack of them, about one's sexual partner and about contraception. The virtuous woman (which here of course does not mean simply "chaste woman" but "woman with the virtues") has such character traits as strength, independence, resoluteness, decisiveness, self-confidence, responsibility, serious-mindedness, and self-determination—and no one, I think, could deny that many women become pregnant in circumstances in which they cannot welcome or cannot face the thought of having *this* child precisely because they lack one or some of these character traits. So even in the cases where the decision to have an abortion is the right one, it can still be the reflection of a moral failing—not because the decision itself is weak or cowardly or irresolute or irresponsible or light-minded, but because lack of the requisite opposite of these failings landed one in the circumstances in the first place. Hence the common universalized claim that guilt and remorse are never appropriate emotions about an abortion is denied. They may be appropriate, and appropriately inculcated, even when the decision was the right one.

Comprehension Questions

1. What does Hursthouse mean when she says that, from the perspective of virtue theory, the right to have an abortion and "the status of the fetus" are irrelevant to whether it's moral to have an abortion?
2. Why does Hursthouse say that it would be "callous and light-minded" to think of abortion as killing something that doesn't matter?
3. Why, on Hursthouse's view, does it matter whether an abortion occurs earlier or later in the pregnancy?
4. Hursthouse says that pregnancy isn't just one among many physical conditions, but she also says that it isn't always vicious to think of pregnancy that way. Why?
5. Hursthouse thinks that abortion can be the right decision, and yet there can be a sense in which it's still wrong. How does she reconcile these two ideas?

Discussion Questions

1. Hursthouse says that the status of the fetus doesn't matter. But you might think that the virtuous person would care about the status of the fetus. Is this a serious problem for Hursthouse? Why or why not?

2. Of the college students who have abortions, many probably think, "I am not ready for motherhood yet." Would Hursthouse say that this is always a good reason for a college student to have an abortion? Why or why not?

3. On Hursthouse's view, it seems that you can have a moral right to act wrongly. Does this seem plausible to you? Why or why not?

4. Hursthouse says that it isn't always an expression of a vice to regard pregnancy as one among many physical conditions, and in support of that claim she discusses women who live very hard lives. Then, she says that if those women view pregnancy as one among many physical conditions, it shows "that something is terribly amiss in the conditions of their lives, which make it so hard to recognize pregnancy and childbearing as the good that they can be." What is Hursthouse trying to say here? When might her point be relevant to the lives of college students?

Case

Consider this case:

It was my junior year of college. I was completely in love and actually living with my (then) boyfriend, Chris. We had officially moved away from the seemingly typical shacking-it-up college couple and were actually playing house. We split the bills and every night I made us dinner. We had made the decision that down the line a sparkly ring, white dress and penguin suit were in our future. A baby fit perfectly into that little dream—later.

Never in a million years did I think going to the doctor over Christmas break for a stomachache would mean finding out I was pregnant. Until reality came into play. We were poor. Unmarried. Still in college. Jobless. Not exactly how I pictured my life—especially not with a baby. But I had a decision to make.

I was a practicing Catholic—I had been raised Catholic and had attended Catholic school for most of my life. . . . The "a" word was not something that was even a part of the conversation. But could I really be a mother before I turned 21? I was already playing house, so how much harder could adding a baby be? . . . I knew I could do it. But there was that small voice in the pit of my gut, the one that always seems to say, . . . "Yes, you'd make it work and be an excellent mother. But are you really, really sure you want to do this? Are you really, really, sure you are prepared?" At this point, I knew I was going to struggle; I felt so selfish. I wasn't worried about what my sorority sisters would say, or my friends back home, or even my professors. I struggled with what I would tell my baby, if I kept it, about how it came into this world. This was such a charged situation for both Chris and me. We both struggled. We wanted to be independent, but at the same time we wanted to be kids. We wanted to be grown-ups, but I wanted to fully celebrate turning twenty-one and drinking twenty-one shots and trying to not puke all over my best friend.

Having a baby at our age would have meant taking a lot of help from others. I think Chris was too proud to let that happen. I knew my parents would help me raise the baby; they would offer emotional and financial support. . . . Chris and I would get married and his parents would help out as well. He was about to graduate from college, so he could get a job quickly, and we could make it work. But, the question became, did we really have to? . . .

[We gave ourselves a month to make a decision.] During that month, my thoughts drowned me. I couldn't focus on my sister, married, age thirty, desperately trying to get pregnant. I couldn't focus on the lessons that the Church had beaten into me for years. I couldn't focus on any of that. So instead I ate chicken queso burritos and thought irrationally. I looked at baby clothes online. I read abortion support group forums.

Chris dealt with it privately. He never really shared his thoughts with me. He simply said, "I support you 100 percent either way. It's not my body, it's not fully my choice." I knew he was a solid man. I knew, from watching him with our dog and the children we knew, that he would be a good father. His father had taught him well. But I also knew he wasn't ready; he, too, wanted to simply be twenty-two, wild and free.

At almost nine weeks, I made my decision. . . . We were going to have a termination.[1]

How might Hursthouse approach this case? What do you think about it?

Note

1. http://www.hercampus.com/health/sexual-health/her-story-i-had-abortion-college

PART III

Sexism, Gender, and Racism

12

§

Sexism

Ann E. Cudd and Leslie E. Jones

....

Cudd and Jones distinguish three varieties of sexism. The first is institutional, which refers to the explicit rules and implicit norms that govern oppressive social institutions. The second is interpersonal, which concerns the way that individuals create or sustain social inequalities. The third is unconscious, which has to do with the psychological mechanisms that promote social inequalities, even when we don't realize that they're at work. Finally, Cudd and Jones highlight one disagreement between feminists. "Equality" feminists think that men and women are basically the same, and that social institutions are to blame for inequality. Change the institutions, fix inequality. "Difference" feminists disagree. They see unjust institutions as the product of interpersonal and unconscious sexism, so merely changing institutions won't work. Moreover, they're open to the possibility that women and men are importantly different from one another, and that those traits unique to women are deeply undervalued.

....

It is a pervasive, long-standing, and deeply disturbing fact that, by many ways of measuring well-being, women around the globe live lesser lives than men. In much of the world they are less well

Cudd, Ann E., and Leslie E. Jones. 2003. "Sexism." In *A Companion to Applied Ethics*, ed. R. G. Frey and C. H. Wellman, 102–117. Malden, MA: Blackwell. Reprinted with permission of John Wiley & Sons.

nourished, less healthy, and less well educated (UNIFEM, 2000). Everywhere they are vulnerable to violence and abuse by men. It has been estimated that as a result of these facts, and because in many places girl babies are disproportionately aborted or killed, there are one billion missing women (Dreze and Sen, 1989). Many more women in the world lack access to education and many more are illiterate. Jobs that are high paying are much less likely to be held by women. Tedious and menial work is much more likely to be done by women. Women in the workforce are paid less than their male counterparts, are more often harassed and intimidated in work, and are far more often responsible for childcare and housework "after work." Independently of their participation in the paying workforce, women suffer from domestic violence at much greater rates, bear primary responsibility for childrearing and housework, and are much more likely to be sick and poor in their old age. In much of the world women do not have access to safe abortion, or sometimes even to contraception, further putting women's health and well-being at risk. Women everywhere bear almost the full burden of unplanned pregnancies. Women in many nations of the world lack full formal equality under the law. Where they have it, they are less likely to be able to access the judicial system, and so still lack substantive equality. And almost nowhere in the world do women hold high government offices at anywhere near the rates of men. In short, when we compare the life prospects of women and men, we find that a woman is far more likely to be poor, unhealthy, abused, and politically disenfranchised, even while she works longer hours and is largely responsible for the primary care of future generations.

Two general explanations could account for this remarkable disparity in life prospects: (1) women are by nature inferior to men, and so less worthy of concern or less able to benefit from equal concern, or (2) women are systematically disadvantaged by society. Under the first we include explanations based on psychology, biology, socio-biology, and so on that maintain that natural differences between men and women are sufficient to justify the comparatively sadder life prospects of women. . . .

In what follows we proceed on the assumption that the more plausible course is to take some version of the second as true. . . .

What Is Sexism?

It is important to note at the outset that sexism is a highly complex notion. . . .

In its widest sense the term "sexism" can be used to refer to anything that creates, constitutes, promotes, sustains, or exploits an unjustifiable distinction between the sexes (Frye, 1983: 18). In this wide sense the term "sexism" (and its nominative "sexist") can be used to refer to any purported though mistaken difference between the sexes. This neutral descriptive use of the term, however, is deeply unsatisfactory. . . .

One catalyst for the identification of sexism was women's participation in struggles against racism. In fact, the first wave of the women's movement began with the participation of a number of thoughtful women in the abolition movement of the nineteenth century (Stanton and Anthony, 1981), and the "second wave" can likewise trace its resurgence to the women of the civil rights movement in the twentieth century (Evans, 1979). When contemplating a name for "the problem that has no name," as Betty Friedan (1983: ch. 1) put it, there is little doubt that for many feminists the parallels with racism made the term "sexism" appealing. . . . Perhaps the most important difference is that racism is based on dubious theories about the differences between the races, while sexual difference can hardly be denied. Racism seems often to be motivated by a hatred or fear of the other from which the conclusion comes that other "races" than one's own are inferior, a kind of racism that Kwame Anthony Appiah has called "intrinsic racism." Sexism, by contrast, is typically akin to what he calls "extrinsic racism," where the judgment that the other is inferior derives from the judgment that aspects or abilities of the other are inferior (Appiah, 1990). . . . However, there are many parallels between racism and sexism. For one thing, both are pervasive and have a high human cost. But, more importantly, the psychological mechanisms that make sexism and racism possible and desirable are similar: namely, our penchant for categorizing by social group, and making invidious distinctions between in-group and out-group members (Cudd, 1998). Furthermore, the social mechanisms that maintain sexism and racism are similar. Both sexism and racism are maintained through systematic violence and economic disadvantage. Both are difficult to pinpoint, but can be statistically documented and are much more readily perceived by the victims than by the respective dominant social groups. Both sexism and racism can have devastating psychological effects on individuals. And both inspire enormously powerful backlash when they are publicly challenged. . . .

. . .

One important effect of the practice of excluding women in these ways is, of course, that women are made more dependent on others, usually men. By reducing the opportunities women have available to them, women are less able to clearly establish, both to themselves and to others, their general ability to accomplish high-paying (or high-status) tasks. Where these patterns are left unchallenged there is thus little to counter the claim that women are, by nature, more dependent. Moreover, these effects of sexist hiring practices are reinforced in a number of ways. They are reinforced by patterns of language which mark and delimit appropriate activities and attitudes on the basis of sex, and relegate the activities and attitudes of women to a lower status (i.e. sexist language). And they are reinforced by systems of education and enculturation which support, if not create and coerce, discrete proclivities for girls and boys, and relegate the proclivities of girls to a lower status. These social aspects of sexism are further mirrored in psychological dispositions, desires, and self-concepts. Accepting the activities, attitudes, and proclivities which are typically associated with men as "normal" or "standard" for human beings (i.e. the man standard) would render the activities, attitudes, and proclivities which are typically associated with women, when different, abnormal or substandard. For instance, women will appear "highly emotional" or "hysterical" when they display more emotion and concern than men, or "brooding" and "moody" when less. . . .

. . . On our view sexism is a systematic, pervasive, but often subtle, force that maintains the oppression of women, and that is at work through institutional structures, in interpersonal interactions and the attitudes that are expressed in them, and in the cognitive, linguistic, and emotional processes of individual minds. . . .

. . .

Levels of Sexism

Sexism can be seen as a force responding to and molding human interactions. As a force, it can be seen, roughly, to operate at three levels: institutional sexism, which works on and through the level of social institutions; interpersonal sexism, which works on and through interactions among individuals who are not explicitly mediated by institutional structures; and unconscious sexism, which works at the personal level of the cognitive and affective processes of individuals. It is helpful to sort out these levels in order to explain why some charges of sexism are relatively uncontroversial, while others are difficult to see or evidence conclusively.

Institutional Sexism

Institutional sexism refers to invidious sexual inequalities in the explicit rules and implicit norms governing and structuring social institutions. Religious institutions provide a useful example of how explicit rules and implicit norms structure institutions. In the Catholic Church, for instance, it is an explicit rule that all priests are men and all nuns are women. Only priests can run the church hierarchy, and priests outrank nuns in most decision-making situations. While it is clear how explicit rules can govern and structure institutions, this example can also help us to see that implicit norms also structure Catholic experience and create sexual inequality. While it is no longer widely accepted as an explicit rule that in heterosexual marriage the man is the head of the household and the woman is the helpmeet, it is implied by the relative rank of priests and nuns in the church and by its sacred writings. This implicit norm positions men above women in marriage (as in all other social institutions in which both sexes are present), clearly an invidious sexual inequality. In addition to the more explicitly rule-governed institutions of government, religion, family, health care, and education, there are crucially important informally or implicitly structured institutions, prime among them being language, and the sites of cultural and artistic production. . . .

Interpersonal Sexism

Whereas institutional sexism involves the explicit rules and their implicit norms that sustain oppressive social institutions, interpersonal sexism involves interactions between persons that are not governed by explicit rules. Interpersonal sexism comprises actions and other expressions between persons that create, constitute, promote, sustain, and/or exploit invidious sexual inequalities.

The person who is acting in a sexist way or making a sexist expression need not intend sexism; there are intentional and unintentional forms of interpersonal sexism. Here are some examples from our experiences:

- As a child, the girl is not allowed the free play of her brothers; she is prevented by her parents and teachers from engaging in rough-and-tumble play, not included in activities involving building, transportation, etc., not encouraged to try or expected to succeed at sports, mathematics, or leadership activities, and required, unlike her brothers, to do domestic chores.

. . .

- In sports she sees males and manhood extolled, females and woman-hood ridiculed. Coaches and teammates insult male athletes by call-ing them "woman" or "girl," and praise them with the term "man."

. . .

- In conversations between colleagues men are routinely deferred to while women's remarks are ignored. When a male colleague re-peats what a female has said, he is complimented for his good idea.

Sexism is a key motif that unifies this otherwise seemingly disparate set of personal experiences. This list could, of course, be greatly expanded, and much feminist work has been devoted to increasing our stock of ex-ample experiences. This work is important because sexism is such an in-tegral but unspoken part of the everyday world that both men and women have a difficult time recognizing it. For society's ground of legitimacy seems to require that injustice be recognized and socially opposed. Yet the injustice of sexism is built into the very fabric of everyone's everyday experiences from infancy on.

Unconscious Sexism

"Unconscious sexism" refers to the psychological mechanisms and tacit beliefs, emotions, and attitudes that create, constitute, promote, sustain, and/or exploit invidious sexual inequalities. . . .

The key to recognizing unconscious motivations, especially unsavory ones that persons are reluctant to acknowledge in themselves, is to look for decisions or actions that could not be justified by a reasonable assess-ment of the available evidence. What counts as "reasonable" and "avail-able" are crucial issues here, of course. By "reasonable" we mean consistent with one's other explicitly held beliefs and widely shared, non-sexist, knowledge in the community. We insist on explicit beliefs here because, of course, if one has tacit sexist beliefs the action could be reasonable but sexist, and yet not counted as unconscious. By "available evidence" we are referring to reports that would be made by a member of the community who does not have sexist beliefs or attitudes, or whose sexist beliefs played no role in the reports, or to widely shared, non-sexist, knowledge in the community. Of course, there may be no non-sexist members of any com-munity. The practices of sexism affect one's self-conception. Internal critique may not be enough to free oneself from identification with those practices. But we must begin to identify sexist practices somewhere. Granting that it is possible that we will not recognize all unconscious (or, indeed, all conscious) sexism, we can still begin by finding the more obvious cases. Consider the following examples:

- A philosophy department is looking to hire a new faculty member. One-third of the applicants are women. One-third of the interview list is made up of women. In the interviews the women are judged as doing worse than the men. The comments afterwards are that they don't seem "as polished" or "professional" as the men. The fact is that the women do not meet the interviewers' expectations of what a philosopher or a faculty member is supposed to look like, a stereotype that includes being a man.
- A department is considering how to advise a female colleague and a male colleague concerning their chances for tenure. They have equal but modest publishing records, and roughly equal but modest teaching records. However, the female colleague has far more service. Both colleagues have been active participants in the departmental politics and have voiced strong opinions in departmental meetings. The male is judged to be an excellent colleague, while the female is judged to be uncollegial. They give the male colleague a very positive report for his tenure prospects, and the female is warned that she must publish more and improve her teaching to get tenure. In fact, the department has judged her to be worse because they feel uncomfortable with a strong, active woman, while the man is judged to have leadership qualities.
- A drug is being tested for its effectiveness in preventing heart disease. All the research subjects are men. When asked to account for this the research team leader responds that women's hormones would interfere with the study. While it is surely true that the drug could affect women differently from men as a result of female hormones, it is equally true that it could affect men differently from women as a result of male hormones. This symmetry is lost on the research team, who, like most of us, tend to think of women as the ones with the "interfering" or abnormal hormones.

Unconscious sexism often seems to be innocent, in the sense that the beliefs or feelings that make it up are never voiced, and often based on widely shared stereotypes. Whether or not it is innocent surely depends on the degree to which the individual has access to information that counters the unconscious sexist beliefs and attitudes, a condition that depends on larger social factors. Although we do believe that "sexism" names not only a mistake but a prima facie wrong, there are cases where one can commit this wrong and yet not be culpable.

. . .

Two Feminist Views of Sexism

Though feminists agree that sexism structures our very experience of the world, feminist theories of sexism vary considerably. Nonetheless, they can be very roughly divided into two categories. First, what can be labeled "equality feminism" maintains that social institutions are the primary medium of sexism. Men and women do not differ markedly in their potential capacities, interests, and abilities. Given similar training, men and women would develop fairly similar talents, at least as similar as those between men or between women. Thus if we are to transform society it will require that we resist and undermine those institutions that enforce sex differences and disproportionately deprive women of opportunities to develop highly valued social skills. Equality feminists need not accept what we have above called "the man standard." Rather, most contemporary equality feminists employ measures of social value such as utility, respect for human rights, or hypothetical agreement in order to develop gender-neutral standards by which to judge the opportunities, activities, and proclivities of men and women.

Alternatively, "difference feminists" maintain that unconscious desires are the primary medium of sexism. Accordingly, social institutions are the result, rather than the cause, of sexism. Recently a variety of feminists holding this view have attempted to both articulate the differences between men and women and re-evaluate equality feminism. Some, like Carol Gilligan (1982), Nel Noddings (1984), and Sara Ruddick (1989), have argued that women's "different voice" involves a greater emphasis on responsiveness, caring, and the maintenance of particular, concrete relationships. This voice is undervalued in society, they argue, because of the dominance of "responsibility" a notion which involves a strict adherence to principle and which, they argue, typifies the male point of view. Others skeptical of gender neutrality are also skeptical of the idea that caring and relationship maintenance best characterize women's difference. They thus seek to identify a different difference. Catherine MacKinnon (1987: 39) writes: "women value care because men have valued us according to the care we give them, and we could probably use some." In her view, since women's subordinate position in society informs their experience of the world, and so requires concrete critical evaluation, it can also give them a unique, and privileged, position from which to criticize our social traditions. Somewhat similarly, Luce Irigaray argues that the critical revaluation of women should neither reassert what has traditionally been taken to be women's nature, nor strive for equality with men. She maintains that the law has a duty to "offer justice to *two genders that differ* in their needs, their desires, their properties" (Irigaray, 1993: 4).

. . .

References

Appiah, A. (1990). "Racisms." In D. T. Goldberg (ed.), *Anatomy of Racism*. Minneapolis: University of Minnesota Press.

Cudd, A. E. (1998). "Psychological Explanations of Oppression." In C. Willett (ed.), *Theorizing Multiculturalism*. Malden, MA: Blackwell.

Dreze, J. and Sen, A. (1989). *Hunger and Public Action*. Oxford: Clarendon Press.

Evans, S. (1979). *Personal Politics: The Roots of Women's Liberation in the Civil Rights Movement and the New Left*. New York: Vintage Books.

Friedan, B. (1983). *The Feminine Mystique*, 20th anniv. edn. New York: Dell.

Frye, M. (1983). *The Politics of Reality*. Trumansburg, NY: The Crossing Press.

Gilligan, C. (1982). *In a Different Voice: Psychological Theory and Women's Development*. Cambridge, MA: Harvard University Press.

Irigaray, L. (1993). *Sexes and Genealogies*, trans. Gillian Gill. New York: Columbia University Press.

MacKinnon, C. (1987). *Feminism Unmodified: Discourses on Life and Law*. Cambridge, MA: Harvard University Press.

Noddings, N. (1984). *Caring: A Feminine Approach to Ethics and Moral Education*. Berkeley, CA: University of California Press.

Ruddick, S. (1989). *Maternal Thinking: Toward a Politics of Peace*. New York: Basic Books.

Stanton, E. C. and Anthony, S. B. (1981). *Correspondence, Writings, Speeches*, ed. E. C. DuBois. New York: Schocken Books.

UNIFEM (2000). *Progress of the World's Women 2000*. New York: United Nations.

Comprehension Questions

1. What are the similarities and differences between sexism and racism?
2. How do sexist attitudes become self-reinforcing?

3. How are explicit and implicit norms related to sexism supposed to differ from one another?

4. How do Cudd and Jones think we can discern instances of unconscious sexism?

5. Why do equality feminists and difference feminists disagree about the possibility of gender-neutral moral standards?

Discussion Questions

1. Cudd and Jones say that some institutions (governments, religious organizations, schools, etc.) sometimes have implicit sexist norms. Can you think of some instances of implicit sexist norms that illustrate their claim?

2. Cudd and Jones provide several examples of attitudes that are sexist without being consciously so. Can you come up with some additional examples?

3. What is the significance of "care" for some versions of difference feminism? Why do other feminists disagree about the moral significance of care?

4. Given that sexism can take so many forms, how much of it can be addressed through legislative or judicial means? Be sure to consider objections to your answer.

Case

Consider this:

A young woman approaches a closed door. Suddenly a young man dashes in front of her and opens the door. Her mother's and grandmother's generations would no doubt have commented approvingly on such a gallant act and on such an apparently well-bred young man. Yet the young woman responds quite differently. She either does not acknowledge the gesture or she acts offended. The young man looks bemused or possibly angry.

Why do the actors in this commonplace drama respond [as] they do? She apparently sees in the gesture some insult; and he feels wronged by this accusation, even if it remains unspoken, because he is sure that his intentions were pure, that no insult was meant. Is there an insult here or is the woman merely behaving in an ungracious manner? Can there be an insult if the man did not intend one? . . .

[Yes.] Gallantry is degrading inasmuch as the gallant feigns enormous respect for the character or desires or other characteristics of the woman, properties which he would probably disdain or ignore in himself or in other men [such as being dainty or "feminine"]. And it is dehumanizing inasmuch as it fails to distinguish women from one another and men from one another, simply assuming that any woman is the inferior of any man. It is insulting to the woman who feels herself socially, physically, and mentally equal or superior to the man who treats her gallantly.[1]

If gallantry is indeed a form of sexism, what kind is it? And what do you make of the charge that it *is* a form of sexism? If holding doors is problematic, then what else might be? What conventions are there in the dating world, for example, that distinguish people based on sex?

Note

1. Linda Bell, "Gallantry: What It Is and Why It Should Not Survive," *The Southern Journal of Philosophy* 22 (1984), 165, 170.

13

A Sensible Antiporn Feminism

A. W. Eaton

....

Eaton clarifies and nuances the feminist case against pornography.
She specifies first that her target is pornography that depicts inegalitarian treatment of women, and not necessarily pornography in general. She then develops an argument that such pornography poses a
threat to women's interests by making inegalitarian treatment seem
desirable. Eaton further explains that there are pertinent differences
in the causal factors and outcomes associated with such harms that
can make a difference in both how we evaluate them and how we determine the sort of response they merit.

....

. . . Nowadays "antiporn feminism" [ATP] conjures images of imperious
and censorial finger-waggers who mean to police every corner of our
erotic imaginations. Their insistence that pornography is harmful to
women is considered overly simplistic, while their proposed remedy for
this putative harm is taken to flagrantly violate the First Amendment.

In some instances this caricature is well deserved. However, I make
the case that on certain key issues this criticism rests on a misunderstand-
ing. It is part of the point of this article to critically examine the terms in
which the pornography debate is framed and to expose confusions

---

Eaton, A. W. 2007. "A Sensible Antiporn Feminism." *Ethics* 117(4): 674–715. Reprinted with
permission of the University of Chicago Press and the author.

resulting from lack of precision on many levels. . . . In so doing, I hope to convince you that ATP can be a sophisticated and reasonable position that is both supported by a powerful intuitive argument and sensitive to the complexities of the empirical data regarding pornography's effects. It can be, in a word, "sensible."

. . .

I. The Harm Hypothesis

Let's begin with the vexing term "pornography."[1] Some antiporn feminists construe the term so broadly as to encompass all forms and genres. This position has been justly criticized for ignoring the often liberatory power dynamics that characterize much gay and lesbian pornography, S/M (sadomasochistic) pornography, and pornography made by and for women.[2] To account for such differences, a sensible APF restricts itself to *inegalitarian pornography*: sexually explicit representations that as a whole eroticize relations (acts, scenarios, or postures) characterized by gender inequity.[3] Although this category overlaps significantly with violent pornography, the two are not coextensive, since some pornography eroticizes sexual relations that are violent but not inegalitarian, while other pornography is deeply degrading to women but not at all violent.

Antiporn feminism connects inegalitarian pornography (hereafter simply "pornography") to harm in several ways. First, it distinguishes the harms occurring in the production of pornography (e.g., the various kinds of coercion, brutality, rape, and other exploitation sometimes inflicted upon women in making porn) from those that occur postproduction. Second, among postproduction harms, some antiporn feminists distinguish the charge that pornographic materials themselves constitute harm, in the manner of hate speech, from the claim that exposure to such representations causes harm. This article focuses on this last kind of harm, which is always indirect, that is, it is always mediated through a second party, namely, the consumer of pornography. The basic idea is that pornography shapes the attitudes and conduct of its audience in ways that are injurious to women. I shall refer to this as the "harm hypothesis."

The best argument for the harm hypothesis can be summed up in just a few steps as follows:

i) Our society is marked by gender inequality in which women (and girls, although I shall say only "women" for ease of exposition) suffer many disadvantages as compared with men (and boys). This inequality is evident in both individuals' attitudes and conduct and in institutional practices.[4]

ii) This is a grave injustice.

iii) Whether or not it is natural, the subordination of women is not inevitable but rather is sustained and reproduced by a nexus of social factors that range from the explicit (as in the denial of rights and privileges and other overt discrimination) to the very subtle. An important example of these more subtle means of subordination are the many ways in which children are socialized from an early age to "appropriate" gender roles, according to which boys should be masculine (i.e., self-confident, independent, courageous, physically strong, assertive, and dominant) and girls should be feminine (i.e., demure, passive, submissive, delicate, and self-sacrificing). The modi operandi of this socialization include religion, the household division of labor, and the influence of various representational forms such as advertisements, television, movies, popular music and music videos, fashion magazines, and high art, all of which often promote masculinity and femininity as ideals for men and women, respectively. Violence and force (as well as the threat of violence and force) also play a significant active role in maintaining gender norms and the subordination of women; that is, sexual assault enforces gender inequality and is not merely a symptom of it.

iv) Aspects of gender inequality have erotic appeal for many people. This can be seen, for example, in the way that gender stereotypes, such as dominance and strength for men and softness and submissiveness for women, standardly serve as markers of sexiness. At the extreme end of the spectrum of gender inequality, nonconsensual violence against women is sexually stimulating for many.

v) Like gender inequality itself, the erotic appeal of unequal relations between the sexes is not inevitable, regardless of whether it is natural. Rather, this particular form of sexual desire is fostered by various kinds of representations, from fashion magazines to high art.

vi) Eroticizing gender inequality—its mechanisms, norms, myths, and trappings—is a particularly effective mechanism for promoting and sustaining it.[5] Its efficacy stems from several factors: (a) Transforming gender inequality into a source of sexual gratification renders this inequality not just tolerable and easier to accept but also desirable and highly enjoyable. (b) This pleasure to which gender subordination is linked is one in which nearly all humans are intensely invested, thereby strengthening gender inequality's significance and broadening its appeal. (c) This eroticization makes gender inequality appealing to men and women alike. Insofar as women want to be attractive to men, they internalize the subordinating norms of attractiveness and thereby collaborate in their own oppression. (*d*) Finally, sexualizing gender inequality enlists our physical appetites and sexual desires in favor of sexism. Since these are rarely, if ever, amenable to control via rational scrutiny, harnessing our appetites and desires to gender inequality is an effective way of psychologically embedding it.

vii) Pornography eroticizes the mechanisms, norms, myths, and trappings of gender inequality. Its fusing of pleasure with subordination has two components: (*a*) it does so in terms of its representational content by depicting women deriving sexual pleasure from a range of inegalitarian relations and situations, from being the passive objects of conquest to scenarios of humiliation, degradation, and sexual abuse; (*b*) inegalitarian pornography presents these representations of subordination in a manner aimed to sexually arouse.

The argument concludes that, by harnessing representations of women's subordination to a ubiquitous and weighty pleasure, pornography is especially effective at getting its audience to internalize its inegalitarian views. This argument trades on a conviction dating back to Aristotle that still has currency in the philosophy of art today, namely, that understanding and appreciating representations often requires an imaginative engagement that can have lasting effects on one's character.[6] Many representations enlist from their audience emotional responses that are ethically relevant. In so doing, they activate our moral powers and enlarge our ethical understanding by training our emotions to respond to the right objects with the proper intensity. Such representations not only affect the audience during actual engagement with the representation but may also have lasting effects on one's character by shaping the moral emotions. A similar conviction appears to underlie modern-day sex therapy, where pornographic representations are prescribed in order to mold patients' sexual inclinations and thereby treat various sexual dysfunctions. If representations can in this way improve one's character, then we should also expect them to be capable of deforming it by "perverting the sentiments of the heart," as Hume puts it.[7] Antiporn feminists hold that pornography perverts the emotional life of its audience by soliciting very strong positive feelings for situations characterized by gender inequality and in so doing plays a role in sustaining and reproducing a system of pervasive injustice.

. . .

II. A Taxonomy of Harms

Without further specification, the harm hypothesis remains futilely vague. To begin with, the alleged cause ranges from something as indefinite as prolonged exposure to pornography to something as specific as a single encounter with a particular representation. And the indirect post-production harms are a motley assortment of adverse effects that differ significantly in their character, severity, and even kind of victim. When discussing pornography's purportedly harmful consequences, antiporn feminists have typically ignored such distinctions and treated the harms en masse, but this undermines the plausibility of the harm hypothesis and leads to confusions regarding what would count as evidence for it. . . .

As noted earlier, the harm hypothesis is concerned with the third-party harms that pornography purportedly causes. This little-noted yet conspicuous fact means that there are actually two stages of cause and effect. . . .

A. Stage 1 Causes

Exposure to pornography is of two sorts: a specifiable and limited number of discrete encounters with particular pornographic representations, which I call *singular* causes, and processes of wider temporal duration, such as prolonged exposure to a variety of pornographic representations, which I call *diffuse* causes. Several variables apply to each sort of encounter. First, one must consider the "strength" of the pornography, or the degree to which it is inegalitarian. Second, one must consider the duration of each encounter and, with respect to singular Stage 1 causes, the total number of encounters. In the case of diffuse causes, one must also consider the frequency of encounters and the total period of pornography use. Finally, it is important to distinguish cases where pornography use is relatively localized in a population from those where it is widespread (the significance of this distinction will become clear when we turn to Stage 2 effects).

Putting these Stage 1 causal variables together begins to reveal the complexities involved in specifying the first term of the harm hypothesis. If pornography has an effect on its consumers, it will likely take the form of a dose-response relationship, where an increase in the level, intensity, duration, or total level of exposure to the cause increases the risk of an effect. Consider an analogy with smoking. When predicting a person's health, it is important to know not simply whether she is a regular smoker, as opposed to only having tried cigarettes a few times, but also how often she smokes, whether she smokes the entire cigarette, what strength of cigarette she prefers, and how long she has been a smoker. Whereas certain combinations of these variables will significantly raise a person's chances of getting cancer, others will not. We should think of pornography along the same lines: whereas one person might have occasionally encountered mildly inegalitarian pornography at some point in his life, another might have been a regular consumer of the most violent and inegalitarian pornography for years. Antiporn feminists and their critics have both overlooked the dose-response relationship,

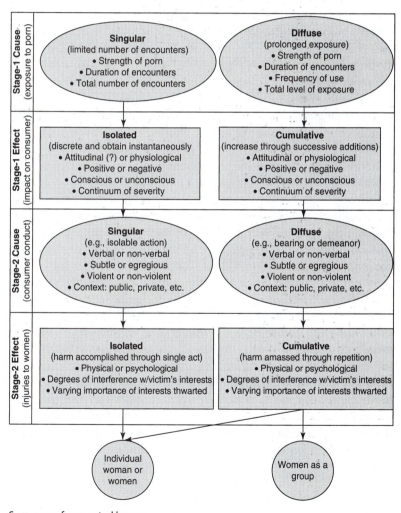

Summary of purported harms

commonly speaking of exposure to pornography as if it were an all-or-nothing phenomenon. This fails to capture the subtlety of human interaction with representations and leads to extreme and implausible formulations of the harm hypothesis. A sensible APF begins by recognizing the many variables at play in the Stage 1 causes.

B. Stage 1 Effects

Stage 1 effects (on consumers of pornography) also admit of many distinctions. *Singular* Stage 1 causes, namely, particular encounters with individual works, yield isolated effects that are disconnected from other effects and obtain in an instant rather than amassing cumulatively. Most physiological responses to pornography are examples of such isolated effects (although, as we shall see below, there is dispute about whether discrete and limited encounters with pornography can yield isolated attitudinal effects). *Cumulative* effects which result from diffuse Stage-1 causes, by contrast, increase gradually through successive encounters such that not any one encounter with pornography suffices to produce them. To return to our smoking analogy, ill effects like emphysema, heart disease, and lung cancer do not result from smoking just one or two cigarettes but instead are the aggregative result of long-term smoking. (The disanalogy here is that smoking is cumulatively harmful for the person who smokes, whereas pornography is purportedly harmful to a third party. Although this disanalogy is irrelevant to the isolated/ cumulative distinction, it will become important in the last section of this article.)

Cutting across the distinction between isolated and cumulative Stage 1 effects are a range of variables pertaining to the quality of these purported effects on consumers of pornography. First, we can distinguish *physiological* effects, such as training sexual responses to inegalitarian representations, from *attitudinal* effects. The latter can be well defined, as in conscious and explicit beliefs about women's inferiority, or diffuse, such as inclinations toward sexual situations where women are subordinate. Attitudes can be further divided into conscious and unconscious and positive and negative (e.g., positive attitudes toward rape as opposed to the breakdown of inhibitions against rape . . .).[8] Finally, Stage 1 effects lie on a continuum of severity from mildly sexist attitudes to violent conduct.

C. Stage 2 Causes

A Stage 2 cause is the outward public manifestation of a Stage 1 effect that can be perceived by, and so affect, another. It is, in a word, conduct. As one might expect, pornography's purported Stage 2 causes reflect the diversity and complexity of the alleged Stage 1 effects. First, as with Stage 1 causes, they can be *singular*, as in an isolable action or series of actions, or *diffuse*, as with a general demeanor or bearing. Second, they vary tremendously in character: They can be verbal or nonverbal, violent or nonviolent, subtle or egregious. Third, they can appear in a variety of public and private contexts: from the family to the workplace, from sexual relations to a court of law. This broad spectrum of conduct ranges from something like a habit of openly glancing at women's bodies in professional contexts,[9] to an unconscious disposition to be lenient with rapists on trial,[10] to an inability to distinguish coerced from consensual sex.

D. Stage 2 Effects

Finally we come to pornography's alleged injuries. As we have seen, antiporn feminists charge that pornography harms women by indirectly impairing or thwarting their interests. As one might expect, given the diversity and complexity in the chain of causes and effects seen thus far, these purportedly harmful effects vary significantly. First, the harms can result from particular acts or from dissipated activities without exact limits that do not lend themselves to precise measurement and definition; that is, in terms used earlier, the Stage 2 effect can be *isolated* or *cumulative*. Second, the harms can be physical or psychological or both. Third, there are degrees of interference with women's interests, from mild interference to complete impairment. Finally, the interests that pornography purportedly thwarts vary in importance. Sexism is not an all-or-none phenomenon but rather exists on a continuum of severity. Sexual assault is an example of a severe injury that is accomplished through a single, isolable act. Constantly being treated as a sex object is considerably less severe cumulative harm: a few isolated instances rarely do lasting damage but regular uninvited sexual attention, however subtle, restricts a woman's participation in public life.[11]

Cutting across the variables just mentioned is a distinction between two kinds of injured party: individual women and women as a group. *Individual harms* occur when a particular person's interests are thwarted or set back. *Group harms*, by contrast, are not merely the aggregate of harms to individual women but instead result from diminishing the status of the group as a whole.[12] The status of women is diminished when simply being a woman is sufficient to make one a potential target for harm—from underestimation of one's intellect to sexual assault.

Although few feminists make this distinction explicitly, many attribute both individual and group harms to pornography. It is important to note that if group harms obtain, it is almost certainly only if pornography use is widespread in a society.

E. Why a Taxonomy of Harms Matters

Pornography's allegedly harmful effect—gender inequality—has a broad range of manifestations and severities. Distinguishing between these is essential for a careful, nuanced, and verifiable formulation of the harm hypothesis in the following ways.

First, it helps us to assess APF's plausibility. Since, as we have seen, the variables of the harm hypothesis are manifold and complex, one should not assume that each kind of cause yields each kind of effect. Certain causal claims—for example, that one man's isolated encounter with a single piece of pornography could by itself lead to rape or to the diminished status of women as a whole—are so unlikely as to seem preposterous, and yet it is for such unreasonable connections that APF is routinely criticized. To avoid such misunderstandings, a sensible APF should clearly delineate the various purported causes and effects so as to correlate them correctly.

A second reason to stress these distinctions between kinds of harms is that they greatly affect the nature of APF's proposed remedies. There are at least four options for preventing and redressing pornography's purported harms: (*a*) criminalization, (*b*) civil action, (*c*) restrictions and other forms of state regulation, or (*d*) moral condemnation. Whereas the first three are matters of state regulation, the last has no necessary legal implications. If pornography is found to be on balance harmful in the ways that antiporn feminists allege,[13] then it merits moral condemnation and perhaps even its public expression. On this point all antiporn feminists should agree. The question is whether pornography's harms license anything more, and the answer depends entirely on just which sorts of harms pornography causes. If pornography's harms are limited to things such as men's underestimation of women's intellects, then, although we should condemn this as genuine harm, our condemnation would not license state intervention of any sort. Many things that are harmful and wrong have no policy implications, for example, bigotry, selfishness, lying, needlessly hurting others' feelings, adultery, and name-calling. It is, then, a mistake to assume—as so many do—that feminist opponents of pornography necessarily support legal remedies, much less censorship.

. . .

Comprehension Questions

1. What is inegalitarian pornography, and how is it related to violent pornography?
2. What is the harm hypothesis?
3. What does Eaton mean when she speaks of pornography "eroticizing" gender inequality?
4. How might eroticized gender inequality harm those who watch that sort of pornography?
5. Eaton suggests that there might be a "dose-response" between viewing inegalitarian pornography and its negative effects. What does this mean?
6. How does Eaton differentiate the aggregation of harms against women from a group harm against women?
7. Why is it important to distinguish the various types of harms of inegalitarian pornography?

Discussion Questions

1. If pornography "need not actively solicit rape" to cause gender inequality, how else might it cause it?
2. What, in your view, are the most morally significant harms discussed by Eaton? Are these harms the sort that warrant judicial or legal action? Why or why not?
3. Explain the analogy that Eaton draws between viewing inegalitarian pornography and smoking cigarettes. What is the upshot of that, and do you think it's a good analogy?

Case

In 2014, a freshman at Duke University—Belle Knox—was outed as a porn star. In response, she wrote the following:

> For me, shooting pornography brings me unimaginable joy. When I finish a scene, I know that I have done so and completed an honest day's work. It is my artistic outlet: my love, my happiness, my home. I can say definitively that I have never felt more empowered or happy doing anything else. In a world where women are so often robbed of their choice, I am completely in control of my sexuality. As a bisexual woman with many sexual quirks, I feel completely accepted. It is freeing, it is empowering, it is wonderful, it is how the world should be. It

is the exact opposite of the culture of slut-shaming and rape apology which I have experienced from certain dark corners of the Internet since being recognized on campus a few months ago. . . .

I did not expect that I would be brutally bullied and harassed online. I did not expect that every private detail about my life would be dissected. I did not expect that my intelligence and work ethic would be questioned and criticized. And I certainly did not expect that extremely personal information concerning my identity and whereabouts would be so carelessly transmitted through college gossip boards. I was called a "slut who needs to learn the consequences of her actions," a "huge fucking whore," and, perhaps the most offensive, "a little girl who does not understand her actions."

Let's be clear about one thing: I know exactly what I'm doing. What about you?

. . . We must question in this equation why sex workers are so brutally stigmatized. Why do we exclude them for jobs, education, and from mainstream society? Why do we scorn, threaten and harass them? Why do we deny them of their personhood? Why does the thought of a woman having sexual experiences scare us so much? The answer is simple. Patriarchy fears female sexuality.

It terrifies us to even fathom that a woman could take ownership of her body. We deem to keep women in a place where they are subjected to male sexuality. We seek to rob them of their choice and of their autonomy. We want to oppress them and keep them dependent on the patriarchy. A woman who transgresses the norm and takes ownership of her body—because that's exactly what porn is, no matter how rough the sex is—ostensibly poses a threat to the deeply ingrained gender norms that polarize our society.

I am well aware: The threat I pose to the patriarchy is enormous. That a woman could be intelligent, educated and CHOOSE to be a sex worker is almost unfathomable. . . . No, all we are is "whores and bimbos."

. . . To the anti-pornography feminists out there: I very much respect your opinion. Nevertheless, I want you to consider how you marginalize a group of women by condemning their actions. Consider that when you demean women for participating in sex work, you are demeaning THEM, and consequently, YOU become the problem.[14]

What do you make of Knox's argument? How might Eaton respond to Knox? Is there a way to reconcile these two views?

Notes

1. There are important debates about how to define the concept of "pornography" and distinguish it from neighboring categories like "erotic art." For treatments of the difficulties in distinguishing works of pornography from works of art, see Lynda Nead, *The Female Nude: Art, Obscenity, and Sexuality* (London:

Routledge, 1992), and "'Above the Pulp-Line': The Cultural Significance of Erotic Art," in *Dirty Looks: Women, Pornography, Power,* ed. Pamela Church Gibson and Roma Gibson (London: British Film Institute, 1993), 144–55; Susan Kappeler, *The Pornography of Representation* (Minneapolis: University of Minnesota Press, 1986); Walter Kendrick, *The Secret Museum: Pornography in Modern Culture* (Berkeley: University of California Press, 1996); and Lynn Hunt, ed., *The Invention of Pornography: Obscenity and the Origins of Modernity* (New York: Zone, 1996). For a recent definition of pornography in the philosophical literature, see Michael Rea, "What Is Pornography?" *Nous* 35 (2001): 118–45.

2. For discussions of varieties of pornography that do not fit the standard antiporn feminist picture, see Richard Dyer, "Idol Thoughts: Orgasm and Self-Reflexivity in Gay Pornography," in *More Dirty Looks: Gender, Pornography, and Power,* ed. Pamela Church Gibson (London: British Film Institute, 2004), 102–9; Claire Pajaczkowska, "The Heterosexual Presumption," in *The Sexual Subject: A Screen Reader in Sexuality,* ed. Terry Threadgold and Annette Kuhn (London: Routledge, 1992), 184–96; Cindy Patton, "Visualizing Safe Sex: When Pedagogy and Pornography Collide," in *inside/out: Lesbian Theories, Gay Theories,* ed. Diana Fuss (London: Routledge, 1991), 373–86; Becki Ross, "'It's Merely Designed for Sexual Arousal': Interrogating the Indefensibility of Lesbian Smut," in *Feminism and Pornography,* ed. Drucilla Cornell (Oxford: Oxford University Press, 2000), 264–317; and Ann Snitow, "Mass Market Romance: Pornography for Women Is Different," in *Passion and Power: Sexuality in History,* ed. Kathy Peiss and Christina Simmon (Philadelphia: Temple University Press, 1989), 245–63.

3. A few points of clarification. A work that includes a few scenes that eroticize inegalitarian relations but in which these are balanced or outweighed by other kinds of scenes—imagine, e.g., a story of a heterosexual couple who take turns in submissive roles while the partner plays the dominant role—would not count as "inegalitarian pornography." Also, I use "gender inequality" in the standard way to refer to the subordination of women; it does not refer to situations where men are subordinate to women. Thanks to an anonymous referee for pressing me to clarify these points.

4. For example, women are discriminated against in employment and are on average paid less than men; they typically bear the greater burden of child care and household chores; their reproductive freedom is restricted or constantly under threat of restriction; they are subject to various forms of sexual harassment in the workplace and other public arenas; and they endure, or at the very least are under the constant threat of, rape, battery, and incest both inside and outside the home. These are just some of the ways that women, simply because they are women, occupy a subordinate position in our society.

5. This idea was first suggested by John Stuart Mill in *The Subjection of Women* (1869; Indianapolis: Hackett, 1988).

6. Aristotle presents these ideas in the *Rhetoric* and the *Politics*, and David Hume expresses something similar in "Of the Standard of Taste," in *Essays Moral, Political, and Literary* (1777), ed. Thomas Hill Green and Thomas Hodge Grose (Indianapolis: Liberty Fund, 1985), 226–49.

7. Hume, "Of the Standard of Taste," 247.

8. For research on pornography's purported disinhibitory effects, see Neil Malamuth, Maggie Heim, and Seymour Feshbach, "Sexual Responsiveness of College Students to Rape Depictions: Inhibitory and Disinhibitory Effects," *Journal of Personality and Social Psychology* 38 (1990): 399–408.

9. It is extremely difficult to systematically measure such subtle and diffuse manners of comportment, much less correlate them with pornography consumption, although some have tried. One study that examines the effects of exposure to pornography on interactions between opposite-gender strangers tries to discern this very sort of nebulous harmful effect. The study exposed male college students to either nonviolent pornography or a nonsexual video and then subjected them to an interview by a female research assistant. (The interview did not involve questions pertaining to sex.) The female assistant, who did not know which type of video the subject had seen, recorded the subjects' apparent sexual interest in her. She was asked to consider, e.g., how much he looked at her body and how close he moved his chair to hers during the interview. The results showed that the research assistant could readily and reliably distinguish men who had seen the pornographic video from those who had watched the nonsexual video (Doug McKenzie-Mohr and Mark Zanna, "Treating Women as Sex Objects: Look to the (Gender Schematic) Male Who Has Viewed Pornography," *Personality and Social Psychology* 16 [1990]: 296–308). There are several problems with such studies. First, they rely at least in part on impressions of behavior that are quite difficult to isolate and measure. Second, the control is nonsexual material rather than egalitarian pornography, so the study proves too much for the feminist thesis. Perhaps any erotic material would have this effect.

10. Andrew Taslitz has convincingly shown the ways that narratives marked by gender hierarchy shape trial outcomes and, in particular, how they undermine justice for rape victims. He examines representations (from high art, popular culture, and pornography) and argues that these influence how jurors gauge a rape survivor's truthfulness, complicity in the rape, and harm incurred by the rape. See Andrew E. Taslitz, *Rape and the Culture of the Courtroom* (New York: New York University Press, 1999).

11. For an excellent description of the role of sexual objectification in maintaining male dominance, see Sandra Bartky, "On Psychological Oppression," in her *Femininity and Domination: Studies in the Phenomenology of Oppression* (New York: Routledge, 1990), 22–32.

12. For a discussion of group-based harms, see Larry May and Marilyn Friedman, "Harming Women as a Group," in *Social Theory and Practice* 11 (1985): 207–34.

13. That is, if pornography injures women in at least some of the ways delineated above and if it does not have counterbalancing positive effects and outward moral condemnation would be beneficial, this would justifiably lead one to do things like write articles condemning it, protest against it, boycott stores that sell it, and so forth . . .

14. http://www.xojane.com/sex/duke-university-freshman-porn-star

14

What Makes a Woman?

Elinor Burkett

Elinor Burkett challenges the claim that transgender individuals are women. Of those born with male sex characteristics who self-identify as women, some maintain their womanhood derives from neurological makeup, while others say they experience themselves as women, despite possessing apparently incongruent biological characteristics. Burkett argues that neither of these facts is a sufficient qualification for being a woman, and that having the lifelong experience of being viewed and treated as a woman is an indispensable requirement of womanhood. She further criticizes as paradoxical demands of certain transgender individuals and advocates to alter the way we talk about gender in a variety of cultural and political contexts.

Do women and men have different brains?

Back when Lawrence H. Summers was president of Harvard and suggested that they did, the reaction was swift and merciless. Pundits branded him sexist. Faculty members deemed him a troglodyte. Alumni withheld donations.

Burkett, Elinor. "What Makes a Woman?" *The New York Times*. June 6, 2015. Reprinted with permission from the author.

But when Bruce Jenner said much the same thing in an April interview with Diane Sawyer, he was lionized for his bravery, even for his progressivism.

"My brain is much more female than it is male," he told her, explaining how he knew that he was transgender.

This was the prelude to a new photo spread and interview in *Vanity Fair* that offered us a glimpse into Caitlyn Jenner's idea of a woman: a cleavage-boosting corset, sultry poses, thick mascara, and the prospect of regular "girls' nights" of banter about hair and makeup. Ms. Jenner was greeted with even more thunderous applause. ESPN announced it would give Ms. Jenner an award for courage. President Obama also praised her. Not to be outdone, Chelsea Manning hopped on Ms. Jenner's gender train on Twitter, gushing, "I am so much more aware of my emotions; much more sensitive emotionally (and physically)."

A part of me winced.

I have fought for many of my sixty-eight years against efforts to put women—our brains, our hearts, our bodies, even our moods—into tidy boxes, to reduce us to hoary stereotypes. Suddenly, I find that many of the people I think of as being on my side—people who proudly call themselves progressive and fervently support the human need for self-determination—are buying into the notion that minor differences in male and female brains lead to major forks in the road and that some sort of gendered destiny is encoded in us.

That's the kind of nonsense that was used to repress women for centuries. But the desire to support people like Ms. Jenner and their journey toward their truest selves has strangely and unwittingly brought it back.

People who haven't lived their whole lives as women, whether Ms. Jenner or Mr. Summers, shouldn't get to define us. That's something men have been doing for much too long. And as much as I recognize and endorse the right of men to throw off the mantle of maleness, they cannot stake their claim to dignity as transgender people by trampling on mine as a woman.

Their truth is not my truth. Their female identities are not my female identity. They haven't traveled through the world as women and been shaped by all that this entails. They haven't suffered through business meetings with men talking to their breasts or woken up after sex terrified they'd forgotten to take their birth control pills the day before. They haven't had to cope with the onset of their periods in the middle of a crowded subway, the humiliation of discovering that their male work partners' checks were far larger than theirs, or the fear of being too weak to ward off rapists.

For me and many women, feminist and otherwise, one of the difficult parts of witnessing and wanting to rally behind the movement for transgender rights is the language that a growing number of trans individuals insist on, the notions of femininity that they're articulating, and their disregard for the fact that being a woman means having accrued certain experiences, endured certain indignities and relished certain courtesies in a culture that reacted to you as one.

Brains are a good place to begin because one thing that science has learned about them is that they're in fact shaped by experience, cultural and otherwise. The part of the brain that deals with navigation is enlarged in London taxi drivers, as is the region dealing with the movement of the fingers of the left hand in right-handed violinists.

"You can't pick up a brain and say 'that's a girl's brain' or 'that's a boy's brain,' " Gina Rippon, a neuroscientist at Britain's Aston University, told *The Telegraph* last year. The differences between male and female brains are caused by the "drip, drip, drip" of the gendered environment, she said.

The drip, drip, drip of Ms. Jenner's experience included a hefty dose of male privilege few women could possibly imagine. While young "Bruiser," as Bruce Jenner was called as a child, was being cheered on toward a university athletic scholarship, few female athletes could dare hope for such largess since universities offered little funding for women's sports. When Mr. Jenner looked for a job to support himself during his training for the 1976 Olympics, he didn't have to turn to the meager "Help Wanted—Female" ads in the newspapers, and he could get by on the $9,000 he earned annually, unlike young women whose median pay was little more than half that of men. Tall and strong, he never had to figure out how to walk streets safely at night.

Those are realities that shape women's brains.

By defining womanhood the way he did to Ms. Sawyer, Mr. Jenner and the many advocates for transgender rights who take a similar tack ignore those realities. In the process, they undermine almost a century of hard-fought arguments that the very definition of female is a social construct that has subordinated us. And they undercut our efforts to change the circumstances we grew up with.

The "I was born in the wrong body" rhetoric favored by other trans people doesn't work any better and is just as offensive, reducing us to our collective breasts and vaginas. Imagine the reaction if a young white man suddenly declared that he was trapped in the wrong body and, after using chemicals to change his skin pigmentation and crocheting his hair into twists, expected to be embraced by the black community.

Many women I know, of all ages and races, speak privately about how insulting we find the language trans activists use to explain themselves. After Mr. Jenner talked about his brain, one friend called it an outrage and asked in exasperation, "Is he saying that he's bad at math, weeps during bad movies and is hard-wired for empathy?" After the release of the *Vanity Fair* photos of Ms. Jenner, Susan Ager, a Michigan journalist, wrote on her Facebook page, "I fully support Caitlyn Jenner, but I wish she hadn't chosen to come out as a sex babe."

For the most part, we bite our tongues and do not express the anger we openly and rightly heaped on Mr. Summers, put off by the mudslinging match that has broken out on the radical fringes of both the women's and the trans movements over events limited to "women-born women," access to bathrooms and who has suffered the greater persecution. The insult and outright fear that trans men and women live with is all too familiar to us, and a cruelly marginalized group's battle for justice is something we instinctively want to rally behind.

But as the movement becomes mainstream, it's growing harder to avoid asking pointed questions about the frequent attacks by some trans leaders on women's right to define ourselves, our discourse and our bodies. After all, the trans movement isn't simply echoing African-Americans, Chicanos, gays, or women by demanding an end to the violence and discrimination, and to be treated with a full measure of respect. It's demanding that women reconceptualize ourselves.

In January 2014, the actress Martha Plimpton, an abortion-rights advocate, sent out a tweet about a benefit for Texas abortion funding called "A Night of a Thousand Vaginas." Suddenly, she was swamped by criticism for using the word "vagina." "Given the constant genital policing, you can't expect trans folks to feel included by an event title focused on a policed, binary genital," responded @DrJaneChi.

When Ms. Plimpton explained that she would continue to say "vagina"— and why shouldn't she, given that without a vagina, there is no pregnancy or abortion?—her feed overflowed anew with indignation, Michelle Goldberg reported in *The Nation*. "So you're really committed to doubling down on using a term that you've been told many times is exclusionary & harmful?" asked one blogger. Ms. Plimpton became, to use the new trans insult, a terf, which stands for "trans exclusionary radical feminist."

In January, Project: Theatre at Mount Holyoke College, a self-described liberal arts college for women, canceled a performance of Eve Ensler's iconic feminist play "The Vagina Monologues" because it offered an "extremely narrow perspective on what it means to be a woman," explained Erin Murphy, the student group's chairwoman.

Let me get this right: The word "vagina" is exclusionary and offers an extremely narrow perspective on womanhood, so the 3.5 billion of us who have vaginas, along with the trans people who want them, should describe ours with the politically correct terminology trans activists are pushing on us: "front hole" or "internal genitalia"?

Even the word "woman" has come under assault by some of the very people who claim the right to be considered women. The hashtags #StandWithTexasWomen, popularized after Wendy Davis, then a state senator, attempted to filibuster the Texas Legislature to prevent passage of a draconian anti-abortion law, and #WeTrustWomen, are also under attack since they, too, are exclusionary.

"Abortion rights and reproductive justice is not a women's issue," wrote Emmett Stoffer, one of many self-described transgender persons to blog on the topic. It is "a uterus owner's issue." Mr. Stoffer was referring to the possibility that a woman who is taking hormones or undergoing surgery to become a man, or who does not identify as a woman, can still have a uterus, become pregnant and need an abortion.

Accordingly, abortion rights groups are under pressure to modify their mission statements to omit the word woman, as Katha Pollitt recently reported in *The Nation*. Those who have given in, like the New York Abortion Access Fund, now offer their services to "people" and to "callers." Fund Texas Women, which covers the travel and hotel expenses of abortion seekers with no nearby clinic, recently changed its name to Fund Texas Choice. "With a name like Fund Texas Women, we were publicly excluding trans people who needed to get an abortion but were not women," the group explains on its website.

Women's colleges are contorting themselves into knots to accommodate female students who consider themselves men, but usually not men who are living as women. Now these institutions, whose core mission is to cultivate female leaders, have student government and dormitory presidents who identify as males.

As Ruth Padawer reported in *The New York Times Magazine* last fall, Wellesley students are increasingly replacing the word "sisterhood" with "siblinghood," and faculty members are confronted with complaints from trans students about their universal use of the pronoun she—although Wellesley rightly brags about its long history as the "world's pre-eminent college for women."

The landscape that's being mapped and the language that comes with it are impossible to understand and just as hard to navigate. The most theory-bound of the trans activists say that there are no paradoxes here, and that anyone who believes there are is clinging to a binary view of gender that's hopelessly antiquated. Yet Ms. Jenner and Ms. Manning, to mention just two, expect to be called women even as the abortion providers are being told that using that term is discriminatory. So are those who have transitioned from men the only "legitimate" women left?

Women like me are not lost in false paradoxes; we were smashing binary views of male and female well before most Americans had ever heard the word "transgender" or used the word "binary" as an adjective. Because we did, and continue to do so, thousands of women once confined to jobs as secretaries, beauticians or flight attendants now work as welders, mechanics and pilots. It's why our daughters play with trains and trucks as well as dolls, and why most of us feel free to wear skirts and heels on Tuesday and blue jeans on Friday.

In fact, it's hard to believe that this hard-won loosening of gender constraints for women isn't at least a partial explanation for why three times as many gender reassignment surgeries are performed on men. Men are, comparatively speaking, more bound, even strangled, by gender stereotyping.

The struggle to move beyond such stereotypes is far from over, and trans activists could be women's natural allies moving forward. So long as humans produce X and Y chromosomes that lead to the development of penises and vaginas, almost all of us will be "assigned" genders at birth. But what we do with those genders—the roles we assign ourselves, and each other, based on them—is almost entirely mutable.

If that's the ultimate message of the mainstream of the trans community, we'll happily, lovingly welcome them to the fight to create space for everyone to express him-, her- or, in gender neutral parlance, hir-self without being coerced by gendered expectations. But undermining women's identities, and silencing, erasing or renaming our experiences, aren't necessary to that struggle.

Bruce Jenner told Ms. Sawyer that what he looked forward to most in his transition was the chance to wear nail polish, not for a furtive, fugitive instant, but until it chips off. I want that for Bruce, now Caitlyn, too. But I also want her to remember: Nail polish does not a woman make.

Comprehension Questions

1. Burkett likens Caitlyn Jenner's rationale for her claim to be a woman to certain remarks of Lawrence H. Summers. Why?
2. On what basis does Burkett distinguish her own female identity from that of transgender individuals like Caitlyn Jenner?
3. Why is Burkett critical of transgender individuals who claim to be born in the wrong body?
4. How does Burkett think the transgender movement differs from apparently similar anti-discrimination movements?
5. Why do some people object to using terms like "vagina" or "woman" in reproductive rights activism?
6. What does Burkett find paradoxical about the call by some transgender activists to drop talk of vaginas or even the term "woman"?

Discussion Questions

1. Do you think transgender activists are right to pressure reproductive rights groups to cease using terms like "vagina" and "woman"?
2. Burkett discusses several different things that go into being a woman. Can you think of any important aspects of being a woman that she has overlooked? If so, are they more consistent with the claims of transgender people like Jenner? Or do they fit with Burkett's view?
3. Burkett touches on the issue of women's colleges and whether they should admit transgender students. Is it right for such colleges to deny them admission? Is it right for them to deny it of some transgender students but not others?

Case

In the summer of 2015, there was a great deal of discussion about Rachel Dolezal—the president of the NAACP chapter in Spokane, Washington, and a part-time professor of Africana studies. Dolezal identifies as black; her parents, however, are white. The Dolezal case is complicated for all sorts of reasons, the most notable being that she may have stood to gain from her self-identification, which raises questions about its sincerity. But consider this case:

> Terrance was born to white parents. However, they decided that they weren't in a position to raise him, and he was soon adopted by a black couple. This couple raised Terrance in a predominantly

African-American neighborhood, where he later attended predominantly African-American schools. As he grew up, he never thought of himself as white, and in middle school, he began taking steps to adjust his appearance to fit into his community. Eventually, Terrance comes to see himself as black, he openly identifies that way, and he usually passes as black. (He passes well enough that, unfortunately, he's been subject to racial profiling: on the suspicion that he might be there to shoplift, he's been followed while browsing in stores at the mall.) However, since he's aware that others might contest his identification, and he doesn't want to be accused of pretending, he indicates that he is Caucasian on official documents and, when it comes time to pay for college, avoids applying for scholarships that are designated for African Americans.

Is Terrance black? If so, why? If not, why not? How does Terrance avoid some of the criticisms that Burkett levels toward Jenner? Is he vulnerable to any of them? Does this sort of case show that we need to be more open to trans identities *other* than gender?

15

Trans Persons, Cisgender Persons, and Gender Identities

Christine Overall

Are trans people that different from cisgender people? Overall doesn't think so. She explains the meaning of relevant terms like "transgender," "cisgender," "gender," and "sex," arguing that we shouldn't just regard gender as a social identity, but also sex. This sets her up to clarify how the gender identities of transgender and cisgender persons are alike insofar as their identities fit within the same (male/female) gender categories, realize those identities in roughly the same ways, and are similarly susceptible to discontinuity in their gender identities.

Sex (female or male) and gender (girl/woman or boy/man) are among the most important characteristics of human persons. Most people assume that (1) a person's sex is fixed and invariant; (2) gender is constant, although some variations in gender display may be recognized and permitted; and (3) a person's gender is congruent with the person's sex at birth; that is, girls and women are female while boys and men are male. Individuals who conform to these assumptions constitute the usually unnamed, default norm

Overall, Christine. 2012. "Trans Persons, Cisgender Persons, and Gender Identities." In *The Philosophy of Sex: Contemporary Readings* 6E, edited by Nicholas Power, Raja Halwani, Alan Soble, 251–267. Lanham, MD: Rowman & Littlefield. Reprinted with permission.

not only statistically but also normatively: it is considered healthy, normal, and inevitable for one's sex to be fixed and invariant, one's gender constant, and one's gender congruent with one's sex at birth. These individuals are *cisgendered*. A cisgendered person, then, is someone whose gender identity and gender presentation are conventionally congruent with her or his sex assigned at birth (usually on the basis of genitalia).

The existence of trans[1] individuals challenges all these assumptions. A trans person is someone whose gender identity (and usually[2] also gender presentation) is not conventionally congruent with the sex assigned at birth. A trans person's gender is not consistent with the individual's sex at birth; hence, (3) is violated. If the trans person undertakes significant bodily modifications, then (1) is violated. And (2) is violated because the person may start out, at least as a small child and sometimes into adulthood, with a gender presentation congruent with the sex at birth but then change gender presentation. Because trans persons violate some or all of assumptions (1), (2), and (3), people generally believe that trans persons are very different from cisgendered persons and that trans persons' relationship to the characteristics of sex and gender is very different from that of cisgendered persons. . . .

This paper aims to dispel this belief about the alleged differences between cisgendered and trans persons by demonstrating the ways in which, with respect to their gender and sex identities, trans persons and cisgendered persons are similar. In making this case, I am not saying (1) that all trans persons—or all cisgendered persons, for that matter—are alike; (2) that there are no significant differences between trans persons and cisgendered persons; or (3) that social and political contexts are the same for both trans and cisgendered persons. . . .

. . .

In order to see this similarity, it is first necessary to recognize that both gender and sex are social identities. By "social identity" I mean a shared understanding of who an individual is that is derived from the individual's membership in a group category.

Gender as Social Identity

While the rigidity with which gender stereotypes is held continues to decline, there can be no denying that there are still gender-based differences in how we are expected to present ourselves and to act. Gender-validating forms of self-presentation include, first, forms of bodily styling, such as tattoos, make-up, hair (including length, color, condition, placement, and style), shaving, waxing, tanning, muscle building, the cultivation of "fitness," and various forms of so-called cosmetic surgery. Second, they include certain ways of dressing, talking, walking, sitting, running, throwing, and dancing.

Gender is socially required to be deeply definitive of each of us. Because of—and in some cases regardless of—our individual bodily configurations, a clear gender identification and presentation are socially compulsory; one does not have much, if any, choice about *whether* to have a gender, although one may have some choice about what kind of gender to have. . . . As everyone knows, gender is socially defined in terms of its association with sex (usually genitalia and so-called secondary sex characteristics like breasts and body hair distribution). The girl/woman gender is associated with female genitalia and secondary sex characteristics; the boy/man gender is associated with male genitalia and secondary sex characteristics. Sometimes, especially when people are trying to be what they think of as scientific, gender is defined in terms of its association with specific kinds and combinations of hormones or chromosomes. But in everyday practice, gender is mostly likely to be associated with relatively easily perceived genitalia and secondary sex characteristics. . . .

[. . .]

Sex as Social Identity

While gender is clearly a social identity, it is often thought that sex is thoroughly biological. But the very fact that there are such processes as sex transitions provides evidence that sex is indeed a social identity. It is by means of social processes, not biological determinism, that an individual's sex gets defined in historically specific ways and becomes almost always the most significant way of categorizing her or him (indeed, a necessary condition for personhood itself),[3] and that the genitalia are seen as representative or even determinative of who and what an individual is. In reality, however, what sex is thought to be varies from one society to another and one historical era to another; there is no ahistorical, acultural concept of sex. . . .[4] For example, sometimes the sex identity of athletes who consider themselves to be female on the basis of their genitalia and participate in athletic events as women is challenged on the grounds that their chromosomes indicate that they are "really" male. In addition, what it means to have a sex also depends upon cultural understandings of the structure of and relationships between female and male genitalia. For example, Thomas Laqueur has shown that before the eighteenth century, males and females were thought to be two different forms of just one sex. Women were believed to have the same genitalia as men, with men's genitalia being outside the body and women's inside the body.[5] And what it means to have a sex also depends on how many sexes are assumed to exist, what the relationships among those sexes are thought to be (whether, for example, they are taken to vary as a matter of degree or of kind), and whether or not the culture recognizes or denies the existence of genital and other physiological configurations that do not conform to the prevailing male or female social norm. . . .

Moreover, in the twenty-first century, one's sex can now be changed, and the ability to change it is the result of social factors, not biological ones. Thanks to scientific and medical research, genitals and breasts can be surgically enhanced, rebuilt, or removed altogether. So-called secondary sex characteristics such as hair distribution and muscle mass can be modified chemically via hormones. The body structure can be reshaped via fitness and nutrition regimes and even through the surgical reconstruction of bones.

A transition from one sex to another is, of course, undertaken not for its own sake but in order to enhance and express the person's gender identity by making the body more closely match the individual's sense of gender. Thus, an individual labeled a boy at birth may both identify and want to publicly present as a woman; the individual may then undergo surgery to create breasts or alter the genitalia to cohere with that felt sense of self. Individuals who undertake sex or gender transitions show, perhaps more than anyone else, that in important ways belonging to a sex is a social, not a biological, phenomenon; that one's sex is not inevitably fixed and immutable; and that one's genitalia (or any other body characteristics) do not inevitably represent, let alone determine through biological inevitability, who or what one is.

Acquired and Aspirational Identities

For the purposes of my argument, I suggest that there are, generally speaking, two kinds of social identities. I call them "acquired identities" and "aspirational identities." An acquired identity is a notable personal characteristic that has been permanently ascribed or earned and requires no further action on the part of its possessor in order to be maintained. For example, one of my acquired identities is being the birth mother of two children. I gestated and delivered them, and whatever may happen in their lives or mine, I remain their birth mother.[6]

Other identities are not acquired but are ongoing and what I call "aspirational." An aspirational identity is a notable personal characteristic such that, if its possessor values it, she must maintain and reinforce it through ongoing action. One example is the identity of being a mother, not in the sense of having gestated and given birth but in the social sense of caregiver for one or more children. The individual who values her identity as a mother in the social sense must continue to engage in what are considered culturally appropriate mothering behaviors. If she fails to do so, she is in danger of losing her identity, as when people say, "She's no mother" or "She's not a real mother." [. . .] With respect to aspirational identities, their possessor is always at risk during her lifetime, if not of failure, then at least of inadequacy; the possessor of an aspirational identity must always and continually prove herself.[7]

To say that an identity is aspirational, however, is not to say that it is necessarily a matter of free choice. In a given culture, some aspirational identities may be compulsory, some may be voluntary, and others may be forbidden. These requirements and constraints may be enforced in the usual ways—through training, validation, reinforcement, the absence of other options, ridicule, shaming, and abuse. [. . .]

Gender as Aspirational Identity

In my sense of the term, gender is an aspirational identity. In that respect, it is the same for everyone. I call gender "aspirational" to acknowledge that gender identity is never complete and never finished; it is something that one renews each day. . . .

One can aspire to exemplify a gender through the aforementioned bodily styling, self-presentation, and gendered activities, all of which must be ongoing for gender identity maintenance.[8] One learns how to aspire to one's gender through cultural tutelage that includes role models, advertising, media representations, parental socialization, peer pressure, gender-segregated activities and facilities, and so on. . . .

At least in theory it is possible to aspire to either of the two genders— the gender socially defined as congruent with one's sex or the gender socially defined as incongruent with it. What one aspires to may or may not match the social expectation of what a person with one's particular body should aspire to, and it may or may not match the gender assignment one was given at birth. A cisgendered person is someone who aspires to a gender identity that is socially considered to be consistent with her or his genitalia of birth and so-called secondary sex characteristics. A trans person is someone who does not aspire to a gender identity that is socially considered to be consistent with her or his genitalia of birth and so-called secondary sex characteristics.

. . .

Trans and Cisgender: Not So Different

The main contention of this essay is that with respect to sex and gender identities, trans persons and cisgendered persons are similar. We are now in a position to see what those similarities are. I shall describe four areas of similarity and then respond to what might seem to be an impediment to my claim about the similarity between trans persons and cisgendered persons.

1. Immersion in the System of Compulsory Gender

Even though some trans and cisgendered persons may be critical or skeptical of gender conventions, all trans and cisgendered persons are, of social necessity, deeply immersed in the system of compulsory gender. That immersion means that both trans and cisgendered persons are expected to validate their gender identity through all the means mentioned earlier—bodily styling; ways of dressing, talking, walking, sitting, running, throwing, and dancing; and gendered activities considered appropriate for men or for women.

In addition, both cisgendered and trans persons may in some cases decide to seek surgery in order to perform their gender identity (although the conditions, requirements, and criteria of access to such treatments are not the same for trans and cisgendered persons). For example, some trans people seek surgery in order to remove their genitalia or to surgically develop genitalia conventionally associated with persons of the gender to which they aspire. Similarly, some cisgendered women seek surgery to enlarge the size of their breasts or to reshape their genitalia (an operation called labiaplasty) in ways they believe to be desirable for authenticating and enhancing their membership in the gender to which they aspire. And some cisgendered men seek treatments and processes to enlarge their genitals. Moreover, some cisgendered and trans persons may seek hormonal treatments of various sorts in order to enhance their experiences or confirm their membership in the gender to which they aspire. For example, cisgendered women may use, at different times in their lives, contraceptive pills and so-called hormone replacement therapy. Cisgendered men may take testosterone. Trans men may take androgens and trans women may use estrogens and progestogens.

The growing demand by both cisgendered and trans persons for substances, operations, and processes to change the genitalia and secondary sex characteristics suggests that although sex is conventionally an identity that is *acquired* at birth (or even before, if fetal sex is identified through prenatal diagnostic tests) on the basis of visible genitalia, it is nonetheless becoming, in the service of achieving gender aspirations, more and more malleable for both trans and cisgendered persons. There is therefore reason to believe that sex is becoming, at least for some cisgendered and trans persons, an *aspirational* identity.

2. Constraints and Opportunities

Both trans and cisgendered persons also experience constraints upon, and find opportunities for, their gender aspirations. The constraints exist because, as I noted earlier, there are only two socially recognized, approved, and permissible genders in this culture, and their expression is still regulated. The opportunities arise, first, because trans people, and some cisgendered people, have the motivation, courage, and creativity to enact gender in ways that are not recognized, approved, and permissible from the point of view of mainstream society, and second because there are more and more cracks in the once-rigid façade of gender as a social institution, cracks that make gender nonconformity possible.

By definition, cisgendered persons aspire to a gender considered congruent with the socially recognized sex of their physical body. But the borderlines of what is considered congruent are still heavily patrolled and are inflected by expectations related to age, race, sexuality, and class. At the same time, with the relaxation over the last half-century of gender stereotypes, cisgendered persons have some freedom as to how they exemplify their gender; what kinds of gendered bodily styling, self-presentation, and activities they engage in; and what kind of man or woman they want to be.

Similarly, trans persons also have constraints and opportunities. For example, in addition to all the gender constraints that cisgendered people experience, some trans persons may be expected and required by the medical establishment to follow particularly strict gender norms considered consistent with the genitalia of members of the other sex in order to gain access to the medical treatments some may desire.[9] Moreover, trans persons' gender aspirations often confront what Bettcher calls "identity enforcement," a form of transphobia that explicitly denies and rejects the trans person's deeply felt identity in favor of what the enforcer believes is the individual's "real" identity.[10]

In terms of opportunities, some trans persons choose to identify explicitly as trans women or trans men, identities that are validated in their own right in trans subcultures and are not mere "qualification[s] of the dominant notion[s]" of woman or man.[11] Other trans persons reject what they see as the limitations associated with both genders as they are conventionally understood. Patrick Califia, for example, describes himself as "Not wanting to be female, but not having much enthusiasm for the only other option our society offers."[12] . . .

Similarly, a few trans persons may simply aim not to live as a member of one gender or another, not to exemplify a socially authorized version of manhood or womanhood, not to be gendered at all. In doing so, they challenge the nonoptional nature of the bi-gender system. A recent example is Australian norrie mAy-Welby [sic], who requested and received from the state of New South Wales an official certificate with the description "sex not specified." mAy-Welby was registered as male at birth, but at age twenty-three began hormone treatment and construction of a vagina. But mAy-Welby did not feel comfortable living as a female, ceased treatment, and decided to live as neither male nor female.[13] (mAy-Welby's change in legal status was subsequently revoked.)[14]

3. Continuity and Discontinuity

It may appear that a difference between the cisgendered person and the trans person has to do with the continuity or discontinuity of their gender aspirations. There is continuity, it might be thought, in the cisgendered person's gender aspirations, whereas there is discontinuity in the gender aspirations of the trans person, who changes her gender presentation and behavior.

This belief is mistaken. In many cases both the continuity of cisgendered people's lives and the discontinuity of trans people's lives may be only apparent. Both cisgendered and transgendered persons may vary, over the course of their lives, in terms of their affiliation to their gender as assigned on the basis of their sex at birth and of their aspirational gender. For example, while some trans persons adopt their new gender identity part way through life, there are others who say they have always felt, or have felt for a long time, that the gender assigned to them on the basis of their genital characteristics was a mistake. They remember a lifetime of aspiring to and acting on a gender that is not consistent with the gender stereotype imposed on persons with their genitalia. Hence, ostensibly new manifestations of their gender are the result of aspirations that have been growing and developing for many years. For them, there is no discontinuity in aspirational gender, and their rejection of their assigned gender does not represent a change in aspiration but rather their taking action on their aspirational gender, which has not changed.

On the other hand, while some cisgendered persons never question the nature of their gender affiliation, others do. A cisgendered woman who does not reject her assigned label of "woman" may nonetheless change, maybe even substantially, her womanly aspirations. That is, over the course of her life, she may make big changes in the kind of woman she wants to be. I think this is the case, for example, with many women whose lives were profoundly changed by feminism at various points in its history. There have also been cases where persons with the assigned gender of woman have chosen to go off to war, to have a sexual relationship with a woman, to work in a "man's" occupation, or to get an education—all behaviors that were incompatible with their assigned gender at the time and therefore represent a kind of gender discontinuity, even when such individuals did not cease to identify as women. Thus, there may be continuity in some trans persons' gender aspirations and discontinuity in some cisgendered persons' gender aspirations.

. . .

So cisgendered and transgendered persons do not necessarily and always differ, as groups, with respect to the continuity or discontinuity of their gender aspirations or the degree of their commitment to their gender.

. . .

Conclusion

I have attempted to demonstrate what I consider to be the similarities, with respect to gender and sex identities, between trans persons and cisgendered persons. Contrary to the assumption that cisgendered and trans persons are very different and that hence to be trans is to be abnormal, disordered, and unhealthy, an examination of the gender aspirations of cisgendered and trans persons reveals significant similarities. It is because of the very nature of gender—a "nature" that is, I assume, mostly social—that there are so many important resemblances between trans and cisgendered persons.

. . . I hope that making this case helps to reduce the "othering" of trans persons by cisgendered persons and hence is a small step toward ending the oppression of trans people.

Comprehension Questions

1. How do transgender persons make certain common assumptions about sex and gender problematic?
2. What is the difference between sex and gender, and in what sense are these social identities?
3. What are some examples that capture the distinction between acquired and aspirational differences?
4. How, according to Overall, do transgender and cisgender persons' respective gender identities relate to their sex identities?
5. What are some constraints and opportunities that face the gender aspirations of transgender and cisgender persons?
6. For cisgender persons, what possible discontinuities can occur as they work out their gender identities?

Discussion Questions

1. Overall is arguing that cisgender and transgender people are not as different in their gender identities as they might appear to be. Can you think of any important differences besides the ones she discusses?
2. Just suppose that Overall's argument fails, and that the gender identities of transgender and cisgender persons *are* different in the ways she considers. Would these differences be morally significant? In other words, if Overall is wrong, would that make any difference as to whether transgender people should be treated differently than cisgender people?
3. Overall speaks of constraints and opportunities you might encounter in carrying out your gender identity. Her usage of these terms seems to have moral weight. Do you think that those constraints are somehow bad and that those opportunities are somehow good (or vice versa)?

Case

Some athletes struggle to balance their desire to excel with expectations about their appearance:

> While most celebrities go incognito behind a hat and sunglasses, Serena Williams uses a different tactic to blend into a crowd: long sleeves.... "My arms are really fit, but I wanted to cover them, because when I do people don't recognize me as much," she said.
>
> Williams ... has large biceps and a mold-breaking muscular frame, which packs the power and athleticism that have dominated women's tennis for years. Her rivals could try to emulate her physique, but most of them choose not to.
>
> Despite Williams's success ... body-image issues among female tennis players persist, compelling many players to avoid bulking up.... Andrea Petkovic, a German ranked fourteenth, said she particularly loathed seeing pictures of herself hitting two-handed backhands, when her arm muscles appear the most bulging. "I just feel unfeminine," she said. "I don't know—it's probably that I'm self-conscious about what people might say. It's stupid, but it's insecurities that every woman has, I think.... Women, when we grow up we've been judged more, our physicality is judged more, and it makes us self-conscious."
>
> ... Williams, 33, who has appeared on the cover of *Vogue*, is regarded as a symbol of beauty by many women. But she has also been gawked at and mocked throughout her career, and she said growing confident and secure in her build was a long process.
>
> "I don't touch a weight, because I'm already super fit and super cut, and if I even look at weights, I get bigger," she said. "For years I've only done Thera-Bands and things like that, because that's kind of how I felt. But then I realized that you really have to learn to accept who you are and love who you are. I'm really happy with my body type, and I'm really proud of it. Obviously it works out for me. I talk about it all the time, how it was uncomfortable for someone like me to be in my body."[15]

How do these examples fit with what Overall says? Do male athletes face the same challenges? How might things be especially complicated for trans athletes?

Notes

1. Although there is a linguistic distinction between "transgender" and "transsexual," I use the general term "trans" to refer to all individuals who go through transitions in sex or gender. I use the term "transition" to refer to the changes trans people undergo. Bobby Noble writes, "The pedantic distinction between

'transgender' and 'transsexual' cannot hold, especially for female to male transsexual men for whom surgeries are always already incomplete" ("Our Bodies Are Not Ourselves: Tranny Guys and the Racialized Class Politics of Embodiment," in *Trans/Forming Feminisms: Trans-Feminist Voices Speak Out,* edited by Krista Scott-Dixon [Toronto: Sumach Press, 2006], 95–104, at 102, note 2). That is, not all trans persons undertake surgery, and even when they do, not all trans persons follow the same path. Trans people vary in their choices about the types, degrees, and extent of body modification they want to undergo.

2. I say "usually" because for reasons such as danger and oppression trans persons sometimes do not self-present in the gender with which they identify.

3. Naomi Scheman, "Queering the Center by Centering the Queer," in *Feminists Rethink the Self,* edited by Diana Tietjens Meyers (Boulder, CO: Westview Press, 1997), 124–62, at 132–33 and 140.

4. John Stoltenberg, *Refusing to Be a Man: Essays on Sex and Justice* (Portland, OR: Breitenbush Books, 1989), 30.

5. Thomas Laqueur, *Making Sex: Body and Gender from the Greeks to Freud* (Cambridge, MA: Harvard University Press, 1990).

6. I am not claiming to be infallible about this identity. It is possible that I could learn that one of my children had been accidentally switched after birth with another infant. My point, instead, is that acquired identities attach to a person because of *past* actions, either her own or those of others, and there is nothing she need (or even can) do now in order to maintain those identities.

7. In some cases we can also distinguish between descriptive and normative aspirational identities, between being an *A* and being a good *A*. Being a professor is an aspirational identity; having passed all educational requirements and acquired an academic position, one must still work to maintain the identity by doing the job of professor with a minimum of competence. Being a good professor requires additional work to achieve excellence in teaching and research. Both being an *A* and being a good *A* require work in order to achieve and maintain the identity. If one slacks off enough, one will not only not be a good *A* but may even lose being an *A* altogether. However, in the case of gender as an aspirational identity, what matters for one's social survival is to succeed in earning and sustaining the descriptive label "woman" or "man." The terms *"good* woman" and *"good* man" (unlike "good professor") do not suggest special expertise in gender presentation, above and beyond mere competence, but instead are terms of moral approbation.

8. Sandra Bartky, *Femininity and Domination: Studies in the Phenomenology of Oppression* (New York: Routledge, Chapman and Hall, 1990).

9. Dean Spade, "Mutilating Gender," in *The Transgender Studies Reader,* edited by Susan Stryker and Stephen Whittle (New York: Routledge, 2006), 314–32.

10. Talia Mae Bettcher, "Without a Net: Starting Points for Trans Stories," *American Philosophical Association Newsletter on Philosophy and Lesbian, Gay, Bisexual, and Transgender Issues* 10:2 (2011): 2–5, at 3.

11. Bettcher, "Without a Net," 3.
12. Patrick Califia, "Manliness," in *The Transgender Studies Reader,* edited by Susan Stryker and Stephen Whittle (New York: Routledge, 2006), 434–38, at 435.
13. "Sex Not Specified: Australia Leads the Way with Legal Document," *Scavenger* (www.thescavenger.net/glbsgdq/sex-not-specified-australia-leads-the-way-in-legal-document-756345-206.html; accessed February 13, 2012).
14. Jane Fae, "Australian Government Withdraws Non-Specified Gender Status," *Pink News: Europe's Largest Gay News Service* (http://www.pinknews.co.uk/2010/03/19/australian-government-withdraws-non-specified-gender-status; accessed February 13, 2012).
15. http://www.nytimes.com/2015/07/11/sports/tennis/tenniss-top-women-balance-body-image-with-quest-for-success.html

16

The Pressure to Cover

Kenji Yoshino

....

Covering is playing down characteristics that are associated with an avowed but stigmatized identity (for example, embracing your identity as a black person, but trying to "act white"). Yoshino explains the difference between covering and the more well-known concept of passing, and describes a number of legal cases to motivate his contention that covering is a serious civil rights issue. Yoshino argues that admitting the importance of sociocultural assimilation is compatible with individuals having the right to assert their identities against excessive demands to cover. Yoshino is critical of the tendency not to scrutinize the warrant for covering demands, suggesting that we should reverse this trend both within and outside of formal legal settings.

....

When I began teaching at Yale Law School in 1998, a friend spoke to me frankly. "You'll have a better chance at tenure," he said, "if you're a homosexual professional than if you're a professional homosexual." Out of the closet for six years at the time, I knew what he meant. To be a "homosexual professional" was to be a professor of constitutional law who "happened" to be gay. To be a "professional homosexual" was to be a gay professor who made gay rights his work. . . .

I didn't experience the advice as antigay. The law school is a vigorously tolerant place, embedded in a university famous for its gay student population. . . . I could see that research related to one's identity—referred to in the academy as "mesearch"—could raise legitimate questions about scholarly objectivity.

. . .

It wasn't long before I found myself resisting the demand to conform. . . . What bothered me was the felt need to mute my passion for gay subjects, people, culture. At a time when the law was transforming gay rights, it seemed ludicrous not to suit up and get in the game. "Mesearch" being what it is, I soon turned my scholarly attention to the pressure to conform. What puzzled me was that I felt that pressure so long after my emergence from the closet. When I stopped passing, I exulted that I could stop thinking about my sexuality. This proved naive. Long after I came out, I still experienced the need to assimilate to straight norms. But I didn't have a word for this demand to tone down my known gayness.

Then I found my word, in the sociologist Erving Goffman's book "Stigma." Written in 1963, the book describes how various groups—including the disabled, the elderly and the obese—manage their "spoiled" identities. After discussing passing, Goffman observes that "persons who are ready to admit possession of a stigma . . . may nonetheless make a great effort to keep the stigma from looming large." He calls this behavior covering. He distinguishes passing from covering by noting that passing pertains to the visibility of a characteristic, while covering pertains to its obtrusiveness. He relates how F.D.R. stationed himself behind a desk before his advisers came in for meetings. Roosevelt was not passing, since everyone knew he used a wheelchair. He was covering, playing down his disability so people would focus on his more conventionally presidential qualities.

As is often the case when you learn a new idea, I began to perceive covering everywhere. Leafing through a magazine, I read that Helen Keller replaced her natural eyes (one of which protruded) with brilliant blue glass ones. On the radio, I heard that Margaret Thatcher went to a voice coach to lower the pitch of her voice. Friends began to send me e-mail. Did I know that Martin Sheen was Ramon Estevez on his birth certificate, that Ben Kingsley was Krishna Bhanji, that Kirk Douglas was Issur Danielovitch Demsky and that Jon Stewart was Jonathan Leibowitz?

. . .

It was only when I looked for instances of covering in the law that I saw how lucky I had been. Civil rights case law is peopled with plaintiffs who were severely punished for daring to be openly different. Workers were fired for lapsing into Spanish in English-only workplaces, women were fired for behaving in stereotypically "feminine" ways and gay parents lost custody of their children for engaging in displays of same-sex affection. These cases revealed that far from being a parlor game, covering was the civil rights issue of our time.

The New Discrimination

In recent decades, discrimination in America has undergone a generational shift. Discrimination was once aimed at entire groups, resulting in the exclusion of all racial minorities, women, gays, religious minorities and people with disabilities. A battery of civil rights laws—like the Civil Rights Act of 1964 and the Americans with Disabilities Act of 1990—sought to combat these forms of discrimination. The triumph of American civil rights is that such categorical exclusions by the state or employers are now relatively rare.

Now a subtler form of discrimination has risen to take its place. This discrimination does not aim at groups as a whole. Rather, it aims at the subset of the group that refuses to cover, that is, to assimilate to dominant norms. And for the most part, existing civil rights laws do not protect individuals against such covering demands. The question of our time is whether we should understand this new discrimination to be a harm and, if so, whether the remedy is legal or social in nature.

Consider the following cases:

1. Renee Rogers, an African-American employee at American Airlines, wore cornrows to work. American had a grooming policy that prevented employees from wearing an all-braided hairstyle. When American sought to enforce this policy against Rogers, she filed suit, alleging race discrimination. In 1981, a federal district court rejected her argument. It first observed that cornrows were not distinctively associated with African-Americans, noting that Rogers had only adopted the hairstyle after it "had been popularized by a white actress in the film *10*." As if recognizing the unpersuasiveness of what we might call the Bo Derek defense, the court further alleged that because hairstyle, unlike skin color, was a mutable characteristic, discrimination on the basis of grooming was not discrimination on the basis of race. Renee Rogers lost her case.

2. Lydia Mikus and Ismael Gonzalez were called for jury service in a case involving a defendant who was Latino. When the prosecutor asked them whether they could speak Spanish, they answered in the affirmative. The prosecutor struck them, and the defense attorney then brought suit on their behalf, claiming national-origin discrimination. The prosecutor responded that he had not removed the potential jurors for their ethnicity but for their ability to speak Spanish. His stated concern was that they would not defer to the court translator in listening to Spanish-language testimony. In 1991, the Supreme Court credited this argument. Lydia Mikus and Ismael Gonzalez lost their case.

3. Diana Piantanida had a child and took a maternity leave from her job at the Wyman Center, a charitable organization in Missouri. During her leave, she was demoted, supposedly for previously having handed in work late. The man who was then the Wyman Center's executive director, however, justified her demotion by saying the new position would be easier "for a new mom to handle." As it turned out, the new position had less responsibility and half the pay of the original one. But when Piantanida turned this position down, her successor was paid Piantanida's old salary. Piantanida brought suit, claiming she had been discharged as a "new mom." In 1997, a federal appellate court refused to analyze her claim as a sex-discrimination case, which would have led to comparing the treatment she received to the treatment of "new dads." Instead, it found that Piantanida's (admittedly vague) pleadings raised claims only under the Pregnancy Discrimination Act, which it correctly interpreted to protect women only while they are pregnant. Diana Piantanida lost her case.

4. Robin Shahar was a lesbian attorney who received a job offer from the Georgia Department of Law, where she had worked as a law student. The summer before she started her new job, Shahar had a religious same-sex commitment ceremony with her partner. She asked a supervisor for a late starting date because she was getting married and wanted to go on a celebratory trip to Greece. Believing Shahar was marrying a man, the supervisor offered his congratulations. Senior officials in the office soon learned, however, that Shahar's partner was a woman. This news caused a stir, reports of which reached Michael Bowers, the attorney general of

Georgia who had successfully defended his state's prohibition of sodomy before the United States Supreme Court. After deliberating with his lawyers, Bowers rescinded her job offer. The staff member who informed her read from a script, concluding, "Thanks again for coming in, and have a nice day." Shahar brought suit, claiming discrimination on the basis of sexual orientation. In court, Bowers testified that he knew Shahar was gay when he hired her, and would never have terminated her for that reason. In 1997, a federal appellate court accepted that defense, maintaining that Bowers had terminated Shahar on the basis of her conduct, not her status. Robin Shahar lost her case.

Simcha Goldman, an Air Force officer who was also an ordained rabbi, wore a yarmulke at all times. Wearing a yarmulke is part of the Orthodox tradition of covering one's head out of deference to an omnipresent god. Goldman's religious observance ran afoul of an Air Force regulation that prohibited wearing headgear while indoors. When he refused his commanding officer's order to remove his yarmulke, Goldman was threatened with a court martial. He brought a First Amendment claim, alleging discrimination on the basis of religion. In 1986, the Supreme Court rejected his claim. It stated that the Air Force had drawn a reasonable line between "religious apparel that is visible and that which is not." Simcha Goldman lost his case.

These five cases represent only a fraction of those in which courts have refused to protect plaintiffs from covering demands. In such cases, the courts routinely distinguish between immutable and mutable traits, between being a member of a legally protected group and behavior associated with that group. . . .

This distinction between being and doing reflects a bias toward assimilation. Courts will protect traits like skin color or chromosomes because such traits cannot be changed. In contrast, the courts will not protect mutable traits, because individuals can alter them to fade into the mainstream, thereby escaping discrimination. If individuals choose not to engage in that form of self-help, they must suffer the consequences.

The judicial bias toward assimilation will seem correct and just to many Americans. Assimilation, after all, is a precondition of civilization— wearing clothes, having manners and obeying the law are all acts of assimilation. . . .

. . .

The Case Against Assimilation

The flaw in the judiciary's analysis is that it casts assimilation as an un-adulterated good. Assimilation is implicitly characterized as the way in which groups can evade discrimination by fading into the mainstream—after all, the logic goes, if a bigot cannot discriminate between two individuals, he cannot discriminate against one of them. But sometimes assimilation is not an escape from discrimination, but precisely its effect. When a Jew is forced to convert to Protestantism, for instance, we do not celebrate that as an evasion of anti-Semitism. . . .

Take the cornrows case. Initially, this case appears to be an easy one for the employer, as hairstyle seems like such a trivial thing. But if hair is so trivial, we might ask why American Airlines made it a condition of Renee Rogers's employment. What's frustrating about the employment discrimination jurisprudence is that courts often don't force employers to answer the critical question of why they are requiring employees to cover. If we look to other sources, the answers can be troubling.

John T. Molloy's perennially popular self-help manual "New Dress for Success" also tells racial minorities to cover. Molloy advises African-Americans to avoid "Afro hairstyles" and to wear "conservative pinstripe suits, preferably with vests, accompanied by all the establishment symbols, including the Ivy League tie." He urges Latinos to "avoid pencil-line mustaches," "any hair tonic that tends to give a greasy or shiny look to the hair," "any articles of clothing that have Hispanic associations" and "anything that is very sharp or precise."

Molloy is equally frank about why covering is required. The "model of success," he says, is "white, Anglo-Saxon and Protestant." Those who do not possess these traits "will elicit a negative response to some degree, regardless of whether that response is conscious or subconscious." . . .

. . .

We can see a similar dynamic in the termination of Robin Shahar. Michael Bowers, the state attorney general, disavowed engaging in first-generation discrimination when he said he had no problem with gay employees. This raises the question of why he fired Shahar for having a religious same-sex commitment ceremony. Unlike American Airlines, Bowers provided some answers. He argued that retaining Shahar would compromise the department's ability to deny same-sex couples marriage licenses and to enforce sodomy statutes.

Neither argument survives scrutiny. At no point did Shahar seek to marry her partner legally, nor did she agitate for the legalization of same-sex marriage. The Georgia citizenry could not fairly have assumed that Shahar's religious ceremony would entitle the couple to a civil license. Bowers's claim that Shahar's wedding would compromise her ability to enforce sodomy statutes is also off the mark. Georgia's sodomy statute (which has since been struck down) punished cross-sex as well as same-sex sodomy, meaning that any heterosexual in the department who had ever had oral sex was as compromised as Shahar.

. . .

So the covering demand presents a conundrum. The courts are right to be leery of intervening in too brusque a manner here, as they cannot risk playing favorites among groups. Yet they also cannot ignore the fact that the covering demand is where many forms of inequality continue to have life. We need a paradigm that gives both these concerns their due, adapting the aspirations of the civil rights movement to an increasingly pluralistic society.

The New Civil Rights

The new civil rights begins with the observation that everyone covers. . . .

Contemporary civil rights has erred in focusing solely on traditional civil rights groups—racial minorities, women, gays, religious minorities and people with disabilities. This assumes those in the so-called mainstream—those straight white men—do not also cover. They are understood only as obstacles, as people who prevent others from expressing themselves, rather than as individuals who are themselves struggling for self-definition. No wonder they often respond to civil rights advocates with hostility. They experience us as asking for an entitlement they themselves have been refused—an expression of their full humanity.

Civil rights must rise into a new, more inclusive register. . . .

This does not mean discrimination against racial minorities is the same as discrimination against poets. American civil rights law has correctly directed its concern toward certain groups and not others. But the aspiration of civil rights—the aspiration that we be free to develop our human capacities without the impediment of witless conformity—is an aspiration that extends beyond traditional civil rights groups.

To fulfill that aspiration, we must think differently both within the law and outside it. With respect to legal remedies, we must shift away from claims that demand equality for particular groups toward claims that demand liberty for us all. This is not an exhortation that we strip protections from currently recognized groups. Rather, it is a prediction that future courts will be unable to sustain a group-based vision of civil rights when faced with the broad and irreversible trend toward demographic pluralism. In an increasingly diverse society, the courts must look to what draws us together as citizens rather than to what drives us apart.

As if in recognition of that fact, the Supreme Court has moved in recent years away from extending protections on the basis of group membership and toward doing so on the basis of liberties we all possess. In 2003, the court struck down a Texas statute that prohibited same-sex sodomy. It did not, however, frame the case as one concerning the equality rights of gays. Instead, it cast the case as one concerning the interest we all—straight, gay or otherwise—have in controlling our intimate lives. Similarly, in 2004, the court held that a state could be required by a Congressional statute to make its courthouses wheelchair accessible. Again, the court ruled in favor of the minority group without framing its analysis in group-based equality rhetoric. Rather, it held that all people— disabled or otherwise— have a "right of access to the courts," which had been denied in that instance.

. . .

If the Supreme Court protects individuals against covering demands in the future, I believe it will do so by invoking the universal rights of people. I predict that if the court ever recognizes the right to speak a native language, it will protect that right as a liberty to which we are all entitled, rather than as a remedial concession granted to a particular national-origin group. If the court recognizes rights to grooming, like the right to wear cornrows, I believe it will do so under something akin to the German Constitution's right to personality rather than as a right attached to racial minorities. And I hope that if the court protects the right of gays to marry, it will do so by framing it as the right we all have to marry the person we love, rather than defending "gay marriage" as if it were a separate institution.

. . . While I have great hopes for this new legal paradigm, I also believe law will play a relatively small part in the new civil rights. . . .

As an initial matter, many covering demands are made by actors the law does not—and in my view should not—hold accountable, like friends, family, neighbors, the "culture" or individuals themselves. When I think of the covering demands I have experienced, I can trace many of them only to my own censorious consciousness. And while I am often tempted to sue myself, I recognize this is not my healthiest impulse.

Law is also an incomplete solution to coerced assimilation because it has yet to recognize the myriad groups that are subjected to covering demands even though these groups cannot be defined by traditional classifications like race, sex, orientation, religion and disability. . . . The law may someday move to protect some of these identities. But it will never protect them all.

. . . The primary solution lies in all of us as citizens, not in the tiny subset of us who are lawyers. People confronted with demands to cover should feel emboldened to seek a reason for that demand, even if the law does not reach the actors making the demand or recognize the group burdened by it. These reason-forcing conversations should happen outside courtrooms—in public squares and prayer circles, in workplaces and on playgrounds. They should occur informally and intimately, in the everyday places where tolerance is made and unmade.

What will constitute a good-enough reason to justify assimilation will obviously be controversial. We have come to some consensus that certain reasons are illegitimate—like racism, sexism or religious intolerance. Beyond that, we should expect conversations rather than foreordained results—what reasons count, and for what purposes, will be for us all to decide by facing one another as citizens. My personal inclination is always to privilege the claims of the individual against countervailing interests like "neatness" or "workplace harmony." But we should have that conversation.

Such conversations are the best—and perhaps the only—way to give both assimilation and authenticity their due. They will help us alleviate conservative alarmists' fears of a balkanized America and radical multiculturalists' fears of a monocultural America. The aspiration of civil rights has always been to permit people to pursue their human flourishing without limitations based on bias. Focusing on law prevents us from seeing the revolutionary breadth of that aspiration. It is only when we leave the law that civil rights suddenly stops being about particular agents of oppression and particular victimized groups and starts to become a project of human flourishing in which we all have a stake.

. . .

This just brings home to me that the only right I have wanted with any consistency is the freedom to be who I am. I'll be the first to admit that I owe much of that freedom to group-based equality movements, like the gay rights movement. But it is now time for us as a nation to shift the emphasis away from equality and toward liberty in our debates about identity politics. Only through such freedom can we live our lives as works in progress, which is to say, as the complex, changeful and contradictory creatures that we are.

Comprehension Questions

1. What is covering and what distinguishes it from passing?
2. What is the rationale offered in the cases discussed by Yoshino for enforcing covering demands?
3. Why does Yoshino think covering should not be accepted as part of cultural assimilation?
4. Why isn't it best to think about the civil rights issue of covering in terms of social groups?
5. How should the problem of covering be addressed in informal settings?

Discussion Questions

1. Summarize the various cases briefly laid out by Yoshino. Do you agree that these are all civil rights violations? Could someone plausibly argue that one of them is different in a significant way from the others?
2. Yoshino's discussion of covering is not meant to license every form of individual self-expression. How would you draw a principled line between when individuals ought to conform and when they ought to assert their freedom of self-expression?
3. Yoshino proposes that covering is a civil rights issue, but also one that individuals must grapple with themselves, and he recommends dialogue about the reasons for covering demands. How else can individuals responsibly address the problem of covering demands?

Case

In his book-length discussion of covering, Yoshino discusses the double-bind that women face in the workplace:

> . . . [L]ong after traditionally male institutions admit women, they retain cultures favoring men. . . . [For example,] women at [the

University of Pennsylvania Law School] experienced pressure to de-sexualize themselves, to eschew stereotypically feminine traits, and to avoid feminist activism. In the words of one professor, women were told: "To be a good lawyer, behave like a gentleman." On the other hand, women were pressed in the opposite direction. Women who spoke out in class were subjected to hissing, public humiliation, and gossip. Women who did not conform to stereotypically feminine be-havior were called "man-hating lesbians" or "feminazi dykes."

. . . In many workplaces, women are pressured to be "masculine" enough to be respected as workers, but also to be "feminine" enough to be respected as women. . . . I could easily imagine two lists of behaviors that represent these expectations. Here are some of the ways in which a woman could say she acts "masculine":

I avoid pastels. I avoid floral designs. I do not wear my hair too long. I do not cry. I am aggressive. I am ambitious. I am analytical. I am asser-tive. I am athletic. I am competitive. I am individualistic. I am self-reliant. I work in a traditionally male-dominated field. I am childless. If I have children, I made my pregnancy "invisible." I built up stores of goodwill in anticipation of my pregnancy. I never admit it when I leave work to take care of my children. I do not have photographs of my children at the office. I do not self-identify as a feminist. I do not make women's issues part of my work. I am told I am exceptional, not like a typical woman. I dissociate myself from other women.

Here are some of the ways in which a woman—and in many cases it could be the same woman—could say she acts "feminine":

I wear earrings. I wear makeup. I do not wear my hair too short. I am never unkempt. I am affectionate. I am cheerful. I am compassionate. I am gentle. I am loyal. I am sensitive. I am soft-spoken. I am sympa-thetic. I am tender. I am understanding. I am warm. I am yielding. I listen. I do not yell at work. I express vulnerability. I perform "nurture" functions at work, like counseling and mentoring. I perform "house-keeping" functions at work, like arranging office events. I work in a "pink-collar" ghetto.[1]

Can you think of other arenas of life in which women face such double-binds? How, for example, do they have to cover to be accepted in their homes, churches, and various social settings?

Note

1. Kenji Yoshino (2007). *Covering: The Hidden Assault on Our Civil Rights*. New York: Random House, Part II.

==== ☙ ====

17

Racism

What It Is and What It Isn't

Lawrence Blum

People use the word "racist" to refer to all sorts of race-related moral failings. Should they? Blum argues that they shouldn't. Instead, he contends that we should reserve the term "racist" for those who have specific negative beliefs or attitudes toward people of other races. Then, we should distinguish between several different race-related problems, such as racial insensitivity, failure to recognize racial identity, racial ignorance, racial anxiety, racial injustice, and racial homogenization. Since these issues require different remedies, keeping them separate helps us think more clearly about how to make moral progress.

We in the United States are notoriously poor at communicating about racial matters. . . . For the past several years I have taught courses on race and racism to undergraduates, graduate students in education, and high school students. Most of my classes are quite racially and ethnically diverse. In my experience a range of reasons accounts for the lack of productive conversation. People are afraid of giving offense. They are afraid of revealing prejudices they know are not

Blum, Lawrence. 2002. "Racism: What It Is and What It Isn't." *Studies in Philosophy and Education* 21: 203–218. Copyright © 2002, Springer. Reprinted with permission.

socially acceptable. They are afraid of *appearing* prejudiced, even if they are actually not. They feel ignorant of groups other than their own and are afraid to risk revealing their ignorance and trying to remedy it. The whole idea of "race" just carries unpleasant associations with them, and they would rather avoid it. They may think we should all be "color-blind," that it is somehow wrong even to take notice of or make reference to other people's racial identity. . . .

The words "racism" and "racist" have become deeply entrenched in the moral vocabulary of the United States and Western Europe. . . . "Racist" has become the standard way to condemn and deplore people, actions, policies, symbols, and institutions for malfeasance in the racial domain.

In serving as a term of moral reproach, "racism" has joined more time-honored vices such as "dishonesty," "cruelty," "cowardice," and "hypocrisy." Apart from a small number of avowed white supremacists, most Americans wish very much to avoid being called "racist." In this regard, "racist" operates similarly to "cruel." Few admit to being cruel. Persons who are cruel might say the target of their cruelty deserved it, or they might simply fail to recognize the harm caused by their actions. Similarly, no one admits to being racist. Those who are, or are thought to be, might say their remarks were just a joke; they did not intend any harm; people are just being oversensitive; it was a personal, not a racial, thing; and the like. . . .

Overusing "Racism"

. . . [T]he widely-shared reproach carried by "racist" is threatened by a current tendency to overuse the term. Some feel that the word is thrown around so much that anything involving "race" that someone does not like is liable to castigation as "racist"—for example, merely mentioning someone's race (or racial designation), using the word "Oriental" for Asians without recognizing its origins and its capacity for insult, or socializing only with members of one's own racial group. . . . A few observers go even further and suspect that the word has lost all significant meaning. "Racism is . . . what black activists define it to be. . . . When words lose coherent meaning, they also lose the power to shame. 'Racism,' 'sexism,' and 'homophobia' have become such words. Labels that should horrify are simply shrugged off" (Nuechterlein, 1996, p. B9). . . .

A major reason for what Robert Miles calls the "conceptual inflation" (Miles, 1989, pp. 41–68), to which the idea of "racism" has been subject is its having become the central or even only notion used to mark morally suspect behavior, attitude, and social practice regarding race. The result— either something is racist, or it is morally in the clear. In Boston a white police officer, as a bizarre joke and apparently with no malice intended, placed a hangman's noose on the motorcycle of a black police officer. "Police probe sees no racism in noose prank," says the headline of an article reporting the findings of an investigation into the incident. Perhaps the white officer was not "a racist," nor operating from racist motives; but, as the victim in the incident said, "You cannot hang a noose like that near any black man who knows his history and say it does not have tremendous significance" (*Boston Globe*, p. B1). [The black officer seemed clearly to be referring to lynching.] If our only choices are to label an act "racist" or "nothing to get too upset about," those who seek to garner moral attention to some racial malfeasance will be tempted to call it "racist." That overuse in turn feeds a diminishing of "racism's" moral force, and thus contributes to weakened concern about racism and other racial ills.

Not all racial incidents are racist incidents. Not every instance of racial conflict, insensitivity, discomfort, miscommunication, exclusion, injustice, or ignorance should be called "racist." This more varied and nuanced moral vocabulary needs to be more fully utilized, complementing "racist" and "racism." All forms of racial ills should elicit concern from responsible citizens. If someone displays racial insensitivity, but not racism, people should be able to see that straightforwardly as a matter of moral concern. In a soccer game, a nine-year-old white boy said, "Boy, pass the ball over here" to one of his black teammates, and "was virtually accused of being a racist by the father of one of his teammates," says an article on the incident. (That description may itself reflect the loss of an evaluative vocabulary other than "racist" and "racism," rather than what the black boy's father actually said.) In any case, the white boy was almost surely not "a racist" and the article itself goes on to express more accurately the racial ill involved in his remark: "The word 'boy' is a tripwire attached to so much charged racial baggage that it is no longer safely used as a term for a prepubescent male." . . .

Defining "Racism"

. . . "Racism" was first used by German social scientists in the 1930s to refer to the ideology of race superiority central to Nazism, and its core historical meaning broadened out to other systems of racial domination

and oppression, such as segregation, South African apartheid, and European colonialism. In this light, I want to suggest that all forms of racism can be related to either of two general "themes"—*inferiorization*, and *antipathy*. Inferiorizing is treating the racial other as inferior or of lesser value and, secondarily, viewing the racial other as inferior. Racial antipathy is simply a strong dislike, often tinged with hostility, toward individuals or groups because of their race. Of the two modes, inferiorization is more obviously linked to historical racist doctrines and social systems. Slavery, segregation, imperialism, apartheid, and Nazism all involved certain groups being regarded as and treated as inferior to other groups.
. . .

Inferiorizing and antipathy racism are distinct. Some superiority racists do not hate the target of their beliefs. They may have a paternalistic concern and feelings of kindness for persons they regard as their human inferiors. This form of racism was prevalent among slave owners, and characterized many whites' views of blacks during the segregation era in the United States. The concern and kindness are misdirected, and demeaning, because the other is not seen as an equal, or even as a full human being; it is a racist form of concern. Nevertheless such attitudes are distinct from antipathy and hatred.

On the other side, not every race hater regards the target of her hatred as inferior. In the U.S. antipathy toward Asians and Jews often accompanies, and is in part driven by, a kind of resentment of those seen as in some ways superior (e.g., more successful). And some whites who hate blacks do not really regard blacks as inferior; they may fear and be hostile to them, but fear and hostility are not the same as contempt and other forms of inferiorizing. (Again, antipathy and contempt may accompany one another.) Survey research suggests that pure superiority racism toward blacks has substantially decreased since segregation, more so than hostility-based racism (Schuman et al., pp. 156–157). Nevertheless, the great and persistent racial inequalities in our society provide a standing encouragement to advantaged groups to see disadvantaged groups as somehow deserving their lower status.

However, antipathy and inferiorizing racism are not entirely separate either. The paternalistic inferiorizing racist (e.g. a white segregationist) often hates those members of the racial group who do not accept the inferior social position he regards as appropriate to their inferior natures—for example, blacks who do not engage in the deference behavior the paternalistic racist expects. Emmett Till was lynched in 1955 out of hatred directed toward a young black man who had transgressed the rules of racial deference and constraint defining him as an inferior being. In addition, many racists both hate *and* regard as inferior members of a particular racial group (and not only a particular subcategory of such members, such as those who do not "stay in their place").

Racial and Racist Stereotypes

If we confine racism to manifestations or representations of racial antipathy or racial inferiorizing, we can see that many things can go wrong in the area of race without being racist. Consider two objectionable stereotypes of blacks, for instance—blacks as intellectually deficient, and blacks as good dancers. The first is a straightforwardly racist stereotype; it portrays blacks as inferior in regard to a fundamental human attribute. The second, however, is not racist, on my account. It attributes a positive rather than a negative quality. It is a far less objectionable stereotype than the inferiority stereotype.

Nevertheless, the stereotype of blacks as good dancers is still an objectionable one. Like any stereotype, it wildly overgeneralizes about a group; it blinds us to the internal diversity of the group—some blacks are bad dancers, some are good, some are so-so (and this is so of every racial group). Also, all stereotyping discourages recognizing the individuality of members of the group.

The stereotype of blacks as good dancers is also objectionable in a more specific, historically contextual sense, which can be recognized in the more variegated moral vocabulary revealed by loosening our fixation on "racism" and "racist." This stereotype hearkens back to the slave era, when viewing blacks as good dancers was bound up with their being seen as mentally inferior. While this direct implication is no longer clearly attached to the "good dancer" stereotype, stereotypes must be viewed historically as well as contemporarily, and a given stereotype's resonance with a much more distinctly racist stereotype renders it objectionable in a way that stereotypes without such historical resonance would not be. Other stereotypes lacking such historical resonance are, for example, Asians as poor drivers, blacks as poor swimmers, and whites as not being able to jump. All are objectionable, racial (race-based) stereotypes. But it is moral overload to call them *racist* stereotypes, and to do so contributes to a cheapening of the moral force of the idea of "racism."

Racial Discomfort or Anxiety

Another application of the definition of racism is the difference between racial antipathy and what I will call "racial discomfort" or "racial anxiety." Consider the following example.

Ms. Verano is a white fourth grade teacher. She feels comfortable with all the children in her very racially-mixed class. She holds all students to equally high standards of performance. But, though she has never admitted this to herself, she is not really comfortable with most of the black parents. She does not dislike blacks, nor does she think they are inferior. However, she is not particularity familiar with African-American culture, knows very few blacks other than her students, and is not confident about her ability to communicate with blacks other than her students, and is not confident about her ability to communicate with black adults. As a result Ms. Verano is somewhat defensive when speaking with black parents in parent conferences, and is not able to listen to their concerns and viewpoints about their children as well as she does with parents in other racial groups. Because she does not glean as much information from the black parents about their children as she does from the other parents, she is not able to serve these children as well as the other children in her class. Ms. Verano does not have antipathy or inferiorizing attitudes toward blacks. To call her a "racist" would be conceptual inflation. She bears no antipathy toward blacks; I have built this feature into the example. Nor does she regard blacks as inferior.

Ms. Verano's situation is best described by saying that she is uncomfortable with black adults (not children). She has "racial discomfort" or "racial anxiety."

Racial anxiety is quite common in the United States, especially, I believe, among whites, although it can be found in any racial group. Racial anxiety can stem from different sources, and one of them can be anxiety that one's racist prejudices be revealed. In this case racial anxiety would be a manifestation of racism. However, racial anxiety is not always racist in its genesis. We can realize that a group of persons is different from us in some socially important way, and we can feel that we are just not knowledgeable enough about this group to feel comfortable in the presence of its members. We can be anxious that we will embarrass ourselves by saying or doing the "wrong thing." We may worry that the group will dislike or reject us if we attempt to approach it. This social anxiety is perfectly familiar regarding cultural differences; the individual is anxious approaching a culture about which she lacks knowledge. Members of different racial groups are also often quite ignorant of one another's modes of life (sometimes but not always because cultural and racial differences correspond), even if they interact in schools and workplaces. In a sense racial anxiety is even *more* likely than mere cultural anxiety, since differences in "race" are more socially charged than are cultural differences. If one is equally ignorant of the other group, there is more reason to be anxious that one will violate some unforeseen norm with regard to a racially different group than a culturally different one.

In itself, racial anxiety or discomfort is not racism. Nor is racial discomfort the sort of thing for which its possessor is subject to moral criticism. It is not morally bad to be racially anxious, as it is morally bad to be racially prejudiced. However, racial discomfort is still a bad thing, and an individual who recognizes her racial anxiety should not rest content with it just because it is not a moral blot on her character. This is so, in part, because, as in Ms. Verano's case, it can lead to acts of a discriminatory character. Ms. Verano is unlikely to be able to educate her black pupils to the same degree as she does her other students, since she will lack information pertinent to them. . . .

Race, Identity, and Recognition

Another race-related ill distinct from racism is illustrated in the following example. A Haitian-American girl is one of two black students in her class. When a race-related issue arises in discussion, the teacher turns to her and asks her what "the black point of view" is on the question at hand.

There seem several distinct though related wrongs this teacher has committed. He has failed to recognize Haitian-Americans as a distinct ethnic group within the larger "black" umbrella. He has treated a racial group in an overly homogeneous manner, implying that there could be something that could coherently be called "the black point of view" on an issue. Finally, he has failed to recognize the student as an individual, with her own individual views.

These three related forms of misrecognition are directed toward an individual or a group of which the individual is a member. The latter two—racial homogenization, and not acknowledging individuality—are particularly serious failings in a teacher. However, that is not to say that they are "racist." The teacher's behavior need not imply that he harbors animus toward blacks, or regards them as inferior.

Racial Motives and Racial Stereotypes

Confusion about both the location and the meaning of racism infected public understanding of a particularly tragic event that took place in Providence, Rhode Island, in January, 2000. Several women were fighting in a late-night diner. The night manager threw the patrons out of the diner, at which point some male friends got involved, one of whom drew a gun. Inside the diner, an off-duty patrolman, Cornel Young, Jr., an African American, was waiting for a take-out order. Meanwhile, the police had been called to the scene outside. Officer Young, after warning the patrons to get down, rushed outside to help the two officers on the scene, his gun drawn. (Providence police are required to carry their firearms when off duty.)

The two officers had ordered the male friend to drop his gun, which he did, and they then turned to Officer Young and ordered him to do so as well. It is not clear whether Young heard the order, but in any case he did not comply, and the two officers, who were white, shot and killed him. It emerged that, despite the officers' failing to recognize Officer Young, one of the officers had been a police academy classmate of Young's, and both had graduated in the same class three years earlier.

The killing sparked community outrage and anguish. Charges of racism were made. It was said that the killing was "racially motivated." Eventually a federal civil rights investigation took place, and the two officers were cleared of having intended to deprive Officer Young of his civil rights, or of acting out of racial animosity.

It is impossible to know whether the two officers were racially biased against blacks. However, their behavior is perfectly consistent with their lacking any form of racial prejudice or racial motivation. It is not likely that they shot at Young because they disliked black people. Some people, recognizing this, then felt some relief. The incident turned from one involving racism to a (mere) "tragic accident."

But this response oversimplifies. Racism may be absent in motivations and attitudes but be present elsewhere. In this situation, it is much more plausible to think that it lay in the stereotypes that the officers carried in their minds about blacks. That is why, or part of why, they reacted to a black man with a gun in plain clothes as if he were a perpetrator, even though they actually knew him as a fellow officer. In another widely-reported case around the same time, four white officers in New York City killed an innocent black man whom they wrongly took to be reaching for a gun. Treating blackness as if it were an indicator of suspiciousness or criminality is referred to as "racial profiling" and has come in for a good deal of public criticism as a result of these and similar incidents, not only ones involving fatalities.

The white officers who killed Officer Young were apparently genuinely remorseful and upset by their having unwittingly killed a fellow officer. But this does not mean they were not prey to racial stereotypes linking blackness to criminality. Officer Young's mother was surely correct when she said that her son would be unlikely to have been shot had he been white. But it is important to be careful about what we mean if we say that he was killed "because he was black." If does not necessarily mean "out of hostility or animosity toward black persons." It could mean "because he was seen in the moment as a dangerous person and this was so in part because he was black." I believe it is also plausible to refer to this racial stereotype as "racist." But my point here is not so much to defend that position as to encourage clarity as to the location of what is, or was, racially objectionable in the situation. It was in the stereotype, not in the motives of the white officers. And it shows the tremendous danger that can accompany racist stereotypes even in the absence of racial antipathy; they can be life threatening. . . .

Conclusion

Gaining some clarity about what "racism" means will help us engage in productive conversations about racial matters—conversations that are too infrequent, both inside and outside classroom settings. We have seen three ways by which we might gain that clarity. First, within a given category (actions, jokes, stereotypes, remarks, stereotypes, persons), we should confine "racism" to especially egregious wrongs in that category. Not every stereotype is racist. Not every remark that is racially offensive is racist. Not every racially insensitive action is a racist action. I have suggested that the distinct opprobrium attaching to "racism" and "racist" can be retained and protected if we recognize that racism refers to racial inferiorization or racial antipathy, and that the different categorical forms of racism can all be related to either of those two definitions.

Second, we should not confuse racism in one category with racism in another. A person who is prey to a racist stereotype is not necessarily "a racist"; nor does she necessarily operate from racist motives. A remark can be unquestionably racist without the person making the remark being a racist, or making the remark for a racist reason, or motive.

Finally, in endeavoring to protect the distinct moral opprobrium of the accusation of "racism" from conceptual inflation and moral overload, as well as from categorical drift and confusion, we must at the same time recognize that "racism" by no means captures all of what can go wrong in the domain of race. There is a much larger terrain of moral ills in the racial domain than racism itself, and we should draw on our manifold linguistic resources—racial insensitivity, failure to recognize racial identity, racial ignorance, racial anxiety, racial injustice, racial homogenization, and so on—to express and describe moral disvalue in this domain. Moral concern is appropriately directed toward this wider domain, and should not be confined to racism appropriately so called.

References

"Black, White Officers Cited in Noose Incident," *Boston Globe*, April 29, 1999, B1.

Miles, R. (1989). *Racism*. London: Routledge.

Nuechterlein, J. (1996). In *First Things*, August–September, from *Chronicle of Higher Education*, September 6.

Schuman, H., Steeh, C., Bobo, L., and Krysan, M. (1997). *Racial attitudes in America: Trends and interpretation*, revised edn. Cambridge: Harvard University Press.

Shipler, D. K. (1997). *A Country of Strangers: Blacks and Whites in America*. New York: Vintage Books.

Comprehension Questions

1. Blum thinks we use the words "racism" and "racist" to talk about everything that's race-related and morally problematic. Why shouldn't we?
2. What's the difference between a "racial" incident and a "racist" incident?
3. What's the difference between the two "themes" of racism—inferiorization and antipathy?
4. What's wrong with *positive* stereotypes about members of a particular racial group?
5. Why isn't "racial anxiety" racism?
6. Why aren't you racist if you employ a racist stereotype?

Discussion Questions

1. What sorts of things do your peers describe as "racist"? Do you agree that the term is overused? Why or why not?

2. Can you think of any arguments *for* describing most race-related moral failings as racism? What are the benefits of using "racism" to cover a lot of race-related moral issues?

3. Blum thinks we shouldn't just talk about racism—we should also talk about racial insensitivity, failure to recognize racial identity, racial ignorance, racial anxiety, racial injustice, and racial homogenization. But you might just think that these are different *dimensions* or *aspects* of racism. How might Blum respond to this?

4. Go through the stories that Blum discusses—the hangman's noose on the motorcycle; saying, "Boy, pass the ball over here"; Emmett Till's lynching; describing blacks as "good dancers"; the teacher's discomfort with black parents; asking for "the black point of view"; the killing of Officer Young. Do you agree with Blum about how to characterize what's wrong about each case? Why or why not?

Case

Woodrow Wilson—the USA's twenty-eighth president—was also a Princeton alum and Princeton's president. Unfortunately, he didn't have a great track record on matters of race. During his time in the White House, he segregated the federal offices in Washington (which meant firing some black employees), he banned interracial marriage in the District of Columbia, and he required people to submit photographs with their applications for federal jobs. Due to Woodrow's relationship with Princeton, his name is featured prominently at that university. In 2015, however, many black students objected to this fact, and they made this demand of the administration:

> WE DEMAND the university administration publicly acknowledge the racist legacy of Woodrow Wilson and how he impacted campus policy and culture. We also demand that steps be made to rename Wilson residential college, the Woodrow Wilson School of Public Policy and International Affairs, and any other building named after him. Furthermore, we would like the mural of Wilson to be removed from the Wilcox dining hall.[1]

Many historically significant figures are now symbols on college campuses. They are remembered in the names of buildings, in statues, in artwork. How should we think about the presence of these symbols? Does someone deserve to be called racist for placing them there? Is someone racist for *keeping* them there? If "racist" isn't the right term, then what is? Moreover, how should we go forward? Should these symbols be removed? If so, what should happen to them? If not, then how should we address the concerns of those who are troubled by them?

Note

1. http://princetonprogressive.com/2015/11/19/black-justice-league-demands-addressed-to-president-eisgruber-and-princeton-university-staff/

18

Latino/as, Asian Americans, and the Black-White Binary

Linda Martín Alcoff

· ·

Linda Martín Alcoff argues that it is problematic, both conceptually and practically, to take anti-black racism as paradigmatic for all types of racism—that is, "the black-white paradigm." She attempts to reveal the paradigm's inadequacy by analyzing racism directed at Latinos and Asian Americans. After clarifying the core features of the paradigm and its history, she identifies several reasons not to use it as a general model for understanding racism. She then makes some suggestions for how we might conceive of racism such that it would capture the unique varieties of racism directed toward Latinos and Asian Americans. Alcoff ends by showing how her proposed reconception of racism can be put to work making sense of the issue of affirmative action in a way that is sensitive to differences in groups such as African Americans, Latinos, and Asian Americans.

· ·

. . . This chapter argues that even if we try to build coalition around what might seem to be our most obvious common concern—reducing racism— the black-white paradigm that dominates racial discourse in the United

---

Alcoff, Linda. 2006. "Latinos, Asian Americans, and the Black-White Binary." In *Visible Identities: Race, Gender, and the Self*, 247–263. New York: Oxford University Press.

States inhibits our comprehension of the variety of racisms and racial identities and thus proves more of an obstacle to coalition building than an aid. I will use the situation of Latinos and Asian Americans to explore the black-white binary, what it is, how it operates, and how it is limiting. . . .

Perhaps because of their similar genealogy as sources of cheap and vulnerable labor, there are some important commonalities between the ideological justifications and legal methods that have been used to persecute and discriminate against Latinos and Asian Americans (Bender and Braveman 1995). Both have been the main victims of "nativist" arguments that advocate limiting the rights of immigrants or foreign-born Americans, and both have often been portrayed as ineradicably "foreign" no matter how many generations they have lived here. . . .

The Black/White Paradigm

The discourse of social justice in regard to issues involving race has been dominated in the United States by what many theorists call the "black/white paradigm," which operates to govern racial classifications and racial politics in the United States, most clearly in the formulation of civil rights law but also in more informal arenas of discussion. Juan Perea defines this paradigm as "the conception that race in America consists, either exclusively or primarily, of only two constituent racial groups, the Black and White. . . . In addition, the paradigm dictates that all other racial identities and groups in the United States are best understood through the Black/White binary paradigm" (1998, 361). Openly espousing this view, Mary Frances Berry, former chair of the US Civil Rights Commission, has stated that the United States comprises "three nations, one Black, one White, and one in which people strive to be something other than Black to avoid the sting of White Supremacy" (quoted in Wu 2002, 34). To understand race in this way is to assume that white supremacy targets only black identity. Others can be affected by racism, on this view, but the dominance of the black/white paradigm works to interpret all other effects as "collateral damage" ultimately caused by the same phenomena, in both economic and psychological terms, in which the given other, whether Latino, Asian American, or something else, is placed in the category of "black" or "close to black." In other words, there is basically one form of racism, and one continuum of racial identity, along which all groups will be placed.[1]

. . .

Legal Puzzles

I want to start with a story that exemplifies the close association between Latinos and Asians in the ideological traditions embedded in the legal history of the United States. In 1854 the California Supreme Court defined Chinese Americans as Indians, that is, Native Americans. This ruling came about after a white man, George W. Hall, was convicted of murder based upon the eyewitness testimony of a Chinese American. Hall's defense lawyer appealed the conviction by invoking the law that said "no black or mulatto person, or Indian, shall be allowed to give evidence in favor of, or against a white man" (Okihiro 1994, 50; see also Lyman 1994). In support of his claim that this law was relevant to Hall's case, the defense lawyer cited the hypothesis that all native peoples of the Americas were originally from Asia and traveled to the Western hemisphere over the Bering Straights. Thus, he argued, the Chinese American man was actually the racial ancestor of Native Americans, and because the latter were lawfully excluded from giving testimony in court, this Chinese man should be excluded also. The California Supreme Court was delighted by this argument, upheld the appeal, freed Hall, and thus linked the legal status of Asian Americans and all those with indigenous American ancestry, a category that includes many or most Latinos.

The story does not end there. The California Supreme Court was concerned that as a scientific hypothesis the Bering Straights theory might one day be disproved, which would then destroy the basis for Chinese exclusion in the courts and allow them to give testimony. Wanting to avoid this outcome, however unlikely it might be, the court decided to embellish on the arguments made in appeal. Justice Charles J. Murray interpreted legal precedent to argue that the terms "black" and "white" are oppositional terms, from which he concluded that black must mean nonwhite and white must exclude all people of color. Thus, by the law of binary logic, Chinese Americans, after having become Native American, then also became black.

Of the many questions that one might like to go back and pose to Charles Murray, perhaps the most obvious is the following: If black and white are oppositional terms, then, instead of black meaning nonwhite, doesn't it just as logically follow that white could mean nonblack, in which case all people of color except African Americans would be white? This conclusion is no more or less fallacious or absurd than Murray's conclusion that black means nonwhite. . . . On the other hand, the borders of other identities—their distinctiveness from each other—are not important for the law to define and maintain. . . .

Asian Americans and Latinos have been tossed back and forth across this black/white binary for 150 years (see Haney López 1996; Lee 1993; G. Martinez 1998; Okihiro 1994; Omi and Winant 1986; C. Rodríguez, 2000). . . .

Contrary to what one might imagine, it has not always or even generally been to the advantage of Asian Americans and Latinos to be legally classified as white. An illustration of this is found in another important legal case decided by the US Supreme Court in 1954, just two weeks before they issued the decision in *Brown vs. Board of Education*. The case of *Hernandez v. Texas* involved a Mexican-American man convicted of murder by an all-white jury and sentenced to life imprisonment (G. Martinez 1998; Suro 1999). His lawyer appealed the conviction by arguing that the absence of Mexican Americans on the jury was discriminatory, making reference to the famous Scottsboro case in which the US Supreme Court overturned (after many years) the conviction of nine African American men on the grounds of an absence of African Americans from the jury. But in the Hernandez case, the Texas Supreme Court ruled that Mexicans were white people of Spanish descent, and therefore that there was no discrimination in the all-white makeup of the jury. . . .

In fact, in Texas not only were Mexicans subject to Jim Crow in public facilities from restaurants to bathrooms, they were also excluded from business and community groups, and children of Mexican descent were required to attend a segregated school for the first four grades, whether they spoke fluent English or not. Thus, when they were classified as nonwhite, Latinos were overtly denied certain civil rights; when they were classified as white, the de facto denial of their civil rights could not be appealed.

. . .

Criticisms

Critics of the black/white paradigm have argued that, although all communities of color have shared the experience of political and economic disenfranchisement in the United States, there are significant differences between the *causes* and the *forms* of this disenfranchisement. . . .

Put in more general terms, these arguments can be summarized as follows:

1. The black/white paradigm has disempowered various racial and ethnic groups from being able to define their own identity, to mark their difference and specificity beyond what could be captured on this limited map. . . .

2. Asian Americans and Latinos (among others) have historically been ignored or marginalized in the public discourse in the United States on race and racism. This is a problem for two reasons, first, because it is simply unfair to be excluded from what concerns one, and second, because it has considerably weakened the analysis of race and racism in the mainstream discussions. . . .

3. By eliminating specificities within the large "black" or nonwhite group, the black/white binary has undercut the possibility of developing appropriate and effective legal and political solutions for the variable forms that racial oppression can take. . . .

4. Eliminating specificities within the large "black" or nonwhite group also makes it difficult to understand or address the real conflicts and differences within this amalgam of peoples. . . .

5. For all these reasons, the black/white paradigm seriously undermines the possibility of achieving coalitions. It is obvious that keeping us in conflict with each other and not in coalition is in the interests of the current power structure.

I would add to these arguments the following two.

6. The black/white binary and the constant invocation of all race discourses and conflicts as between blacks and whites has produced an imagery of race in this country in which a very large white majority confronts a relatively small black minority. This imagery has the effect of reinforcing the sense of inevitability to white domination.

This is not the reality of racial percentages in almost any major urban center in the country today. Nonwhites outnumber whites in New York, Miami, Chicago, Atlanta, and Los Angeles, and come very close in San Francisco, Dallas, and Washington, DC. There is thus a real potential for a major shift in political power, . . . *The numbers and concentrations of people of color in the United States means that we are quickly moving past the politics of recognition, in which people of color must clamor for recognition from the all-powerful majority, and reaching the politics of power negotiation, in which we can negotiate from a position of power rather than having to rely exclusively on moral appeals.* . . . [2] . . .

Thus, thinking of race only in terms of black and white produces a sense of inevitability to white domination and thus a sense of fatalism, even though the facts call for the opposite. . . .

The next argument that I would make in regard to the black/white binary is that it mistakenly configures race imagistically as exclusively having to do with color, as if color alone determines racial identity and is the sole object of racism. Equating race with color makes it seem as if all the races other than black and white must be lined up between them since they clearly represent the polar extremes. There is certainly a racist continuum of color operating in this and in many countries, but my point is that this continuum is not the *only* axis by which racism operates.

. . . Related to this idea is the claim that Asian Americans and Latinos are closer to white and will eventually "become" white. Let me address this latter idea first. . . .

There are three major differences between the groups who have had "success" in becoming white and Latinos and Asian Americans. The groups I am referring to here, and about whom there is some very good historical research emerging, are the Irish Americans and (white Anglo) Jews. . . .

In regard, however, to the differences between Irish Americans and Jews on the one hand and Asian Americans and Latinos on the other, the first obvious significant difference is in color and physical appearance. The Irish and Jews can "blend in" to US society in a way that Asian Americans and most Latinos cannot. The admission of the Irish and Jews into the category "white" did not require challenging the idea that superior characteristics come from European societies, and that superior characteristics are correlated to light skin color. . . .

The second difference concerns historical memory. The Irish and Jews represent bad memories within Europe, memories of colonialism and genocide, and thus they operate as the symbolic representation of Europe's moral failings. The Irish and Jews do not have that symbolic meaning in the United States and in fact may carry the opposite symbolic meaning by representing the idea that "anyone" can make it and be accepted here, even those who were despised in Europe. In contrast, African Americans and Mexican Americans and Native Americans, most notably, among others, represent a symbolic reminder of the hollowness of claims to white moral superiority. The Irish and Jews are not a psychic threat to the ideological supremacy of white identity in the same way that many Latinos, Asian Americans, and certainly African Americans are.

A third major difference concerns perceived assimilability, although here the Irish and Jews must separate. The Irish are perceived as entirely assimilable, Jews only partly so because of religion (which is another reason Jews tend to be moved back and forth). Latinos, to the extent they are European, come from a Spanish Catholic culture considered premodern and less civilized, and to the extent they are also indigenous, come from a culture perceived as totally different than Anglo-European. The symbolic opposition between "East" and "West," or the Orient and the Occident, is a major prop of the Anglo-European self-image fomenting a plethora of such dichotomies as between "individualism versus collectivism," "democracy versus despotism," and future-oriented versus static societies. These binary formulations rule out the possibility of synthesis and present assimilation as a doubtful project at best. . . .

. . .

Racisms

What makes all of these diverse examples of vilification forms of racism is the fact that the threats each group poses flow from group attributes. In other words, it is not that each member of these groups *chooses* to exemplify or pursue the negative quality attributed to them. Racism denies that kind of individual agency. Rather, racism sees each member of the racialized and despised group as harboring tendencies and manifesting character traits as a result of their genealogical identity. To consider Christianity a higher religion than Islam would be a form of cultural chauvinism; to consider Muslims as all potential suicide bombers is a form of racism.

. . .

Racial oppression works on multiple axes, I would argue, with color being the most *dominant* and currently the most *pernicious*. But color is not *exhaustive* of all the forms racial oppression can take. The most pejorative terms used against Asian Americans often have a racial connotation but one without a color component— "Chinks," "slant-eyes," and, for the Vietnamese, "gooks." These terms denigrate a whole people, not a particular set of customs or a specific history, and thus parallel the essentializing move of racist discourse that universalizes negative value across a group. The two most pejorative terms widely used against Latinos in this country have been the terms "spic"—a word whose genealogy references people who were heard by Anglos as saying "no spic English"—and "wetback."

The first invokes the denigration of language, the second denigrates both where people came from and how they got here: from Mexico across the Rio Grande. Mexican Americans were also called "greasers," which connoted the condition of their hair, not their skin color. . . . We might think of these as two independent axes of racialization that operate through physical features other than color, and through genealogies of cultural origin. There is, then, the color axis, the physical-characteristics-other-than-color axis, and the cultural-origin axis.

The discrimination against Asian Americans and Latinos has also operated very strongly on a fourth axis, "nativism." Nativism is a prejudice against immigrants; thus it is distinct, though often related to, xenophobia or the rejection of foreigners. Acuña explains that historical nativism is also distinct from anthropological nativism, which refers to a "revival of indigenous culture," because historical nativism refers to the belief of some Anglo-Americans that they are "the true Americans, excluding even the Indian" because they represent in their cultural heritage the "idea" of "America" (1988, 158).[3] On this view, the problem with Asian Americans and Latinos is not just that they are seen as foreign; they are seen as ineluctably foreign. Their cultures of origin are seen as so inferior (morally and politically if not intellectually), they are incapable of and unmotivated toward assimilation to the superior mainstream white Anglo culture. They want to keep their languages, demand instruction in public schools in their primary languages, and they often maintain their own holidays, cuisines, religions, and living areas (the latter sometimes by choice). Despite the fact that Mexican Americans have been living within the current US borders for longer than most Anglo-Americans, they are all too often seen as squatters on US soil, interlopers who "belong" elsewhere.

. . .

What's at Stake

I want to end with an example that links the false homogenization of people of color with the recent demise of affirmative action programs in higher education, which I think will show how much is at stake in our need to recognize the complexity of our differences. Dana Takagi argues persuasively that the recent disabling of affirmative action policies "grew out of fluid discourse(s) on racial minorities in higher education in which the main issues were pivotally constructed in, and encapsulated by, the debate over Asian admissions" and specifically the debate over claims that Asian Americans were overrepresented in American universities (1992, 7). In other words, the alleged overrepresentation of Asian Americans in colleges and universities was used to argue that the problem of minority underrepresentation in higher education is not caused by race, and therefore an affirmative action based on race is neither helpful nor justifiable.

What I would argue here is that the black/white binary is operating in this case to obscure the real problems. Conservatives argued that Asian Americans are nonwhite so that their case can be used to dismantle affirmative action for all: if they can get in, we all can get in. But this would follow only if the category "nonwhite" is undifferentiated in terms of how racism operates. Others wanted to argue that Asian Americans are being treated here as white, and thus have no interest in an antiracist coalition.

It is certainly true that it is a white power structure that privileges such things as test scores. But Asian Americans were still not actually being treated as whites. Takagi points out that the claims of overrepresentation conveniently ignored the large disparity between Asian American admission rates and white admission rates (the percentage of admissions in relation to the pool of applicants), a disparity that cannot be accounted for by SAT scores or grades. That is, holding scores and grades constant, white individuals were more likely to be admitted than Asian Americans, even if in real numbers on some campuses Asian American acceptances outnumbered whites. (To give one example of this, the Asian American Student Association at Brown University discovered that between 1979 and 1987 there was a 750 percent increase in Asian applications, even while there was a steadily declining admission rate—from 44 percent in 1979 to 14 percent in 1987) (1992, 28). So there has been a covert quota system operating against Asian American applicants in many university systems, which is covered over by their high numbers of admission and is no doubt motivated by the same fears of "yellow peril" that were used to justify discrimination in the 1800s. Asian Americans are not seen as white despite the fact that they have so-called "white" attributes because they are seen as unassimilable; they are suspected of retaining loyalty to Asian countries and thus of being a threat to "the nation." The concern about overrepresentation targeted Asian Americans exclusively; the only people similarly targeted in the past were Jews, and these cases are clearly attributable to anti-Semitism. This concern certainly has not been raised in regard to the poor, who are underrepresented, or to the children of alumni or to athletes, both of whom are overrepresented.

Takagi traces the empirical studies, public discourse, and policy changes prompted by this concern over overrepresentation to the argument that affirmative action should ignore race and address only class, even though the claim that racism can be addressed in this way can be easily empirically disproved given the disparity of SAT scores within classes across racial difference.[4]

What this case demonstrates is not that all nonwhites should be grouped together in all cases of attempts to redress social inequities, but precisely the opposite: They should not be lumped together. The problems of discrimination that Asian Americans face in higher education in the United States have had to do with overt policies that apply quotas based on specific forms of racism directed against them. The problem of discrimination that African Americans and Latinos have faced in higher education has to do with the use of SAT scores and the quality of their public education, which is vastly unequal to that received by whites. Racism is the culprit in each case, but the means and ideology vary, and thus the effective redress will have to vary.

Takagi recounts that some Asian American activists who wanted to end the unfair quotas on their admission rates called for a meritocracy of admissions based on SAT scores and grades. But this would block only one form of racism, leaving others not only intact but ideologically reinforced. Meritocracy is still an illusion highly disadvantageous to African Americans and Latinos. Thus, strategies that seek to eliminate discrimination, including argumentative strategies used to defend affirmative action, must either be made specific to certain historically disadvantaged groups or, if they are general, must consider their possible effects on other groups. Only a rich knowledge of the specific and variable forms of racism in the United States will make such considerations possible.

References

Acuña, Rodolfo. 1988. *Occupied America: A History of Chicanos.* 3rd ed. New York: Harper Collins.

Bender, Leslie and Daan Braveman. 1995. *Power, Privilege, and Law: A Civil Rights Reader.* St. Paul, Minnesota: West Publishing Company.

Gordon, Lewis. 1995. *Bad Faith and Antiblack Racism.* Atlantic Highlands, N.J.: Humanities Press.

Haney López, Ian F. 1996. *White by Law: The Legal Construction of Race*. New York: New York University Press.

Lee, Sharon M. 1993. "Racial Classifications in the U.S. Census: 1890–1990." *Ethnic and Racial Studies*, Volume 16, Number 1, January: 75–94.

Lyman, Stanford. 1994. *Color, Culture, Civilization: Race and Minority Issues in American Society*. Chicago: University of Illinois Press.

Martinez, George A. 1998. "Mexican Americans and Whiteness," in *The Latino Condition*, edited by Richard Delgado and Jean Stefancic. New York: New York University Press, 175–79.

Okihiro, Gary. 1994. *Margins to Mainstreams: Asians in American History and Culture*. Seattle: University of Washington Press.

Omi, Michael, and Howard Winant. 1986. *Racial Formations in the United States: From the 1960s to the 1980s*. New York: Routledge.

Perea, Juan. 1998. "The Black/White Binary Paradigm of Race" in *The Latino Condition*, edited by Richard Delgado and Jean Stefancic. New York: New York University Press, pp. 359–68.

Rodriguez, Clara E. 2000. *Changing Race: Latinos, the Census, and the History of Ethnicity in the United States*. New York: New York University Press.

Suro, Roberto. 1999. *Strangers among Us: Latino Lives in a Changing America*. New York: Random House.

Takagi, Dana Y. 1992. *The Retreat from Race: Asian-American Admissions and Racial Politics*. New Brunswick, N.J.: Rutgers University Press.

Wu, Frank. 2002. *Yellow: Race in America beyond Black and White*. New York: Basic Books.

Comprehension Questions

1. What does Alcoff mean by "the black/white paradigm" of racism?

2. Recall the account of George W. Hall's trial and its aftermath. What does that show about historical racism directed against Asian Americans?

3. What does *Hernandez v. Texas* show about historical racism directed against Asian Americans?

4. Why does Alcoff claim that the black/white paradigm provides an inadequate understanding of racism?

5. Why does Alcoff think racism against Latinos and Asian Americans will not go away by these groups "becoming white"?

6. What are the four axes Alcoff identifies as distinct variables for making sense of various forms of racism?

7. What recommendations does Alcoff make for sensibly dealing with the issue of affirmative action?

Discussion Questions

1. Alcoff illustrates the limits of the black/white paradigm for understanding racism by discussing racism against Latinos and Asian Americans. Can you think of additional groups whose treatment would challenge or bolster Alcoff's position?
2. Alcoff identifies four types ("axes") of racism. Do you think her classification is complete? Is each type really distinct from each other?
3. Racism, as Alcoff generically defines it, is when negative characteristics are attributed to some group and used as grounds for treating its members differently from everyone else. This practice is obviously immoral. However, why should we think that it's immoral? What argument can we develop against it?

Case

Consider this:

> When [Donald] Trump announced his [presidential] candidacy, on June 16th, [2015,] he vowed to build a two-thousand-mile-long wall to stop Mexico from "sending people that have lots of problems." He said, "They're bringing drugs. They're bringing crime. They're rapists. And some, I assume, are good people." Three of the statements had no basis in fact—the crime rate among first-generation immigrants is lower than that for native-born Americans—but Trump takes an expansive view of reality. "I play to people's fantasies," he writes in *The Art of the Deal*, his 1987 memoir. "I call it truthful hyperbole. It's an innocent form of exaggeration—and a very effective form of promotion." Trump's campaign announcement was mocked and condemned—and utterly successful. His favorability among Republicans leaped from 16 percent to 57 percent, a greater spike than that of any other candidate's début. Immigration became the centerpiece of his campaign.[5]

> How can you use Alcoff's framework to understand Trump's rhetoric? Also, when trying to make sense of what Trump said, how should we factor in his comments from *The Art of the Deal*? Is it ever OK for politicians to engage in "truthful hyperbole"?

Notes

1. The use of terms such as "antiblack racism," used for example by Gordon (1995), helpfully specifies the kind of racism one is discussing and leaves open the possibility that there are other forms of racism.

2. This surely explains the jockeying for position among the Democrats and Republicans for African American and Latino voters, respectively. If those groups unite with opposing sectors of the white majority, white majority rule is ensured.

3. It is also distinguished from "indigenism," or the view that only those peoples indigenous to a land have moral rights to its occupation.

4. Just to give one example, there is an 80 point difference between blacks and whites in mean SAT scores, even when both come from families making $70,000 or more, and similar cases apply to Puerto Ricans and other groups.

5. http://www.newyorker.com/magazine/2015/08/31/the-fearful-and-the-frustrated

19

=== 🐎 ===

Racial Cognition and the Ethics of Implicit Bias

Daniel Kelly and Erica Roedder

．．．

Daniel Kelly and Erica Roedder examine the nature and morality of implicit racial bias in their essay. First they review some of the evidence for the idea that implicit racial bias, that is, the implicit association of negative traits with people of certain races, is a widespread phenomenon and one that may influence a person's behavior. Next, Kelly and Roedder delve into the problem of how to morally assess implicit racial bias. They suggest that there are good reasons for thinking that even having such a bias is morally wrong, and that if you can reasonably suppose that you're biased, you should attempt to correct for it in practice, even in the absence of empirical evidence for it.

．．．

1. Introduction

．．．

The aim of this paper is two-fold. Our first goal is to call philosophical attention to some of the most provocative empirical work on racial cognition. Accordingly, the first half of the paper will discuss one portion

Kelly, Daniel, and Erica Roedder. 2008. "Racial Cognition and the Ethics of Implicit Bias." *Philosophy Compass* 3(3): 522–540. Reprinted with permission of John Wiley and Sons.

of this large literature: work regarding implicit racial biases. Our second goal is to raise a number of philosophical questions about the proper normative assessment of behaviors and judgments linked to those implicit biases. In the second half of the paper, then, we will assume these implicit racial biases are roughly as current research depicts them to be, and go on to sketch a few of the most promising avenues of philosophical research that we believe are opened up by the psychological complexities revealed in this work on racial cognition.

2. Implicit Racial Bias

Rather ingenious strategies have uncovered subtle forms of racial discrimination that still exist in real world settings. One recent study investigated the effect of race on hiring practices in two U.S. cities. Researchers sent out fabricated résumés to Help Wanted ads appearing in major newspapers in Boston and Chicago. Half of the résumés were headed by a very Black sounding name (e.g., Lakisha and Jamal), while the other half were headed by a very White sounding name (e.g., Emily and Greg).[1] The results were remarkable: overall, résumés bearing White names received an astonishing 50 percent more callbacks for interviews than their Black counterparts. Furthermore, an interesting pattern emerged for highly qualified résumés. For White sounding names, résumés with highly qualified credentials received 30 percent more callbacks than their less qualified White counterparts; in contrast, employers did not differentiate nearly as much between highly qualified Black résumés and their less qualified Black counterparts. The amount of discrimination was fairly consistent across occupations and industries. Of particular interest was the fact that employers who explicitly listed "Equal Opportunity Employer" in their ad discriminated just as much as other employers (Bertrand and Mullainathan).

. . .

. . . One of the most sophisticated and widely used windows into racial cognition is an experimental measurement technique called the Implicit Association Test, or IAT for short. More than any other technique, the IAT has been used to establish the existence and shed light on the character of implicit racial biases. In short, the IAT has been used to show that a great many people, including those who genuinely profess themselves to be racially impartial and explicitly disavow any form of racial prejudice, display subtle signs of racial bias in controlled experimental settings. . . .

The Implicit Association Test (IAT)

The IAT was designed by psychologists to probe aspects of thought that are not easily accessible or immediately available to introspection.[2] . . .

. . . The core idea behind . . . IATs is that stronger associations between items will allow them to be grouped together more quickly and easily.[3] For instance, faster and more accurate performance on iterations when good and White items are to be grouped together than on iterations when good and Black are to be grouped together indicates a stronger association between good and White. Stronger associations between good and White, in turn, are taken to indicate an implicit bias towards Whites over Blacks. As should be evident, this test does not use self-report or explicitly ask subjects about their attitudes about race. Unlike those more direct tests that are based on self report, and which are often used in conjunction with IATs (e.g. McConahay), the IAT requires subjects to make snap judgments that must be made quickly, and thus without moderating influence of introspection and deliberation and often without conscious intention. Biases revealed by an IAT are often thought to implicate relatively automatic processes.

IAT and Race

. . . In using tools like the IAT in conjunction with more direct, self-report methods, researchers have further found that even those who sincerely profess tolerant or anti-racist views can nevertheless harbor implicit racial biases (often to their own surprise and chagrin).[4] Counterintuitive as it may seem, this robust pattern of results shows that a person's avowed views on race and racism are not a reliable guide to whether or not they are implicitly biased.

. . .

We will conclude with a final example that speaks to both the influence of IAT results on behavior and real world relevance. . . . many important judgments must be made almost instantaneously and in high pressure situations. Such split second decisions have been shown to be sensitive to race in other ways as well. A number of studies have asked people to make snap decisions about whether a presented object is a gun or some other harmless object. Researchers found that when first shown a picture of a Black face, both White and Black Americans become more likely to misidentify a harmless object as a gun (Payne, "Weapon Bias"). Not only is this "weapon bias" found in people who explicitly try to avoid racial biases, but the weapon bias is highly correlated with the indirect measures of racial biases, including the IAT (Payne, "Conceptualizing

Control"). The relevance of such findings is difficult to deny, especially in light of tragedies such as the 1999 shooting of Amadou Diallo, who was shot forty-one times by police officers who thought he was drawing a gun; he was actually just reaching for his wallet.

3. Normative Questions

So far, we have discussed the psychology of racial cognition, focusing on the implicit attitude test. Such findings introduce new and significant normative questions. In the rest of this article, we'll briefly survey some of the normative questions that we think are fruitful areas for future research on racial cognition, and consider attempts to answer questions similar to them. . . .

Is It Morally Problematic to Harbor Implicit Racial Bias?

One major question is whether it is morally problematic, in and of itself, to have an implicit bias against members of a particular race.[5] Obviously, implicit racial bias is problematic insofar as it leads to harmful or unfair consequences. For instance, suppose implicit bias forms part of the explanation of why an innocent Black man is shot by a police officer. In this case, implicit bias is clearly a bad thing: It partly caused a *harmful* consequence, i.e., the death of a young man. Similarly, implicit racial bias is clearly bad insofar as it leads to *unfair* consequences, e.g., the unequal promotion of White versus Black employees within a company.

Let us set aside such consequences for a moment and consider the question of the implicit attitude itself—is this attitude intrinsically a bad thing? . . .

. . . consider an *explicitly* racist person. We might ask of him, is his explicitly racist attitude, in and of itself, a bad thing? Suppose, for instance, that a man were never to act on his explicit racial beliefs, keeping his racist thoughts and feelings to himself. Perhaps he secretly seethes with disgust after drinking from water fountains used by Blacks and often has thoughts like, "It's so obvious that Black children aren't as smart as White children."[6]

Most Westerners, we suspect, would disapprove of such a person. Even if the man never acts on these racist thoughts and feelings, and even if he is morally upright in all the other aspects of his life (e.g., he goes to church, is faithful to his wife, etc.), there is still something morally problematic about his attitudes. While it's good that the man refrains from acting on these racist thoughts and feelings, it is unfortunate and morally condemnable that he has such attitudes at all.

. . .

. . . If this is right, can the same be said about *implicit* thoughts and feelings? For instance, what exactly *are* implicit attitudes? Are they akin to Freudian unconscious states, occupying some deep core of our psyche? Or are they more minimal and peripheral? . . . Let us consider, for a moment, an extremely minimal construal of implicit attitudes suggested by this: an implicit attitude is simply a tendency to associate one concept with another, in the way that, for instance, the concept *salt* might prime the concept *pepper*. A high IAT score, on this understanding, means that a person strongly associates, e.g., Black faces with handguns. Assuming that this is an exhaustive description of the implicit attitude—a tendency to associate one concept with another—can a tendency to associate certain concepts, in and of itself, be morally problematic?

One way to approach this question is through the lens of rationality. While it is clear that explicitly racist beliefs are mostly irrational, in addition to being immoral (e.g., the thought that Black children are less smart than White children), there seems to be room to argue that some implicit racial associations are (to a *limited extent*) rational. . . .

To see why someone might argue that implicit attitudes are sometimes rational, let's first consider a different case, i.e., gender. IAT results suggest that most people strongly associate men with science, more so than they do women with science (see Nosek and Banaji). But if the implicit attitude really is *just* an association of concepts, might it be rational to make such associations? Women, as a matter of fact, are not as well-represented in the sciences. . . . With respect to the issue of rationality, our point is that if implicit attitudes are construed in this very minimal way—as indicating only that a person associates two concepts—it appears they can be rational in some sense (e.g., insofar the association between concepts accurately reflects a correlation or statistical regularity that holds among those referents of the concepts).

Let us now return to the racial example. Consider the tendency to associate the faces of young, Black men with handguns. Someone might analogously suggest that, were it true that young Black men carry guns at a higher rate than White men, then it would be rational to associate Black faces with handguns. This is important because, as we mentioned earlier, it might be thought that rationality and morality go hand-in-hand: . . .

. . .

We suspect this is not the right way to think about rationality and implicit attitudes. First, we think that a rational attitude may still be an *immoral* one. Rationality and morality are different virtues, so it should be expected that a person can have the one without the other. . . .

Our point is that it can sometimes be unkind or uncompassionate to believe ill of a person, even if it is rational to do so. Thus it can sometimes be immoral to hold a belief that is, in fact, rational.

As a second point, suppose we were to grant, for the sake of argument, the suggestion that rational attitudes are moral and irrational ones are immoral. Even on this supposition, a case can still be made that implicit racial biases are morally problematic. We suspect that such associations (such as those found in studies on the weapon biases) almost always extend beyond what is rational, and there will almost always be a "remainder": an implicit association that goes beyond what rationality endorses. If this is right, then even on the supposition that morality and rationality are tightly bound together, implicit attitudes will remain morally problematic to the extent that they outstrip what is rationally justifiable. . . .

. . . In the remainder of this section, we'll examine . . . the work of two authors: Garcia's account of racism and Blum's account of stereotyping.

Garcia's analysis of racism stresses the intrinsic features of certain attitudes. He writes that someone is a racist when they have certain affective and volitional attitudes:

> [W]hat makes someone a racist is her disregard for, or even hostility to, those assigned to the targeted race . . . [S]he is hostile to or cares nothing (or too little) about some people because of their racial classification . . . [H]ate and callous indifference (like love) are principally matters of *will* and desire: what does one want, what would one choose, for those assigned to this or that race? (43)

Importantly, Garcia construes racism as a deformation of affect and the will, and this informs his account of why it is morally problematic: racist attitudes, in themselves, are "inherently contrary to the moral virtues of benevolence and justice" (43). Such attitudes, he argues, are hateful and ill-willed, and are thus opposed to benevolence by their very nature. On Garcia's account, the question of whether it is wrong to harbor an *implicit* attitude will therefore boil down to whether the attitude is intrinsically opposed to benevolence, e.g., whether it is an attitude of hate or one of ill will.

Determining whether implicit attitudes are intrinsically opposed to benevolence, however, will require progress on two fronts. First, there are issues tied to empirical work and how to interpret evidence provided by indirect tests. Implicit attitudes (or some implicit attitudes) may turn out to be *merely cognitive* associations, in which case they would be neither affective nor volitional. Such attitudes, on Garcia's account, would not be intrinsically opposed to benevolence, and so would not be morally problematic.[7]

Suppose, on the other hand, some implicit attitudes are indeed affectively laden, as a growing body of empirical research suggests (e.g., Vanman et al.; Phelps et al.; Amodio, Harmon-Jones, and Devine; see also Payne et al.). This possibility raises a different kind of difficulty, which turns on whether such implicit attitudes should be thought of as "inherently contrary to the moral virtue of benevolence." While it is obvious that explicit, hate-filled racial rage is intrinsically opposed to benevolence, it is far less clear whether the more subtle attitudes measured by the IAT ought to be categorized in this way. . . .

Let us turn now to Blum's account of racial stereotyping. . . .

In much of his article, Blum analyzes what stereotypes *do*. Two of the most important features he describes are that they mask individuality (the stereotyper fails to be sensitive to an individual's quirks and characteristics) and that they lead to what he calls *moral distancing*. In moral distancing, the stereotyper sees a stereotypee as more "other" than he or she really is, and this corrodes her sense of a common, shared humanity. Here, we think Blum's account can be usefully and straightforwardly generalized to implicit attitudes. One must simply ask: do implicit attitudes have these deleterious effects? Do implicit biases mask individuality and lead to moral distancing? These sound like clear-cut empirical questions. If implicit racial biases do lead thinkers to fail to appreciate the individuality of others or to morally distance themselves, then it follows from Blum's account that those implicit biases are morally reprehensible.

. . .

As a final note, it seems to us that ethicists working on implicit racism might be well-served by making a distinction between what is wrong and what is morally blameworthy. Particularly in the case of implicit attitudes, it is salient that their acquisition may be rapid, automatic, and uncontrollable.[8] These features, it might be thought, are related to features that establish blameworthiness—such as identification (Frankfurt) or reasons-responsiveness (Fischer and Ravizza). For instance, it might be said that the implicitly racist person doesn't identify with his implicit attitude, or that the attitude isn't responsive to reasons; thus we cannot hold a person fully accountable for those implicit attitudes. If this is right, one might say that such attitudes are morally wrong—and condemnable—but that the person himself cannot be blamed for having them. . . .

Might I Be Racially Biased?

One of the remarkable features of *implicit* bias is the possibility that individuals may not be aware of their own bias. Neither introspection nor honest self-report are reliable guides to the presence of such mental states, and one may harbor implicit biases that are diametrically opposed to one's explicitly stated and consciously avowed attitudes. Because of this, thinkers face a thorny, real-life epistemological problem: Given that a large proportion of the population is implicitly racially biased, is it reasonable to conclude that I, myself, am racially biased? And if I believe I might be, how should that belief affect my deliberation and behavior?

The possibility that you, yourself, may harbor implicit biases has implications for your concrete beliefs about everyday matters. For instance, suppose you are a White professor grading a Black student's paper, and you are initially inclined to give the paper an 89/100. Does the possibility of implicit racial bias give you good reason to think the paper actually deserves slightly better, e.g., 90 or 91 points? Let's call this example *the savvy grader*, since the problem arises when a thinker is psychologically savvy and is thus aware of the prevalence of implicit racial bias (the example is discussed in Roedder).

An analogy will be helpful here. Suppose you learn of psychological research showing that most people are inclined to underestimate the size of circles when set across a hatched background. Suppose you are later asked to judge the size of a circle on a hatched background. In deciding the size of the circle, it is most rational to estimate it to be slightly larger than you are initially inclined to guess. . . .

With this in mind, let us return to the case of the savvy grader. Assume for a moment that experiments uncovered a racial bias in the grading of student papers. . . . We maintain that by parity of reasoning, it would be wise to make a similar adjustment for the implicit bias in grading, just as you would correct for the visual bias in judging the size of a circle.[9] In both cases, one is acting for purely *epistemic* reasons; in order to give the most accurate grade, i.e., in order to grade the paper based on its merits, it is reasonable for the savvy grader to correct for the effects of racial biases.[10]

. . .

There is much more to say here. In particular, we might wonder how much evidence of implicit racial bias a savvy grader needs before it is reasonable for her to adjust how she assigns grades. Roedder argues that the epistemic requirements are strikingly low: It is enough if she knows that, ceteris paribus, the bias exists *on average*. Consider the visual analogy again. If one were told that, *on average*, people see the circle as 25 percent smaller than it really is, most of us would take that as a reason to increase our original estimate of its size by 25 percent. Here, too, the epistemic factors relevant to grading papers do not appear substantially different from those of the visual case. . . .

Of course, we don't yet have evidence that directly bears on the question of whether or not normal thinkers are implicitly biased against their Black students when grading papers; to date there has not been a systematic effort to look for racial bias in essay grading at the college level. . . .

Thus the important question is this: Knowing what you know now about implicit bias in other domains (perhaps from reading this very article!), and if you had to place a bet, would you bet that there *is* a racial bias in grading or that there *isn't*?[11] If you find yourself inclined to think that (more likely than not) there is a racial bias in grading, and if the line of reasoning sketched here is correct, then merely having this empirical hunch is enough to rationally compel you to make some sort of compensatory adjustment in your Black students' grades.[12] . . .

. . . Implicit racial bias is just one example where psychological science shows our *reasoning* capacities to be impaired, and where we have *no introspective access to our own impairment*. Whenever this is the case, and wherever thinkers are savvy enough to learn about the psychology of such biases, similar epistemological challenges concerning self-assessment and proper adjustment are likely to arise.

References

Amadio, D., E. Harmon-Jones, and P. Devine. (2003). "Individual Differences in the Activation and Control of Affective Race Bias as Assessed by Startle Eyeblink Response and Self-Report." *Journal of Personality and Social Psychology* 84 (4), 738–53.

Blum, Lawrence. (2004). "Stereotypes and Stereotyping: A Moral Analysis." *Philosophical Papers* 3, 251–89.

Cunningham, W., K. Preacher, and M. Banaji. (2001). "Implicit Attitude Measures: Consistency, Stability, and Convergent Validity." *Psychological Science* 12 (2), 163–70.

Devine, P., et al. (2002). "The Regulation of Explicit and Implicit Race Bias: The Role of Motivations to Respond Without Prejudice." *Journal of Personality and Social Psychology* 82 (5), 835–48.

Fischer, J. and M. Ravizza. (1998). *Responsibility and Control: A Theory of Moral Responsibility.* Cambridge: Cambridge University Press.

Garcia, J. L. A. (2004). "Three Sites for Racism: Social Structures, Valuings and Vice." In *Racism in Mind*, eds. M. P. Levine and T. Pataki. Ithaca, NY: Cornell University Press, 36–55.

Greenwald, A., D. McGhee, and J. Schwartz. (1998). "Measuring Individual Differences in Implicit Cognition: The Implicit Association Test." *Journal of Personality and Social Psychology* 74 (6), 1464–80.

Greenwald, A. and A. Nosek. (2001). "Health of the Implicit Association Test at age 3." *Zeitschrift für Experimentelle Psychologie* 48, 85–93.

McConahay, J. (1986). "Modern Racism, Ambivalence, and the Modern Racism Scale." In *Prejudice, Discrimination, and Racism*, eds. J. F. Dovidio and S. L. Gaertner. Orlando, FL: Academic Press.

Nosek, B. A., A. G. Greenwald, and M. R. Banaji. (2007). "The Implicit Association Test at Age 7: A Methodological and Conceptual Review." In *Automatic Processes in Social Thinking and Behavior*, ed. J. A. Bargh. Philadelphia, PA: Psychology Press.

Nosek, B. A., A. G. Greenwald, and M. R. Banaji. (2005). "Understanding and Using the Implicit Association Test: II. Method Variables and Construct Validity." *Personality and Social Psychology Bulletin* 31 (2), 166–80.

Payne, B. K. (2005). "Conceptualizing Control in Social Cognition: The Role of Automatic and Controlled Processes in Misperceiving a Weapon." *Journal of Personality Social Psychology* 81, 181–92.

Payne, B. K. (2006). "Weapon Bias: Split-Second Decisions and Unintended Stereotyping." *Current Directions in Psychological Science* 15, 287–91.

Payne, B. K., et al. (2005). "An Inkblot for Attitudes: Affect Misattribution as Implicit Measurement." *Journal of Personality and Social Psychology* 89 (3), 277–293.

Phelps, E., et al. (2000). "Performance on Indirect Measures of Race Evaluation Predicts Amygdala Activation." *Journal of Cognitive Neuroscience* 12 (5), 729–38.

Roedder, E. (2010). "Savvy Thinking" and "The Epistemology of Self-Correction for Implicit Bias." *Beings Like Us: Deliberating in Light of Psychological Theory.* Ph.D. dissertation, New York University, Department of Philosophy.

Vanman, E. J., et al. (1997). "The Modern Face of Prejudice and Structural Features that Moderate the Effect of Cooperation on Affect." *Journal of Personality and Social Psychology* 73, 941–59.

Comprehension Questions

1. What does the study about the fabricated résumés show about people's attitudes regarding race?

2. How does the Implicit Association Test work, and what does it tell us about people's attitudes regarding race?
3. Why might it be wrong to have an explicit racist attitude, even if you don't act on it?
4. In what sense might some implicit racial biases be rational?
5. Regardless of its rationality, why do you think that it's wrong to have implicit racial biases?
6. What reason do Kelly and Roedder give for thinking that you should correct for implicit racial bias in yourself, given adequate evidence of it?
7. Why do Kelly and Roedder think you ought to correct for implicit racial bias in yourself even without having adequate evidence for it?

Discussion Questions

1. Kelly and Roedder focus on implicit racial bias and discuss the case of a white instructor making corrections for that bias when evaluating the work of black students. What types of implicit bias might you be susceptible to, and do you think you ought to correct for it somehow?
2. There are several different reasons discussed by Kelly and Roedder for thinking having implicit racial biases is morally wrong. Which do you think is the strongest? Can you think of any additional reasons?
3. Kelly and Roedder suggest that even if it is morally wrong to have implicit racial biases, it might nevertheless not be morally blameworthy to have them. Do you think the distinction between wrongness and blameworthiness should apply in this case?

Case

Here's a summary of a troubling study:

> Two hundred ten Princeton University undergraduates . . . were assigned to one of 105 same-sex pairs. A white student was assigned the role of instructor; a second student, who could be either black or white, played the student. "Instructors first completed an ostensible cognitive flexibility task that, in reality, was a subliminal priming task inconspicuously assessing implicit racial bias," the researchers write. . . . The teachers were supplied with materials for creating their lesson—on Byzantine history—and given eighteen minutes to prepare. The instructors then met their students, and proceeded to teach a seven-minute lesson. Two coders watched videotapes of these encounters

and graded each teacher for nervousness, discomfort, awkwardness, and stiffness. They also rated the quality of the lesson, grading it for, among other things, clarity and the coherence of the material.

Following the lesson, while the instructor completed a test designed to measure conscious, explicit bias, the student took a test on the material he or she was just taught, which included recalling important names, dates, and other relevant facts.

The result: Once explicit bias was removed from the equation, greater unconscious bias on the part of an instructor predicted lower test scores for black, but not white, students. "Our evidence suggests this was due to higher bias instructors being more anxious, and therefore giving less effective lessons," the researchers write.[13]

What should we say about these instructors in light of Kelly and Roedder's arguments? What should instructors do with this information? What should students do with it?

Notes

1. Throughout, we will simplify the discussion by considering just two groups, and using the capitalized terms "Black" and "White" to refer to those putative racial groups and their members. Other terminology, e.g., "African-American," is less suitable for our purposes because it is overly restrictive. For example, it does not appear that implicit racial biases against Blacks apply only to Black *Americans*, or only to Americans of specifically *African* descent.

2. See Greenwald, McGhee, and Schwartz for the first presentation of the IAT itself, as well as the initial results obtained with it. Also see Greenwald and Nosek; Lane et al.; Nosek, Greenwald, and Banaji, "Implicit Association Test" for more recent reviews of data gathered using IATs, and for useful discussions of the methodological issues surrounding the test.

3. More precisely: "the logic of the IAT is that this sorting task should be easier when the two concepts that share a response are strongly associated than when they are weakly associated" (Nosek, Greenwald, and Banaji, "Implicit Association Test" 267).

4. Similar dissociations have been found using a wide variety of other indirect measures, including evaluative priming (Cunningham, Preacher, and Banaji; Devine et al.), the startle eyeblink test (Phelps et al.; Amodio, Harmon-Jones, and Devine), and EMG measures (Vanman et al.).

5. We know of no efforts to answer this question, although it is posed in Jolls and Sunstein.

6. In stating these examples, we felt *extremely* uncomfortable, and we anticipate that our readers will feel the same way. However, we think concrete examples are needed in order to make salient our point: In general, explicitly racist attitudes—even if they are not acted upon—are morally damnable.

7. At least, they would not be morally problematic *in the way* that racist attitudes are problematic. Garcia offers an account of racism, not a complete moral theory.
8. See Gregg, Seibt, and Banaji. We have stated that it is more *salient* that implicit attitudes are uncontrollable. That's because, arguably, the acquisition of most *explicit* attitudes is uncontrollable as well; it's just not salient at first glance. One does not control one's acquisition of, for instance, one's beliefs about plants, one's attitudes towards pets, etc. So one will need to appeal to more complex or carefully delineated features—perhaps identification or reasons-responsiveness—if one wants to claim that implicit attitudes are not proper subjects of blame, but that explicit attitudes are.
9. There are, of course, many ways one might go about compensating for implicit racial bias. Most obviously, one might use conscious rules, e.g., "Bump up borderline grades of Black students." In addition, there are various psychological techniques which seem to mitigate implicit racial bias, such as entertaining counterstereotypic thoughts (e.g., imagining a positive Black role model, or a female scientist).
10. People sometimes question the idea that grades are apt to be "accurate" at all. In many ways, this is irrelevant—most of us want to avoid having the race of a student affect their grading. That desire is enough to motivate the problems we raise here: If one has this desire, it seems that one is rationally compelled to correct for possible influence of race in deliberation.
11. To add to the case we are making, one can appeal to expert opinion. In that vein, we have discussed this issue with two members of Banaji's lab at Harvard, both of whom said they'd be "very surprised" if there wasn't implicit racial bias in the domain of grading.
12. This version of epistemic argument is highly compressed, thus there isn't room to respond to a number of important objections. Roedder contains a much fuller exploration and defense of these claims.
13. http://www.psmag.com/books-and-culture/unconscious-teacher-bias-harms-black-college-students

20

===== 📖 =====

How Not to Accuse Someone of Prejudice

Emrys Westacott

. . . .

In discussions of racism, sexism, and other forms of prejudice, two kinds of fallacious reasoning sometimes appear: the "appeal to subjective response" and the "accusation of privilege." The first fallacy treats someone's subjective response to a comment as sufficient evidence of prejudice or insensitivity. This fails to acknowledge that the reasonableness of the response is always an open question. The second fallacy involves dismissing what people accused of prejudice say in their defense on the grounds that the privileged always speak that way. This insultingly treats what is said as an effect of causes rather than the result of rational reflection. Both forms of specious reasoning risk bringing the worthy cause of combatting prejudice into disrepute.

. . . .

A colleague recently responded to a memo I circulated by telling me they considered it unintentionally heterosexist. I didn't agree. After a brief exchange of e-mails that served only to sandpaper

Westacott, Emrys. 2015. "How Not to Accuse Someone of Prejudice." *Think* 14(41): 21–29. Copyright ©2015 The Royal Institute of Philosophy. Reprinted with the permission of Cambridge University Press. doi:10.1017/S1477175615000275 *Think* 14(41) (Autumn 2015) © The Royal Institute of Philosophy, 2015.

each other's sore spots, they called my attention to the following passage in Allen Johnson's book *Privilege, Power, and Difference*:

> If someone confronts you with your own behavior that supports privilege, step off the path of least resistance that encourages you to defend and deny. Don't tell them they're too sensitive or need a better sense of humor . . . Listen to what's being said. Take it seriously. Assume for the time being it's true, because given the power of paths of least resistance, it probably is. (Allen Johnson, *Privilege, Power, and Difference* [New York: McGraw-Hill, 2nd ed., 2005] 141.)

The passage is well-intended and, up to a point, reasonable. But in my opinion it should be read with caution, since it can easily encourage fallacious thinking and thereby harm the very cause it hopes to advance—a cause with which I fully sympathize. Of course, the tenor of the passage is to encourage a self-critical attitude, and we're all in favor of that. But the same kind of reasoning could also be used to fend off the advice being given. After all, one can easily imagine rewriting the passage to put the boot on the other foot:

> If someone tells you you're being hypersensitive or unreasonable, step off the path of least resistance that encourages you to defend and deny. Don't tell them their behavior supports privilege. Listen to what's being said. Take it seriously. Assume for the time being it's true, because given the power of the paths of least resistance, it probably is.

As my colleague and I found, navigating these shoals in our everyday interactions, achieving the proper admixture of knowledge, understanding, self-awareness, sensitivity, and reason, can be difficult. Still, I believe that in our attempts to manage this, it is important that we recognize and respect basic logical parameters. If we fail to do this, we do our cause a disservice.

In discussions of sexism, racism, heterosexism, heteronormativism, and other forms of prejudice, I have sometimes encountered two particular forms of specious reasoning. I will label these the *appeal to subjective response* and the *accusation of privilege*. My purpose here is simply to explain what these are and what is wrong with them.

The *appeal to subjective response* involves inferring that an action or statement expresses some sort of prejudice solely on the grounds that someone is hurt or offended by it. Reasoning in this fashion is unsupportable and leads to all kinds of problems. To see how this is so, let us consider two specific examples.

Example 1: A teacher says to a class: "Imagine a doctor and nurse who work together and fall in love. Should he continue as her boss?"

This statement is possibly both sexist and heterosexist. I say "possibly" because context in such cases is everything. It need not be objectionable if, for instance, it is just one of many varied scenarios thrown out by a creative writing instructor to illustrate plot possibilities. But if it belongs to a persistent pattern of stereotyped thinking, then it is open to criticism.

How would we justify the claim that the utterance is sexist? The standard procedure is to define the relevant concept and then show how a particular instance falls under it. So in this case, we would offer a definition of sexism that includes the act of presupposing harmful gender stereotypes or oppressive notions of normality and argue that the teacher in Example 1 is doing just that. The charge of heterosexism would be supported in a similar way.

Now contrast that with the following:

Example 2: A teacher says to a class: "Imagine a doctor and a nurse who work together and fall in love. Should they keep working together?'

This seems unobjectionable: no sexist or heterosexist assumptions are being made. But suppose a student did object, saying that when they hear talk of a "doctor and nurse" relationship, this conjures up in their mind—and makes them painfully aware of—a long history of hierarchical doctor-nurse relationships in which the doctors are male and dominant, the nurses are female and subservient, and gay relationships of any kind are excluded from the picture. So although what the teacher says may not explicitly reinforce oppressive stereotypes, it may still be judged sexist and heterosexist in some sense—namely, relative to this student's subjective response informed by her particular experiences.

Is this a reasonable argument? Absolutely not. Yet some accusations of prejudice take essentially this form. One well-known example concerns the use of the word "niggardly." In 1999 a student at the University of Wisconsin–Madison complained to the faculty senate about a professor of English who had used the word while teaching a class on Chaucer. She charged the professor with using racially offensive language. It is, of course, possible to imagine someone using this word, perhaps emphasizing it repeatedly in remarks directed at African-Americans in a manner designed to produce discomfort. In that case, its use could certainly be judged racist. And if I was aware that my audience might dislike the term, perhaps because they mistakenly believed it to contain a racial slur, then my decision to use it could perhaps be criticized as insensitive. But notice, in both these situations we look at more than just the audience's reaction to decide whether the speaker is at fault. We also consider the speaker's intentions, or at least the speaker's levels of self-awareness and sensitivity. To conclude that the speaker's use of the word is racist—or blameworthy in some other way—*solely* on the basis of the listener's subjective response is a serious error.

In fact this sort of reasoning is not just unsound; it is harmful. For if we give it credence we will be forced to embrace a shifting, unstable notion of what constitutes prejudice, a concept that will be far less useful as a tool for criticizing real prejudice when we encounter it. Defining racist, sexist, or heterosexist speech solely, or even primarily, by reference to audience responses means that the same utterance made by the same person to the same audience can be innocent one day and prejudiced the next simply because, in the meantime, the listener has had experiences that affect the way he or she responds. It means that *any* statement whatsoever could be deemed prejudiced, since if someone sincerely claims to be offended, oppressed, demeaned, or marginalized by something said, then that emotional response, in itself, validates their complaint.

This is not to imply that audience response is irrelevant. Obviously, one important indicator that something you've said might be objectionable is that someone objects to it; and if this happens repeatedly and with various audiences, it behooves you to reflect critically on the charges being made against you. After all, accusations of prejudice usually are prompted by words or deeds that express prejudice. But the mere fact that your listeners object or feel offended does not prove that their response is justified. They may have misunderstood your meaning or intention. They may be overreacting. Their reaction may be irrational.

The key point here is easily demonstrated. The subjective response of a listener or reader is *never* sufficient evidence that someone's words are racist, sexist, or heterosexist since one can always ask the question: Is the response reasonable? Of course, this question itself does not always have a clear-cut answer, for the parties in dispute are likely to disagree here, too. But that is a different problem. The point still holds that the reasonableness of a person's response is always an open question.

Often, when there is a disagreement over this question, a secondary quarrel ensues about whether an apology is in order and, if so, what form it should take. Suppose you say something that I find hurtful or offensive and I tell you this. How should you respond? Unless you are going out of your way to be aggressively dismissive of my feelings, you will probably say that you are sorry. But "sorry" can be said in many ways. You could be:

a) Expressing *remorse*—You're sorry that you said something objectionable or insensitive, and you're asking for forgiveness.
b) Expressing *sympathy*—You're sorry that I am suffering in some way.
c) Expressing *regret*—You're sorry that what you said hurt or annoyed me. If you had known it would have this effect you might not have said it.

Notice that neither the expression of sympathy nor the expression of regret need carry any admission of wrong-doing. Both are, in fact, quite compatible with your belief that my reaction is unreasonable.

The wounded party naturally wants to hear an expression of remorse—in effect, an admission of guilt. But should you offer this if it is not sincere? Admitting guilt when we don't believe we've done anything wrong is something most of us find very hard to do. And any moral credit we might receive for our apparently self-critical receptivity to the perspective of others is more than offset by our insincerity. One could even speak here of a lack of integrity.

Faced with this dilemma—torn between wanting to be responsive yet also wanting to be sincere—we typically say we are sorry in one of the other two senses. The word "sorry" then seems to convey the *form* of an apology; but in truth it merely expresses sympathy or regret. For the person offended, of course, this is not good enough. In fact, it seems to compound the initial offense by being patronizing. To them we seem to be saying: "Yes, yes, I know you're offended, but there's really nothing to be offended about," rather as we'd say to a child, "I know you're afraid, but trust me, there's nothing to be afraid of." Yet what is one supposed to do? To express indifference would be callous. To admit guilt would be insincere. Their asking me to try to understand why they might be offended is all very well; but shouldn't they, by the same token, try to understand why I don't feel able to apologize in good faith?

This secondary exchange leads us to the second fallacy mentioned earlier, the *accusation of privilege*, which might arise in something like the following way. Imagine Pat to be a straight white male, and Kim to be someone who doesn't have one or more of these attributes. Pat says something that Kim criticizes as racist, sexist, or heterosexist. The conversation proceeds as follows:

PAT: I just don't get it. I don't see anything wrong with what I said.

KIM: That's because you don't know what it's like to be unprivileged, oppressed, and marginalized.

PAT: Well I just think you're being hypersensitive and unreasonable.

KIM: That's what the voice of privilege always says. Your attitude is dismissive.

Now Kim's claim that privilege often defends itself by accusing others of hypersensitivity or illogicality is undoubtedly true. But that doesn't make her riposte appropriate. On the contrary, it is misguided for at least two reasons.

First of all, it is logically irrelevant. Pat is denying that what he said is sexist. The appropriate response to this—to say it again—is to define the concept of sexism clearly and then show how what has been said falls under it. But in the above exchange, Kim evades this task. Instead, Kim first offers an explanation of why Pat "doesn't get it" in terms of Pat's life story, and then tries to account for his charge of unreasonableness by claiming it is typical of his type. The explanations may be psychologically and sociologically astute, but they still evade rather than engage the issue at hand.

Recall a key point made earlier: it is always possible that one's subjective response to what another says or does is unreasonable. This is relevant here, too; it means that Pat might be right. Imagine, for instance, this extreme situation. A female student tells a male teacher that she finds his wearing a tie threatening: It smacks of authority, privilege, bondage, and ultimately, she says, threatens her subtly and symbolically with the noose. His response is to say, "I don't get it. How can my wearing a tie suggest a threat to harm you? I think you're being unreasonable."

Now if something like this occurs in normal circumstances, the chances are that the student is mentally ill. Yet she can still respond to the charge that she's being unreasonable by saying, "That's what privilege always says." But the fact that privilege very often does defend itself in this way is obviously beside the point here. It isn't a valid piece of reasoning or an additional bit of evidence that helps to justify her initial complaint. It's a *substitute* for a justification, a big fat red herring.

A second objection to the statement "that's what privilege typically says" is that it closes down discussion. Moreover, it does so in a pernicious way.

How is Pat supposed to respond to the observation that he is saying "what privilege typically says"? Presumably by stopping in his tracks, reflecting on things, and becoming more self-aware, more culturally sensitive, and so on. These would doubtless be excellent outcomes: We could all benefit from enhanced self-awareness and sensitivity. And pointing out to someone that what they are saying is what members of a group to which they belong typically say can certainly sometimes be useful. This is no doubt how Kim would defend her remark.

But Kim's observation moves the debate from a discussion about reasons to one about causes. This is what makes it pernicious. It says to Pat: "I'm not going to bother showing how your claim is false or unjustified. Instead, I'm just going to point out what is causing you to speak as you do—viz. your position of privilege."

Treating someone's utterances as mere effects of causes is one way of showing that person a profound lack of respect. The subtle implication is that what they say is not the result of reason or reflection but merely a consequence of other forces at work on them. Exactly the same strategy has been used countless times by men against women, whenever an idea has been dismissed as "exactly the sort of thing women would say." This move is insulting. Just how insulting can be gauged by considering the sort of occasion when we might consider it appropriate. One instance that comes to mind is when we are dealing with people who are mentally deranged. Then there may, sadly, be times when we would be justified in ignoring the content of what they say and choose to focus, instead, on the condition responsible for their utterances ("It's not he who's saying those terrible things—it's the illness.").

Thus, whatever the intention behind an observation like "that is what privilege typically says," such responses are more likely to insult than to persuade. And they are more likely to produce frustration than a renewed commitment to self-criticism. The accused, after all, is in a position akin to that of Joseph K. in Kafka's *The Trial* who, when he protests to a priest that he is innocent, is told, "But that is how the guilty speak."

It is a wonderful thing that we have reached a point in history when sophisticated critiques of prejudice, injustice, and oppression in their many and often subtle forms abound. It is a fine thing to cultivate awareness of the many ways that we unwittingly participate in forms of speech and behavior that perpetuate prejudice. But just as we try to avoid prejudice, we must also be careful to avoid specious reasoning which risks bringing a good cause into disrepute.

Comprehension Questions

1. What's the point of the quotation from Allen Johnson and Westacott's way of reworking it?
2. What's the "appeal to subjective response," and why does Westacott think that such appeals are misguided?
3. What should be done instead of making an appeal to subjective response?
4. Why is it wrong to define the harm of discriminatory speech by the subjective response it causes in its victims?
5. What are some differences in how people use the word "sorry"?
6. On Westacott's view, how does the "accusation of privilege" work? What's wrong with it?
7. In what way can the accusation of privilege be disrespectful?

Discussion Questions

1. Have you ever been accused of being privileged? If so, what happened?
2. For Westacott, it should always be possible for two people to exchange reasons when one of them is accused of discriminatory speech. Can you imagine any scenarios where you think this isn't the case? What's special about them?
3. How do you think Westacott's positive proposal would work in practice? Are you optimistic about people's reasonableness? Do you think it matters for Westacott's proposal whether or not it actually helps people resolve disagreements?
4. Suppose that, in general, being privileged makes you prone to discriminatory speech. Moreover, suppose that being offended by a remark is good evidence that the remark is discriminatory. Does it follow that privilege and offense are good evidence of actual discrimination? Why or why not?

Case

Robin DiAngelo argues that there are many factors that make it difficult for white people to have open conversations about racial prejudice and injustice. She claims that the following things can trigger "race-based stress" in white people, leading them to ignore or downplay the challenge to their view of race in the United States:

1. Suggesting that a white person's viewpoint comes from a racialized frame of reference (challenge to objectivity);
2. People of color talking directly about their own racial perspectives (challenge to white taboos on talking openly about race);
3. People of color choosing not to protect the racial feelings of white people in regards to race (challenge to white racial expectations and need/entitlement to racial comfort);
4. People of color not being willing to tell their stories or answer questions about their racial experiences (challenge to the expectation that people of color will serve us);
5. A fellow white not providing agreement with one's racial perspective (challenge to white solidarity);
6. Receiving feedback that one's behavior had a racist impact (challenge to white racial innocence);
7. Suggesting that group membership is significant (challenge to individualism);
8. An acknowledgment that access is unequal between racial groups (challenge to meritocracy);
9. Being presented with a person of color in a position of leadership (challenge to white authority);
10. Being presented with information about other racial groups through, for example, movies in which people of color drive the action but are not in stereotypical roles, or multicultural education (challenge to white centrality).[1]

Suppose that DiAngelo is correct. If so, then it's worth noting that many discussions of privilege involve hitting multiple triggers for race-based stress. It would be very surprising if people who became defensive for these reasons were in a position to have a frank conversation about their own privilege—or even recognize it. How does this affect Westacott's argument?

Note

1. http://www.huffingtonpost.com/good-men-project/why-its-so-hard-to-talk-to-white-people-about-racism_b_7183710.html

PART IV

Affirmative Action in Admissions

The Meaning of "Merit"

William G. Bowen and Derek Bok

Affirmative action in college admissions—that is, the practice of using not only applicants' academic track records, but also factors like race, ethnicity, or gender, to evaluate their applications—is still hotly debated. At bottom, Bowen and Box see it as a question of merit. Some say affirmative action policies in higher education would keep deserving students from rightful admission, while others, like Bowen and Bok, believe affirmative action actually helps better identify deserving applicants. First, they argue against the idea that an applicant's track record is necessarily a good measure of merit. The point of affirmative action, they insist, is not that race *per se* should count positively in an applicant's favor. Rather, it can serve as an indirect measure to pick out students of high potential who are well positioned to contribute to the enrichment of campus culture and, in the course of time, contribute to society by remedying the scarcity of high-ranking professionals who are racial minorities.

"Merit," like preference" and "discrimination," is a word that has taken on so much baggage we may have to reinvent it or find a substitute.

Still, it is an important and potentially valuable concept because it reminds us that we certainly do not want institutions to admit candidates who lack merit, however the term is defined. Most people would agree that rank favoritism (admitting a personal friend of the admissions officer, say) is inconsistent with admission "on the merits," that no one should be admitted who cannot take advantage of the educational opportunities being offered, and that using a lottery or some similar random numbers scheme to choose among applicants who are over the academic threshold is too crude an approach.

One reason why we care so much about who gets admitted "on the merits" is because . . . admission to . . . selective schools . . . pays off handsomely for individuals of all races, from all backgrounds. But it is not individuals alone who gain. Substantial additional benefits accrue to society at large through the leadership and civic participation of the graduates and through the broad contributions that the schools themselves make to the goals of a democratic society. These societal benefits are a major justification for the favored tax treatment that colleges and universities enjoy and for the subsidies provided by public and private donors. The presence of these benefits also explains why these institutions do not allocate scarce places in their entering classes by the simple expedient of auctioning them off to the highest bidders. The limited number of places is an exceedingly valuable resource—valuable both to the students admitted and to the society at large—which is why admissions need to be based "on the merits."

Unfortunately, however, to say that considerations of merit should drive the admissions process is to pose questions, not answer them. There are no magical ways of automatically identifying those who merit admission on the basis of intrinsic qualities that distinguish them from all others. Test scores and grades are useful measures of the ability to do good work, but they are no more than that. They are far from infallible indicators of other qualities some might regard as intrinsic, such as a deep love of learning or a capacity for high academic achievement. . . . Moreover, such quantitative measures are even less useful in answering other questions relevant to the admissions process, such as predicting which applicants will contribute most in later life to their professions and their communities.[1]

Some critics believe, nevertheless, that applicants with higher grades and test scores are more deserving of admission because they presumably worked harder than those with less auspicious academic records. According to this argument, it is only "fair" to admit the students who have displayed the greatest effort. We disagree on several grounds.

To begin with, it is not clear that students who receive higher grades and test scores have necessarily worked harder in school. Grades and test scores are a reflection not only of effort but of intelligence, which in turn derives from a number of factors, such as inherited ability, family circumstances, and early upbringing, that have nothing to do with how many hours students have labored over their homework. Test scores may also be affected by the quality of teaching that applicants have received or even by knowing the best strategies for taking standardized tests, as coaching schools regularly remind students and their parents. For these reasons, it is quite likely that many applicants with good but not outstanding scores and B+ averages in high school will have worked more diligently than many other applicants with superior academic records.

More generally, selecting a class has much broader purposes than simply rewarding students who are thought to have worked especially hard. The job of the admissions staff is not, in any case, to decide who has earned a "right" to a place in the class, since we do not think that admission to a selective university is a right possessed by anyone. What admissions officers must decide is which set of applicants, *considered individually and collectively*, will take fullest advantage of what the college has to offer, contribute most to the educational process in college, and be most successful in using what they have learned for the benefit of the larger society. Admissions processes should, of course, be "fair," but "fairness" has to be understood to mean only that each individual is to be judged according to a consistent set of criteria that reflect the objectives of the college or university. Fairness should not be misinterpreted to mean that a particular criterion has to apply—that, for example, grades and test scores must always be considered more important than other qualities and characteristics so that no student with a B average can be accepted as long as some students with As are being turned down.

Nor does fairness imply that each candidate should be judged in isolation from all others. It may be perfectly "fair" to reject an applicant because the college has already enrolled many other students very much like him or her. There are numerous analogies. When making a stew, adding an extra carrot rather than one more potato may make excellent sense—and be eminently "fair"—if there are already lots of potatoes in the pot. Similarly, good basketball teams include both excellent shooters and sturdy defenders, both point guards and centers. Diversified investment portfolios usually include some mix of stocks and bonds, and so on.

To admit "on the merits," then, is to admit by following complex rules derived from the institution's own mission and based on its own experiences educating students with different talents and backgrounds. These "rules" should not be thought of as abstract propositions to be deduced through contemplation in a Platonic cave. Nor are they rigid formulas that can be applied in a mechanical fashion. Rather, they should have the status of rough guidelines established in large part through empirical examination of the actual results achieved as a result of long experience. . . .

Above all, merit must be defined in light of what educational institutions are trying to accomplish. In our view, race is relevant in determining which candidates "merit" admission because taking account of race helps institutions achieve three objectives central to their mission—identifying individuals of high potential, permitting students to benefit educationally from diversity on campus, and addressing long-term societal needs.

Identifying Individuals of High Potential

An individual's race may reveal something about how that person arrived at where he or she is today—what barriers were overcome, and what the individual's prospects are for further growth. Not every member of a minority group will have had to surmount substantial obstacles. Moreover, other circumstances besides race can cause "disadvantage." Thus colleges and universities should and do give special consideration to the hard-working son of a family in Appalachia or the daughter of a recent immigrant from Russia who, while obviously bright, is still struggling with the English language. But race is an important factor in its own right, given this nation's history and the evidence presented in many studies of the continuing effects of discrimination and prejudice. Wishing it were otherwise does not make it otherwise. It would seem to us to be ironic indeed—and wrong—if admissions officers were permitted to consider all other factors that help them identify individuals of high potential who have had to overcome obstacles, but were proscribed from looking at an applicant's race.

Benefiting Educationally from Diversity on the Campus

Race almost always affects an individual's life experiences and perspectives, and thus the person's capacity to contribute to the kinds of learning through diversity that occur on campuses. This form of learning will be even more important going forward than it has been in the past. Both the growing diversity of American society and the increasing interaction with other cultures worldwide make it evident that going to school only with "the likes of oneself" will be increasingly anachronistic. The advantages of being able to understand how others think and function, to cope across racial divides, and to lead groups composed of diverse individuals are certain to increase.

To be sure, not all members of a minority group may succeed in expanding the racial understanding of other students, any more than all those who grew up on a farm or came from a remote region of the United States can be expected to convey a special rural perspective. What does seem clear, however, is that a student body containing many different backgrounds, talents, and experiences will be a richer environment in which to develop. In this respect, minority students of all kinds can have something to offer their classmates. The black student with high grades from Andover may challenge the stereotypes of many classmates just as much as the black student from the South Bronx. . . .

Addressing Long-Term Societal Needs

Virtually all colleges and universities seek to educate students who seem likely to become leaders and contributing members of society. Identifying such students is another essential aspect of admitting "on the merits," and here again race is clearly relevant. There is widespread agreement that our country continues to need the help of its colleges and universities in building a society in which access to positions of leadership and responsibility is less limited by an individual's race than it is today. . . .

Fundamental judgments have to be made about societal needs, values, and objectives. When a distinguished black educator visited the Mellon Foundation, he noted, with understandable pride, that his son had done brilliantly in college and was being considered for a prestigious graduate award in neuroscience. "My son," the professor said, "needs no special consideration; he is so talented that he will make it on his own." His conclusion was that we should be indifferent to whether his son or any of the white competitors got the particular fellowship in question. We agreed that, in all likelihood, all of these candidates would benefit from going to the graduate school in question and, in time, become excellent scientists or doctors. Still, one can argue with the conclusion reached by the parent. "Your son will do fine," another person present at the meeting said, "but that isn't the issue. *He may not need us, but we need him!* Why? Because there is only one of him."

That mild exaggeration notwithstanding, the relative scarcity of talented black professionals is all too real. It seemed clear to a number of us that day, and it probably seems clear to many others, that American society needs the high-achieving black graduates who will provide leadership in every walk of life. This is the position of many top officials concerned with filling key positions in government, of CEOs who affirm that they would continue their minority recruitment programs whether or not there were a legal requirement to do so, and of bar associations, medical associations, and other professional organizations that have repeatedly stressed the importance of attracting more minority members into their fields. In view of these needs, we are not indifferent to which student gets the graduate fellowship.

Neither of the authors of this study has any sympathy with quotas or any belief in mandating the proportional representation of groups of people, defined by race or any other criterion, in positions of authority. Nor do we include ourselves among those who support race-sensitive admissions as compensation for a legacy of racial discrimination.[2] We agree emphatically with the sentiment expressed by Mamphela Ramphele, vice chancellor of the University of Cape Town in South Africa, when she said: "Everyone deserves opportunity; no one deserves success." But we remain persuaded that present racial disparities in outcomes are dismayingly disproportionate. At the minimum, this country needs to maintain the progress now being made in educating larger numbers of black professionals and black leaders.

Selective colleges and universities have made impressive contributions at both undergraduate and graduate levels. To take but a single illustration: Since starting to admit larger numbers of black students in the late 1960s, the Harvard Law School has numbered among its black graduates more than one hundred partners in law firms, more than ninety black alumni/ae with the title of chief executive officer, vice president, or general counsel of a corporation, more than seventy professors, at least thirty judges, two members of Congress, the mayor of a major American city, the head of the Office of Management and Budget, and an assistant U.S. attorney general. . . . If, at the end of the day, the question is whether the most selective colleges and universities have succeeded in educating sizable numbers of minority students who have already achieved considerable success and seem likely in time to occupy positions of leadership throughout society, we have no problem in answering the question. Absolutely.

We commented earlier on the need to make clear choices. Here is perhaps the clearest choice. Let us suppose that rejecting, on race-neutral grounds, more than half of the black students who otherwise would attend these institutions would raise the probability of acceptance for another white student from 25 percent to, say, 27 percent at the most selective colleges and universities. Would we, as a society, be better off? Considering both the educational benefits of diversity and the need to include far larger numbers of black graduates in the top ranks of the business, professional, governmental, and not-for-profit institutions that shape our society, we do not think so.[3]

How one responds to such questions depends very much, of course, on how important one thinks it is that progress continues to be made in narrowing black-white gaps in earnings and in representation in top-level positions. As the United States grows steadily more diverse, we believe that Nicholas Katzenbach and Burke Marshall are surely right in insisting that the country must continue to make determined efforts to "include blacks in the institutional framework that constitutes America's economic, political, educational and social life." This goal of greater inclusiveness is important for reasons, both moral and practical, that offer all Americans the prospect of living in a society marked by more equality and racial harmony than one might otherwise anticipate.

We recognize that many opponents of race-sensitive admissions will also agree with Katzenbach and Marshall, but will argue that there are better ways of promoting inclusiveness. There is everything to be said, in our view, for addressing the underlying problems in families, neighborhoods, and primary and secondary schools that many have identified so clearly. But this is desperately difficult work, which will, at best, produce results only over a very long period of time. Meanwhile, it is important, in our view, to do what can be done to make a difference at each educational level, including colleges and graduate and professional schools.

The alternative seems to us both stark and unworthy of our country's ideals. Turning aside from efforts to help larger numbers of well-qualified blacks gain the educational advantages they will need to move steadily and confidently into the mainstream of American life could have extremely serious consequences. Here in the United States, as elsewhere in the world, visible efforts by leading educational institutions to make things better will encourage others to press on with the hard work needed to overcome the continuing effects of a legacy of unfair treatment.

Comprehension Questions

1. Why is merit supposed to matter so much in the process of college admissions?
2. Why are Bowen and Bok skeptical about simply using grades to identify students worthy of admission?
3. According to Bowen and Bok, how should the admissions process be kept "fair"?
4. Why do Bowen and Bok think that taking race into account in college admissions can better help them select high-potential individuals, and what benefits do they think doing so can have for the student body at large?
5. How is it, according to Bowen and Bok, that letting race factor in college admissions could serve society in the long run?

Discussion Questions

1. Bowen and Bok contend that making race a factor in admissions decisions could enrich the learning experience of the broader student body. In your experience, what difference does it make to have a diverse student body? Are the benefits significant enough to support Bowen and Bok's view?
2. In your view, how should college admissions committees evaluate applicants? What makes an applicant deserving of admission? Compare your view with that of Bowen and Bok. If your view differs from theirs, why is yours preferable?
3. Bowen and Bok dismiss the idea that race should be a factor in college admissions in the United States as a matter of restitution for historical injustices against African Americans. Why do you suppose they reject this view? Are the reasons that come to mind compelling ones? Why or why not?

Case

In 2003, the US Supreme Court upheld the University of Michigan Law School's admissions policy, which took race into account. Interestingly, however, the justices didn't think that race-conscious policies could be defended forever. After acknowledging the current legitimacy of the Law School's practices, they wrote:

> We are mindful, however, that "[a] core purpose of the Fourteenth Amendment was to do away with all governmentally imposed discrimination based on race." *Palmore v. Sidoti*, 466 U. S. 429, 432 (1984). Accordingly, race-conscious admissions policies must be limited in time. This requirement reflects that racial classifications, however compelling their goals, are potentially so dangerous that they may be employed no more broadly than the interest demands. Enshrining a permanent justification for racial preferences would offend this fundamental equal protection principle. We see no reason to exempt race-conscious admissions programs from the requirement that all governmental use of race must have a logical end point. . . .
>
> The requirement that all race-conscious admissions programs have a termination point "assure[s] all citizens that the deviation from the norm of equal treatment of all racial and ethnic groups is a temporary matter, a measure taken in the service of the goal of equality itself." *Richmond v. J. A. Croson Co.*, 488 U. S., at 510 (plurality opinion); see also Nathanson & Bartnik, *The Constitutionality of Preferential Treatment for Minority Applicants to Professional Schools*, 58 Chicago Bar Rec. 282, 293 (May–June 1977) ("It would be a sad day indeed, were America to become a quota-ridden society, with each identifiable minority assigned proportional representation in every desirable walk of life. But that is not the rationale for programs of preferential treatment; the acid test of their justification will be their efficacy in eliminating the need for any racial or ethnic preferences at all").[4]

Do you agree with the justices' view that race-conscious admissions programs should eventually be phased out? Why or why not? If you think they *should* be phased out, then how would we know when the time is right? Some of the justices thought that we'd be there in twenty-five years—that is, in 2028. Does it seem plausible to you that we're a decade or so away from the time when it won't be possible to defend race-conscious admissions programs?

Notes

1. Martin Luther King, Jr., now regarded as one of the great orators of this century, scored in the bottom half of all test takers on the verbal GRE.

2. Justice Thurgood Marshall made such an argument in the *Bakke* case in urging his colleagues on the Supreme Court to uphold the racial quotas provided by the University of California Davis School of Medicine; in his view, such programs were simply a way "to remedy the effects of centuries of unequal treatment . . . I do not believe that anyone can truly look into America's past and still find that a remedy for the effects of that past is impermissible" (438 U.S. at p. 402). Understandable as this argument may seem against a historical background of slavery and segregation, it did not prevail because the remedy is not precise enough to be entirely just in its application. Not every minority student who is admitted will have suffered from substantial discrimination, and the excluded white and Asian applicants are rarely responsible for the racial injustices of the past and have sometimes had to struggle against considerable handicaps of their own. For these reasons, a majority of justices in the *Bakke* case rejected Marshall's reasoning, although similar arguments continue to be heard.

3. This emphasis on the consequences of rejecting race-neutral policies will seem misplaced to some of the most thoughtful critics of affirmative action, who will argue that their objection to race-based policies is an objection in principle: In their view, no one's opportunities should be narrowed, even by an iota, by reference to the individual's race. We respect this line of argument. However, we do not agree, "in principle," that colleges and universities should ignore the practical effects of one set of decisions or another when making difficult decisions about who "merits" a place in the class. The clash here is principle versus principle, not principle versus expediency. As we argued earlier in the chapter, in making admissions decisions, what is right in principle depends on how one defines the mission of the educational institution involved. For us, the missions of colleges and universities have strong educational and public policy aspects and do not consist solely of conferring benefits on particular individuals.

4. https://supreme.justia.com/cases/federal/us/539/306/case.html

22

Does Your "Merit" Depend upon Your Race?

A Rejoinder to Bowen and Bok

Stephan Thernstrom and Abigail Thernstrom

It's only natural to want everyone to succeed in life and reap all of its potential benefits. Since a college education is so valuable in our society, and since racial minorities are less likely than their white counterparts to receive a college education, the efforts of proponents of affirmative action in higher education are at least understandable. Stephan and Abigail Thernstrom share the desire for all to fare well, but they disagree with people like William Bowen and Derek Bok who advocate for taking applicants' race into account when making college admissions decisions. Making race part of an applicant's merit creates a double standard and makes the concept of merit too subjective. Moreover, the Thernstroms maintain that affirmative action in college admissions is degrading to all parties concerned, even beneficiaries of the practice, and is morally no different than old racist practices limiting how many Jewish applicants were admitted into institutions of higher education. They recommend instead that we focus on improving the quality of primary and secondary education to enable racial minorities to gain admittance to college on their own merits.

Thernstrom, Stephan, and Abigail Thernstrom, "Does Your 'Merit' Depend upon Your Race? A Rejoinder to Bowen and Bok," in Steven M. Cahn, *The Affirmative Action Debate* (New York: Routledge, 2nd edition, 2002). Reprinted with permission of Taylor and Francis Group.

In his *Reflections of an Affirmative Action Baby*, Stephen Carter tells us that his academic record as an undergraduate at Stanford was strong, but not good enough to win him admission to Harvard Law School. Shortly after he got a rejection letter from Harvard, though, he received a telephone call informing him that there had been a mistake in the review of his application. The admissions committee had somehow failed to notice that Mr. Carter was an African American, and that made all the difference. As an ordinary applicant, Carter did not make the grade. But Harvard Law School had a lower standard for black applicants, so it was eager to have him.

Stephen Carter felt patronized and demeaned by Harvard Law School, and chose to go elsewhere for his law education. He recognized that his race may well have given him a boost at the other schools that admitted him, but he could not be sure how much. Only Harvard made it crystal clear, inadvertently making the racial basis of its judgment completely transparent. He was not being admitted because of his personal achievements; he was not unequivocally outstanding, but merely outstanding compared with other African-American applicants.

Derek Bok, once the dean of Harvard Law School, and William G. Bowen cannot grasp why a Stephen Carter might feel deflated and diminished by such treatment. Although they claim to be making the case for nuanced, holistic, highly individualized admissions decisions, in fact what they defend are crude judgments that reduce applicants to members of racial categories. From their perspective, society needs more black attorneys, and the elite law schools have to do their part. If energetic recruitment efforts do not yield enough minority applicants who would win admission strictly on the basis of their individual qualifications, schools must do their duty by accepting black and Latino applicants with weaker credentials. What's the problem? After all, everyone they admit is qualified. That many whites and Asians whom they reject are better qualified doesn't matter, because "society" already has enough white and Asian attorneys.

Bowen and Bok, of course, once headed two of the most distinguished universities in the United States—indeed, in the world. Bowen was president of Princeton University, and Bok was president of Harvard. The shining reputations of Princeton and Harvard derive primarily from the excellence of their faculties and their student bodies, and that excellence has been the result of a commitment to meritocratic selection procedures. They admit the very best students from their applicant pools, and they hire the best scholars they can find to teach them.

It was not always so. Before World War II, both Harvard and Princeton held Jewish applicants to a higher standard than Gentiles, and kept the numbers of Jews in the student body severely limited, in order to leave ample room for alumni sons who were more notable for their social graces than for their intelligence. They also were extremely reluctant to hire Jews as faculty members.[1]

Bowen and Bok's effort to relativize the "meaning of merit" drains the concept of any clear meaning and echoes the arguments made by proponents of the Jewish quotas in the bad old days. Test scores and grades are but very limited measures of individual potential, they claim. Such objective measures of academic performance may not identify applicants who have "a deep love of learning" or "a capacity for high academic achievement," much less those who "will contribute most in later life to their professions and their communities," they say. Earlier Ivy League presidents would have added "character" to the list, but the notion of judging who will contribute most to "their professions and their communities" may amount to the same thing.

These are disturbingly subjective criteria, and it is well to recall that in the past they were applied in a manner that few would defend today. Isaac Levine from P.S. 164 in Brooklyn had a straight-A record and 1480 on the SATs, but Yale would have had too many Jews if it took him. Bowen and Bok tell us that "adding an extra carrot rather than one more potato" to the stew "may make excellent sense—and be eminently 'fair'—if there are already lots of potatoes in the pot." This metaphor is profoundly revealing—more revealing than its authors realize. Winthrop Brooks IV of Andover Academy might be the extra carrot that was needed. Despite his mediocre academic qualifications, he would likely "contribute" more to society when he joined his father's investment banking firm after graduation. Doubtless he had a better "character" as well, at least as character was rated by Yale admissions officers. Yale had enough students of Levine's "kind," and needed more of Brooks's kind. A supposedly nuanced judgment of competing individuals, in this instance, would have been made on the basis of gross ethnic and social class stereotypes.

Decisions like these amounted to naked discrimination against Jews, and were indefensible. And yet we wonder what Bowen and Bok would have to say about the matter. Their very long book about admissions to elite schools never mentions this unsavory history, although it seems extremely pertinent. It may seem difficult to deny that Jewish quotas were discriminatory, but that conclusion rests on the assumption that grades and test scores are a reasonable measure of the qualifications of an applicant to college—a reasonable gauge of his or her "merit." Once you relativize and racialize merit, as Bowen and Bok do, it is impossible to say that any unsuccessful candidate has been treated unfairly. "Sure, Levine was a good potato, but we had enough potatoes. We really needed more carrots in the pot."

Fortunately, academic merit as measured by high school grades and test scores matters far more to admissions officers at Harvard, Princeton, and other elite schools than Bowen and Bok would have us believe. Their stew metaphor implies that such institutions don't want too many students with exceptional academic qualifications—a stew with nothing but beef would not be very tasty. Presumably the carrots, potatoes, bay leaf, and thyme are people with weaker grades and lower SATs but other outstanding characteristics. However, a glance at any of the standard guides to colleges and universities will reveal that the average student admitted to such schools has SAT scores in the top 2 to 3 percent and ranks at or very close to the top of his or her high school class. Princeton cannot be accepting significant numbers of applicants whose grades and test scores are merely average or below average because it is convinced they nonetheless have a "deep love for learning," a "special rural perspective," or some other equally fuzzy attribute.

The authors' scorn for standardized tests even leads them to remark in a footnote that "Martin Luther King, Jr., now regarded as one of the great orators of this century, scored in the bottom half of all test-takers" on the verbal portion of the Graduate Record Examination. But of course no one defends SATs and GREs on the grounds that they identify people with Dr. King's remarkable talents. These tests, however, do a good job in predicting academic performance, numerous studies have shown.

All of Bowen and Bok's rhetoric about how "merit" is a multifaceted, relative, many-splendored thing is designed to obscure a simple and regrettable fact. If students were admitted to the most selective colleges and universities strictly on the basis of their academic merit, the number of African Americans and Hispanics who would be successful in the competition would be very small.

Some figures from California illustrate the problem vividly. Admission to a campus of the University of California, the best state university system in the country, is guaranteed to state residents who rank in the top eighth of their high school graduating class. Grades are the primary criterion, but SAT scores are also considered in determining the list of students deemed to have the merit to make them "UC-eligible."

What is the racial mix among the UC-eligibles? The most recent data available are for 1999, and indicate that just 2.8 percent of African-American public high school seniors in the state had strong enough records to be guaranteed a place at the University of California. The proportion was only slightly higher—3.8 percent—for Latino students. This did not mean, though, that non-Hispanic whites had more than their proportional share of places in the top-eighth group. In fact, 12.4 percent of California's white 12th-graders ranked in the top 12.5 percent. The only group of overachievers was Asian Americans. An astonishing 31.5 percent met the requirements for admission. Asian-American students were 2.5 times more likely than their white classmates to qualify for admission to the University of California—a stunning achievement. At the two most prestigious and competitive schools in the UC system—Berkeley and UCLA—four out of ten students are Asian American. Remarkably, they outnumber whites on both campuses, even though there are four times as many whites as Asians in the population of California as a whole.

These huge racial disparities, it should be noted, cannot be blamed on the allegedly discriminatory nature of the SATs.[2] A 1997 study by the UC administration demolishes that common argument.[3] It found that if grades alone determined who is UC-eligible, the number of Hispanic students admitted would rise slightly—by 5 percent. The proportion of Asians would decline a bit—by 3 percent. The two groups most affected would be blacks and whites, but the effects would be precisely the opposite of what SAT critics maintain. The number of blacks admitted would *decline* by 18 percent if the SAT were eliminated from consideration, and the number of whites would *rise* by 17 percent. The racial mix of the entering class would have looked even less balanced racially than it actually was with SAT scores factored in.

Suppose that we wanted to make the student body of the University of California more representative of the population of the state. Proportional representation is the norm implicit in all proposals for engineering "diversity" by means of racial double standards in admissions. Bowen and Bok, we believe, are being disingenuous when they deny that they advocate proportional representation at elite schools. They may not insist upon going all the way to precise racial and ethnic proportionality, and indeed the pool of "qualified" black and Hispanic applicants, even by their expansive definition, is too small to attain proportionality. But the central theme of their long book is that without racial preferences, not enough non-Asian minorities would attend elite colleges, although it's not clear how they can conclude that a freshman class that is, say, 2 to 3 percent black does not have enough African Americans without some standard of what a sufficient share would be. And what could that standard be except the black share of the total population?

California could make the UC student body match the racial mix of the state's population by taking Bowen and Bok's relativistic conception of merit to its logical conclusion. It could simply declare that the top 12.5 percent of students *from each racial group* are qualified. If merit is relative to social circumstances, why not? That would quadruple black enrollment, triple Latino enrollment, and leave the white share of UC-eligibles completely unchanged.

The only losers would be Asian Americans, whose share would be cut by nearly two-thirds (dropping from 31.5 percent to 12.5 percent). The performance of an Asian-American high school student who hoped to attend the University of California would then be appraised not in comparison to all other students in the state but relative to that of other Asian Americans. People of Asian descent would be rejected even though their academic records were far stronger than those of whites, as well as blacks and Hispanics.[4] What principled objection could Bowen and Bok make to that? For them, after all, "fairness" in admissions does not mean that "grades and test scores must always be considered more important than other qualities and characteristics, so that no student with a B average can be accepted as long as students with As are being turned down."

Employing racial double standards in admissions, we have demonstrated in detail, elsewhere, does not have the benign effects Bowen and Bok attribute to them, and has many unintended negative consequences we lack the space to spell out here.[5] Suffice it to say that racial preferences reinforce the dreadful stereotype that blacks just aren't academically talented. And they involve the arbitrary assignment of individuals to racial and ethnic categories, and assume it is legitimate to offer them different opportunities depending upon the group to which they have been assigned. They state that race-neutral admissions are "unworthy of our country's ideals" and seem to believe that the sorting of American citizens along lines of race and ethnicity is what the framers of the Fourteenth Amendment had in mind. It is true that judging citizens by the color of their skin is indeed as American as apple pie. But the civil rights warriors of the 1950s and 1960s did not put their lives on the line to perpetuate such terrible habits of mind, we firmly believe, and their vision of a color-blind society was embodied in the Civil Rights Act of 1964.

In the concluding pages of their book, Bowen and Bok issue a warning. If forced to choose, today's educational leaders will see creating a certain racial mix on campus as more important than maintaining intellectual standards. Here we have a breathtakingly candid statement of the priorities of two of the most distinguished figures in higher education today—priorities that reflect those of the higher education establishment as a whole. Intellectual excellence should be sacrificed on the altar of diversity.

This repugnant trade-off would not be necessary, of course, if we concentrated our efforts on closing the yawning racial gap in educational performance among elementary and secondary school pupils. The massive database compiled by the National Assessment of Educational Progress reveals that the average African-American high school senior today reads at the same level as the average white or Asian in the eighth grade, and Hispanics do little better. Racial differentials are even sharper at the extremes of the distribution. Black and Latino high school graduates with academic records that would qualify them for admission to elite colleges and universities are in pathetically short supply, as the California evidence cited above makes clear.

As long as the average black high school senior reads at the eighth-grade level, efforts to engineer parity in the academy are doomed to failure. For a generation now, racial preferences in higher education have been a pernicious palliative that has deflected our attention from the real problem: the need for much better schooling in the pre-K–12 years. That desperate need is *the* civil rights issue of our time.

Comprehension Questions

1. What does the account of Stephen Carter suggest about race as a factor in college admissions?
2. What is Bowen and Bok's attitude about the issue of race in college admissions?
3. How does Bowen and Bok's proposal resemble anti-Jewish discrimination in college admissions in the early twentieth century?
4. In what way does using race as a criterion in college admissions make the idea of merit subjective or relative?

5. The Thernstroms think that there are problems with trying to make the racial makeup of a collegiate student body representative of the larger population. What are they?
6. What negative effects do the Thernstroms attribute to the practice of using race to evaluate college applicants?
7. How do the Thernstroms think we should deal with the relative lack of racial minorities in higher education?

Discussion Questions

1. The Thernstroms compare using race to evaluate college applicants with quotas for admitting Jewish applicants into higher education in the early twentieth century. Both cases obviously involve discrimination. Is discrimination immoral in both cases, as they claim? Why or why not?
2. Letting race influence admissions decisions will make evaluating applicants subjective, the Thernstroms say. How do you imagine someone like Bowen and Bok would respond? Do you agree that taking race into account must make such judgments subjective? Why or why not?
3. Imagine you were a close friend of Stephen Carter, and that he related his story (as portrayed by the Thernstroms) to you right after receiving the phone call regarding his admittance to Harvard and asked for your advice. Would you recommend that he go to Harvard or not? What reasons would you give him?

Case

After losing in a number of lower courts, the US Supreme Court is going to consider Abigail Fisher's lawsuit against the University of Texas at Austin. Fisher—who is white—has accused UT of having a racially discriminatory admission policy. (By the time this book makes it to your hands, the case may well have been decided. Google it!) Her case raises the question of whether race should have *any* role in admission decisions. Here's a summary of the situation:

> If you want entrance to UT Austin and you live in Texas, you have three options: You can score in the top 10 percent of your high school class, which grants you automatic entry; you can try for the non–top 10 slots; or, if your grades are weak, you can attend a satellite campus and transfer, provided [that you have] good grades and a strong course load.

When Fisher applied in 2008 . . . the UT Austin filled 92 percent of its in-state spots with students from the top 10 program. She wasn't among them. With a 3.59 grade-point average and a modest SAT score of 1180 out of 1600, she was a solid student but not a great one, not for a school with . . . an extremely low acceptance rate (comparable to Harvard's) for in-state students admitted outside of top 10.

For the remaining 8 percent of in-state spots, UT Austin used a comprehensive approach that weighed grades and test scores along with essays, leadership, activities, service to the community, and "special circumstances." Those ranged from socioeconomic status and school quality, to family background and race. As the university's director of admissions explained . . . "[R]ace provides—like language, whether or not someone is the first in their family to attend college, and family responsibilities—important context in which to evaluate applicants, and is only one aspect of the diversity that the University seeks to attain."

Neither special circumstances nor grades were determinative. Of the 841 students admitted under these criteria, 47 had worse AI/PAI scores (a combination of the holistic measure, grades, and test scores) than Fisher, and 42 of them were white. On the other end, UT rejected 168 black and Latino students with scores equal to or better than Fisher's.[6]

As those 168 black and Latino students might point out, it's clear that race isn't a *decisive* factor in UT's admission policy. You don't get in just based on that factor. Given this, do you think that Fisher has the right to complain? Is it wrong to give race *any* weight? Why or why not?

Notes

1. The history of Jewish admissions quotas at Harvard, Yale, and Princeton is well told in Marcia Graham Synnott, *The Half-Opened Door: Discrimination and Admissions at Harvard, Yale, and Princeton* (Westport, CT: Greenwood Press, 1979). Synnott's account is too soft on Harvard, though, because key internal Harvard documents were not open to scholars when her research was being conducted. For the full story, based upon much newly available evidence, see Morton Keller and Phyllis Keller, *Making Harvard Modern: The Rise of America's University* (New York: Oxford University Press, 2001), which also includes disturbing evidence of Harvard's reluctance to appoint Jews to the faculty in the 1930s and 1940s.

2. See our critical appraisals of the most popular recent book attacking the SATs, Nicolas Lemann's *The Big Test* (1999); Stephan Thernstrom, "Status Anxiety," *National Review*, December 6, 1999, and Abigail Thernstrom, "Shooting the Messenger," *Times Literary Supplement*, June 9, 2000.

3. University of California, Office of the President, Student Academic Services, *University of California Follow-up Analyses of the 1996 CPEC Eligibility Study*, 1997.

4. If this seems too fanciful, it should be noted that for many years the best public high school in San Francisco, Lowell High, operated a racial quota that worked exactly this way. An examination was used to sift out applicants, and Chinese-American students had to get a higher score than other Asians, with a lower cutoff score for whites and a still lower one for blacks and Hispanics. The San Francisco Unified School District was forced to abandon the system in 1999, after it was sued by Chinese parents complaining that the system deprived their children of the equal protection of the laws guaranteed them by the Fourteenth Amendment.

5. For a detailed and highly critical evaluation of Bowen and Bok's work, see Stephan Thernstrom and Abigail Thernstrom, "Reflections on *The Shape of the River*," *UCLA Law Review* 46, June 1999. A somewhat shorter version of this paper that includes newer evidence is "Racial Preferences in Higher Education: An Assessment of the Evidence," in *One America? Political Leadership, National Identity, and the Dilemmas of Diversity*, ed. Stanley A. Renshon (Washington, DC: Georgetown University Press, 2001).

6. http://www.slate.com/articles/news_and_politics/politics/2015/06/fisher_v_university_of_texas_the_supreme_court_might_just_gut_affirmative.html

PART V

Speech and Protest

23

≡ 𝕓 ≡

Words That Wound

Richard Delgado and Jean Stefancic

In the following excerpts from Richard Delgado and Jean Stefancic's book *Understanding Words That Wound*, the authors take care first to untangle the knot of conceptual distinctions connected to the phenomenon of hate speech—distinctions concerning its target, how it's embodied, and the type of harm it can cause. They describe the physical, psychological, and economic damage hate speech can do to its victims, as well as the potential harm suffered by its perpetrators and society at large. Delgado and Stefancic explain what makes hate speech an especially important issue in the college and university setting, as well as the constitutional principles that generate conflicting judgments about the legitimacy of hate speech regulation. Lastly, they entertain—but ultimately reject—the worry that hate speech regulation tends to have an undesirable "chilling effect" on campus discourse.

What Is Hate Speech?

Many people speak loosely about hate speech, without specifying what they mean or distinguishing the various types of utterance that might be under consideration. This is a sure recipe for analytical unclarity and policy disaster.

One can consider hate speech along various axes, including direct and indirect, veiled or overt, single or repeated, backed by authority and power or not, and accompanied by threat of violence or not. One can also consider hate speech based on the characteristic of the person or group at which it is aimed, such as race, sex, sexual orientation, or national origin. Hate speech can be targeted against one individual ("Smith, you goddamn African American, you are a . . ."). It can be directed against a small group (such as a black fraternity at a college campus). Or it can be aimed at a group in general ("I hate Xs; they should be thrown out of this country"). It can be delivered orally, in writing, or on the Internet. It can even take tangible form, such as a monument, flag, or sports logo.

Finally, one should differentiate hate speech in terms of who is doing the speaking—a teacher, a passerby, a public speaker, three hoodlums surrounding a small victim on a dark night, or an educated, genteel author who writes about the "X problem," making clear that the problem with Xs is not the way they are treated but their culture or genes. . . .

Individual Harms of Hate Speech

The harms of hate speech include its adverse impacts—sometimes devastating ones—on the victim, the speaker, and society at large. The harms vary, of course, according to the type of hate speech. The more diffuse kind—for example, "All niggers are inferior and should go back to Africa"—is apt to be more harmful to society in general. The more targeted variety—"You goddamn nigger, go back to Africa"—harms society as well, particularly cumulatively, but its principal impact is felt by the individual victim.

Physical Harms

Hate speech is not merely unpleasant or offensive. It may leave physical impacts on those it visits, particularly when uttered in one-on-one situations accompanied by at least an implicit threat—that is, by someone taller, larger, older, or more powerful than the victim or in a position of authority vis-à-vis him or her. The same is true when the hate speaker is a member of a group engaged in taunting a single member of a disempowered minority faction. Then, the response is internalized, as it must be, for talking back will be futile or even dangerous. In fact, many hate crimes have taken place when the victim did just that—spoke back to the aggressor and paid with his or her life.

The immediate, short-term harms of hate speech include rapid breathing, headaches, raised blood pressure, dizziness, rapid pulse rate, drug-taking, risk-taking behavior, and even suicide.[1] The stresses of repeated racial abuse may have long-term consequences, including damaged self-image, lower aspiration level, and depression.[2] Scientists suspect that the high blood pressure many African Americans suffer is associated with inhibited, constrained, or restricted anger, in addition to genetic factors.[3] American blacks exhibit higher rates of high blood pressure and higher death rates from hypertension, hypertensive disease, and stroke than do similarly situated whites.[4] . . .

Psychological Harms

In addition to the immediate physical harms—flinching, clenching, tightening of muscles, adrenaline rush, and the other somatic consequences of a sudden verbal assault—hate speech can cause mental and psychological effects. These include fear, nightmares, and withdrawal from society—what Joe Feagin and his collaborator call an impotent despair.[5] The victim of hate speech, especially the one who fears more of the same, may behave circumspectly, avoiding the situations, places, and company where it could happen again. Needless to say, this "cultural mistrust," a mild form of healthy paranoia, has implications for both the mental health and professional chances of minority workers.[6] Other victims will respond with anger, either internalized or acted out (neither of which is calculated to make things better).[7] They are also likely to curtail their own speech, so as not to provoke more ridicule, put-downs, or revilement. Self-esteem may wither.

Victims may reject identification with their own race, the very feature that brought about the verbal attack.[8] Or, conversely, they may affect a kind of false bravado, in which they try to convince themselves "It doesn't get to me—I just let it roll off my back." Alternatively, the person may rationalize—the speaker was just ignorant, or targeted him or her not because of race but some other feature. . . .

Some victims may take refuge in alcohol, drugs, or other self-defeating escapes.[9] This is true not only for blacks; three recent studies of Mexican Americans have found that experience with discrimination is associated with increased levels of stress, suffering, depression, and life dissatisfaction.[10] Finally, social scientists who have studied the effects of disrespectful treatment and labeling have demonstrated that speech that communicates low regard for an individual because of race tends, over time, to create in the victim the very traits of inferiority that it assigns.[11]

Scholars who have studied the effects of racism and racist epithets on children believe that youthful victims are among the most easily damaged by racial epithets and name-calling. Children as young as three develop consciousness of race; they know, furthermore, that race makes a difference, and that it is better to be of some races than others.[12]

... Children who bear the brunt of such language can respond in one of two ways. They can respond aggressively, such as by shouting back at or striking the one who insulted them. Or, they can behave passively and pretend to ignore the aggression. Neither response is successful. Children who behave aggressively in school or elsewhere are marked as troublemakers, adding to their alienation and rejection. . . . Children who behave passively in the face of their own scapegoating turn the harm inward; robbed of confidence and a sense of ease, these children become defensive, morose, and introverted. This effect is compounded when the parents, who may suffer discrimination themselves, bring their problems home so that they have less energy to devote to their children.[13]

Tangible and Economic Harms

The harms of hate speech go beyond damage to the psyches and bodies of its victims. It can also affect their pecuniary prospects and life chances. Recent studies show that minority students at white-dominated universities may earn lower GPAs and standardized test scores as a result of the stress of studying and living in racially charged environments.[14] The person who is timid, bitter, tense, or defensive as a result of frequent encounters with racism is likely to fare poorly in employment and other settings as well.[15] Claude Steele's pioneering experiments with "stereotype threat" show that the bearers of stereotypes perform poorly when placed in competitive situations that remind them of society's expectation that they will fail.[16] . . . Finally, racism closes off career options. Many minority youths are apt to favor careers, such as the army, the post office, public school teaching, or social work, where prejudice is low, rather than ones—business, accounting, journalism— where prejudice is much more likely to affect one's chances.[17]

Is a racial insult or epithet more serious than one based on other characteristics, such as weight, age group, or physical appearance? Yes.

Unlike those other personal characteristics, a person can do nothing to change his or her race. Moreover, race cuts closer to the core of a person's identity than does physique, age, or hair color. Thus, an insult like "You damn nigger. Why don't you . . ." is apt to cause more distress and be less easily shrugged off than "You damn woman driver (student driver, old fart driver), why don't you get off the road!" The driver may feel bad about the insult, especially if it was deserved. But the driver knows that he or she spends only part of the day driving and that in other areas of life he or she may be unusually competent.[18]

Also, racial insults and name-calling evoke and call up a specific history—including violence, lynching, Indian wars, and signs barring Latinos and blacks—that ones based on fatness or clumsiness do not. The recipient of a racial epithet is likely to know of this history and recognize the cultural weight—and maybe the veiled threat—behind it.[19]

Harms to the Perpetrator and to Society as a Whole

Finally, racial hate speech harms the perpetrator and society as a whole.[20] Bigots suffer when their narrow, categorical thinking etches in a little deeper. They fail to develop a universal moral sense that extends to all persons. They can easily develop a mildly paranoid mentality with respect to the group they routinely disparage. . . . They will fail to learn one of life's most useful lessons—that people of other races and types are just like [the people of] my own: some good, some bad.[21]

Society at large suffers, as well, when hate speech goes unpunished. It is a visible, dramatic breach of one of our most deeply felt ideals, that "all men are created equal." A society in which some, but not all, must run a gauntlet of racial abuse and stigmatization scarcely exemplifies this ideal. A racial insult conveys to all who hear or learn about it that equality and equal respect are of little value. Even those who do not take part in the system of racist speech may find themselves demoralized when they realize how often social norms of equality and brotherhood are breached and how far we are, as a group, from living in an egalitarian, humane society.[22]

Racism, including the verbal kind, also contributes to a class system, one in which some regularly confront hurdles and road blocks that others do not in obtaining a job, taking out a loan, or simply walking down the street.[23] At a minimum, every person of color expends an enormous amount of energy dealing with discrimination, including the many daily decisions of what to confront and what to let go.[24] It goes without saying that American democracy is, by its nature, antithetical to a class society.

The injuries inflicted by racist hate speech are neither minimal nor unserious. Social scientists who have studied hate crime know that the effects are more long-lasting than they are when the same crime is committed without a racial or similar motivation.[25] Any crime shatters one's self-confidence and sense of personal security. A person who is assaulted and robbed on the sidewalk in front of his or her home will take months, if not years, to recover. But one who is assaulted and robbed by a perpetrator who shouts racial abuse at the same time and makes clear that the victim was selected because of race will brood about the event longer and take longer to return to a normal level of self-confidence in going about the world. The same is true of hate speech.

College and University Students: The Case of Campus Hate Speech (and Conduct) Codes

College and university students . . ., particularly seventeen- and eighteen-year-old freshmen, may be traversing the final stages of personality development and are still vulnerable to assaults on their personhood and self-esteem. College hate speech brings all these issues into play, plus a powerful countervailing First Amendment interest, since colleges and universities are places of intellectual and academic inquiry where speech, ideally, should be as free as possible.

Literally hundreds of colleges and universities have enacted some type of hate speech code.[26] Some regulate hate speech directly, by means of a specific regulation designating it as a campus offense and providing some form of sanction. Others regulate it under a general provision—that is, without naming it directly—such as a rule requiring that members of the campus community treat each other with respect or desist from interfering with each other's ability to study, work, or enjoy the privileges of campus life.[27]

Why the great interest in regulating hate speech on campus, and why do campuses often rely on before-the-event regulations, as opposed to (for example) tort actions or suits for harassment or hostile environment brought after the fact? Colleges have not been shy about explaining their reasons. Campus hate speech is ubiquitous, and increasing . . . [The] average undergraduate of color experiences hate speech (depending on how narrowly or broadly it is defined) frequently, as often as once a day.[28] These experiences have measurable effects: Students of color may drop out, feeling threatened and demoralized. Others hear about incidents of unredressed hate speech at a given college and choose not to go there. "I have to deal with racism the rest of my life," one said. "Why should I deal with that in college?"[29] . . . Another study showed that tolerating a hostile environment for minority students caused them to earn lower grades.[30] One professor described the role of "racial microaggressions" in keeping minority students on edge.[31] Professors of color, too, consider the climate of a school in deciding where to apply for a teaching position.

In addition to these consequences, hate speech simply looks bad, especially when it takes the form of mediacentric events, such as the following, that attract the press and TV cameras.

- At a major Western university, concern for the safety of Muslims became a prominent issue when hate-filled messages appeared on the pillars of the campus library and anonymous hate messages were left on the voice recorder of the Muslim Students Association.[32]
- At a famous military academy, five white cadets, clad in white sheets and cone-shaped masks, awoke a black cadet who was sleeping in his room. After shouting obscenities, they fled, leaving behind a charred cross made of newspaper. After reporting the incident, the black cadet suffered further harassment for having gone to the authorities, and later resigned from the academy. The school took no action other than recommending ethnic awareness classes for all cadets.[33]

  . . .

- At another elite public university, a drunk fraternity member shouted epithets at a group of passing black students; later a campus disc jockey told black students who had demanded that the station play rap music to go back where they came from. Still later, members of a gay and lesbian group reported that an anonymous caller had left a phone message urging that people like them should be taken out and gassed as Hitler did with the Jews. The campus responded by stepping up awareness training and enacting a policy prohibiting "those personally abusive epithets which, when directly addressed to any ordinary person, are likely to provoke a violent reaction whether or not they actually do so."[34]

  . . .

Why do events like these happen? What is going on in the minds of the perpetrators? . . . [I]gnorance certainly cannot account for more than a small fraction of campus hate speech, including some of the more glaring examples in the list immediately above. A leading authority, Lu-in Wang, wrote that much hate behavior is opportunistic and dependent on context or setting. The perpetrator finds himself in a situation—perhaps in the company of others of his race and seeing a lone member of an out-group—in which he knows that a push, shove, blow, or epithet will go unpunished. It may bring rewards, enabling the hate speaker/actor to bond with his peer group or terrorize the member of the out-group, thereby enhancing his own group's standing. Relatively few hate incidents are planned and intentional, beginning with a perpetrator who consciously decides to go looking for a member of a minority group to oppress. The hardcore, animus-driven perpetrator is the exception, not the rule. Many hate speakers and actors hardly know why they act or speak as they do. They never calculate in advance; they may gain little from the act; afterward, they may be astonished at what they did.[35]

. . .

The Structure of the Campus Hate Speech Code Controversy

The campus hate speech controversy contains a few elements that are not present elsewhere in the discourse on hate speech, in part because hate speech codes, unlike tort or criminal law rules, operate before, not after, the fact. The latter approaches punish speech in familiar ways that cut across large categories of conduct. Like rules against conspiracy, threat, false advertising, and copyright infringement, they punish speech and communication. But they are familiar and uncontroversial; no one today suggests that laws against plagiarism, for example, are unconstitutional, even if sometimes it is a black, brown, or low-income plaintiff who charges a white, privileged defendant with violating a general norm.

Scholars (including us) have pointed out that the campus hate speech controversy features two constitutional narratives in collision.[36] Both narratives, equality and free speech, are deeply rooted in our traditions. Equality proponents point out, with considerable justification, that campus hate speech offends values of equal citizenship and equal dignity.[37]

Especially when concerted, hate speech marginalizes its victims and relegates them to second-class roles.[38] But, by the same token, laws against hate speech diminish the free-speech interests of the hate speaker; they limit speech, another value of high importance in our scale of constitutional rights.[39] Without a code of some sort, free speech would violate equality; but, with a code, equality interests intrude on free speech—on what people can say. Striking the right balance between equality and speech is, to say the least, a delicate and value-laden task.[40]

Another feature present in the campus hate speech situation is incessancy. Campus administrators worried about hate speech, and victims filing charges under the codes, are not worried so much about the damage from a single incident as the compounding or aggregate effect of many such incidents.[41] A victim who experienced just one attack of hate speech might laugh it off, or wonder what on earth the speaker meant. The problem is that the victim of hate speech—for example, a black or gay undergraduate—is apt to experience many such offenses, in a nearly daily rain of insults, aspersions, loaded language, anonymous e-mail messages, and social exclusion. Like water dripping on limestone, hate speech scars through its frequent repetition. How to curtail the underlying behavior, not to mention apportion punishment, is a challenging task.

The Backlash: Reverse Victimization and the "Diversity Hoax" Argument

Not only is the task challenging, it is by its nature misguided, according to some critics of hate speech regulation. These critics argue that hate speech guidelines are political correctness gone amok, that they curtail campus discussion, and that conservative or independent-minded maverick speakers are their main victims. A 1999 book by several graduates and students at the University of California (Boalt Hall) law school argued that hate speech codes, like affirmative action and other liberal measures, constitute a diversity hoax.[42] One aspect of this hoax is that conservative speakers end up silenced in the classroom and elsewhere. They are now the main victims of liberal and civil rights orthodoxy....[43]

How seriously should we take this argument? Despite the book's laments about political correctness, hate speech seems not at all to have been silenced ... but is growing in frequency and severity. The same is true for its more sophisticated, civilized counterparts—books such as *The Bell Curve*, call-in radio, and Web sites touting white supremacy are growing in numbers. Most campuses, executive boardrooms, and the officer ranks of the military are predominantly white. White thoughts, ideas, and power are in little danger of being suppressed. How many white readers, for example, could name more than three famous historical figures who are black, Latino, or Asian? Minority persons of the most minimal level of literacy could name many more—as well as dozens of famous figures who are white.

Comprehension Questions

1. What physical harms can hate speech cause for its victims?
2. How does hate speech psychologically affect its recipients?
3. In what ways does hate speech negatively impact its targets' economic prospects?
4. Why do Delgado and Stefancic think hate speech isn't just harmful for its victims, but also both for those who perpetrate it and for society as a whole?
5. Why do universities adopt measures to regulate hate speech themselves rather than relying on the legal system?
6. What two constitutional principles are most pertinent to the issue of hate speech, and what stance do they recommend toward it?
7. What negative affects do some claim that hate speech regulation has caused, and what do Delgado and Stefancic make of that claim?

Discussion Questions

1. Delgado and Stefancic give numerous examples of physical, psychological, and economic harms that hate speech can cause. What additional examples can you come up with?
2. It is sometimes suggested that campus hate speech regulation might have the unfortunate consequence of inhibiting people's legitimate self-expression. Do you think that is true? Can you think of any instances where this has happened at your institution?
3. Does your institution have a policy specifically dealing with hate speech? What is it? In light of the different approaches to the issue discussed by Delgado and Stefancic, do you think your institution's policy is acceptable? Would you recommend any changes?

Case

Consider this story:

> Yik Yak is a location-based, anonymous social media app that's all the rage among college students—including those who like to spread a little hate, sexism and other joys. . . . But the thing about Yik Yak . . . that makes it worthy of America's collective attention right now is that the young men who founded it actually had what they considered a pretty noble social mission. It turns out it just might not have been one suited for the modern age. . . .

> Yik Yak, the founders said in early interviews, was the app for that guy (or girl) who may be the funniest or the smartest person in the room but doesn't, for whatever reason, feel that he or she can speak up. The combination of anonymity and the chance to post to a running feed available in its entirety only to people on or near specific college campuses would free that silenced person to make salient and sometimes really hilarious observations about the world.

> Yik Yak's founders later told the New York Times that they envisioned a "democratic" social media app. This would be the place where the quality of the comment and the community's response to it would determine how long it remained visible. They wanted to create Twitter without the risk of the cool-kids-with-lots-of-followers club.

> They hadn't expected that members of a Rowan University frat would use it to post a sex tape filmed—or at the very least posted—without the consent of a woman involved. They hadn't anticipated that female and minority professors would face particular challenges with the kind of commentary posted about them on Yik Yak. They hadn't anticipated that users in places as wide-ranging as Mississippi, Vermont, Alabama, and New York would use the app to post threats of bombings and mass shootings or to suggest other forms of coordinated violence.

> They hadn't anticipated the intense online bullying on Yik Yak at high schools (high school access has since been disabled). They hadn't expected that flippant comments about sexual violence and other danger would be directed at women so often that a group of seventy-two feminist organizations would file a Title IX civil rights complaint with the US Department of Education in October. The complaint claims that the failure of schools to in some way regulate the app or limit access to it violates the responsibility of educational institutions to foster environments where everyone can learn and participate without the damaging influence of threats and harassment. They didn't expect to see Yik Yak mentioned in connection with a story about a Washington murder.[44]

Given the arguments that Delgado and Stefancic make, what should individuals—and colleges—do about Yik Yak? Should you boycott it, given how people have been using it? Should colleges ask Yik Yak to create a geo-fence that prohibits use on campus? Alternately, should they simply discourage the use of Yik Yak without trying to enforce a ban? Finally, can some technologies foster hate speech, and if so, can they be blamed for that?

Notes

1. See, e.g., Richard Delgado and Jean Stefancic, *Must We Defend Nazis? Hate Speech, Pornography, and the New First Amendment*, 5–10 (1997); Joe R. Feagin and Karyn D. McKinney, *The Many Costs of Racism*, 6–38, 65–93 (2003) [hereinafter, *Many Costs of Racism*]; Joe R. Feagin, Kevin E. Early, and Karyn D. McKinney, *The Many Costs of Discrimination: The Case of Middle-Class African Americans*, 34 Ind. L. Rev. 1313, 1323–1328, 1346–1357 (2001) [hereinafter, *Many Costs*].
2. E.g., *Many Costs*, supra, at 1328–1346, 1354–1356.
3. *Defend Nazis?*, supra, at 6; *Many Costs*, supra, at 1350–1352.
4. *Defend Nazis?*, supra, at 6.
5. *Many Costs*, supra, at 1328–1334.
6. Ibid. at 1323 et seq.
7. Ibid. at 1323–1328.
8. Ibid. at 1334–1335; *Defend Nazis?*, supra, at 5, 10.
9. *Defend Nazis?*, supra, at 6, 91–92, 133.
10. *Many Costs*, supra, at 1335.
11. *Defend Nazis?*, supra, at 5, 7, 9.
12. *Defend Nazis?*, supra, at 6, 8; Debra Van Ausdale and Joe R. Feagin, *The First R: How Children Learn Race and Racism* (2001).
13. *First R*, supra; *Defend Nazis?*, supra, at 8, 10; *Many Costs*, supra, at 1354–1357.
14. See Chapter 6, this volume; text and notes immediately supra.
15. *Defend Nazis?*, supra, at 5–7.
16. Claude M. Steele and Joshua Aronson, *Stereotype Threat and the Intellectual Test Performance of African Americans*, 69 J. Personality and Soc. Psychol. 797 (1995).
17. See, for example, the extensive writing of scholar Charles Moskos on this subject.
18. *Defend Nazis?*, supra, at 5–10.
19. Ibid. at 4–10; *Many Costs*, supra, at 23–25, 52–53. On this history, see Juan Perea et al., *Race and Races* (2000).
20. *Defend Nazis?*, supra, at 4, 7.
21. Ibid. at 7.
22. Ibid.
23. Ibid. at 7–8.
24. Ibid.; *Many Costs of Racism*, supra, at 39–64, 119–146.

25. Frederick M. Lawrence, *The Punishment of Hate: Toward a Normative Theory of Bias-Motivated Crimes*, 93 Mich. L. Rev. 320, 342–343 (1994).
26. See, e.g., Jon B. Gould (2001). "The Precedent that Wasn't: College Hate Speech Codes and the Two Faces of Legal Compliance," 35 *L. & Soc. Rev.* 35, 352–53 (2001).
27. Ibid.
28. See Chapter 2; David Glenn, "Scholars Present Data in Hopes of Bolstering Legal Defense of Affirmative Action," *Chronicle of Higher Education*, August 20, 2002 (online edition, on file with author).
29. Isabel Wilkerson, "Racial Harassment Altering Blacks' Chances in College," *New York Times*, May 9, 1990, at A1.
30. "Scholars Present Data," supra.
31. Ibid.
32. Jessika Fruchter, "U. Colorado Students Deface Library with Anti-Arab Graffiti," *U. Wire*, September 20, 2001.
33. Richard Delgado and Jean Stefancic, *Must We Defend Nazis? Hate Speech, Pornography, and the New First Amendment*, 49–50 (1997).
34. Ibid. at 51.
35. See Lu-in Wang. (1999). "The Complexities of 'Hate,'" *Ohio St. L.J.* 60, 799.
36. *Defend Nazis?* supra, at 46–49, 62–66.
37. Ibid. at 47–48, 65–67.
38. Ibid. at 66–68.
39. Ibid. at 62–65.
40. *See* Richard Delgado and Jean Stefancic, *Hateful Speech, Loving Communities: Why Our Notion of "A Just Balance" Changes So Slowly*, 82 Cal. L. Rev. 851 (1994).
41. *Defend Nazis?*, supra, at 66–68.
42. David Wienir and Marc Berley, eds., *The Diversity Hoax: Law Students Report from Berkeley* (1999).
43. Ibid.
44. https://www.washingtonpost.com/news/the-fix/wp/2015/11/12/yik-yak-might-not-encourage-racism-and-threats-but-it-certainly-enables-them/

24

Campus Speech Restrictions

Martin Golding

....

We consider our First Amendment right to free speech so fundamental that we are rightly suspicious of anything that looks like an infringement of it. At the same time, we recognize that some forms of speech can be very damaging. Think of racist, sexist, and, in general, discriminatory speech. In recent decades there has been a great deal of discussion about restricting such speech on campus. Can discriminatory speech be so damaging that it ought to be prohibited? In taking up this question Martin Golding opts to answer, with some hesitation, in the negative. Discriminatory speech is surely immoral, but he denies that college or university professionals are in any position to evaluate such psychological injuries. Golding worries, moreover, that if, for instance, racist insults deserve restricting, then racist opinion more generally also does. Hence, he doubts restrictions of discriminatory speech can be clearly separated from unjustified censorship, and must therefore be avoided.

....

Varieties of Speech Restrictions

The campus speech code movement is declared by Samuel Walker to be the most successful American effort to restrict speech.[1] But Walker also

Golding, Martin P. 2000. "Campus Speech Restrictions." In *Free Speech on Campus*. Lanham, MD: Rowman & Littlefield. Reprinted with permission.

suggests that the success was short-lived. He bases this judgment mainly on three court cases, two of them involving campus speech codes, and one, a city ordinance penalizing "hate" crimes.[2] The main constitutional defects found in the codes were vagueness (what does "stigmatizes or victimizes" mean?), overbreadth (reaching protected speech as well as some possibly unprotected speech), and violations of content- and viewpoint-neutrality (prohibiting some speech because of disagreement with its message). We shall not review these cases here.[3] Instead, we shall be looking at . . . articles that support speech codes. These articles give what I take to be the most powerful arguments, but I find them problematic nonetheless. . . .

Campus "atmosphere" and the mere existence of a speech code, as we have seen, can have the effect of inhibiting free trade in ideas, by chilling the expression of unacceptable or unpopular thoughts. Atmosphere can deter taking up controversial or "touchy" topics, even in law school classes, where one would expect them.[4] In 1993, one university (Minnesota) went so far as to offer to provide students and instructors, on request, with a "campus climate adviser" who would be present in the classroom to oversee discussions of race, gender, and diversity, to ensure that they are respectful and not insulting.[5] . . . Few people today are aware that in the 1960s members of the John Birch Society, a far-right group, tape-recorded professors' class lectures. Such actions clearly can have an intimidating effect on the expression, however respectful, of dissident or unpopular views.

Aside from speech codes, other speech-restricting devices are available. Many student activities receive funding through mandatory fees collected by a school, and they are dispersed to various groups by student councils and student governments. Some groups, however, may be highly benefited because their aims are favored, and others far less benefited because their aims are not favored. So, for example, there are instances of the defunding of dissident, usually conservative, student newspapers or organizations. At one time it was the defunding or deprivation of official recognition of radical, leftist groups such as the Students for a Democratic Society, the notorious SDS.[6] In contrast to such "nonofficial" speech restrictions as theft of newspapers and tearing down posters, these have a kind of official status.

University and college administrations have also moved against student publications and groups that are critical of them. Posters, flyers, and skits . . . that make fun of administration policies, but which arguably are expressions of ideas, have been ordered removed by administrations in knee-jerk reactions. Some of these policies concern such contentious topics as race, gender, and multiculturalism. The president of George Washington University stated that, while he supported freedom of the press, it was wrong to use student tuition dollars "to print newspapers that offend us."[7] So much for the vaunted importance of diversity, at least as far as diversity of ideas goes.[8]

Preliminaries on Speech Codes

We now have to examine arguments for speech codes and other such expression-restricting devices more directly, particularly, though not exclusively, as they might affect students. We shall focus on a group of writers, Critical Race Theorists, who make a powerful case for campus as well as noncampus speech restrictions. If their case does not succeed, it is not likely that any other case will.

But we should begin by agreeing on one thing: a "zero tolerance" code, a code that would prohibit *anything* that *anyone* finds offensive, is clearly unacceptable.

It would make campus life unbearable were it strictly enforced; it would prevent the discussion of any topic that might be "unwelcome" to any individual. And it's not just that people would have to think before they speak—ordinarily not a bad thing. In fact, though, such a code would not be uniformly enforced; certain occasions of speech would be punished and others not (often for ideological reasons), which is plainly unfair. Second, "merely offensive" expressions shouldn't be speech code violations. Such a rule would clearly be too restrictive and would contravene the university's own constitutional free speech provision, let alone the First Amendment.[9] And it probably won't help to say that "very offensive" speech should be prohibited. Burning the American flag in protest is very offensive to very many people but few defenders (faculty and students) of speech restrictions would want it to be a crime. To ask, then, what degree or kind of offensiveness one wants to prevent, requires that one consider *why* some forms of speech should be interdicted and others not.

And it is not just speech codes as such that are at issue. Some campuses do not have a code that is explicitly called a speech code. For example, Duke University prides itself on not having a speech code. But virtually all campuses have conduct codes, as student handbooks show, and these generally forbid *harassing* behavior, under which "verbal harassment" may be subject to punishment. . . .

When we speak of speech codes here, we mean to cover harassment codes that impinge on speech as well. Speech codes vary in their details, with too much variety to list here. The University of Michigan code covered classroom expressions while the University of Wisconsin code explicitly exempted the classroom, and it was also not applicable to faculty, which has its own code.[10] Some codes require that the proscribed language be used "intentionally," others allow for "strict liability." . . .

The writers we shall examine want to contextualize the First Amendment and to some extent I find this aspect of their thought congenial. I believe that the law should be interpreted and applied in a fact-sensitive way, that courts should take into account the social consequences of their decisions, and that interests have to be balanced. I think this is especially true with respect to the judicially developed common law, though too much fact-sensitivity can lead to the erosion of legal rules and principles. Nevertheless, I think that the case for contextualization is harder to make regarding the civil liberties enshrined in the Bill of Rights, and especially the liberties in the First Amendment. Only the most compelling case should allow us to intrude on these liberties. And because the freedom of speech is so vital to the work of universities, the same holds for the free speech provision of the university's constitution. In fact, the freedom of speech is so central to the activity of the university, the pursuit of knowledge, that it may be more important there than in society generally.

Words That Wound

[T]wo main, and interrelated, motivations for campus speech restrictions [are] promotion of a "comfortable learning environment" and protection from "verbal behavior" that may cause hurt. Students need to be protected from demeaning and denigrating speech if they are to be—and feel—equal on campus. Furthermore, punishing "hate speech" teaches people that racism or other prejudice is unacceptable and can bring about tolerance and sensitivity. It is also said, depending on how a code is formulated, that no legitimate campus speech is in fact prohibited.

On the other side, there is the objection, as a matter of principle, that a university has no business determining which ideas or expressions are acceptable and which groups or individuals deserve protection by limiting the speech of others; moreover, that speech codes suffer from difficulties in formulation in that they are vague and overly broad; and finally, that they allow too much discretion to those charged with their administration. All these points, pro and con, raise contentious matters.

Perhaps the most important academic writing in favor of speech restrictions, and not just in campus codes, comes from Critical Race Theory, written by authors of Asian, African-American, and Chicano descent, whose articles are reprinted in an important collection, *Words That Wound*.[11] These articles make a powerful case for campus speech restrictions. Their focus often tends to be narrow, that is, on race. As stated earlier, if their case does not succeed, it is not likely that any other case will. . . .

Drawing on the social sciences and their own life experience as minorities, the critical race theorists want to "contextualize" First Amendment jurisprudence, which they otherwise regard as "absolutist" and "extremist." They want to abandon . . . the liberal pretense of "neutrality," and to openly endorse a value-laden approach. Consider, for example, state and local laws that prohibit parading in masks or hoods. Everyone knows that these laws are aimed at the Ku Klux Klan. Why not be honest about it? A law specifically prohibiting only Klansmen probably would fail the test of viewpoint-neutrality; the law would be aimed at the Klan's message.

. . . Most important is the fact that these writers want us to look at offensive speech from the point of view of the recipient, the victim. This idea is expressed in the very title of Professor Mari Matsuda's article, "Public Response to Racist Speech: Considering the Victim's Story."[12]

. . .

The "words that wound" . . . position is strongly in line with the motivations we've discussed for campus speech restrictions. These writers begin by pointing to the numerous racial affronts experienced by blacks in recent years.

Insult as Assault

Although Richard Delgado is not primarily concerned with campus speech, he introduces some influential ideas to the "critical race theory" position on codes.[13] He focuses, in particular, on the harm caused by racist speech. While it hardly needs demonstration that racial insults are detestable, Professor Delgado maintains that a racial insult is a kind of assault and that restriction of racist speech can pass constitutional muster under the First Amendment.[14] Delgado argues that the traditional torts (legally actionable civil wrongs) of defamation and intentional infliction of emotional distress are inadequate to deal with hate speech, particularly that directed against blacks. . . .

Delgado surveys the social science literature on the psychologically damaging effects of verbal racism and argues for an "action for racial insult," an independent tort for racial slurs. Racial insults are qualitatively different from mere insults because they "conjure up the entire history of racial discrimination in this country."[15] The racial insult is a kind of assault, a verbal slap in the face, as some writers have put it. Second, Delgado argues that a tort for racial insult can overcome constitutional free speech objections. Racial insults are not very different from other kinds of speech that may be constitutionally restricted, such as obscenities and "fighting words." A racial insult, unlike the slogan in *Cohen* ("Fuck the Draft"), is not political speech; "its perpetrator intends not to discover truth or advocate social action."[16] As an assault, racist speech approaches a physical blow, which is subject to restriction by the law. . . .

Delgado, then, apparently maintains that the racial insult is "nonspeech," not really speech at all, not the expression of an idea. . . .

Professor Delgado's argument is applicable to campus speech: racial slurs are subject to restriction and discipline in campus codes. Quite obviously, he maintains that such insults are not "merely offensive." They are words that cause substantial harm to their recipients. It is in any case significant that for Delgado the distinctive quality of the insult is its *racial* component understood in a particular way. "You dumb honkey" directed to a white would be legally actionable only in the "unusual situation" where the recipient suffers substantial harm. . . . On the other hand, "You damn nigger," said by a white, would almost always be actionable, and damages could be awarded presumably even in the absence of harm to the recipient in order to deter speech insulting to blacks, according to Delgado.[17] Although campus speech codes are not about instituting a special tort action, slurs directed to black students similarly may be proscribed in campus speech codes and be subject to disciplinary action.[18]

I find myself torn by Professor Delgado's position, not so much by his argument itself, but because I think that racial and ethnic slurs deliberately directed against *any* group are vile, loathsome, and morally contemptible. I am not a moral relativist. Yet his approach gives rise to a number of questions that trouble me. These questions also arise regarding other critical race theorists. We shall therefore consider some of them here, keeping in mind that they apply to other writers.

Some Questions on Delgado's Approach

Delgado's article deals almost entirely with single *words,* epithets and slurs, and his position rests on an empirical claim about the psychologically damaging effects of racial insults and their symbolic nature, that they "conjure up the entire history of racial discrimination in this country." How would "other groups" fare on this analysis? And what about ideas that demean? Are these tortious too? Or are expressions of demeaning ideas speech that is protected by the First Amendment?[19] Let us consider an example involving a different group.

American Jews experience the smearing of swastikas on synagogues as offensive and outrageous. Such acts are punishable as vandalism, but Jews are highly troubled by them, given the history of anti-Semitism in the United States and elsewhere. Admittedly, anti-Semitism has declined in America, though it continues to surface, even in universities. The symbolic meaning of the swastika is too obvious to need an explanation. In 1977 there began a year-long controversy over whether a neo-Nazi group, the National Socialist Party of America, could hold a march through the Village of Skokie, a suburb of Chicago where many Holocaust survivors lived. At one point the American Jewish Congress argued for prohibiting only the display of the swastika as a "deliberately provocative and abusive symbol." Others stressed that the demonstration itself would inflict "psychic trauma" on the Holocaust survivors.[20]

It seems, then, that other groups may also have a plausible claim for a tort of racial assault or some similar dignitary or civility tort. Thus, displays of swastikas arguably should be assaults for which Jews who experience distress ought to receive compensation. Granted, blacks have suffered from a long history of racial discrimination, as Delgado says. However, once a claim for racial assault, by the display of a hateful word or symbol, is recognized, other groups are sure to stand in line with an equally good, or nearly equally good, claim as a result of the fact-sensitive contextualization of the First Amendment. One very reputable writer, whose name I won't mention, thinks that blacks experience greater suffering from an insult than members of religious groups. This empirical claim is at least debatable. It should not be forgotten that Jews have been castigated as a "race"—recall German "racial science."[21] And the brunt of anti-Semitism is not that Jews merely are an "inferior" race but something worse: that they are "evil." Even the word "Jew" often has a derogatory connotation. In any case, the Holocaust survivors in Skokie would have experienced severe psychic stress from the display of swastikas in a neo-Nazi march.

Now it should be noticed that the elements of the cause of action for racial insult (see n. 17) are not formulated with reference to a particular race; yet Delgado's entire argument turns on the uniqueness of the black experience and fails, therefore, to support his general proposal. On the other hand, to confine the concept of assault by insult to blacks seems too narrow. Surely, other groups would complain that they are being unfairly left out, whether in a civil action or in a campus speech code. But where do we draw the line? May other groups claim "victim" status? . . . Extending assault by insult to other groups contains a major difficulty, namely, the evaluation of the evidence on the psychologically damaging effects of verbal assault against this or that group. Such a task is beyond the competence of courts.

And it is also beyond the competence of university administrators who have instituted speech codes that prohibit speech that purportedly denigrates students on the basis of their race, religion, sexual orientation, Vietnam veteran status, HIV status, political affiliation, pregnancy status, etc. . . .

. . .

Even more difficult, and problematic for campus speech, than insults are "sanitized" racism and anti-Semitism, that is, racism and anti-Semitism presented as "scholarship." College courses that promote sanitized racism and anti-Semitism tend to be highly "politicized," in the sense used earlier, and as such are academically questionable.[22] Holocaust denial is a case in point: for Jews it "conjures up the entire history of anti-Semitism," to use Delgado's phrase.[23] Also very highly troubling to Jews are anti-Semitic expressions by such black figures as Minister Louis Farrakhan (Judaism is a "gutter religion") and Khallid Muhummad, inflammatory and exaggerated claims about Jewish involvement in the slave trade, claims about the responsibility of Jews for AIDS among blacks, and the distribution of *The Protocols of the Elders of Zion* at meetings of some black student groups in universities.[24] All these are, of course, expressions of ideas, which in fact are potentially more damaging than the isolated epithet, slur, or insult. These ideas may stimulate actions that have disastrous consequences. The same is true of "scholarly" claims about the alleged intellectual inferiority of blacks and the gross sexuality of black males. But shall expression of such ideas be actionable, on Delgado's approach?

Probably not. For as Delgado apparently holds, the racial epithet is invoked as an assault, not as a statement of fact that may be proven true or false. And if this is correct, utterance of a racial epithet in the logically appropriate context is arguably not an expression of an idea, and so arguably is not protected by the First Amendment. Ideas, "sanitized racism," on the other hand, even if detestable, are protected speech, he may hold. But should they be, once the liberal pretense of "neutrality" is abandoned and the First Amendment is "contextualized" . . .? If one wants to penalize "wounding words" it makes no sense to single out gutter epithets, as the African American academic Henry Louis Gates Jr., says.[25]

And there is another issue. Is it the case that epithets or slurs have no intellectual content, do not convey ideas? The display of the Confederate flag may be just as offensive to blacks as the swastika is to Jews, and isn't this so because of what these objects *symbolize*, the messages or ideas that they convey? And doesn't the use of such emotive terms as "nigger" and "kike" convey a message? Of course, it is often difficult to tell what the message is or to disentangle the cognitive component from the emotive. The epithet/idea distinction is not easy to make; ideas and beliefs are central to most slurs. For example, the imperative sentence, "Get away from me you dirty nigger [kike]," cannot be true or false, but it does probably connote the speaker 's belief that blacks [Jews] are inferior to him. Moreover, it seems wrong to say that an advocate of racial and religious tolerance, such as Delgado, may use such words, but an opponent may not.

Because epithets and slurs can have an intellectual or ideational component, penalizing their use may have the effect of suppressing the expression of ideas. This conclusion, however, makes me uneasy because I do not think that racial, ethnic, or religious slurs have a place on the college campus, which is committed to rational thinking, especially in the classroom. But punishment is something else. I believe that the overwhelming majority of members of the academic community, faculty and students, don't like vilifiers; their nasty words make us angry and to want to punish the user. A punitive approach, however, forces us—and the courts—to take sides on whose speech is palatable. In particular, it also creates an atmosphere in which people hesitate to express controversial ideas, and not just on matters of race. It doesn't please me that "sanitized" racism and anti-Semitism, which can be more damaging than slurs, should not be punishable; these, however, have to be countered by argument. In any case, if Delgado doesn't think so, other critical race theorists do seem to allow that demeaning ideas could be suppressed.

. . .

Comprehension Questions

1. What are some ways that speech can be restricted on college campuses?
2. What is a zero tolerance policy?
3. How can campus conduct codes relate to speech restriction on campus?
4. What does Golding mean when he says critical race theorists want to contextualize the First Amendment?
5. What, as Golding reports it, is Delgado's rationale for restricting racist speech?
6. Why does Golding think that Delgado's focus on race is problematic?
7. What is sanitized racism, and what challenge does it pose to Delgado's view?
8. How, according to Golding, does Delgado's view conflict with the aim of content-neutrality?

Discussion Questions

1. What kind of speech rules are there on your campus? Do you know of any cases where people violated those rules? If so, what happened?
2. Do you agree more with Delgado that there is something especially damaging about discriminatory speech directed against African Americans, or with Golding's criticism of that view? Explain your position.
3. Based on Golding's discussion, do you think any form of discriminatory speech should be restricted on college campuses? Why or why not?
4. Suppose Golding is right, and that discriminatory speech should not be restricted on campus. Are speech restrictions the only way to deal with the problem? What other approaches to the problem can you think of?

Case

Here are the first few paragraphs of an op-ed in the *Duke Chronicle*:

> I am thinking a lot about speech. I am thinking about how an urgent and overdue conversation about racism—on our campus and across our country—has been derailed by a diversionary and duplicitous obsession with the First Amendment. I am thinking about how quickly the conversation has shifted from white supremacy to white fragility—and how this shift is itself an expression of white supremacy.
>
> White fragility refers to a range of defensive behaviors through which white people (or more accurately, people who believe they are white) deflect conversations about race and racism in order to protect themselves from race-based stress. Because white people tend to live in environments where whiteness is both dominant and invisible, they grow accustomed to racial comfort, as a result of which even a small amount of racial stress becomes intolerable. This helps explain why talking about white supremacy can feel more painful to white people than white supremacy itself, why the ostensible "stifling" of debate can feel more pressing than the literal strangulation of Eric Garner and how "free speech" seems more important than black lives.
>
> Needless to say, it requires an astounding degree of narcissism, ignorance and—yes—fragility to scan headlines detailing the daily, state-sanctioned slaughter of people of color and somehow conclude that speech is the real problem. White fragility weighs the minimal discomfort of being confronted with painful realities about race and racism against the literal death of black and brown bodies and decides that the latter matter less than white discomfort.[26]

The author, Bennett Carpenter, isn't necessarily advocating for restrictions on speech, but he is calling into question our commitment to the value of free speech. What might Golding say in response? How should Carpenter's challenge lead us to rethink Golding's arguments—if at all?

Notes

1. Samuel Walker, *Hate Speech: The History of an American Controversy* (Lincoln: University of Nebraska Press, 1994), 133. The essential factor in this success was that the movement had more or less organized advocates. On the other side, strong advocacy groups, e.g., the American Civil Liberties Union, are the reason why the United States has its extensive constitutional free speech protections, according to Walker.

2. *Doe v. Univ. of Michigan,* 721 F. Supp. 852 (E.D. Mich. 1989) (speech code effectively declared unconstitutional); *UMW Post v. Board of Regents of the Univ. of Wisconsin,* 774 F. Supp. 1163 (E.D. Wis. 1991) (speech code effectively declared unconstitutional); *R.A.V. v. City of St. Paul,* 505 U.S. 377 (1992) (hate crime ordinance declared unconstitutional).

3. For a study of the cases, see Timothy C. Shiell, *Campus Hate Speech on Trial* (Lawrence: University of Kansas Press, 1998).

4. This has been told me by a number of law professors, though law schools are just the place for taking up touchy issues. A notorious instance was the moot court competition at NYU Law School in 1990. The issue assigned for argument was whether a father could obtain custody of his child on the grounds that its mother was a lesbian. As is typical, some students were assigned to argue on one side and some on the other, but those assigned for the petitioner objected: The question, it was said, is not even debatable. The Moot Court Board decided that the issue was not "appropriate." In fact, it is the sort of issue that lawyers confront in the real world. For a description of the incident, see Nat Hentoff, *Free Speech for Me—But Not for Thee* (New York: HarperCollins, 1992), 202–16.

5. Documented in A. C. Kors and H. A. Silverglate, *The Shadow University: The Betrayal of Liberty on America's Campuses* (New York: Free Press, 1998), 176. The stifling of expression by "atmosphere" is well documented in Hentoff, *Free Speech*.

6. See *Healy v. James,* 408 U.S. 169 (1972) (upholding, on First Amendment grounds, the SDS's right to official recognition at Central Connecticut State College).

7. "Protest THIS!" is a university-funded student humor newspaper that offended racial and gender sensibilities. The issue had fake advertisements (for "MastaCard" and for the "Asian Student Alliance," with pictures of blacks and Asians). The paper's staff is racially and ethnically diverse, and the ads were done by minorities. An earlier issue ran a fictitious story saying rape counselors were tired of victims' "whining." University President Trachtenberg opposed continued funding of "Protest THIS!", but also said that it probably deserves "a chance to do better." *Washington Post,* May 17, 1998, B10.

8. The notorious 1997 SUNY/New Paltz Women's Studies conference, "Revolting Behavior: The Challenges of Women's Sexual Freedom," had a workshop on sadomasochism, which was recommended as an alternative way of loving. The president of the school defended it on grounds of academic freedom. But suppose a group of men had put on a pornography conference. I doubt very much that it would have received the same defense. Ironically, the New Paltz conference would have violated provisions of the Indianapolis anti-pornography ordinance inspired by the feminists Catharine MacKinnon and Andrea Dworkin. This ordinance banned sexually explicit works in which "women are presented as sexual objects who enjoy pain or humiliation." The ordinance was

struck down in *American Booksellers Ass'n v. Hudnut,* 771 F.2d 323 (7th Cir. 1985). It has been reported to me that in some Duke women's studies courses men have been made the subject of ribald humor. I cannot vouch for the truth of the report, but I doubt that a course in which women were similarly treated would escape serious administrative objection.

9. The Supreme Court has gone beyond protection of merely offensive speech. In 1949 it upheld the right of a racist to give a speech that "vigorously, if not viciously" insulted various racial and political groups. *Tenninielo v. Chicago,* 337 U.S. 1 (1949).

10. The code, instituted in 1981, restricts faculty speech as part of its rules banning harassment. It forbids faculty members from slurring students according to race, gender, ethnicity, etc., and also makes punishable the use of teaching techniques that make "the instructional setting hostile or intimidating, or demeaning" to students according to their group. Although no faculty member has been disciplined under the code, some have been subjected to long investigations for possible violations—which is enough to make others wary. In contrast to the student code, which was held unconstitutional in 1991 (see n. 2), the faculty code has not been challenged in the courts. See "U. of Wisconsin Considers Proposal to Ease Limits on Faculty Speech," *Chronicle of Higher Education,* October 2, 1998, A14. On March 1, 1999, the faculty voted 71–62 to abolish the code provisions relating to instructional settings.

11. M. J. Matsuda, C. R. Lawrence III, R. Delgado, and K. W. Crenshaw, *Words That Wound: Critical Race Theory, Assaultive Speech and the First Amendment* (Boulder, CO: Westview Press, 1993). With slight editorial changes and the elimination of some footnotes, this book reprints previously published articles by the first three authors. The introduction describes the origins and aims of Critical Race Theory. Quotations are from this book.

12. *Michigan Law Rev.* 87 (1989), 2320–81. This article is reprinted in *Words That Wound,* 17–52.

13. Regarding campus speech, see Richard Delgado, "Campus Anti-Racism Rules: Constitutional Narratives in Collision," *Northwestern Univ. Law Rev.* 85 (1991), 343–87. This article describes a clash between a First Amendment narrative, marketplace interpretations of law and politics, and an equal protection one. Racial slurs, says Delgado, "contribute little to the discovery of truth" (379). I don't think that this article adds anything fundamentally new to the article cited in the next footnote, which is discussed in the text. Professor Delgado helped draft the University of Wisconsin policy, invalidated in *UMW Post,* cited in n. 2.

14. See Richard Delgado, "Words That Wound: A Tort Action for Racial Insults, Epithets, and Name-Calling," *Harvard Civil Rights-Civil Liberties Law Rev.* 17 (1982), 138–81. This article is reprinted in *Words That Wound,* 89–110.

15. *Words That Wound,* 100.

16. *Words That Wound,* 107.

The leading proponent of the high-value/low-value distinction is Cass R. Sunstein. See Sunstein, "Pornography and the First Amendment," *Duke Law J.* (1986), 589–627, especially 602–08. Among the factors relevant to determining low-value speech are its distance from the "central concern" of the First Amendment and its non-cognitive appeal. Sunstein is criticized in Larry Alexander, "Low Value Speech," *Northwestern Univ. Law Rev.* 83 (1989), 547–54. See also Kent Greenawalt, *Fighting Words* (Princeton, NJ: Princeton University Press, 1995), 87f., 102ff.

17. The elements of the cause of action for racial insult are not formulated with reference to a particular race: "In order to prevail in an action for a racial insult, the plaintiff should be required to prove that language was addressed to him or her by the defendant that was intended to demean through reference to race; that the plaintiff understood and intended to demean through reference to race; and that a reasonable person would recognize as a racial insult." *Words That Wound,* 109. The word "demean," which occurs in many campus speech codes too, is not defined. But the last provision may take care of the problem. Still, how is the speaker to know whether something will be taken as demeaning?

18. Presumably, there must be a definite audience; "Niggers be damned" would not be enough to satisfy the criteria for a cause of action or a campus violation unless said in the presence of a black or, if put on a poster, it is seen by a black. It is sometimes said that some people can't be insulted, apparently because they have such a low opinion of themselves that they do not perceive the remark as denigrating, or because they *are* contemptible. It seems to be Delgado's position that a racial slur makes black recipients *feel* bad, as objects of contempt.

19. See Walker, *Hate Speech,* 46ff. Though there are earlier group libel laws, the only hate speech law enacted in the 1930s was a 1934 New Jersey law, enacted as a result of clashes between Nazi and anti-Nazi groups. The law prohibited "propaganda or statements creating or tending to create prejudice, hostility, hatred, ridicule, disgrace or contempt of people . . . by reason of their race, color, creed or manner of worship." It was used to prosecute a Jehovah's Witness who distributed anti-Catholic literature. In an opinion that invoked Holmes's "marketplace of ideas," the law was overturned on constitutional free speech grounds (*State v. Klapprott,* 22 A. 2d 877 (1941)). A number of speech cases have involved members of the Jehovah's Witnesses, on which see Walker's book.

20. There are continuous calls to punish anti-Semitic and anti-black vandalism as hate crimes, but the *R.A.V.* case (n. 2) undercuts the effort. On the legal wrangling over the Skokie march, see Walker, *Hate Speech,* 120–25. The National Socialist Party eventually won its case but didn't hold the march; it did get what it wanted: publicity.

21. The term "anti-Semitism" was invented by Wilhelm Marr (1818–1902), the founder of the German League of Anti-Semites in 1879. Marr's opposition to

Jews was not on religious grounds, but rather that they were an "alien" race, a charge that goes back to the ancient world. In current American white-supremacist literature, Jews are said to be not a religious group, but an Asiatic race, "locked in mortal combat with Aryan man." See Adolph Hitler, *Mein Kampf*, trans. Ralph Mannheim (Boston: Houghton Mifflin, 1943), Vol. I, Chapter 11. On December 9, 1998, the fiftieth anniversary of the convention against genocide, the UN General Assembly decided to list anti-Semitism as a form of racism.

22. Politicization is "the practice of misstating or distorting or denying a truth or judgment for which adequate grounds can be given, in behalf of a partisan political cause, whether it be a revolutionary or a counterrevolutionary one." Politicization is different from partisanship, taking sides on a controversial issue.

23. A number of anti-Semitic Web sites purporting to be based on "scholarship" are devoted to Holocaust denial. This is not to say that there aren't open issues about its interpretation, its causes, etc. See www.hatewatch.org, which also has links to all sorts of hate organizations (anti-black, anti-Catholic, anti-Muslim, etc.). White-supremacist groups tend to be anti-Semitic as well as anti-black.

24. "To what extent the whole existence of this people is based on a continuous lie is shown incomparably by the *Protocols of the Wise Men of Zion*, so infinitely hated by the Jews." Hitler, *Mein Kampf*, 307. This work is an anti-Semitic forgery aimed at showing the existence of an international Jewish conspiracy bent on world domination. Its latest version was concocted in Paris at the end of the nineteenth century by an unknown author working for the Russian secret police. Translated into many languages, the work received wide circulation, and was sponsored in the United States by Henry Ford until 1927. Nazi propaganda heavily relied on it and it has been reissued in Arab states.

25. Henry Louis Gates, Jr., "Let Them Talk," *New Republic*, September 20–27, 1993, 37–49, at 45. This article is a review of *Words That Wound*.

26. http://www.dukechronicle.com/article/2016/01/free-speech-black-lives-and-white-fragility

§

25

The Coddling of the American Mind
Greg Lukianoff and Jonathan Haidt

Greg Lukianoff and Jonathan Haidt take a critical look at concern over offensive speech and behavior in higher education, especially as embodied in calls for trigger warnings and condemnation of some speech and behavior as microaggressions. While acknowledging the need for sensitivity and respect toward students, they argue that many expressions of this recent trend are misguided, using concepts from cognitive behavioral therapy to show that they actually foster distorting and harmful habits of the mind. Mining the resources of both cognitive behavioral therapy and certain venerable intellectual traditions, Lukianoff and Haidt sketch an alternative general approach to coping with offensive speech and behavior and offer some practical recommendations aimed at lawmakers, administrators, and students.

Something strange is happening at America's colleges and universities. A movement is arising, undirected and driven largely by students, to scrub campuses clean of words, ideas, and subjects that might cause discomfort or give offense. Last December, Jeannie Suk wrote in an online article for *The New Yorker* about law students asking her fellow professors at Harvard not to teach rape law—or, in one case, even use the word *violate* (as in "that violates the law") lest it cause students distress. In February, Laura Kipnis, a professor at Northwestern University, wrote an essay in *The Chronicle of Higher Education* describing a new campus politics of sexual paranoia—and was then subjected to a long investigation after students who were offended by the article and by a tweet she'd sent filed Title IX complaints against her. In June, a professor protecting himself with a pseudonym wrote an essay for Vox describing how gingerly he now has to teach. "I'm a Liberal Professor, and My Liberal Students Terrify Me," the headline said. . . .

Two terms have risen quickly from obscurity into common campus parlance. *Microaggressions* are small actions or word choices that seem on their face to have no malicious intent but that are thought of as a kind of violence nonetheless. For example, by some campus guidelines, it is a microaggression to ask an Asian American or Latino American "Where were you born?," because this implies that he or she is not a real American. *Trigger warnings* are alerts that professors are expected to issue if something in a course might cause a strong emotional response. For example, some students have called for warnings that Chinua Achebe's *Things Fall Apart* describes racial violence and that F. Scott Fitzgerald's *The Great Gatsby* portrays misogyny and physical abuse, so that students who have been previously victimized by racism or domestic violence can choose to avoid these works, which they believe might "trigger" a recurrence of past trauma.

. . .

The press has typically described these developments as a resurgence of political correctness. That's partly right, although there are important differences between what's happening now and what happened in the 1980s and 1990s. That movement sought to restrict speech (specifically hate speech aimed at marginalized groups), but it also challenged the literary, philosophical, and historical canon, seeking to widen it by including more diverse perspectives. The current movement is largely about emotional well-being. More than the last, it presumes an extraordinary fragility of the collegiate psyche, and therefore elevates the goal of protecting students from psychological harm. The ultimate aim, it seems, is to turn campuses into "safe spaces" where young adults are shielded from words and ideas that make some uncomfortable. And more than the last, this movement seeks to punish anyone who interferes with that aim, even accidentally. You might call this impulse *vindictive protectiveness*. . . .

... The dangers that these trends pose to scholarship and to the quality of American universities are significant; we could write a whole essay detailing them. But in this essay we focus on a different question: What are the effects of this new protectiveness *on the students themselves*? Does it benefit the people it is supposed to help? ...

...

The Thinking Cure

For millennia, philosophers have understood that we don't see life as it is; we see a version distorted by our hopes, fears, and other attachments. The Buddha said, "Our life is the creation of our mind." Marcus Aurelius said, "Life itself is but what you deem it." The quest for wisdom in many traditions begins with this insight. Early Buddhists and the Stoics, for example, developed practices for reducing attachments, thinking more clearly, and finding release from the emotional torments of normal mental life.

Cognitive behavioral therapy is a modern embodiment of this ancient wisdom. It is the most extensively studied non-pharmaceutical treatment of mental illness, and is used widely to treat depression, anxiety disorders, eating disorders, and addiction. ...

The goal is to minimize distorted thinking and see the world more accurately. You start by learning the names of the dozen or so most common cognitive distortions (such as overgeneralizing, discounting positives, and emotional reasoning . . .). Each time you notice yourself falling prey to one of them, you name it, describe the facts of the situation, consider alternative interpretations, and then choose an interpretation of events more in line with those facts. Your emotions follow your new interpretation. In time, this process becomes automatic. When people improve their mental hygiene in this way—when they free themselves from the repetitive irrational thoughts that had previously filled so much of their consciousness—they become less depressed, anxious, and angry.

The parallel to formal education is clear: cognitive behavioral therapy teaches good critical-thinking skills, the sort that educators have striven for so long to impart. By almost any definition, critical thinking requires grounding one's beliefs in evidence rather than in emotion or desire, and learning how to search for and evaluate evidence that might contradict one's initial hypothesis. But does campus life today foster critical thinking? Or does it coax students to think in more distorted ways?

Let's look at recent trends in higher education in light of the distortions that cognitive behavioral therapy identifies. We will draw the names and descriptions of these distortions from David D. Burns's popular book *Feeling Good*, as well as from the second edition of *Treatment Plans and Interventions for Depression and Anxiety Disorders*, by Robert L. Leahy, Stephen J. F. Holland, and Lata K. McGinn.

Higher Education's Embrace of "Emotional Reasoning"

Burns defines *emotional reasoning* as assuming "that your negative emotions necessarily reflect the way things really are: 'I feel it, therefore it must be true.'" Leahy, Holland, and McGinn define it as letting "your feelings guide your interpretation of reality." But, of course, subjective feelings are not always trustworthy guides; unrestrained, they can cause people to lash out at others who have done nothing wrong. . . .

. . .

There have always been some people who believe they have a right not to be offended. Yet throughout American history—from the Victorian era to the free-speech activism of the 1960s and 1970s—radicals have pushed boundaries and mocked prevailing sensibilities. Sometime in the 1980s, however, college campuses began to focus on preventing offensive speech, especially speech that might be hurtful to women or minority groups. The sentiment underpinning this goal was laudable, but it quickly produced some absurd results.

Among the most famous early examples was the so-called waterbuffalo incident at the University of Pennsylvania. In 1993, the university charged an Israeli-born student with racial harassment after he yelled "Shut up, you water buffalo!" to a crowd of black sorority women that was making noise at night outside his dorm-room window. Many scholars and pundits at the time could not see how the term *water buffalo* (a rough translation of a Hebrew insult for a thoughtless or rowdy person) was a racial slur against African Americans, and as a result, the case became international news.

Claims of a right not to be offended have continued to arise since then, and universities have continued to privilege them. In a particularly egregious 2008 case, for instance, Indiana University–Purdue University at Indianapolis found a white student guilty of racial harassment for reading a book titled *Notre Dame vs. the Klan*. The book honored student opposition to the Ku Klux Klan when it marched on Notre Dame in 1924.

Nonetheless, the picture of a Klan rally on the book's cover offended at least one of the student's coworkers (he was a janitor as well as a student), and that was enough for a guilty finding by the university's Affirmative Action Office.

These examples may seem extreme, but the reasoning behind them has become more commonplace on campus in recent years. . . .

. . .

Since 2013, new pressure from the federal government has reinforced this trend. Federal antidiscrimination statutes regulate on-campus harassment and unequal treatment based on sex, race, religion, and national origin. Until recently, the Department of Education's Office for Civil Rights acknowledged that speech must be "objectively offensive" before it could be deemed actionable as sexual harassment—it would have to pass the "reasonable person" test. To be prohibited, the office wrote in 2003, allegedly harassing speech would have to go "beyond the mere expression of views, words, symbols or thoughts that some person finds offensive."

But in 2013, the Departments of Justice and Education greatly broadened the definition of sexual harassment to include verbal conduct that is simply "unwelcome." Out of fear of federal investigations, universities are now applying that standard—defining unwelcome speech as harassment—not just to sex, but to race, religion, and veteran status as well. Everyone is supposed to rely upon his or her own subjective feelings to decide whether a comment by a professor or a fellow student is unwelcome, and therefore grounds for a harassment claim. Emotional reasoning is now accepted as evidence.

If our universities are teaching students that their emotions can be used effectively as weapons—or at least as evidence in administrative proceedings—then they are teaching students to nurture a kind of hypersensitivity that will lead them into countless drawn-out conflicts in college and beyond.

Schools may be training students in thinking styles that will damage their careers and friendships, along with their mental health.

Fortune-Telling and Trigger Warnings

Burns defines *fortune-telling* as "anticipat[ing] that things will turn out badly" and feeling "convinced that your prediction is an already-established fact." Leahy, Holland, and McGinn define it as "predict[ing] the future negatively" or seeing potential danger in an everyday situation.

The recent spread of demands for trigger warnings on reading assignments with provocative content is an example of fortune-telling.

The idea that words (or smells or any sensory input) can trigger searing memories of past trauma—and intense fear that it may be repeated—has been around at least since World War I, when psychiatrists began treating soldiers for what is now called post-traumatic stress disorder. But explicit trigger warnings are believed to have originated much more recently, . . . seemingly overnight, students at universities across the country have begun demanding that their professors issue warnings before covering material that might evoke a negative emotional response.

In 2013, a task force composed of administrators, students, recent alumni, and one faculty member at Oberlin College, in Ohio, released an online resource guide for faculty (subsequently retracted in the face of faculty pushback) that included a list of topics warranting trigger warnings. These topics included classism and privilege, among many others. The task force recommended that materials that might trigger negative reactions among students be avoided altogether unless they "contribute directly" to course goals, and suggested that works that were "too important to avoid" be made optional.

It's hard to imagine how novels illustrating classism and privilege could provoke or reactivate the kind of terror that is typically implicated in PTSD. Rather, trigger warnings are sometimes demanded for a long list of ideas and attitudes that some students find politically offensive, in the name of preventing other students from being harmed. This is an example of what psychologists call "motivated reasoning"—we spontaneously generate arguments for conclusions we want to support. Once *you* find something hateful, it is easy to argue that exposure to the hateful thing could traumatize some *other* people. . . . Preventing that devastation becomes a moral obligation for the whole community. Books for which students have called publicly for trigger warnings within the past couple of years include Virginia Woolf's *Mrs. Dalloway* (at Rutgers, for "suicidal inclinations") and Ovid's *Metamorphoses* (at Columbia, for sexual assault).

. . .

However, there is a deeper problem with trigger warnings. According to the most basic tenets of psychology, the very idea of helping people with anxiety disorders avoid the things they fear is misguided. A person who is trapped in an elevator during a power outage may panic and think she is going to die. That frightening experience can change neural connections in her amygdala, leading to an elevator phobia. If you want this woman to retain her fear for life, you should help her avoid elevators.

But if you want to help her return to normalcy, you should take your cues from Ivan Pavlov and guide her through a process known as exposure therapy. You might start by asking the woman to merely look at an elevator from a distance—standing in a building lobby, perhaps—until her apprehension begins to subside. If nothing bad happens while she's standing in the lobby—if the fear is not "reinforced"—then she will begin to learn a new association: elevators are not dangerous. (This reduction in fear during exposure is called habituation.) Then, on subsequent days, you might ask her to get closer, and on later days to push the call button, and eventually to step in and go up one floor. This is how the amygdala can get rewired again to associate a previously feared situation with safety or normalcy.

Students who call for trigger warnings may be correct that some of their peers are harboring memories of trauma that could be reactivated by course readings. But they are wrong to try to prevent such reactivations. Students with PTSD should of course get treatment, but they should not try to avoid normal life, with its many opportunities for habituation. Classroom discussions are safe places to be exposed to incidental reminders of trauma (such as the word *violate*). . . .

The expansive use of trigger warnings may also foster unhealthy mental habits in the vastly larger group of students who do not suffer from PTSD or other anxiety disorders. . . . The psychiatrist Sarah Roff pointed this out last year in an online article for *The Chronicle of Higher Education*. "One of my biggest concerns about trigger warnings," Roff wrote, "is that they will apply not just to those who have experienced trauma, but to all students, creating an atmosphere in which they are encouraged to believe that there is something dangerous or damaging about discussing difficult aspects of our history."

In an article published last year by *Inside Higher Ed*, seven humanities professors wrote that the trigger-warning movement was "already having a chilling effect on [their] teaching and pedagogy." They reported their colleagues' receiving "phone calls from deans and other administrators investigating student complaints that they have included 'triggering' material in their courses, with or without warnings." A trigger warning, they wrote, "serves as a guarantee that students will not experience unexpected discomfort and implies that if they do, a contract has been broken."

When students come to *expect* trigger warnings for any material that makes them uncomfortable, the easiest way for faculty to stay out of trouble is to avoid material that might upset the most sensitive student in the class.

Magnification, Labeling, and Microaggressions

Burns defines *magnification* as "exaggerat[ing] the importance of things," and Leahy, Holland, and McGinn define *labeling* as "assign[ing] global negative traits to yourself and others." The recent collegiate trend of uncovering allegedly racist, sexist, classist, or otherwise discriminatory microaggressions doesn't *incidentally* teach students to focus on small or accidental slights. Its *purpose* is to get students to focus on them and then relabel the people who have made such remarks as aggressors.

The term *microaggression* originated in the 1970s and referred to subtle, often unconscious racist affronts. The definition has expanded in recent years to include anything that can be perceived as discriminatory on virtually any basis. For example, in 2013, a student group at UCLA staged a sit-in during a class taught by Val Rust, an education professor. The group read a letter aloud expressing their concerns about the campus's hostility toward students of color. Although Rust was not explicitly named, the group quite clearly criticized his teaching as microaggressive. In the course of correcting his students' grammar and spelling, Rust had noted that a student had wrongly capitalized the first letter of the word *indigenous*. Lowercasing the capital *I* was an insult to the student and her ideology, the group claimed.

. . .

What are we doing to our students if we encourage them to develop extra-thin skin in the years just before they leave the cocoon of adult protection and enter the workforce? Would they not be better prepared to flourish if we taught them to question their own emotional reactions, and to give people the benefit of the doubt?

Teaching Students to Catastrophize and Have Zero Tolerance

Burns defines *catastrophizing* as a kind of magnification that turns "commonplace negative events into nightmarish monsters." Leahy, Holland,

and McGinn define it as believing "that what has happened or will happen" is "so awful and unbearable that you won't be able to stand it." Requests for trigger warnings involve catastrophizing, but this way of thinking colors other areas of campus thought as well.

Catastrophizing rhetoric about physical danger is employed by campus administrators more commonly than you might think— sometimes, it seems, with cynical ends in mind. For instance, last year administrators at Bergen Community College, in New Jersey, suspended Francis Schmidt, a professor, after he posted a picture of his daughter on his Google+ account. The photo showed her in a yoga pose, wearing a T-shirt that read I WILL TAKE WHAT IS MINE WITH FIRE & BLOOD, a quote from the HBO show *Game of Thrones*. Schmidt had filed a grievance against the school about two months earlier after being passed over for a sabbatical. The quote was interpreted as a threat by a campus administrator, who received a notification after Schmidt posted the picture; it had been sent, automatically, to a whole group of contacts. According to Schmidt, a Bergen security official present at a subsequent meeting between administrators and Schmidt thought the word *fire* could refer to AK-47s.

Then there is the eight-year legal saga at Valdosta State University, in Georgia, where a student was expelled for protesting the construction of a parking garage by posting an allegedly "threatening" collage on Facebook. The collage described the proposed structure as a "memorial" parking garage—a joke referring to a claim by the university president that the garage would be part of his legacy. The president interpreted the collage as a threat against his life.

. . .

What Can We Do Now?

Attempts to shield students from words, ideas, and people that might cause them emotional discomfort are bad for the students. They are bad for the workplace, which will be mired in unending litigation if student expectations of safety are carried forward. And they are bad for American democracy, which is already paralyzed by worsening partisanship. When the ideas, values, and speech of the other side are seen not just as wrong but as willfully aggressive toward innocent victims, it is hard to imagine the kind of mutual respect, negotiation, and compromise that are needed to make politics a positive-sum game.

Rather than trying to protect students from words and ideas that they will inevitably encounter, colleges should do all they can to equip students to thrive in a world full of words and ideas that they cannot control. One of the great truths taught by Buddhism (and Stoicism, Hinduism, and many other traditions) is that you can never achieve happiness by making the world conform to your desires. But you can master your desires and habits of thought. This, of course, is the goal of cognitive behavioral therapy. With this in mind, here are some steps that might help reverse the tide of bad thinking on campus.

The biggest single step in the right direction does not involve faculty or university administrators, but rather the federal government, which should release universities from their fear of unreasonable investigation and sanctions by the Department of Education. Congress should define peer-on-peer harassment according to the Supreme Court's definition in the 1999 case *Davis v. Monroe County Board of Education*. The *Davis* standard holds that a single comment or thoughtless remark by a student does not equal harassment; harassment requires a pattern of objectively offensive behavior by one student that interferes with another student's access to education. Establishing the *Davis* standard would help eliminate universities' impulse to police their students' speech so carefully.

Universities themselves should try to raise consciousness about the need to balance freedom of speech with the need to make all students feel welcome. Talking openly about such conflicting but important values is just the sort of challenging exercise that any diverse but tolerant community must learn to do. Restrictive speech codes should be abandoned.

Universities should also officially and strongly discourage trigger warnings. They should endorse the American Association of University Professors' report on these warnings, which notes, "The presumption that students need to be protected rather than challenged in a classroom is at once infantilizing and anti-intellectual." Professors should be free to use trigger warnings if they choose to do so, but by explicitly discouraging the practice, universities would help fortify the faculty against student requests for such warnings.

Finally, universities should rethink the skills and values they most want to impart to their incoming students. At present, many freshman-orientation programs try to raise student sensitivity to a nearly impossible level. Teaching students to avoid giving unintentional offense is a worthy goal, especially when the students come from many different cultural backgrounds. But students should also be taught how to live in a world full of potential offenses. . . .

Comprehension Questions

1. What are microaggressions and trigger warnings?
2. What sets apart present discourse about microaggressions and trigger warnings from the more familiar one about political correctness?
3. What's the general lesson that Lukianoff and Haidt think we can learn from cognitive behavioral therapy?
4. How does emotional reasoning show up in higher education, and why do Lukianoff and Haidt think we should be worried about it?
5. Why do Lukianoff and Haidt suggest those calling for trigger warnings are "fortune telling"?
6. How do Lukianoff and Haidt think we can remain sensitive to students without using trigger warnings?
7. What do Lukianoff and Haidt mean when they say that labeling speech and behavior as microaggressions often involves catastrophizing?
8. According to Lukianoff and Haidt, what should Congress and universities do rather than being more restrictive about offensive speech and behavior?

Discussion Questions

1. Lukianoff and Haidt think that calls for trigger warnings are misguided, and they discuss some actual cases where such demands seem unreasonable. Can you think of a case (real or imagined) where it might be legitimate to provide a trigger warning and make the material optional?
2. Lukianoff and Haidt seem to suggest that speech and behavior commonly deemed to be microaggressions are often not real harms, but only perceived harms. Do you agree with their assessment? Are there any microaggressions that you think really are harms?
3. According to Lukianoff and Haidt, recent attempts to deal with offensive speech and behavior by restricting it are often not helpful but harmful. Do you agree that these attempts really are harmful? Can you think of additional harms they cause not mentioned by Lukianoff and Haidt?

Case

Consider this story from Columbia University:

> [In the Fall 2014 semester], a student shared an experience with an audience of instructors and fellow students. This experience, she said, came to define her relationship to her Lit Hum class and to Core material in general. During the week spent on Ovid's *Metamorphoses*, the class was instructed to read the myths of Persephone and Daphne, both of which include vivid depictions of rape and sexual assault. As a survivor of sexual assault, the student described being triggered while reading such detailed accounts of rape throughout the work. However, the student said her professor focused on the beauty of the language and the splendor of the imagery when lecturing on the text. As a result, the student completely disengaged from the class discussion as a means of self-preservation. She did not feel safe in the class. When she approached her professor after class, the student said she was essentially dismissed, and her concerns were ignored.[1]

What went wrong here? How could it have gone better? Would a trigger warning have helped?

Note

1. http://columbiaspectator.com/opinion/2015/04/30/our-identities-matter-core-classrooms

====== ⚹ ======

26

Why I Use Trigger Warnings

Kate Manne

....

Some people argue that trigger warnings aren't beneficial and are instead possibly harmful. Others contend that trigger warnings ought to be required and that triggering material should be optional. Kate Manne tries to chart a course between these two extremes. Manne agrees with the critics that what's at stake is students' ability to rationally engage with course material. Yet, against certain critics, she suggests that providing trigger warnings can aid rather than inhibit this. On the other hand, while she agrees that instructors do well to voluntarily give trigger warnings to their students, she argues that the case for trigger warnings is not so strong as to justify making them compulsory or to require that triggering material be optional.

....

Trigger warnings have been getting a lot of pushback lately. Professors who have adopted the practice of alerting their students to potentially disturbing content in a text or class are being accused of coddling millennials. And the students who request them are being called "infantile," or worse. In a recent story in *The Atlantic*, the authors Greg Lukianoff and Jonathan Haidt describe them as part of a movement,

Manne, Kate. 2015. "Why I Use Trigger Warnings." *The New York Times*, September 19, 2015. Reprinted with permission from the author.

"undirected and driven largely by students, to scrub campuses clean of words, ideas, and subjects that might cause discomfort or give offense."

I happen to be both a millennial and, for the past two years, an assistant professor of philosophy. I've been using trigger warnings in my teaching—in cases when they seem appropriate—since I began to lecture.

Trigger warnings are nothing new. The practice originated in Internet communities, primarily for the benefit of people with post-traumatic stress disorder. The idea was to flag content that depicted or discussed common causes of trauma, like military combat, child abuse, incest, and sexual violence. People could then choose whether or not to engage with this material.

But trigger warnings have been adapted to serve a subtly different purpose within universities. Increasingly, professors like me simply give students notice in their syllabuses, or before certain reading assignments. The point is not to enable—let alone encourage—students to skip these readings or our subsequent class discussion (both of which are mandatory in my courses, absent a formal exemption). Rather, it is to allow those who are sensitive to these subjects to prepare themselves for reading about them, and better manage their reactions. The evidence suggests that at least some of the students in any given class of mine are likely to have suffered some sort of trauma, whether from sexual assault or another type of abuse or violence. So I think the benefits of trigger warnings can be significant.

Criticisms of trigger warnings are often based on the idea that college is a time for intellectual growth and emotional development. In order for this to happen, students must be challenged. And they need to learn to engage rationally with ideas, arguments, and views they find difficult, upsetting or even repulsive. On this count, I agree with the critics, and it is in fact the main reason that I do issue warnings.

In philosophy, we often draw a distinction between responses based on reasons and those that are merely *caused*. In the first case, our response has a basis in rational reflection. We can cite reasons that we think justify our opinion. But in the latter case, we find ourselves involuntarily caused—or triggered—to have a certain reaction.

Triggered reactions can be intense and unpleasant, and may even overtake our consciousness, as with a flashback experienced by a war veteran. But even more common conditions can have this effect. Think, for example, about the experience of intense nausea. It comes upon a person unbidden, without rational reflection. And you can no more reason your way out of it than you reasoned your way into it. It's also hard, if not impossible, to engage productively with other matters while you are in the grip of it. You might say that such states temporarily eclipse our rational capacities.

For someone who has experienced major trauma, vivid reminders can serve to induce states of body and mind that are rationally eclipsing in much the same manner. A common symptom of PTSD is panic attacks. Those undergoing these attacks may be flooded with anxiety to the point of struggling to draw breath, and feeling disoriented, dizzy and nauseated. Under conditions such as these, it's impossible to think straight.

The thought behind trigger warnings isn't just that these states are highly unpleasant (although they certainly are). It's that they temporarily render people unable to focus, regardless of their desire or determination to do so. Trigger warnings can work to prevent or counteract this.

As teachers, we can't foresee every instance of potentially triggering material; some triggers are unpredictable. But others are easy enough to anticipate, specifically, depictions or discussions of the very kinds of experiences that often result in post-traumatic stress and even, for some, a clinical disorder. With appropriate warnings in place, vulnerable students may be able to employ effective anxiety management techniques, by meditating or taking prescribed medication.

To me, there seems to be very little reason not to give these warnings. As a professor, it merely requires my including one extra line in a routine email to the class, such as: "A quick heads-up. The reading for this week contains a graphic depiction of sexual assault." These warnings are not unlike the advisory notices given before films and TV shows; those who want to ignore them can do so without a second thought. The cost to students who don't need trigger warnings is, I think, equally minimal. It may even help sensitize them to the fact that some of their classmates will find the material hard going. The idea, suggested by Professor Haidt and others, that this considerate and reasonable practice feeds into a "culture of victimhood" seems alarmist, if not completely implausible.

Mr. Lukianoff and Professor Haidt also argue in their article that we shouldn't give trigger warnings, based on the efficacy of exposure therapy—where you are gradually exposed to the object of a phobia, under the guidance of a trained psychotherapist. But the analogy works poorly. Exposing students to triggering material without warning seems more akin to occasionally throwing a spider at an arachnophobe.

Of course, all this still leaves the questions of how and when to give trigger warnings, and where to draw the line to avoid their overuse. There is no formula for this, just as there is no formula for designing classes, for successful teaching and meaningful communication with students. As teachers we use our judgment and experience to guide our words and actions in the entire act of teaching. We should be trusted, without legislation from college administrators, to decide, ideally in dialogue with our students—whose voices are eerily silent in these discussions in the media—when (and when not) to use these warnings.

Common sense should tell us that material that is merely offensive to certain people's political or religious sensibilities wouldn't merit a warning. True, politics and religion can make people irrationally angry. But unlike a state of panic, anger is a state we are able to rein in rationally—or at least we should be able to.

There are several difficult issues that still need to be hashed out. For example, although I see a willingness to use trigger warnings as part of pedagogical best practices, I don't believe their use should be mandatory. There is already too much threat to academic freedom at the moment because of top-down interference from overreaching administrators. But when it comes to the bottom-up pressure from students on professors to adopt practices like giving trigger warnings, I am sympathetic. It's not about coddling anyone. It's about enabling everyone's rational engagement.

Comprehension Questions

1. How is the current practice of using trigger warnings in universities unlike its origins on the Internet?
2. What common ground does Manne share with critics of trigger warnings like Greg Lukianoff and Jonathan Haidt?
3. What, on Manne's view, should we use trigger warnings to prevent?
4. Manne is dissatisfied with Lukianoff and Haidt's claim that presenting potentially triggering material in a course without warning is akin to exposure therapy. Why?
5. What guidance does Manne offer about when it is appropriate to give trigger warnings?

Discussion Questions

1. Manne suggests that trigger warnings prevent a negative effect of triggering material—namely, that of limiting students' ability to rationally engage with course material. Can you think of other negative

effects that she doesn't mention? How would taking those into account affect her argument?

2. In defending trigger warnings, Manne says that all she recommends is giving students advance notice. She does not recommend, for instance, allowing students to opt out of the triggering material. Given Manne's argument for using trigger warnings, can you think of any accommodations that would be appropriate other than the one she suggests?

Case

In 2015, some students at Duke objected to the summer reading selection:

Several incoming freshmen decided not to read *Fun Home* because its sexual images and themes conflicted with their personal and religious beliefs. Freshman Brian Grasso posted in the Class of 2019 Facebook page July 26 that he would not read the book "because of the graphic visual depictions of sexuality," igniting conversation among students. The graphic novel, written by Alison Bechdel, chronicles her relationship with her father and her issues with sexual identity. "I feel as if I would have to compromise my personal Christian moral beliefs to read it," Grasso wrote in the post . . . [Moreover,] several freshmen agreed with Grasso that the novel's images conflicted with their beliefs. Freshman Bianca D'Souza said that while the novel discussed important topics, she did not find the sexual interactions appropriate and could not bring herself to view the images depicting nudity. Freshman Jeffrey Wubbenhorst based his decision not to read the book on its graphic novel format. "The nature of *Fun Home* means that content that I might have consented to read in print now violates my conscience due to its pornographic nature," he wrote in an email. Grasso said that many students privately messaged him thanking him for the post and agreeing with his viewpoint. He explained that he knew the post would be controversial but wanted to make sure students with similar Christian beliefs did not feel alone, adding that he also heard from several students with non-Christian backgrounds who chose not to read the book for moral reasons.[1]

Should these students have been warned about the content of *Fun Home*? If so, why? If not, why not? Does Manne's reasoning support warning them? Why or why not?

Note

1. http://www.dukechronicle.com/article/2015/08/freshmen-skipping-fun-home-for-moral-reasons

===== 🐦 =====

27

Self-Respect and Protest

Bernard R. Boxill

....

Perhaps nothing seems more obvious than the idea that when you are treated unjustly, you have a right to complain publicly about it. In other words, you can—and perhaps ought to—protest when you've been wronged. But, as Bernard Boxill shows, there are some reasons to doubt this. These reasons become apparent when we examine the famous debate between civil rights leaders Booker T. Washington and W. E. B Dubois about whether African Americans can have self-respect while protesting their unjust treatment. Boxill summarizes some key points in that debate and then presents his own argument. On his view, it is not only consistent with self-respect to protest injustice, you often *will* protest to prove that you respect yourself.

....

M ust a person protest his wrongs? Booker T. Washington and W. E. B. Dubois debated this question at the turn of the century. They did not disagree over whether protesting injustice was an effective way to right it, but over whether protesting injustice, when one could do nothing to right it oneself, was self-respecting. Washington felt that it was not. Thus, he did not deny that protest could help ameliorate

Boxill, Bernard R. 1976. "Self-Respect and Protest." *Philosophy & Public Affairs* 6(1): 58–69. Reprinted with permission of John Wiley & Sons.

conditions or that it was sometimes justified; what he did deny was that a person should keep protesting wrongs committed against him when he could not take decisive steps to end them. By insisting on "advertising his wrongs" in such cases, he argued, a person betrayed a weakness for relying, not on his "own efforts" but on the "sympathy" of others. Washington's position was that if a person felt wronged, he should do something about it; if he could do nothing he should hold his tongue and wait his opportunity; protest in such cases is only a servile appeal for sympathy; stoicism, by implication, is better. Dubois strongly contested these views. Not only did he deny that protest is an appeal for sympathy, he maintained that if a person failed to express openly his outrage at injustice, however assiduously he worked against it, he would in the long run lose his self-respect. Thus, he asserted that Washington faced a "paradox" by insisting both on "self-respect" and on "a silent submission to civic inferiority,"[1] and he declared that "only in a . . . persistent demand for essential equality . . . can any people show . . . a decent self-respect."[2] Like Frederick Douglass, he concluded that people should protest their wrongs. In this essay I shall expand upon and defend Dubois' side of the debate. I shall argue that persons have reason to protest their wrongs not only to stop injustice but also to show self-respect and to know themselves as self-respecting.

Washington always failed to press the claim that black people are victims of America's racial injustice. He frequently implied, and sometimes stated explicitly, that the white perpetrators of injustice were economically and, especially, morally the people most hurt and maimed by racial injustice and that, by comparison, the black victims of injustice suffered only "temporary inconvenience."[3] From this kind of reasoning it is easy to conclude that the morally compelling ground for reform is to save, not so much the victims of injustice, but its perpetrators, because their "degradation" places them in greatest need.

What is pertinent is that this was the consideration he thought prudent to present to America and that he hoped would be efficacious in motivating reform. This consideration, though urged insistently, did not arouse resentment. America apparently did not mind being accused of degradation—as long as its affairs, its advancement, and its moral salvation remained the center of moral concern. For, as I have indicated, Washington did explicitly draw the conclusion that the morally compelling ground for reform was the moral salvation of white America.[4]

The idea that being a perpetrator is worse than being a victim is, of course, true in the sense that the person guilty of perpetrating injustice is morally worse than the person who must endure it. But, it does not follow from this that the perpetrator of injustice suffers greater evil than his victim or that the ground for seeking justice is to save the unjust man, if the victim has rights then the perpetrator's duty is not to avoid degrading himself but to respect those rights. To claim that the victim of injustice has rights is thus to challenge the transgressor's arrogant assumption that his own advancement, economic or moral, is the sole legitimate object of social policy.

Because protest emphasizes the wrongs of the victim and declares that redress is a matter of the highest urgency, a person who insistently protests against his own condition may seem to be self-centered and self-pitying. He appears to dwell self-indulgently on his grievances and to be seeking the commiseration of others. Washington, for example, criticized Frederick Douglass for constantly reminding black people of "their sufferings"[5] and suspected that persistent protesters relied on "the special sympathy of the world" rather than on "their own efforts."[6] This is an important charge since the self-respecting person is self-reliant and avoids self-pity. It is not answered by the claim that people have rights, for having rights does not necessarily justify constant reiteration that one has them. The charge is answered, however, by a closer consideration of what is involved in claiming a right. The idea that the protester seeks sympathy is unlikely, since in claiming his rights he affirms that he is claiming what he can demand and exact, and sympathy cannot be demanded and exacted. The idea that the protester is self-pitying is likewise implausible, since a person who feels pity for himself typically believes that his condition is deplorable and unavoidable, and this is not at all what the protester affirms. On the contrary, he affirms that his condition is avoidable, he insists that what he protests is precisely the illegitimate, and hence avoidable, interference by others in the exercise of his rights, and he expresses the sentiment, not of self-pity, but of resentment. Protest could be self-indulgent if it were a demand for help, and it could show a lack of self-reliance if it claimed powerlessness. But, in insisting on his rights, the protestor neither demands help nor claims powerlessness. He demands only noninterference. What Frederick Douglass protested against, for example, was interference. He scorned supererogatory help. "Do nothing with us," he exclaimed, "And, if the Negro cannot stand on his own legs, let him fall."[7]

It follows from the above that when a person protests his wrongs, he expresses a righteous and self-respecting concern for himself. If, as we assume, the self-respecting person has such a concern for himself, it follows that he will naturally be inclined to protest his injuries. Would he always have good reason actually to give vent to his indignation? Protest, it seems, is the response of the weak. It is not a warning of retaliation. The strong man does not waste too much time protesting his injuries; he prevents them. Why then should the weak, but self-respecting, person protest his wrongs? Surely if either protest or whining will prevent injury, the self-respecting person will protest rather than whine. For protest is self-respecting. Though it cannot compel the transgressor to reform, it tells him that he should be compelled to reform and that he is being asked no favors. But, if as Washington's defenders aver, protest often provokes persecution, why should a weak and vulnerable people protest? If it will help, why can't a self-respecting people pretend servility? But it seems that people do protest their wrongs, even when it is clear that this will bring no respite and, instead, cause them further injury. W. E. B. Dubois exhorted black people, "even when bending to the inevitable," to "bend with unabated protest."[8] Is this mere bravado? Or does a person with self-respect have a reason to protest over and above the hope that it will bring relief?

It may be argued that he does; that he should protest to make others recognize that he has rights. But, though a person who believes he has a right not to be unjustly injured also believes that others wrong him if they injure him unjustly and that they should be restrained from doing so, it is not clear that he must want them to share his conviction that he has this right. Why should he care what they believe?

It may be proposed that the self-respecting person will want others to respect him because he wants to remain self-respecting. For unopposed injustice invites its victims to believe that they have no value and are without rights. This confident invitation may make even the self-respecting fear that their sense of their own value is only prejudiced self-love. It may therefore be argued that since protest is an affirmation of the rights of the victim, the self-respecting victim of injustice will protest to make others recognize, and in that way reassure him, that he has rights. Frederick Douglass, for example, once referred to this acknowledgment as the "all important confession."[9] But, though the self-respecting need to reassure themselves that they have rights, they would disdain this kind of reassurance. It is not self-respecting because it shows a lack of self-reliance.

The self-respecting person cannot be satisfied to depend on the opinions of others. This is not to question the proposition that it is difficult to believe what everyone denies and easy to believe what everyone affirms. It is to say that, even while he concedes this, the self-respecting person will want to have his conviction of his worth rationally based.

But it is not clear that the self-respecting person has good reason to protest, even if he does want others to respect him. Washington, for example, understood that social acknowledgment was important but condemned protest. He argued that to be acknowledged as worthy citizens black people would do better to develop the qualities and virtues that would make them economically valuable members of society. Washington was right. For though protest is an uncompromising claim that the victim of some injury has a right not to be injured, it does not follow that protest is therefore a likely way of getting others to agree.

It may be objected that though protest is not plausibly designed to persuade others that the victim of some injury has value or rights, it is designed to compel them to acknowledge that he is a moral being. This issue is raised by Orlando Patterson in his essay "Toward a Future That Has No Past."[10] Speaking of a slave's stealing as "an assertion of moral worth"—that is, as protest—Patterson points out that by screaming, "You are a thief," the master admits that the slave is a moral being, since it is in the act of punishing him as a thief that the master most emphatically avows the slave to be a moral being. Since what the slave wants to hear is that he is a thief, his aim is surely not to be acknowledged as an economically valuable asset but as a being who is responsible for his acts. Finally, though this concession is made loudly and publicly and, by all accounts, sincerely, it is nevertheless absurd and paradoxical. For though the master calls the slave a thief, and thus a moral being, he continues to treat him as a piece of property. Still, it may seem that the slave wins a victory. At least, even if it is painful, he enjoys the satisfaction of forcing a most unwilling agent to treat him as a moral being. This argument has considerable force. For a self-respecting person no doubt desires to be treated as a moral being. But it is not clear that a master must, in consistency, deny that a slave is a moral being. If he wants to justify himself, what he must deny is that the slave has rights.

It may finally be argued that affirming one's rights may be necessary to keeping the sense of one's value simply because doing so is an essential part of having self-respect. It may be false that one believes that one has rights. The argument must therefore be that protest is necessary to keeping the sense of one's value if one believes that one has rights. But why should one affirm what one believes, however deeply and firmly one believes it?

Besides meting out injury incommensurate with the victim's worth and rights, uncontested and unopposed injustice invites witnesses to believe that he is injured just because he is wicked or inferior. Oppressors, no doubt, desire to be justified. They want to believe more than that their treatment of others is fitting; they want those they mistreat to condone their mistreatment as proper, and therefore offer inducements and rewards toward that end. Thus, even the self-respecting person may be tempted at least to pretend servility for some relief. But he will find that such pretense has its dangers; it shakes his confidence in his self-respect. I shall argue that the self-respecting person in such straits must, in some way, protest to assure himself that he has self-respect.

Since self-respect is valuable, it contributes to an individual's worth. But a person can have self-respect and few other good qualities. Since all men have inalienable rights, there is always a rational basis for self-respect, but a person may have an inflated and false sense of his worth. He may be mean and cowardly and cut an absurd figure, but insofar as he has faith in himself, he has self-respect. Consequently, when an individual desires to know whether he has self-respect, what he needs is not evidence of his worth in general but evidence of his faith in his worth. I argued earlier that protest is an indifferent way of getting others to acknowledge and thus to confirm that one has worth. But it may be an excellent way of confirming that one has faith in one's worth. For, as the preceding discussion should suggest, evidence of faith in one's worth is different from evidence of one's worth in general.

A person with a secure sense of his value has self-respect. This does not mean that he cannot lose it. It is a contradiction in terms, however, to suppose that anyone with self-respect would want to lose it. A person would want to lose his self-respect only if he feared that his belief in his worth was false or irrational, or, for some other reason, undesirable. But a person cannot be securely convinced of what he fears is false or irrational. And if a person believes that something has worth, he cannot believe that it is desirable to be ignorant of it. Hence, the person with self-respect cannot want to lose it.

Moreover, the self-respecting person cannot be oblivious to, or unconcerned about, the question of his self-respect. He must be aware that he believes he has value and that this is important. A person can have a belief and be unaware of having it, or have a sense of security and be unable to specify what he feels secure about. But the self-respecting person does not merely believe in his worth or have a vague sense of security. He feels secure about his belief in his worth. Thus, since a person cannot feel certain about something and be unaware of what he feels certain about, the self-respecting person must be aware that he believes he has value. And, for reasons already stated, he must believe that this belief is desirable. People sometimes do lose their self-respect. Thus to the extent that he is reflective, the person with self-respect will concede the possibility of losing it. And, though he may be confident of retaining it, he need not be. Though he may not be servile, a person may properly fear that, because of what he is doing or because of what is happening to him, he will become servile.

He may also fear that he is already servile. If he has self-respect he will be aware that he entertains the belief that he has worth and that he should be convinced of it, though he need not be sure that he is convinced of it. For he will probably also know that servile people too can value and persuade themselves that they have the self-respect which they lack. Thus, not only may a person with self-respect fear losing it; he may fear not having it.

Hence, the self-respecting person wants to know that he is self-respecting.

To know this he needs evidence. The need for such evidence must be especially poignant to the self-respecting person when, to prevent injury, he pretends servility. Observers often cannot agree on how to interpret such behavior. The "Sambo" personality, for example, is supposed to typify the good humored, ostensibly servile black slave. Sambo was apparently very convincing. In *Slavery: A Problem in American Institutional Life*, Stanley Elkins suggests that Sambo's "docility" and "humility" reflected true servility. On the other hand, other historians suspect that Sambo was a fraud. Patterson, for example, argues that Sambo's fawning laziness and dishonesty was his way of hitting back at the master's system without penalty. Thus, Patterson sees Sambo's "clowning" as a mask, "to salvage his dignity," a "deadly serious game," in which "the perfect stroke of rebellion must ideally appear to the master as the ultimate act of submission." Patterson is persuasive, but true servility is possible. Sambo could have been genuinely servile. Certainly every effort was made to make him so. There is therefore room for uncertainty.

It may be pointed out that if Sambo's ostensible servility was his way of "hitting back," he was providing evidence of self-respect all along. But this must be qualified. Unless it is already known to be pretense, apparent servility is evidence of servility. If Sambo gave a perfect imitation of servility, neither he nor his master could have any reason to think he was anything but servile. If his pretense is to provide him with evidence of his self-respect it must, to some discernible extent, betray him. Patterson may be right that the "perfect stroke of rebellion must seem to the master as the ultimate act of submission,"[11] but the deception must succeed, not because it is undetectable, but because the master is so blinded by his own arrogance that he cannot see that what is presented as abasement is really thinly disguised affront.

If the above argument is sound, only consummate artistry can permit a person continuously and elaborately to pretend servility and still know that he is self-respecting. Unless it is executed by a master, the evidence of servility will seem overwhelming and the evidence of self-respect too ambiguous. But, as I have argued, the self-respecting person wants to know he is self-respecting. He hates deception and pretense because he sees them as obstacles to the knowledge of himself as self-respecting. If only occasionally, he must shed his mask.

This may not be so easy. It is not only that shedding the mask of servility may take courage, but that if a person is powerless it will not be easy for him to make others believe that he is taking off a mask. People do not take the powerless seriously. Because he wants to know himself as self-respecting, the powerless but self-respecting person is driven to make others take him seriously. He is driven to make his claim to self-respect unmistakable. Therefore, since nothing as unequivocally expresses what a person thinks he believes as his own emphatic statement, the powerless but self-respecting person will declare his self-respect. He will protest. His protest affirms that he has rights. More important, it tells everyone that he believes he has rights and that he therefore claims self-respect. When he has to endure wrongs he cannot repel and feels his self-respect threatened, he will publicly claim it in order to reassure himself that he has it. His reassurance does not come from persuading others that he has self-respect. It comes from using his claim to self-respect as a challenge.

Thus, even when transgressors will not desist, protest is nevertheless directed at them. For the strongest challenge to a claim to self-respect and one which can consequently most surely establish it as true will most likely come from those most anxious to deny that it has any basis.

Comprehension Questions

1. What positions do Booker T. Washington and W. E. B. Dubois take on the issue of whether a self-respecting person ought to protest injustice done to them?
2. Why, according to Boxill, is protest not equivalent to a form of self-pity?
3. What challenges face the idea that one should, as a self-respecting person, protest unjust treatment in order to convince others of one's individual worth?
4. How is it supposed to be the case that protest can bring an unjust person to acknowledge his or her victim's moral status?
5. What is the connection between certainty in one's self-worth and having self-respect, as Boxill describes the issue?
6. How, on Boxill's account, does protest show self-respect?

Discussion Questions

1. Boxill's discussion of protest is illustrated throughout by the case of African Americans' protest of systematic racial injustice. Looking to the present, what injustices can you think of that might warrant protest? Does Boxill's argument easily extend to these contexts?
2. If Boxill is right, there are some cases where protest against injustice is morally permissible. What sort of protest do you suppose his account justifies? Would it justify protesting in the form of civil disobedience? Would it only justify nonviolent protest, or also violent protest?
3. Boxill's discussion centers on the connection between self-respect and protest. Setting aside self-respect, are there any other personal ideals that might support or clash with the idea of protesting?

Case

Boxill seems to think that the self-respecting person will protest, but he doesn't say anything about how the person will protest. And sometimes, it isn't *that* people are protesting, but *how* they're protesting that gets criticized. Consider this, for example:

> [The students who have been involved in recent protests—the ones] who seek to combat real structural inequities by renaming buildings,

sheltering undergraduates from texts that make them feel unsafe, subjecting faculty and staff to mandatory sensitivity training, or imposing ideological litmus tests on campus speakers—might believe that their cause is rooted in the student experience of the 1960s, when protests over civil rights and the Vietnam War roiled American campuses. In some ways it is: Today, as in the 1960s, a collegiate generation raised with an expansive understanding of its own rights and entitlements is fusing macro political issues to personal, everyday experience and demanding changes both in the halls of government and in the college dining hall.

But there is a startling inversion of logic in the progression from the 1960s and today. Fifty years ago, college students self-identified with repressed minorities at home and abroad and demanded freedom from the shackles of in loco parentis supervision and stewardship. They clamored to be treated as emancipated adults and foisted on their elders a noisy and disruptive free speech culture. Today's students, who are certainly no less politically minded than their forbearers, are demanding the opposite. Far from freeing themselves of stewardship, they demand faculty "create a home" in which they remain children in the protection of more powerful elders. They insist on protection from ideas and voices that upset them and require a nurturing and therapeutic environment that bears no relationship to the real world of politics (or, for that matter, of business, technology, art, or culture).

Today's protesters may think they are marching in the footsteps of those who came before. In fact, they are undoing much of that generation's enduring accomplishment.[12]

Is there anything that Boxill might say to defend today's student protesters? How might self-respect lead today's students to make different demands than those of earlier generations?

Notes

1. W. E. B. Dubois, "Of Mr. Booker T. Washington and Others," in *Negro Social and Political Thought 1850–1920*, ed. Howard Brotz (New York, 1966), p. 514. Hereafter cited as Brotz.
2. *W. E. B. Dubois*, ed. William M. Tuttle, Jr. (New Jersey, 1973), p. 48.
3. Booker T. Washington, "Democracy and Education," in Brotz, p. 370.
4. Ibid.
5. Booker T. Washington, "The Intellectuals and the Boston Mob," in Brotz, p. 425.
6. Ibid., p. 429.
7. Frederick Douglass, "What the Black Man Wants," in Brotz, p. 283.
8. *W. E. B. Dubois*, p. 43.

9. Frederick Douglass, "What Are the Colored People Doing for Themselves?" in Brotz, p. 208.

10. Orlando Patterson, "Toward a Future That Has No Past: Reflections on the Fate of Blacks in the Americas," in *The Public Interest* 27 (Spring 1972), p. 43.

11. Ibid.

12. http://www.politico.com/magazine/story/2015/12/campus-protests-1960s-213450

Symbolic Protest and Calculated Silence

Thomas E. Hill, Jr.

....

One natural reason for protesting injustice is that protesting makes things better. Perhaps it can prevent future injustice, or encourage the victims of injustice. It is much harder to understand why you ought to protest injustice from a deontological perspective. From a deontological perspective, you can't appeal to the good consequences of protesting to justify it, and more important, you can be obligated to protest even when protest won't bring about any good consequences at all. Thomas Hill considers some standard deontological principles—for example, that you ought to tell the truth and that you shouldn't harm innocents—and finds that they don't yield any strong obligation to protest injustice, though they do make protest permissible in some cases. However, he argues that we sometimes have a duty to dissociate ourselves from groups or individuals that perpetrate serious injustice. In this way, you can more closely associate yourself with the good by severing your ties with evil.

....

Hill, Thomas E. 1979. "Symbolic Protest and Calculated Silence." *Philosophy & Public Affairs* 9(1): 83–102. Reprinted with permission of John Wiley & Sons.

The reasons for protesting a serious injustice are usually not hard to find. One wants to put an end to the wrongdoing, to prevent its recurrence, or at least touch some consciences in a way that may prove beneficial in other contexts. But sometimes there seems to be no reasonable hope of achieving these ends. The perpetrators of injustice will not be moved, protest may be inconvenient or risky to oneself, and its long-range effects on others may be minimal or may include as much harm as help. To protest in these circumstances seems at best a symbolic gesture. But is it a gesture worth making? Attitudes about this diverge sharply. Some say that, despite the consequences, protest is called for: "One cannot stand silently by." To denounce injustice at a risk to oneself is morally admirable, they say, whether or not it produces a positive net utility. Others see symbolic protest as pointless and at times reprehensible. If the overall effects for others are not better and it entails harm or risk to oneself, is it not foolish? And isn't the motive simply a self-righteous desire to be, or appear, morally "pure"?

These conflicting attitudes pose a problem of understanding for moral philosophy. The point of view behind the second attitude is clear enough: Acts, including speech acts, are to be evaluated by their probable consequences; no one is morally required to take risks unless the probable consequences are beneficial; what is commendable is regard for the best results, not futile gestures. If silence, even compromise, is well calculated to produce the best consequences, then that is the course one should take. This consequentialist attitude is familiar and, in the absence of cogent alternatives, very appealing. In reflecting on sample cases, however, many of us, I think, will find ourselves drawn to the first attitude, which regards symbolic protest as commendable despite the risks. But what can be said for it? Why should we feel that symbolic protest is often appropriate and admirable rather than foolish and self-righteous?

I

It may be well to begin by fixing attention on some examples. Consider first an old woman in Nazi Germany. She lives on modest savings and offers no support to the Nazi regime either physically or morally. When the latest discriminatory laws against Jews are enforced, she is moved to protest. As a non-Jew she could have remained silent and thereby avoided much subsequent harassment. She is regarded as a silly eccentric and so cannot expect to make an impact on others, much less to stop the Nazi machinery. She still feels that she should speak up, but she wonders why. Next consider a liberal businessmen at a racist dinner party. Invited by business acquaintances, he is shocked to find that the conversation on all sides is openly and grossly contemptuous of certain minorities on grounds of racial bias alone. The guests try to outdo one another with tales about how they manage to circumvent equal opportunity laws. Polite opposition yields nothing but cynical laughter. The indignant liberal is convinced at last that nothing he can say will have any good effect on this company. He wonders then whether it is best to finish the dinner quietly, for the sake of his business interests, or to walk out in protest.[1]

These cases exemplify certain conditions which I shall take as paradigmatic of the problem of symbolic protest, at least of the sort I intend to discuss: (a) the protest is of a serious injustice done to others; (b) the protest cannot reasonably be expected to end the injustice, to prevent its recurrence, or to rectify it in any way; (c) the protest may cause some harm, but not disaster, to the protestor; (d) the effects of the protest on others' welfare can reasonably be expected to be minimal or to include a balance of benefit and harm. In real cases, of course, the facts may be disputed, but for present purposes let us take these conditions as given. . . .

The examples have been deliberately constructed to set aside familiar utilitarian arguments for protest. . . .

In setting aside utilitarian considerations, however, we do not necessarily limit our conclusions to cases in which they do not apply. For if, by focusing on the restricted cases, we can find non-utilitarian arguments for protest, these may reinforce whatever utilitarian arguments there are for protest.

II

Having set aside utilitarian considerations, it is natural to look for reasons for protest among the principles commonly held by deontologists. These would include prohibitions of promise-breaking, deliberate deception, killing of innocents, and the like. In special cases of symbolic protest these principles might be applicable. Suppose, for example, that I have made a solemn promise to a friend that I will not stand by while his good name is slandered by his enemies after his death. Then, as soon as he dies, greedy and malicious biographers try to make a quick profit by inventing scandalous stories about him. Suppose that I know that the stories are false, but I cannot prove it. Even if I cannot prevent their publication or force retractions, it seems I should protest and tell the truth as I know it. This seems so, even if the effort is inconvenient to me and the effect on others is insignificant.

There may also be times when protest is necessary to avoid deception. Suppose, for example, that a group of people is doing what I regard quite wrong, say, amusing themselves by slaughtering polar bears with rifles from helicopters. But imagine that these are wealthy, influential people, with whom for selfish reasons I want to be associated. If I let my true feelings show, they may break off the association; and I am reasonably convinced that I cannot change them. Avoiding the issue, let us say, is impossible: I must pretend to condone their activities or else let them know my objections. As they, assuming our mutual respect, come to count me as a friend, surely I should not persist in the deception.

. . . In other special situations deontological principles come into play in a rather more complex way. Consider the judge in Nazi Germany who is ordered to sign death warrants for political prisoners whom he believes innocent. To refuse will only result in his replacement by someone else who will sign the warrants. . . . He figures that he can bring about some good results by keeping quiet, signing the warrants, and trying to help others secretly later. But this path of calculated silence is blocked if there is an absolute, or at least quite stringent, moral principle against killing innocent people. His only remaining choices are to resign without protest or to resign (or be dismissed) with protest. The principle against killing does not itself require protest but it rules out the only appealing alternative.

. . .

Sometimes the relevant deontological principle may be, not a direct prohibition of deception, killing, slandering, and the like, but a more indefinite proscription of complicity in such activities. Although rhetoric often treats any association with corrupt people or institutions as complicity, I have in mind a narrower sense of the term. The paradigm is a direct and substantial contribution to wrongdoing, made freely with acceptable options available and with the knowledge that one is so contributing. . . .

Like the previous principles, a principle against moral complicity can undermine the rationale for suppressing a protest even though it provides no direct reason to protest. Consider the worker in a factory recently converted from automobile-making to the production of tanks for use in an unjust war. He knows that if he resigns, he will be replaced easily; and if he protests the war, he will be fired. Losing the job would be a personal hardship, and, because he is of an unpopular and suspect race, he believes that no one would be influenced by his protest. Sabotage is out of the question, as it has been repeatedly detected and suppressed. To hold back his objections to the war and quietly continue to build the tanks seems to involve him in moral complicity. The only remaining options are to resign without giving reasons or to protest. The prohibition of complicity does not demand protest, but it blocks off as illegitimate a choice to reap the maximum benefits of remaining silent.

. . .

IV

If the purpose of symbolic protest is not to satisfy familiar deontological principles . . ., what is the point? One conception worth exploring is that the point, at least the immediate point, is to disassociate oneself from evil. . . . While committing no injustice himself, a person can nevertheless associate himself with those who do by condoning their activities; and a person can disassociate himself from a corrupt group both by acting to prevent their unjust acts and also, in appropriate contexts, by protesting, denouncing what they do, and taking a symbolic stand with the victims. "Who one is" for moral purposes—e.g., a Nazi, a racist, a Christian, a humanist—is determined not simply by substantive contributions to various good or evil causes but to some extent by what and whom one associates oneself with, and in some contexts this depends importantly on the symbolic gestures one is prepared to make.

. . .

First consider disassociation from organizations or groups that are deeply involved in injustice and prove to be beyond reform. To refuse all commerce and communication with corrupt groups would be foolish and dangerous; and to proclaim repeatedly, "I am not one of them!" seems self-righteous and unnecessary. But a more limited disassociation in special contexts is often regarded as morally appropriate and even commendable. Suppose, for example, that a person finds himself a member of an organization that has just become, or is just discovered to be, thoroughly corrupt, reaping profits from all manner of harmful and unjust practices. The organization might be a social club, an athletic team, a political party, a business firm, or any voluntary group capable of joint action, incurring obligations, and having common interests and principles. . . . Often the offensive part of the organization can be isolated and opposed without complete withdrawal; but sometimes not. The corruption may be so severe and so deeply entrenched that to remain a member, especially a non-protesting member, seems morally intolerable. . . .

Sometimes, of course, a person can disassociate himself from a group without making a protest. If the group is highly structured, there may be formal procedures for severing the connection: resigning, refusing to pay dues, getting rid of one's stock holdings, and so on. Sometimes, however, the group is so loosely bound by ties of sentiment, mutual expectations, common aims, and the like, that there are no official procedures for getting out. One must make one's objections explicit or be counted a continuing member. The membership conditions may even be so vague that without an overt act of disassociation one will still *be* a member. Suppose, for example, you have deliberately but informally associated yourself with "whites" in a racially polarized community; with a certain social set; with an unstructured group of fans of a team or a politician; or with a revolutionary movement. As there are no dues, membership lists, and the like, there can be no formal resignation. . . . to dissociate at once you may have to say something or do something to express your new attitude of opposition.

. . .

. . . [D]isassociation is not simply an inward disapproval or secret resolve to oppose; these amount to only a wish or plan to disassociate. Again, disassociation is not simply a matter of words or symbolic gestures; for the person who *says* that he disassociates himself, even turns in a formal resignation, is not always convincing. If he continues to favor the group and secretly gives it aid, then he has only pretended to disassociate himself or has done so only in form. To disassociate, one needs both an appropriate attitude, including a disposition to refuse support, and some outward manifestation of that attitude, for example, opposition or refusal of support when the occasion allows or, at least, tokens of one's intention to oppose or refuse support if nothing more is possible.

The principle that one should disassociate from irreparably corrupt groups, if accepted, would favor symbolic protest in many cases. If, to alter my previous examples, the woman in Nazi Germany had voted for the Nazis, or was a party member or government employee, she might reasonably regard herself as associated with the leadership even though she came to disapprove of their policies. Lacking an opportunity for effective opposition, she might well think that a symbolic protest was necessary to disassociate her, so far as possible, from them. Again, if my liberal businessman was in partnership with other guests and if their racist attitudes affected joint policy, he would naturally feel that a symbolic protest was the least he could do. But the examples as originally described were not so clear-cut. The old woman was a German but not otherwise associated with the Nazis, and the liberal was acquainted with the other guests but not in partnership with them. These associations lie at best on the border of the class of voluntary groups we have considered; and so the argument for symbolic protest as a way of disassociating from evil groups is blurred in these cases. Moreover, a slight shift in the cases would make this rationale for symbolic protest even more dubious. Suppose, for example, that the old woman was not even a German but a foreigner just passing through Nazi Germany. As she is not associated with the Nazis, she has no need to disassociate herself in the sense we have been considering. Similarly, if the liberal businessman had overheard racist talk from strangers on a bus, rather than from partners or fellow guests, he had no need to break off an association. The principle that one ought to disassociate from irreparably corrupt organizations is also of limited application for another reason, noted earlier: one can often disassociate without protesting. For example, one can resign from a company without giving reasons, divest oneself of stock in a morally dubious enterprise without explaining why, and run away from military induction without stating one's moral objections to it or the war it supports.

Another principle which, I suspect, is widely held in some form or other is that one should refuse to associate oneself with individuals who are thoroughly corrupt. This would apply in contexts where one had no previous association with the individuals, such as friendship or membership in the same clubs. The idea is that when a person reaches an extreme point of corruption, and seems to offer no hope of reform, one should not merely deplore what he does but deny him much of what is normally extended to those with whom one associates oneself: for example, loyalty, trust, respect as an individual, social amenities, readiness to cooperate and compromise, and the various signs of being pleased to share in mutual projects. The principle, no doubt, is acceptable to most only if suitably qualified. There may be overriding reasons of state which require some association with the worst of leaders. Some would say that everyone is owed respect as a human being, and others might add that all should be loved. Organizations can be abandoned as worthless and beyond repair without anyone necessarily being the worse for it, but when the same attitude is generally taken toward a person it seems inevitable that at least one person will be hurt. Refusal to associate with someone can easily be hypocritical; people in glass houses should hesitate to throw stones, and most of our houses are to some extent brittle. Nevertheless, if these matters are taken into account, many would still say that there are times when one should refuse to associate with corrupt people and [that there are] morally appropriate ways to do it. A European prince was widely applauded, for example, when he literally turned his back on a notorious African tyrant, and a late presidential candidate was roundly condemned by many for posing for photographs with his arm around the man who had come to symbolize hostility to civil rights.

The principle that one should refuse to associate oneself with extraordinarily corrupt people would favor symbolic protest in situations where silence creates a presumption of normal social relations, giving the impression that what is really outrageous is in fact overlooked or condoned. The businessman, for example, would give an impression of being ready to associate himself with the racists if he finished his dinner quietly listening to their stream of bigotry. And even a visitor in Nazi Germany would seem ready to associate with the Nazis if she went through the motions of the happy tourist while Jews were being rounded up for deportation. In these circumstances a person who wanted not to associate himself with extreme racists would naturally see vigorous protest as at least a partial way of expressing this and of preventing association from developing.

The principles just considered favor symbolic protest only in extreme cases, in which the protestor wants to get out of a corrupt group altogether or avoid becoming associated with extraordinarily corrupt individuals. There are many other situations, however, in which the symbolic protest may seem appropriate: for example, when one belongs to a basically good organization which is seriously unjust in some limited aspect, or when one has important overriding moral reasons to remain a part of a basically bad organization, or when for good reasons one does not wish to shun an unjust individual but only deplore what he does. In these cases too symbolic a protest might be motivated by a desire to disassociate oneself, in a sense, from evil. The idea would be not to break or avoid an association with an individual or group but to put oneself on record as opposed to the sort of acts and policies that are protested . . . .

. . .

V

Even if these principles are intuitively appealing, we still naturally wonder *why* we should disassociate ourselves from evil in the various ways we have considered. By hypothesis, protest will not put an end to the injustice or have, on balance, beneficial consequences. One familiar response, suggested by both critics and advocates of symbolic protest, is that the purpose is "to keep one's hands clean." This view can take many forms, most of which do little to support our initial intuitive feelings for symbolic protest.

It is sometimes said, for example, that by his silence the non-protestor shares the guilt of the wrongdoer or, more dramatically, that the blood of the victims will stain his hands as well as the oppressor's. But this requires interpretation. On one reading, the contention reflects a confused idea of moral guilt. It treats guilt as something which can pass from one person to another by contact, like the stains of fresh blood or dye, or by social intercourse, like reputation and stigma. . . . But on any standard view of guilt which implies a wrong on the part of the guilty, guilt cannot be transferred in these ways. If the non-protestor is guilty, it is for something he himself has done (or omitted), not for what others have done (or omitted). . . .

. . .

There is, I think, a more charitable reading of the "clean hands" rationale for symbolic protest. On this interpretation, the protestor's attempts to disassociate himself are not so much efforts to avoid responsibility as expressions of the high value he places on justice. Normally one who cares for justice can show it not only by refraining from unjust acts but also by constructive efforts to reform unjust institutions, and the like. But in the contexts under discussion there are no opportunities for such constructive activity. One is faced with gross injustice and is powerless to stop it. Deploring it intensely, one would naturally prefer not to be surrounded by it, to live amiably with those who perpetuate it, and to suppress one's feelings about it. Those who care deeply about aesthetic standards will similarly want to disassociate themselves in various ways from groups and individuals who perpetuate ugliness, even when they cannot effect a change, and they will naturally want to speak out when confronted with the most blatant offenses against taste. Civility requires more restraint in this case, but the feelings can be similar. What makes symbolic protest commendable on this view is not intended results but the underlying values expressed. . . .

While this may help to explain why those who make symbolic protests are sometimes admired and commended, it does not offer much of an argument to a person who is wondering whether or not he should make a symbolic protest. Should we say to him, "Disassociate yourself because you will thereby give natural expression to your deep concern for justice, which is something commendable to have"? If he lacks the deep concern, protest would only fool others and make him no better. But if he has it and knows that this is what makes him *want* to disassociate himself from corrupt groups or individuals, he may wonder why he would be more commendable if he decides to act on this desire. To express a commendable desire just to show others that one has it is not an especially worthy motive. . . .

The idea that one should disassociate oneself from evil in order to "keep one's hands clean" focuses attention on what disassociation is supposed to do for the protestor. . . . An alternative conception, suggested by Kant, would turn attention in another direction. The point, on this view, is not so much to keep one's own hands clean as to avoid white-washing the bloody deeds of others. In answer to the question of whether or not one is permitted to associate with the wicked, Kant says . . . that any decent self-respecting person has more to offer individuals (and groups, causes, and so on) than whatever effective action he can take on their behalf. He can also give it "honor," credit, and acclaim; and he does this not just by explicit praise but by identifying himself publicly with those individuals (groups, causes, and so on). That such intangibles are regarded important is evident in all sorts of contexts where morality is not at issue. For example, in friendships, families, well-knit teams, and social clubs, we value not only the time, money, and other substantive support that our associates give us; we also care about their good opinion and the honor they do us by identifying with us. But a person who is indiscriminate about whom and what he associates himself with debases his currency, so to speak, and so makes his choice to associate no honor at all. . . . The point of disassociation, on this view, is not so much to gain benefits for oneself or to punish the corrupt but to enable one to honor the persons, groups, and causes that, from a moral point of view, most deserve it. One would disassociate from evil so that one could more meaningfully associate with good.

...

Comprehension Questions

1. How do consequentialists and non-consequentialists differ in their views about protesting injustice?
2. What kind of support do deontological duties—such as the duty to tell the truth, or not to deceive—lend to the person who protests injustice?
3. What are some typical features of the act of dissociating oneself from a corrupt group?
4. What limitations are there on the applicability of the duty to dissociate oneself from corrupt groups?
5. What makes the principle that one should dissociate from corrupt groups different from the principle that one should dissociate from corrupt individuals?
6. Why does Hill reject the "clean hands" rationale for refusing to associate with corrupt groups or individuals, and what's his alternative?

Discussion Questions

1. Have you ever participated in a protest? If so, what was it? Would you do it again? If not, is there a protest that you think you would participate in? If so, which one? Otherwise, why not?
2. Recall the two cases with which Hill starts his discussion—the old woman in Nazi Germany and the businessman at a racist dinner party. After introducing a principle in favor of protesting injustice, he suggests it's unclear whether it applies to these cases. In light of his arguments, do you think these two have a duty to protest? Why or why not?
3. Hill mentions that there are constraints on our ability to dissociate from individuals. What are these constraints? Do you think they are legitimate? Can you think of any other constraints that Hill doesn't mention?

Case

In 2013, *Rolling Stone* published an eye-opening piece on what it's like to be a chicken in an industrial farm (which is the situation of over 95 percent of the nine *billion* chickens that are raised and killed in the United States each year):

> You are a typical egg-laying chicken in America, and this is your life: You're trapped in a cage with six to eight hens, each given less than a square foot of space to roost and sleep in. The cages rise five high and run thousands long in a warehouse without windows or skylights. You see and smell nothing from the moment of your birth but the shit coming down through the open slats of the battery cages above you. It coats your feathers and becomes a second skin; by the time you're plucked from your cage for slaughter, your bones and wings breaking in the grasp of harried workers, you look less like a hen than an oil-spill duck, blackened by years of droppings. Your eyes tear constantly from the fumes of your own urine, you wheeze and gasp like a retired miner, and you're beset every second of the waking day by mice and plague-like clouds of flies. If you're a broiler chicken (raised specifically for meat), thanks to "meat science" and its chemical levers—growth hormones, antibiotics and genetically engineered feed—you weigh at least double what you would in the wild, but lack the muscle even to waddle, let alone fly. Like egg-laying hens—your comrades in suffering—you get sick young with late-life woes: heart disease, osteoporosis. It's frankly a mercy you'll be dead and processed in forty-five days, yanked from your floor pen and slaughtered. The egg-layers you leave behind will grind on for another two years or so (or until they're "spent" and can't produce any more eggs), then they're killed too.[2]

Now let's be honest: there's very little you can do about this. You can opt out of eating chicken, of course, and perhaps you should. But that may not make much difference—if any—given how large and complex the market is. According to Hill, that doesn't matter. Do you agree? If so, what does that mean for your diet?

Notes

1. Walking out, like refusing a handshake and turning one's back, can be means of protesting without words. So when, in the title of this paper, calculated silence is contrasted with protest, this must not be taken too literally. For the purpose of protest, symbolic actions often speak louder than words.
2. http://www.rollingstone.com/feature/belly-beast-meat-factory-farms-animal-activists

PART VI

Drugs and Drinking

29

An Argument for Drug Prohibition

Peter de Marneffe

We know that drugs are highly valuable to those who use them, and that prohibition would involve infringing on personal liberties, which is generally undesirable. We also know that they often have serious negative consequences, both physical and psychological, for their users. Weighing these and other considerations, Peter de Marneffe argues that the harms of drug use (and indirectly caused by drug manufacturing and sales) are significant enough to justify prohibition. As he reasons, failing to prohibit drugs—he focuses on the case of heroin—would inevitably lead to greater drug abuse, harming drug users and their families (especially any young or adolescent children they may have). He addresses, further, several common reasons for worrying that prohibition will be ineffective.

The General Argument

There is only one good reason for drug prohibition, which is that some of us will be worse off if drugs are legalized. Why would any of us be worse off? With drug legalization there will be more drug abuse, and drug abuse is bad for people.

de Marneffe, Peter. 2005. "An Argument for Drug Prohibition." In *The Legalization of Drugs: For and Against*, Douglas Husak and Peter de Marneffe, pp. 109–118. New York: Cambridge University Press. Copyright © 2005 Doug Husak and Peter de Marneffe. Reprinted with the permission of Cambridge University Press.

By "drug abuse" I mean use that (a) harms others or oneself or creates a risk of harm that is great enough either to constitute a wrong to others or to be imprudent. Within the range of harms I mean to include the loss of valuable opportunities and resources as well as damage to a person's physical or psychological health, functioning, or well-being.

Since drug prohibition itself makes drug use harmful in a number of ways—by creating significant risks of criminal liability, for example—it is necessary to distinguish legally created harms from what I will call *independent harms*, which are those that drug use would produce even if drugs were legal. Drug prohibition can be justified only as reducing independent harms since legally created harms would be eliminated by legalization. What independent harms, then, does drug prohibition reduce? This depends on the drug in question, but grouping all currently illegal drugs together we can say that drug prohibition now reduces risks of premature death, accidental bodily injury, violence, vandalism, marital instability, child neglect, and failure at important educational and occupational tasks. This is the argument for drug prohibition, and so against drug legalization.

By *drug legalization* I mean a policy under which there are no criminal penalties for the *manufacture* and *sale* of drugs (to adults). If drugs were legalized, the law would therefore treat drugs such as heroin and cocaine in roughly the same way that it now treats alcohol and cigarettes. Drug legalization in this sense is different from "drug decriminalization," which is the removal of criminal penalties for the *use* of drugs and for the possession of small quantities. In supporting drug *prohibition* here, I oppose drug *legalization*, but not necessarily drug *decriminalization*.

Drug prohibition is justified, in my view, as reducing the independent harms of drug abuse. But it is commonly objected that drug laws "don't work." Does this mean that drug laws do not *eradicate* drug abuse? If so, it is no argument for drug legalization. In this sense laws against murder and theft do not work either, but this does not mean that we should abolish them. The question in evaluating drug prohibition, as in evaluating any coercive policy, is whether it reduces harm to individuals *enough* to justify the burdens imposed on individuals by its system of penalties. We think this is true of laws against murder and theft. So we think they are justified. If this were likewise true of drug prohibition, this policy would likewise be justified.

Does the objection that drug laws do not work mean, then, that they do absolutely *nothing* to reduce drug abuse? If so, this is hard to believe. The main reason people use drugs is that they are enjoyable. If an activity is enjoyable, we can safely predict that more people will engage in it and that individuals will engage in it more often as it becomes easier and less expensive to do. If drugs are legal, they will be easier to acquire because they will be sold at local stores. They will be less expensive because they will be more plentiful and their price will no longer reflect the risks of selling an illegal product: the risks of violence, incarceration, confiscation of property, and so on. Drugs will be safer because they will be sold in standard dosages. Furthermore, the psychological cost of having to deal with unsavory characters in unsafe parts of town in order to buy drugs will be eliminated, as well as the stigma involved in buying an illegal product.

Admittedly it does not follow logically from the premise that drug *use* will increase with legalization that drug *abuse* will also increase. It is *possible* that everyone who is disposed to abuse drugs already uses them illegally and abuses them as much as he or she would if they were legal. Since, however, drug legalization would make it easier to use drugs, it would also make it easier to abuse them. If we assume, then, that a person is more likely to do something she or he is tempted to do the easier and less costly it is, we may reasonably conclude that a person is also more likely to abuse drugs if they are legal. To this we may add that if the manufacture and sale of drugs are legal, drug manufacturers will market them in the same way that alcohol and cigarettes are now marketed. Assuming, then, that such marketing results in people's drinking and smoking more than they otherwise would, we can predict that similar advertising of currently illegal drugs would result in people's using drugs more than they otherwise would, and so in this way also [lead] to an increase in drug abuse.

What any honest defender of drug prohibition must still concede is that the mere fact that drug prohibition works to *some* degree is not enough to justify it. It must work *well enough* to justify the burdens it imposes on people. That is, it must decrease the independent harms of drug abuse *enough* to justify the legally created harms it creates. In what follows I will assume that drug prohibition functions to reduce these independent harms *substantially*. I make this assumption because it is what I believe, but I concede that it cannot be proved. I believe that no one is justified in feeling certain *one way or the other* about the degree to which drug prohibition reduces the independent harms of drug abuse. What I aim to do, then, is to offer a philosophical defense of drug prohibition that is consistent with what we know for sure about drug use; that is based on plausible assumptions about human nature; and that represents a morally defensible balancing of the interests of individuals on certain empirical assumptions.

Heroin

Different drugs have different effects. Some, although they may be subject to abuse, are not nearly as harmful as others. So we must always evaluate the policy of prohibition drug by drug. For this reason I begin my defense of drug prohibition by stating an argument for heroin prohibition. I start here because I believe it is easier to make a persuasive case for prohibiting heroin than for prohibiting any other drug, with the possible exception of alcohol. If I am right about this, and the case for heroin prohibition fails, then this is a powerful argument for drug legalization in general. If, on the other hand, the case for heroin prohibition succeeds, then this will provide a good vantage point from which to consider whether good arguments might also be made for prohibiting other drugs.

Heroin has two properties that make it the appropriate object of special concern. One of these is that heroin offers a unique and very intense form of pleasure.[1] This is especially true when heroin is injected, but smoking heroin, which has become more common as purer forms of heroin have become available on the black market, also produces intense pleasure. Not everyone who tries heroin enjoys it, but a high proportion of those who try it say they do.[2] Moreover, heroin users commonly say that heroin is far more pleasurable than anything else they have experienced and sometimes describe an almost religious devotion to it.[3] Because such a high proportion of those who try it enjoy it, and because it is so much more pleasurable to many of them than anything else they might do, we can safely predict an increase in heroin use, and so in heroin abuse, if heroin is legalized.

Why would this be a bad thing? The other important property of heroin is that, as a particularly strong form of opium, it has the effect on some people of sharply depressing their motivation to achieve worthwhile goals and to meet their responsibilities and commitments to others, to go to school or go to work, for example, or to take care of their children. If heroin depresses motivation in this way, then an increase in heroin abuse will result in more children being neglected by their parents and more adolescents neglecting their education and other important developmental tasks.

Children need parents who are attentive and involved. If parents are oblivious to their children's needs, the effects on their children's future welfare, and indirectly on the rest of society, constitute significant harms. Adolescence, too, is a time when we learn important social and cognitive skills, habits, and forms of self-discipline that are crucial to our future ability to work, to succeed financially and professionally, to sustain important relationships, and to meet important family commitments, such as those to our children. If a person spends the adolescent years getting high on heroin instead of going to class, meeting the emotional challenges of growing up, and developing constructive relationships with adults in positions of authority, he or she is likely to be permanently hobbled.

Heroin may not necessarily have this negative effect on motivation. Drug researchers have observed that the effects of a drug vary with "set and setting": the social group in which the drug is used, their expectations and values, and the occasions on which the drug is used.[4] If, for example, alcohol is drunk in drams throughout the day as a refreshment for the purpose of giving workers a mental lift, it will predictably have a different psychological effect than if it is drunk after work in bars for the purpose of lowering one's inhibitions against making sexual advances or getting into fights. Within our society, however, heroin use is not part of any formal social setting, and its use is not regulated by conventional norms. Furthermore, it is widely understood to depress motivation and concern with conventionally defined success. So it is reasonable to expect that if heroin were now legalized, heroin use would continue to have this psychological effect, at least for the foreseeable future.

Since alcohol is currently legal, and this condition is not likely to change soon, it is necessary to defend the prohibition of any drug against the background of legalized alcohol. Observe, then, that an increase in the use of some drug as a result of legalization might actually result in a net decrease in the independent harms of drug and alcohol abuse taken together. To understand why, suppose that people who are now deterred from abusing a drug by its relative scarcity and danger typically abuse alcohol instead. If so, then legalizing this drug might not result in a net increase in overall drug and alcohol abuse. It might only make drugs that are now illegal the "drug of choice" of those who now abuse alcohol. This is significant because alcohol abuse is arguably worse—the cause of more independent harms—than the abuse of any currently illegal drug. Heroin use, for example, does not cause liver cirrhosis or have the same apparent tendency to lead to violence. So if the legalization of heroin were to lead those who now abuse alcohol to abuse heroin instead, this might result in a net *reduction* of independent harms.

To be justified in supporting drug prohibition, while leaving current alcohol policy in place, we must therefore be justified in believing that the abuse of drugs that are now illegal would increase and that the number of

independent harms overall would increase as a result. I think we are justified in believing this about heroin partly because of the uniquely intense
form of pleasure it offers, which leads some of those who use it to "fall in
love" with it in ways that they would never fall in love with alcohol or any
other drug, and partly because habitual heroin use has a greater negative
impact on motivation than habitual drinking typically does. For these
reasons I believe that the independent harms of drug abuse would increase substantially if heroin were legalized. To fill in this picture, imagine that anyone older than eighteen or twenty-one may buy heroin from
the local liquor store or the local pharmacy, in safe and inexpensive doses.
Under these conditions we can safely predict that the amount of heroin
use among the general population will rise, and that the amount of heroin
abuse among parents and adolescents will rise proportionately. If heroin
is legal, parents can buy and use it legally. Some of them will abuse it.
Parental abuse of heroin will lead to the neglect of children, resulting in
feelings of low self-esteem and a lack of direction. Parental drug use is
also a model for child drug use. The greater availability of heroin will
mean, too, greater availability to one's peers, and so more peer acceptance
of heroin use, and so greater influence within peer groups to use it.[5] True,
no one younger than eighteen or twenty-one will be able to purchase
heroin legally, but we can safely predict that this restriction will do no
more to discourage underage heroin use than it does now to discourage
underage drinking or smoking.[6] This is because, as is now the case with
alcohol and cigarettes, some stores will not be particularly vigilant about
to whom they sell their heroin, and many teenagers will be able to get
heroin from older siblings or friends, or to steal it from their parents, or
to have strangers buy it for them.

For these reasons, if heroin is legalized, some individuals will be at a
much higher risk of heroin abuse than they otherwise would be: Those
whose parents and peers use it who would not otherwise use it, who have
low self-esteem and a lack of direction as a result of parental neglect resulting from heroin abuse, who are struggling emotionally and academically, and who would therefore welcome this means of escape. To this we
can add that adolescence is often a difficult period, as individuals struggle
to form an independent identity and to accomplish important tasks amid
an array of psychological distractions. For this reason, heroin will be
tempting to adolescents in many different situations. Get high, and you
can stop worrying about being unpopular, or unattractive, or bad at
sports or worrying about your parents' finances or marital troubles.

Given the relief from anxiety and worry that heroin temporarily provides, as well as the simple pleasure, the belief that *many* adolescents will be at a substantially higher risk of heroin abuse if it is legalized is thus reasonable. Perhaps most adolescents who abuse drugs have other problems beforehand, but legalization would only increase the likelihood that those with other problems would abuse drugs, thus exacerbating whatever other problems they already had. . . .

The Costs of Prohibition

The argument I have just sketched for heroin prohibition depends on a number of empirical assumptions that might be questioned. But even if they are sound, it does not directly follow that heroin prohibition is justifiable since this policy itself imposes substantial burdens. The most serious of these is the substantial risk of criminal liability that it imposes on those who are tempted to manufacture and sell heroin. If this risk of criminal liability is too great, then the benefits of reducing heroin abuse among parents and teenagers will not be great enough to justify prohibition. A defensible policy of prohibition therefore rests on the assumption that heroin abuse can be reduced substantially—enough to make the policy worthwhile—even with a gradual and proportionate system of penalties that does not impose an unacceptably high risk of imprisonment on anyone.

What would such a system look like? First, the possession of small quantities of heroin would be a misdemeanor, not a felony. (Whether this amounts to *decriminalization* depends on whether legal penalties for misdemeanors and even less serious administrative violations are counted as "criminal" penalties.) Second, although the manufacture, sale, and possession of larger quantities would be a felony, the penalties would be gradual and proportionate. No one would be incarcerated for a first offense, unless he or she refused to meet the conditions of probation, such as counseling and community service, and penalties for second and third offenses would remain relatively light. Although it seems fair to confiscate supplies and other assets even for first offenses, long prison sentences for those involved in the drug trade are unjustifiable, even after the second or third conviction, because these sentences are themselves so destructive of a person's life prospects.

. . .

Drug prohibition is justifiable only because we think that people, especially young people, do not always act in their own best interest and therefore need some protection from the worst possible consequences of their potentially imprudent decisions. Since this is equally true of many people who decide to deal drugs, especially young people, they likewise need protection in the form of a gradual and proportionate system of penalties. Some may contend here that heroin prohibition will be ineffective without a harsher system, but there is no compelling reason to believe that prohibition is made any more effective by harsh penalties than it would be by lighter penalties more reliably and consistently enforced.[7] In fact, the effectiveness of prohibition might be *increased* by lightening the penalties, since this might increase the chances of conviction for drug offenses by compassionate juries. The risk of criminal liability is not the only significant burden imposed by a policy of drug prohibition. The drug trade is also violent because it is illegal, and so theft, breach of contract, unfair trade practices, and other disputes cannot be settled in court. Drug prohibition thus increases the risk of violence to those involved in the drug trade and to innocent bystanders. For this reason a policy of heroin prohibition will be fully justifiable only if the government is committed to reducing the neighborhood violence that the black market creates, where this will require, among other things, increased funding for neighborhood policing.

That the drug trade also produces huge profits for those willing to break the law has had grave political consequences in some countries, such as Colombia and Afghanistan, where drug lords wield tremendous political influence and inflict terrible violence on those who oppose them.[8] For this reason a policy of heroin prohibition will be fully justifiable only if the governments of the developed world are willing to offer financial incentives to less developed countries to grow other crops and to help them suppress money laundering activities. In some cases it may also be necessary for the governments of the developed world to use their military forces against drug lords, with the consent of local governments, in order to protect local government officials from intimidation and violence, and, in some places such as Afghanistan, actively to engage in a policy of "nation-building."

Another significant cost of drug prohibition is that its effective enforcement creates a risk of civil liberty violations by the police and others. If heroin prohibition is to be fully justifiable, drug enforcement agencies must therefore be trained to respect civil liberties scrupulously and institutional incentives must not be created for breaking the law in ways that violate the civil rights of innocent citizens.

Still another cost of drug prohibition is that it increases the risk of fatal overdose to those who now use drugs because illegal drugs are commonly sold in unpredictable and unregulated doses. To be fully justified in enforcing a policy of heroin prohibition, the government must therefore also be committed to reducing the risk of fatal overdose by effective public information activities. And, in order to reduce the risks of contracting hepatitis, HIV, and AIDS, the government should in any case make clean needles available to drug users who want them.

Another burden of heroin prohibition as it is currently enforced is that it prohibits the possession of heroin for the treatment of pain. Heroin is thought by some to be more effective than other drugs in treating chronic pain caused by diseases such as cancer because it relieves a person's misery while allowing her to maintain relatively clear conscious contact with the world. If so, then a defensible policy of heroin prohibition must also allow the prescription of heroin for use in hospitals and hospices.

In sum, heroin prohibition as it is now enforced imposes many burdens. Some of these, such as overly harsh penalties, are unjustifiable, but these unjustifiable burdens are not *necessarily* imposed by a policy of heroin prohibition. What I maintain, then, is that if the unnecessary burdens of heroin prohibition are eliminated, and the necessary burdens are therefore lightened as much as possible, the benefits of reducing heroin abuse among parents and young people can justify a policy of heroin prohibition. . . .

Comprehension Questions

1. What is de Marneffe's overall argument for drug prohibition, and what does he mean by "independent harm"?
2. How does de Marneffe respond to the claim that drug prohibition does not work?
3. What is the strategic value of focusing on heroin in particular?
4. What harms are associated with heroin use, and in what ways do they differ from those associated with alcohol use?
5. Why does de Marneffe think legalizing heroin would increase risk of its use and abuse?
6. How does de Marneffe propose to alter existing penalties for drug use, sale, and production? Why should we accept these alterations?
7. What costs are associated with drug prohibition, and how does de Marneffe think they can be handled?

Discussion Questions

1. De Marneffe focuses on heroin based on the idea that his argument for heroin's prohibition can serve as a model for arguments targeting other drugs. Do you think his argument for heroin prohibition can legitimately be extended to cover other drugs? Why or why not?

2. De Marneffe's claim is that the harms associated with drugs outweigh the harms of their prohibition. When you compare the two, do you draw the same conclusion as de Marneffe does? Why or why not?

3. Has de Marneffe failed to mention any harms or benefits related to drug use or its prohibition? Would it affect his argument significantly to take these into account?

Case

Whether or not drugs should be prohibited, most of them *are* prohibited. Still, colleges have some discretion as to how they deal with drug violations. Consider:

> In 2012 and 2013, 521 Wesleyan students were referred to campus officials for disciplinary action involving drug use on campus. Only four students were arrested.... Between 2011 and 2013, 537 students at the University of California at Berkeley were arrested for drug use on campus, and 254 were referred for disciplinary action.... At the University of Georgia, 42 students received disciplinary referrals, while there were nearly 200 arrests. During that same three-year time span, Florida State University referred just 32 of its 40,000 students for disciplinary action for drug use on campus. More than 400 students were arrested.
>
> Kevin Kruger, president of a higher education administrator's association, explains the difference this way: "There is a philosophy for minor drug offenses on some campuses that emphasizes the educational process of helping students learn from their mistakes without the outcome of a criminal record." At Florida State, by contrast, the chief of police said: "Our process is to enforce the laws as they are outlined with each chapter of our Florida statute.... We try not to apply uneven discretion in drug cases. It's pretty straightforward. We're there to enforce the laws."[9]

Which approach should colleges take to drug offenses on campus? Why?

Notes

1. James Q. Wilson, "Heroin," in *Thinking about Crime* (New York: Basic Books, 1975), p. 132.
2. Erich Goode, *Drugs in American Society*, 5th ed. (New York: McGraw-Hill, 1999), pp. 95, 333.
3. Ibid., pp. 333–4.
4. See Norman Zinberg, *Drug, Set, and Setting: The Basis for Controlled Intoxicant Use* (New Haven, CT: Yale University Press, 1984).
5. See Denise B. Kandel, Ronald C. Kessler, and Rebecca Z. Margulies, "Antecedents of Adolescent Initiation into Stages of Drug Use: A Developmental Analysis," in Denise B. Kandel, ed., *Longitudinal Research on Drug Use: Empirical Findings and Methodological Issues* (Washington, DC: Hemisphere, 1978). For the relative influence of peers and parents in drug use, see Denise B. Kandel, "Adolescent Marijuana Use: Role of Parents and Peers," *Science* 181 (September, 14, 1973), 1067.
6. See Substance Abuse and Mental Health Services Administration (SAMHSA), *Results from the 2002 National Survey on Drug Use and Health: National Findings* (Rockville, MD: Office of Applied Studies, 2003) (henceforth NSDUH 2002), figures 3.1 and 4.2.
7. See James Q. Wilson and Richard J. Hernstein, *Crime and Human Nature* (New York: Simon & Schuster, 1985), p. 62.
8. For the negative effects of drug prohibition on other countries, see Jorge Chabat, "Mexico's War on Drugs: No Margin for Maneuver," *Annals of the American Academy of Political and Social Science* 582 (July 2002), p. 134; Marlyn J. Jones, "Policy Paradox: Implications of U.S. Drug Control Policy for Jamaica," *Annals of the American Academy of Political and Social Science* 582 (July 2002), p. 117; and Fransico E. Thoumi, "Illegal Drugs in Colombia: From Illegal Economic Boom to Social Crisis," *Annals of the American Academy of Political and Social Science* 582 (July 2002), p. 102.
9. https://www.insidehighered.com/news/2015/02/27/how-institutions-handle-drug-violations-varies-greatly

30

=== 🐦 ===

Drug Prohibition Is Both Wrong and Unworkable

Tibor R. Machan

There are no doubt negative consequences to using drugs, and it is entirely possible that legalizing illicit drugs might lead to higher rates of drug abuse. Tibor Machan makes a strong case that despite certain possible harmful outcomes, the thing to do is to legalize drugs. In fact, Machan goes so far as to argue that all presently illegal drugs—even "hard drugs" like cocaine or heroin—ought to be made legal. He offers a number of reasons for thinking this, pointing out, for instance, that just as permitting drug use has negative consequences, so likewise does drug prohibition. When we weigh the two options, the scale tips in favor of legalization, which Machan thinks involves far fewer significant costs. Further, he urges that apart from restrictive drug policies' negative outcomes, they are also objectionable because they unnecessarily limit individual decision making and undermine individuals' ability to take responsibility for their own choices.

Machan, Tibor. 2012. "Drug Prohibition Is Both Wrong and Unworkable." *Think* 11(30): 85–92. Copyright © 2012 The Royal Institute of Philosophy. Reprinted with the permission of Cambridge University Press.

Introduction

Many are growing increasingly skeptical of the claims by government officials about winning the war against drugs. Should this war be supported because a smaller percentage of teenagers use marijuana, or should it be opposed because a larger percentage of teenagers and young adults use cocaine and crack in the USA? Should people be optimistic when multi-billion dollar shipments of cocaine are confiscated, or pessimistic that seizures continue to increase yet have such little impact on price and consumption? Drug prohibition was doomed to failure from the start, no less so than alcohol prohibition, and the best alternative is an immediate return to complete legalization of such drugs.

Suppression of voluntary trade mostly drives the market underground and adds a criminal element, or so history teaches. So, the trade and use of drugs should not be prohibited and any abuse must be dealt with by means of education, moral fortitude, willpower, and social institutions, without benefit of coercive force of arms. Unfortunately this proposition is not obvious in our so-called "free" societies—perhaps due to the widespread conviction that individual responsibility is merely a relic of ancient philosophy and religion; and the modern, scientific age has superseded the need for these. But this is wrong and shortly it will be obvious why.

The war on drugs received several major increases in funding during the 1980s, and the U.S. military is now heavily involved in drug law enforcement. Despite these increased resources we are no closer to success with drug prohibition than communism is at creating a "new economic man." The fact that a full array of illegal drugs is available for sale throughout the federal prison system, the Pentagon, and in front of the Drug Enforcement Administration building in Washington, DC, demonstrates that little has been accomplished.

One lofty goal of drug prohibition was to prevent crime by removing access to mind-altering drugs. The great tragedy is that prohibition has created a vast new area of criminal activity—crimes such as robbery, burglary, and prostitution committed in order to pay for the high prices of illegal drugs. It is well documented that drug users commit crimes to pay the high prices brought on by prohibition and that wealthy addicts do not. And of course the vast smuggling operations on the United States–Mexican border have involved murders galore. Yet the futile "war" is continued.

The rate of crimes with victims increased during the alcohol prohibition of the 1920s only to decline rapidly in 1933, the year Prohibition was repealed. Crime continued to decline until the mid-1960s and has been increasing ever since. For instance, the prison population increased by 35 percent between 1984 and 1988 in the USA. During that period the "criminals on parole" population increased by over 50 percent! More innocent bystanders are being killed, more school systems are infected, and more neighborhoods are destroyed by the growing problems of prohibition.

The 1990 arraignment of Washington, DC, Mayor Marion Barry was a notorious media event, but in fact drug prohibition has been corrupting the political process for a very long time. This corruption is not confined to the United States. A look around the globe shows that countries that produce, process, and sell illegal drugs are also afflicted with corrupt political systems—consider several of them in Southeast Asia, Lebanon, Mexico, Afghanistan, and many in South America.

The American government occasionally reports with great pride that a smaller percentage of teenagers are regular marijuana smokers. What is left out of such press releases is that consumption of virtually every other type of drug has increased and that the number of reported deaths associated with illegal drug use continues to skyrocket. New types of drugs such as smokable cocaine and synthetic opiates are being introduced onto the streets at an alarming rate. The switch from marijuana to the more potent and dangerous drugs is arguably directly attributable to the enforcement of drug laws.

Prohibition forces black market suppliers to take precautions against detection. This ever present profit-making incentive takes on several forms such as:

1. Producing only the most potent form of a drug.
2. Switching from low potency drugs, such as marijuana, to high potency drugs, such as cocaine and heroin.
3. Inventing and producing more potent drugs, such as "designer drugs," which are synthetic opiates thousands of times more potent than opium.

These results have been labeled accurately in the popular press the "Iron Law of Prohibition."

The history of drug prohibitions reveals that black markets produce low quality, high potency, and extremely dangerous products. The most powerful weapon of these black marketeers is not the gun, but the ability to stay at least one step ahead of law enforcement.

The population of the United States is growing older and more affluent. Normally these demographic changes would reduce drug use and addiction. Even habitual heroin users stabilize their habits and mature out of addiction if they survive the war on drugs. However, these beneficial trends have been far outweighed by the increased severity of the effects of prohibition. In fact, we would be surprised if prohibition actually did work. Any law or program that undermines individual responsibility and liberty has little chance of enhancing a democratic and free market society.

Most people now agree that prohibition is not working—the dispute is over what to do about it. Many argue that we don't have the right people in charge, but we have been changing the guard (and the law) now for over 150 years. Others argue that we just haven't done enough, but things have only become worse as we devote more of our resources and surrender our liberties to this cause. The support for prohibition rests on the fact that people cannot contemplate the obvious alternative—legalization.

The most important point to make is that if one has the right to his or her life, this implies that one also has the right to do with it what one will provided this doesn't involve aggression. And while it is possible that drug—as well as, of course, alcohol—consumption has side effects that can spill over on others who may be injured by junkies and traders, most such side effects are more sensibly attributed to prohibition itself. The high profits from illegal drug trade make such trade appealing to young people, especially members of poor minorities. That, too, would vanish once legalization occurred.

This is not the place to defend the right to one's life and the implied right to the liberty to live as one chooses if it is done peacefully, but the crux of the argument is that everyone has the responsibility to conduct himself or herself morally, and this would be impossible if other people had the authority to interfere with one's peaceful conduct. Thus the sovereignty of individuals is fundamental and that implies that how one uses or abuses oneself is a basic right of everyone. (Those who dispute this have a fundamentally different conception of social life, construing everyone to be the property of the community or state!)

The Benefits of Legalization

Legalization has many obvious benefits. The first is of course that it will place responsibility for drug abuse within the private sector, that is, the individuals who will make free choices as to whether to indulge or abstain. Then, also, anticipated lower prices would mean that drug users would no longer have to resort to crime to pay for their habits. With the tremendous profits gone, corruption of public officials would be reduced, and because Westerners and, especially, Americans constitute a bulk of world consumption, political corruption worldwide would be reduced.

Government budgets at the Federal, state, and local levels could be cut as entire programs are dismantled. However, one thing legalization would *not* do is balance government budgets. There is no way that tax rates on drugs could be raised high enough to offset the enormous federal deficit. Furthermore, high tax rates would encourage the black market to continue, people would still commit crimes to pay the high prices, and politicians would still be involved in corruption.

Legalization will create jobs in the private sector. People will be employed making heroin, cocaine, and marijuana for recreational, medical, and other legitimate users. All of these products have legitimate uses and may have as-yet-undiscovered ones. Marijuana (hemp) will be a valuable (and environmentally safe) source of products such as paper, fiber, fuel, budding materials, clothing, animal and bird food, medicine and medicinal preparations, and a protein source for humans. It can be grown in a variety of climates and sod types and grows well without chemical fertilizers or pesticides.

The repeal of drug prohibitions will allow police, courts, and prisons to concentrate on real criminals while at the same time greatly reducing the number of crimes committed to pay for drugs. No longer will judges be forced to open prison doors because of overcrowding. The courts and police will be better able to serve and protect—crime will pay a lot less! Street gangs will deteriorate without their income from illegal drug sales.

The people involved and methods of producing and selling drugs will change dramatically. The current dealers of drugs will not survive in a competitive marketplace. Large companies will produce and distribute these drugs on a national scale. In such an environment the drugs will be less potent and less dangerous. Consumers will be safer and better informed—changes in the product will be consumer-driven. The producers will face many legal constraints such as negligence and product liability laws. The threat of wrongful death suits and class action lawsuits will also constrain their behavior.

It is not surprising that these products were much safer before drug prohibition. The makers of Bayer Aspirin sold heroin pills that were safe enough to prescribe to babies, and the Coca-Cola Company used cocaine in its product. These products were generally non-poisonous, non-toxic, and non-lethal. The three major free market drugs—alcohol, caffeine, and nicotine—are substantially safer today than they were ten or thirty years ago. The average potency of all three continues to decrease over time.

Constructive debate can overcome political and ideological maneuvering only if people clearly understand the differences between prohibition and legalization. Prohibition is simply a piece of legislation enforced by use of law officers, guns, and prisons. Prohibition is *not* drug education, drug treatment centers, rehabilitation centers, self-help programs such as Alcoholics Anonymous, religion, family, friends, doctors, help hot-lines, and civic organizations. "Just Say No" does not have to leave because we say goodbye to prohibition.

"Private Prohibitions"

In discussing the problems of drug abuse many people feel that legalization would only reduce the prices of drugs and therefore only increase the amount and severity of drug abuse. People would be smoking marijuana in McDonald's, the school bus driver would be shooting up heroin, and airplane pilots would be snorting cocaine before takeoff. This confusion results from a failure to distinguish between prohibition and private contractual regulations.

Restaurants could prevent people from smoking marijuana just as they have the right to prevent people from smoking cigarettes or from entering without shoes or a shirt. Airlines, railroads, and nuclear power plants have the right and incentive to contract with their workers, for example, not to drink alcohol on the job. These "private prohibitions" are generally aimed at the most significant problems of drug use such as safety. Not only are they specifically targeted, they are better enforced—co-workers, customers, unions, insurance companies, and management also benefit from such restrictions and therefore contribute to enforcement. The use of private restrictions and drug testing will be enhanced after the repeal of prohibition.

While not all aspects of prohibition and legalization are discussed here, enough has been said to refute many of the myths of legalization and to make the question of quantity consumed a non-issue. Re-legalization is the admission of government's failure in pursuit of a lofty goal, not a ringing endorsement of drug abuse.

Legalization has been labeled immoral by prohibitionists, but nothing could be further from the truth. Reliance on individual initiative and responsibility is no sin. It is not only the key to success in the battle against drug abuse, it is also a reaffirmation of traditional American values. How can someone make a moral choice when one is in fact forced into a particular course of action? How is the fabric of society strengthened when we rely on guns and prisons to enforce behavior rather than letting behavior be determined by individual responsibility and family upbringing?

The sooner we move toward re-legalization, the sooner we can begin the process of healing the scars of prohibition, solving the problems of drug abuse, and curing this nation's addiction to drug laws.

Comprehension Questions

1. What harmful consequences does Machan attribute to restrictive drug policies?
2. How does drug prohibition affect the use and production of illicit drugs?
3. How does Machan link the issue of individual rights with the permissibility of drug use?
4. What benefits does Machan expect would follow from drug legalization?
5. What are "private prohibitions," and what potential role might they play after drugs are made legal?

Discussion Questions

1. Often, people assume that those who support drug legalization want to use the drugs that would become legal. Is that a fair assumption? Why or why not?
2. Machan thinks that one drawback of drug prohibition is that it discourages individual initiative. Do you think individuals are any less likely to take initiative in making their own decisions as a result of restrictive drug laws?
3. According to Machan, the negative consequences of drug use stem largely from drug prohibition and not drug use as such. What harms can you think of that are associated with drug use, setting aside the effects of prohibition? Do you think these are weighty enough to justify our drug policies?
4. Imagine that Machan's argument wins the day: Drugs are legalized. Would it be wrong for you to use any of them? What moral principles might be relevant here? Explain your position and the reasoning behind it.

Case

There's some evidence that drug legalization is undermining the Mexican drug cartels:

> Agents on the 2,000-mile United States border have [been] unable to stop the northward flow of drugs and southward flow of dollars and guns. But the amount of one drug—marijuana—seems to have finally fallen. US Border Patrol has been seizing steadily smaller quantities of the drug, from 2.5 million pounds in 2011 to 1.9 million pounds in 2014. Mexico's army has noted an even steeper decline, confiscating 664 tons of cannabis in 2014, a drop of 32 percent compared to the year before.
>
> This fall appears to have little to do with law enforcement, however, and all to do with the wave of US marijuana legalization. The votes by Colorado and Washington State to legalize marijuana in 2012, followed by Alaska, Oregon and D.C. last year have created a budding industry . . . Analysts are still trying to work out the long-term effect this shift will have on Mexican cartel finances and violence. The legal marijuana industry could be the fastest growing sector of the US economy. It grew 74 percent in 2014 to $2.7 billion, according to the ArcView group, a cannabis investment and research firm. This includes revenue from both recreational drug stores and from medical marijuana, which has been legalized in 23 states. The group predicts the industry will top $4 billion by 2016.[1]
>
> This means less cash for Mexican cartels to buy guns, bribe police and pay assassins. Coinciding with legalization, violence has decreased in Mexico. Homicides hit a high in 2011, with Mexican police departments reporting almost 23,000 murders. Last year, they reported 15,649.

If all drugs were to be legalized, this could be devastating for the cartels, and would almost certainly save Mexican lives. This raises a very important question. Let's suppose that drug legalization would slightly *increase* the total number of drug-related deaths in the United States—say, by an additional 5,000 per year. However, it would *decrease* deaths related to the drug war in Mexico by 10,000 per year. Should the United States legalize in those circumstances? Or does the country have an obligation to protect its own, even if (a) the policy is paternalistic and (b) it results in a greater number of deaths elsewhere?

Note

1. http://time.com/3801889/us-legalization-marijuana-trade/

The Morning After
Hangovers and Regrets
Thomas Vander Ven

· ·

What are some of the consequences of heavy drinking, and how do students navigate them? These are the questions that Vander Ven takes up in "The Morning After." On the basis of extensive student interviews, he shows how students justify and downplay hangovers, bond through post-binging misery, and try to manage experiences of disappointment, embarrassment, and shame. Though Vander Ven doesn't draw any moral conclusions from his research, it clearly raises plenty of hard moral questions. How responsible are people for the decisions they make when drunk? What should we make of the strategies people use to excuse some of those decisions? What are some of the ways that people downplay the consequences of heavy drinking, and when is that a problem?

· ·

I proceeded to become quite drunk, loud and aggressive like I usually become. From there, the enjoyment of the bar was waning so we concluded the night briefly at Paddy's [a bar]. We then went back to my apartment, ordered food, watched a movie, then

Vander Ven, Thomas. 2011. "The Morning After." In *Getting Wasted: Why College Students Drink Too Much and Party So Hard*. New York: NYU Press. Reprinted with permission.

proceeded to smoke a joint. After that I passed out for a while then proceeded to sleep with my friend's little sister (no sex was involved). . . . While I had a fun night, I have to now deal with the fact that I hooked up with my friend's little sister and must deal with this situation as it is. This excessive night of drinking resulted in me achieving nothing for the next day except for lying around and watching TV till I went to sleep. [twenty-two-year-old male]

I drank a few more there and ended up wrestling around with a friend. I made an idiot of myself. I woke up the next morning feeling sick and ashamed. I knew I drank too much and I have not been in that condition in over a year. [twenty-one-year-old male]

Clearly, after a night of serious drinking there is often work to be done. Regretful or hungover partiers must develop strategies to repair the damages wrought by intoxication. An ailing or regretful drinker, for example, might find ways to justify his or her behavior; he or she may employ rhetorical strategies to suggest that no harm was done after all. . . . [A] severely hungover individual must develop strategies to reframe his or her flawed experience or he or she is not likely to continue to drink to excess. If the ailing drinker is not able to put the "best face" on the consequences of drinking, he or she may decide that the alcohol intoxication is not worth the trouble. . . . When college drinkers are able to put a positive "spin" on problematic drinking, it helps to perpetuate serial intoxication. . . .

Hangover Management

Painful, slightly uncomfortable, or totally debilitating hangovers can be a compelling reminder of the recklessness of the night before. But the unpleasantness of an alcohol hangover may or may not compel one to change one's drinking behavior. . . . Hangovers, then, must be made tolerable or defined in ways by drinkers and their peers as "worth it" given the pleasure they experienced during the drinking episode. Methods of defining, treating, tolerating, and justifying the hangover may be learned and practiced, then, in order for alcohol abuse practices to continue after a challenging encounter with a post-intoxication illness. Recent empirical studies have demonstrated that young alcohol abusers may not "learn their lesson" from a negative experience with alcohol intoxication. In fact, one study suggested that the heaviest drinkers in a college sample did not learn from their mistakes, but instead they overestimated the level of alcohol

consumption that it would take to experience a similarly negative consequence.[1] Other investigators have found that negative expectancy outcomes
are sometimes reported as motivations for future alcohol use.[2] These findings suggest that alcohol abusers develop strategies to justify or neutralize
the negative consequences delivered by alcohol abuse. . . .

The Irrelevant Hangover

. . . [One] way to define a hangover is to consider its effects on your obligations on the morning following a bout with intoxication. According to
some accounts, a hangover does not really "count" if you have no important
tasks or responsibilities to accomplish on the day after a drinking episode.
The following respondent embraces her hangover but denies that it had any
tangible consequences: "The next morning I did have a hangover but I'm
used to it. I didn't have anything that I had to do that day" [twenty-year-old
female]. This nineteen-year-old male agrees with this summation about the
irrelevancy of an alcohol hangover: "I was tired the next morning and had
a little bit of a hangover. It went away after I slept a little longer. I didn't have
anything else to do the next day so it didn't really affect anything."

Other accounts suggest that a hangover is relatively less compelling if
the student is able to meet his or her responsibilities in spite of the dis-
comforts associated with the morning-after ordeal. This nineteen-year-old
male recognizes that the night of drinking negatively affected his ability
to make good on his obligations as a student, but he comes through in the
end: "When I got home, I went to bed and forgot to set my alarm for my
12:00 class. I woke up at about 12:10 and was late to my class. I still went
to class, though, so that is the main thing." That he was able to attend his
class was enough validation for this student that the drinking episode
had little consequence. Never mind that he was late and was unlikely to
be prepared to participate in the class or to fully comprehend the material
covered. In his mind, he was there and that was enough.

The approach described above might be characterized as a technique
of neutralization. In 1957, groundbreaking criminologists Gresham Sykes
and David Matza argued that juvenile delinquents use linguistic devices
to neutralize the guilt that they may feel when contemplating the violation of laws. According to the authors, one common neutralization technique is the denial of injury:

> For the delinquent . . . wrongfulness may turn on the question of
> whether or not anyone has clearly been hurt by his deviance . . . and

this matter is open to a variety of interpretations. Vandalism, for example, may be defined by the delinquent as simply "mischief"—after all, it may be claimed, the persons whose property has been destroyed can well afford it. . . . [W]e are arguing that the delinquent frequently, and in hazy fashion, feels that his behavior does not really cause any great harm despite the fact that it runs counter to the law.[3]

Having a hangover is not against the law, but drinking yourself into a lethargic, sickly mess has the potential to generate guilt and self-disappointment. The most proximate victim of a hangover is the hangover sufferer himself or herself. Moreover, drunkenness itself is a victimless offense unless it is considered as self-harm (i.e., bodily harm, damage to one's life chances) or a threat to the functioning of the social order. The popular conception of the "problem drinker" points to someone who has allowed his or her drinking to get in the way of his or her social institutional obligations. . . . By this definition, most college drinkers are unlikely to define their heavy drinking as "problematic" since it is not clear that it interferes with their . . . institutional demands. University students may be in a particularly good structural position to deny the injury of a hangover since, in many cases, going to class is their only formal responsibility and, furthermore, classroom expectations of the student may be minimal at best. . . . [One] need not be in top physical or mental condition to sit silently through a class. . . .

Hangovers: No Pain, No Gain!

The hangover experience, as physically and mentally taxing as it may be, might simply be regarded as a small price to pay for a night of laughter and unbridled adventure. College drinking may result in a blistering headache and sick stomach the next morning, but, hey, it was worth it. This sentiment was commonly reported by respondents who acknowledged having a painful or uncomfortable post-drinking experience but were able to minimize it by arguing that the pain was worth it considering what a great time they had during their drinking episode: "Although I felt terrible in the morning, I had a great time being with all my friends and having some laughs" [twenty-one-year-old female]; "The morning after was miserable cuz I always feel yucky the morning after I drink. I drank lots of water and just rested during the day till I felt better. It was worth it though cuz I had so much fun on Friday" [eighteen-year-old female].

Furthermore, being hungover may in fact be regarded as part of the fun. When co-drinkers wake up next to one another in similar states of disrepair, the hangover becomes a pleasant, collective experience that involves commiserating over their mutual sickness, telling war stories from the night before, and laughing at the sorry shape they are in. A shared hangover can take a lot of the "bite" out of the aches and pains associated with alcohol withdrawal. In the following story, Macy, a twenty-year-old female, describes her drinking group's struggle with a collective hangover and demonstrates how easy it was for them to plan their next party:

> But the next day we sat around and discussed what happened. We tried to piece together the night and we all agreed that we would never play that game again [strip beer pong]. We were so hung over that we were the biggest wastes of space. All we did was lie on our couches and watch football. It was a battle to get up to eat and go to the bathroom. Even though we did things that soberly we would not even think about and we could not function properly the next day, you can be sure that this weekend will be filled with alcohol. We are already planning on making mixed drinks and having people over again. We figure since we work so hard during the week, we owe it to ourselves to let loose on the weekends. It's dumb logic I know, but it works for us. . . .

Apparently, being sick together is part of the co-drinking experience. In everyday life, sharing an illness and all of its attendant symptoms with close friends is uncommon. But for drinking partners—especially those who live together—the morning after a drinking episode is a time for friends to wallow in their misery together while reconstructing the fun parts of the previous evening together. Being hungover together also provides an opportunity for friends to care for one another and express genuine empathy. Waking up in a contorted mess in the clothes you wore the night before might not make your parents proud, but sharing this experience with an empathetic friend may help to redefine the situation as a positive one. . . .

Post-Intoxication Regrets: The Experience and Management of Disappointment, Embarrassment, and Shame

Hangovers may be relatively easy to brush off. The passage of time may be the best remedy for a hangover, and the clock never stops ticking. But the psychic pains that heavy drinkers sometimes face on the morning after a drinking episode may not be so easily discharged. While pulsating headaches fade away and ravenous thirst can eventually be quenched, it is more difficult to wash away the overwhelming regrets related to engaging in risky or unprotected sex, behaving in ways that destroyed a valued relationship, or acting foolishly or out of character in public. Regrets linger. Consider the case of Carmen, a twenty-two-year-old female:

> Two nights ago [Saturday night] I went to a party with my friends. The people at the party had beer and almost a full bar. I drank mixed drinks (liquor) outside. . . . Later we went downtown to the bars where I continued to drink mixed drinks and shots and I ended up getting pretty wasted. I'll also say it was one of the most fun nights at the bar. I was walking around talking to several people and having a very good time. I also received several drinks that were just given to me. I left the bar with this guy I like and drove to his apartment. That was stupid! At his apartment we engaged in sexual acts (not intercourse). Also at his apartment I realized I had way too much because I started to feel spinny. That wore off. I drove back to my place at about 4:00 A.M. and got a call from a guy that works at the bar I was at that likes me. He came over at about 5:00 A.M. and we engaged in sexual intercourse. That was stupid also! I did not go to bed until about 6:00 A.M. and did not awake until 1:00 P.M. I felt kind of jittery all day the next day. I had a hangover but it wasn't until last night and this morning that I started feeling really bad about sleeping with some guy I hardly know. Alcohol is no excuse for my actions but I think those things would not have happened if it weren't for all the alcohol I drank. Now for all I know I could've contracted some sort of STD which is the worst thing that could happen. Now I have stress and anxiety about that.

Carmen's sober self judges the behavior of her intoxicated self as "stupid." She engaged in casual sexual relations with two different men in one night[4] (one of whom she "hardly knew") and got behind the wheel of her car after a night of heavy drinking. Her post-intoxication experience is shadowed by a looming sense of disappointment, shame, stress, and anxiety. In hindsight, Carmen sees her behavior as ill-advised and acknowledges that she could have gotten a sexually transmitted disease, which according to her is "the worst thing that can happen." She wrote this account two days after the events occurred and she continued to wrestle with regret, a feeling often reported by many of my respondents.

Regrets are defined by psychologists as negative emotions connected to thoughts about how past actions might have achieved better outcomes.[5] Furthermore, feeling regret serves as an informal form of social control because it functions as sort of a self-administered punishment for the commission of wayward behavior.[6] The regretful person might say to himself or herself, "I shouldn't have done that. That's not me. I'm better than that." Thus, the regretful college drinker may devise plans for the future to behave more in line with his or her values and self-concept. On the other hand, the behaviors that stimulate regret may be redefined in ways that allow the regretful person to disavow his or her actions (e.g., "That wasn't me doing and saying those things. That was the alcohol"). College drinkers often find ways to distance themselves from drunken misdeeds, thereby perpetuating the behavior.

My respondents' regrets varied by degree and according to the kinds of behaviors they were regretful about. Regrets are associated with, or perhaps driven by, feelings of disappointment and shame. In the most minor cases, regretful drinkers were merely disappointed about the manner in which their alcohol consumption affected their ability to achieve valued goals. According to psychologists, people experience disappointment when negative outcomes disconfirm positive expectations.[7] When college drinkers disappoint themselves, it is because they feel as though they have let themselves down by being unable to accomplish their goals or to meet their role requirements. The disappointed drinker says, "I'm better than that. I had good intentions and I let alcohol get in the way." . . .

Acting a Fool: Shame-Producing Drunken Performances

. . . Many of my respondents spoke of feeling extremely embarrassed about their drunken behaviors. Grace, a twenty-year-old female, regrets her intoxicated habit of repeating herself when she's polluted with alcohol:

Q: [After a night of drinking,] do you talk about what happened the night before?
A: Yeah, like if someone remembers something that someone else doesn't. It's, "Do you remember when you did that?' and they're going, "No, I did what?" and you know, it's just, usually it's all harmless things, so it's funny. We don't have any like vandals or serious kleptomaniacs or anything but . . .

Q: Okay, so do you ever say, "Do you remember what you said last night?"

A: That usually happens to me. . . . I repeat myself a lot when I'm drunk and people say, "You know how many times you told me this?" I'm like, "probably about eight" and they're like, "Yep" and I'm like, "Oh." Yeah, usually it's me that, I get really embarrassed because, even though I drink on a fairly regular basis, I still get embarrassed because I feel like it's not how I should act. I need to be more disciplined; I need to be more distinguished. I, this image, this pristine image of myself is tarnished when I do that. And granted, people don't see me like, you know, this pristine image that I have for myself, you know, it's, I don't know . . .

As her remark demonstrates, Grace claims to feel embarrassed on the morning *after* an awkward public display. But is this *really* embarrassment that she is feeling? What is embarrassment? Most sociologists seem to agree that embarrassment is an almost immediate, overwhelming, psychological and physiological response to a sense of failing to meet the expectations of a social situation. According to sociologists Weinberg and Williams, embarrassment is "[s]ignified by embodied emotional signs such as blushing, fumbling, sweating, etc. Embarrassment occurs when we fail to project an acceptable self before others in the social situation."[8] Thus, embarrassment is an immediate emotional and physical response to a situation where one has failed to behave in line with the identity that one claims for oneself. Grace, on the other hand, feels emotional distress on the *following day* after hearing about her behavior. According to sociologists of emotion, then, this is not embarrassment. If Grace had been truly embarrassed, she would have felt uncomfortable *that* night immediately after being told that she repeated herself about "eight times." But for heavy drinkers, the psychic pain is delayed until they are sober again and see their behavior with a more critical eye. . . . College drinkers don't feel embarrassed while they are intoxicated because they "don't care" if they meet social expectations or because social expectations are different in the drinking scene. The next morning, however, they become reengaged with their more critical self. Now they care. When the sober self sees the drunken self as an object, dark feelings emerge. Debilitating emotions arrive the next day when drinkers evaluate their alcohol-fueled behavior from a sober, more conventional perspective. What the regretful drinker feels is *shame*.

Drunk Behavior and Shame

Since college drinkers have temporarily disabled their ability to feel embarrassed, they often end up behaving in ways that, upon reflection, produce distress the next day. A common regret for college drinkers relates to the drunken use of cell phones to contact love interests while intoxicated, known as a "drunk dial" or "drunk text." Intoxicated students feel emboldened to communicate electronically with ex-partners or romantic interests in ways that they normally would not if they were sober. This twenty-year-old female appears to feel only a mild sense of regret after a "drunk dial": "Then I started drunk dialing my friends and called a boy and told him I wanted to make out with him on his voicemail. . . . The night was so much fun overall, except I was a little embarrassed about that voicemail I had left.". . .

Although drunken messaging may deliver some anxiety the next morning, other intoxicated performances trigger more powerful feelings during the post-intoxication period. Regret is particularly punishing when the drinker experiences shame. According to sociologist Thomas Scheff, shame is the most powerful *social* emotion:

> By shame I mean a large family of emotions that includes many cognates and variants, most notably embarrassment, humiliation, and related feelings such as shyness that involve reactions to rejection or feelings of failure or inadequacy. What unites all these cognates is that they involve the feeling of a *threat to the social bond*. . . . If, as proposed here, shame is a result of threat to the bond, shame would be the most social of the basic emotions.[9]

Feelings of shame are overpowering because it seems to the shame holder that he or she has created a massive gulf between himself or herself and the social body to which he or she wishes to belong. When college drinkers experience shame it is much worse than feeling immediately embarrassed over a social faux pas; shame can feel like a dramatic sense of social distance, alienation, and isolation. . . .

According to my informants, one of the most common forms of shame-producing drunken behavior involves an ill-advised or casual sex act. Gretchen, a twenty-year-old female, describes her post-intoxication consternation after a regrettable sexual encounter:

> This party ended horribly for me. I kissed one of my guy friend's brothers and while eating at Wendy's with friends got in an argument

with my roommate that ended up with her staying at the sorority house for the night and me going back to my dorm crying. At my dorm, my best guy friend and I spent a lot of time complaining about my roommate (his ex-girlfriend). We were both drunk and angry and we ended up sleeping together. I cheated on my boyfriend with my roommate's ex/my boyfriend's friend all because I was drunk and temperamental. Until then, my boyfriend had been the only person I'd slept with. I felt like a dumb, drunk slut—your typical college sorority girl. I was hung over and ashamed the next day.

Gretchen's shame is connected to her failure to act appropriately towards her social relationships. She was disloyal to her boyfriend *and* to her roommate. Her shame reflects her temporary sense of social distance from relationships that mattered to her. In addition, according to Gretchen, her drunken misbehavior transformed her into a walking, talking stereotype (e.g., "a dumb drunk slut"; a "typical sorority girl"). . . .

What *are* you going to do when your behavior delivers you such shame that you feel that you cannot face the social world? . . . [Regretful] college drinkers often find ways to explain away their indiscretions. The most simplistic strategy involves putting all of the blame on alcohol. In this case, a troubled drinker denies responsibility for the behavior in question by acting as if the alcohol drained him or her of free will and personal agency. Offering an excuse or justification for objectionable behavior is known by sociologists as "giving an account." Marvin Scott and Stanford Lyman, two revered American sociologists, articulated their original theoretical statement concerning accounts in the 1960s. According to Scott and Lyman an account is "a statement made by a social actor to explain unanticipated or untoward behavior—whether that behavior is his own or that of others and whether the proximate cause for the statement arises from the actor himself or from someone else."[10] The authors described two types of accounts, excuses and justifications: "Excuses are accounts in which one admits that the act in question is bad, wrong, or inappropriate but denies full responsibility. . . . Justifications are accounts in which one accepts responsibility for the act in question, but denies the pejorative quality associated with it."[11]

Most humans use accounts frequently, maybe even daily. The function of an account—especially an excuse or denial of responsibility—is to protect and preserve the identity one desires to claim for oneself. If I claim to be a level-headed, anti-violent pacifist, but then get into a drunken fistfight over a beer pong game, I've got some explaining to do. When college drinkers go searching for an excuse for their drunken buffoonery, they do not need to look very far—alcohol is a ready-made, convenient excuse. Let's return to Carmen's story for a simple example of the "drunk excuse." The reader will recall that Carmen had casual sexual relations with two men in a matter of hours. Feeling regretful about her sexual encounters, she offers the following account: "It wasn't until last night and this morning that I started feeling really bad about sleeping with some guy I hardly know. Alcohol is no excuse for my actions but I think those things would not have happened if it weren't for all the alcohol I drank." Carmen's account features the use of a common rhetorical game. She makes a socially acceptable statement about her belief that alcohol is "no excuse for my actions" but then goes right ahead and blames the alcohol anyway. Carmen is claiming that she is not the kind of person who would normally engage in reckless sex acts with virtual strangers. She will not own those behaviors because she would not typically choose them. In other words, Carmen's behavior was not the result of some moral failing or something essentially pathological about her—it was the alcohol that caused it.

Comprehension Questions

1. What is neutralization? How do people neutralize hangovers?
2. Why might someone think that a hangover was worth it?
3. What's the difference between regret, embarrassment, and shame?
4. What's the connection between shame and "social distance"?
5. What's an "account"?

Discussion Questions

1. Do Vander Ven's students sound like people you know? Why or why not?
2. In your experience, what are some common regrets after a night of heavy drinking? Relatedly, what are some common sources of shame?
3. People are very good at downplaying the costs of their drinking. Do you think that people are *too* good at downplaying the costs of their drinking?
4. When we drink heavily, we give up some control over ourselves. Can it be wrong to do that? If so, when and why?

Case

Consider this:

> University of Maryland students have long complained that school rules deter them from calling for help when they are concerned about the health or safety of a student who has been drinking heavily. If they have been drinking themselves, or have alcohol in their rooms, underage students risk being booted from campus housing or receiving a permanent mark on their academic transcripts—major penalties for undergraduates. Schools across the country are addressing the same issue as they try to avoid sending a message of permissiveness about illegal underage alcohol use and binge drinking without scaring students into inaction when a situation becomes dangerous. About one hundred colleges, including George Washington University and the University of Virginia, have Good Samaritan rules that provide either a break or amnesty to students who seek help in a medical emergency....
>
> Maryland students told a committee researching the policy last month that they had seen friends flee a dorm party after someone downed eight to ten shots, slammed his head and was gushing blood. One student with emergency medical training said his friends called him, instead of an ambulance, after a friend drank eleven shots in four minutes. Another described blacking out for two hours, saying friends waited ninety minutes before calling an EMT. "There were times when students were unconscious and nobody ever called. I wouldn't have expected anyone to call for help for me," a student said at a public forum where undergraduates were promised anonymity. "Our rationale for making those decisions was that there was a 95 percent chance that they'll sleep it off."
>
> Now a good Samaritan proposal, pushed by students for the past two years, is making its way to the university senate, which is scheduled to vote on it tomorrow. The proposal could lessen the penalties for violating university alcohol rules if a student is caught because he called authorities out of concern for someone's safety. The proposal would not protect students who break the law or engage in egregious conduct, but disciplinary or residence hall charges would be dismissed if the student met with administrators and completed an alcohol intervention program, if necessary, said John Zacker, director of student conduct.[12]

The co-drinkers in this story are called "friends." Do they sound like friends? What does it say about a friend if he or she would abandon you were you to be seriously injured? Does being drunk excuse that behavior? Moreover, should colleges implement Good Samaritan policies like the one being discussed here? Why or why not? Are there any foreseeable downsides?

Notes

1. Wechsler, Henry, and Bernice Wuethrich. 2002. *Dying to Drink: Confronting Binge Drinking on College Campuses*. New York: Rodale.
2. Zamboanga, Byron L. 2006. From the Eyes of the Beholder: Alcohol Expectancies and Valuations as Predictors of Hazardous Drinking Behaviors among Female College Students. *American Journal of Drug and Alcohol Abuse* 32: 599–605.
3. Sykes, Gresham, and David Matza. 1957. Techniques of Neutralization: A Theory of Delinquency. *American Sociological Review* 22: 664–70.
4. Would Carmen judge herself so harshly if she were a man? Though gender-specific social norms about sexual promiscuity ("casual, no-strings-attached sex") have changed some over time, women continue to be held to a higher standard.
5. Roese, Neal, Kai Epstude, Florian Fessel, Mike Morrison, Rachel Smallman, Amy Summerville, Adam Galinsky, and Suzanne Segerstrom. 2009. Repetitive Regret, Depression, and Anxiety: Findings from a Nationally Representative Survey. *Journal of Social & Clinical Psychology* 28 (6): 671–688.
6. Cameron, Anthony. 2009. Regret, Choice Theory, and Reality Therapy. *International Journal of Reality Therapy* 28 (2): 40–42.
7. Carroll, Patrick J., James A. Shepperd, Kate Sweeny, Erika Carlson, and Joann P. Benigno. 2007. Disappointment for Others. *Cognition & Emotion* 21 (7): 1565–76.
8. Weinberg, Martin S., and Colin J. Williams. 2005. Fecal Matters: Habitus, Embodiments, and Deviance. *Social Problems* 52: 316.
9. Scheff, Thomas. 2000. Shame and the Social Bond: A Sociological Theory. *Sociological Theory* 18 (1): 96–97.
10. Scott, Marvin B., and Stanford M. Lyman. 1968. Accounts. *American Sociological Review* 33: 45.
11. Scott, Marvin B., and Stanford M. Lyman. 1968. Accounts. *American Sociological Review* 33: 47.
12. http://www.washingtonpost.com/wp-dyn/content/article/2009/04/21/AR2009042103689.html

The Dark Power of Fraternities

Caitlin Flanagan

....

Plenty of drinking happens at fraternities. Partly as a result, plenty of injuries and assaults happen too. However, although fraternities were once seriously threatened by lawsuits, Flanagan shows how they've worked to limit legal liability for the people who party in their houses—including their own members. The upshot is that fraternities seem to create environments that lead to serious harms, but they often aren't legally responsible for them. Is this ethical? That, in short, is the question Flanagan raises in this essay.

....

College fraternities—by which term of art I refer to the formerly all-white, now nominally integrated men's "general" or "social" fraternities, and not the several other types of fraternities on American campuses (religious, ethnic, academic)—are as old, almost, as the republic. In a sense, they are older: They emanated in part from the Freemasons, of which George Washington himself was a member. When arguments are made in their favor, they are arguments in defense of a foundational experience for millions of American young men, and of a system that helped build American higher education as we know it.

Fraternities also provide their members with matchless leadership training. While the system has produced its share of poets, aesthetes, and Henry James scholars, it is far more famous for its success in the powerhouse fraternity fields of business, law, and politics. An astonishing number of CEOs of *Fortune* 500 companies, congressmen and male senators, and American presidents have belonged to fraternities. Many more thousands of American men count their fraternal experience—and the friendships made within it—as among the most valuable in their lives. The organizations raise millions of dollars for worthy causes, contribute millions of hours in community service, and seek to steer young men toward lives of service and honorable action. They also have a long, dark history of violence against their own members and visitors to their houses, which makes them in many respects at odds with the core mission of college itself.

Lawsuits against fraternities are becoming a growing matter of public interest, in part because they record such lurid events, some of them ludicrous, many more of them horrendous. . . . A recent series of articles on fraternities by Bloomberg News's David Glovin and John Hechinger notes that since 2005, more than sixty people—the majority of them students— have died in incidents linked to fraternities, a sobering number in itself, but one that is dwarfed by the numbers of serious injuries, assaults, and sexual crimes that regularly take place in these houses. Many people believe that violent hazing is the most dangerous event associated with fraternity life, but hazing causes a relatively small percentage of these injuries. Because of a variety of forces, all this harm—and the behaviors that lead to it—has lately been moving out of the shadows of private disciplinary hearings and silent suffering, and into the bright light of civil lawsuits, giving us a clear picture of some of the more forbidding truths about fraternity life. While many of these suits never make it to trial, disappearing into confidential settlements . . . or melting away once plaintiffs recognize the powerful and monolithic forces they are up against, the narratives they leave behind in their complaints—all of them matters of public record—comprise a rich and potent testimony to the kinds of experiences regularly taking place on college campuses. Tellingly, the material facts of these complaints are rarely in dispute; what is contested, most often, is only liability.

I have spent most of the past year looking deeply into the questions posed by these lawsuits, and more generally into the particular nature of fraternity life on the modern American campus. Much of what I found challenged my beliefs about the system, assumptions that I came to see as grossly outdated, not because the nature of fraternity life has changed so much, but rather because life at the contemporary university has gone through such a profound transformation in the past quarter century. I found that the ways in which the system exerts its power—and maintains its longevity—in the face of the many potentially antagonistic priorities in contemporary higher education commanded my grudging respect. Fraternity tradition at its most essential is rooted in a set of old, deeply American, morally unassailable convictions, some of which—such as a young man's right to the freedom of association—emanate from the Constitution itself. . . .

But it's impossible to examine particular types of campus calamity and not find that a large number of them cluster at fraternity houses. . . . [Moreover, the] notion that fraternities are target defendants did not hold true in my investigation. . . . Why are so many colleges allowing students to live and party in such unsafe locations? And why do the lawsuits against fraternities for this kind of serious injury and death—so predictable and so preventable—have such a hard time getting traction? The answers lie in the recent history of fraternities and the colleges and universities that host them.

What all of these lawsuits ultimately concern is a crucially important question in higher education, one that legal scholars have been grappling with for the past half century. This question is perhaps most elegantly expressed in the subtitle of Robert D. Bickel and Peter F. Lake's authoritative 1999 book on the subject, *The Rights and Responsibilities of the Modern University: Who Assumes the Risks of College Life?*

The answer to this question has been steadily evolving ever since the 1960s, when dramatic changes took place on American campuses, changes that affected both a university's ability to control student behavior and the status of fraternities in the undergraduate firmament. During this period of student unrest, the fraternities—long the unquestioned leaders in the area of sabotaging or ignoring the patriarchal control of school administrators—became the exact opposite: representatives of the very status quo the new activists sought to overthrow. Suddenly their beer bashes and sorority mixers, their panty raids and obsession with the big game, seemed impossibly reactionary when compared with the mind-altering drugs being sampled in off-campus apartments where sexual liberation was being born and the Little Red Book proved, if nothing else, a fantastic coaster for a leaky bong.

American students sought to wrest themselves entirely from the disciplinary control of their colleges and universities, institutions that had historically operated *in loco parentis*, carefully monitoring the private behavior of undergraduates. The students of the new era wanted nothing to do with that infantilizing way of existence, and fought to rid themselves of the various curfews, dorm mothers, demerit systems, and other modes of institutional oppression. If they were old enough to die in Vietnam, powerful enough to overthrow a president, groovy enough to expand their minds with LSD and free love, then they certainly didn't need their own colleges—the very places where they were forming their radical, nation-changing ideas—to treat them like teenyboppers in need of a sock hop and a chaperone. It was a turning point: American colleges began to regard their students not as dependents whose private lives they must shape and monitor, but as adult consumers whose contract was solely for an education, not an upbringing. The doctrine of *in loco parentis* was abolished at school after school. Through it all, fraternities—for so long the repositories of the most outrageous behavior—moldered, all but forgotten. Membership fell sharply, fraternity houses slid into increasing states of disrepair, and hundreds of chapters closed.

Animal House, released in 1978, at once predicted and to no small extent occasioned the roaring return of fraternity life that began in the early 1980s and that gave birth to today's vital Greek scene. The casting of John Belushi was essential to the movie's influence: No one had greater credibility in the post-1960s youth culture. If something as fundamentally reactionary as fraternity membership was going to replace something as fundamentally radical as student unrest, it would need to align itself with someone whose bona fides among young, white, middle-class males were unassailable. In this newly forming culture, the drugs and personal liberation of the 1960s would be paired with the self-serving materialism of the 1980s, all of which made partying for its own sake—and not as a philosophical adjunct to solving some complicated problem in Southeast Asia—a righteous activity for the pampered young collegian. Fraternity life was reborn with a vengeance.

It was an entirely new kind of student who arrived at the doors of those great and crumbling mansions: at once deeply attracted to the ceremony and formality of fraternity life and yet utterly transformed by the social revolutions of the past decades. These new members and their countless guests brought with them hard drugs, new and ever-developing sexual attitudes, and a stunningly high tolerance for squalor (never had middle- and upper-middle-class American young people lived in such filth as did 1960s and 1970s college kids who were intent on rejecting their parents' bourgeois ways). Furthermore, in 1984 Congress passed the National Minimum Drinking Age Act, with the ultimate result of raising the legal drinking age to twenty-one in all fifty states. This change moved college partying away from bars and college-sponsored events and toward private houses—an ideal situation for fraternities. When these advances were combined with the evergreen fraternity traditions of violent hazing and brawling among rival frats, the scene quickly became wildly dangerous.

Adult supervision was nowhere to be found. Colleges had little authority to intervene in what took place in the personal lives of its students visiting private property. Fraternities, eager to provide their members with the independence that is at the heart of the system—and responsive to members' wish for the same level of freedom that non-Greek students enjoyed—had largely gotten rid of the live-in resident advisers who had once provided some sort of check on the brothers. With these conditions in place, lawsuits began to pour in.

The mid-1980s were a treacherous time to be the defendant in a tort lawsuit. Personal-injury cases had undergone a long shift to the plaintiff's advantage; the theory of comparative negligence—by which an individual can acknowledge his or her own partial responsibility for an injury yet still recover damages from a defendant—had become the standard; the era of huge jury verdicts was at hand. Americans in vast numbers— motivated perhaps in part by the possibility of financial recompense, and in part by a new national impetus to move personal suffering from the sphere of private sorrow to that of public confession and complaint— began to sue those who had damaged them. Many fraternity lawsuits listed the relevant college or university among the defendants, a practice still common among less experienced plaintiffs' attorneys. These institutions possess deep reservoirs of liability coverage, but students rarely recover significant funds from their schools. . . . [A] great deal of time and money can be spent seeking damages from institutions of higher learning, which can be protected by everything from sovereign immunity and damage caps (in the case of public universities), to their limited ability to monitor the private behavior of their students. But for the fraternities themselves, it was a far different story.

So recently and robustly brought back to life, the fraternities now faced the most serious threat to their existence they had ever experienced.

A single lawsuit had the potential to devastate a fraternity. In 1985, a young man grievously injured in a Kappa Alpha–related accident reached a settlement with the fraternity that, over the course of his lifetime, could amount to some $21 million—a sum that caught the attention of everyone in the Greek world. Liability insurance became both ruinously expensive and increasingly difficult to obtain. The insurance industry ranked American fraternities as the sixth-worst insurance risk in the country—just ahead of toxic-waste-removal companies. "You guys are nuts," an insurance representative told a fraternity CEO in 1989, just before canceling the organization's coverage; "you can't operate like this much longer."

For fraternities to survive, they needed to do four separate but related things: take the task of acquiring insurance out of the hands of the local chapters and place it in the hands of the vast national organizations; develop procedures and policies that would transfer as much of their liability as possible to outside parties; find new and creative means of protecting their massive assets from juries; and—perhaps most important of all—find a way of indemnifying the national and local organizations from the dangerous and illegal behavior of some of their undergraduate members. . . .

Self-insurance was an obvious means for combating prohibitive insurance pricing and the widening reluctance to insure fraternities. In 1992, four fraternities created what was first called the Fraternity Risk Management Trust, a vast sum of money used for reinsurance. Today, thirty-two fraternities belong to this trust. In 2006, a group of seven other fraternities bought their own insurance broker, James R. Favor, which now insures many others. More important than self-insurance, however, was the development of a risk-management policy that would become—across these huge national outfits and their hundreds of individual chapters—the industry standard. This was accomplished by the creation of something called the Fraternal Information and Programming Group (FIPG), which in the mid-1980s developed a comprehensive risk-management policy for fraternities that is regularly updated. Currently thirty-two fraternities are members of the FIPG and adhere to this policy, or to their own even more rigorous versions. One fraternity expert told me that even non-FIPG frats have similar policies, many based in large measure on FIPG's, which is seen as something of a blueprint. In a certain sense, you may *think* you belong to Tau Kappa Epsilon or Sigma Nu or Delta Tau Delta—but if you find yourself a part of life-changing litigation involving one of those outfits, what you really belong to is FIPG, because its risk-management policy (and your adherence to or violation of it) will determine your fate far more than the vows you made during your initiation ritual—vows composed by long-dead men who had never even heard of the concept of fraternity insurance.

FIPG regularly produces a risk-management manual—the current version is fifty pages—that lays out a wide range of (optional) best practices. If the manual were *Anna Karenina*, alcohol policy would be its farming reform: the buzz-killing subplot that quickly reveals itself to be an authorial obsession. For good reason: The majority of all fraternity insurance claims involve booze—I have read hundreds of fraternity incident reports, not one of which describes an event where massive amounts of alcohol weren't part of the problem—and the need to manage or transfer risk presented by alcohol is perhaps the most important factor in protecting the system's longevity. Any plaintiff's attorney worth his salt knows how to use relevant social-host and dramshop laws against a fraternity; to avoid this kind of liability, the fraternity needs to establish that the young men being charged were not acting within the scope of their status as fraternity members. Once they violated their frat's alcohol policy, they parted company with the frat. It's a neat piece of logic: The very fact that a young man finds himself in need of insurance coverage is often grounds for denying it to him.

So: alcohol and the fraternity man. Despite everything you may think you know about life on frat row, there are actually only two FIPG-approved means of serving drinks at a frat party. The first is to hire a third-party vendor who will sell drinks and to whom some liability—most significant, that of checking whether drinkers are of legal age—will be transferred. The second and far more common is to have a BYO event, in which the liability for each bottle of alcohol resides solely in the person who brought it. If you think this is in any way a casual system, then you have never read either the FIPG risk-management manual or its sister publication, an essay written in the surrealist vein titled "Making Bring Your Own Beverage Events Happen."

The official BYO system is like something dreamed up by a committee of Soviet bureaucrats and Irish nuns. It begins with the composition—no fewer than twenty-four hours before the party—of a comprehensive guest list. This guest list does not serve the happy function of ensuring a perfect mix of types and temperaments at the festivity; rather, it limits attendance—and ensures that the frat is in possession of "a witness list in the event something does occur which may end up in court two or more years later." Provided a fraternity member—let's call him Larry—is older than twenty-one (which the great majority of members, like the great majority of all college students, are not), he is allowed to bring six (and no more) beers *or* four (and no more) wine coolers to the party. (FIPG's admiration for the wine-cooler four-pack suggests that at least some aspects of the foundational document—including its recommendation for throwing a *M*A*S*H*-themed party as recently as 2007—have not received much of an overhaul since its first edition, published in the mid-1980s.) Okay, so Larry brings a six-pack. The first stop, depending on which fraternity he belongs to: a "sober check point," at which he is subjected to an examination. Does he appear to have already consumed any alcohol? Is he in any way "known" to have done so? If he passes, he hands over his ID for inspection. Next he must do business with a "sober monitor." This person relieves him of the six-pack, hands him a ticket indicating the precise type of beer he brought, and ideally affixes a "non-breakable except by cutting" wristband to his person; only then can Larry retrieve his beers, one at a time, for his own personal consumption. If any are left over at the end of the party, his fraternity will secure them until the next day, when Larry can be reunited with his unconsumed beers, unless his frat decided to "eliminate" them overnight. Weaknesses in the system include the fact that all of these people coming between Larry and his beer—the sober monitors and ID checkers and militarized barkeeps—are Larry's fraternity brothers, who are among his closest buddies and who have pledged him lifelong fealty during candlelit ceremonies rife with Masonic mumbo jumbo and the fluttering language of nineteenth-century romantic friendship. Note also that these policies make it possible for fraternities to be the one industry in the country in which every aspect of serving alcohol can be monitored and managed by people who are legally too young to drink it.

Clearly, a great number of fraternity members will, at some point in their undergraduate career, violate their frat's alcohol policy regarding the six beers—and just as clearly, the great majority will never face any legal consequences for doing so. But when the inevitable catastrophes do happen, that policy can come to seem more like a cynical hoax than a real-world solution to a serious problem. When something terrible takes place—a young man plummets from a roof, a young woman is assaulted, a fraternity brother is subjected to the kind of sexual sadism that appears all too often in fraternity lawsuits—any small violation of policy

can leave fraternity members twisting in the wind. Consider the following scenario: Larry makes a small, human-size mistake one night. Instead of waiting for the slow drip of six warm beers, he brings a bottle of
Maker's Mark to the party, and—in the spirit of not being a weirdo or a
dick—he shares it, at one point pouring a couple of ounces into the passing Solo cup of a kid who's running on empty and asks him for a shot.
Larry never sees the kid again that night—not many people do; he ends
up drinking himself to death in an upstairs bedroom. In the sad fullness
of time, the night's horror is turned into a lawsuit, in which Larry becomes a named defendant. Thanks in part to the guest/witness list,
Larry can be cut loose, both from the expensive insurance he was required to help pay for (by dint of his dues) as a precondition of membership, and from any legal defense paid for by the organization. What will
happen to Larry now?

. . . "I've recovered millions and millions of dollars from homeowners' policies," a top fraternal plaintiff's attorney told me. For that is how
many of the claims against boys who violate the strict policies are paid:
from their parents' homeowners' insurance. As for the exorbitant cost of
providing the young man with a legal defense for the civil case (in which,
of course, there are no public defenders), that is money he and his parents
are going to have to scramble to come up with, perhaps transforming the
family home into an ATM to do it. The financial consequences of fraternity membership can be devastating, and they devolve not on the
eighteen-year-old "man" but on his planning-for-retirement parents.

Like the six-beer policy, the Fraternal Information and Programming
Group's chillingly comprehensive crisis-management plan was included
in its manual for many years. But in 2013, the plan suddenly disappeared
from its pages. When asked why this was so, Dave Westol, a longtime
FIPG board member, said, "Member organizations prefer to establish
their own procedures, and therefore the section has been eliminated."
However, many fraternities continue to rely on the group's advice for in-
house risk management, and it is well worth examining if you want to
know what takes place in the hours following many fraternity disasters.
As it is described in the two most recent editions that I was able to obtain
(2003 and 2007), the plan serves a dual purpose, at once benevolent and
mercenary. The benevolent part is accomplished by the clear directive
that injured parties are to receive immediate medical attention, and
that all fraternity brothers who come into contact with the relevant

emergency workers are to be completely forthright about what has taken place. And the rest? The plans I obtained recommend six important steps:

1. In the midst of the horror, the chapter president takes immediate, commanding, and inspiring control of the situation: "In times of stress, leaders step forward."

2. A call is made to the fraternity's crisis hotline or the national headquarters, no matter the hour: "Someone will be available. They would much rather hear about a situation from you at 3:27 A.M. than receive an 8:01 A.M. telephone call from a reporter asking for a comment about 'The situation involving your chapter at ____.'"

3. The president closes the fraternity house to outsiders and summons all members back to the house: "Unorthodox situations call for unorthodox responses from leaders. Most situations occur at night. Therefore, be prepared to call a meeting of all members and all pledged members as soon as possible, even if that is at 3 A.M."

4. One member—who has already received extensive media training—is put in charge of all relations with the press, an entity fraternities view as biased and often unscrupulous. The appointed member should be prepared to present a concise, factual, and minimally alarming account of what took place. For example: "A new member was injured at a social event."

5. In the case of the death of a guest or a member, fraternity brothers do not attempt direct contact with the deceased's parents. This hideous task is to be left to the impersonal forces of the relevant professionals. (I know of one family who did not know their son was in any kind of trouble until—many hours after his death, and probably long after his fraternity brothers had initiated the crisis-management protocol—their home phone rang and the caller ID came up with the area code of their boy's college and a single word: coroner). If the dead person was a fraternity member who lived in the house, his brothers should return any borrowed items to his room and temporarily relocate his roommate, if he had one. Members may offer to pack up his belongings, but "it is more likely the family will want to do this themselves." Several empty boxes might thoughtfully be left outside the room for this purpose.

6. Members sit tight until consultants from the national organization show up to take control of the situation and to walk them through the next steps, which often include the completion of questionnaires

explaining exactly what happened and one-on-one interviews with the fraternity representatives. The anxious brothers are reminded to be completely honest and forthcoming in these accounts, and to tell the folks from national absolutely everything they know so that the situation can be resolved in the best possible manner.

As you should by now be able to see very clearly, the interests of the national organization and the individual members cleave sharply as this crisis-management plan is followed. Those questionnaires and honest accounts—submitted gratefully to the grown-ups who have arrived, the brothers believe, to help them—may return to haunt many of the brothers, providing possible cause for separating them from the fraternity, dropping them from the fraternity's insurance, laying the blame on them as individuals and not on the fraternity as the sponsoring organization. Indeed, the young men who typically rush so gratefully into the open arms of the representatives from their beloved national—an outfit to which they have pledged eternal allegiance—would be far better served by not talking to them at all, by walking away from the chapter house as quickly as possible and calling a lawyer.

So here is the essential question: In the matter of these disasters, are fraternities acting in an ethical manner, requiring good behavior from their members and punishing them soundly for bad or even horrific decisions? Or are they keeping a cool distance from the mayhem, knowing full well that misbehavior occurs with regularity ("most events take place at night") and doing nothing about it until the inevitable tragedy occurs, at which point they cajole members into incriminating themselves via a crisis-management plan presented as being in their favor?

Comprehension Questions

1. What does it mean to have the freedom of association?
2. What's the doctrine of *in loco parentis*?
3. What was one effect of raising the legal drinking age to twenty-one in all fifty states?
4. What were the four things that fraternities needed to do to survive in the 1980s? How did fraternities accomplish these goals?
5. What is the "BYO System"?
6. Why might someone think that the FIPG crisis management plan serves the interests of the national organization, and not those of the local members?

Discussion Questions

1. Greek parties have a reputation for being wilder than other college parties. In your experience, is this true? If so, what might explain this?

2. It probably seems strange that colleges used to operate *in loco parentis*, and you might be glad that your college isn't interested in your private life. But what might have been some of the *benefits* of colleges having such obligations to students? You certainly gain freedom in the new model, but what was lost?

3. Is it reasonable for fraternities to expect people to follow the rules at a BYO event? Why or why not? And if not, what does that imply—if anything—about whether fraternities should be held responsible for what happens in their houses?

Case

Consider this:

A West Virginia University freshman who died at a fraternity house in November had a blood alcohol level of 0.49, police said Tuesday. Nolan Burch, eighteen, was one of twenty Kappa Sigma pledges attending an initiation ritual on November 12, 2014, when he was blindfolded and taken to another location where he consumed a large amount of liquor, according to a news release from Morgantown police.

Burch was later taken back to the Kappa Sigma house "due to his very high level of intoxication and was laid on a table," police said. According to the release, fraternity members noticed Burch's face had turned blue and they could not detect a pulse. They called 911 at 11:50 p.m, and Burch was taken to a hospital where he died. Burch's BAC at the time of his death was six times the state limit for drinking and driving (for those of legal drinking age).

The afternoon of the initiation event, Burch tweeted: "It's about to be a very eventful night to say the least—Nolan Burch (@NolanBurch9) November 12, 2014."

The national fraternity said the WVU chapter of Kappa Sigma had lost its charter on Nov. 10—prior to the night Burch died—for previous, unrelated violations of the organization's code of conduct. "When a chapter's operations are suspended and/or closed, the chapter is directed to no longer host or otherwise participate in any functions associated with the fraternity," said Derald Dryman, spokesman for the Kappa Sigma national fraternity. "The events that took place the night of November 12, 2014 were after the chapter had been informed of their closing and therefore not approved or otherwise supported by the Fraternity." Dryan added the Burch family "and all the young men and women affected by this tragic event remain in our thoughts and prayers."[1]

A fellow student was later arrested for hazing Burch; the student had given him a bottle of liquor as part of a big/little event. In any case, the national organization was able to avoid any liability for what happened to Burch. Of course, the prior suspension ensured no liability, but they would have avoided it anyway, as the hazing broke the fraternity's rules. This raises a few important questions. First, if the national organization knows full well that students are going to haze one another—and that they're going to create situations like this one, where excessive drinking leads to a tragic death—are they partially *morally* responsible for what happens, even if they aren't *legally* responsible? Second, some hazing seems pretty harmless. But it sometimes goes seriously wrong. Why does that happen, and what could be done to prevent it?

Note

1. http://www.huffingtonpost.com/2015/01/27/west-virginia-fraternity-pledge_n_6557238.html

PART VII

Consumer Ethics

33

Download This Essay
A Defense of Stealing E-Books
Andrew T. Forcehimes

It's tempting to think that downloading digital content online, like e-books, is just like stealing an item from a brick-and-mortar retailer. Both acts seem to wrongfully deprive someone of something, so they're both instances of theft. Andrew Forcehimes holds that the analogy is not as apt as it seems. He introduces another analogy to show why. He compares online sources for downloading e-books to public libraries' sharing of copyrighted content to the broader public. The function of the two being so similar, Forcehimes suggests that any reason backing the latter practice ought to likewise count as support for the former. And by the same token, any reason for not sharing e-books online ought also to count against public libraries' sharing copyrighted material. Forcehimes considers some popular objections to sharing e-books and finds them lacking, concluding that, just like public libraries, online sources for downloading e-books ought to be permissible and even viewed as providing a valuable service to the public.

Forcehimes, Andrew. 2013. "Download This Essay: A Defence of Stealing Ebooks." *Think* 12 (34):109–115. Copyright © 2013 The Royal Institute of Philosophy. Reprinted with the permission of Cambridge University Press.

Philosophers write essays. Nowadays most of them are highly technical and argumentative. They have titles like "A Rejoinder to So and So" or "A Critique of Such and Such." This is somewhat understandable. Like others in my field, as a philosopher, my work is predicated on having interlocutors—all of whom, with a few exceptions, I have never met. This is the beauty of the written word combined with public libraries. Because of printing I can engage the ideas of others from a different time or place; because of libraries I am not excluded from the conversation because of social or economic class.

Public libraries are a wonderful resource. However, not too long ago I realized that I could greatly supplement the service libraries offer. To put it bluntly, I steal books online. This descriptive claim leads to two normative questions, which I often pose to my ethics class: "Can one give an argument in favor of public libraries (in the bricks and paper sense) that is not also an argument in favor of stealing books online? Or, can one give an argument against this kind of stealing that would not also be an argument against libraries?" I contend that the answer to both questions is no.[1]

Let's begin by looking at what public libraries are exactly and the arguments in favor of them. Public libraries are institutions that buy books and then allow members of the community to freely borrow them. If we were not so accustomed to this process, it would seem quite odd (or at least it should). Libraries get to buy a copyrighted book, the content of which is the property of either a publisher or author, and give it out for free. Not only this but the person borrowing it, under fair-use law, can photocopy the book or article in its entirety and keep it forever. Recently, in order to meet rising demand with decreasing budgets, libraries have started engaging in interlibrary loan. By this process, I can request and receive a book, which my particular library does not own, through another library. I can, by this same process, also request and receive photocopies of journal articles and chapters of books that my library neither has access to nor owns, and I can keep these copies indefinitely.[2]

It is important to keep in mind that all of this material is someone else's copyrighted property, so what would justify libraries in providing this kind of service? The standard argument hinges on the claim that no one should be deprived of information because of morally arbitrary contingencies such as race, sex, class, and age. But regardless of this, one might still ask, why should individuals have public access to information? The responses here may vary, but at the core all seem to hold that open access to information plays a pivotal role in a well-functioning society. For instance, an informed citizenry seems to be the best (if not the only) way of holding lawmakers accountable, which is why effective tyranny requires propaganda, silencing of dissent, and information distortion— all of which are thwarted by access to public libraries.

Beyond leveling the playing field between citizens and lawmakers, libraries attempt to mitigate the epistemic disparity among citizens. That is, we can eliminate inequalities in the amount of knowledge citizens have based on privileges that not all share. Minimally, it seems clear that acquiring information through reading books requires both time and money. Eliminating even one of these obstacles for the least well off members of society is surely a worthy endeavor, which is precisely what libraries attempt to do. Libraries prevent people from looking down on those who did not have certain educational advantages; they make, borrowing an expression from Philip Pettit, citizens capable of looking one another in the eye. Hence, insofar as libraries facilitate in meeting the twin goals of promoting a well-informed and equally-informed citizenry, we have good *prima facie* reasons for their existence and promotion.

But we should pause here to spell out why libraries are so peculiar in terms of their relation to property rights, specifically, intellectual property rights. Intellectual property is protected by copyright, and here lies the conflict: Libraries provide access to information; copyrights attempt to limit access to information. We have briefly looked at the argument in favor of libraries, what then is the argument in favor of copyrights?

To take a familiar case, the United States Constitution holds that congress has the power "[t]o promote the Progress of Science and useful Arts, by securing for limited Times to Authors and Inventors the exclusive Right to their respective Writings and Discoveries" (art.I, §8, cl.8.). The idea here is that progress in science and arts is motivated by economic incentives, and authors will be less motivated to produce work if they are deprived of this incentive. Thus, if one copies or steals a work, the author is harmed in virtue of the economic loss, and society is harmed because of the decreased incentive to innovate. I do not want to judge the merits of this argument quite yet, although I think it rests on two questionable assumptions (which I will return to below). Rather, I want to highlight that if one is in favor of libraries, one must hold something like the following premise: The cost of making every member of society pay to gain access to information—what seems to be an obvious implication of copyrights—is outweighed by the benefits that society receives by providing that information for free. But how is this not also an argument, consistently applied, for the theft of books online?

That is, if one is on board with the benefits libraries provide to societies, then one should be on board with the electronic distribution of books (indeed even rejoice in its speed and ease of access). If I can walk into a library, check out a book and scan it to my computer (or better, have someone else do the scanning for me through interlibrary loan), how is this relevantly different from logging on to a website and downloading a scanned version of the book? Do I mix my labor with the PDF while I am scanning so that it now becomes my property in some Lockean sense? If this counts, then so does moving around my mouse and typing. The important point here is that if access to certain information trumps copyright and justifies libraries, then it looks like access to the same information trumps copyright and justifies downloading books online. And the fact that one can access this information more efficiently is a *virtue*, not a vice.

But let us now examine how tight the connection is between libraries and stealing books online by looking at the argument from the other direction. Is there any argument that could be leveled against stealing books online that would not also impugn libraries?

With few exceptions (extreme want or necessity), it is considered morally blameworthy to steal another's property. In the most obvious cases, I have harmed you in some way by taking what is yours. For example, if you own a pear and I come along and steal your pear, then I have deprived you of some good that was rightfully yours. You can no longer enjoy it. If you worked for it, then your work was for naught. And this highlights one of the key features of property rights—physical excludability.

But intellectual property is relevantly different. If you work to write a book and I come along to copy it after its publication, I have not excluded you from selling future copies the way I could exclude you from selling your pear. I can, at least in one sense, leave you with exactly as much and as good as you previously had—intellectual property is nonrivalrous. But, it is argued, something seems to have gone awry. If you write a book, then you should be entitled to profit from it. So instead of physical excludability, copyrights step in and legally provide exclusive rights—barring others, without permission, from using the product—that is, legal excludability. Again, this idea rests on the notion that an author would be unable to secure royalties and hence overall production of work would decline because of decreased incentives.

Here it is worth noting that this point seems to ride on the following two claims: First, that those who copy or steal a work would have been willing to pay for it, and second that authors will not be self motivated. So, first, is it fair to say that if I steal a book I have harmed the author by depriving her of some good? This first claim must assume that if I were prevented from stealing the book, I would have purchased it. Only under these conditions can one safely assume that the stealing of a book would result in the harm of lost revenue for the author.

I would like a newer translation of Plato's *Five Dialogues* but if it is going to cost me $75, then I am willing to stick with the G. M. A Grube version. But if I did happen to steal a newer version, this fact does not entail that I would have otherwise purchased it. In fact, most people steal *because* they cannot afford to purchase. So we cannot assume that there is a one to one ratio between books that are stolen and books that would have otherwise been purchased, hence we cannot assume that stealing deprives the author of a good they would have otherwise received.

The second claim has more intuitive appeal. It seems at least plausible that increased economic incentives are linked to increased production of new works. However, England was the first to pass copyright laws in the early eighteenth century, and there is a large body of works that predates this. Taking this fact into account, we can make a distinction between works that would not have come into existence if not for royalties and those that would have come into existence regardless of royalties (and recall that the justification for copyrights assumes that royalties have to be the *primary* incentive, not just one among many). Certainly, however, there are a host of incentives that motivate authors, arguably taking primacy over royalties—for example, fame, tenure, and humanitarian ends, among others. And even if this is not convincing, here I am willing (although I do not think required) to opt for a narrower version of the argument, focusing only on those books that would be produced regardless of the incentives provided by copyright. Although one may think there are few books that meet this criterion, virtually *all* academic books do (with the exception of a few textbooks). And this nicely connects up to the first half of the argument, which shows that libraries and the electronic distribution of books are justified in the first place by the educational benefits they provide to societies, for it seems uncontroversial to assert that academic books (whose purpose it is to educate), fulfill this requirement much more than books that seek royalties above all (e.g., romance novels). In short, it seems there is an *inverse* relationship between the information that would be useful for a well-functioning society and a book's creation hinging on royalties.

Perhaps, one might challenge again, even if most (academic) authors are not in it for the money, the publishers are, and in the same way that one makes her holdings less secure by stealing from others, stealing and copying books make the production of future books less secure. But here's the rub, if this argument is correct it should also be an argument against libraries, especially those that do not buy all of their books, relying instead on interlibrary loan. If it is the case that it is morally wrong to upload a book because the unlimited number of downloads that might follow could jeopardize future publishing, then it should be equally wrong for a place to exist where anyone is allowed to walk in and do effectively the same thing. Or, to put it differently, how is a library buying one copy of a book and then distributing it to multiple individuals any different from one individual buying a book and distributing it to multiple individuals online?

The argument put forth here does not resist copyrights wholesale, rather it shows that the way we think about copyrights is inconsistent. Let's conclude then explicitly with what I take to be the most interesting upshot of this argument: There is a kind of willful taking of another's property—stealing books online—that is not morally wrong, and if it is morally wrong, then operating or using a library is also morally wrong.

Comprehension Questions

1. In what ways does sharing e-books resemble the practice of public libraries?
2. What reasons are there for thinking public libraries should be able to share copyrighted material with the broader public?
3. Why do some people think that authors' copyrights ought to be protected?
4. How, according to Forcehimes, does theft of physical property differ in its effects from theft of intellectual property?
5. Why doesn't Forcehimes think that stealing e-books is vulnerable to objections that appeal to diminished incentive?

Discussion Questions

1. Do you have friends who pirate e-books? If so, what proportion of your friends are doing it?
2. Suppose Forcehimes is right and it is morally OK to steal e-books. As a citizen, you also have an obligation to abide by the law. Does your moral permission trump your duty as a citizen?

3. Forcehimes seems to suggest that his argument has the most force when the stolen e-book in question is an academic one. Why think he's right? Do you find that his case is significantly weaker for, say, popular fiction?

4. The argument Forcehimes presents is limited to the morality of stealing e-books. What about other types of digital content? Could a similar argument be made for stealing digital music or movies? Would it be as strong in these cases?

Case

Apparently, some of your peers aren't buying their books:

> The cost to students of college textbooks skyrocketed 82 percent between 2002 and 2012, according to a 2013 report by the U.S. General Accountability Office, the research arm of Congress. As a result, students have been looking for less expensive options, such as renting books—and, now, finding them on the Internet, uploaded by other students. . . . [In 2013], a student wrote on a Tumblr blog called "Children of the Stars" complaining about a professor who insisted that students buy an online version of a specific paperback sociology book for more than $200—which the professor wrote himself—and would not allow them to purchase "an older, paperback edition of the same book for $5." The student continued: "This is why we download," and "Don't ever, EVER buy the newest edition of a book," which is followed by a list of Web sites with pirated books. As of 2:20 p.m. Eastern on [September 10, 2014], the post had 780,942 views.[3]

Is stealing an e-book permissible in these circumstances? If so, why? If not, why not? Could any of Forcehimes's arguments be used to defend downloading an e-book in this situation?

Notes

1. Recently (March 2012), seventeen publishing companies filed an injunction which shut down a website called library.nu—the most efficient and well-stocked resource for stealable electronic books.

2. See §107–108 of the United States Copyright Act, which holds that "it is not an infringement of copyright for a library or archives, or any of its employees acting within the scope of their employment, to reproduce no more than one copy or phonorecord of a work." Since it is not a violation of copyright there are no royalties involved with photocopying a book that a library holds.

3. https://www.washingtonpost.com/news/answer-sheet/wp/2014/09/17/more-students-are-illegally-downloading-college-textbooks-for-free/

34

A Response to Forcehimes's "Download This Essay: A Defense of Stealing E-Books"

Sadulla Karjiker

....

This essay is a reply to Andrew Forcehimes's argument that stealing e-books is morally the same as checking out a book from a public library. Like Forcehimes, Karjiker agrees that the main issue is whether or not stealing e-books has the economic effect of lowering the incentive for authors to publish their work. That result is obviously undesirable, given that their work is widely valued by society. Unlike Forcehimes, Karjiker thinks this effect on authors is substantial; so much so that it justifies copyright protection. He sets out a careful economic analysis leading to this conclusion, responding in detail to Forcehimes's argument in order to show the value of copyright protection and the relevant dissimilarities between stealing e-books and using public libraries.

....

Karjiker, Sadulla. 2014. "A Response to Forcehimes' 'Download This Essay: A Defence of Stealing Ebooks.'" *Think* 13(38): 51–57. Copyright © 2014 The Royal Institute of Philosophy. Reprinted with the permission of Cambridge University Press.

In his article, [which appears as the previous chapter in this book], Andrew Forcehimes contends that any argument concerning copyright law which favors the existence of public libraries will necessarily also justify the stealing of e-books. It is submitted that, at least economically, there is a qualitative and quantitative difference between permitting public libraries and allowing the online distribution of e-books for free download without the copyright holders' consent. This difference justifies the different legal treatment of these activities: the former being lawful, and the latter unlawful.

Debates about social institutions, such as copyright protection, almost unavoidably concern the issue of their purpose, that is, the goods they allocate or the conduct they incentivize. Forcehimes correctly notes that the rationale, and, it is submitted, the only coherent justification, for copyright protection, is an economic one. Due to their intangible nature, copyright works, economically, are *public goods*. Public goods have the quality of being both *non-rivalrous* and *non-excludable*. A non-rivalrous good can be consumed or enjoyed by an additional person without diminishing the enjoyment of others, at negligible, or no extra, cost. The claimed nonexcludability of copyright works means that persons cannot be prevented from using or enjoying it.

In the absence of copyright protection, the public-good nature of copyright works gives rise to the so-called free-rider problem: non-paying users of the public good. A public good creates benefits—positive externalities—which others can enjoy, without the producer of the good having the ability to prevent such enjoyment. This results in market failure because, despite the enjoyment of the good by a large number of people, they have no incentive to pay any amount for such benefit. The market price of a product serves as a signal to influence future behavior. Despite enjoying the benefits of the public good, consumers will, rationally, under-state their actual price preferences for such goods, which will cause producers to receive skewed signals about the actual demand for such goods, resulting in an insufficient supply of such goods. It also results in the producer of the good being unable to charge a price from all those who benefitted from the good, which reflects the benefit they derive from the good.

Thus, the rationale for the legal protection of copyright works is based on the perceived need to encourage the creation of such works, which are considered to be socially beneficial. By awarding authors proprietary rights in their creations, copyright law allows authors the ability to earn direct financial returns (and potentially profit) from their efforts;

copyright law provides the required incentives for authors to create copyright works. This system of proprietary copyright protection is considered to be more socially efficient than other possible alternative solutions to the public-good problem, such as the public financing of production, patronage, or seeking to rely on contractual restrictions. However, affording such proprietary rights to authors imposes costs on society. After all, if it costs (almost) nothing for others to utilize and enjoy a copyright work, why should they be prevented from doing so? The value of intellectual property, such as copyright works, to society is considered to generally exceed the costs of their protection. It is because of this perceived social benefit of copyright works that it becomes necessary to address the problem of market failure which impedes, or deters, their creation.

It is as a consequence of the recognition that copyright imposes social costs that the law permits exceptions, to reduce the social costs, while still creating sufficient incentives for authors. The purpose of copyright protection is not to exclude any segment of society from conversation or to allow people to claim proprietary rights in ideas. Copyright law does not protect ideas or commonplace facts, and the law makes provision for fair-dealing (or fair-use) exceptions for activities such as the use of copyright works for study, review, criticism, or reporting current events. In fact, unlike the UK and South Africa, US copyright law (as Forcehimes appears to use US law as the basis for his article) has an open-ended approach to the permissible exceptions (§107 of the US Copyright Act), which expressly recognizes the economic basis for copyright protection. One of the factors which a court has to consider whether a particular use of a copyrighted work is fair is "the effect of the use upon the potential market for or value of the copyrighted work." It is irrelevant whether some of the illegal copiers of copyright work would not have been willing to pay for it. Provided that others were prepared to pay for the work, but now no longer have to because it is freely available, it most definitely financially harms an author who seeks to earn money from his or her creation. It is disingenuous to suggest that an author would only suffer harm if every one of the illegal downloaders of an e-book was prepared to pay for it.

The effect, economically, of making an e-book available online for free download without the copyright owner's consent is vastly different than making physical copies of that work available in a public library. What has made the development of the Internet and digitization of content such a significant, and disruptive, problem—more so than the copying of copyright works that had taken place to date—are the following: First, the copying of digital content does not result in any degradation of the quality of the content, and, second, the scope of the sharing of copyright works is no longer confined by physical restrictions. Works online are now infinitely copyable, and are no longer required to be distributed by physical means. Until the emergence of digital reprographic technology, copying of library material was expensive, and the distribution of such copies was confined to relatively small groups.

While it is certainly true that you may make a copy of a work which you obtained at a public library for research or for private use, this permitted exception was considered as a justifiable limitation on the proprietary rights of the copyright owner. Accessing a copyright work from a library imposes costs on the individual doing so, which do not have to be incurred when downloading an e-book online; for example, it requires a physical visit to the library to collect and return the work (not to mention the time having to wait for an interlibrary loan), and it requires you to physically make the copy, by photocopying or scanning the work. In the pre-Internet era, any circulation of such copies would have been confined to a relatively small group of people who had actual contact with each other. While this type of bootlegging of copyright works—which is perhaps quite familiar to those of us who shared music on compact cassettes—does harm the potential market for the copyrighted work, it is, economically, orders of magnitude less damaging than online copyright infringement. If I make a copyright work—particularly a perfect digital copy—available on the Internet, it is available for download by any person, regardless of where they are, or if we know each other. It is not hyperbole to describe the Internet as "the most efficient copying machine built by man." The availability online of perfect, unauthorized copies of a copyright work would lead to the market failure described above.

Yes, Forcehimes is correct that creative works were created before copyright protection existed, and, indeed, continue to be created by *some* authors who do not require, or seek, an economic incentive. This, however, does not undermine the economic rationale for copyright protection. Some of the most well-known and influential creations, such as Homer's *Iliad*, and Leonardo Da Vinci's *Vitruvian Man*, were created without the incentives provided by copyright law. Prior to the invention of the printing press, creative works, such as books, were of limited economic value as goods, and, hence, there was little point in seeking any copyright-type legal protection. The reasons why the printing press transformed the economic value of cultural assets such as literary works were the following: First, prior to the invention of the printing press there was very little demand for such works as the majority of the population was illiterate. Second, the creators of such works were generally affluent and motivated by nonfinancial interests such as cultural advancement, producing the works in their leisure time—sometimes anonymously. Another reason why some creators were not directly motivated by financial concerns was the fact that works were often created under a system of patronage. Third, the costs of reproducing works before the printing press were very high because they were manuscripts. The reason these copies were so expensive was that it involved the time-consuming task of producing another manuscript. These copies would almost certainly be of an inferior quality because of human error, which reduced their value. In other words, the quality-adjusted cost of copies was very high.

At present, too, not all authors seek to rely directly on the proprietary rights which copyright law affords authors, and which permits them to earn the usual financial returns from their efforts. We have, for example, seen the emergence of alternative licensing schemes such as the Creative Commons and the various open-source software licenses. However, the mere fact that these authors have forgone the direct reward which copyright protection enables authors to earn as an incentive does not necessarily mean that these authors lack financial incentives to create such works. They may have simply opted to choose an alternative business model, and this flexibility is something which copyright protection facilitates. More importantly, while it may be the case that *some* people will author works without requiring the direct financial incentive which copyright permits (which Forcehimes seeks to rely on as one of his bases for justifying the illegal downloading of e-books), others may still require such financial incentives; provided that the social benefits of encouraging the creation of such works outweigh the costs of affording copyright protection, copyright protection is, from an economic perspective, justified. It is also telling that most authors still seek to rely on the direct rewards which copyright protection provides for, rather than opting for one of the more liberal-licensing regimes.

Although Forcehimes clearly recognizes the economic rationale, he also seeks to justify the unauthorized copying or dissemination of copyright works on a Lockean theory of property law. The moral justifications for copyright protection, such as the Lockean natural rights theory, the Hegelian personality theory, or utilitarianism, while intuitively appealing, are largely unconvincing. This is not to suggest that laws do not have any moral content or that the moral justifications do not, or should not, have any bearing on copyright policy. We could, for example, decide that, in a particular context, moral considerations should trump the economic arguments. However, there is nothing to suggest that this has in fact occurred in relation to copyright policy: The principles, and, indeed, the fair-dealing exceptions permitted by copyright law, satisfy the economic justifications for copyright protection.

For completeness, in order to address some of Forcehimes's overly-broad statements about copyright protection, it is necessary to clarify any misconceptions that may exist concerning copyright protection. First, copyright's purpose is not to limit access to information. It has always been lawful to lend a copy of a book that you bought to a friend. Your friend is not denied the access to the information because she was not prepared to pay, or could not afford to pay, for the book. Public libraries make use of the same principle to benefit society generally, which tends to offset any unnecessary social cost imposed by copyright protection. Second, unlike some of the moral justifications, the economic justification for copyright protection is not premised on rewarding, nor enriching, authors *per se*. It merely provides authors with the necessary incentives by ensuring that they have an adequate *opportunity* to earn a financial return from works which are considered to be, on balance, socially beneficial. In fact, it is arguable that the purpose of copyright protection is, paradoxically, to increase the size of the public domain, as the protection is for a limited period of time.[1] From this perspective, copyright protection is only permissible to the extent that it incentivizes creation and enlarges the public domain.

While copyright law, and the permissible fair-dealing exceptions, have to be updated periodically to take account of, among other things, technological changes in order to ensure that they attain the desired purpose, at present, there appears to be no inherent contradiction in prohibiting the online distribution of e-books without the copyright holders' consent, and permitting access to physical books via public libraries.

Comprehension Questions

1. What's the argument to which Karjiker is responding?
2. What economic considerations support the conclusion that copyright protection is legitimate?

3. How does copyright law accommodate the importance of making information publicly available?

4. In what ways does Karjiker think using public libraries differs from stealing e-books?

5. Why does Karjiker disagree with Forcehimes's view about authors' incentive to publish?

Discussion Questions

1. What are the comparative costs to you of using the library versus stealing an e-book? In your experience, is it true that there are greater costs to using the library (as Karjiker says)?

2. Karjiker claims that the best way to ensure that authors produce works is to protect the market economy where authors pursue financial incentives. What other arrangements are possible? Which one do you think is best?

3. Karjiker says that one difference between sharing library material versus the unauthorized sharing of e-books is the "degradation of content." Do you agree that this is a significant difference? Why?

Case

Consider this news report:

Piracy may be the bane of the music industry but according to a new study, it may also be its engine. A report from the BI Norwegian School of Management has found that those who download music illegally are also ten times more likely to pay for songs than those who don't.

Everybody knows that music sales have continued to fall in recent years, and that filesharing is usually blamed. We are made to imagine legions of Internet criminals, their fingers on trackpads, downloading songs via BitTorrent and never paying for anything. One of the only bits of good news amid this doom and gloom is the steady rise in digital music sales. Millions of Internet do-gooders, their fingers on trackpads, pay for songs they like—purchasing them from Amazon or iTunes Music Store. And yet according to Professor Anne-Britt Gran's new research, these two groups may be the same.

The Norwegian study looked at almost two thousand online music users, all over the age of fifteen. Researchers found that those who downloaded "free" music—whether from lawful or seedy sources—were also ten times more likely to pay for music. This would make music pirates the industry's largest audience for digital sales.

Wisely, the study did not rely on music pirates' honesty. Researchers asked music buyers to prove that they had proof of purchase.[2]

The study came out in 2009, and similar ones have confirmed its findings.
Of course, this study is about music, not e-books. Still, you might wonder
whether it casts doubt on Karjiker's idea about the economic costs of digital theft. Does it? And that issue aside, what does this study imply about
the ethics of stealing music? If you ultimately spend more than you would
otherwise, does that make it morally OK?

Notes

1. The ratcheting up of the term of protection for copyright works in the United
   States and Europe is regrettable and unwarranted, and is not defendable in
   accordance with the economic justification for copyright protection.
2. http://www.theguardian.com/music/2009/apr/21/study-finds-pirates-buy
   -more-music

≡≡≡ 🐦 ≡≡≡

35

The Singer Solution to World Poverty

Peter Singer

....

If you stopped buying things you don't need, you could save a child's life. Given this, is it wrong for you to get a new phone when your old one works? Or a new pair of shoes when you've got several already? Peter Singer thinks so. In fact, he thinks you should be giving away everything you earn that doesn't go toward necessities. You might think that this is unreasonable, but Singer argues that the facts about global poverty—and our own moral convictions—suggest otherwise.

....

In the Brazilian film "Central Station," Dora is a retired schoolteacher who makes ends meet by sitting at the station writing letters for illiterate people. Suddenly she has an opportunity to pocket $1,000. All she has to do is persuade a homeless nine-year-old boy to follow her to an address she has been given. (She is told he will be adopted by wealthy foreigners.) She delivers the boy, gets the money, spends some of it on a television set and settles down to enjoy her new acquisition. Her neighbor spoils the fun, however, by telling her that the boy was too old to be adopted—he will be killed and his organs sold for transplantation. Perhaps Dora knew this all along, but after her neighbor's plain speaking, she spends a troubled night. In the morning Dora resolves to take the boy back.

Suppose Dora had told her neighbor that it is a tough world, other people have nice new TVs too, and if selling the kid is the only way she can get one, well, he was only a street kid. She would then have become, in the eyes of the audience, a monster. She redeems herself only by being prepared to bear considerable risks to save the boy.

At the end of the movie, in cinemas in the affluent nations of the world, people who would have been quick to condemn Dora if she had not rescued the boy go home to places far more comfortable than her apartment. In fact, the average family in the United States spends almost one-third of its income on things that are no more necessary to them than Dora's new TV was to her. Going out to nice restaurants, buying new clothes because the old ones are no longer stylish, vacationing at beach resorts—so much of our income is spent on things not essential to the preservation of our lives and health. Donated to one of a number of charitable agencies, that money could mean the difference between life and death for children in need.

All of which raises a question: In the end, what is the ethical distinction between a Brazilian who sells a homeless child to organ peddlers and an American who already has a TV and upgrades to a better one—knowing that the money could be donated to an organization that would use it to save the lives of kids in need?

Of course, there are several differences between the two situations that could support different moral judgments about them. For one thing, to be able to consign a child to death when he is standing right in front of you takes a chilling kind of heartlessness; it is much easier to ignore an appeal for money to help children you will never meet. Yet for a utilitarian philosopher like myself—that is, one who judges whether acts are right or wrong by their consequences—if the upshot of the American's failure to donate the money is that one more kid dies on the streets of a Brazilian city, then it is, in some sense, just as bad as selling the kid to the organ peddlers. But one doesn't need to embrace my utilitarian ethic to see that, at the very least, there is a troubling incongruity in being so quick to condemn Dora for taking the child to the organ peddlers while, at the same time, not regarding the American consumer's behavior as raising a serious moral issue.

In his 1996 book, *Living High and Letting Die*, the New York University philosopher Peter Unger presented an ingenious series of imaginary examples designed to probe our intuitions about whether it is wrong to live well without giving substantial amounts of money to help people who are hungry, malnourished, or dying from easily treatable illnesses like diarrhea. Here's my paraphrase of one of these examples:

> Bob is close to retirement. He has invested most of his savings in a very rare and valuable old car, a Bugatti, which he has not been able to insure. The Bugatti is his pride and joy. In addition to the pleasure he gets from driving and caring for his car, Bob knows that its rising market value means that he will always be able to sell it and live comfortably after retirement. One day when Bob is out for a drive, he parks the Bugatti near the end of a railway siding and goes for a walk up the track. As he does so, he sees that a runaway train, with no one aboard, is running down the railway track. Looking farther down the track, he sees the small figure of a child very likely to be killed by the runaway train. He can't stop the train and the child is too far away to warn of the danger, but he can throw a switch that will divert the train down the siding where his Bugatti is parked. Then nobody will be killed—but the train will destroy his Bugatti. Thinking of his joy in owning the car and the financial security it represents, Bob decides not to throw the switch. The child is killed. For many years to come, Bob enjoys owning his Bugatti and the financial security it represents.

Bob's conduct, most of us will immediately respond, was gravely wrong. Unger agrees. But then he reminds us that we, too, have opportunities to save the lives of children. We can give to organizations like Unicef or Oxfam America. How much would we have to give one of these organizations to have a high probability of saving the life of a child threatened by easily preventable diseases? (I do not believe that children are more worth saving than adults, but since no one can argue that children have brought their poverty on themselves, focusing on them simplifies the issues.) Unger called up some experts and used the information they provided to offer some plausible estimates that include the cost of raising money, administrative expenses, and the cost of delivering aid where it is most needed. By his calculation, $200 in donations would help a sickly two-year-old transform into a healthy six-year-old—offering safe passage through childhood's most dangerous years. To show how practical philosophical argument can be, Unger even tells his readers that they can easily donate funds by using their credit card and calling one of these toll-free numbers: (800) 367-5437 for UNICEF; (800) 693-2687 for Oxfam America.

Now you, too, have the information you need to save a child's life. How should you judge yourself if you don't do it? Think again about Bob and his Bugatti. Unlike Dora, Bob did not have to look into the eyes of the child he was sacrificing for his own material comfort. The child was a complete stranger to him and too far away to relate to in an intimate, personal way. Unlike Dora, too, he did not mislead the child or initiate the chain of events imperiling him. In all these respects, Bob's situation resembles that of people able but unwilling to donate to overseas aid and differs from Dora's situation.

If you still think that it was very wrong of Bob not to throw the switch that would have diverted the train and saved the child's life, then it is hard to see how you could deny that it is also very wrong not to send money to one of the organizations listed above. Unless, that is, there is some morally important difference between the two situations that I have overlooked.

Is it the practical uncertainties about whether aid will really reach the people who need it? Nobody who knows the world of overseas aid can doubt that such uncertainties exist. But Unger's figure of $200 to save a child's life was reached after he had made conservative assumptions about the proportion of the money donated that will actually reach its target.

One genuine difference between Bob and those who can afford to donate to overseas aid organizations but don't is that only Bob can save the child on the tracks, whereas there are hundreds of millions of people who can give $200 to overseas aid organizations. The problem is that most of them aren't doing it. Does this mean that it is all right for you not to do it?

Suppose that there were more owners of priceless vintage cars— Carol, Dave, Emma, Fred and so on, down to Ziggy—all in exactly the same situation as Bob, with their own siding and their own switch, all sacrificing the child in order to preserve their own cherished car. Would that make it all right for Bob to do the same? To answer this question affirmatively is to endorse follow-the-crowd ethics—the kind of ethics that led many Germans to look away when the Nazi atrocities were being committed. We do not excuse them because others were behaving no better.

We seem to lack a sound basis for drawing a clear moral line between Bob's situation and that of any reader of this article with $200 to spare who does not donate it to an overseas aid agency. These readers seem to be acting at least as badly as Bob was acting when he chose to let the runaway train hurtle toward the unsuspecting child. In the light of this conclusion, I trust that many readers will reach for the phone and donate that $200. Perhaps you should do it before reading further.

Now that you have distinguished yourself morally from people who put their vintage cars ahead of a child's life, how about treating yourself and your partner to dinner at your favorite restaurant? But wait. The money you will spend at the restaurant could also help save the lives of children overseas! True, you weren't planning to blow $200 tonight, but if you were to give up dining out just for one month, you would easily save that amount. And what is one month's dining out, compared to a child's life? There's the rub. Since there are a lot of desperately needy children in the world, there will always be another child whose life you could save for another $200. Are you therefore obliged to keep giving until you have nothing left? At what point can you stop?

Hypothetical examples can easily become farcical. Consider Bob. How far past losing the Bugatti should he go? Imagine that Bob had got his foot stuck in the track of the siding, and if he diverted the train, then before it rammed the car it would also amputate his big toe. Should he still throw the switch? What if it would amputate his foot? His entire leg?

As absurd as the Bugatti scenario gets when pushed to extremes, the point it raises is a serious one: Only when the sacrifices become very significant indeed would most people be prepared to say that Bob does nothing wrong when he decides not to throw the switch. Of course, most people could be wrong; we can't decide moral issues by taking opinion polls. But consider for yourself the level of sacrifice that you would demand of Bob, and then think about how much money you would have to give away in order to make a sacrifice that is roughly equal to that. It's almost certainly much, much more than $200. For most middle-class Americans, it could easily be more like $200,000.

Isn't it counterproductive to ask people to do so much? Don't we run the risk that many will shrug their shoulders and say that morality, so conceived, is fine for saints but not for them? I accept that we are unlikely to see, in the near or even medium-term future, a world in which it is normal for wealthy Americans to give the bulk of their wealth to strangers. When it comes to praising or blaming people for what they do, we tend to use a standard that is relative to some conception of normal behavior. Comfortably off Americans who give, say, 10 percent of their income to overseas aid organizations are so far ahead of most of their equally comfortable fellow citizens that I wouldn't go out of my way to chastise them for not doing more. Nevertheless, they should be doing much more, and they are in no position to criticize Bob for failing to make the much greater sacrifice of his Bugatti.

At this point various objections may crop up. Someone may say: "If every citizen living in the affluent nations contributed his or her share I wouldn't have to make such a drastic sacrifice, because long before such levels were reached, the resources would have been there to save the lives of all those children dying from lack of food or medical care. So why should I give more than my fair share?" Another, related, objection is that the government ought to increase its overseas aid allocations, since that would spread the burden more equitably across all taxpayers.

Yet the question of how much we ought to give is a matter to be decided in the real world—and that, sadly, is a world in which we know that most people do not, and in the immediate future will not, give substantial amounts to overseas aid agencies. We know, too, that at least in the next year, the United States government is not going to meet even the very modest United Nations–recommended target of 0.7 percent of gross national product; at the moment it lags far below that, at 0.09 percent, not even half of Japan's 0.22 percent or a tenth of Denmark's 0.97 percent. Thus, we know that the money we can give beyond that theoretical "fair share" is still going to save lives that would otherwise be lost. While the idea that no one need do more than his or her fair share is a powerful one, should it prevail if we know that others are not doing their fair share and that children will die preventable deaths unless we do more than our fair share? That would be taking fairness too far.

Thus, this ground for limiting how much we ought to give also fails. In the world as it is now, I can see no escape from the conclusion that each one of us with wealth surplus to his or her essential needs should be giving most of it to help people suffering from poverty so dire as to be life-threatening. That's right: I'm saying that you shouldn't buy that new car, take that cruise, redecorate the house, or get that pricey new suit. After all, a $1,000 suit could save five children's lives.

So how does my philosophy break down in dollars and cents? An American household with an income of $50,000 spends around $30,000 annually on necessities, according to the Conference Board, a nonprofit economic research organization. Therefore, for a household bringing in $50,000 a year, donations to help the world's poor should be as close as possible to $20,000. The $30,000 required for necessities holds for higher incomes as well. So a household making $100,000 could cut a yearly check for $70,000. Again, the formula is simple: Whatever money you're spending on luxuries, not necessities, should be given away.

Now, evolutionary psychologists tell us that human nature just isn't sufficiently altruistic to make it plausible that many people will sacrifice so much for strangers. On the facts of human nature, they might be right, but they would be wrong to draw a moral conclusion from those facts. If it is the case that we ought to do things that, predictably, most of us won't do, then let's face that fact head-on. Then, if we value the life of a child more than going to fancy restaurants, the next time we dine out we will know that we could have done something better with our money. If that makes living a morally decent life extremely arduous, well, then that is the way things are. If we don't do it, then we should at least know that we are failing to live a morally decent life—not because it is good to wallow in guilt but because knowing where we should be going is the first step toward heading in that direction.

When Bob first grasped the dilemma that faced him as he stood by that railway switch, he must have thought how extraordinarily unlucky he was to be placed in a situation in which he must choose between the life of an innocent child and the sacrifice of most of his savings. But he was not unlucky at all. We are all in that situation.

Comprehension Questions

1. Why, exactly, does Singer think you should be giving money to aid organizations?
2. Lots of people could donate to aid organizations—not just you. Why, according to Singer, doesn't that matter?
3. Most people won't give as much as Singer says we should. Does he think that that's a problem for his view?
4. "If everyone else did more, no one would have to give very much at all. So, it's unfair to ask anyone to give away everything that isn't going toward a necessity." What's Singer's response to this objection?
5. Singer says that Bob wasn't unlucky. What does he mean by this?

Discussion Questions

1. How much do you know about global poverty? Just how bad is it to live in certain parts of the developing world?
2. On Singer's view, how much should you *personally* be giving away? (That is, how much of your money is going to things that aren't necessities?)
3. "It's my money, and I can do what I want with it." Is this a good objection to Singer? Why or why not?
4. Some people agree with Singer that they *ought* to give away most of their money, but they admit that they just don't want to be that generous. If that describes you, then how do you make sense of your situation? Are we just dealing with plain old selfishness? Or is there some other explanation?

Case

No one would do what Singer suggests . . . would they? As it turns out, some people do:

Julia and her partner, Jeff Kaufman, met in college. They had little space or money, and much of their enjoyment came from spending time with their friends. When they married in 2009, they talked about how they would live and agreed that they would continue to live modestly so they could give something, even on a low income, and as their earnings increased they would give more. Julia is a social worker, and Jeff is a computer programmer. Their combined income was under $40,000 in 2008, but since then a sharp increase in Jeff's earnings has brought it to $261,416 for the year ending July 2014. In each of these years from 2008 to 2014, with one exception when Julia was saving to pay her way through graduate school, Julia and Jeff have donated at least a third of their income, and as their income rose they have given half. . . .

Julia and Jeff saved money by using public transit rather than owning a car. Their housing expenses are low because they rent part of a house, but they expect these costs to go up once they buy their own house. They are saving for that and also for retirement and future expenses related to their child. Nevertheless, they were able to donate half their income and plan to continue doing that in future. . . .

As a small child, Julia Wise grasped that although she did not lack anything she needed, there were others who did. Ever since, she has seen every dollar she spends as a dollar taken out of the hands of someone who needs it more than she does. So the question she asks herself is not how much she should give, but how much she should keep.[1]

Do people like Julia and Jeff affect your thinking about giving? If so, how? Why don't more people live like they do? Why are we so resistant to what seems like a very powerful argument?

Note

1. Peter Singer, *The Most Good You Can Do* (New York: Yale University Press, 2015), Chapter 3.

36

Women Shopping and Women Sweatshopping
Individual Responsibility for Consumerism

Lisa Cassidy

There are some good arguments against shopping the way so many of us do. After summarizing two of them—one due to Peter Singer, the other due to Thomas Pogge—Lisa Cassidy considers why we don't feel responsible for wrongdoing, explaining Samuel Sheffler's hypothesis that our intuitions about responsibility are shaped by living in small communities, not global and hyper-connected ones. Cassidy then explores three conceptions of responsibility that might help us live morally in the twenty-first century. Ultimately, she argues that we should ask ourselves two questions: "How should I manage my lifestyle?" and "How might I care about others around the world?"

As American women toil in climate-controlled malls to choose just the right outfits, some women in the Global South work in sweatshop conditions to produce those consumer goods.[1] Shoppers

Cassidy, Lisa. 2011. "Women Shopping and Women Sweatshopping: Individual Responsibility for Consumerism." In Fashion—Philosophy for Everyone: Thinking with Style, ed. Jessica Wolfendale and Jeanette Kennett, 186–198. Malden, MA: Blackwell. Reprinted with permission of John Wiley & Sons.

"here" wonder about sweatshop workers "there." Though facts are murky, any reasonably well-informed American consumer has reason to at least *suspect* that the clothes or shoes she is purchasing may have been produced in inhumane conditions.

This leaves a consumer with a moral dilemma of some complexity: Is shopping for a new pair of party shoes a harmless hobby, or is it an act of capitalist imperialism? By buying these shoes am I actually hurting someone in some far corner of the world? Must I do research on every bit of clothing I buy to have a clean conscience? If I personally boycott brands or stores that I suspect may use sweatshops, is that an effective response to the problem? Should I splurge on eco-luxury brands because they are "certified" fair-trade or sweatshop-free? But if everyone stopped buying from the local malls wouldn't women in the Global South actually be worse off than they are right now because their incomes would be even more meager?

This essay will first review what philosophers Peter Singer and Thomas Pogge have said about the responsibilities of those who hail from wealthy nations. Then the focus will shift to individual responsibility for consumerism in the global age. . . . My own argument will be that individual responsibility for consumption is best understood when we attend to the three different senses of the term "responsibility.". . .

Do Prestigious, Ivy League, Male Philosophers Ever Think About Clothes? Yes! (Well, Sort Of)

In 1971 philosopher Peter Singer wrote a now-landmark essay called "Famine, Affluence, and Morality." In it Singer worried about the then-developing humanitarian crisis in Bangladesh, where thousands were going hungry as the world idled. Singer maintains that *every one of us* who can help the starving by donating funds to poverty relief has a moral duty to do so. (If you've bought a new hoodie this past week, he means you!) To illustrate his point he devised this analogy: "If I am walking past a shallow pond and see a child drowning in it, I ought to wade in and pull the child out. This will mean getting my clothes muddy, but this is insignificant, while the death of the child would presumably be a very bad thing."[2] The fact that the children in Bangladesh are far away—and not literally in a pond before you—makes no moral difference in terms of your obligation. He says to let the child drown because you wish to save your clothes from the mud is monstrous. By extension, the money spent on my patent-leather ballet flats, belted trench coat, and Lucky Brand jeans could have been used to save the lives of distant strangers.

Today the core of Singer's position remains unchanged: We in the Global North should cut unnecessary consumer and government spending to donate funds to relieve world poverty because suffering is bad, and we should do what we can to eliminate it. Notice here that Singer does not assume that citizens of the "Global North" (North America, Europe, or Australasia) have actually done anything to particularly impoverish citizens of the "Global South" (Latin America, Africa, or Asia). Instead Singer finds that we should be invested in ensuring the well-being of the poor for utilitarian reasons, because they are equal to us in every moral way and suffering is inherently bad.

Enter rival philosopher Thomas Pogge. He actually wants a similar sort of economic justice for the world's poor, but Pogge's reasoning is much more of an indictment against the Global North. Pogge's analysis finds that the rich folks of the Global North actually have created the dire poverty in the South by not actively correcting past economic and political injustices.[3] In contrast to Singer, Pogge thinks the child drowning in the pond is dying because we broke his leg and put him in there.[4] Average people contribute to ongoing injustices by harming the world's poor with our political and economic policies. For Pogge, we have an obligation to alleviate global poverty because of a *you break it, you buy it* policy: We broke the Global South, now we need to pay to make it right. . . .

Individual Responsibility Only Seems to Fit in Extra Small

Most people, I suppose, like to think of themselves as reasonably decent people, and they usually, I hope, are right. But Singer's and Pogge's arguments imply that those of us who bought this year's must-have cardigan sweater (guilty!) are in serious moral failure because we did not donate those fifty bucks to world poverty relief instead. A concern about Singer and Pogge is that they have set the moral bar too high for ordinary people to successfully scale. Philosopher Samuel Scheffler can explain this concern about Singer's and Pogge's accounts. Scheffler suggests that people in our society share a common-sense view of individual responsibility.[5] This common-sense view has two features: First, duties not to harm others take priority over duties to help others (this is called negative duties trumping positive duties); second, it is morally right to prefer our friends and loved ones over strangers.[6] He says this understanding of responsibility is *restricted* in that it makes our moral world seem quite small. Scheffler goes on to show how in our society we are accustomed to giving primacy to acts (rather than omissions), to weighing near effects over distant ones, and to counting individual effects over group effects.[7] So we imagine that we are members of a small community, where what we do matters more than what we fail to do, the impacts of our actions are directly experienced, and our actions are measured individually rather than collectively. In such a social setting, responsibility that is restricted to not harming others and looking out for loved ones first makes good sense. The problem for us now is the global age; we no longer live in the small communities which gave rise to this understanding of moral agency. "[It is] more difficult than ever to sustain the conception of human social relations as consisting primarily of small scale interactions among single individuals. The earth has become an increasingly crowded place."[8]

Scheffler might say that Singer's and Pogge's proposals are implausible because most of us simply don't think of individual responsibility as they do. Singer and Pogge want to alter individual responsibility to be (as Scheffler would say) non-restrictive: Positive duties to help others would matter as much as negative duties not to hurt, and caring for strangers would matter to us as much as caring for loved ones. But such a drastically revised conception of responsibility will be psychologically and morally difficult to accept. This is not to say that Singer or Pogge is *wrong* about our obligations to relieve Southern poverty. Not wrong exactly, but perhaps *ill-fitting*. . . . Scheffler says it just feels so natural (not that it is natural, but it feels like it is) to give count to acts rather than omissions, weigh near effects over distant ones, and concentrate on individual effects over group effects. We think to ourselves, "Well, I don't *see* anyone being hurt when I buy this sweater for Dad, but if I came empty-handed to his birthday party it really would disappoint him.". . .

Am I Responsible for the Suffering of the World's Poor?

So far I have reviewed Singer's and Pogge's attempts to expand individual responsibility for alleviating suffering in the Global South [and] Scheffler's explanation that individual responsibility will have to be rethought for the global age. . . . Still, the question remains: In what way am I *responsible for* and *to* the world's poor, particularly the low-wage laborers in the Global South who make my consumer consumption possible?

Our word "responsibility" comes from the Roman legal proceeding called "the response." When called to testify at a legal proceeding, one would give the response to the charges levied. This response was an account of oneself or one's actions. Hence our understanding of individual responsibility rests largely on this idea of being accountable. And while the above question is posed as a simple yes or no, we soon see that personal accountability has more nuance than that. (My subsequent work here is directly derived from Claudia Card, although her discussion is not about fashion or consumption.[9])

Let's first notice that the question—am I responsible for the suffering of the world's poor?—uses a particular understanding of responsibility. The understanding is a familiar one, the credit sense of responsibility.[10] When we say someone is responsible in the credit-taking sense, we mean this person is the past cause of some current state of affairs. For example, if I attempt to return a garment without its tags the sales clerk may say, "You were responsible for keeping the tags on, and we cannot take the return without them." She is correct of course, and I would have only myself to blame for removing the tags. This credit sense of responsibility therefore looks backwards to the past to find a way of accounting for the present state of things. . . .

When it comes to analyzing the impact of economic globalization, we just don't know if I ought to be blamed for hurting others with the purchase of this season's It-bag. So the short answer to the question at hand is a definite *maybe*. However, the ambiguity of this answer doesn't give me a free pass. Singer's point is that we have a duty to prevent suffering if we can, even if we are not to be blamed with originating it.

One possible option is "sustainable consumption." The *New York Times* reported some time ago that consumers are increasingly interested in buying products that are produced in humane and ecological ways.[11] Nowadays fair trade coffee or sweatshop free garments are widely available for premium prices. For example, when I purchase a pair of TOMS shoes . . . the company will donate a second pair of shoes to a needy child somewhere in the world. In this way, I can take credit for helping a shoeless child.

Relying on sustainable consumption to respond to the shopper's dilemma is a start. But it is worth noting that these products are more expensive, so as to be luxury items. Then again, all fashion purchases that go beyond the basics that we need to keep ourselves minimally clothed and shod are also, when you think about it, "luxuries." TOMS shoes start at $48.00. A plain cotton T-shirt is about $25.00 at the sweatshop-free mall chain American Apparel, compared with ten dollars for a T-shirt from Target. So it seems that consumers must be willing to pay about 30 to 50 percent more for fashions that will leave them free of guilt or impervious to blame. In this way, ethical responsibility itself becomes part of the commodity. Your "vegan yellow/plaid patch woven" TOMS are therefore a double luxury: first, because you likely didn't need any new shoes at all, and second, you have the luxury of feeling like you may be credited with being charitable. A smart business strategy, and it might even be one that actually helps alleviate global poverty. . . .

We can also finesse the question at hand slightly to read: What can I do to act responsibly toward the world's poor? This shift indicates that personal accountability is more than being credited with past deeds. It is also about looking forward to the future.[12] One part of being an ethical person is accounting for your commitments. This is where two additional senses of responsibility come in: management responsibility and caretaking responsibility.

A second sense of responsibility is the management sense. In this sense, we are responsible for sifting through possible courses of action, choosing what is appropriate or desirable, and steering the course to some conclusion. The management sense of responsibility is used when I conduct my back-to-school wardrobe evaluation. I determine what still fits (uh oh!), what is still in style (huh?), what should be donated because I never should have bought it in the first place (yikes!). Then I am ready for autumn, taking responsibility for my wardrobe by sticking to my list and my budget.

The management sense of responsibility might also be employed in deeper ways to analyze consumer consumption. . . . I think a reasonable and well-considered answer to the question "Why do you shop?" is the reply "Because I'm bored."

American ennui needs to be treated seriously in an analysis of what drives consumerist consumption. I think the problem is that we are bored, that boredom wholly infuses many aspects of middle-class American [life, which] is a fundamentally boring experience. To acquire things is, of course, initially exciting, but the excitement is obviously short-lived. And convenience is even more boring. To have things easily at hand is sometimes pleasurable, but more often, in suburban New Jersey surroundings, convenience is beneath remark.

Consumer activity is cyclically undertaken to stave off the national monotony: I am bored, I shop, I buy hip aviator-style sunglasses; I get bored with what I purchased, I shop again for hipper cat-eye sunglasses.

My purse is now crammed with sunglasses. I shop for a new purse. Shopping is not only a form of entertainment, it becomes an expression of personal entitlement. The mall (or the virtual mall) becomes our gym, our kitchen, our doctor's office, our church. This is how we can explain people paying $21.80 for a T-shirt proclaiming, "It's not shopping, it's retail therapy" at Razzle.com—along with more than one hundred other T-shirts merely commemorating *shopping*.

Adopting less consumerist virtues would involve taking responsibility for how we manage our money, our time, and most of all our psychic attentions. It would also involve finding meaning beyond convenience and acquisition. If I am bored with myself I might reasonably decide to change my style and then take steps to manage this transformation. My workaday, staid academic style might be traded in for carefree joie-de-vivre just by squaring my shoulders back to face the world and following through to find a renewed sense of adventure. I could take responsibility for an attitude makeover that wouldn't cost a dime.

The final sense of responsibility is the care-taking sense. This sense of responsibility means being committed to supporting something or someone.[13] I practice the care-taking sense of responsibility, for example, when I accompany my mother to shop for a formal gown. When she asks me to go shopping for her upcoming affair I say, "Sure, I'll take care of you." Now I am committed to standing behind her: I negotiate coupons and discounts with the sales staff, schlep different styles into the dressing room, and give her my unbridled opinions on fit or color. (I have to be cautious with the last bit, or else I won't be taking good care but will simply hurt her feelings.)

Perhaps ethically responsible shoppers will come to see themselves as taking care of others beyond their immediate circle of self, family, and friends. This might require some leap of the imagination, which was Singer's strategy when he placed that imaginary drowning child in the pond. As Scheffler has pointed out, we just don't have the same level of attachment to strangers as we do to loved ones. In ordinary circumstances—say, when I am at the mall—it is simply overwhelming to think of the chains of connection tying me to those who produced the consumer goods on the shelves. I suspect spending less time at the mall and online is part of the answer.

On the face of things it seems improbable to think of me as taking care of the strangers who labored to make my clothes, my pajamas, my wraps and scarves, my running shoes. Perhaps I cannot care for them in the immediate sense of being able to touch them, to look them in the eyes, and to see to their immediate welfare. But there are other ways of taking responsibility for others and standing behind them. I can care *about* them, for example, even if I can't care *for* them.[14] Caring about citizens in the Global South may involve donating funds to poverty relief, as Singer and Pogge variously argue. Or it may involve other activities. Perhaps it means reading the newspaper or becoming politically involved. Perhaps it simply means, as one feminist philosopher has suggested, not placing the trivial amusements of one's own children above the basic needs of others' children.[15]

Unfortunately, I think we too often ignore the ways that we should take responsibility for our consumerism. Perhaps this is because so much of the existing analysis concentrates on the credit sense of responsibility, looking backward to assign blame for our shopping. When consumers do contemplate responsibility for their purchases, I bet these thoughts are quickly dusted away, lest specters of guilt and shame sully the joy of a new purchase. We say: "This might be made in a sweatshop, but I'm not really sure so I just won't think about it now. I am too busy with my own concerns." (This also might be a way of saying, "It bores me to think about sweatshop labor.")

We can instead focus on taking responsibility for ourselves and others. I have argued that the management and care senses of responsibility are helpful, given the haziness of globalization's impact on world poverty. The questions we could ask ourselves are: How should I manage my lifestyle, and how might I care about others around the world? Answers to these questions will be deeply personal and individualized; some might make great changes in their lives and others may blithely shop away the same as before.

Comprehension Questions

1. Why, exactly, does Singer think that each of us is *obligated* to help relieve global poverty?
2. Why, exactly, does *Pogge* think that each of us is obligated to help relieve global poverty?
3. On Scheffler's view, what are the features of our "common-sense" view of individual responsibility?
4. What's Cassidy's point when she says that Singer and Pogge's conception of individual responsibility is "ill-fitting"?
5. What are Cassidy's three senses of responsibility, and how do they differ?
6. What is "American ennui"?

Discussion Questions

1. Think about the clothes in your closet. What do you know about their origins? Would it surprise you to find out that some of them were made in sweatshops? Do you think that some of them *were* made in sweatshops?
2. Pogge thinks that we in wealthy countries are collectively responsible for global poverty because we haven't corrected economic and political injustices. What sorts of injustices might he be talking about?
3. Do you feel somehow responsible for—or any responsibility to—the people who made your clothing (and other consumer goods)? Why or why not?
4. Cassidy suggests that, sometimes, we might find it *boring* to think about sweatshop labor. Do you think she's right? If she's right, then what does that say about us?

Case

This is how GiveDirectly describes what it does:

1. *Target.* We first locate extremely poor communities using publicly available data. We then send field staff door-to-door to digitally collect data on poverty and enroll recipients. We target households using criteria that vary by region—including aggregating a range of factors or looking at housing materials.
2. *Audit.* We use a set of independent checks to verify that recipients are eligible and did not pay bribes, such as physical back-checks, image verification, and data consistency checks. For example, we use GPS coordinates, satellite imagery, and crowdsourced labor to detect irregularities.
3. *Transfer.* We transfer recipient households roughly $1,000, or around one year's budget for a typical household. We use electronic payment systems; typically, recipients receive an SMS alert and then collect cash from a mobile money agent in their village or nearest town.
4. *Monitor.* We call each recipient to verify receipt of funds, flag issues, and assess our own customer service. We also staff a hotline for inbound calls and in some cases staff follow up in person.[16]

GiveDirectly also has third parties study the results of its work:

Rigorous, experimental evaluation of impacts is rare among nonprofits. GiveDirectly collaborates with third-party researchers to measure the impacts of cash transfers and answer complex design questions. Researchers are fully independent and independently-funded. We report the results of our evaluations and also announce studies in progress before the data are in, so that we can be held accountable for the results. How do our transfers affect recipient households? [A study has] documented large, positive, and sustainable impacts across a wide range of outcomes including assets, earnings, food security, mental health, and domestic violence.[17]

Cassidy wants to consider becoming *responsible for* the people who make our consumer goods. Is donating to GiveDirectly an example of what she means? Why or why not? If it isn't what Cassidy means, then what does that show about the difference between Cassidy's view and Singer's?

Notes

1. The "Global South" has replaced the term "Third World." The poorest nations in the world are in the Southern Hemisphere; the exception is the nations of Australasia (Australia and New Zealand). The Global North includes the wealthiest nations: Canada, the United States of America, the European Union, Switzerland, and Australasia.
2. Peter Singer, "Famine, Affluence and Morality," *Philosophy and Public Affairs* 1 (1972): 229–243.
3. Thomas Pogge, *World Poverty and Human Rights: Cosmopolitan Responsibilities and Reforms* (London: Polity Press, 2002).
4. Thomas Pogge, "'Assisting' the Global Poor," in *Global Ethics: Seminal Essays*, Thomas Pogge and Keith Horton, eds. (London: Paragon House Publishers, 2008), p. 552.
5. Samuel Scheffler, "Individual Responsibility in a Global Age," *Social Philosophy and Policy* 12 (1995): 219–236.
6. Scheffler, "Individual Responsibility in a Global Age," p. 223.
7. Scheffler, "Individual Responsibility in a Global Age," p. 227.
8. Scheffler, "Individual Responsibility in a Global Age," pp. 228–229.
9. Claudia Card, *The Unnatural Lottery: Character and Moral Luck* (Philadelphia: Temple University Press, 1996).
10. Card, *The Unnatural Lottery*, p. 28.
11. Rob Walker, "Brewed Awakening?" *The New York Times*, June 6, 2004: Magazine section.
12. Card, *The Unnatural Lottery*, p. 28.
13. Card, *The Unnatural Lottery*, p. 28.
14. Nel Noddings, *Caring: A Feminine Approach to Ethics and Moral Education*, (Berkeley: University of California Press, 1984).
15. Virginia Held, *Feminist Morality* (Chicago: University of Chicago Press, 1993).
16. https://www.givedirectly.org/operating-model
17. https://www.givedirectly.org/research-at-give-directly

Puppies, Pigs, and People
Eating Meat and Marginal Cases
Alastair Norcross

....

What did you have for lunch today? Chicken salad? A hamburger?
A BLT? Whatever it was, the story behind the meat is probably
pretty dark. (If you doubt this, go to YouTube and search for "factory
farm.") Of course, many people already know how badly animals
are treated in industrial agriculture, and they enjoy eating meat
anyway. Should they? Is it wrong to eat products from factory farms?
Norcross argues that it is. He compares us to Fred, who tortures
puppies for the sake of gustatory pleasure. As he shows, it's harder
than you might think to distinguish between our behavior and Fred's.

....

1. Fred's Basement

Consider the story of Fred, who receives a visit from the police one day.
They have been summoned by Fred's neighbors, who have been disturbed
by strange sounds emanating from Fred's basement. When they enter the
basement they are confronted by the following scene: Twenty-six small

Norcross, Alastair. 2004. "Puppies, Pigs, and People: Eating Meat and Marginal Cases."
Philosophical Perspectives 18: 229–245. Reprinted with permission of John Wiley & Sons.

wire cages, each containing a puppy, some whining, some whimpering, some howling. The puppies range in age from newborn to about six months. Many of them show signs of mutilation. Urine and feces cover the bottoms of the cages and the basement floor. Fred explains that he keeps the puppies for twenty-six weeks, and then butchers them while holding them upside-down. During their lives he performs a series of mutilations on them, such as slicing off their noses and their paws with a hot knife, all without any form of anesthesia. Except for the mutilations, the puppies are never allowed out of the cages, which are barely big enough to hold them at twenty-six weeks. The police are horrified, and promptly charge Fred with animal abuse. As details of the case are publicized, the public is outraged. Newspapers are flooded with letters demanding that Fred be severely punished. There are calls for more severe penalties for animal abuse. Fred is denounced as a vile sadist.

Finally, at his trial, Fred explains his behavior, and argues that he is blameless and therefore deserves no punishment. He is, he explains, a great lover of chocolate. A couple of years ago, he was involved in a car accident, which resulted in some head trauma. Upon his release from hospital, having apparently suffered no lasting ill effects, he visited his favorite restaurant and ordered their famous rich dark chocolate mousse. Imagine his dismay when he discovered that his experience of the mousse was a pale shadow of its former self. The mousse tasted bland, slightly pleasant, but with none of the intense chocolaty flavor he remembered so well. The waiter assured him that the recipe was unchanged from the last time he had tasted it, just the day before his accident. In some consternation, Fred rushed out to buy a bar of his favorite Belgian chocolate. Again, he was dismayed to discover that his experience of the chocolate was barely even pleasurable. Extensive investigation revealed that his experience of other foods remained unaffected, but chocolate, in all its forms, now tasted bland and insipid. Desperate for a solution to his problem, Fred visited a renowned gustatory neurologist, Dr. T. Bud. Extensive tests revealed that the accident had irreparably damaged the godiva gland, which secretes cocoamone, the hormone responsible for the experience of chocolate. Fred urgently requested hormone replacement therapy. Dr. Bud informed him that, until recently, there had been no known source of cocoamone, other than the human godiva gland, and that it was impossible to collect cocoamone from one person to be used by another. However, a chance discovery had altered the situation. A forensic veterinary surgeon, performing an autopsy on a severely abused puppy, had discovered high concentrations of cocoamone in the puppy's brain. It turned out that puppies, who don't normally produce cocoamone, could be stimulated to do so by extended periods of severe stress and suffering. The research, which led to this discovery, while gaining tenure for its authors, had not been widely publicized, for fear of antagonizing animal welfare groups. Although this research clearly gave Fred the hope of tasting chocolate again, there were no commercially available sources of puppy-derived cocoamone. Lack of demand, combined with fear of bad publicity, had deterred drug companies from getting into the puppy torturing business. Fred appeals to the court to imagine his anguish, on discovering that a solution to his severe deprivation was possible, but not readily available. But he wasn't inclined to sit around bemoaning his cruel fate. He did what any chocolate lover would do. He read the research, and set up his own cocoamone collection lab in his basement. Six months of intense puppy suffering, followed by a brutal death, produced enough cocoamone to last him a week, hence the twenty-six cages. He isn't a sadist or an animal abuser, he explains. If there were a method of collecting cocoamone without torturing puppies, he would gladly employ it. He derives no pleasure from the suffering of the puppies itself. He sympathizes with those who are horrified by the pain and misery of the animals, but the court must realize that human pleasure is at stake. The puppies, while undeniably cute, are mere animals. He admits that he would be just as healthy without chocolate, if not more so. But this isn't a matter of survival or health. His life would be unacceptably impoverished without the experience of chocolate.

End of story. Clearly, we are horrified by Fred's behavior, and unconvinced by his attempted justification. It is, of course, unfortunate for Fred that he can no longer enjoy the taste of chocolate, but that in no way excuses the imposition of severe suffering on the puppies. I expect near universal agreement with this claim (the exceptions being those who are either inhumanly callous or thinking ahead, and wish to avoid the following conclusion, to which such agreement commits them). No decent person would even contemplate torturing puppies merely to enhance a gustatory experience. However, billions of animals endure intense suffering every year for precisely this end. Most of the chicken, veal, beef, and pork consumed in the United States comes from intensive confinement facilities, in which the animals live cramped, stress-filled lives and endure unanesthetized mutilations.[1] The vast majority of people would suffer no ill health from the elimination of meat from their diets. Quite the reverse.

The supposed benefits from this system of factory farming, apart from the profits accruing to agribusiness, are increased levels of gustatory pleasure for those who claim that they couldn't enjoy a meat-free diet as much as their current meat-filled diets. If we are prepared to condemn Fred for torturing puppies merely to enhance his gustatory experiences, shouldn't we similarly condemn the millions who purchase and consume factory-raised meat? Are there any morally significant differences between Fred's behavior and their behavior?

2. Fred's Behavior Compared with Our Behavior

The first difference that might seem to be relevant is that Fred tortures the puppies himself, whereas most Americans consume meat that comes from animals that have been tortured by others. But is this really relevant? What if Fred had been squeamish and had employed someone else to torture the puppies and extract the cocoamone? Would we have thought any better of Fred? Of course not.

Another difference between Fred and many consumers of factory-raised meat is that many, perhaps most, such consumers are unaware of the treatment of the animals, before they appear in neatly wrapped packages on supermarket shelves. Perhaps I should moderate my challenge, then. If we are prepared to condemn Fred for torturing puppies merely to enhance his gustatory experiences, shouldn't we similarly condemn those who purchase and consume factory-raised meat, in full, or even partial, awareness of the suffering endured by the animals? While many consumers are still blissfully ignorant of the appalling treatment meted out to meat, that number is rapidly dwindling, thanks to vigorous publicity campaigns waged by animal welfare groups. Furthermore, any meat-eating readers of this article are now deprived of the excuse of ignorance.

Perhaps a consumer of factory-raised animals could argue as follows: While I agree that Fred's behavior is abominable, mine is crucially different. If Fred did not consume his chocolate, he would not raise and torture puppies (or pay someone else to do so). Therefore Fred could prevent the suffering of the puppies. However, if I did not buy and consume factory-raised meat, no animals would be spared lives of misery. Agribusiness is much too large to respond to the behavior of one consumer. Therefore I cannot prevent the suffering of any animals. I may well regret the suffering inflicted on animals for the sake of human enjoyment. I may even agree that the human enjoyment doesn't justify the suffering. However, since the animals will suffer no matter what I do, I may as well enjoy the taste of their flesh.

There are at least two lines of response to this attempted defense. First, consider an analogous case. You visit a friend in an exotic location, say Alabama. Your friend takes you out to eat at the finest restaurant in Tuscaloosa. For dessert you select the house specialty, "Chocolate Mousse a la Bama," served with a small cup of coffee, which you are instructed to drink before eating the mousse. The mousse is quite simply the most delicious dessert you have ever tasted. Never before has chocolate tasted so rich and satisfying. Tempted to order a second, you ask your friend what makes this mousse so delicious. He informs you that the mousse itself is ordinary, but the coffee contains a concentrated dose of cocoamone, the newly discovered chocolate-enhancing hormone. Researchers at Auburn University have perfected a technique for extracting cocoamone from the brains of freshly slaughtered puppies, who have been subjected to lives of pain and frustration. Each puppy's brain yields four doses, each of which is effective for about fifteen minutes, just long enough to enjoy one serving of mousse. You are, naturally, horrified and disgusted. You will certainly not order another serving, you tell your friend. In fact, you are shocked that your friend, who had always seemed to be a morally decent person, could have both recommended the dessert to you and eaten one himself, in full awareness of the loathsome process necessary for the experience. He agrees that the suffering of the puppies is outrageous, and that the gain in human pleasure in no way justifies the appalling treatment they have to endure. However, neither he nor you can save any puppies by refraining from consuming cocoamone. Cocoamone production is now Alabama's leading industry, so it is much too large to respond to the behavior of one or two consumers. Since the puppies will suffer no matter what either of you does, you may as well enjoy the mousse.

If it is as obvious as it seems that a morally decent person, who is aware of the details of cocoamone production, couldn't order Chocolate Mousse a la Bama, it should be equally obvious that a morally decent person, who is aware of the details of factory farming, can't purchase and consume factory-raised meat. If the attempted excuse of causal impotence is compelling in the latter case, it should be compelling in the former case. But it isn't.

The second response to the claim of causal impotence is to deny it. Consider the case of chickens, the most cruelly treated of all animals raised for human consumption, with the possible exception of veal calves.

In 1998, almost 8 billion chickens were slaughtered in the United States,[2] almost all of them raised on factory farms. Suppose that there are 250 million chicken eaters in the United States, and that each one consumes, on average, twenty-five chickens per year (this leaves a fair number of chickens slaughtered for nonhuman consumption, or for export). Clearly, if only one of those chicken eaters gave up eating chicken, the industry would not respond. Equally clearly, if they all gave up eating chicken, billions of chickens (approximately 6.25 billion per year) would not be bred, tortured, and killed. But there must also be some number of consumers, far short of 250 million, whose renunciation of chicken would cause the industry to reduce the number of chickens bred in factory farms. The industry may not be able to respond to each individual's behavior, but it must respond to the behavior of fairly large numbers. Suppose that the industry is sensitive to a reduction in demand for chicken equivalent to 10,000 people becoming vegetarians. (This seems like a reasonable guess, but I have no idea what the actual numbers are, nor is it important.) For each group of 10,000 who give up chicken, a quarter of a million fewer chickens are bred per year. It appears, then, that if you give up eating chicken, you have only a one in ten thousand chance of making any difference to the lives of chickens, unless it is certain that fewer than 10,000 people will ever give up eating chicken, in which case you have no chance. Isn't a one in ten thousand chance small enough to render your continued consumption of chicken blameless? Not at all. While the chance that your behavior is harmful may be small, the harm that is risked is enormous. The larger the numbers needed to make a difference to chicken production, the larger the difference such numbers would make. A one in ten thousand chance of saving 250,000 chickens per year from excruciating lives is morally and mathematically equivalent to the certainty of saving twenty-five chickens per year. We commonly accept that even small risks of great harms are unacceptable. That is why we disapprove of parents who fail to secure their children in car seats or with seat belts, who leave their small children unattended at home, or who drink or smoke heavily during pregnancy. Or consider commercial aircraft safety measures. The chances that the oxygen masks, the lifejackets, or the emergency exits on any given plane will be called on to save any lives in a given week, are far smaller than one in ten thousand. And yet we would be outraged to discover that an airline had knowingly allowed a plane to fly for a week with nonfunctioning emergency exits, oxygen masks, and lifejackets. So, even if it is true that your giving up factory raised chicken has only a tiny chance of preventing suffering, given that the amount of suffering that would be prevented is in inverse proportion to your chance of preventing it, your continued consumption is not thereby excused.

But perhaps it is not even true that your giving up chicken has only a tiny chance of making any difference. Suppose again that the poultry industry only reduces production when a threshold of 10,000 fresh vegetarians is reached. Suppose also, as is almost certainly true, that vegetarianism is growing in popularity in the United States (and elsewhere). Then, even if you are not the one, newly converted vegetarian, to reach the next threshold of 10,000, your conversion will reduce the time required before the next threshold is reached. The sooner the threshold is reached, the sooner production, and therefore animal suffering, is reduced. Your behavior, therefore, does make a difference. Furthermore, many people who become vegetarians influence others to become vegetarian, who in turn influence others, and so on. It appears, then, that the claim of causal impotence is mere wishful thinking, on the part of those meat lovers who are morally sensitive enough to realize that human gustatory pleasure does not justify inflicting extreme suffering on animals.

Perhaps there is a further difference between the treatment of Fred's puppies and the treatment of animals on factory farms. The suffering of the puppies is a necessary means to the production of gustatory pleasure, whereas the suffering of animals on factory farms is simply a by-product of the conditions dictated by economic considerations. Therefore, it might be argued, the suffering of the puppies is *intended as a means* to Fred's pleasure, whereas the suffering of factory raised animals is merely *foreseen* as a side-effect of a system that is a means to the gustatory pleasures of millions. The distinction between what is intended, either as a means or as an end in itself, and what is "merely" foreseen is central to the Doctrine of Double Effect. Supporters of this doctrine claim that it is sometimes permissible to bring about an effect that is merely foreseen, even though the very same effect could not permissibly be brought about if intended. (Other conditions have to be met in order for the Doctrine of Double Effect to judge an action permissible, most notably that there be an outweighing good effect.) . . .

[However,] neither the doctrine itself, nor the alleged moral distinction between intending and foreseeing can justify the consumption of factory-raised meat. The Doctrine of Double Effect requires not merely that a bad effect be foreseen and not intended, but also that there be an outweighing good effect. In the case of the suffering of factory-raised animals, whatever good could plausibly be claimed to come out of the system clearly doesn't outweigh the bad. Furthermore, it would be easy to modify the story of Fred to render the puppies' suffering "merely" foreseen. For example, suppose that the cocoamone is produced by a chemical reaction that can only occur when large quantities of drain-cleaner are forced down the throat of a conscious, unanesthetized puppy. The consequent appalling suffering, while not itself a means to the production of cocoamone, is nonetheless an unavoidable side effect of the means. In this variation of the story, Fred's behavior is no less abominable than in the original.

One last difference between the behavior of Fred and the behavior of the consumers of factory-raised meat is worth discussing, if only because it is so frequently cited in response to the arguments of this paper. Fred's behavior is abominable, according to this line of thinking, because it involves the suffering of *puppies*. The behavior of meat eaters, on the other hand, "merely" involves the suffering of chickens, pigs, cows, calves, sheep, and the like. Puppies (and probably dogs and cats in general) are morally different from the other animals. Puppies *count* (morally, that is), whereas the other animals don't, or at least not nearly as much. So, what gives puppies a higher moral status than the animals we eat?

Presumably there is some morally relevant property or properties possessed by puppies but not by farm animals. Perhaps puppies have a greater degree of rationality than farm animals, or a more finely developed moral sense, or at least a sense of loyalty and devotion. The problems with this kind of approach are obvious. It's highly unlikely that any property that has even an outside chance of being ethically relevant[4] is both possessed by puppies and not possessed by any farm animals. For example, it's probably true that most puppies have a greater degree of rationality (whatever that means) than most chickens, but the comparison with pigs is far more dubious. Besides, if Fred were to inform the jury that he had taken pains to acquire particularly stupid, morally obtuse, disloyal and undevoted puppies, would they (or we) have declared his behavior to be morally acceptable? Clearly not. This is, of course, simply the puppy version of the problem of marginal cases. . . . The human version is no less relevant. If their lack of certain degrees of rationality, moral sensibility, loyalty, devotion, and the like makes it permissible to torture farm animals for our gustatory pleasure, it should be permissible to do the same to those unfortunate humans who also lack those properties.

Since the latter behavior isn't permissible, the lack of such properties doesn't justify the former behavior.

Perhaps, though, there *is* something that separates puppies, even marginal puppies (and marginal humans) from farm animals—our sympathy. Puppies count more than other animals, because we care more about them. We are outraged to hear of puppies abused in scientific experiments, but unconcerned at the treatment of laboratory rats or animals on factory farms. Before the 2002 World Cup, several members of the England team sent a letter to the government of South Korea protesting the treatment of dogs and cats raised for food in that country. The same players have not protested the treatment of animals on factory farms in England. This example, while clearly illustrating the difference in attitudes towards cats and dogs on the one hand, and farm animals on the other, also reveals one of the problems with this approach to the question of moral status. Although the English footballers, and the English (and United States) public in general, clearly care far more about the treatment of cats and dogs than of farm animals, the South Koreans, just as clearly, do not. Are we to conclude that Fred's behavior would not be abominable were he living in South Korea, where dogs and cats are routinely abused for the sake of gustatory pleasure? Such relativism is, to put it mildly, hard to swallow. Perhaps, though, we can maintain the view that human feelings determine the moral status of animals, without condoning the treatment of dogs and cats in South Korea (and other countries). Not all human feelings count. Only the feelings of those who have achieved exactly the right degree of moral sensibility. That just so happens to be those in countries like the United States and Britain who care deeply for the welfare of dogs and cats, but not particularly for the welfare of cows, chickens, pigs, and other factory-raised animals. Dog and cat eaters in South Korea are insufficiently sensitive, and humane farming advocates in Britain and the United States are overly so. But, of course, it won't do simply to insist that this is the right degree of moral sensibility. We need an explanation of why this is the right degree of sensibility. Moral sensibility consists, at least in part, in reacting differently to different features of situations, actions, agents, and patients. If the right degree of moral sensibility requires reacting differently to puppies and to farm animals, there must be a morally relevant difference between puppies and farm animals. Such a difference can't simply consist in the fact that (some) people do react differently to them. The appeal to differential human sympathy illustrates a purely descriptive psychological difference between the behavior of Fred and that of someone who knowingly consumes factory-raised meat. It can do no serious moral work.

I have been unable to discover any morally relevant differences between the behavior of Fred, the puppy torturer, and the behavior of the millions of people who purchase and consume factory-raised meat, at least those who do so in the knowledge that the animals live lives of suffering and deprivation. If morality demands that we not torture puppies merely to enhance our own eating pleasure, morality also demands that we not support factory farming by purchasing factory-raised meat.

Comprehension Questions

1. Why does Norcross have Fred produce cocoamone? Why is that important for the analogy he's developing?
2. Most of us don't actually raise or slaughter animals, but Norcross says that that doesn't matter. Why not?
3. If you don't eat meat from factory farms, it might be the case that no animal is spared. However, Norcross says that this doesn't make it OK to eat meat from factory farms. Why not?
4. Fred is hurting *puppies*. You, however, are only involved in hurting *cows*. Norcross says that this doesn't matter either. Why not?
5. You might think that puppies are *smarter* than traditional farm animals. Norcross isn't impressed by this objection. Why not?
6. Is Norcross arguing that you should be a vegetarian or a vegan? If so, then what's his argument for this conclusion? If not, then what *is* he arguing for?

Discussion Questions

1. How much do you know about standard practices in concentrated animal feeding operations and slaughterhouses?
2. People feel very differently about puppies than they do about traditional farm animals. Why? And do you think that this matters morally? Why or why not?
3. Lots of people know about how badly animals are treated in factory farms, and yet this knowledge doesn't affect how they eat. Why do you think that is?
4. If it's wrong to eat products from factory farms, then the vast majority of Americans are acting wrongly. Is it plausible that most people are doing the wrong thing? Or should we assume that, if most people are doing it, it's morally OK?

Case

Norcross is going after those who support factory farms. In response, you might want to shop at places that sell more humane animal products. But how confident can we be about where our food comes from? Consider this story, which broke in November of 2015:

> For [shoppers who want meat from humanely-raised animals,] optimistic messages offered by Whole Foods . . . provide assurance that they're making an ethical food choice. "Our birds live in harmony with the environment and we allow them plenty of room to roam," explains a Diestel Turkey Ranch brochure, prominently displayed at many Whole Foods meat counters. Diestel turkeys raised at the Ranch's main farm earn a 5+ welfare mark—the highest—from the nonprofit Global Animal Partnership. . . . Diestel is one of only a handful of Whole Foods meat suppliers out of about 2,100 to achieve this remarkable distinction. So, along with the Diestel's promise that "on our ranch a turkey can truly be a turkey," it seems safe to assume that the Diestel turkeys sold at Whole Foods lived a decent life.
>
> But a recent undercover investigation by the animal advocacy group Direct Action Everywhere tells a more complicated story. Located in Sonora, California, Diestel's showcase farm gives every appearance of being a model operation. . . . Yet, as investigators discovered, the birds roaming in Sonora may be at best a token sampling of Diestel's overall turkey population. The main source of Diestel's turkey output appears to be an industrial operation with twenty-six barns (housing about 10,000 birds each) located 3.5 miles down the highway. . . . [Investigators] became suspicious in part because of a 2013 water discharge report—something the regional water board filed in response to complaints that toxic waste from a Diestel facility was making its way into local drinking water. The report also revealed that the Sonora farm produced about 1 percent of Diestel's turkeys. . . .
>
> Visits to Diestel's Jamestown facility [conducted over nine months] revealed horrific conditions, even by the standards of industrial agriculture. The group saw turkeys that had been jammed into over-crowded barns, trapped in piles of feces, and afflicted with swollen eyes and open sores. Technically, the birds were allowed outdoor access, but investigators said they saw only one bird outside over the course of the nine-month investigation—an escaped turkey at that. In some cases investigators found dead turkeys strewn across the barn floor. In others, they were overwhelmed by noxious odors and had to leave. Company records (posted on the side of the barn) showed that up to 7 percent of the birds died in a single week.[3]

Given this, does Norcross's argument support cutting out nearly *all* animal products? After all, if you can't be sure, why take the risk of being like Fred?

Notes

1. For information on factory farms, see, for example, Jim Mason and Peter Singer, *Animal Factories*, 2nd ed. (New York: Harmony Books, 1990), Karen Davis, *Prisoned Chickens, Poisoned Eggs: An Inside Look at the Modern Poultry Industry* (Summertown, TN: Book Publishing Co., 1996), John Robbins, *Diet for a New America* (Walpole, NH: Stillpoint, 1987).
2. *Livestock Slaughter 1998 Summary*, NASS, USDA (Washington, DC: March 1999), 2; and *Poultry Slaughter*, NASS, USDA (Washington, DC: February 2, 1999), 1f.
3. http://www.slate.com/blogs/moneybox/2015/11/24/whole_foods_turkeys_supplier_diestel_ranch_raises_birds_in_horrible_factory.html

38

It's Not *My* Fault

Global Warming and Individual Moral
Obligations

Walter Sinnott-Armstrong

....

Global warming is real, and climate change is the result. The consequences of climate change are likely to be enormous, and if we don't
act soon, they'll be even worse. So *we* ought to do something. But
does that mean that *you* ought to do something? More specifically,
do you have an obligation to act in environmentally responsible ways?
If so, do you have an obligation to act in environmentally responsible
ways *all the time*? Sinnott-Armstrong takes up these questions and
answers them negatively. He does this by considering a number of ways
that you might criticize taking a joyride in a gas-guzzling vehicle.
Ultimately, he concludes that none of them is satisfying.

....

... [E]ven if scientists establish that global warming is occurring, even if economists confirm that its costs will be staggering, and even if political theorists agree that governments must do something about it, it is still not clear what moral obligations regarding global warming devolve upon individuals like you and me. That is the question to be addressed in this essay.

1. Assumptions

To make the issue stark, let us begin with a few assumptions. I believe that these assumptions are probably roughly accurate, but none is certain, and I will not try to justify them here. Instead, I will simply take them for granted for the sake of argument.[1]

First, global warming has begun and is likely to increase over the next century. We cannot be sure exactly how much or how fast, but hot times are coming.

Second, a significant amount of global warming is due to human activities. The main culprit is fossil fuels.

Third, global warming will create serious problems for many people over the long term by causing climate changes, including violent storms, floods from sea level rises, droughts, heat waves, and so on. Millions of people will probably be displaced or die.

Fourth, the poor will be hurt most of all. The rich countries are causing most of the global warming, but they will be able to adapt to climate changes more easily. Poor countries that are close to sea level might be devastated.

Fifth, governments, especially the biggest and richest ones, are able to mitigate global warming. They can impose limits on emissions. They can require or give incentives for increased energy efficiency. They can stop deforestation and fund reforestation. They can develop ways to sequester carbon dioxide in oceans or underground. These steps will help, but the only long-run solution lies in alternatives to fossil fuels. These alternatives can be found soon if governments start massive research projects now.

. . .

2. The Problem

Even assuming all of this, it is still not clear what I as an individual morally ought to do about global warming. That issue is not as simple as many people assume. I want to bring out some of its complications.

It should be clear from the start that *individual* moral obligations do not always follow directly from *collective* moral obligations. The fact that your government morally ought to do something does not prove that *you* ought to do it, even if your government fails. Suppose that a bridge is dangerous because so much traffic has gone over it and continues to go over it. The government has a moral obligation to make the bridge safe. If the government fails to do its duty, it does not follow that I personally have a moral obligation to fix the bridge. It does not even follow that I have a moral obligation to fill in one crack in the bridge, even if the bridge would be fixed if everyone filled in one crack, even if I drove over the bridge many times, and even if I still drive over it every day. Fixing the bridge is the government's job, not mine. While I ought to encourage the government to fulfill its obligations, I do not have to take on those obligations myself.

. . .

What about global warming? If the government fails to do anything about global warming, what am I supposed to do about it? There are lots of ways for me as an individual to fight global warming. I can protest against bad government policies and vote for candidates who will make the government fulfill its moral obligations. I can support private organizations that fight global warming, such as the Pew Foundation, or boycott companies that contribute too much to global warming, such as most oil companies. Each of these cases is interesting, but they all differ. To simplify our discussion, we need to pick one act as our focus.

My example will be wasteful driving. Some people drive to their jobs or to the store because they have no other reasonable way to work and eat. I want to avoid issues about whether these goals justify driving, so I will focus on a case where nothing so important is gained. I will consider driving for fun on a beautiful Sunday afternoon. My drive is not necessary to cure depression or calm aggressive impulses. All that is gained is pleasure: Ah, the feel of wind in your hair! The views! How spectacular! Of course, you could drive a fuel-efficient hybrid car. But fuel-efficient cars have less "get up and go." So let us consider a gas-guzzling sport utility vehicle. Ah, the feeling of power! The excitement! Maybe you do not like to go for drives in sport utility vehicles on sunny Sunday afternoons, but many people do.

Do we have a moral obligation not to drive in such circumstances? This question concerns driving, not "buying" cars. To make this clear, let us assume that I borrow the gas guzzler from a friend. This question is also not about "legal" obligations. So let us assume that it is perfectly legal to go for such drives. Perhaps it ought to be illegal, but it is not. Note also that my question is not about what would be *best*. Maybe it would be better, even morally better, for me not to drive a gas guzzler just for fun. But that is not the issue I want to address here. My question is whether I have a *moral* obligation not to drive a gas guzzler just for fun on this particular sunny Sunday afternoon.

. . .

I admit that I am *inclined* to answer, "Yes." To me, global warming does *seem* to make such wasteful driving morally wrong.

Still, I do not feel confident in this judgment. . . . My moral intuition might be distorted by overgeneralization from the other cases where I think that other entities (large governments) do have moral obligations to fight global warming. I also worry that my moral intuition might be distorted by my desire to avoid conflicts with my environmentalist friends. The issue of global warming generates strong emotions because of its political implications and because of how scary its effects are. It is also a peculiarly modern case, especially because it operates on a much grander scale than my moral intuitions evolved to handle long ago when acts did not have such long-term effects on future generations (or at least people were not aware of such effects). In such circumstances, I doubt that we are justified in trusting our moral intuitions alone. We need some kind of confirmation.[2]

One way to confirm the truth of my moral intuitions would be to derive them from a general moral principle. A principle could tell us why wasteful driving is morally wrong, so we would not have to depend on bare assertion. And a principle might be supported by more trustworthy moral beliefs. The problem is *which* principle?

3. Actual Act Principles

One plausible principle refers to causing harm. If one person had to inhale all of the exhaust from my car, this would harm him and give me a moral obligation not to drive my car just for fun. Such cases suggest:

The harm principle: We have a moral obligation not to perform an act that causes harm to others.

This principle implies that I have a moral obligation not to drive my gas guzzler just for fun *if* such driving causes harm.

The problem is that such driving does *not* cause harm in normal cases. If one person were in a position to inhale all of my exhaust, then he would get sick if I did drive, and he would not get sick if I did not drive (under normal circumstances). In contrast, global warming will still occur even if I do not drive just for fun. Moreover, even if I do drive a gas guzzler just for fun for a long time, global warming will not occur unless lots of other people also expel greenhouse gases. So my individual act is neither necessary nor sufficient for global warming.

. . .

Another argument leads to the same conclusion: The harms of global warming result from the massive quantities of greenhouse gases in the atmosphere. Greenhouse gases (such as carbon dioxide and water vapor) are perfectly fine in small quantities. They help plants grow. The problem emerges only when there is too much of them. But my joyride by itself does not cause the massive quantities that are harmful.

Contrast someone who pours cyanide poison into a river. Later someone drinking from the river downstream ingests some molecules of the poison. Those molecules cause the person to get ill and die. This is very different from the causal chain in global warming, because no particular molecules from my car cause global warming in the direct way that particular molecules of the poison do cause the drinker's death. Global warming is more like a river that is going to flood downstream because of torrential rains. I pour a quart of water into the river upstream (maybe just because I do not want to carry it). My act of pouring the quart into the river is not a cause of the flood. Analogously, my act of driving for fun is not a cause of global warming.

Contrast also another large-scale moral problem: famine relief. Some people say that I have no moral obligation to contribute to famine relief because the famine will continue and people will die whether or not I donate my money to a relief agency. However, I could help a certain individual if I gave my donation directly to that individual. In contrast, if I refrain from driving for fun on this one Sunday, there is no individual who will be helped in the least.[3] I cannot help anyone by depriving myself of this joyride.

The point becomes clearer if we distinguish global warming from climate change. You might think that my driving on Sunday raises the temperature of the globe by an infinitesimal amount. I doubt that, but, even if it does, my exhaust on that Sunday does not cause any climate change at all. No storms or floods or droughts or heat waves can be traced to my individual act of driving. It is these climate changes that cause harms to people. Global warming by itself causes no harm without climate change. Hence, since my individual act of driving on that one Sunday does not cause any climate change, it causes no harm to anyone.

The point is not that harms do not occur from global warming. I have already admitted that they do. The point is also not that my exhaust is overkill, like poisoning someone who is already dying from poison. My exhaust is not sufficient for the harms of global warming, and I do not intend those harms. . . . I admit that some harms can be imperceptible because they are too small or for other reasons. Instead, the point is simply that my individual joyride does not cause global warming, climate change, or any of their resulting harms, at least directly. . . .

4. Internal Principles

. . . Maybe we can do better by looking inward.

Kantians claim that the moral status of acts depends on their agents' maxims or "subjective principles of volition"[4]—roughly what we would call motives or intentions or plans. This internal focus is evident in Kant's first formulation of the categorical imperative:

The universalizability principle: We have a moral obligation not to act on any maxim that we cannot will to be a universal law.

The idea is not that universally acting on that maxim would have bad consequences. (We will consider that kind of principle below.) Instead, the claim is that some maxims "cannot even be thought as a universal law of nature without contradiction."[5] However, my maxim when I drive a gas guzzler just for fun on this sunny Sunday afternoon is simply to have harmless fun. There is no way to derive a contradiction from a universal law that people do or may have harmless fun. Kantians might respond that my maxim is, instead, to expel greenhouse gases. I still see no way to derive a literal contradiction from a universal law that people do or may expel greenhouse gases. There would be bad consequences, but that is not a contradiction, as Kant requires. In any case, my maxim (or intention or motive) is not to expel greenhouse gases. My goals would be reached completely if I went for my drive and had my fun without expelling any greenhouse gases. This leaves no ground for claiming that my driving violates Kant's first formula of the categorical imperative.

Kant does supply a second formulation, which is really a different principle:

The means principle: We have a moral obligation not to treat any other person as a means only.[6]

It is not clear exactly how to understand this formulation, but the most natural interpretation is that for me to treat someone as a means implies my using harm to that person as part of my plan to achieve my goals. Driving for fun does not do that. I would have just as much fun if nobody were ever harmed by global warming. Harm to others is no part of my plans. So Kant's principle cannot explain why I have a moral obligation not to drive just for fun on this sunny Sunday afternoon.

. . .

Another inner-directed theory is virtue ethics. This approach focuses on general character traits rather than particular acts or intentions. It is not clear how to derive a principle regarding obligations from virtue ethics, but here is a common attempt:

The virtue principle: We have a moral obligation not to perform an act that expresses a vice or is contrary to virtue.

This principle solves our problem if driving a gas guzzler expresses a vice, or if no virtuous person would drive a gas guzzler just for fun.

How can we tell whether this principle applies? How can we tell whether driving a gas guzzler for fun "expresses a vice"? On the face of it, it expresses a desire for fun. There is nothing vicious about having fun. Having fun becomes vicious only if it is harmful or risky. But I have already responded to the principles of harm and risk. Moreover, driving a gas guzzler for fun does not always express a vice. If other people did not produce so much greenhouse gas, I could drive my gas guzzler just for fun without anyone being harmed by global warming. Then I could do it without being vicious. This situation is not realistic, but it does show that wasteful driving is not essentially vicious or contrary to virtue.

Some will disagree. Maybe your notions of virtue and vice make it essentially vicious to drive wastefully. But why? To apply this principle, we need some antecedent test of when an act expresses a vice. You cannot just say, "I know vice when I see it," because other people look at the same act and do not see vice, just fun. It begs the question to appeal to what you see when others do not see it, and you have no reason to believe that your vision is any clearer than theirs. But that means that this virtue principle cannot be applied without begging the question. We need to find some reason why such driving is vicious. Once we have this reason, we can appeal to it directly as a reason why I have a moral obligation not to drive wastefully. The side step through virtue does not help and only obscures the issue.

. . .

5. What Is Left?

We are left with no defensible principle to support the claim that I have a moral obligation not to drive a gas guzzler just for fun. Does this result show that this claim is false? Not necessarily . . . It only shows that we do not *know* whether it is morally wrong. Our ignorance might be temporary. If someone comes up with a defensible principle that does rule out wasteful driving, then I will be happy to listen and happy if it works. However, until some such principle is found, we cannot claim to know that it is morally wrong to drive a gas guzzler just for fun. . . .

This conclusion will still upset many environmentalists. They think that they know that wasteful driving is immoral. They want to be able to condemn those who drive gas guzzlers just for fun on sunny Sunday afternoons. My conclusion should not be so disappointing. Even if individuals have no such moral obligations, it is still morally better or morally ideal for individuals not to waste gas. We can and should praise those who save fuel.

We can express our personal dislike for wasting gas and for people who do it. We might even be justified in publicly condemning wasteful driving and drivers who waste a lot, in circumstances where such public rebuke is appropriate. Perhaps people who drive wastefully should feel guilty for their acts and ashamed of themselves, at least if they perform such acts regularly; and we should bring up our children so that they will feel these emotions. All of these reactions are available even if we cannot truthfully say that such driving violates a moral *obligation*. And these approaches might be more constructive in the long run than accusing someone of violating a moral obligation.

Moreover, even if individuals have no moral obligations not to waste gas by taking unnecessary Sunday drives just for fun, governments still have moral obligations to fight global warming, because they can make a difference. My fundamental point has been that global warming is such a large problem that it is not individuals who cause it or who need to fix it. Instead, governments need to fix it, and quickly. Finding and implementing a real solution is the task of governments. Environmentalists should focus their efforts on those who are not doing their job rather than on those who take Sunday afternoon drives just for fun.

This focus will also avoid a common mistake. Some environmentalists keep their hands clean by withdrawing into a simple life where they use very little fossil fuels. That is great. I encourage it. But some of these escapees then think that they have done their duty, so they rarely come down out of the hills to work for political candidates who could and would change government policies. This attitude helps nobody. We should not think that we can do enough simply by buying fuel-efficient cars, insulating our houses, and setting up a windmill to make our own electricity. That is all wonderful, but it neither does little or nothing to stop global warming, nor does this focus fulfill our real moral obligations, which are to get governments to do their job to prevent the disaster of excessive global warming. It is better to enjoy your Sunday driving while working to change the law so as to make it illegal for you to enjoy your Sunday driving.

References

Kant, I. (1959). *Foundations of the metaphysics of morals* (L. W. Beck, Trans.). Indianapolis, IN: Bobbs-Merrill. (Original work published in 1785).

Parfit, D. (1984). *Reasons and Persons*. Oxford: Clarendon Press.

Sinnott-Armstrong, W. (2005). "Moral Intuitionism and Empirical Psychology." In T. Horgan and M. Timmons, eds., *Metaethics after Moore*. New York: Oxford University Press, 339–365.

Comprehension Questions

1. Sinnott-Armstrong says even if scientists establish that global warming is occurring, it isn't clear what moral obligations we have. Why?
2. What's the difference between collective and individual obligations? Why don't the latter follow from the former?
3. Why doesn't driving a gas guzzler violate the harm principle?
4. Why doesn't driving a gas guzzler violate the universalizability principle?
5. Why doesn't driving a gas guzzler violate the means principle?
6. Why doesn't driving a gas guzzler violate the virtue principle?

Discussion Questions

1. Climate change isn't the only area where no individual makes much of a difference, and yet if enough people act, we can make a significant difference together. What are some of those other areas?
2. Sinnott-Armstrong says that the case for contributing to famine relief is actually *better* than the case for refraining from wasteful driving. Why? And do you think he's right?

3. How can Sinnott-Armstrong say both (a) that it's not wrong to drive wastefully and yet (b) that people who drive wastefully should feel guilty for doing so?
4. Some people will react to Sinnott-Armstrong's argument by saying: "Who cares? Climate change isn't real anyway." Unfortunately, this response flies in the face of a clear scientific consensus. How should we explain skepticism about climate change?

Case

In "A Perfect Moral Storm," Stephen Gardiner writes this:

> [Here is] a very unpleasant thought: perhaps there is a problem of corruption in the theoretical [debate about global warming. . . .] [Global warming's] complexity may turn out to be perfectly convenient for us, the current generation, and indeed for each successor generation as it comes to occupy our position. For one thing, it provides each generation with the cover under which it can seem to be taking the issue seriously—by negotiating weak and largely substanceless [international agreements], for example, and then heralding them as great achievements—when really it is simply exploiting its temporal position [i.e., opting to make only a few minor sacrifices now, even though that will force future generations to make many drastic sacrifices later]. For another, all of this can occur without the exploitative generation actually having to acknowledge that this is what it is doing. By avoiding overtly selfish behavior, earlier generations can take advantage of the future without the unpleasantness of admitting it—either to others, or, perhaps more importantly, to itself.[7]

The upshot: We ought to be very skeptical of reasoning that gets us off the hook, so to speak, when it comes to climate change. Do you think that Gardiner is right? Why or why not? And if he *is* right, what does that skepticism imply about how we should read Sinnott-Armstrong's essay?

Notes

1. If you do not share my bleak view of global warming, treat the rest of this essay as conditional. The issue of how individual moral obligations are related to collective moral obligations is interesting and important in its own right, even if my assumptions about global warming turn out to be inaccurate.
2. For more on why moral intuitions need confirmation, see Sinnott-Armstrong (2005).
3. Another difference between these cases is that my failure to donate to famine relief is an inaction, whereas my driving is an action. As Bob Fogelin put it in

conversation, one is a sin of omission, but the other is a sin of emission. But I assume that omissions can be causes. The real question is whether my measly emissions of greenhouse gases can be causes of global warming. I do not seem to have the same moral obligation to teach my neighbors' children when our government fails to teach them. Why not? The natural answer is that I have a special relation to my children that I do not have to their children. I also do not have such a special relation to future people who will be harmed by global warming.

4. Kant (1785/1959, p. 400, n. 1).

5. Ibid, 424. According to Kant, a weaker kind of contradiction in the will signals an imperfect duty. However, imperfect duties permit "exception in the interest of inclination" (421), so an imperfect obligation not to drive a gas-guzzler would permit me to drive it this Sunday when I am so inclined. Thus, I assume that a moral obligation not to drive a gas-guzzler for fun on a particular occasion would have to be a perfect obligation in Kant's view.

6. Ibid, 429. I omit Kant's clause regarding treating others as ends because that clause captures imperfect duties, which are not my concern here (for reasons given in the preceding note).

7. Stephen M. Gardiner, "A Perfect Moral Storm: Climate Change, Intergenerational Ethics and the Problem of Moral Corruption," *Environmental Values* 15 (2006): 408–409.

Climate, Collective Action, and Individual Ethical Obligations

Marion Hourdequin

In Sinnott-Armstrong's view, governments ought to do something about climate change. However, *you* don't necessarily have to do anything about it. Or, at least, it's sometimes OK for you to act in ways that are environmentally irresponsible. By contrast, Hourdequin argues that the virtue of integrity requires us to bring our political and individual lives into alignment. On her view, if you think that carbon emissions ought to be limited, then *you* ought to limit your own carbon emissions, even if this means sacrificing some things that you'd otherwise enjoy.

I. Introduction

. . . Walter Sinnott-Armstrong (2005) [has] argued that under current circumstances, individuals do not have obligations to reduce their personal contributions to greenhouse gas (GHG) emissions. . . . Sinnott-Armstrong argues that with respect to climate change, there is nothing

Hourdequin, Marion. 2010. "Climate, Collective Action and Individual Ethical Obligations." *Environmental Values* 19: 443–464. Republished with permission of The White Horse Press.

morally wrong with driving one's SUV for fun on a Sunday afternoon. Sinnott-Armstrong argues that one's personal choice to drive or not drive has little to no effect on the course of global climate change. Therefore, driving causes no (climate) harm and is morally permissible. Each of us does, however, have an obligation to work toward governmental policies that will mitigate climate change by reducing greenhouse gas emissions. This paper [argues] that although we have moral obligations to work toward collective agreements that will slow global climate change and mitigate its impacts, it is also true that individuals have obligations to reduce their personal contributions to the problem. The paper thus explores rationales for the view that individuals should reduce their personal greenhouse gas emissions. [To do this, I discuss] the idea of moral integrity, which recommends congruence between one's actions and positions at the personal and political levels. . . .

. . . Rather than attempt to provide a principled positive case for the lack of personal obligation, Sinnott-Armstrong surveys a number of candidate arguments *for* such an obligation and finds each of them inadequate. The conclusion that we lack an obligation to reduce our personal emissions, or more precisely, that there is no clear ground for a personal obligation to reduce emissions, thus depends on the comprehensiveness of the survey. Since Sinnott-Armstrong does not provide a comprehensive review of all the potential grounds of a personal obligation to reduce emissions (or even of all the plausible grounds: The grounds I discuss below are not considered as a part of the survey), his argument is far from decisive. . . .

In the [case of] climate change . . . one might think that [it is] wrong to emit excessive quantities of greenhouse gases, because: 1) emitting greenhouse gases is in itself morally wrong, and 2) by emitting an excess of greenhouse gases, one is making the problem of climate change worse. However, according to . . . Sinnott-Armstrong, emitting greenhouse gases is not in itself morally wrong. Sinnott-Armstrong argues that an individual's fossil fuel emissions alone have virtually no effect on climate change, nor do they create any kind of harm to humans or animals. [. . . Only] the aggregate emissions of greenhouse gases . . . causes harm. . . . Yet given that others are exploiting the commons as well, is it not true that a particular individual's emissions make climate change *worse*? This, again, Sinnott-Armstrong denies, because an individual's contribution is negligible and cannot, in itself, raise or lower the temperature of the planet.[1]

. . .

There are clearly a number of assumptions built in to these arguments that one might question. . . . [However,] I want to consider whether there might be any reason to reduce one's personal emissions even if [Sinnott-Armstrong is] right that doing so has no direct consequentialist payoff, that is, even if they are right that a reduction in emissions on one person's part will result in a nonexistent or negligible net change in greenhouse gas emissions overall.

II. Integrity as a Ground for an Obligation to Reduce Personal Emissions

One ground for [a personal obligation to reduce one's greenhouse gas emissions] stems from the acceptance of an obligation that . . . Sinnott-Armstrong defend[s], plus the requirements of moral integrity. Although [Sinnott-Armstrong believes] that individuals have no obligation to reduce their personal emissions, [he thinks] that individuals *do* have obligations to respond to climate change. More specifically, individuals have obligations to work toward a collective solution to the problem. For Sinnott-Armstrong, this means that individuals have obligations to work toward the election of political candidates who will enact policies to reduce emissions at the national scale. . . .

If one accepts the existence of these obligations, then I believe that one must also accept some degree of personal obligation to control one's emissions. The common sense ground for this latter obligation involves an obligation to avoid hypocrisy. However, the ground may be framed more positively as one of moral integrity. Before explaining why integrity, in conjunction with a commitment to mitigating the effects of climate change, entails an individual obligation to reduce emissions, I discuss briefly the ideal of integrity more generally.

Integrity is a frequently-cited virtue. The ideal of integrity figures widely in discussions of business ethics, for example, and in public life, integrity is widely regarded—despite its rarity—as a desired characteristic of politicians. From a philosophical perspective, however, integrity is difficult to pin down. In a recent paper, Audi and Murphy observe the dearth of explicit discussion of integrity in the literature on virtue ethics. They find, further, that "integrity" is used to express diverse and often vague ideas: "In a great many cases, 'integrity' is a specific-sounding term for something like moral soundness, whose exact character is left quite unspecified" (Audi and Murphy, 2006: 8). In other words, "integrity" is a "blunt instrument," one that lacks precision and in many cases could be replaced by a more specific term (Audi and Murphy, 2006: 8).

Nevertheless, Audi and Murphy do not think that the concept of integrity should be abandoned, and they set out to clarify some of the term's central meanings, focusing on the ideas of *integration* and *being integral*. Both of these ideas are important to thinking about integrity in the context of our obligations regarding global climate change. *Integrality* (or *being integral*) involves the internalization of certain commitments, such that these commitments are central to an individual's identity. When a commitment is fully integral, the individual typically honors it without deliberation (Audi and Murphy, 2006: 9). This sense of integrity clearly bears some relationship to the other sense, for if a commitment is to be integral to an individual's thought and action, it should be *well integrated* with other commitments the individual holds. *Integration* helps the individual avoid conflicts among her various commitments; it involves "a kind of unity among the elements in which they form a coherent, ideally a harmonious, structure" (Audi and Murphy, 2006: 9).

These two aspects of integrity—integration and integrality—are important to understanding an individual's obligations to address climate change. A person who is truly concerned about climate change and is committed to alleviating it to the best of her ability must make some effort to effect social change. . . . However, a person of integrity who has this commitment will act also on a personal level to reduce her own emissions and will, in general, avoid frivolous emissions of greenhouse gases: her actions at the political level will be integrated with those at the personal level.

It may be too strong to say that someone who is working on the political level to reduce collective greenhouse gas emissions, but is not doing anything as an individual to reduce her emissions, is practically inconsistent; yet it certainly seems that an individual who worked for emissions-limiting policies while steadily and frivolously increasing her own emissions would be working at cross purposes. The kind of unity that integrity recommends requires that an individual work to harmonize her commitments at various levels and achieve a life in which her commitments are embodied not only in a single sphere, but in the various spheres she inhabits.

. . . Sinnott-Armstrong might object at this point that integrity does not require personal action to reduce one's GHG emissions, even in light of a more general commitment to abate climate change, because the moral valence of one's actions at the personal and the political level is different. At the political level, one's efforts to support climate change policy have a positive moral valence because they are likely to have positive consequences with respect to climate change mitigation, whereas at the personal level one's efforts have a neutral moral valence because they are likely to have no consequences whatsoever with respect to climate change mitigation.

This assessment is problematic. It is dubious that one's riding a bike instead of driving will lower gas prices such that more people drive or that some people drive more. Although this *could* happen, what actually happens is probably highly context dependent, and there is an equally strong argument to be made in favor of the view that one's commitment to cycling to work might actually cause others to reconsider their own driving habits. Even if such a reconsideration does not lead these individuals to take up biking themselves, they might think more carefully about how they utilize their cars, and perhaps even consider GHG emissions as they make their next car purchase.[2]

Furthermore, even if it is sometimes the case that one's personal actions to reduce climate change have little to no effect on the course of climate change, integrity nevertheless requires a kind of synchrony between personal and political action that [Sinnott-Armstrong fails] to acknowledge. Let us grant that there may be cases in which one is justified making tradeoffs between one's actions at the personal and the political level. For example, we might think that Al Gore is morally justified in flying around the country (a greenhouse-gas-intensive activity) in order to promote awareness about climate change impacts and catalyze social change. Even so, integrity at the very least grounds *a prima facie* moral obligation for Al Gore to control his own emissions, such that his flying around the country to promote political action may be justified, but his own household energy use warrants scrutiny. In Gore's case, the tension is particularly stark, because he flies around the country not only to advocate large-scale policy changes, but to advocate that *individuals change their* actions so as to reduce their own contributions to the climate change problem.[3]

Even if Gore were not advocating this kind of individual action, however, it seems to me that being a person of integrity involves reconciling, insofar as one can, one's commitments at various levels. Consequentialist calculations can run counter to such integration (witness the moral valence argument above), but this is often a shortcoming rather than a virtue of such calculations. Consequentialism has long been criticized for its failure to recognize the separateness of persons. In consequentialist arguments against an obligation to reduce one's own emissions, the reasoning fails to recognize the *wholeness* of persons. That is, consequentialism may not only blur the boundaries between individuals, but fail to acknowledge a coherent structure *within* them, as Bernard Williams (1973) has cogently pointed out. To coherently structure one's life around a commitment to mitigate climate change requires that one take this commitment seriously in both one's personal life and one's political action. And unless there is good reason to believe that restricting one's own emissions would undermine larger scale change, those committed to the overall goal of reducing greenhouse gas emissions ought to do so themselves. The virtue of integrity entails that this obligation holds even if one's personal actions are themselves neutral with respect to their direct consequences for climate.

In principle, consequentialist considerations have an important role to play in ethics, so what I have said should not be taken as a general indictment of consequentialist reasoning. However, consequentialist reasoning in the arguments for a political, but not personal, obligation with respect to climate change does not take adequate account of human psychology. Pointing to integrity as a countervailing consideration is valuable in this context because it takes fuller account of psychological considerations that make the stark separation of personal and political obligations unreasonable and undesirable.

Nevertheless, the value of integrity can itself be justified on consequentialist grounds, albeit grounds reflecting sensitivity to human psychology. Integrity is a virtue for both intrapersonal and interpersonal reasons. At the intrapersonal level, integrity is a moral virtue that acknowledges the psychological and agential benefits of integrating one's commitments into a coherent whole, and of bringing one's beliefs, words, and actions into line with one another. Interpersonally, integrity is a virtue from the perspective of intersubjective intelligibility and in affirming to others the authenticity of one's commitments. Where we see in others a lack of coherence between their political commitments and personal choices, we often wonder how to make sense of this apparent mismatch, and we may question the sincerity with which certain commitments are held. A politician's environmental commitments, as embodied in public pronouncements and legislative support, for example, may be called into question if he or she lives a lavish and environmentally damaging lifestyle.

Mark Halfon (1989) suggests another ground for the value of integrity. He describes a case in which an individual is dedicated to political change—in this case, the abolition of institutionalized racism—and suffers significantly as a result of this commitment because she is protesting official government policy. What is more, in the case Halfon describes, it is highly unlikely that the activist's commitment will be effective in inducing a change in government policy. From a consequentialist perspective, then, the activist's commitments make no sense: She is bringing more suffering upon herself than she is likely to alleviate through her commitment. We may nevertheless say that the activist is a person of integrity, and that her integrity is morally admirable. Why? Halfon (1989: 146) says:

> One thing that can be said [about such a person] is that she wants or chooses to be a certain kind of person, or to live a certain way of life, and that her life loses its meaning or point if she fails to actively fight against what she believes to be a demeaning and unjust institution.

In the case of climate change, we might say that a commitment to mitigating climate change should, in general, entail a commitment to being the kind of person who is thoughtful about her greenhouse gas emissions and makes an effort to reduce them. Just as it would be odd and morally problematic for an environmental activist who is fighting for controls on non-point source pollution to dump large quantities of fertilizer on her lawn, it is odd and morally problematic for a climate change activist to be profligate and thoughtless about her GHG emissions. . . .

IV. Conclusion

[There is a type of] individualism that finds its expression in the view that one's only responsibility is to change society without changing oneself. This kind of individualism, which rests on the sort of assumptions that characterize collective action problems, fails to recognize the connections between the personal and the social, the expressive function of personal action, the importance of integrity, the role of individual action in constructing one's moral identity, and the effect of individual action on one's relations with others, and on *their* actions. I have tried, in this paper, to highlight the problems with this latter kind of individualism, and the promise of abandoning it.

References

Audi, R. and P. Murphy. (2006). "The Many Faces of Integrity." *Business Ethics Quarterly* 16 (1), 3–21.

Axsen, J. and K. Kurani. (2009). "Interpersonal Influence Within Car Buyers' Social Networks: Five Perspectives on Plug-in Hybrid Electric Vehicle Demonstration Participants." Research Report UCD-ITS-WP-09-04. Davis, CA: University of California Institute of Transportation Studies.

Christakis, N. A. and J. H. Fowler. (2008). "The Collective Dynamics of Smoking in a Large Social Network." *New England Journal of Medicine* 358 (21), 2249–58.

Christakis, N. A. and J. H. Fowler. (2009). *Connected: The Surprising Power of Our Social Networks and How They Shape Our Lives.* NewYork: Little, Brown, and Co.

Fowler, J. H. and N. A. Christakis. (2010). "Cooperative Behavior Cascades in Human Social Networks." *PNAS* 107 (12), 5334-5338.

Halfon, M. (1989). *Integrity: A Philosophical Inquiry.* Philadelphia: Temple University Press.

Heffner, R., T. Turrentine, and K. Kurani. (2006). "A Primer on Automobile Semiotics." Research Report UCD-ITS-RR-06-01. Davis, CA: University of California Institute of Transportation Studies.

Heffner, R., K. Kurani and T. Turrentine. (2007). "Symbolism in California's Early Market for Hybrid Electric Vehicles." *Transportation Research Part D* 12, 396–413.

Horton, D. (2006). "Environmentalism and the Bicycle." *Environmental Politics* 15 (4), 41–58.

Parfit, D. (1984). *Reasons and Persons.* New York: Oxford University Press.

Sinnott-Armstrong, W. (2005). "It's Not *My* Fault: Global Warming and Individual Moral Obligations." In W. Sinnott-Armstrong and R. Howarth, eds., *Perspectives on Climate Change: Science, Economics, Politics, Ethics.* Amsterdam: Elsevier, 285–307.

Williams, B. (1973). "A Critique of Utilitarianism." In J. C. C. Smart and B. Williams, *Utilitarianism: For and Against.* New York: Cambridge, 77–150.

Comprehension Questions

1. What do Hourdequin and Sinnott-Armstrong agree about? What do they disagree about?
2. What, according to Hourdequin, is integrity?
3. How is integrity relevant to our individual obligations regarding climate change?
4. Why does Hourdequin discuss Al Gore?

5. What does Hourdequin mean when she says that "consequentialist arguments against an obligation to reduce one's own emissions [fail] to recognize the *wholeness* of persons"?
6. Hourdequin identifies three ways in which integrity is valuable. What are they?
7. Why does Hourdequin describe Sinnott-Armstrong's position as a kind of individualism? What does she mean?

Discussion Questions

1. Do you think that most people you know are willing to change their behavior for environmental reasons? When people aren't willing to make changes, why do you think that is?
2. Hourdequin briefly suggests that the flip side of integrity is hypocrisy. The implication here is that Sinnott-Armstrong is *defending* hypocrisy. How would Sinnott-Armstrong reply to that charge?
3. Are *avoiding hypocrisy* and *having integrity* the same thing? If so, why? If not, why not?
4. Suppose that Hourdequin is right both that (a) integrity requires harmonizing our political and personal commitments in the way she discusses and (b) we ought to have integrity. If so, then where *else* might integrity require us to adjust our behavior? In other words, where else do we find the "I don't make a difference" mentality at work, and how would we live differently if we were to stop making that excuse?

Case

According to the Union of Concerned Scientists, here are "the top ten things you can do to help tackle global warming":

1. When you buy your next car, look for the one with the best fuel economy in its class.
2. Make your house more air tight.
3. Buy and USE a programmable thermostat.
4. Eat less meat, especially beef.
5. Use power strips in your home office and home entertainment center.
6. Upgrade your refrigerator and air conditioner.
7. Get an electricity monitor.

8. Change those light bulbs.
9. Wash clothes in cold water.
10. Buy less stuff.[4]

The Natural Resources Defense Council encourages you do some of the same things. In addition, they recommend that you

1. Send a message to your elected officials, letting them know that you will hold them accountable for what they do—or fail to do—about global warming.
2. Pick a Green-e-certified energy supplier that generates at least half of its power from wind, solar energy and other clean sources.
3. [Make] up for your remaining carbon output by purchasing carbon offsets.
4. Choose alternatives to driving such as public transit, biking, walking and carpooling, and bundle your errands to make fewer trips.[5]

Now suppose that we ought to address the problem of global warming. If so, are you morally obligated to do all these things (at least insofar as you can or as far as they apply to you)? Does integrity require that you adjust your lifestyle accordingly? Why or why not? Moreover, if you *do* think that you're morally obligated to do all these things, are these *all* the things you ought to do? Or are there others?

Notes

1. The claim that individual acts cause no climate-related harm is contestable. First, if there are threshold effects on climate change, then one individual's action could move the climate beyond an important "tipping point." Second, Parfit (1984) argues that small or imperceptible harms can be morally wrong, and even *very* wrong. Sinnott-Armstrong (2005: 291) dismisses Parfit's arguments because he insists that the minute changes in climate caused by a single individual's actions are not harms: "No storms or floods or heat waves can be traced to my individual acts of driving." Individuals *qua* individuals do not cause climate harms, asserts SinnottAnnstrong—but he provides little argument to refute Parfit's claims in Chapter 3 of *Reasons and Persons* (1984), which point in the direction of counting individual contributions to climate change as harms.

2. These are hypotheses about how certain individual behaviors (in this case, bicycling) affect the thought and behavior of others. As such, they are subject to investigation using the tools of social scientific research (laboratory experimentation, observation of human behaviors, and theoretical modeling). To my knowledge, there exists no research that specifically investigates bicycle commuters' effects on others' transportation choices and behavior. However,

there is a growing body of evidence supporting the plausibility of the claims made here. For example, Christakis and Fowler (2008, 2009) have shown the importance of social networks in influencing behavior (e.g., smoking cessation shows striking social patterns, where the smoking behavior of close contacts influences strongly the likelihood that a person will quit) and have argued based on experimental evidence that, in the words of a recent article's title, "cooperative behavior cascades in human social networks" (Fowler and Christakis, 2010). This latter work specifically examined behavior in public goods games . . . Other authors find that certain consumer choices (e.g., hybrid vehicle purchases) and individual behaviors (e.g., bicycle commuting) develop important symbolic values for individuals and communities, that conversations among individuals about their transportation choices are important in constructing these meanings, and that individual choices reflect concern for these symbolic values (see Axsen and Kurani, 2009; Heffner et al., 2006; Heffner et al., 2007; Horton, 2006) . . .

3. Gore reportedly purchases carbon offsets to counteract his greenhouse gas emissions; however, substantial controversy exists about whether carbon offsets are of comparable value to individual reductions in consumption.

4. http://www.ucsusa.org/global_warming/what_you_can_do/ten-personal-solutions-to.html

5. http://www.nrdc.org/globalwarming/gsteps.asp

PART VIII

Sports

40

$\overset{\displaystyle =\!=\!=}{\underset{\displaystyle =\!=\!=}{\text{ℬ}}}$

The Role and Value of Intercollegiate Athletics in Universities

Myles Brand

Athletics programs have a complicated status in institutions of higher education. As prominent as they are in the campus community, you don't major in basketball or football, and playing those sports won't count toward your credit hours or satisfy any degree requirements. In fact, some people wonder why institutions of higher education should have athletics programs at all. There are even those who hold that it is detrimental to the aims of higher education to maintain athletic programs as they currently do. Myles Brand weighs in to explain why, in his view, athletics does have a legitimate place in higher education. Partly, he relies on the many similarities between athletics and performance arts like music, arguing that the former has value much in the same way as the latter. At a deeper level, criticisms of athletics in higher education have an inadequate conception of the values higher education should promote, which should, Brand contends, include the virtues of the mind as well as those of the body.

Brand, Myles. 2006. "The Role and Value of Intercollegiate Athletics in Universities." *Journal of the Philosophy of Sport* 33(1): 9–20. Reprinted with permission of Taylor & Francis Group.

. . .

In this article . . . my target is to defeat some of the objections of one crucial constituency, namely the faculty and other members of the academy. In particular, I will argue for the following thesis: The role and importance of intercollegiate athletics are undervalued by the academy.

Intercollegiate athletics has the potential to contribute far more to the academic enterprise than it does currently. The contributions of intercollegiate athletics have failed to be realized because of misconceptions of college sports and preconceptions in the academy. Removal of these impediments provides an opportunity for sports on campus to better support the academic mission of universities and colleges.

. . .

The Standard View

The Standard View conceives of intercollegiate athletics as an extracurricular activity. It resembles participation in student government and protesting against the university administration. It has more educational value than fraternity parties but less than the chess club.

According to the Standard View, college sports may have some redeeming developmental value for students, but they are not part of the educational experience. Intercollegiate athletics can be eliminated from the campus without in any way diminishing the educational mission of the institution. Some critics go beyond the Standard View to claim that intercollegiate athletics detracts from the institution's ability to educate, and it is a strong negative force on campus.

College sports are merely "beer and circuses," as one author puts it, designed to entertain and distract attention from universities' failures (Sperber 2000). The Standard View, though not necessarily this stronger version, is widely held by faculty members, academic administrators, and many external constituents not closely allied with the university. It is not widely held by students, alumni, local community members, and national fans or by many governing-board members. The Standard View tends to pervade the nonstudent campus culture, mostly because of faculty influence.

The main problem with the Standard View is that it misrepresents college sports and the experiences of student-athletes. As a result, it creates problems for the functioning of an athletics department, and it inhibits the positive, constructive values of intercollegiate athletics from influencing campus life and the education of undergraduates. The Standard View is the leading contributor to the undervaluation of college sports.

Let me begin the argument with a seemingly small point. When the educational experience of student-athletes is compared with those studying the performing arts such as music, dance, and theater, as well as the studio arts, it is difficult to find substantive differences. Consider, in particular, music students at universities with major music programs. These students must be accomplished before admission. They have to audition, and the best of them receive scholarships. Those with exceptional talent are often admitted even if their purely academic credentials, demonstrated by their grade-point averages and SAT scores, are below the range of normally admitted students.

Many of the music students admitted to the best music departments and schools have ambitions for professional careers. Once admitted, they practice innumerable hours on their own and as members of the university's symphony orchestras, vocal and choral groups, and jazz ensembles. They perform with these groups on weekends and evenings during the semester, and, on occasion, they miss class to perform at off-campus locations. These performances often involve paid admission. In nearly every case, both performance and practice are intense, highly competitive for lead roles, time demanding, and year-round. . . .

. . .

Of course, the vast majority of music students never have a significant music career. Even in the best university music departments, the proportion of students that become international stars is infinitesimal. Some music graduates teach music; most, however, enter careers that are, at best, indirectly related to their music education. Nonetheless, these individuals benefited from their college education, not only in music but also because of the learning achieved in general-education coursework and because of broadly based intellectual and personal growth.

The similarities of the experience of music students and student-athletes should be apparent. Student-athletes must be accomplished in their sport before enrollment, especially at the National Collegiate Athletic Association (NCAA) Division I institutions, and they must "audition" through game performances and camps.[1] Like musicians, the best are sought by universities and receive scholarships. Some talented prospects are admitted even if their grade-point averages and SAT scores are below the range of the student body. Student-athletes practice on their own and as members of teams, they play on weekends or evenings during the semester, and they travel to off-campus sites. Their games provide entertainment to the college community, and tickets normally must be purchased.

There are rare athletics prodigies, but most attend college. Very few of those who play in college become professionals in their sports. In Division I men's basketball, for example, less than one half of 1 percent of Division I scholarship players each year have an opportunity to play in the professional National Basketball Association (NBA), and the large majority of those have short careers. Some teach their craft after graduation—that is to say become coaches—but most pursue other careers, only some of which are related to college sports.

Like student-musicians, student-athletes receive public praise for the exercise of their abilities. In both cases, their successes—and failures—reflect on their home institutions. Both groups tend to form strong bonds with their mentors—their coaches or master teachers—as well as other students in the program. Student-musicians tend to major in music, though not always. Student-athletes undertake a broad array of majors, with business and the social sciences being the predominant ones, although sometimes their majors reflect their interests in athletics, such as kinesiology and broadcasting.[2]

These similarities point to a convergence of educational experiences between student-athletes and others engaged in certain pre-professional courses of study. Given this convergence, it might be expected that the student-athlete experience and that of students in the performing arts would have similar academic standing, but that is not the case.

In general, music students receive academic credit for learning their instruments, practicing, and playing in the school symphony. In general, student-athletes do not receive academic credit for instruction by coaches, nor do they receive academic credit for team practice or play. Many institutions give credit to members of the general student body to take classes in sports, say golf or tennis instruction. When physical education was required, as it tends not to be now, credit was awarded to non-athletes. But again, at NCAA Division I institutions, students do not receive credit for intercollegiate athletic participation.

What are the reasons for this apparent disparity in academic standing between student-athletes and student-musicians? There appear to be two primary ones. The first is the claim that credit is awarded only when the activity has content and the class (or its equivalent) is taught by a qualified instructor. This reason for the difference between student-musicians and student-athletes is not tenable, however.

How are we to specify content in this instance? In the case of physics, psychology, and philosophy courses, for example, the content is relatively clear. It is the systematic knowledge that is organized and conveyed by the instructor and textbooks and learned by the students. This is factual knowledge, knowledge "that." For example, physics students are expected to know that the speed of light is a constant, and philosophy students are expected to know that Western philosophy began with the ancient Greeks.

Music performance students are expected to gain knowledge "that" in some of their classes, such as music theory, but, by and large, performance students gain knowledge "how." That is, they learn how to do certain things, for example, how to play Bach's Brandenburg concertos. Learning how to do something is to gain a skill or to exercise an acquired skill in specific circumstances (Ryle 1949).

Student-athletes, too, must learn factual knowledge. They must know the rules of the game and about nutrition and exercise. But the most important learning undertaken by student-athletes is to come to know "how." Individual and team practices provide opportunities for student-athletes to learn skills and to apply those skills in specific situations.

Content includes knowing "how," as well as knowing "that," both facts and skills. . . .

Thus, student-athletes and performance students each learn content in the same way. Some content is acquired in cognate courses, and that tends to be factual knowledge. The primary content, however, in both cases is knowledge how, and that is acquired in individual or group settings with a master teacher or coach. It is this knowledge how that enables them to perform in the concert hall or on the playing field.

. . .

This account focuses on learned cognitive skills, whereas the perspective I am stressing is based on learned physical skills. Cognitive-skill learning is, for the most part, gaining knowledge that; physical-skill learning is, for the most part, gaining knowledge how. No doubt, both occur through athletics participation, and both contribute to a student's education, but the main part is that, although athletics participation may well generate learning that is assimilable to the intellectual model of a university education, there is another type of learning that occurs in athletics participation that focuses on physical-skill development and that is a legitimate and worthy part of a university education.

The remaining part of this defense of the Standard View is that there is a difference between learning by student-athletes and performance students because of the differences in qualifications of the instructors.

Here, too, the claim does not stand up to scrutiny. At fine universities and colleges across this nation, we expect a large majority of the instruction of undergraduates to be undertaken by those with terminal degrees or the equivalent in their fields. We do permit those in training—graduate students—to render instruction, but only under the supervision of senior teachers.

In the case of physics, psychology, and philosophy, among other disciplines, the terminal degree is the PhD. That is the appropriate degree when the primary, often exclusive, learning is factual knowledge. In the case of skill-based disciplines, however, such as the performing and studio arts, the PhD is not ordinarily the terminal degree. In these cases, it is usually the MFA, though that, too, might not be required. Rather, in these disciplines, the underlying requirement is that there is a track record of excellence, verified by peers, of teaching the skills appropriate to the activity. Peer judgment in the cases of skill instruction plays at least as important a role in asserting qualifications, and likely more so, than it does in factual knowledge instruction.

In athletic coaching, and to a large degree in the performing and studio arts, there is an apprenticeship system for instructors. Of course, minimal academic credentials are required, usually at least the baccalaureate degree, but after that, one learns from masters. Coaches begin as assistants and, through involvement with successful coaches, emerge, if they are talented, as head coaches. Similar routes to leadership in their fields are followed by performing and studio master teachers. Often, though certainly not always, coaches and master teachers themselves have or had high skill levels in their areas of expertise.

Those who teach in the performing and studio arts tend to be on the tenure track. That often held for coaches in the past, but Division I coaches are not now on the tenure track, except for a few elders who retain their faculty positions. There are some institutions in Divisions II and III that continue the practice of putting coaches on the tenure track, especially when they teach classes to the general student body.

Thus, the first purported reason for the disparity in academic standing between athletics and performance students—namely, differences in instructional content and teacher qualifications—is not defensible.

The second reason for the disparity between athletics and performance disciplines cuts to the heart of the matter. It focuses directly on the role and value of intercollegiate athletics in universities. This reason is that there are unsubstantiated cultural preconceptions within the academy about intercollegiate athletics.

Not all faculty members and academic administrators are anti-athletics. There are many faculty members who are fans and many who work toward the success and proper conduct of intercollegiate athletics, for example, through service as NCAA faculty representatives and on campus-based committees. . . . Aside from these efforts to understand and reform intercollegiate athletics, however, there is serious and growing discontent among faculty members. The underlying reason is that, for the most part, faculty members hold intellectual powers in higher esteem then they do bodily abilities. Put provocatively, the American academy is prejudiced against the body.

Most faculty members are engaged in disciplines that are intellectual. Universities generally are involved in research and scholarship involving factual knowledge. . . . [T]he intellectual, cognitive approach prevails. In it, emphasis on bodily skills is inappropriate; indeed, it subverts the true aim of the university. A focus on bodily skills leads to a vocational or purely professional view of education, and that, it is held, is antithetical to the mission of an institution of higher learning. . . . The core of the university is the study and advancement of the liberal arts.

Music and dance performance, though not purely intellectual, are treated as exceptions because they fall into the category of art. Actually, that is not entirely correct. It depends on what kind of music or dance. Classical music qualifies; rock and roll does not. The art form must relate to high culture. Rock and roll can be studied in a disinterested, intellectual way, and there are college courses on the history and sociology of rock and roll, but playing in a rock band does not ordinarily warrant college credit toward graduation.

In sum, the prejudice against the body, and with it professional studies that emphasize physical skill, is deeply rooted in the American academy. It was not until the middle of the twentieth century that music, even classical music, rose to departmental status in many universities. This bias against the body and toward cognitive and intellectual capacity is the driving force of the disdain by many faculty members for college sports and the acceptance of the Standard View.

. . .

The Integrated View

The Standard View should be replaced by a more balanced view about athletics that integrates it into the mission of the university. Call this the Integrated View. The primary and defining feature of the Integrated View is that athletic programs are made part of the educational mission of the university. Although they are not part of the liberal-arts core, they play the same type of role as music and art and, perhaps, business and journalism.

The Integrated View is based on a different perspective of the role of physical-skill education than that of the Standard View. The Integrated View disposes of the bias against physical-skill development. The Attic Greeks had a good perspective. They believed that the mental and the physical should both be part of a sound education. Even someone as committed to the superiority of the mental as Plato held that physical accomplishment was necessary for successful citizenship. The central idea here is that of harmony. The harmony, the unity, of mind and body is crucial to a happy life (Plato: Book II 376E, Book III 412B, Book VII 521C–541B).[3]

The idea of harmony between mind and body in education comports well with the underlying philosophy of education in this country. America is the only country in the world that includes athletics extensively in its educational system. In Europe, sports are played mostly outside the university. Independent club sports, many of which involve payment to the athletes, substitute for intercollegiate athletics. Some Asian countries are reconsidering the separation of sports and education. Mainland China is reviewing its educational system, and there is some prospect that they will emulate the American system and incorporate athletics directly into it.

By focusing on the harmony between mind and body in education, athletics takes on a more central role. That role is not unlike the role of music in education, once again following the ancient Greeks. Some students specialize in music, but not many. Nonetheless, music is to be appreciated and enjoyed by all. It is considered a valuable part of the curriculum and the campus environment. Similarly, a minority of students are focused on intercollegiate athletics—from less than 2 percent of the general student body at large Division I institutions to 30 percent or more at some highly selective Division III liberal-arts colleges. Nonetheless, athletics and student-athletes should find a central role in university life. Athletics should be a valuable part of the educational environment.

The Integrated View raises a provocative issue. If athletic participation is relevantly similar to music performance with respect to content—namely, in knowledge of skills—as well as instructor qualifications, then if academic credit is provided for music students, should it not also be provided for student-athletes? There are some obvious limitations in providing credit to student-athletes. We should not offer majors in basketball or other sports. But it appears reasonable to provide a small number of credits, one time only, provided that the course has been approved through the normal process by appropriate faculty committees and it has an attendance requirement. There is the potential for abuse and academic fraud but, with faculty oversight, not more so than with some other courses in the university. In any case, the idea of offering credit for students participating in intercollegiate athletics is worthy of consideration, once the Integrated View is established at an institution.

Intercollegiate athletics, at its best, demonstrates positive values. These values include striving for excellence, perseverance, resilience, hard work, respect for others, sportsmanship and civility, and losing—and winning—with grace. Consider for a moment reactions to losing. Most undergraduate students, especially freshmen, have difficulty with failure, but student-athletes, who are accustomed to competition and the failures that accompany it, become good at overcoming adversity. If they lose a big game on Saturday afternoon, they are on the field the next Monday working doubly hard. Many students would do well to embrace this value of resilience and coping with failure early in their college careers.

In general, it would be good if the positive values exhibited by student-athletes were learned and adopted by the general student body. A college education is not only an exercise in gaining factual and skill-based knowledge; it is an opportunity to develop a value system, a set of enduring goals, and a perspective on life. In large part, college is about becoming a productive citizen and a mature person. This developmental aspect of a college education is especially pertinent to traditional-age students who have a residential experience. The positive, constructive values of student-athletes, gained through their experiences in intercollegiate athletics, are apt models.

Given that certain types of physical-skill development have roles to play in an institution of higher education and that intercollegiate athletics is one such type of skill development, intercollegiate athletics should be treated similarly to music education and education in other areas that involve skill development. For example, departments of intercollegiate athletics and schools of music should be relevantly similar in terms of the university's organizational chart.

. . .

The advantage of mainstreaming the athletic department into the mission and structure of the university is that it reflects the balanced approach to education that includes both cognitive and physical capacity. It also has the advantage of removing the impetus for the bias against intercollegiate athletics underlying the Standard View. . . . By placing athletics in the mainstream of the university, its value to the education of undergraduates becomes more apparent.

Students' education may include both intellectual- and physical-skill elements. Although an emphasis on the intellectual certainly has had salutary effects, a university education should not be limited in that skill development is necessarily excluded. The structure of the university, in turn, should reflect this integrated approach. On the defensive side, failure to place adequate operational controls on intercollegiate athletics is a recipe for deep problems, including public exposure by the media. On the constructive side, mainstreaming intercollegiate athletics into the campus structure is likely to yield value for the institution in terms of broadly based developmental educational opportunities.

. . .

References

Bowen, W. G., and Levin, S. A. (2003). *Reclaiming the Game: College Sports and Educational Values*. Princeton, NJ: Princeton University Press.

Brand, M. (2001). "Academics First: Reforming Intercollegiate Athletics." Address delivered to the National Press Club, January 23, 2001. *Vital Speeches of the Day* 67 (12) (April), 367–71.

Brand, M. (1984). *Intending and Acting: Toward a Naturalized Action Theory*. Boston: Massachusetts Institute of Technology, Bradford Press.

Coalition on Intercollegiate Athletics Web site: www.math.umd.edu/~jmc/COIA. *NCAA Division I Manual*, Article 20.

Orszag, J., and Orszag, P. "The Empirical Effects of Collegiate Athletics: An Interim Report," "The Physical Capital Stock Used in College Athletics," and "Division II Intercollegiate Athletics: An Empirical and Case Study Analysis." Available at www.ncaa.org.

Plato. (1951). *The Republic of Plato*. Trans. F. M. Cornford. New York and London: Oxford University Press.

Ryle, G. (1949). "Knowing How and Knowing That." In *The Concept of Mind*. London and New York: Hutchinson's University Library.

Shulman, J. L., and W. G. Bowen. (2001). *The Game of Life: College Sports and Educational Values*. Princeton, NJ: Princeton University Press.

Simon, R. L. (1991). "Do Intercollegiate Athletics Belong on Campus?" In *Fair Play: Sports, Values, and Society*. Boulder, CO: Westview Press.

Sperber, M. A. (2000). *Beer and Circus: How Big-Time College Sports Is Crippling Undergraduate Education*. New York: Henry Holt and Co.

Comprehension Questions

1. What is the "Standard View" about college sports?
2. In what ways are college athletics programs similar to performing arts?
3. What, in Brand's view, is wrong with the two arguments against giving academic credit for participation in college sports?
4. What sort of content do student-athletes learn in their involvement with college sports, and what qualifications do athletics instructors possess?
5. Why does Brand say that "the American academy is prejudiced against the body"?
6. What is the "Integrated View" about college sports?
7. What positive values do intercollegiate sports help promote, and which would be beneficial to the broader student body?

Discussion Questions

1. Think about the reasons Brand discusses for holding the Standard View. Are these *all* the reasons you might give for excluding athletics from higher education? What others can you think of? Are they good reasons?
2. Part of the value of college sports, according to Brand, is that it fosters certain desirable qualities in student-athletes. Does what he says fit with your experience? Even if he's right, is this a good reason to include athletics in higher education?
3. Brand accuses the Standard View of denigrating physical skill. Do you think physical skill is especially valuable? Is it the sort of thing institutions of higher education need to encourage? Why or why not?

Case

Consider this:

> During the past two decades, [Sharon Stoll, a professor of physical education at the University of Idaho and the director of its Center for Ethical Theory and Honor in Competition and Sport,] has measured the moral-reasoning abilities of more than 70,000 college athletes, evaluating their written responses to various scenarios.
>
> Her research has found that, on the whole, athletes have significantly lower moral-reasoning skills than the general student population—and she says that is a direct result of the competitive sports environment. . . . [Moreover, Stoll has found that in recent years

there has been] a sharp decline in athletes' moral reasoning. Team-sport athletes perform worse than any others, with lacrosse players scoring the lowest, followed by ice hockey and football players. Players of individual sports like golf and tennis fare better—but still lower than non-athletes. And although female athletes score higher than men, their moral-reasoning abilities have also dropped; [Stoll] believes they could fall as low as men's scores within five years.

Athletes are worse at moral thinking for several reasons, [Stoll] says. From an early age, many elite players are trained to view their opponents as obstacles to overcome rather than honorable individuals. They also frequently develop a sense of entitlement, are not encouraged to think for themselves, and rarely face consequences for acting irresponsibly. While they may know right from wrong, they often believe they can get away with anything.[4]

Here are two examples of the questions Stoll has asked. In each case, students choose the answer that best describes their views: SA = Strongly agree; A = Agree; N = Neutral; D = Disagree; SD = Strongly disagree.

1. Two rival basketball teams in a well-known conference played a basketball game on Team A's court. During the game, Team B's star player was consistently heckled whenever she missed a basket, pass, or rebound. In the return game on Team B's home court, the home crowd took revenge by heckling Team A's players. Such action is fair because both crowds have equal opportunity to heckle players.
2. During a volleyball game, player A hit the ball over the net. The ball barely grazed off player B's fingers and landed out of bounds. However the referee did not see player B touch the ball. Because the referee is responsible for calling rule violations, player B is not obligated to report the violation.[5]

What do you make of Stoll's conclusions? Do you find them surprising? Why or why not? If Stoll is right, what does that mean for Brand's argument?

Notes

1. The NCAA divides colleges and universities into three divisions reflecting athletic scholarship (grants-in-aid) support, the level of competition, and differences in philosophy. For example, Division III, unlike Divisions I and II, does not offer athletic scholarships. Division I, in turn, is subdivided in football, and only in football, into Divisions I-A, I-AA, and I-AAA. Division I-AAA does not field football teams. Division I-A, which consists of 117 schools, plays at the highest competitive level and receives the lion's share

of fan and media attention. Overall, there are approximately 360,000 current student-athletes in the NCAA competing at more than 1,000 colleges and universities. See www.ncaa.org for details of structure and membership.

2. See Shulman and Bowen for the majors and post-college careers of student-athletes.

3. See Simon 1991: 156ff. Simon quotes A. Bartlett Giamatti, former president of Yale University and commissioner of Major League Baseball: "The Greeks saw physical training and games as a form of knowledge, meant to toughen the body in order to temper the soul, activities pure in themselves, immediate, obedient to the rules so that winning would be sweeter still" (10: 157).

4. http://chronicle.com/weekly/v52/i48/48a03201.htm

5. https://www.webpages.uidaho.edu/center_for_ethics/Measurements/HBVCI/sample.htm

41

On the Role and Value of Intercollegiate Athletics in Universities

J. Angelo Corlett

Suppose that college sports do, in fact, contribute to the goals of higher education. Even if we grant this, there might be other reasons to be concerned about college athletics programs. According to Angelo Corlett, whatever the merit of college athletics, it's just too financially draining. The costs it imposes on colleges and universities far outweigh its purported benefits. Corlett's is an economic argument and it's especially forceful in the aftermath of the 2008 financial crisis, the effects of which linger still. Of course, this worry about financial waste in higher education is not peculiar to college athletics, as Corlett notes. Instead, it's a concern we might have about many areas of higher education, probably to their detriment.

. . .

The late and distinguished Myles Brand, former professor of philosophy at the University of Arizona, president first of the University of

Oregon and then of Indiana University, and president of the NCAA, recently made a distinction between the "Standard View" of intercollegiate athletics according to which intercollegiate athletics is an extracurricular activity (Brand 2006, 9), and the "Integrated View" which holds that athletics should be part of the educational environment and that we ought to eliminate the bias against physical skill development (Brand 2006, 17). Since the publication of Professor Brand's article, an economic crisis has rocked not only the United States but most of the rest of the world, and it is particularly experienced harshly by US colleges and universities. While Professor Brand's defense of the Integrated View is important and insightful, it fails to take into account this fiscal crisis and how it seems to require a different attitude, one of deep fiscal responsibility, toward every aspect of the college and university experience.

In the spirit of creating fruitful dialogue concerning the matter of intercollegiate athletic funding in particular and academic programs in general, I will argue that the global economic crisis makes it obvious that neither the Standard View nor the Integrated View of intercollegiate athletics will suffice. Instead, an economic argument will be marshaled that forces those of us in higher education to become deeply fiscally responsible. While it is primarily an economic argument, it is also a qualitative one in that, I assume, the quality of a higher educational institution is contingent at least in part on how fiscally viable it is able to become and remain over time. I shall refer to it as the "Fiscal Responsibility View" and it relies for its plausibility primarily on an Argument from Fiscal Responsibility which states that every aspect of public higher education must be re-evaluated in terms of its economic efficiency. Where there is significant and more than temporary waste, fraud or corruption, fiscal responsibility requires that budgetary decisions be made to resolve the issue in terms of terminating administrators, faculty or staff and even programs that are doing more fiscal harm than good to the mission of the higher educational institution in question, or those administrators, faculty and staff who are regularly underproductive[1] need to be either demoted, given a greater course load (if teaching faculty[2]) without an increase in compensation, as the case may be. Public higher education is the general target of my discussion. By "higher educational institutions" and "colleges and universities" I specifically mean those that award graduate degrees.

Unlike the Standard View, the Fiscal Responsibility View sidesteps the issue of whether or not athletics is or ought to be part of the core mission of public higher education. For it can hold such a view—indeed, it can even add that each unit of higher education can be construed as having equal weight—and nonetheless hold fast to what Professor Brand calls the "principle of self-support" (Brand 2006, 16) with regard to academic units or programs, thereby differentiating the Fiscal Responsibility View from the Integrated View. The difference between the Standard View and the Integrated View, on the one hand, and the Fiscal Responsibility View, on the other, is that the latter view seeks to hold every program and individual in graduate-degree granting higher educational institutions to a general principle that no significant and ongoing waste, fraud or corruption is to be tolerated or go unpunished (at the very least, it should never be rewarded as is often currently the case). Once this anti-waste, -fraud and -corruption principle is taken seriously, and once it is linked to Professor Brand's principle of self-support within colleges and universities, most administrators, faculty, staff and programs will have to either begin to conform to new standards of efficiency and productivity or face dire consequences. Assumed here is that no legitimate employment contract should respect under-performance (judged by reasonable professional standards) by anyone for more than a short time or in absence of serious illness or injury. So where waste, fraud, corruption or significant under-productivity is evident, significant and more than temporary, then the personnel aligned with them must be terminated, otherwise demoted or otherwise penalized, as the case warrants according to basic considerations of fairness and proportionality.

All of the foregoing is relevant to Professor Brand's statement that "recent studies conducted under the auspices of the NCAA cast serious doubt on the claim that continued increases in expenditures results in improved competitiveness or in an enhanced ability to satisfy the principle of self-support" (Brand 2006, 16, citing Orszag and Orszag 2009). Professor Brand also writes that "[T]here is no correlation between winning teams and funds for operational expenditures. Overall, the studies do not support the rationale often given for increased expenditures on athletics" (Brand 2006, 16). Furthermore, "[F]ewer than two dozen Division I-A schools, perhaps as few as one dozen when everything is taken into account, actually meet the principle of self-support. The 100 or so Division I-A institutions and the remaining 900 other schools with NCAA athletics programs all subsidize them" (Brand 2006, 16).[3] Following such statements, Professor Brand asks: "Is that bad?" and answers, "It is only if one is committed to the Standard View that athletics lies outside the central mission of the university" (Brand 2006, 16).

However, Professor Brand's answer is incorrect. It *is* a bad thing, indeed fiscally irresponsible, that intercollegiate athletic teams for the most part fail to be self-supporting and drain valuable resources from general academic budgets—especially during such devastating economic times wherein state support for higher education is being reduced by hundreds of millions of dollars per year in systems such as the California State University. This is especially the case unless and until academic budgets are able to cover robustly the wide-ranging academic needs of higher educational institutions. So one need not hold the Standard View in order to condemn fiscal irresponsibility in the form of not satisfying the principle of self-support with regard to athletic programs. And any bias against intercollegiate athletic programs can be averted by this standpoint by judiciously applying the principle of self-support and the Argument from Fiscal Responsibility to every other unit in a higher educational institution *in light of the particular circumstances of each unit.* Thus if *reasonable but flexible standards of fiscal responsibility* are applied across the board within higher educational institutions, then based on the NCAA findings cited by Professor Brand himself, not only would most every higher educational institution having athletic programs need to eliminate them insofar as public funding is concerned because they are not self-supporting (thereby constituting a kind of significant waste), but every other department or program in graduate-degree conferring institutions, including under-productive administrators, faculty and staff would need to be eliminated, demoted, or otherwise punished[4] (as the case maybe) insofar as *they* are under-productive or are not self-supporting. In fact, given that a very small number (at best) of intercollegiate athletic programs can and will survive this test of self-support, there will be insufficient numbers of such programs to even justify continuing the NCAA itself, effectively terminating NCAA intercollegiate athletics altogether unless substantial private funding can be garnered for such activities. But the Argument from Fiscal Responsibility has even more dramatic implications, each of which might permit the significant reduction of the costs of tuition and fees in such colleges and universities.

College and university presidents, for example, who fail to raise sufficient sums of external funding for their own institutions as stipulated by reasonable contracts should be terminated or at least have their salaries and benefits lowered commensurate with their level of under-productivity insofar as their job descriptions include garnering substantial funding for their respective universities. It also implies that faculty who do not publish well and often as stipulated by reasonable contracts must teach more courses per year than their colleagues who do publish well and often, saving, as matters currently stand, several million dollars per year per college or university from having to hire additional faculty to teach courses for under-productive faculty who enjoy reduced teaching loads. This assumes, of course, that college and university faculty must publish well and often in order to teach excellent and up-to-date content, as *I assume here that there is a strong correlation between the quality of the academic content of what faculty teach and the quality of the academic content of peer-reviewed published faculty research* (Corlett 2005). Generally, motivated faculty who have solid pedagogical skills who are also regularly engaged in peer-reviewed published research are in better positions than those who are not engaged in such research to pass along their improved knowledge or information gained through their research endeavors to their students as the need arises, both in and out of the classroom or laboratory.

Moreover, professional academic responsibility would encourage (perhaps even obligate) faculty at graduate-degree conferring institutions to do so on a regular basis. I argue that the full-time tenured and tenure-track teaching faculty at such institutions have both institutional and moral obligations to regularly engage in peer-reviewed published research—one of the primary reasons of which is to pass along such improved knowledge to their students. While the statistical correlation between the engagement in peer-reviewed research and quality of teaching might be questioned, my point is a normative one: Regardless of whether or not said faculty in fact effectively and regularly pass along their updated knowledge to their students in and out of the classrooms and laboratories, they have an institutional and moral duty to do so. They ought to do so because it should be construed as being part of their very role responsibility as faculty to do so. This is why, I take it, that faculty who engage in research are said to engage in "faculty *development*." It is vital that faculty regularly engage in research in order to keep their minds alive with updated knowledge and information from their fields of expertise because, again, *the quality of the content of faculty teaching is contingent on the quality of the content of what they publish*. For just as it would be reasonable to question the quality of the content of the teaching of a scientist who taught a contemporary science course based on information that was dated and even incorrect, so too ought other academic areas be subject to the same kind of professional expectation regarding the connection that should exist between the content of faculty research and the content of what they teach.

. . .

. . . John Kekes articulates part of the complex role of university faculty in the following terms: "[A]cademics fail in their responsibility if they do not teach the truth they have arrived at through research and of what they teach is not what research indicates that there is most reason to believe to be true" (Kekes 2006, 132). It is this conception of university faculty as courageous seekers of truth and avoiders of error and as devoted and creative conveyors of such knowledge to students that I have in mind by my reference to the role of such faculty in higher education (Corlett 2005).

So for all of Professor Brand's discussion of the importance of physical training and such, that is not central to the Argument from Fiscal Responsibility generated by the recent and enduring economic crisis. What matters more is the extent to which graduate-degree conferring public higher educational institutions in the United States are willing and able to reduce significant waste, fraud and corruption in order to become more efficient institutions, and thereby to become more responsible ones in order to better serve students and society more generally. By becoming more efficient, such colleges and universities can better protect the overall quality of the public good of higher education.

. . .

The implications of the Fiscal Responsibility View are that, given the truth of Professor Brand's statements about NCAA Division I-A athletic programs not being self-supporting, they ought to be eliminated altogether unless they can be self-supporting by way of, say, private means. But it is not because of some bias against physical training that justifies that elimination of such programs. Rather, it is because they are not self-supporting and it would be fiscally irresponsible to keep them afloat with public funds especially during these tough economic times. After all, it is precisely such waste, fraud and corruption that serve as contributory causes of the current economic crisis to begin with, at least with regard to colleges and universities generally.

It might be argued that universities should build character, moral virtue, fair treatment of others using agreed-upon rules, courage in the face of challenges to one's self-esteem and even physical body, cooperative tasks, and so on; in short, many things that are "essential" for a good human being and to which athletic programs can make a contribution.[5]

While these points are true, this is surely insufficient to justify the massive debt that such programs accrue. Such moral virtues can be taught by universities and colleges by way of far less economically costly physical education courses in team sports for which students pay normal tuition and fees.

. . .

But the waste, fraud, and corruption ought not to stop with underproductive administrators, faculty and staff as such. They extend to administrative decisions to assume multi-million dollar institutional loans for various amenities in order to, it is said, compete to attract the best students. These amenities include but are not limited to such facilities as world-class football stadiums, basketball arenas, gymnasiums, workout facilities, tennis courts, track and field facilities, art museums, chaplain's offices, and the like. While it might be argued with some degree of plausibility that at least some of these kinds of facilities are needed or helpful for a good education, it is surely beyond credulity to argue that the tremendous expenses of constructing and maintaining such facilities are justified when so many of the basics of higher education are suffering (library acquisitions and faculty research funding, for example). And the oft-made assertion that intercollegiate athletics can be used to effectively garner institutional support from alumni is tenuous at best (Hacker and Dreifus 2010, 170–174).

. . .

Thus while it is true that the Standard View is biased against the development of athletic skills in an academic context, it does not follow that the Integrated View is the best one on offer. Nor is the real problem with that of the institution of tenure as so many would have us think (Taylor 2010, 204 f.). The Fiscal Responsibility View must be seen as the best of the three, though of course *fiscal matters do not exhaust what is important in higher education*. It places the responsibility on administrators and faculty to hire and retain and promote the very best possible candidates for hire [those who have excellent (or at least good) records in research, teaching and service], and to refuse to continue to even interview or extend offers to those whose productivity is below minimally decent standards of performance.[6]

Under these circumstances, it is hard to imagine a good reason why intercollegiate athletic programs should be retained by way of public funding given how they generally fail to satisfy the principle of self-support. While this argument saddens me because I truly enjoy watching intercollegiate athletics and I am singularly devoted to writing and teaching philosophy, I must as a fiscally responsible faculty member embrace it unless or until intercollegiate athletics, not unlike many academic departments or programs throughout higher education in the United States, ceases to be a significant drain on higher educational resources more generally.

. . .

References

Brand, M. (2006). "The Role and Value of Intercollegiate Athletics in Universities." *Journal of the Philosophy of Sport* 33, 9–20.

Corlett, J. A. (2005). "The Good Professor." *Journal of Academic Ethics* 3, 27–54.

Corlett, J. A. (2013). "Economic Exploitation in Intercollegiate Athletics." *Sports, Ethics, and Philosophy: Journal of the British Philosophy of Sport Association* (in press).

Hacker, A., and Dreifus, C. (2010). *Higher Education?* New York: Times Books.

Kekes, J. (2006). "Academic Corruption." In R. Barrow & P. Keeney, eds., *Academic Ethics*, 131–43. Aldershot: Ashgate.

Lehrer, K. (2000). *Theory of Knowledge*. Boulder: Westview Press.

Orszag, J., & Orszag, P. (2009). "The Empirical Effects of Collegiate Athletics: An Update Based On 2004–2007 Data." Commissioned by the National Collegiate Athletic Association. Retrieved from http://fs.ncaa.org/ Docs/DI_MC_BOD/ DI_BOD/2009/April/04,%20_Empirical_Effects.pdf.

Poff, D. (2003). "The Duty to Protect: Privacy and the Public University." *Journal of Academic Ethics* 1, 3–10.

Roszak, T. (2006). "On Academic Delinquency." In R. Barrow & P. Keeney, eds., *Academic Ethics* (pp. 65–104). Aldershot: Ashgate.

Searle, J. (2006). "The Prospects for the University." In R. Barrow and P. Keeney, eds., *Academic Ethics*. Aldershot: Ashgate, 105–30.

Shils, E. (2006). The Academic Ethics. In R. Barrow and P. Keeney, eds., *Academic Ethics*. Aldershot: Ashgate, 35–51.

Taylor, M. C. (2010). *Crisis on Campus*. New York: Knopf.

Comprehension Questions

1. What, roughly, is the Fiscal Responsibility View, and how does it relate to the Standard View and the Integrated View?
2. Why, on the Fiscal Responsibility View, is it a bad thing that athletic teams are not financially self-supporting?

3. What other areas of higher education does the Fiscal Responsibility target besides college athletics?

4. What demands does the Fiscal Responsibility View make on teaching faculty? Why?

Discussion Questions

1. On Corlett's view, any program indulging in significant and ongoing waste, fraud, or corruption is problematic. He supposes that college athletics programs fit that description. Why does he think that? Do you agree? Why or why not?

2. Corlett claims that teaching faculty are wasteful and generate inefficiency when they don't publish adequately. Do you agree with him that there is an important connection between instructors' publication record and efficiency? If you aren't sure, then what would you need to know in order to answer this question?

3. Someone might respond to the Fiscal Responsibility View by saying that the value of certain things can't be reduced to their cash value. Do you think that's true of the value of college athletics? Why or why not?

Case

Suppose that Corlett is right about the wastefulness of college athletics. Still, it's clear that a few schools *are* making money from their athletic programs (or, more accurately, a few schools are making money from *some* of their programs). But what happens to that money? Here are six notable results from a 2013 study on poverty among college athletes:

1. College athletes on full scholarship do not receive a "free ride." For the 2009–2010 academic year, the average annual scholarship shortfall (out-of-pocket expenses) for Football Bowl Series (FBS) "full" scholarship athletes was $3,222.

2. The compensation FBS athletes who are on "full scholarship" receive for living expenses (room and board, other expenses) situates the vast majority at or below the poverty level.

3. The percentage of FBS schools whose "full" athletic scholarships leave their players in poverty is 85 percent for those athletes who live on campus; 86 percent for athletes who live off campus.

4. The average FBS "full" scholarship athlete earns less than the federal poverty line by $1,874 on campus and $1,794 off campus.

5. If allowed access to the fair market like the pros, the average FBS football and basketball player would be worth approximately

$121,048 and $265,027, respectively (not counting individual commercial endorsement deals).

6. Football players with the top ten highest estimated fair market values are worth between $345k and $514k in 2009–10. The top spot was held by University of Texas football players. While 100 percent of these players received scholarships that left them living below the federal poverty line and with an average scholarship shortfall of $2,841 in 2010–11, their coaches were paid an average of over $3.5 million each in 2010 excluding bonuses.[7]

What do you make of these results? Even if football makes money, can schools justify the way they distribute their income? Why or why not?

Notes

1. Faculty research under-productivity might well be determined fairly on the basis of, say, average research productivity over the course of one's career up to the time of evaluation. So that those, for instance, who publish in excess of the basic standard (say, one article per year in a range of specified kinds of journals) might be able to "bank" their excess publications above and beyond the standard during years when they are less productive such as their final years nearing retirement or during a time of recovery from serious illness or injury.

2. Of course, I refer here only to full-time tenured and tenure-track teaching faculty in classrooms or laboratories, not to part- or full-time temporary, adjunct, or other contingent faculty who work terribly hard without reasonable compensation for their fine efforts.

3. This evidence is supported by the claim that "The overwhelming majority of those 17,917 teams in all sports and schools end up losing money. In the top football division, which can count on strong ticket sales, 113 of its 118 teams still run a deficit. Of the five that made a profit, only two brought in enough to erase the overall deficit of their schools' athletics departments" (Hacker and Dreifus 2010, 158–159; also see 164–167).

4. One possibility here would be to permanently reduce and cap the salaries of such underproductive personnel, a practice found in some higher educational institutions.

5. I thank an anonymous referee for this journal for making this interesting point.

6. Without a doubt, this approach would place a great deal of pressure on graduate students to publish as graduate students. But perhaps this will eventuate in their becoming more mature thinkers in their respective fields, while simultaneously serving as a good reason for currently underemployed and well qualified Ph.D.s to gain a foothold in the academic job market.

7. http://www.ncpanow.org/research/body/The-Price-of-Poverty-in-Big-Time-College-Sport.pdf

PART IX

Gaming, Music, and Humor

Defending the Morality of Violent Video Games

Marcus Schulzke

....

Do violent video games desensitize people to violence? Do they lead people to act violently? Do their costs outweigh any benefits they might have for those who enjoy them? Schulzke takes up these questions in his essay, arguing that the accusations leveled against violent video games are unfounded.

....

One of the most controversial and practically significant topics in the study of contemporary media is whether there is a connection between violent entertainment and aggressive behavior. In recent years, video games have replaced television, movies, and music as the primary concern. Video game violence has received a great deal of attention, yet for all the discussion of it, we know surprisingly little. The debate seems to be deadlocked, with empirical and theoretical work supporting and attacking violent video games making little progress toward a definitive conclusion. This is for two reasons. First, the empirical studies do not consistently favor one side. Most suggest that simulated violence is

---

Schulzke, Marcus. 2010. "Defending the Morality of Violent Video Games." *Ethics of Information Technology* 12: 127–138. Copyright © 2010, Springer. Reprinted with permission.

harmful, but there is a significant body of work reaching the opposite conclusion, as well as studies showing bias among researchers critical of gaming. More importantly, games seem to have no effect on crime as an increased propensity to aggression suggests that they would. Second, the ongoing debate about video game violence suffers from some problems of framing. Violent gaming is often made out to be a single issue, when in fact there are multiple interrelated questions that must be addressed. This essay will show that violent games are not immoral on . . . utilitarian grounds. . . .

. . . McCormick argues that even if games have the effect of increasing the risk of violent incidents they have a number of positive benefits that may outweigh the potential harm. He cites three primary reasons why games may be positive. First, they are fun and have a clear value in entertaining consumers that can outweigh some costs that they might incur.[1] Reynolds agrees with this in his utilitarian analysis of *Grand Theft Auto 3*, as he argues that games may offend and degrade different groups, but a utilitarian cannot consider this apart from the pleasure they give players. Reynolds argues that the value of the entertainment is greater than that of their harm as these games are responsible for giving what he estimates to be over a billion hours of entertainment to millions of people.[2] . . . While it is difficult to measure the harm done to those offended by the game, it is clear from sales that millions of people derive pleasure from gaming; the time many devote to them is likewise a sign that they are a source of happiness.

McCormick's second and third reasons are that games fuel the economy, directly and indirectly. The direct effect from video game sales keeps a multibillion dollar industry strong. Indirectly, video games help in developing new technologies that are useful outside the entertainment industry, and they are useful in creating simulations for various occupations. . . . To this list of benefits, we can add many others. Among these is that gaming leads to improved visual perception and cognition of space.[3] Action video games were found to be particularly helpful in this respect, as they are able to quickly raise non-gamers to the same proficiency of visual processing as those who played regularly.[4] Jeroen Jansz shows that the heavily criticized *Grand Theft Auto* series is praiseworthy and that it can help gamers understand themselves because of the amount of control that players are given. Adolescents who may feel like their lives are outside their control have complete freedom to decide how their player acts, dresses, and treats others. With this freedom, players are able to better understand their feelings and to confront their own identity in a comfortable setting.[5]

Waddington objects to McCormick's utilitarian argument by saying that we do not know the costs, benefits, and the percentage change in the costs of violent games. Thus, there are three uncertain variables making calculation difficult. However, this is not true. We have a very good idea of the benefits of video games. Their economic impact is quantifiable as is the number of hours of entertainment they bring to gamers. *GTA* alone sold over 66 million games by 2008,[6] evidence that at least this many people derive entertainment from game violence. Other heavily criticized violent games are likewise usually among the top sellers. There are also a number of educational benefits. The improvements in visual perception, hand-eye coordination, and other motor skills from gaming are also well documented.[7] The difficulty only lies in deciding how much these benefits should weigh against any harm that games do, but this is a problem intrinsic to utilitarian theory and should not be counted against violent games. Nevertheless, we can see whether there are negatives that should enter into the utilitarian calculus and that depends on the kind of research examined in the next section.

The Real World Effects of Violent Games

There are three basic empirical questions regarding video game violence. Do they give players the skills to hurt people more effectively? Do they weaken feelings of empathy? Do they motivate players to commit violent acts?

. . .

Training Killers

One of the most common claims made against violent games is that they have the capacity to train players to commit violent acts. As McCormick explains, if video games lead to violence they do not have to have a direct causal link. Instead, they may have an indirect link of creating violent dispositions or giving players the capacity to follow through with violent desires.[8] Many scholars worry that gamers are being trained in how to kill[9] and perhaps even how to kill for the military.[10] This argument is not that video games make players kill, and need not even include the claim that players will be more likely to commit violent acts. The essential point for this criticism is only that games make players more skilled at hurting others. The argument depends on the plausibility of the analogy between actions in a game and the real world. In order for this criticism to work, there must be a high degree of similarity. Galloway describes this reasoning perfectly, and points out that it depends on an assumed similarity between the actions performed in the game and actions in the real world:

> The conventional wisdom on realism in gaming is that, because life today is so computer-mediated, gamers actually benefit from hours of realistic gameplay. The time spent playing games trains the gamer to be close to the machine, to be quick and responsive, to understand interfaces, to be familiar with simulated worlds.[11]

This criticism is most common in the popular literature on video games, but even some scholarly critics argue that games are capable of training players to kill. Dave Grossman, a former soldier, is the most widely cited critic making this claim. His argument, that video games teach players how to use weapons, appears as one of the primary claims made against violent games in many studies.[12] Phil Chalmers makes an assertion typical of this line of reasoning: "Lee Boyd Malvo—one of the snipers responsible for the 2002 shootings in the Washington, DC, area—trained on an Xbox video game called Halo."[13] Similarly, speaking about the Columbine murderer Eric Harris, Gibbs and Roche remark that it is easy to see "how a video-game joystick turned Harris into a better marksman, like a golfer who watches Tiger Woods videos."[14]

This argument is weak because there is too little similarity between the acts of violence in games and in the real world to maintain that the mechanics are the same in each. While there are a number of useful computer training simulations, most casual games do not accurately replicate their subject matter. *Guitar Hero* is a prime example. In these incredibly popular games, players can hold an electronic guitar and push buttons that correspond to notes in a song. The game feels real, but the resemblance is superficial. A master of *Guitar Hero* will have no easier time learning the guitar than a novice because the simulation is so far removed from the activity. In fact, skill in playing the game may hinder guitar playing ability because the transitioning between the two requires retraining. . . . Likewise, using a mouse or a gamepad to punch and shoot is far removed from the activity of fighting. As technology changes there may be some danger of simulations actually teaching players skills they could use to fight. It is certainly possible that in the future first-person shooters might have game guns that look and act like real guns and that can actually serve as training tools. Nevertheless, violent games do not yet give the player the skills to actually carry out acts of violence simulated in the game and until they do, we should not overestimate the power of games to train players. . . .

Destroying Empathy

Another of the central empirical claims is that exposure to violent video games may erode players' capacity to feel empathy. Wonderly argues this from the perspective of David Hume's moral philosophy.[15] In contrast with earlier philosophers who tried to base morality on abstract moral precepts or on individual virtue, Hume understood morality as being rooted in natural identification with others' feelings. Empathy is an intersubjective faculty—our being with others allows us to feel their experiences and we are naturally averse to harming others because of our capacity to empathize with them. If video games destroy our understanding of others, then they will plausibly lead to harmful consequences when seen from a Humean perspective.

. . . Wonderly's Humean approach is primarily an empirical problem. It fits into the utilitarian critique as the erosion of empathy is, if it is real, one harm that can be weighed against violent games when calculating their consequences. The critical point in Wonderly's argument is establishing the link between a degradation of empathy and playing violent video games, but she provides surprisingly little evidence to support this. She only references a handful of studies and these are problematic.

For example, Wonderly's first source of support is a study conducted by Mathiak and Weber in which fMRI scans were taken of players' brains while playing violent video games.[16] During play the limbic orbitofrontal area of the brain is inactive. Wonderly considers this significant because it is this region that controls empathy. The study's usefulness is doubtful. There is a clear methodological failing in that it only involves thirteen players—far too few to make a reliable generalization. Aside from this, it jumps to the unwarranted conclusion that deactivating the same part of the brain that controls empathy during play will have a lasting effect on the brain, and that this will translate into changes in behavior. These problems are typical of many studies of desensitization. One study had subjects play either violent or nonviolent video games for twenty minutes then measured their heart rate and galvanic skin response to a ten minute video containing acts of violence.[17] Researchers concluded that violent video games do desensitize players because those exposed to violent games showed lower heart rates and galvanic skin responses. It assumes that desensitization can be measured by these two scales, that the reduction in them is a significant change to a person's outlook rather than a temporary effect, and, most significantly, the study purports to test the response to real violence, but the "real-life violence" is only a video. At best, the study reveals that violent video games induce temporary changes in subjects' physiological response to violence on television.

Wonderly also cites studies by David Grossman who claims that video games and other violent media are ways of conditioning people to accept violence. Grossman's conclusion that violent media lead to violent behavior is based on dubious empirical and theoretical foundations. His support is the increased rates of violent crimes in the United States, Western Europe, New Zealand, and Australia between 1957 and 1992. The data does indeed indicate a rise in violence over those years and might lend credence to Grossman's conclusions about violent media during that time; however, video games were hardly violent before 1992. Grossman's statistics for the United States are drawn from the FBI, which reports that there has been a dramatic *decrease* in violent crime and crime in general since 1992. In 2008 there were 454.5 violent crimes per 100,000 Americans, down from 757.5 in 1992. Overall crime went from 5,660.2 per 100,000 Americans to 3,667.[18] The numbers indicate a steady and almost uninterrupted downward trend starting around 1992. . . .

Although most studies do conclude that there is some connection between violent video games and actual violence, there are still many that reach the opposite conclusion or even that find that violent games alleviate feelings of hostility.[19] Durkin's argument that violent games decrease violence by providing a safe channel for aggression is particularly interesting as it coincides with Aristotle's thoughts on catharsis. Even many studies that do find some evidence of games increasing aggression show that this is largely dependent on existing aggressive dispositions and, therefore, that games may only aggravate behavior that has its roots elsewhere.[20] We can also find powerful evidence that there is no link between violent video games and real-life violence by looking at the effects of gaming outside the countries that gaming studies usually focus on. Japanese children are even more avid gamers than those in English speaking countries, yet studies of Japanese gamers find little evidence of behavioral changes. Sakamoto concludes that there may be some harmful effects, but that empirical research on Japanese gamers has not found any.[21]

. . .

Assessing Direct Causation

The strongest of the empirical theses—in the sense that it makes the most sweeping claim—is that video games actually lead players to perform violent actions. Proponents of this view argue that they not only give players the skills to carry out their destructive wishes or that they desensitize, but that merely playing a game or seeing it can drive one to reproduce the harmful acts represented in the game. If true, this would be the most worrying of the three hypotheses. It would not only mean that violent games have immense power to undermine social order, it would also be a threat to individual autonomy by compelling gamers to perform actions they would otherwise be averse to. Of the three hypotheses, this one has the least support. Much of the evidence supporting the thesis that games promote violent action is circumstantial—based on isolated cases that ignore contextual factors. Unlike the other two hypotheses, this one is very difficult to test as it is probably impossible to conduct ethical research on whether a given stimuli actually increases the likelihood of harming others. A prime example of this position comes from Peter Singer, who uses Eric Harris and Dylan Klebold as examples of the potential harm of video game violence. The two played *Doom* at "an impressionable age" and compared the shotgun they used in the shooting to the one in the game.[22] While he does acknowledge that this does not prove there is a causal relationship, the fact that he relies on this single case study to determine the effects of violent video games suggests that he thinks there is such a relationship. He also thinks that victims and their families seeking damages from criminals who play video games should use this reasoning as the basis for seeking compensation. Singer's argument is based on the premise that in the absence of compelling evidence for either side, we should assume that video games cause violence. Again, the empirical claim is problematic. The argument that video games inspired Harris and Klebold contradicts in-depth studies of the shooting.[23] The FBI investigation reveals that video games were not a cause of the Columbine shooting[24]; the criminologists and investigators working on the case are certainly in a much better position to understand it than Singer because of their access to information about the murderers.[25]

. . .

Comprehension Questions

1. In the selection you have, Schulzke defends violent games on utilitarian grounds. So what sorts of considerations *aren't* in play?
2. Schulzke spends a while talking about how much pleasure people get from playing violent games. Why?
3. How does Schulzke reply to the "violent games train killers" objection?
4. How does Schulzke reply to the "violent games destroy empathy" objection?
5. How does Schulzke reply to the "violent games lead to actual violence" objection?

Discussion Questions

1. Do you play violent video games? If so, then what effects, if any, do you think they have on you? (And if you don't play them, why not?)
2. Schulzke argues that violent games don't destroy empathy. However, it's widely known that the US military uses video games to train soldiers. Moreover, consider a report like this one:

> One blistering afternoon in Iraq, while fighting insurgents in the northern town of Mosul, Sgt. Sinque Swales opened fire with his .50-cal. That was only the second time, he says, that he ever shot an enemy. A human enemy. "It felt like I was in a big video game. It didn't even faze me, shooting back. It was just natural instinct. *Boom! Boom! Boom! Boom!*" remembers Swales, a fast-talking, deep-voiced, barrel-chested twenty-nine-year-old from Chesterfield, Virginia. He was a combat engineer in Iraq for nearly a year.[26]

3. Are reports like this a problem for Schulzke's argument? Why or why not?
4. In the selection you have, Schulzke defends violent games on utilitarian grounds. How might someone object to these games on nonutilitarian grounds?
5. Are there any costs or benefits of violent games that Schulzke overlooks? If so, what are they, and how do they affect his utilitarian calculations?

Case

In early 2016, NIL Entertainment released a game called *Survival Island 3—Australia Story 3D* on the App Store and Google Play. A Change.org petition got started not long after, which said this:

> *Survival Island 3—Australia Story 3D* . . . promotes violence towards Australia's Indigenous people by allowing and even encouraging the players to kill Indigenous Australians. The game shamelessly promotes the fact that you will "have to fight with aboriginals" and uses warning messages like, "Beware of Aborigines!" when Indigenous people appear on screen. The game portrays Indigenous Australians as violent and aggressive, as well as trying to promote the Indigenous characters as authentic representations of a diverse culture through the description phrasing, "Meet real aboriginals."
>
> Indigenous Australians face daily racism and discrimination. Indigenous Australians are over-policed and continue to die at the hands of the state. This app further perpetuates the denial of Indigenous Australians' humanity. It associates us with flora and fauna of the Australian landscape. By shooting "dangerous Aboriginals," this app makes us inhuman, it reinforces racial violence and lack of punishment for white people taking black lives; it makes fun and sport of massacres and Frontier violence. This App is another colonialist frontier and continues to exploit the deaths of many Aboriginal people without regard to the trauma that it instigates.
>
> The profiting of historical genocide and introducing these genocides as entertainment completely disregards the continual suffering of our people.[27]

There are plenty of problems with *Survival Island 3*. However, if Schulzke is right, what should we make of the claim that the game promotes *actual* violence? Could Schulzke be right about games generally, but wrong about this one? If so, why think that? Moreover, what should we make of the other charges against the game—for example, that it perpetuates the denial of Indigenous Australians' humanity?

Notes

1. Schulzke, M. (2009). "Moral Decision Making in Fallout." *Game Studies* 9 (2), http://gamestudies.org/0902/articles/schulzke, accessed November 1, 2009.
2. Reynolds, R. (2002). *Playing a "Good" Game: A Philosophical Approach to Understanding the Morality of Games.* Paper presented at the International Game Developers Association.
3. Ferguson, C. (2007). "Evidence for Publication Bias in Video Game Violence Effects Literature: A Meta-Analytic Review." *Aggression and Violent Behavior*

12 (1), 470–82; Ferguson, C. (2007)." The Good, the Bad and the Ugly: A Meta-Analytic Review of Positive and Negative Effects of Violent Video Games." *Ethics and Information Technology* 78 (4), 309–16.

4. Green, C. S., and Bavelier, D. (2007). "Action-Video-Game Experience Alters the Spatial Resolution of Vision." *Psychological Science* 18 (1), 88–94.

5. Jansz, J. (2006). "The Emotional Appeal of Violent Video Games for Adolescent Males." *Communication Theory* 15 (3), 219–41.

6. Martin, M. (2008). "Grand Theft Auto Series Has Sold 66 Million Units to Date." *Gamesindustry.biz.*

7. Rosser, J. C. J., Lynch, P. J., Cuddihy, L., Gentile, D. A., Klonsky, J., and Merrell, R. (2007). "The Impact of Video Games on Training Surgeons in the 21st Century." *Archives of Surgery* 142 (2), 181–186.

8. McCormick, M. (2001). "Is It Wrong to Play Violent Video Games?" *Ethics and Information Technology* 3 (4), 277–287.

9. Grossman, D., and DeGaetano, G. (1999). *Stop Teaching Our Kids to Kill: A Call to Action Against TV, Movie, and Video Game Violence.* New York: Crown.

10. Leonard, D. (2007). "Unsettling the Military Entertainment Complex: Video Games and a Pedagogy of Peace." *SIMILE: Studies in Media & Information Literacy Education* 4 (4), 1–8.

11. Galloway, A. (2004). "Social Realism in Gaming." *Game Studies* 4 (1).

12. See, e.g., Gibson, D. (2004). *Communication, Power, and Media.* New York: Nova Publishers.

13. Chalmers, P. (2009). *Inside the Mind of a Teen Killer.* Nashville: Thomas Nelson Inc.

14. Gibbs, N., and Roche, T. (1999). "The Columbine Tapes." *Time Magazine.* December 20.

15. Wonderly, M. (2007). "A Human Approach to Assessing the Moral Significance of Ultra-Violent Video Games. *Ethics and Information Technology* 10 (1), 1–10.

16. Mathiak, K., and Weber, R. (2006). "Toward Brain Correlates of Natural Behavior: fMRI During Violent Video Games." *Human Brain Mapping* 27 (12), 948–56.

17. Carnagey, N. L., Anderson, C. A., and Bushman, B. J. (2007). "The Effect of Violence on Physiological Desensitization to Real-Life Violence. *Journal of Experimental Social Psychology* 43 (4), 489–496.

18. Bureau of Justice Statistics. (2009). http://www.ojp.usdoj.gov/bjs/glance/tables/viortrdtab.htm, Accessed September 20, 2009.

19. Durkin, K., and Barber, B. (2002). "Not So Doomed: Computer Game Play and Positive Adolescent Development." *Journal of Applied Developmental Psychology* 23 (4), 373–92; Fleming, M. J., and Rick Wood, D. J. (2001). "Effects of Violent Versus Nonviolent Video Games on Children's Arousal, Aggressive Mood, and Positive Mood." *Journal of Applied Social Psychology* 31 (10), 2047–71.

20. Anderson, C. A., and Dill, K. E. (2000). "Video Games and Aggressive Thoughts, Feelings, and Behavior in the Laboratory and in Life. *Journal of Personality and Social Psychology* 78 (4), 772–790. Aristotle. (1999). *Nicomachean Ethics*. Upper Saddle River: Prentice Hall.

21. Sakamoto, A. (2000). "Video Games and Violence Controversy and Research in Japan." In C. V. F. U. Carlsson (Ed.), *Children and Media Violence Yearbook 2000: Children in the New Media Landscape*. Goteborg: UNESCO International Clearinghouse on Children and Violence on the Screen.

22. Singer, P. (2007). "Video Crime Peril vs. Virtual Pedophilia." *The Japan Times*.

23. Langman, P. (2009). *Why Kids Kill: Inside the Minds of School Shooters*. New York: Palgrave Macmillan.

24. Kutner, L., and Olson, C. (2008). *Grand Theft Childhood: The Surprising Truth about Violent Video Games and What Parents Can Do*. New York: Simon and Schuster.

25. Singer's claim draws attention to an important oversight in the studies critical of violent games: the cases that are relied on as examples of game-induced aggression are always given different explanations by law enforcement officials. This is true for Singer's use of the Columbine Shooting, Grossman's discussion of Michael Carneal, and Chalmers' example, Lee Boyd Malvo. In each of these cases video games were not found to be significant. Where there is disagreement, we should favor the explanations of investigators who have the training and access to information to form sound judgments.

26. http://www.washingtonpost.com/wp-dyn/content/article/2006/02/13/AR2006021302437.html

27. https://www.change.org/p/amazon-killing-indigenous-australians-is-not-a-game

43

—— 🐿 ——

The Gamer's Dilemma

An Analysis of the Arguments for the Moral Distinction Between Virtual Murder and Virtual Pedophilia

Morgan Luck

Murder is wrong, but virtual murder doesn't seem to be. That is, you shouldn't murder people in real life, but it seems to be OK to murder people in video games. But why? If it's because someone gets hurt in real life, and no one gets hurt in video games, then here's something to mull over. No one gets hurt in virtual pedophilia either—that is, no one is hurt by simulating child molestation in the context of a video game. (Dark, I know.) What should we say about this? Is there some crucial difference between virtual murder and virtual pedophilia? Or are they both wrong? Or are they both OK (even if one—or both—isn't your thing)? Here, Luck argues against the "there's a crucial difference option." On his view, we have to choose between saying that both are OK, or that neither is.

Luck, Morgan. 2009. "The Gamer's Dilemma: An Analysis of the Arguments for the Moral Distinction between Virtual Murder and Virtual Pedophilia." *Ethics and Information Technology* 11: 31–36. Copyright © 2008, Springer. Reprinted with permission.

Introduction

Is it immoral for a player to direct his character to murder another within a computer game? The standard response to this question is no. This is because no one is actually harmed as a result of a virtual harm. Such an outlook seems intuitive, and it explains why millions of gamers feel it is perfectly permissible to commit acts of virtual murder. Yet this argument can be easily adapted to demonstrate why virtual pedophilia might also be morally permissible, as no actual children are harmed in such cases. This result is confronting, as most people feel that virtual pedophilia is not morally permissible. The aim of this paper is to examine whether any good arguments can be produced to reconcile the intuition that virtual murder is morally permissible, with the intuition that virtual pedophilia is not.

Before we outline the arguments for the moral distinction between virtual murder and virtual pedophilia, let us be clear about what is meant by these terms. A player commits an act of virtual murder in those cases where he directs his character to kill another in circumstances such that, were the game environment actual, the actions of his character would constitute actual murder. . . .

Note that our focus is upon murder, rather than killing in general. The difference being that, while the act of killing a person may be morally permissible, murder is not. For example, consider the popular computer game *Battlefield 1942*, which simulates various World War II battles. Presumably a player directing his character, an Allied soldier, to kill an Axis soldier within the context of such a battle, is not committing an act of virtual murder. This is because, were the game environment actual, we would not, by most reasonable accounts, consider the soldier to be a murderer. Compare this case to one involving a game such as *Grand Theft Auto*, which simulates the antics of a car thief. In this game a player may direct her character to run over innocent pedestrians. Such an act does constitute virtual murder, since were the game environment actual, the player's character would be deemed a murderer.

A similar account of virtual pedophilia will also be adopted. A player commits an act of virtual pedophilia in those cases where she directs her character to molest another in circumstances such, were the game environment actual, her character would be deemed a pedophile. Again, for the sake of simplicity we shall concern ourselves only with cases where: The character that is virtually molested is controlled by the computer, rather than another player; the character that is molested clearly represents a child; the game player is an adult; and the game player's character clearly represents an adult. [. . . For] our purposes we shall focus on those computer games, such as *Grand Theft Auto*, where clear instances of virtual murder are apparent.

With the types of cases to which we are concerned introduced, we can now focus our attention upon a dilemma faced by game players who routinely commit acts of virtual murder. Unless such players can identify a morally relevant distinction between virtual murder and virtual pedophilia, they must either accept that committing virtual pedophilia is morally permissible, or that they themselves have often committed morally prohibited acts. This is hardly a dilemma for those game players who are willing to permit virtual pedophilia on the grounds that, like virtual murder, no one is actually harmed.[1] However, for those players who are not prepared to bite this bullet, only one option remains if they wish to continue playing such games in good conscience. They must present an argument for the moral distinction between the acts. Five such arguments will be critically examined in what follows.

Argument 1: Social Acceptability

I consider this first argument if only to quickly set it aside. While it is certainly true that committing virtual murder is, for the most part, socially acceptable, committing virtual pedophilia remains taboo. Some may hope to seize upon this distinction as morally relevant. However, although reference to social conventions may *explain* why it is that people are more comfortable with virtual murder than they are with virtual pedophilia, unless one is willing to reduce morals to conventions, it certainly does not provide a moral *justification* for this outlook. Such an argument would be akin to asserting that, by virtue of the fact slavery was socially acceptable within ancient Rome, it was also, at that time, moral. We shall continue on the assumption that morality is not relative in this sense.

Argument 2: Significant Likelihoods

This argument builds upon the common belief "that violent video games make it more likely, even if only by a small amount, that people will commit harmful acts against others."[2] Let us presume that there is evidence to suggest that people who indulge in virtual pedophilia are more likely to commit acts of actual pedophilia. Let us also presume that the likelihood that virtual murder will result in actual murder is significantly lower than the likelihood virtual pedophilia will result in actual pedophilia. If both such presumptions were true, then a broadly consequentialist argument may be mounted as to why virtual pedophilia, and not virtual murder, should be morally prohibited. The argument would run as follows. Any act which is significantly likely to result in harm is immoral.[3] Committing acts of virtual murder does not significantly raise the likelihood of committing actual murder, whereas committing acts of virtual pedophilia does significantly raise the likelihood of actual pedophilia. Therefore, it is immoral to commit virtual pedophilia, but not necessarily virtual murder.

Although the above argument is valid, whether or not the premises are true is less obvious. For not only must we have good reason to suppose that virtual pedophilia is significantly likely to result in actual pedophilia, we must also have good reason to suppose that virtual murder is not significantly likely to result in actual murder. However, Levy suggests that there is reason to suppose that the "arguments that virtual child pornography will harm actual children are . . . weak."[4] And of course there are numerous studies claiming violence in computer games leads to actual violence.[5] So unless we can find evidence to suggest the opposite, this argument will fail to get off the ground.[6]

Also, this argument allows for situations where *not* committing acts of virtual pedophilia might be immoral. For example, imagine a person who has overwhelming urges to commit pedophilia. She can satisfy these urges if she were to indulge in virtual pedophilia. However, if she does not, she will be driven to commit acts of actual pedophilia. In a similar vein, Levy argues that a strong case can be made for allowing virtual pedophilia, since it may "reduce the amount of harm to actual children, by providing an acceptable outlet for dangerous desires, and by encouraging pornographers to seek alternatives to real children."[7] . . . Consequently, in order for the gamer to utilize this argument, not only may they have to allow for instances where people have a moral obligation to commit acts of virtual pedophilia, but they must also present evidence as to why virtual murder is less likely to result in actual murder than virtual pedophilia is likely to result in actual pedophilia.

Argument 3: Enjoying the Competition, Rather Than the Kill

Rather than focusing on the harm virtual pedophilia may cause to *others*, perhaps a clear moral distinction between virtual pedophilia and virtual murder can be found if we focus upon the harm agents cause *themselves* by indulging in such acts. One might argue that, on those occasions where a player enjoys performing the act of virtual pedophilia, they harm themselves. For were you to enjoy virtual pedophilia, presumably you find something pleasurable about the notion of actual pedophilia. If this were the case, by fostering a pleasure for actual pedophilia you are harming yourself, on the grounds that such a trait injures your character. McCormick considers this argument as a natural extension of Aristotelian virtue ethics, stating that, according to this theory, by "participating in simulations of excessive, indulgent, and wrongful acts . . . you do harm to yourself in that you erode your virtue, and you distance yourself from your goal of eudaimonia."[8] And it is precisely due to this self-harm that virtual pedophilia should be determined as immoral. Putting aside the notion that individuals may have the right to harm themselves (at least to some degree), let us consider how it is that virtual murder might hope to escape this same argument.

When one pawn takes another in a game of chess, it represents one army defeating another. Presumably chess players do not derive much pleasure from this representation of killing. Rather they enjoy the game because of other factors, such as it satisfying their competitive nature. The same might be said for virtual murder within computer games. A player may enjoy a computer game because, for example, it satisfies her competitive nature, not because it allows her to commit acts of virtual murder *per se*. If this were true, then virtual murder may not result in the same type of self-harm as virtual pedophilia. This in turn may explain why virtual murder is usually considered morally permissible, while virtual pedophilia is not. Intuitively, it does seem likely that people who are interested in committing acts of virtual pedophilia do so because they believe there is something enjoyable about actual pedophilia. Also, it does seem likely that most players enjoy computer games for reasons other than their ability to allow them to commit virtual murder. However, according to this view, there is nothing intrinsically wrong with virtual pedophilia. To illustrate this point, imagine you are playing a computer game, the object of which is to steal the Crown Jewels from the Tower of London. One way to achieve this goal is to seduce and sleep with a Beefeater's daughter, who just so happens to be fifteen. A player who commits this act of virtual pedophilia may do so, not because he enjoys the notion of having sex with a child, but because he wishes to complete the game. Given the above argument, this instance of virtual pedophilia will be as permissible as a virtual murder.

One might attempt to counter this argument by suggesting that a player would not knowingly purchase a computer game that entailed virtual pedophilia, unless on some level she enjoyed the act. But, of course, the same argument can be put to the player who knowingly purchases a game entailing virtual murder. In addition, not all acts of virtual murder within computer games are intrinsic to the objectives of the game. For example, within the popular game *Grand Theft Auto*, players routinely go out of their way to drive over innocent pedestrians, despite the fact that doing so does not increase their chances of completing the game. Likewise, it is difficult to suggest that game players do not enjoy committing virtual murder to some extent, since there is a notable trend within computer games to make the act of killing more graphic. As McCormick points out,

> game makers have made some of these games more and more graphic in their portrayals of torture, assault, murder, and other acts of violence. Whereas shooting an opponent from a distance would have once resulted only in the collapse of his or her body, now the shot is accompanied by screams of pain, realistic writhing, blood, specific damage to a part of the body, flying body parts, and death.[9]

Admittedly, enjoying virtual murder may not be the primary aim of game players, but it would be naive to suggest that no enjoyment is derived from such acts. And to whatever extent it is enjoyed, according to this argument, it will be immoral.

Argument 4: Unfairly Singling Out a Group for Harm

This argument for the moral distinction between virtual murder and virtual pedophilia derives from the severity of acts they represent. Although it is clear that murder and pedophilia are both harmful acts, some might argue that pedophilia is far more so. This may not seem immediately apparent, for given that most parents hope to minimize the amount of harm that might befall their children, it is not clear that they would prefer their child to be murdered rather than molested. However, the person making this argument might call our attention to the fact that, while the acts of murder and pedophilia both result in a person being harmed, it is only the pedophile that unfairly singles out a particular group of people for harm. This, they may argue, is what makes pedophilia a far more harmful act overall.

This argument seems to have some merit. For although computer games which entail virtual murder may be socially acceptable, it is doubtful that a game involving, for example, only murdering Jews or homosexuals, would be tolerated. It seems therefore, that unfairly singling out a group for harm is, in itself, additionally harmful. Subsequently, since virtual pedophilia not only represents a harmful act, but also singles out children as the recipients of this harm, it could be seen as more harmful than virtual murder (since virtual murder does not necessarily single out any particular group). Therefore, if this difference in harm were significant, then we might conclude that this is why virtual murder is morally permissible, while virtual pedophilia is not.

Two points should be made in response to this argument. Firstly it does not seem immediately obvious that the act of randomly murdering a number of people is significantly less harmful than the act of molesting this same number of children. Secondly, this argument seems to suggest that if a computer game allowed players to molest people of all different age groups, including children, it would be morally permissible to play such a game. This is because, given that such a game does not single out a particular group of people to molest, it would be just as acceptable as a computer game which does not single out a particular group of people to murder.

Argument 5: The Special Status of Children

Some might argue that it is not the singling out of a group for harm which causes virtual pedophilia to be worse than virtual murder, *per se*, but the fact that virtual pedophilia involves harming children in particular. This argument builds upon the idea that children have a special status. This is because children possess properties such as innocence, defenselessness, etc. . . . which, *ceteris parabis*, make harming a child worse than harming an adult. The gamer might choose to draw upon the special status of children to suggest that, providing virtual murder does not entail virtual *child* murder, it will be less harmful than virtual pedophilia. And if this degree of harm is significant, then we have reason to suppose that virtual *adult* murder is morally permissible, while virtual pedophilia is not.

This argument has some force; for it seems plausible that children do indeed have a special status. However, we must take care not to exaggerate it. The important caveat to bear in mind is the *ceteris parabis* clause. If it is true that, *ceteris parabis*, harming a child is worse than harming an adult, then it is clearly the case that child murder will be more harmful than adult murder; and, likewise, child molestation will be more harmful that adult molestation. However, it does not follow that child molestation is more harmful than adult murder. This is because, within such a comparison, all things are not equal. In other words, murder is not equal to molestation. In order to resurrect this argument the gamer must abandon the *ceteris parabis* clause, and claim that harming a child is worse than harming an adult. Yet this seems far too strong. Do we really wish to suggest that stealing a child's lollipop is worse than torturing an adult? Consequently, unless there is strong evidence to suggest molestation is as harmful as murder, an appeal to the special status of children does not seem to deliver the right results for the gamer.

Deciding Which Virtual Bullet to Bite

None of the five arguments for the moral distinction between virtual murder and virtual pedophilia seem wholly convincing. In which case, barring the existence of further arguments for this distinction, players of such games are left with two options. Either they acknowledge that acts of virtual murder and virtual pedophilia are morally prohibited, or they acknowledge that both are morally permissible.

References

Aristotle. (1968). "The Poetics." In D. W. Lucus, ed., *Aristotle*. Oxford University Press, Oxford.

Brey, P. (1999). "The Ethics of Representation and Action in Virtual Reality." *Ethics and Information Technology* 1: 5–14.

Cisneros., D. (2002). "'Virtual Child' Pornography on the Internet: A 'Virtual' Victim?" *The Law and Technology Review* 19.

Elton, M. (2000). "Should Vegetarians Play Video Games?" *Philosophical Papers* 29 (1): 21–42.

Ferguson, C. J., S. Rueda, A. Cruz, D. Ferguson, S. Fritz, and S. Smith. (2008). "Violent Video Games and Aggression: Causal Relationship or Byproduct of Family Violence and Intrinsic Violence Motivation?" *Criminal Justice and Behavior* 35 (8), 311–32.

Levy., N. (2002). "Virtual Child Pornography: The Eroticization of Inequality." *Ethics and Information Technology* 4, 321.

McCormick, M. (2001). "Is It Wrong to Play Violent Video Games." *Ethics and Information Technology*, 3, 278.

Powers, T. M. (2003). Real Wrongs in Virtual Communities. *Ethics and Information Technology* 5, 191–98.

"Virtual Porn, Real Corruption." (2002). *The National Review*, May 3.

Walton, K. and Tanner, M. (1994). "Morals in Fiction and Fictional Morality." *Proceedings of the Aristotleian Society* 68 (Suppl Vol), 27–66.

Weigman and E. van Schie. (1998). "Video Game Playing and Its Relations with Aggressive and Prosocial Behavior." *British Journal of Social Psychology* 37, 367–78.

Williams, D. and M. Skoric. (2005). "Internet Fantasy Violence: A Test of Aggression in an Online Game." *Communication Monographs* 72, 217–33.

Worth, S. (2004). "Fictional Spaces." *Philosophical Forum* 4 (35), 439–55.

Comprehension Questions

1. What, exactly, does Luck mean by "virtual murder" and "virtual pedophilia"? What sort of actions *wouldn't* count, but kind of sound like they would?

2. When discussing the "social acceptability" argument, Luck draws a distinction between *explanation* and *justification*. What is he talking about? Why don't social conventions justify?

3. Luck brings up people who might *want* to engage in actual pedophilia, but who would be satisfied by engaging in virtual pedophilia. Why?

4. Luck considers the possibility that people who engage in virtual pedophilia might be harming themselves. In what sense, exactly, might they be doing this? Moreover, how, exactly, does Luck argue that people engaging in virtual pedophilia need *not* be harming themselves?

5. Why shouldn't we say that harming a child is always worse than harming an adult?

Discussion Questions

1. Do you think that virtual pedophilia is wrong? Why or why not? (And whatever you do, go beyond, "Yuck!")

2. Do you think that virtual *murder* is wrong? If so, why? (Remember: Something can be wrong without being the worst thing ever.)

3. Suppose that virtual pedophilia is wrong and that there's no way to distinguish it from virtual murder. Given this, what *else* might be wrong? (Think about other things in games—but don't limit yourself to them!)

4. Suppose that virtual pedophilia is wrong. If so, could we justify banning games that involved it? Why or why not?

Case

Consider this story from CNN, which was published in 2010:

> The game begins with a teenage girl on a subway platform. She notices you are looking at her and asks, "Can I help you with something?" That is when you, the player, can choose your method of assault. With the click of your mouse, you can grope her and lift her skirt. Then you can follow her aboard the train, assaulting her sister and her mother. As you continue to play, "friends" join in and in a series of graphic, interactive scenes, you can corner the women, raping them again and again. The game allows you to even impregnate a girl and urge her to have an abortion. The reason behind your assault, explains the game, is that the teenage girl has accused you of molesting her on the train. The motive is revenge.
>
> It is little wonder that the game, titled RapeLay, sparked international outrage from women's groups. Taina Bien-Aime helped yank the game off store shelves worldwide. "This was a game that had absolutely no place on the market," said Taina Bien-Aime of women's rights organization Equality Now which has campaigned for the game to be taken off the shelves. But the controversy that led to stopping sales of the game instead took it viral. . . . It is still readily available on dozens of Web sites, sometimes for free.[10]

How should we think about games like this? Should we accept that, since virtual murder is OK, this is too? Or should we condemn both? Whether or not the game is morally defensible, should we try to regulate developers, preventing them from releasing such games? Why or why not?

Notes

1. Such intuitions were shared by the U.S Supreme Justices, who in 2002 overturned a ban on virtual child pornography on the basis that such material was protected by the First Amendment since it "records no crime and creates no victims by its production." See "Virtual Porn, Real Corruption," *The National Review*, May 3, 2002.
2. M. McCormick, "Is It Wrong to Play Violent Video Games?" *Ethics and Information Technology*, 3: 278, 2001.
3. Of course the usual caveats would have to be added to this premise. For example, the act would have to be avoidable, and were it not performed something worse would not occur.
4. N. Levy, "Virtual Child Pornography: The Eroticization of Inequality," *Ethics and Information Technology*, 4: 321, 2002.

5. C. J. Ferguson, S. Rueda, A. Cruz, D. Ferguson, S. Fritz and S. Smith, "Violent Video Games and Aggression: Causal Relationship or Byproduct of Family Violence and Intrinsic Violence Motivation?," *Criminal Justice and Behaviour*, 35(3): 311–332, 2008; O. Weigman and E. van Schie, "Video Game Playing and Its Relations with Aggressive and Prosocial Behavior," *British Journal of Social Psychology*, 37: 367–378, 1998; D. Williams and M. Skoric, "Internet Fantasy Violence: A Test of Aggression in an Online Game," *Communication Monographs*, 72: 217–233, 2005.

6. This is not to suggest such evidence might not be forthcoming.

7. Levy, p. 321.

8. McCormick, p. 285.

9. McCormick, p. 277.

10. http://www.cnn.com/2010/WORLD/asiapcf/03/30/japan.video.game.rape/

44

The Ethics of Singing Along
The Case of "Mind of a Lunatic"
Aaron Smuts

People like to sing along to songs. Sometimes, though, Smuts thinks that we sing along in a worrisome way. In these cases, we're listening to a song that describes something twisted, we imagine ourselves doing that very thing, and we enjoy it. In other words, we take pleasure in mentally acting out something evil. But Smuts argues that it's wrong to enjoy evil, whether in the imagination or not. So, it's wrong to sing along with songs that way. He defends this view by examining the controversial "Mind of a Lunatic" (1990) by Geto Boys.

I. Introduction

In 1990, a Houston-based rap group called Geto Boys released their third album, *The Geto Boys*, bearing one of the recently introduced parental advisory stickers along with a disclaimer from the record label: "Def American Recordings is opposed to censorship. Our manufacturer and distributor, however, do not condone or endorse the content of this

Smuts, Aaron. 2013. "The Ethics of Singing Along: The Case of 'Mind of a Lunatic'." *The Journal of Aesthetics and Art Criticism* 121–129. Reprinted with permission of John Wiley & Sons.

recording, which they find violent, sexist, racist, and indecent." The album was clearly designed to arouse controversy; critics took the bait. The album went gold. Within a year, it was blamed for at least one death.[1] Two songs on the album, "Mind of a Lunatic" and "Assassins," feature narratives of hideously immoral action—rape, necrophilia, murder, and kidnapping—as well as exaggerated, comically overblown nastiness—stealing from the poor, beating of the blind, and the killing of an innocent grandmother.

Throughout the album, the members of the group—Bushwick Bill, Scarface, and Willie D—tell stories of their evil misadventures. The violence in "Mind of a Lunatic" approaches that of a slasher movie. In the first verse, Bushwick Bill makes explicit reference to the genre. Later in the song, Willie D says that he will leave the listeners with worse nightmares than Freddie Kruger. Midway through, Scarface describes himself as sitting in a candlelit room "Dreaming of the people I've dismantled."[2] What are we to make of this?

Although I think there are reasons to worry about the Geto Boys, on a plausible interpretation their music is not nearly as morally bad as it first appears. Their songs are filled with the typical bravado of the genre amplified by slasher/gore. What could be tougher, more dangerous, and all-around bad than a lunatic-serial-killer-rapist-maniac! I will take a closer look at "Mind of a Lunatic," but my concern is not so much with the morality of the song as with the morality of listening to it.

I am not entirely sure what the prescribed mode of listening might be, but I am sure that a common mode is problematic. Often audiences do not simply listen to popular songs; they sing along. This encourages a curious mode of engagement that is far different from the way people typically approach other kinds of narrative artworks, such as film, theater, and literature. Most important, this mode of engagement is sometimes morally problematic. It is problematic when it involves the enjoyment of evil, more particularly, the enjoyment of imaginatively doing evil. This is morally problematic because it is bad to take pleasure in imagined suffering. And it is even worse to take pleasure in thoughts of doing evil.

II. Listening to "Mind of a Lunatic"

"Mind of a Lunatic" is designed to shock. It features extreme violence, including a brutal rape narrative in the first segment. The song opens with these words: "The sight of blood excites me; shoot you in the head sit down, and watch you bleed to death."[3] The speaker is Bushwick Bill. He is clearly not a very nice guy. Things get much worse. In the second verse, he describes watching a woman through a window. He decides to brutally rape and kill her. As the song progresses, we learn that not only is Bushwick a murdering rapist, he is something straight out of a horror movie. He has sex with the corpse of his victim and writes his name on the wall in blood. On the charts of evil, this is hard to top.

The remainder of the song describes several other violent episodes. Each is recounted in the first person by the various members of the group. They maintain their personas throughout. But when Scarface tells us how he killed the grandmother of his strung-out girlfriend, we learn that "she was screamin' out, 'Brad!' "—Scarface's first name, not his stage name.[4] The song does not merely attribute the violence to the stage-name persona, but to the actual person—Brad Jordan. Similarly, after giving his actual birth date, Willie D closes the song, saying that the events are not fictional. We are dealing with a strange form of slasher fiction. The characters in *Halloween* (John Carpenter, 1978) do not refer to Michael Myers as Tony Moran, the actor playing the adult killer. Nor do we learn that Myers was born on the same day as the actor. The Geto Boys are different. Apparently, they want to be thought of as monsters.

It would be easy to denounce the song as the product of a group of, well, lunatics. Who else would tell stories like this about themselves? On first blush, the music looks like immoral garbage. Maybe the distributor was right. Perhaps they should not have sold the album. But this is too quick, too simple. Although it is plausible that the song might be morally problematic, it depends on how it should be interpreted. And this is not so clear.

"Mind of a Lunatic" is more complex than it might at first appear. I doubt that the Geto Boys intend to endorse, much less encourage, rape, mass murder, and all manner of exaggerated violence. It is inconceivable that they would adopt this as their goal. They are not monsters. Nihilists of this sort could never have produced three albums together! They are not here to promote evil. No, their goals appear to be more innocuous: "Mind of a Lunatic" is part slasher fiction, part persona-boasting, part shock-the-bourgeoisie, and part comment on how white America sees young black men. It implicitly says: So you think we are bad; you could not even imagine just how bad we are.

At times, the song borders on a parody of how white America sees black men. A distinctly white-sounding voice repeats: "That guy is crazy."[5]

Accordingly, one might think that the song is a politically motivated parody. Although it would be nice if we could see it as an extended parody, this is unlikely. The Geto Boys appear to have simply taken certain elements of the genre to their logical extension. The songs are seldom funny. And there is little overt irony. This is not pure parody.

Parody or not, the song clearly uses a horror narrative to develop the personas of the band members. As is common in the genre, the members attempt to play up their putative authenticity. But the fact that Scarface uses his given name does not mean that he has left his persona behind. Scarface (Brad Jordan) is a persona. The song is reputation-building, big talk, of an unprecedented sort. Properly considered, the song does not condone, at least not in any obvious way, rape and murder. Hence, it is not nearly as bad as it first appears.

But my purpose here is not interpretation. Instead, I am principally interested in how people listen to the song. The morality of the song and the morality of listening might diverge. Regardless of how we should interpret a song, not everyone will respond in the intended way. This is not a phenomenon unique to music. Just think of the cult of gangster worship around *Scarface* (Brian De Palma, 1983). My Italian cobbler in Park Slope, Brooklyn, had a small shrine to the movie in 2010! Nearly three decades after the movie was released, gangster-worshiping kids across the country could be seen wearing T-shirts covered with dollar signs featuring Pacino in the final scene holding his "little friend." The lessons have been incorporated into numerous hip-hop songs. Apparently, the most important lesson is the first: "Lesson 1. Don't get high off your own supply."[6] Although the film tells a Cinderella story, it does not idolize the gangsters. Rather, it is a movie about an incestuously jealous drug smuggler who shows a few Greek virtues (and even more vices). This gangster worship is morally problematic. It is equally unexpected. Surely it was not De Palma's intention to develop a subcultural icon.

Regardless, with "Mind of a Lunatic" we do not need to look for aberrant modes of reception. Instead, a common form of listening to the song is morally problematic. Although film and theater audiences may occasionally recite the lines of campy midnight productions, it is common for people to sing along with songs. In the case of "Mind of a Lunatic," the song gives the listener the words to be as bad as the persona, to eloquently express anger and pronounce on their own fierceness with style. The problem is that, unlike merely acting out a part on the stage, this kind of listening encourages a mode of engagement where audiences visualize the content they describe from the first person.

My claim might sound implausible, but it has phenomenological support. This mode of engagement is unlike reading a novel written in the first person. Listeners are not just hearing someone else's thoughts; rather, they assume the persona of the speaker. Singing along is closer to portraying a part onstage, but subtly different. Perhaps it is akin to channeling a demon, at least when the words are those of the Geto Boys. When people engage with songs in this manner, they tend to visualize acting out the content as they talk themselves through the narrative. As a result, the song encourages listeners to imagine doing evil. Moreover, it provides an occasion for listeners to enjoy imaginatively doing evil. To be clear, I do not think that this is the only mode of listening to music in this genre. But it is common. Call it the "angry teenager mode." It is far from unusual and it is morally problematic.

At this point, one may balk. One might be willing to grant the empirical claim that this mode of listening is common, but deny my conclusion. It is not as if the Geto Boys really killed any grandmothers. And it is not as if by reciting the lyrics audience members thereby rape and murder.[7] No one is harmed. No harm, no foul. In the following section, I address this worry. I defend the claim that it is bad to enjoy evil, regardless of whether or not it is merely fictional.

III. Enjoying the Bad

[. . . Someone might think that morality concerns how we think about, feel about (i.e. emotionally respond to), and treat (in action) real things.] According to this claim, merely fictional objects are outside the scope of morality. Although this is prima facie plausible, I think it is wrong. There are compelling reasons to reject this. . . claim. I turn now to show why.

If it is bad to delight in fictional suffering, most likely it will have to be bad to delight in actual suffering. I simply cannot see how it could be bad to take pleasure in fictional suffering otherwise. So this is where I begin. Obviously, it is not a great idea to spend a lot of time taking pleasure in the suffering of others. It requires a rotten character to enjoy suffering in the first place, but it is bound to make a person worse. The habitual enjoyment of evil is likely character destroying. One might even be led to do evil as a result of the corruption. It is plausible that taking pleasure in suffering can be instrumentally bad. But since this is largely an empirical question, I will say nothing more about it here.

My concern here is not with whether our engagement with artworks can be corrupting, nor am I concerned with whether our reactions to fiction can reflect poorly on our characters, for surely they can. Instead, what I want to know is whether it is intrinsically bad to enjoy evil. G. E. Moore thinks so. He argues that there are three principal kinds of evil: (1) enjoying or admiringly contemplating things that are themselves evil, (2) hatred of the good, and (3) pain.[8] We do not have to accept Moore's entire axiology to agree that it is intrinsically bad to enjoy evil. We merely need to consider a few cases to see that Moore is right, at least in this regard.

Imagine slipping on a banana peel at the local supermarket. You spin to brace your fall, but on the way down the corner of your mouth catches on the sharp lip of a shelf. It rips your mouth wide open. Through the gaping flesh of your torn cheek, most of your teeth are visible. You scream in agony. The blood fills your mouth, pours down your face, and pools on the floor. The paramedics arrive quickly. As they tend to your wound, a crowd gathers. Some softly snicker; others just watch. Unbeknownst to you, most of the crowd quietly admires the scene, taking pleasure in your sobs of pain and the sight of the red oozing out of your wound. As with Bushwick Bill, the sight of blood excites them.

This is certainly a scary crowd. We worry that they might be flesh-eating zombies or, worse, psychopaths. But this is not the only source of unease. Even if you did not notice the snickering, even if you falsely believed that the crowd was thoughtfully concerned, their pleasurable reactions would be morally bad. They should feel guilty or, at least, ashamed for having such reactions. We would frown on them for feeling this way. Most plausibly, the crowd is worthy of disesteem.

[. . . Likewise,] consider Moore's thought experiment. To see the badness of enjoying cruelty, he asks us to imagine a world of people solely occupied with cruel thoughts:

> If we then consider what judgment we should pass upon a universe which consisted *solely* of minds thus occupied [with thoughts of cruelty], without the smallest hope that there would ever exist in it the smallest consciousness of any object other than those proper to these passions, or any feeling directed to any such object, I think that we cannot avoid the conclusion that the existence of such a universe would be a far worse evil than the existence of none at all.[9]

Although it is difficult to imagine a universe composed only of minds occupied with cruel thoughts, it is even more difficult to imagine a good reason to think that such a universe would be better than an empty one.

Just as it seems clear that a universe occupied only by a single suffering creature is worse than an empty universe, it likewise seems bad if the universe were occupied solely by someone thinking cruel thoughts. This suggests that enjoying the bad is intrinsically bad. It is not bad merely for what it leads to. No, it is bad in itself.

[Finally,] consider a third scenario: imagine two worlds, each having just one inhabitant, say a sole survivor of a nuclear holocaust.[10] In world A, the survivor spends her free time thinking nice thoughts. She often imagines cats playing with rubber bands on sunny windowsills. In world B, the survivor lives a similar life, but rather than imagine cats, he has the fantasy life of Bushwick Bill: He spends his afternoons imagining torturing children with a pair of pliers and a blowtorch. Is either world preferable?

The cat fancier in world A is a bit precious, but she is not hideously repulsive. In contrast, the survivor in B is repugnant. I doubt that the repulsion stems from worries about the consequences of his fantasizing. Yes, compulsive fantasies of child torture are probably indicative of inclinations that we would rather not see realized. But we can put this aside. We do not have to live in either world. We are merely asked to decide which one is better. If we were given a choice to bring one or the other into existence, we should choose A. Most plausibly world B is worse. Not because we worry that a child might be tortured, or that we might be injured by this freak, but because the child-torturing fantasist enjoys evil. That is bad enough.

Once again, this scenario suggests that it is intrinsically bad to enjoy evil. In fact, the universe of cruel thought and the two worlds examples give us reason to think that enjoying merely imagined evil is bad. Plausibly, engaging with fiction is a kind of guided imagination. Hence, it appears that. . . we found a reason to believe [in the intrinsic badness of] enjoying fictional evil. And the events portrayed in "Mind of a Lunatic" are no less evil than those envisioned by the child-torturing fantasist.

IV. Fiction and Autonomous Fantasy

One might argue that there is an important difference between the kind of imagining found in the previous scenarios and that involved in engaging with fictional works. For instance, in the third case above, we might think that the child-torturing fantasist takes pleasure in what Christopher Cherry calls a "surrogate fantasy."[11] Surrogate fantasies are those that the fantasist would like to take place. They are surrogates for reality. The survivor in world B likely wishes there were children around to torture. But not all fantasies are like this. Some fantasies are "autonomous."

Cherry argues that autonomous fantasies are unlike surrogate fantasies in that the fantasist does not desire the fantasy to be actualized. For instance, as Thomas Hurka notes, it is perfectly conceivable that someone could enjoy rape fantasies, but not want to rape. Nor would he want to witness a rape. He would be horrified by the violence. But he is not horrified by merely imagined violence. On Cherry's taxonomy, his fantasies are autonomous, not surrogate. Autonomous fantasies appear to be far less morally problematic; perhaps they are morally innocuous.

[. . . However, even if first-person listening is autonomous fantasizing, this doesn't show that there is nothing wrong with singing along to "Mind of a Lunatic."] Earlier I offered a compelling account of the badness of enjoying imagined suffering, whether surrogate or autonomous. It is intrinsically bad to enjoy evil. The universe of cruel thought and the two worlds examples show as much. The implications for fiction do not require much elaboration.

[. . . More importantly] listening to songs is often different. While listening to songs, people commonly vocalize. They sing or talk out the lyrics. The words sometimes become their own. In the process, listeners often assume the singer-persona. When this happens, it is not clear if they should be called "listeners," as this is not the principal mode of engagement. Instead, they are more like role-players . . . [And when] the actions portrayed are evil, listeners imagine doing evil. And they often enjoy it. Hence, while listening to songs, sometimes listeners take pleasure in imaginatively doing evil. This is bad. Although I do not know if the angry teenager mode is a form of autonomous or surrogate fantasy, it is morally problematic either way. It is bad to enjoy evil thoughts. And it is likely worse to enjoy thoughts of doing evil.

Comprehension Questions

1. Why does Smuts think that "Mind of a Lunatic" isn't nearly as bad as it first appears to be?
2. What is the "angry teenager mode" of listening?
3. What's the point of the (very disturbing) banana peel example?
4. What's the difference between autonomous and surrogate fantasies?
5. Why, exactly, does Smuts think that some people enjoy evil when listening to "Mind of a Lunatic"?

Discussion Questions

1. "Mind of a Lunatic" was a popular song when it came out. How do you explain its popularity? Why do you think people are attracted to songs that have such dark content?
2. What songs might be thought of as today's "Mind of a Lunatic"?
3. If someone *actually did* the things described in "Mind of a Lunatic," we would probably be disturbed by people who really enjoyed hearing all the gory details. (Imagine someone saying, of an actual rape, "Tell me more! I really want to be able to picture what happened.") Why do you think we'd have that reaction? If these people aren't interested in committing violent acts themselves, then we do we care about what they enjoy hearing?
4. Smuts says that it's wrong to listen to "Mind of a Lunatic" in "angry teenager mode." What other modes of listening are there? (Don't worry about names—just think through the possibilities.)

Case

Consider some of the lyrics from Robin Thicke's "Blurred Lines," which debuted in 2013:

> I know you want it
> You're a good girl
> Can't let it get past me
> You're far from plastic
> Talk about getting blasted
> I hate these blurred lines
> I know you want it
> But you're a good girl
> The way you grab me
> Must wanna get nasty
>> Go ahead, get at me

These lyrics—combined with a video that was often described as "rapey"—led to ample criticism and the song's being banned at several British universities. Of course, lots of pop songs have questionable sexual content; Thicke's certainly isn't the first. But "Blurred Lines" does highlight themes in contemporary music that some people associate with rape culture. How should we think about these sorts of songs in light of Smuts's argument?

Notes

1. R. A. Dyer and Rick Mitchell, "Geto Boys' Music Blamed in a Slaying in Dodge City," *Houston Chronicle*, July 23, 1991.
2. Geto Boys, "Mind of a Lunatic," on *Grip it! On That Other Level* (1990, Rap-A-Lot Records).
3. Geto Boys, "Mind of a Lunatic."
4. Geto Boys, "Mind of a Lunatic."
5. Geto Boys, "Mind of a Lunatic."
6. The Geto Boys sample from the movie extensively throughout the album. Scarface takes his stage name from the movie.
7. Except for, perhaps, Christopher Martinez, who claimed to have been hypnotized by "Mind of a Lunatic" when he killed Bruce Romans in 1991. See Dyer and Mitchell, "Geto Boys' Music Blamed in a Slaying in Dodge City," p. 25.
8. G. E. Moore, *Principia Ethica* (New York: Dover, 2004), pp. 207–214, sections 124–128.
9. Moore, *Principia Ethica*, p. 209, section 125.
10. I assume that fantasy is a species of imagining and use the terms interchangeably.
11. Cherry, "When Is Fantasizing Morally Bad?" p. 113, later uses the label "idle fantasy" to refer to autonomous fantasy.

45

The Negative Ethics of Humor

John Morreall

....

Can it ever be wrong to tell a joke? If so, when? Are there *kinds* of jokes that you just shouldn't tell? If so, which ones? Morreall argues that, if we want to answer these questions, we shouldn't focus on whether the joke happens to trade on a stereotype. Instead, he takes the primary problem with some humor to be that it involves *disengaging* from things with which we ought to be engaged. Sometimes, this takes the form of *irresponsible* humor; we use it to deflect attention from serious issues. In other cases, humor *blocks compassion*, leading us not to empathize when we really should. Finally, humor can *promote prejudice*, discouraging us from respecting the differences between individuals.

....

I will be discussing racist and sexist jokes. . . . as part of a general ethics of humor. And in these moral reflections, I want to pay attention to the special psychological and linguistic features of humor. . . . The central feature here is the playful disengagement of non-bona-fide language and actions.

This non-practical, non-cognitive orientation is something humor shares with play in general and with aesthetic experience. In all three,

Morreall, John. 2009. "The Negative Ethics of Humor." In *Comic Relief: A Comprehensive Philosophy of Humor.* Malden, MA: Blackwell. Reprinted with permission of John Wiley & Sons.

we are for the moment not concerned with gaining knowledge or achieving practical gain.[1] We are disengaged, idle, "distanced." While joking with friends, for example, nothing is urgent, no action is called for. We are not attending to anyone's needs, but are like art lovers strolling through a gallery or music lovers listening to a concert. That is why Ludovici spoke of the "indolence of humor"[2] and Hobbes said, "They that are intent on great designs have not time to laugh."[3]

The practical disengagement of humor . . . helps explain the opposition between amusement and negative emotions. To have practical concern about a situation is to be emotionally involved with it. A situation that does not meet with our approval naturally elicits fear, anger, or hatred, if we are focused on ourselves; and compassion, if someone else is suffering the setback. As Henri Bergson said, "Laughter is incompatible with emotion. Depict some fault, however trifling, in such a way as to arouse sympathy, fear, or pity; the mischief is done, it is impossible for us to laugh."[4]

When we want to evoke anger or outrage about some problem, we don't present it in a humorous way, precisely because of the practical disengagement of humor. Satire is not a weapon of revolutionaries.

Humor involves cognitive as well as practical disengagement. While something is making us laugh, we are for the moment not concerned with whether it is real or fictional. As we have said, the creator of humor puts ideas into our heads not to communicate information, but for the delight those ideas will bring. And so we grant comic license to people telling funny anecdotes, letting them exaggerate the absurdity of real situations, and create extra details. Indeed, someone listening to a funny story who tried to correct the teller—"No, she didn't spill her drink on the mayor *and* the governor, just on the mayor"—will probably be hushed up by the other listeners.

As in play and in aesthetic experience, the practical and cognitive disengagement in humor can have harmful effects. I will focus on three. First, the disengagement can be irresponsible, as we neglect actions that are called for, and do things that should not be done. Secondly, it can block compassion. And thirdly, it can promote prejudice.

First Harmful Effect: Irresponsibility

Humor can disengage us from what we are doing or failing to do. To follow the parallel with play and aesthetic experience, there is nothing intrinsically wrong with playing music, but when Nero played as Rome burned, that was objectionable. There is nothing intrinsically wrong with creating *bons mots*. But when Marie Antoinette responded to reports of famine by saying "Let them eat cake," that was objectionable because, as queen, she was supposed to care about her people.

In our daily lives, we sometimes "laugh off" a problem or criticism instead of taking appropriate action. If my doctor puts me on a special diabetic diet, warning me of blindness or early death if I don't follow it, then I may discount her advice with a quip like "She's fatter than I am" and ignore the diet. Or if my friend needs my help in controlling his alcoholism, and the next time he gets drunk I laugh at his antics instead of helping him restore self-discipline, then my humor is also irresponsible. In Stanley Milgram's famous experiments with obedience to authority figures, where subjects were ordered to give potentially fatal electric shocks to people simply for not remembering word associations, 14 of 40 subjects burst out laughing and then administered the shock.[5] Here laughter seems like whistling in the dark, a way to suppress legitimate concern. In laughing off some problem, we treat it as trivial. It is unimportant, "no big deal," and thus doesn't call for our attention. An extreme case of humor supporting irresponsibility is the "total cynic" who laughs at everything and assumes no responsibility for anything. The MTV program *Beavis and Butt-Head* is based on such characters.

This disengagement fostered by humor is often deliberately used by politicians to deflect criticism. During their famous debates, as Abraham Lincoln began waffling on an important issue, Stephen Douglas accused him of being "two-faced." Lincoln responded, "Ladies and gentlemen, I leave it to you. If I had two faces, would I be wearing this one?" When John Kennedy was criticized for using his father's massive wealth to finance his bid for the presidency, he staged an event at a fund-raising dinner. Pretending to open a telegram, Kennedy said, "I have just received a telegram from my generous daddy: 'Dear Jack, Don't spend a dollar more than is necessary. I'll be damned if I'll pay for a landslide.'" In his first televised debate with Walter Mondale before the 1984 election, incumbent Ronald Reagan sounded uninformed and confused. Critics said that as the oldest presidential candidate in history, he was simply not up to the job. For the next TV debate, therefore, Reagan's handlers prepared a funny line for him to memorize. As soon as a reporter asked about the "age issue," Reagan said, "I am not going to make age an issue in this campaign. I am not going to exploit for political gain my opponent's youth and inexperience." The audience laughed, the age issue evaporated, and Reagan went on to win by one of the greatest margins in history.

He was probably in the early stages of Alzheimer's disease, as we now know, but this joke made it impossible for anyone to bring up such a possibility.

Second Harmful Effect: Blocking Compassion

Another way the disengagement in humor can cause harm is by blocking compassion for those who need help. In such cases, humor can harm in two ways—by displacing action, and by insulting those who are suffering, thus increasing their suffering. Suppose that I am walking along an icy sidewalk and see someone awkwardly slip and fall into a puddle, breaking his wrist. If I stand back and laugh, then not only have I not helped him, but my treating his accident as mere material for my amusement has demeaned him, belittled him, made him feel that he doesn't matter. From the way I am laughing, it seems that his suffering is no more important than the pain of Wile E. Coyote in Roadrunner cartoons. As Peter Jones put it, "The victim of laughter is confronted by the reaction of a mere spectator."[6]

In cases of mild suffering, we call such humor insensitive or callous; in more serious cases we call it cruel. Consider the cover of the July 1974 "Dessert Issue" of *National Lampoon* magazine. In 1971 George Harrison and others had done a charity concert to benefit victims of a famine in Bangladesh. That was made into the record album *Concert for Bangladesh*, whose cover was a photograph of a starving child. The cover of *National Lampoon's* "Dessert Issue" looked almost identical to that photograph, only it was of a *chocolate sculpture* of a starving child, with part of the head bitten off.

A good deal of humor in past centuries was similarly cruel. Laughing at dwarves and people with deformities, and at the mentally retarded and the insane, was common. In ancient Roman slave markets, deformed and idiotic children often brought high prices because buyers found them amusing. Cruelty also grew into sadism, as people caused the suffering that they enjoyed. The Roman emperor Trajan celebrated a military victory in 106 CE by having five thousand pairs of gladiators fight to the death. In fifteenth-century Paris, burning cats was a form of home entertainment. Before the French Revolution, members of the nobility would visit insane asylums to taunt the inmates, by clanking their canes across the bars, for example. In Britain, bear-baiting was popular until the nineteenth century. For a special royal festival attended by Elizabeth I in 1575, thirteen chained bears were torn to death by dogs. Idi Amin is said to have cut off the limbs of one of his wives and sewn them onto the opposite sides of her body, for his own amusement. A more recent example of sadistic humor is the humiliation of prisoners by Americans in Abu Ghraib prison in Iraq. When asked why they made the men pile on top of one another naked, soldiers said that it was a joke, "just for fun."

Even when such fun does not involve the suffering of someone present, so that it does not directly humiliate people and increase their suffering, humor can promote insensitivity, callousness, or cruelty toward those being laughed about. The *National Lampoon* cover was probably not seen by starving children in Bangladesh or their parents, but still, it tended to inure readers of the magazine to their suffering, the suffering of other famine victims, and, generally, human beings needing help. . . .

Perhaps the most widely accepted moral rule is to not cause unnecessary suffering. From that it follows that we should not laugh at someone's problem when compassion is called for.

Third Harmful Effect: Promoting Prejudice

The two harmful effects of humor we have seen so far—blocking action and blocking compassion—are based on the way humor disengages us *practically* from what we are laughing about. A third harmful effect is based on the way it disengages us *cognitively* from the object of amusement. Here we will finally get to what is wrong with racist and sexist jokes. . . .

. . . [S]exist and racist jokes, like jokes in general, are known to be fictional by tellers and audience alike. We often introduce jokes with play signals such as, "Have you heard the one about . . .?" and we use the present instead of the past tense to indicate that what we are saying is not a report of a real event.

Adding to this unreality, what characters in jokes say and do is unlike what real people say and do. When these characters are stupid, lazy, or sexually promiscuous, the degree of those shortcomings is usually exaggerated far beyond what they are in any real human being. In the Polish astronaut joke, the man's belief that flying to the sun at night would keep him cool isn't just stupid, but more stupid than any real person's beliefs. This fantastic exaggeration found in so much humor is ignored by virtually all ethicists writing about ethnic jokes, who treat those jokes as if they were assertions that Poles are stupid, black people are lazy, etc.

Such bald assertions, however, are not funny and are easy to falsify. When people are communicating information, listeners often think that what a speaker is saying or implying is false, and so they question or contradict that person. But we don't question or contradict joke tellers. No one hearing the joke above would say, "There *are* no Polish astronauts," or "Most Poles *are not* stupid." Neither those telling this joke nor their listeners are committed to a belief in the existence of Polish astronauts, or to a belief that Poles in general are stupid.

Indeed, we could enjoy this joke even though we had no beliefs at all about Poles. The first time I heard a version of this joke, at a humor conference in the Netherlands, it was told about a *Frisian* astronaut. I had no idea who Frisians were, but I still enjoyed the picture of the astronaut saying that traveling at night would solve the problem of the sun's heat. The next day when I learned that the Frisians are an ethnic group living in the northern part of the Netherlands, I still did not *believe* that Frisians are stupid, any more than I *believe* that Poles are stupid when I laugh at Polish jokes.

The stupidity of the character in this joke, I suggest, is not a piece of information being communicated, but a fantastic idea being presented for playful enjoyment. What most people enjoy in hearing this joke is not a belief that they are superior to Poles or Frisians, but the mental gymnastics they go through in making sense of the line "I'll go at night"—all the while knowing that no real person would say such a thing in earnest. Whatever might be objectionable about telling standard sexist and racist jokes, then, it is not that they *assert* or *imply* that certain groups of people have preposterous degrees of stupidity, sexual promiscuity, etc. But that does not let the tellers of such jokes off the moral hook, for there are other ways to promote prejudice. Those who circulate racist and sexist jokes do it, I suggest, not by making truth-claims but by being *indifferent* to the truth. They are disengaged cognitively and practically from the stereotypes in what they are saying, and they don't care about the harm that circulating those stereotypes may cause.

What usually makes these jokes harmful is that they present characters with exaggerated degrees of undesirable traits who represent groups that some people believe actually have those traits. Indeed, we sort such jokes into genres largely by naming the ethnic or gender group and the shortcoming, that is, the stereotype being exaggerated. There is the Dumb Blonde joke, the Flighty Fag joke, the Dishonest Greek joke, etc. To write a new joke of one of these types, you create a story about members of the target group that attributes an exaggerated degree of the shortcoming to those characters.

The fun in these jokes is based on stretching negative stereotypes. Whether the tellers of sexist and racist jokes accept those stereotypes or not, their playing with them through exaggeration converts morally objectionable ideas into palatable ones. Putting a "play frame" around stereotypes in a joke aestheticizes them, removing them, at least temporarily, from moral scrutiny. As listeners enjoy sexist and racist jokes, they let harmful stereotypes in under their moral radar. A straightforward assertion might quickly draw criticism, but an exaggerated version of a stereotype presented in a clever way will probably be simply enjoyed.

Humor's play frame allows prejudicial ideas to be slipped into people's heads without being evaluated. It even allows for the creation of stereotypes that any reasonable person would reject out of hand were they asserted. In the 2006 comedy *Borat: Cultural Learnings of America for Make Benefit Glorious Nation of Kazakhstan*, Sacha Baron Cohen plays a Kazakh journalist who is a crude, boorish, incestuous, anti-Semitic, racist, Gypsy-hating, sexist boor, as are the other Kazakhs in this fake documentary. Borat introduces the "town rapist" and boasts that his sister is the "Number Four prostitute in our country."

In reality, no Kazakhs appear in the film: Cohen based his new stereotype on people he met in southern Russia. The village shown and its inhabitants are Rumanian. Real Kazakhs are not Slavic but a mix of Turkic and Mongolian, and they don't look like Cohen or the people in the film. In the nineteenth century the Kazakhs were invaded by Russia; thousands died resisting colonization and conscription into the Russian army. Under Stalin and Khruschev, huge tracts of their grazing land were converted to agriculture to feed Russians. For resisting, a million and a half Kazakhs died, along with 80 percent of their livestock. Russian settlers were brought in to displace Kazakhs, until by the 1970s Kazakhstan was the only Soviet republic in which the native people were in the minority. In creating his new fictitious stereotype of Kazakhs, with negative features often attributed to Russians, Cohen insulted Kazakhs twice. He portrayed them as having vices they don't have: Anti-Semitism was never widespread in Kazakhstan, nor was the persecution of Gypsies; women have rights equal to men's. And secondly, the vices he attributes to Kazakhs he took from stereotypes of their Russian oppressors. The deep offense here was obvious in a four-page advertisement taken out by the government of Kazakhstan in the *New York Times* before the release of the film, to counteract the stereotype Cohen had created. A simple question asked by critics was why Cohen had not thought up a fictitious country to go with his fictitious stereotype....

What is objectionable about sexist and racist stereotypes, of course, is that they categorize all members of a group as being interchangeable and as having certain shortcomings. Instead of respecting group members as individual persons, those who think in stereotypes tend to write them all off as inferior. They belittle, demean, dismiss them. To use the archaic verb from which we get "contempt," they contemn the whole group—they treat its members as low, worthless, beneath notice. As Richard Mohr has said of anti-gay jokes, "The individual as distinctive is erased, dissolved into a prejudged type which determines in society's eyes all of his or her significant characteristics. The jokes . . . presume that a gay person is nothing but his sexual orientation and its efflorescences."[7]

[. . . So] nothing as cognitively sophisticated as belief is required for such jokes to do harm. Mere repeated thinking of groups in negative stereotypes is enough to prompt us to treat real individuals not according to their actual merits and shortcomings, and so justly, but as automatically inferior because they belong to those groups. In milder cases, this mistreatment may involve only condescension, but in other cases, as under Jim Crow, South African apartheid, and homophobia, it involves malicious distrust, hatred, oppression, and even murder. That's why groups who have suffered from such mistreatment often show resentment for the humor that stereotyped them—American blacks for Jim Crow humor, women for sexist jokes, and gays for "fag jokes."[8]

The objectionableness of jokes based on stereotypes, I suggest, is not all-or-nothing, but is proportional to the harm those stereotypes are likely to cause. . . .

[Consider a joke about] lawyers:

> Two lawyers on a fishing trip in Alaska awake one morning to see a grizzly bear running toward their tent. One hurriedly starts putting on his running shoes.
> "Don't be a fool," the other lawyer says. "You can't outrun a grizzly bear."
> "I don't have to outrun *him*," the first lawyer says, "I only have to outrun *you*."

This joke is based on the image of lawyers as tough-minded and uncaring, and retelling it helps keep that stereotype alive. But does the joke or the stereotype lead to the mistreatment of lawyers? Do people act condescendingly toward lawyers, insult them, or deny them jobs because of that stereotype? Hardly. Lawyers are a powerful and respected group in our society, and the stereotype of the tough-minded, unsentimental lawyer enhances rather than threatens their power and position. In fact, lawyers even put that stereotype to work in TV commercials and Yellow Pages advertising for law firms. . . .

All this contrasts sharply with the harm black people, women, and homosexuals have endured because of the stereotypes circulated about them. Not only have they been insulted, but they have suffered discrimination in voting, in buying real estate, and in the courts. Racist and sexist stereotypes cost them money, respect, status, and power. That is precisely why so many people object to sexist and racist jokes, while not objecting to lawyer and doctor jokes. . . .

The stereotypes perpetuated by jokes are more objectionable, then, when they are about people who lack social status and power, and when those stereotypes are part of the social system that marginalizes them and "keeps them in their place."

Comprehension Questions

1. What does Morreall mean by the "practical disengagement of humor"?
2. In what sense did Lincoln, Kennedy, and Reagan each use humor irresponsibly?
3. When we laugh, we usually aren't feeling compassion at the same time. However, Morreall doesn't think that *all* humor is problematic. So when is "blocking compassion" supposed to be a concern?
4. Morreall clearly thinks that it can be OK to make jokes that play on ethnic, gender, and racial stereotypes. So when are those jokes problematic? When do they "promote prejudice"?
5. On Morreall's view, what's the difference between jokes about African Americans or the LGBTQ community, on the one hand, and lawyers on the other?

Discussion Questions

1. We sometimes laugh at jokes and then say, "That was wrong." What's going on in those cases?
2. How have you seen humor used irresponsibly, or in ways that block compassion, or in ways that promote prejudice?
3. Morreall says that "[when] we want to evoke anger or outrage about some problem, we don't present it in a humorous way." You might

think that the work of people like Stephen Colbert, John Stewart, Larry Wilmore, and John Oliver are counterexamples to this claim. Are they? Why or why not?

4. It sounds like Morreall is saying that no joke is *inherently* wrong. Jokes *become* wrong when they're used irresponsibly, or block compassion, or promote prejudice. Is he right about that? Are there jokes that are morally problematic whether or not they have these consequences?

5. Is there any humor that's *always* irresponsible, or *always* blocks compassion, or *always* promotes prejudice? Consider, for example, rape jokes. Might they always be guilty of one of these charges? Why or why not?

Case

In 2015, *The Guardian* posted an article that included this passage about Amy Schumer, a popular comic:

> Schumer's stand-up repeatedly delves into racial territory tactlessly and with no apparent larger point. Her standup special features jokes like "Nothing works 100% of the time, except Mexicans" and much of her character's dumb slut persona is predicated on the fact that the men she sleeps with are people of colour. "I used to date Latino guys," she says in an older stand-up routine. "Now I prefer consensual."

Schumer responded on Twitter:

> I am a comic. I am so glad more people are laughing at me and with me all of a sudden. I will joke about things you like and I will joke about things you aren't comfortable with. And that's OK. Stick with me and trust I am joking. I go in and out of playing an irreverent idiot. That includes making dumb jokes involving race. I enjoy playing the girl who from time to time says the dumbest thing possible and playing with race is a thing we are not supposed to do, which is what makes it so fun for comics.
>
> You can call it a "blind spot for racism" or "lazy" but you are wrong. It is a joke and it is funny. I know that because people laugh at it. Even if you personally did not. I am not going to start joking about safe material. And don't ask that of me. I love what I do and won't let anyone take that away. I ask you to resist the urge to pick me apart. Trust me. I am not a racist. I am a devout feminist and lover of all people. My fight is for all people to be treated equally. So move on to the next person who is more deserving of your scrutiny and not the girl in your corner.
>
> Sincerely Amy (a dirty half Jew)[9]

What might Morreall say about Schumer's jokes? And what do you make of Schumer's defense of herself?

Notes

1. See Roger Scruton, in *The Philosophy of Laughter and Humor*, ed. John Morreall (Albany: State University of New York Press, 1987), 170–1.

2. Anthony Ludovici, *The Secret of Laughter* (New York: Viking, 1933), 11–13.

3. Thomas Hobbes, *English Works of Thomas Hobbes*, 11 vols. (London: Bohn, 1845), vol. 4, 455.

4. Henri Bergson, *Laughter: An Essay on the Meaning of the Comic*, trans. by C. Brereton and F. Rothwell (New York: Macmillan, 1913), 139.

5. Stanley Milgram, *Obedience to Authority: An Experimental View* (New York: HarperCollins, 1974).

6. Peter Jones, "Laughter," in *Proceedings of the Aristotelian Society*, Supplementary Volume 56 (1982), 225.

7. Richard Mohr, "Fag-ends and Jokes' Butts," from "Gays and Equal Protection," unpublished manuscript.

8. For an historical examination of the use of humor to keep American blacks "in their place," see Joseph Boskin, *Sambo: Rise and Demise of an American Jester* (Oxford: Oxford University Press, 1986).

9. https://twitter.com/amyschumer/status/615182173570633728/photo/1?ref_src =twsrc%5Etfw

PART X

Dishonesty, Enhancement, and Extra Credit

Why Is Cheating Wrong?

Mathieu Bouville

....

Most of us assume that cheating—such as copying another student's work for a homework assignment—is wrong. On closer examination, though, Bouville argues that this assumption isn't so plausible—or, at least, the idea that cheating is wrong because it's unfair doesn't hold up under critical reflection. For starters, many assignments are not competitive in nature, and so worries about unfairness don't apply. Further, even when assignments are competitive in nature, cheating is just one of many factors that create a mismatch between a student's grade and what they deserve, and no one raises worries about the other factors. Bouville thinks that there's a better reason to be morally concerned about cheating: It harms the cheater as a learner. Nevertheless, he doubts this is reason enough to justify the strong moral condemnation and harsh penalties that cheaters often receive.

....

Asking why cheating is wrong may seem silly or gratuitously provocative. . . . Yet, if one does not know why cheating is wrong one cannot set policies that would respond sensibly to it.

When seen as unconnected, problems are often easy to solve: increase retirement age to reduce the deficit of public pension schemes, and decrease it to reduce unemployment. Educational policy can be likewise flawed when

Bouville, Mathieu. 2010. "Why Is Cheating Wrong?" *Studies in the Philosophy of Education* 29:67–76. Copyright © 2009, Springer. Reprinted with permission.

questions are answered one by one without paying attention to the inconsistencies in the answers. Cheating is generally treated as if it were independent of the nature and purpose of exams, independent of grading, and so on. I will try to show that when one takes several questions together instead of answering one without considering others, what used to be obvious no longer is.

. . .

False Starts

A common view is that cheating is forbidden and cheaters break a rule. . . . However, Kohn (2007) draws attention to those "cases where what is regarded as cheating actually consists of a failure to abide by restrictions that may be arbitrary and difficult to defend." Breaking a rule is illegitimate only if the rule is legitimate. Either the rule has a rational justification and this rather than breaking a rule makes cheating wrong, or the rule is arbitrary and there is no reason to endorse it. . . .

As Drake (1941) pointed out, cheating can be frustrating to the instructors, who may "interpret such behavior as a direct affront to themselves." . . . While this may explain better than genuine arguments why teachers dislike cheating it does not show that cheating is wrong. . . . It is interesting to note that this is generally not offered as an argument in articles looking at cheating in a "cold" objective way but can be found in more personal papers, such as that of Johnston. . . .

Another possibility is that cheating is morally wrong because cheaters treat their teachers as mere means, rather than as ends in themselves.[1] But this claim does little to address the important issue . . . of the relation between cheating and sanctions: expelling a student for treating a teacher only as a means seems absurdly disproportionate.[2] (Would one dismiss teachers who treat students as mere means to a salary?)

Cheating as Unfair Advantage

In this section, I will focus on a popular argument against cheating: the relationship between cheating and grades—cheaters receive undeservedly high grades and thus an unfair advantage over other students.

Grades as a Proxy of How Good a Student Is

A fairly common view equates grades and value of the students (how knowledgeable, talented, competent they are). . . . the issue with such a view is that it implies that efficient cheaters are good students, since they get good grades. Plainly, if anything is to be said against cheating, one must recognize that grades are but a *proxy* for how good students are, an approximation of what they know, what they can do. It is thus possible for grades and worth to be different; every teacher has given grades that did not seem right, that did not correspond to what the students "were worth"—some students are not good at taking tests, a student may have made a silly and costly mistake, and so on (also see Bouville 2009b). Cheating may be just another source of discrepancy.

Cheating and the Future Success of the Students

Since it is of the nature of grades to describe student performance, a grade that is a poor description is a poor quality grade. Such a grade is like a map of a city that does not actually represent the streets of this city. But if no one ever were to use this map, the problem would be a purely abstract one: inaccurate grades matter only if someone somehow acts upon them, otherwise I could just as well assign -p as a grade. Naturally grades are concretely used: they are a proxy for what students know and can do, which is in turn used as a proxy for what students may be able to do in the future. In other words, grades are used as predictors of future success: high school grades are used for admission to universities, law school grades to infer how good a lawyer the student will be, and so on. In admissions, one looks at grades only in order to guess how well students may do in the future. . . . Therefore, any time grades do not correspond to how well students can be expected to perform a poor decision will be made. Such decisions can be called unfair since they advantage less deserving students.

. . .

Unfair Advantage Without Cheating

It is common for teachers to knowingly give a student a grade that is evidently inadequate: for instance, they commonly give a bad grade to a student they know to be good. If one does not see a major problem with grades being decorrelated from how good students are then the fact that the grades of cheaters do not reflect their actual value should not be a problem either. In other words, there are cases in which no cheating is involved yet a grade is clearly a bad estimate of how good a student is, that is, an unfair (dis)advantage. It is then unclear, if teachers are not bothered by such incongruities, why similar discrepancies would be problematic when due to cheating.

Picture a student who has an essay proofread by his parents or a personal tutor; the student did all the writing but received help that contributed to improving his work (e.g. that section is unclear, this book should be of help). He will get a better grade than a student of equal intelligence and talent who cannot receive or afford any such help. This is an unfair advantage but one would not call it cheating (whatever one thinks of the unfairness of the situation, the favored student did nothing wrong). If grades are used to decide who should be admitted to a top university, a smart and talented student, a student with a tutor, and a cheater will look the same even though the first is superior to the other two. Cheating and tutoring both create an unfair advantage.

Cheating May Be a Trifle

Cheating can give an unfair advantage only in cases of direct competition between students. Entrance exams and other "high stakes" tests are an example. Homework is not. Paradoxically there is more empirical work on cheating on homework than on high stakes exams, that is, the greatest knowledge about the extent of cheating lies where it is of least importance from the viewpoint of unfair advantage. A consequence is that, for all we know, there may not be a single situation where cheating does massively occur and provides an important edge: Homework is irrelevant to this competition and the most important exams are also the most heavily proctored. In other words, it is quite possible that cheating may not in fact provide a major advantage.

What Teachers Say, What Teachers Do

It is not uncommon for teachers to give a good student a bad grade, fully aware that the student deserves better—but the grade that came out of the exam is the grade that came out of the exam. And they do not really mind doing so. When a grade is a poor assessment of the value of the student, it is the grade that wins; for instance, it is this faulty assessment that will be part of transcripts, not the actual worth of the student.[3] Regardless of what they say, teachers who do not see a major problem with grades not matching how good students are—i.e., grades that give an unfair (dis) advantage—should not either mind the fact that the grades of cheaters do not reflect their actual value.

How teachers see cheating is an interesting clue of how they see education. Taking cheating to be essentially a matter of unfair advantage means that education is seen as a race of all against all. . . . If asked, the vast majority of teachers would shun such an idea. . . . . . . Treating cheating on homework as essentially a matter of a student getting an unfair advantage means losing sight of what one is trying to accomplish. Not only is the focus generally on grades rather than on learning, grades rather than learning are seen as the issue in cases where grades are mostly irrelevant.

Cheating and Learning

Of course there is no need to act as if school were just a race of all against all (even when one claims that school is precisely not that). One could instead point out that students copying from others or a book do not learn anything in the process. In other words, cheating interferes with education.

Cheating Undermines Feedback

Passow et al. (2006) argue that "acts of academic dishonesty undermine the validity of measures of student learning": If teachers do not know that there is something the students do not understand (if they cheat it may seem that they understand) then it is impossible for them to know whether to accelerate or slow down, on what to focus, or how to redesign their lectures next year—in the long term, cheating hurts the students. It also prevents teachers from providing students with relevant feedback.

One should remark that this argument is more relevant to homework than to exams (especially final exams) because the latter are used more for grading or ranking and less for feedback, making cheating on homework worse than cheating on finals. Moreover, cheating on entrance exams would not be wrong at all since these are not meant to provide any feedback at all. In other words, this argument forces us to hold as worst the instances of cheating that would generally be seen as mildest. This is not surprising since feedback (either way) is not genuinely seen as of prime importance; that grades matter more is clearly reflected in the far greater importance given (by both students and teachers) to exams compared to homework. Finally, one should point out that if the only problem with cheating is merely that it hinders feedback then it is a very venial detail, and would not justify the outrage and dismissals one witnesses.

The applicability of this argument depends deeply on the actual practice of the teachers. In particular, it is not a universal truth that teachers use graded assignments for feedback to the students. Were it so, grades would be less ubiquitous and written comments far more numerous and extensive. Also, many teachers have taught the same class the same way for decades without ever changing their course based on the specifics of their current audience; so the fact that cheaters create noise on the feedback is irrelevant when this feedback is not taken into account anyway. In other words, not all instructors can claim that cheating interferes with their teaching. . . .

Cheating Undermines Learning

A more important issue with cheating is that it can directly get in the way of learning. For instance, students who copy homework assignments instead of doing them themselves will not learn what they should. . . . For cheaters to be punished because cheating hinders learning, the following four conditions are necessary (the last of them—that sanctioning cheaters must actually have a positive consequence—will be addressed in the next section).

First, the assignment on which the student cheated must teach this student something worthwhile. The best students may have little need for homework, some teachers assign work which has little pedagogical value, and so on. Can students who would not learn anything by doing the homework copy it? It makes no sense to make certain students fail a class because they were so good that they did not need homework (also see Kohn 2007). Moreover, if the problem is that the teacher assigns work that does not contribute much to student learning one may wonder why the students are punished rather than the teacher.

A second condition is that cheating on this assignment must hinder learning. One should remark that it may be the absence of cheating, rather than cheating, that is bad. For instance, Stephens (2005) found that "only 18 percent [of high school students] believed that 'working on an assignment with other students when the teacher asked for individual work' was cheating." This is because "students regarded this forbidden collaboration as furthering their knowledge and understanding, and therefore saw it as an act of learning rather than a form of cheating" (also see Kohn 2007).

Third, anything that hinders learning as much as cheating does must be sanctioned as much as cheating. Since, in terms of learning, not doing one's homework at all and copying it are on a par, the argument of hindrance to learning cannot justify treating cheaters more harshly than those who simply ignore their homework. One can also remark that hobbies, working for tuition money, and so on can adversely affect learning as well—yet one would not expel students just because they have a part-time job or a boyfriend.[4] . . .

. . . Take three students. One is bright and learns nothing from doing a given assignment, another did not do the assignment and the last one copied it from a friend. . . . none of these three students got anything out of the assignment. From the viewpoint of learning there is no difference between them—why should one of them be sanctioned?

Should One Reduce Cheating?

Cheating has a negative impact on education inasmuch as students cheat rather than study. But this justifies trying to curb cheating only if doing so actually has a positive impact on learning. In particular, the sanction must not hamper learning more than cheating does. . . . Expelling students so they do not fail later classes and eventually drop out is as meaningless as making suicide liable to the death penalty because suicide is wrong.

Does Less Cheating Mean Better Education?

. . . Cole and Kiss (2000) found that "students are most likely to cheat when they think their assignments are pointless, and less likely to cheat when they admire and respect their teachers and are excited about what they are learning." . . . Some students are not motivated by what they are taught and they copy the assignments so they do not waste their time on something of no interest to them—while at the same time getting good enough grades to stay out of trouble. . . .

Stephens and Nicholson (2008) interviewed a student who is "simply not very interested in learning (or working hard at it) and he isn't much emotionally affected by his cheating, which he acknowledges is wrong." It is far from obvious that if this student stopped cheating he would study hard instead. When you can get something for free, you just take it; if it is no longer free, either you pay for it or you give it up. What would students do if they could no longer get good grades for free? Some would certainly do the homework assignments and study for the exams (to maintain their high grades), but other students would not study more (to maintain their low workload).

Curbing cheating may not necessarily make students study more, that is, it may not have a positive impact on learning. . . .

. . .

Conclusion

. . .

Several issues have been raised repeatedly in the course of the discussion. One is whether cheating on homework is worse than cheating on exams (especially the "high stakes" kind). Homework is meant to contribute to learning, unlike entrance exams, but the latter are more important in the competition for admissions. Since most teachers and students take cheating on exams to be far worse, they must take cheating to be about competition rather than about education.

A second issue is that of sanctions. In particular, if the fight against cheating is a fight for education then expelling cheaters is wrong because this hurts their education far more than cheating itself. Once more it appears that, no matter what teachers would claim, their usual policies do not focus on education.

Another issue regarding the prevention of cheating is that the fact that cheating hinders education does not mean that putting an end to it will automatically improve education. Those students who want to get passable grades with as little work as possible are unlikely to start studying hard just because they can no longer cheat. What hinders education is not cheating but the underlying lack of motivation: Fighting cheating may only address a superficial symptom. And if curbing cheating does not have a major positive impact on learning then the fact that cheating hinders learning cannot justify fighting it.

A last problem is consistency. This is especially clear with the claim that cheating provides an unfair advantage. Indeed, cheating is not the only way to dissolve the link between grades and future success, so that one cannot take it for granted that a given instance of cheating will get a student something undeserved in a way chance or some widely accepted practice could not. For instance, it is common for teachers to knowingly give a good student a bad grade. But if they are not bothered by such incongruities, why would similar discrepancies be problematic when due to cheating? It would also make sense that, if the problem with cheating is that it prevents learning, then anything that hampers learning (not just cheating) be likewise sanctioned.

References

Anderman, E. M., Griesinger, T., and Westerfield, G. (1998). "Motivation and Cheating During Early Adolescence." *Journal of Educational Psychology* 90, 84–93.

Blankenship, K. L., and Whitley, B. E. (2000). "Relation of General Deviance to Academic Dishonesty." *Ethics and Behavior* 10, 1–12.

Bouville, M. (2008). "Plagiarism: Words and Ideas." *Science and Engineering Ethics* 14, 311–322. Bouville, M. (2009a). "Crime and Punishment in Scientific Research." Available at http://arxiv.org/abs/0803.4058.

Bouville, M. (2009b). "Exam Fairness." Available at http://www.mathieu.bouville.name/education-ethics/Bouville-exam-fairness.pdf.

Burkill, S., and Abbey, C. (2004). "Avoiding Plagiarism." *Journal of Geography in Higher Education* 28, 439–446.

Butler, R. (1988). "Enhancing and Undermining Intrinsic Motivation." *British Journal of Educational Psychology* 58, 1–14.

Butler, R., and Nissan, M. (1986). "Effects of No Feedback, Task-Related Comments, and Grades On Intrinsic Motivation and Performance." *Journal of Educational Psychology* 78, 210–216.

Cole, S., and Kiss, E. (2000). "What Can We Do About Student Cheating?" *About Campus* 5, 5–12.

Collier, H. W., Perrin, R., and McGowan, C. B. (2004). "Plagiarism: Let the Policy Fix the Crime." In *Fourth Asia Pacific Interdisciplinary Research in Accounting Conference*, Singapore, July 4–6, 2004, 1226–45.

Covington, M. (1992). *Making the Grade: a Self-Worth Perspective on Motivation and School Reform.* Cambridge: Cambridge University Press.

Drake, C. A. (1941). "Why Students Cheat." *Journal of Higher Education* 12, 418–420.

Guyau, J.-M. (1884). *Esquisse d'une morale sans obligation ni sanction.* Paris: Félix Alcan (G. Kapteyn, Trans. [1898]. "A Sketch of Morality Independent of Obligation or Sanction." London: Watts & Co).

Hall, C. W., Bolen, L. M., and Gupton, R. H. (1995). "Predictive Validity of the Study Process Questionnaire for Undergraduate Students." *College Student Journal* 29, 234–239.

Jensen, L. A., Arnett, J. J., Feldman, S. S., and Cauffman, E. (2002). "It's Wrong, but Everybody Does It: Academic Dishonesty Among High School and College Students." *Contemporary Educational Psychology* 27, 209–228.

Johnston, D. K. (1991). "Cheating: Reflections on a Moral Dilemma." *Journal of Moral Education* 20, 283–291.

Kohn, A. (1994). "Grading: The Issue Is Not How but Why." *Educational Leadership* 52 (2), 38–41.

Kohn, A. (2007). "Who's Cheating Whom?" *Phi Delta Kappan* 89, 88–97.

Lingen, M. W. (2006). "Tales of Academic Dishonesty and What Do We Do About It?" *Oral Surgery, Oral Medicine, Oral Pathology, Oral Radiology, and Endodontology* 102, 429–30.

McCabe, D. L. (1997). "Classroom Cheating Among Natural Science and Engineering Majors." *Science and Engineering Ethics* 3, 433–45.

McCabe, D. L., Treviño, L. K., and Butterfield, K. D. (1996). "The Influence of Collegiate and Corporate Codes of Conduct On Ethics-Related Behavior in the Workplace." *Business Ethics Quarterly* 6, 461–76.

McKeachie, W. J. (2002). *Teaching Tips*. Boston, MA: Houghton Mifflin.

Murdock, T. B., Miller, A., and Kohlhardt, J. (2004). "Effects of Classroom Context Variables on High School Students' Judgments of the Acceptability and Likelihood of Cheating." *Journal of Educational Psychology* 96, 765–77.

Mustaine, E. E., and Tewksbury, R. (2005). "Southern College Students' Cheating Behaviors: An Examination of Problem Behavior Correlates. *Deviant Behavior* 26, 439–61.

Parmley, W. W. (2000). "Plagiarism—How Serious Is It?" *Journal of the American College of Cardiology* 36, 953–954.

Passow, H. J., Mayhew, M. J., Finelli, C. J., Harding, T. S., and Carpenter, D. D. (2006). "Factors Influencing Engineering Students' Decisions to Cheat by Type of Assessment." *Research in Higher Education* 47, 643–84.

Roig, M., and Caso, M. (2005). "Lying and Cheating: Fraudulent Excuse Making, Cheating, and Plagiarism." *Journal of Psychology* 139, 485–94.

Roth, N. L., and McCabe, D. L. (1995). "Communication Strategies for Addressing Academic Dishonesty." *Journal of College Student Development* 36, 531–41.

Stephens, J. M. (2005). "Justice or Just Us? What to Do About Cheating." In A. Lathrop and K. Foss, eds., *Guiding Students from Cheating and Plagiarism to Honesty and Integrity: Strategies for Change*. Westport, CT: Libraries Unlimited, 32–34.

Stephens, J. M., and Nicholson, H. (2008). "Cases of Incongruity: Exploring the Divide Between Adolescents' Beliefs and Behaviors Related to Academic Cheating." *Educational Studies* 34, 361–76.

Comprehension Questions

1. What criticisms of cheating does Bouville consider to be false starts? Why?

2. Given that many things besides cheating keep grades from reflecting students' quality, what does that mean about the purported unfairness of cheating?

3. Why does Bouville think worries about the unfairness of cheating are apt for "high-stakes exams," but not for homework?

4. How can cheating negatively affect teachers' ability to provide feedback to students, and why does this matter?

5. What are the three initial conditions Bouville suggests must be met in order for cheating to deserve punishment?

6. Why might it be a bad idea to punish cheaters even if cheating harms them by keeping them from learning?

Discussion Questions

1. Suppose you are regularly assigned homework that you can reasonably judge to be just busy work, with no learning benefit for you. Do you agree with Bouville's suggestion that it might not be wrong for you to cheat here? Why or why not?

2. Bouville claims that the practice of expelling students for cheating because cheating hinders learning is self-defeating. Do you think that's right? Why or why not? Is some other punishment more appropriate?

3. Imagine that you're a good student and that you studied intensely for an exam, but your grade suffered because you misunderstood a part of the exam instructions. Also, suppose that cheaters shouldn't get to keep the good grades they received because the grades don't reflect their own competence. If so, what does that imply about your case?

Case

Consider this case:

> [Sam Eshaghoff] took college-entrance exams for cash. . . . The 19-year-old whiz kid says his bustling business started with a casual proposal from a classmate. "He's like, 'Yo, you're good on your SATs and I'm not. And you know [it's possible for you to take the test for me]. How much is it going to take?'" The answer was a cool $2,500. Eshaghoff told "60 Minutes" that he took the tests—both the SAT and the ACT—roughly 20 times for score-starved clients. "My whole clientele were based on word of mouth and, like, a referral system," Eshaghoff said. He offered up his SAT wizardry gratis only once, for his then-girlfriend. With his business booming, Eshaghoff began to feel like he was performing a noble public service... "I mean, a kid who has a horrible grade-point average, who no matter how much he studies is gonna totally bomb this test, by giving him an amazing score, I totally give him this . . . new lease on life. He's gonna go to a totally new college. He's gonna be bound for a totally new career and a totally new path on life."[5]

This scheme got Eshaghoff arrested. Do you think that it should have? What do you make of Eshaghoff's defense of cheating?

Notes

1. One can notice that all students who seek good grades (even those studying hard) basically see the teacher as a distributor of grades, not as an end. In fact, it is not clear to me how students can avoid treating teachers as means: Teachers are essentially means to an education. (This is true whatever your job: if you were not a means to anyone, who would accept to remunerate you?)

2. Even if cheating *is* wrong, this does not automatically imply that it must be harshly punished. Guyau (1884, p. 168) even claims that moral judgment "cannot pass the limits of the moral world to be transformed into the least kind of coercive and penal action. This affirmation 'You are good, you are bad' ought never to become this: 'You must be made to enjoy or to suffer.' " In any case, the harsher the sanction, the more uncontroversial the crime should be.

3. The reason why grades trump one's intuition of the value of students is probably that they are objective and thus deemed superior to the subjective opinion of a teacher. But if grades claim that good students are bad, of what exactly are they an objective measure? Grading based on the number of points the student's name would get in Scrabble is objective as well; it is also completely silly (also see Bouville 2009b). Saying that the objectivity of grades is their main quality means that what they actually measure is of secondary importance. "What grades offer is spurious precision" (Kohn 1994). This, again, undermines the meaning of grades as a measure of the value of the students.

4. One should also remark that grades (which one so dearly wants to protect from cheating) are bad for education as well. Ruth Butler (1988) found that students who received feedback in the form of grades did worse than those who received written comments but no grade. Butler and Nissan (1986) note that "grades may encourage an emphasis on quantitative aspects of learning, depress creativity, foster fear of failure, and undermine interest." According to Anderman et al. (1998), "students who reported cheating in science perceived their classrooms as being extrinsically focused and perceived their schools as being focused on performance and ability"—that is, the emphasis on grades favors cheating.

5. http://nypost.com/2011/12/30/sat-taker-for-hire-tells-60-minutes-it-was-easy-to-cheat/

Enhancement and Cheating

Rebecca Roache

....

There are lots of reasons to be concerned about the use of pharmacological cognitive enhancers like Ritalin. They could be unsafe or addictive, for instance. Rebecca Roache tackles the separate issue of
whether using these drugs is a form of cheating. If we think of cheating as an unfair advantage one has over others, then using cognitive
enhancers looks like cheating, since it gives one greater odds of success
in the educational competition for qualifications and ultimately jobs.
Using cognitive enhancers would be wrong, she concedes, if their only
consequence was to give a competitive edge over one's peers. But that
picture, Roache argues, is simplistic. On the one hand, she suggests
that using pharmaceutical cognitive enhancers is no different in principle from the morally unquestionable use of nonpharmaceutical cognitive enhancers like tutoring services. On the other hand, she claims
that recognizing the good these drugs can do to help students achieve
should be enough to eliminate worries about unfair advantages.

....

A common worry expressed about the use of pharmacological cognitive enhancements such as Modafinil and Ritalin is that using
them constitutes cheating (Fukuyama 2002; Henderson 2008).
Those who enhance in this way are better placed to beat their unenhanced

Roache, Rebecca. 2008. "Enhancement and Cheating." *Expositions* 2(2): 153–156. Reprinted
with permission.

peers to the top educational qualifications and jobs; accordingly, enhancing is unfair. Is this worry justified?

The worry about cheating is often bound up with other worries about enhancement. These include concerns about safety, addictiveness, and accessibility. These concerns can be addressed independently of the concern about cheating, and so, to avoid complicating matters, let us assume that cognitive enhancement is safe to use, that it is non-addictive, and that it is accessible to everyone, not just the rich. Ought we still to be worried about the fairness of cognitive enhancement? Well, in the absence of these ancillary concerns, one of the issues that remain is that those who choose not to enhance will be at a disadvantage, left behind in the race for the best qualifications and jobs by their enhanced peers. Is this fair? Should people be free to use drugs like Modafinil and Ritalin to get ahead, or should education authorities and employers ban such enhancement, perhaps introducing urine tests to ensure that this ban is enforced, as Cambridge neuroscientist Sir Gabriel Horn has recently been quoted to suggest (Henderson 2008)?

We can start with a terminological point. Whether or not the use of cognitive enhancement drugs constitutes cheating depends on whether the use of such drugs is forbidden in the rules of the game. Currently, the rules to which students and employees must adhere typically forbid activities like plagiarism, forging references, and lying about one's educational and employment history—and those students and employees who break these rules can expect to be punished. Rules against the use of cognitive enhancement drugs are not currently widespread. Ought they to be?

The answer to this question depends on what we think is more important: a level playing field on which students and employees can compete equally for qualifications and jobs, or the value of the achievements made through such competition. In some areas of life, the main purpose is to advance knowledge, and so maximizing the achievements made is plausibly more important than having a level playing field. As Anders Sandberg has commented, "that many of the theorems of the mathematician Paul Erdös were proven under the influence of amphetamines does not diminish their intellectual brilliance or importance" (Sandberg 2008). And, in the quest for a cure for cancer, if it turns out that cognitively enhanced scientists would be able to discover a cure more quickly than unenhanced scientists, then using cognitive enhancement could result in millions of lives being saved. In other areas of life, it is extremely important to remain alert and focused. For those working as airline pilots or surgeons, the consequences of a lapse in concentration could be dire. Cognitive enhancement could help prevent such lapses. These examples demonstrate that, while fairness is important, avoidably slowing the advancement of scientific knowledge or reducing the alertness of airline pilots and surgeons is too high a price to pay to ensure that those who do not wish to enhance are able to compete on a level playing field.

In other areas of life, however, competition is more important. A key purpose of education in schools and universities is to enable students to compete for the best qualifications. Should cognitive enhancement be banned in such contexts? There are at least two good reasons to answer "no" to this question. First, even if competition for qualifications is a valuable aspect of education, it is not the only valuable aspect. As well as enabling one to gain educational qualifications, studying also enables students to understand more about the world and the people in it, and to enrich themselves intellectually and culturally. If it turns out that cognitive enhancement enables students to increase the extent to which they understand the world and enrich themselves, then banning it in the interest of ensuring fairer competition for qualifications would be too hasty. In order to decide whether or not to ban it, we would first need to assess whether the value to be gained from banning it and thereby ensuring a fair competition would outweigh the value to be gained from allowing students to enjoy the noncompetitive aspects of education more intensely with the aid of cognitive enhancement.

However, banning cognitive enhancement in education would not ensure that students are able to compete on a level playing field. This is the second reason to answer "no" to the question posed above. Consider that, even without access to drugs like Modafinil and Ritalin, most students have to compete with other students who are naturally more intelligent, disciplined, alert, and focused. As such, most students are already at a disadvantage. It may be objected that, in aiming at a level playing field, we should ignore such "natural" advantages, and concentrate only on ensuring that students have equal opportunities to achieve the best grades given their existing abilities. However, even this does not leave us with a level playing field. Some students are able and willing to employ personal tutors; others are not. Some students spend most of their time out of school studying; others spend their time out of school relaxing or working to earn money. Some students use caffeine or computer software to aid their studying—both of which are types of cognitive enhancement—others do not. Such practices ensure that, even without novel methods of cognitive enhancement, students do not compete on a level playing field. And, that schools and universities do not currently outlaw the use of personal tutors, caffeine, and studying outside of school suggests that maximizing the extent to which students compete on a level playing field is not as important as some opponents of enhancement suggest. An uneven playing field may even be seen as advantageous, in that it can drive students to work harder as they attempt to beat their peers. As such, it is far from obvious that we should aim to create a level playing field by limiting the ways in which students can compete. At the very least, opponents of enhancement need to demonstrate exactly why using drugs like Modafinil and Ritalin is relevantly different from employing a personal tutor or drinking coffee to remain alert.

There is something important to learn from the worry about unfair competition, however. As far as possible, it is desirable to discourage the pursuit of what the economist Fred Hirsch has called "positional goods": those goods whose value to those who have them depends on others not having them. This is because the collective pursuit of positional goods is a waste of time and resources: As Hirsch remarked, "if everyone stands on tiptoe, no one sees better" (Hirsch 1977, 5). If the value of cognitive enhancement rests solely on its ability to enable one to compete better than others for things like educational qualifications, then its use should be discouraged. However, it is unlikely that the value of cognitive enhancement is exhausted by the positional goods it confers. We have seen that it may have value in enabling people like scientists, airline pilots, and surgeons to do their jobs more effectively. And, even in education, where competition for qualifications plays a central role, cognitive enhancement could add value by enabling students to make the most of the noncompetitive elements. There is a clear case for banning cognitive enhancement in education only if the value of education is exhausted by the competition for qualifications, because only in such a case is cognitive enhancement a purely positional good when used in the context of education. There may be some who wish to argue that the value of education is indeed exhausted by the competition for qualifications, and that anyone who believes otherwise is an academic fantasist. However, if this is the case, then the qualifications for which students compete are themselves purely positional goods, and so the argument to ban cognitive enhancement also works to ban educational qualifications.

The worry about cheating is not, as a result, sufficient justification for banning the use of cognitive enhancement drugs. Arguably, the worry about enhancement and cheating is usually overblown. The most important concerns about such enhancement are perhaps those that I initially disregarded: safety, addictiveness, and accessibility. Since these concerns are also among the most philosophically uninteresting, it should not be surprising that philosophical debate about enhancement gravitates instead towards issues like cheating. As in many debates in applied philosophy, however, we must take care not to allow what is most interesting to distract us from what is most important.

References

Fukuyama, F. (2002). *Our Posthuman Future*. New York: Farrar, Straus and Giroux.

Henderson, M. (2008). "Academy of Medical Sciences Suggests Urine Tests to Detect Smart Drugs." *The Times*, May 22, 2008.

Hirsch, F. (1977). *Social Limits to Growth*. London: Routledge and Kegal Paul.

Sandberg, A. (2008). "Brain Boosting and Cheating in Exams: Four Responses." *Practical Ethics: Ethical Perspectives on the News* blog (http://blog.practicalethics.ox.ac.uk/2008/05/brain-boosting-and-cheating-in-exams-four-responses/).

Comprehension Questions

1. What are some possible causes for concern over the use of cognitive enhancement drugs?
2. Why might someone choose to take cognitive enhancers, apart from outcompeting peers?
3. What reasons does Roache provide for thinking higher education is not a level playing field?
4. What is a positional good, and why does Roache deny cognitive enhancement drugs are just positional goods?

Discussion Questions

1. People often talk about doping in sports, but they don't talk so much about cognitive enhancement in academic contexts. How similar are they? Do you think that one might be wrong and the other OK, or do they stand or fall together?
2. In her discussion, Roache sets aside the issues of whether cognitive enhancement drugs are safe, addictive, and available for all. If it turned out that they were unsafe, addictive, or not accessible to all, would any of these be good enough reasons to ban use of cognitive enhancers?

3. Roache compares the use of cognitive enhancement drugs to "cognitive enhancers" like caffeine and tutoring services. Is Roache right to think that there is no morally significant difference between them? Why or why not?

4. Try to think of as many qualifications students typically compete for as you can. In your mind, when you compare these with the other benefits Roache mentions of taking cognitive enhancers, which do you find to be morally more significant, and why?

Case

Consider the following argument:

> It isn't unfair for students to use cognitive enhancers. In fact, we *ought* to provide cognitive enhancers for some students. Through no fault of their own, some students have a much harder time focusing and remaining motivated to finish their school work. In some cases, this difficulty has a genetic basis; in others, it's because of features of their environment. Either way, they shouldn't be punished for having certain parents or having been born in a certain place. Instead, we should give them drugs that allow them to compete on a level playing field— or, at least, as level a playing field as we can make it. So rather than study drugs being unfair, it's unfair *not* to give study drugs to disadvantaged students.
>
> To be clear, the claim isn't that we should *force* some students to take study drugs. Rather, the claim is that public institutions ought to make them accessible to students who want them. They should be easy to get (perhaps through the health center), they should be free (the cost could be covered by a health service fee), and students should know that they're available (the school might provide information about them at orientation). These drugs won't allow disadvantaged students to outperform their peers, but that was never the point. Instead, these drugs should help make disadvantaged students more successful in individual courses and in their college careers overall.[1]

Is this a good argument? Why or why not?

Note

1. Thanks to Keisha Ray for the general line of thought, though I take responsibility for any shortcomings of this particular way of developing it.

48

===== 🐝 =====

Ideals of Student Excellence and Enhancement

Gavin G. Enck

....

Your natural cognitive abilities can only carry you so far, and it is tempting, in some circumstances, to want to enhance them. Perhaps you've used the caffeine of coffee to stay awake while studying late into the night. That seems innocent enough. Besides caffeine, there are also prescription drugs (Ritalin and Adderall, for instance) that have a significant cognitive enhancement effect. The use of these drugs for academic purposes when you have no cognitive deficiency is highly controversial. But Gavin Enck argues that sometimes taking pharmaceutical cognitive enhancers is morally OK—and even virtuous! Enck discusses several fictional scenarios to highlight when the choice to use cognitive enhancers is virtuous and when not, suggesting that if a student is motivated by a sincere desire for learning and self-improvement, then taking cognitive enhancers is blameless.

....

. . .

Discussions about the permissibility of students using enhancements in education are often framed by the question, "Is a student who uses

Enck, Gavin. 2013. "Ideals of Student Excellence and Enhancement." *Neuroethics* 6: 155–164.
Copyright © 2012, Springer. Reprinted with permission.

cognitive-enhancing drugs cheating?" . . . While the question of cheating is interesting, it is but only one question concerning the permissibility of enhancement in education. Another interesting question is, "What kinds of students do we want in our academic institutions?" I suggest that one plausible answer to this question concerns the ideals of human excellence or virtues. The students we want in our academic institutions are virtuous or, at least minimally, possess certain virtues. I argue that a virtuous student may choose to use cognitive-enhancing drugs for reasons of self-improvement.

That a virtuous student may choose to use cognitive-enhancing drugs for reasons of self-improvement illustrates that under certain conditions motivation can determine the permissibility of using enhancements. . . .

. . .

My focus is cognitive-enhancing drugs, which I refer to as *cognitive enhancers* when they are used to augment a person's capacities of focus and concentration to higher functioning levels and for a longer period, as they are being used in an educational system. . . . For simplicity, I limit the scope of my project to the academic institutions of colleges and universities, which I refer to as *academia*, and focus on undergraduate education. Among undergraduate students (and graduate students) surveyed, 20 percent reported using cognitive enhancers, out of which 90 percent indicated that the use was for enhancement, not for treatment (White et al 2006). To illustrate some of the context and considerations for undergraduate students' use of cognitive enhancers, I begin the following section with three cases of undergraduate students using cognitive enhancers.

I

Undergraduate students Teresa, Edith, and Oliver are all studying Ludwig Wittgenstein's *Philosophical Investigations* in a philosophy class (Wittgenstein 1953). When studying Wittgenstein, which involves the academic tasks of researching, reading, and writing, Teresa takes 10 mg of dextroamphetamine every four to six hours. Teresa has a cognitive condition or disorder and this cognitive enhancer allows her capacities of focus and concentration to function at proficient levels. While studying Wittgenstein, Edith also takes 10 mg of dextroamphetamine every four to six hours, but unlike Teresa, Edith does not have a condition or disorder; instead, she uses a cognitive enhancer because of her passion for philosophy. Using cognitive enhancers enables her capacities of focus and concentration to function at higher levels, allowing her to not only work efficiently and effectively on these academic tasks but, also, to devote more of her time to learning philosophy. The last student, Oliver, also takes 10 mg of dextroamphetamine every four to six hours, but he does not take this cognitive enhancer as treatment for a cognitive condition or disorder or because of a passion for learning philosophy. Oliver takes the cognitive enhancer because he spent the majority of the lectures and discussion sections posting pithy comments on Facebook and not paying attention. He doesn't understand the material and is using the cognitive enhancer to improve his capacities of focus and concentration while he pulls an "all-nighter" to write his final paper.

In the broadest terms, the cases of Teresa, Edith, and Oliver describe some, but certainly not all, the considerations and contexts involved in the use of cognitive enhancers. While these three cases do not account for all considerations and contexts pertaining to the use of cognitive enhancers, they can be used to illustrate the sort of cases that fall outside the range of my project's interest. I take Teresa's use of cognitive enhancer as being treatment and will not consider her case. My interest is on cases like Oliver and Edith, the 90 percent of students using cognitive enhancers in academia where the use is strictly for enhancement. Moreover, my interest specifically is on Edith's case since, generally speaking, one would think her motivation for using a cognitive enhancer is a good reason.

First, let's compare Oliver and Edith's cases in respect to motivation. Oliver's motivation for using cognitive enhancers is to make-up an assignment because of improper study habits. This, typically, is not a good reason and does not reflect well on Oliver's attitude or character. Even if the use of cognitive enhancers in academia is wrong based on an all-things-considered judgment, one can still hold that Oliver's motivations reflect poorly on his attitude and character. Now contrast Oliver's motivation with Edith's motivation: Edith uses the cognitive enhancer in order to devote all her spare time to learning philosophy. One, generally speaking, would consider this a good reason and indicate that Edith has a good attitude and character. Again, even if the use of cognitive enhancers in academia is wrong based on an all-things-considered judgment, one can still hold that Edith's motivation reflects a good attitude and character. I think that motivation is a significant and relevant consideration because it not only differentiates Edith's use of cognitive enhancers from Oliver's but, importantly, also is indicative of her possessing a good attitude and character. In the following section, I attempt to offer an approach to enhancement in academia that encapsulates this significance.

II

[Let's] begin by asking, "What kinds of students do we want in our academic institutions?" One plausible answer concerns the ideals of human excellence or virtues. . . . One kind of student we want in our academic institutions is a student that is virtuous or, at least minimally, possesses certain virtues. In the following I offer an account of virtue that serves as an outline in which my account of virtuous students fills in the details.

Conceptually, virtues are the properties of a person that make their possessor an ideal of human excellence (Aristotle 1984; Adams 2006; Wallace 1978; Tzun 1963; Zagzebski 1999). These virtues, broadly speaking, are character traits, emotional tendencies, or dispositions to think, feel, and act in certain ways. The motivational structures (character traits or emotional tendencies) are stable and enduring, and the dispositions (thoughts, feeling, and actions) are regular and reliable. A virtue requires a strong connection between a person's motivational structures and dispositions. A person with the virtue of compassion has a character trait to comfort those in need and is successful in providing such comfort. This person *consistently* thinks, feels, and acts in ways to comfort other people, so a single compassionate action does not mark a person as having the virtue of compassion. Although one may have several reasons for consistently acting compassionately, to have the virtue of compassion requires that at least one of the reasons for acting compassionately is to provide sympathy or alleviate suffering. One cannot attribute the virtue of compassion to someone who does not reliably think, feel, and act to provide comfort, or to someone who lacks the sufficient motivation of sympathy (or alleviation of suffering) for their actions.

. . .

One reason we want virtuous students in academia is that it is of great importance in our lives that a person's actions and motivations are strongly and appropriately connected. We place great value on a person's having good character. When raising children, parents not only want them to think, act, and feel in certain ways but, importantly, to do so for the right reasons, as a matter of character. . . . Consider the cases of Vincent and Mark, two students in a course on Buddhism. Vincent wants to understand Buddhism's tenets of *Four Noble Truths* and *anatta* (concept of no-self) because these tenets challenge Vincent's belief system. For Vincent, learning about a multiplicity of viewpoints provides a wider and deeper range of options for assessing his own life. Mark also wants to understand Buddhism's tenets of *Four Noble Truths* and *anatta* but not because these views challenge his belief system or because they permit a wider and deeper range of options for self-assessment. Instead, Mark wants to understand Buddhism's system of beliefs simply to pass the course with a good grade. In this case, while we would typically regard both Vincent and Mark's dispositions as being permissible, one would prefer a student with Vincent's motivation since the desire to understand a challenging belief system is indicative of character. Therefore, when considering the kind of student we would want in academia, the motivations students have for their academic projects connote their character. Our belief in the importance of character is a reason for wanting students in academia to be virtuous or possess certain virtues.

. . .

In respect to virtuous students, I think at a minimum one would want students to possess the virtues of *seeking understanding* and *seeking accurate beliefs*. The first virtue, seeking understanding, is a structuring virtue: a character trait that organizes and configures one's activities (Adams 2006). For seeking understanding, a student has the motivational structure to organize and configure their dispositions to seek greater comprehension of the human experience. This virtue motivates a student to structure activities so that the student can draw upon and make connections about accurate beliefs between diverse academic domains and disciplines. One of the goals of academia is to expose students to the various disciplines in the sciences, arts, and humanities to develop their intellectual capacities so students with this virtue can draw upon and make connections between many diverse disciplines.

A second virtue is that of seeking accurate beliefs. By seeking accurate beliefs, I mean "accurate belief(s)" as in "belief(s) that correctly represent(s)/depict(s) the world/reality."[1] A student with this virtue has the character trait to actively pursue accurate beliefs. Seeking accurate beliefs is usually considered a good thing: scientists, police detectives, physicists, and historians are nearly universally commended for seeking accurate beliefs. So it seems quite natural to think that one would also want students, as a matter of character, to seek accurate beliefs since accurate beliefs are often a mark of excellence in thought but also conducive to the goal of academia.

. . .

III

Returning to the issue of student-use of cognitive enhancers, one can ask whether a virtuous student would use cognitive enhancers or not. . . . [It] seems likely that in many situations a virtuous student may choose to use cognitive enhancers for self-improvement. The augmentation of one's capacities of focus and concentration to higher functioning levels, in general, is an improvement. Typically, enhancements result in 10–20 percent improvement in a given task (Sandberg 2011). For virtuous students, this 10–20 percent improvement is significant because with their capacities of focus and concentration operating at higher functioning levels, these students could more efficiently and effectively work on academic activities. . . .

Now imagine that in Teresa, Edith, and Oliver's Wittgenstein's class there happens to be a virtuous student, Vivian. Vivian wants to take as many classes as possible on a wide variety of topics. Her course workload is large, and she also has a part-time job. Vivian wants to make the most of her academic career, and for these reasons of self-improvement she uses cognitive enhancers. These cognitive enhancers improve her capacities of focus and concentration to higher functioning levels, resulting in her being able to efficiently and effectively work through her course workload, which is important because her part-time job limits the amount of time she is able to study. The use of cognitive enhancers also allows Vivian to pursue, improve, and develop her overall intellectual capacities, further allowing her to appreciate and connect with her and others' life experiences. So Vivian may choose to use cognitive enhancers in academia for reasons of self-improvement.

An objection against my account of virtuous students and their use of cognitive enhancers for self-improvement is that the use of cognitive enhancers cheapens the experience of academia. Since cognitive enhancers allow a student's intellectual capacities to function at higher levels, these students—even if virtuous—are bypassing or "shortcutting" the academic workload. In bypassing the academic workload, the cognitive enhancers cheapen a student's experience of academia (President's Council 2003; Sandel 2007). . . .

However, this objection is misguided because it rests on the presupposition that using cognitive enhancers directly augments a person's cognition. Cognition is the complex interaction between a multiplicity of mental functions and neurological processes. In respect to overall cognition, the use of cognitive enhancers . . . augment the capacities of focus and concentration (Smith and Farah 2011; O'Reilly 2010). Yet, cognitive enhancers do not bypass or "shortcut" the workload or the experience of academia. A student using cognitive enhancers still has to do the same amount of academic work, but in augmenting his or her capacities of focus and concentration, they are simply using these capacities more efficiently and effectively. Achievement in academia ultimately rests upon the student. A student, whether using cognitive enhancers or not, still has to make a decision to actually do the work. . . . Simply using cognitive enhancers or any enhancement does not guarantee academic success. . . . [T]hus, this student will still have to work through an academic workload, experiencing certain highs and lows, and have a full—not cheapened—experience of academia. Furthermore, that the student is virtuous entails that their reasons for using cognitive enhancers are not as an attempt to bypass or shortcut the academic experience but for reasons of self-improvement.

IV

I have argued, rather broadly, that virtuous students may choose to use cognitive enhancers for reasons of self-improvement. . . . If a virtuous student, or one possessing the virtues of seeking understanding and accurate beliefs, chooses to use cognitive enhancers, does that make the use of cognitive enhancers in academia permissible? I think that, in fact, it does make the use of cognitive enhancers permissible.

. . . My claim is not that a virtuous student would always choose to use cognitive enhancers, but that the situations and reasons a virtuous student would consider as justifying the use of cognitive enhancers are rather limited. In academia, a virtuous student has the practical wisdom for judging the situations and the reasons for when to use or not use cognitive enhancers. There are many rules, consequences, and motivations that a virtuous student would judge as reasons against using cognitive enhancers.

Imagine that Vivian is preparing to write her final paper for the Wittgenstein course. There are many rules, consequences, and motivations that Vivian would judge as reasons against using cognitive enhancers. She may choose not to use cognitive enhancers if these enhancements were illegally obtained from acquaintances, family members, other students, or ordered on the Internet. The potential harmful side effects, withdrawal symptoms, and the lack of long-term, empirical medical evidence concerning the health risks might be reasons Vivian chooses not to use cognitive enhancers. Alternatively, it could turn out that the use of cognitive enhancers is likely to result in little or no enhancement for her. Finally, Vivian may choose not to use cognitive enhancers if she lacks good motivations for using them. As a virtuous student, Vivian would not think of using cognitive enhancers to rectify irresponsible study habits, or to competitively beat other students like Oliver and Teresa, or to overcome the ennui of academic activity. . . .

. . . [A] virtuous student chooses to use cognitive enhancers after assessing the relevant information and considerations in a situation and for reasons of self-improvement. [The] use of cognitive enhancers is permissible under certain conditions in academia, [and this] permissibility rests upon the central tenet of my virtuous student account: the connection between motivational structures and dispositions necessitates that a virtuous student has a sufficiently appropriate reason for acting. . . Put otherwise, a student's reason for using cognitive enhancers determines the permissibility of using cognitive enhancers.

To illustrate how a student's reasons for using cognitive enhancers determines whether their use is permissible, let's re-evaluate Oliver and Edith's cases. In Oliver's case, his reason for choosing to use cognitive enhancers is to make up an assignment because of improper study habits. Making up an assignment because of improper study habits does not seem to be a good reason for a student to use cognitive enhancers. Because Oliver's reason for acting, his motivation, does not reflect well on his character and is not indicative of human excellence, it is possible to consider his use of cognitive enhancers as impermissible. Now consider Edith's case: her reasons for using cognitive enhancers are to gain a better understanding of Wittgenstein and for her love of philosophy. Wanting to better comprehend the material and for intellectual development does seem to be a good reason for a student to use cognitive enhancers. Edith's reasons for using cognitive enhancers reflect good character and, importantly, are indicative of human excellences. . . .

. . .

References

Adams, Robert Merrihew. (2006). *A Theory of Virtue*. Oxford: Oxford University Press.

Annas, Julia. (2006). "Virtue Ethics." In *The Oxford Handbook of Ethical Theory*, ed. David Copp, 515–36. Oxford: Oxford University Press.

Annas, Julia. (2011). *Intelligent Virtues*. Oxford: Oxford University Press.

Aristotle. (1984). In *The Complete Works of Aristotle: The Revised Oxford Translation*, ed. Jonathan Barnes. Princeton: Princeton University Press.

McDowell, John. (1997). "Virtue and Reason." In *Virtue Ethics*, ed. Roger Crisp and Michael Slote, 141–62. Oxford: Oxford University Press.

O'Reilly, Randall C. (2010). "The What and How of Prefrontal Cortical Organization." *Trends in Neurosciences* 33: 355–361.

President's Council on Bioethics. (2003). *Beyond Therapy: Biotechnology and the Pursuit of Happiness*. New York: Regan Books.

Sandberg, Anders. (2011). "Cognition Enhancement: Upgrading the Brain." In *Enhancing Human Capacities*, ed. Julian Savulescu, Ruud ter Meulen, and Guy Kahane, 71–91. Oxford: Blackwell Publishing Ltd.

Sandel, Michael J. (2007). *The Case Against Perfection: Ethics in the Age of Genetic Engineering*. Cambridge: Harvard University Press.

Smith, M. Elizabeth and Martha J. Farah. (2011). "Are Prescription Stimulants 'Smart Pills'? The Epidemiology and Cognitive Neuroscience of Prescription Stimulant Use by Normal Healthy Individuals." *Psychological Bulletin* 137, 717–41.

Tzun, Hsun. (1963). "Encouraging Learning." In *Basic Writings of Mo Tzu, Hsun Tzu, and Han Fei Tzu* (trans: Watson, Burton), 15–23. New York: Columbia University Press.

Wallace, James D. (1978). *Virtues and Vices*. New York: Cornell University Press.

White, B.P., K.A. Becker-Blease and K. Grace-Bishop. (2006). "Stimulant Medication Use, Misuse, and Abuse in an Undergraduate and Graduate Student Sample." *Journal of American College of Health* 54, 261–8.

Wittgenstein, Ludwig. (1953). *Philosophical Investigations* (trans: Anscombe, G. E. M.). Upper Saddle River: Prentice Hall.

Zagzebski, Linda. (1999). "What is Knowledge?" In *The Blackwell Guide to Epistemology*, ed. John Greco and Ernest Sosa, 92–116. Oxford: Blackwell.

Comprehension Questions

1. What, generally speaking, is Enck's approach to the morality of cognitive enhancement drugs?

2. How do the cases of Teresa, Edith, and Oliver differ from one another?

3. What is a virtue and how is it relevant to the moral evaluation of actions?

4. What virtues does Enck think it's good for college students to have?

5. Why does Enck say that Vivian's behavior is morally permissible?

6. How does Enck respond to the worry that using cognitive enhancers cheapens the educational experience?

7. What limits are there, on Enck's view, to the permissible use of cognitive enhancers?

Discussion Questions

1. Do you know people who use study drugs? Have you ever respected someone *because* he or she was using such a drug? Why or why not?
2. In reply to the objection that cognitive enhancers cheapen the educational experience, Enck insists that these students must still choose to do their work and follow through with it. Are you convinced by Enck's response? Why or why not?
3. Of the cases Enck discusses (i.e., Edith, Oliver, and Vivian), which do you think is most typical? If there were very few virtuous users of cognitive enhancers, should colleges and universities ban them? Explain your view.
4. Can you think of any virtuous motivations for taking cognitive enhancers besides the ones Enck mentions? What are they?

Case

Consider this:

> As the school year winds down, it's safe to assume that many college students used stimulants such as Ritalin and Adderall to get through finals. While the students may have been motivated to improve their odds of getting good grades, a new study suggests that students' reasons for taking simulants aren't so blatantly opportunistic. . . . After several conversations, the students said that stimulants . . . enhanced their experience of studying—making it easier for them to face the work and making the work less forbidding and even more enjoyable . . . Many talked about feeling overwhelmed at exam time, which in turn lowered their self-confidence and made them procrastinate. Ben, a graduate student, said that Adderall eliminated that fear and gave him the "confidence that the work will get done." Harrison, another graduate student who used stimulants to help overcome self-doubt and procrastination, told the researchers that "that sounds kind of bad." But he also emphasized the benefits he experienced: being able to "engage in a task and feel good" and not be "disrupted by what your misery or insecurity might do to interfere with completing the task."[2]

Is there a moral difference between (a) using study drugs to help you focus and (b) what Ben and Harrison are doing, which seems to be using those drugs to get over certain psychological hang-ups? If so, what is it? If not, then think about Harrison's point of view. Why might he say that his reason "sounds kind of bad"?

Notes

1. If, however, one disagrees with this conception of "seeking accurate beliefs," it is possible to instead consider "accurate beliefs" as meaning "beliefs that broaden a student's intellectual horizons by exposure to a multiplicity of disciplines." Either definition is consistent not only with seeking accurate beliefs being a virtue, but something one would want students to possess.

2. http://www.thehastingscenter.org/Bioethicsforum/Post.aspx?id=7446 &blogid=140

The Role of Cultural Values in Plagiarism in Higher Education

Nina C. Heckler and David R. Forde

The practice of plagiarism is a problem that plagues higher education, and it has only increased in recent decades. But what do students make of the issue? In the hope that better understanding the phenomenon will lead to better ways of dealing with it, Heckler and Forde present their study of undergraduate students and their attitudes toward plagiarism. They find that while it's widely agreed by students that plagiarizing is immoral, students were able to provide a substantial list of motivations to do so—with complaints about instructors at the top of the list. Further, students identified numerous cultural values that they took to be possible sources of support for or opposition to cheating. In light of this information, Heckler and Forde make several recommendations about how those in higher education can counteract the prevalence of plagiarism, ranging from efforts to help freshmen better manage their time to reducing the relative importance of research for faculty in favor of a greater emphasis on educational practice.

. . .

Plagiarism—the copying of others' work or ideas without attribution, treating the material as if it were one's own—can occur in any number of areas, including the copying of art, music, lab work, computer programming, and technology. However, the focus of this research is on *textual* plagiarism. Specifically, this is the "reproduction of text from other academic sources, such as journal articles, books, or lecture notes without adequate acknowledgment of the source, copying some or all of other students' assignments and even having assignments 'ghost-written' by other authors" (Selwyn 2008, p. 465). Investigators point to evidence that plagiarism and other forms of academic misconduct are in part supported by a culture that both encourages and facilitates the practice (Callahan 2004). The present work reports on the role of cultural values in university students' perceptions of and behavior regarding textual plagiarism. Accordingly, a class of 538 introductory sociology students were administered a questionnaire regarding their understanding of what constitutes plagiarism, how widespread it is, whether or not they consider the practice a part of the collegiate culture, how it might differ in its ethical implications from other forms of plagiarism, and the possible role of student cultural values in its practice and justification.

. . .

The Present Study

[A] primary goal [of this research] was to gain an understanding of students' perspectives regarding plagiarism. The objective was to assist instructors in higher education in their efforts to communicate norms about the practice of plagiarism and to reduce its incidences. Accordingly, the study sought to determine: (a) whether students know the meaning of plagiarism and of Internet plagiarism; (b) whether students perceive plagiarism to be a widespread problem on college campuses; (c) whether students perceive Internet plagiarism and traditional plagiarism differently in terms of their ethical implications; (d) whether students perceive plagiarism to be a part of the culture on their campus; (e) what rationale students have heard to justify plagiarism; and (f) what American cultural values students think contribute to or deter plagiarism.

Methodology

Participants

Five hundred thirty-seven online undergraduate *Introduction to Sociology* students from a public state university in the southern region of the United States were invited to participate.

. . . The students had completed a chapter within the previous month on culture—the concept, key elements, and applications. . . .

Procedure

. . . Students were presented by the instructor with an opportunity to complete a questionnaire about plagiarism as an extra credit assignment to be turned in online. . . . For those students who did not want to complete the survey, an alternative assignment was provided. Either assignment required approximately 20 minutes to complete. . . . In order to receive credit, names were included either on the questionnaire or in the email. They were advised that completion of the assignment would garner full extra credit, and content from the survey would not be graded.

Instrument

The research instrument consisted of a questionnaire designed to elicit students' cultural perspectives and understandings of plagiarism on college campuses. Note that students were not asked to report on their own use of plagiarism but they were indirectly asked their perceptions of it. The use of an indirect question is a commonly used method when a respondent may be uneasy about reporting their own behavior. It also is a direct question about the social norms of plagiarism. The survey included seven open-ended questions developed based on the course textbook "Chapter 2, Culture" assignment. The textbook used for the course was *Society: The Basics*, 10th Edition (Macionis 2008).

In Question One, students were asked to define both plagiarism and Internet plagiarism. Responses were coded as to whether or not they could define such terms accurately. An accurate definition had to include elements of the following: reproduction or inclusion of another person's creative work into one's own work without proper attribution whether from the Internet or other sources. Question Two asked if they thought plagiarism was widespread on college campuses. The responses were coded as yes or no. Question Three asked if students think plagiarism is a part of the dominant culture, subculture, popular culture or not a part of their college campus culture. Responses were coded as dominant, subculture, popular or none. Question Four asked if there is a difference in ethical implications between Internet plagiarism and traditional plagiarism. Responses were coded as Internet and traditional plagiarism having the same ethical implications, Internet plagiarism having more ethical implications, or Internet plagiarism having less ethical implications. Question Five asked what justifications students have heard for plagiarizing. Students were able to include as many justifications as they had heard.

Questions Six and Seven asked whether there were any American cultural values that could contribute to or deter plagiarizing, respectively. Students were asked to list as many values as they deemed appropriate. The eleven American cultural values as defined by Williams (1970) discussed in the chapter were used to code responses, including: individualism, activity and work, practicality and efficacy, progress, equal opportunity, material comfort, democracy and free enterprise, freedom, racism and group superiority, science, and leisure.

. . .

Results

Definition, Extent, and Ethical Implications

Table 1 shows that 100 percent of the 240 students who responded to the questionnaire were able to define plagiarism and Internet plagiarism. In

Table 1 Students' Perceptions Regarding Plagiarism

VARIABLE	n (%)
Define *plagiarism*	240 (100.0%)
Believe widespread problem	189 (84.0%)
Part of collegiate culture	
Popular	72 (34.8%)
Subculture	60 (29.0%)
Dominant	23 (11.1%)
None	52 (25.1%)
Ethical implications: Internet vs. traditional	
Same	207 (87.7%)
Internet more	2 (0.8%)
Internet less	27 (11.4%)

addition, the vast majority of students perceived plagiarism to be a widespread problem on college campuses. While there was considerable variation in students' perceptions of plagiarism as a part of collegiate culture, a strong majority of students (74.9 percent) perceived it to be a part of their collegiate culture and that it was not just a subcultural view. In terms of its ethical implications, 87.7 percent of students felt that there was no difference in the ethical implications between traditional and Internet plagiarism.

Justifications for Plagiarism

A large range of responses were given as justifications that students have heard for plagiarism: Everyone does it, won't get caught by faculty, student is too busy, student didn't have time to complete assignment, easier to get assignment done, it wasn't the entire paper, forgot until last minute, had same idea with different wording, to get a better grade, paraphrased, didn't know how to cite, if on the Internet it is public/not copyrighted, faculty didn't explain assignment, paid for it, and couldn't find enough material. We collapsed these responses into eight categories (Table 3).

The most common justification for plagiarism students stated was that it was the *faculty's fault* (43.7 percent). In the longer narratives, students said things such as an assignment was not being explained clearly, faculty expectations were too high, or that faculty would not be able to catch them. In this latter category, students alluded to the large number of papers the professor had to grade, big classes and resulting student anonymity, and the instructor not being computer savvy. Some students perceived that the professor simply "did not care." "If the professor cared they would check the sources and tell us we would be caught and punished—I think that would decrease the problem, but they really don't care. . . .

Many students also acknowledged that students were at fault for plagiarizing because of their own failings (40.3 percent). In the narratives, students gave justifications for plagiarism such as lack of *time management* skills (e.g., "I am too busy." "I ran out of time.") to self-handicapping explanations (e.g., "I lost my syllabus and didn't know until I ran into a girl from class at a party the night before it was due." "Had a big date the night before—homework can be late").

A large number of students (34.9 percent) justified plagiarism by "blaming society" for developing the Internet *as* a public or "open" forum for information. In their words: "Stuff on the Internet is not copyrighted or published so it isn't theft." ". . . If they didn't want someone to use their words and ideas, they wouldn't put it on the Internet."

The notion that plagiarism is simply an easier way of completing assignments or getting better grades, or simply as a *means to an end*, was given by 34.9 percent of respondents. Responses ranged from "needing to graduate" to "I'm paying for it," to not disappointing parents.

The results in Table 2 were limited to the most frequently endorsed categories (30 percent or more agreement) . . .

Influence of Cultural Values

Table 3 shows an alphabetic list of American cultural values that may contribute to or deter plagiarism. Multiple response data were used to help us to understand factors that may be related to these cultural values.

Contributing Values

About one third of all respondents (32.9 percent) indicated *individualism* as a value contributing to the prevalence of plagiarism. The concept of *personal success* was addressed in statements coded as individualism where a student may say, "Our culture tells us to do whatever it takes to be successful even if it means cheating." The individual achievement at all costs concept was evident as another student stated, . . . "Instead of valuing the process by which an education is obtained, and the information learned through the process, our cultural value of individual achievement means that rewards are only based on grades."

Over 18 percent of students' responses indicated that *science* as a cultural value contributes to the prevalence of plagiarism. Reasons cited included the society's science and technology emphasis as "the hope for the

Table 2 Rationales Students Have Heard for Justifying Plagiarism

RATIONALE	*n* (%)
Faculty's fault	104 (43.7%)
Time management	96 (40.3%)
Means to an end	83 (34.9%)
Internet is public	83 (34.9%)
Did not know	69 (29.0%)
Same idea	65 (27.3%)
Not whole paper	23 (9.7%)
Everyone does it	22 (9.2%)
Have not heard any	17 (7.1%)

future," and growing up with the Internet. A respondent stretched it so far as to say: "Our culture focuses on the use of technology to better our lives so we think that using the Internet to copy and paste information into our paper is bettering our lives."

Freedom was included in 17.5 percent of answers. To this population of students, freedom meant, ". . . we don't have parents looking over our shoulder anymore; we get to do whatever we want." This value was followed closely by *race/group superiority* at 16.3 percent. One of these students . . . alluded to intelligence and inferiority motives: "Students who feel 'dumber' than other students may think they have the right to plagiarize because of being inferior." Other students went so far as to say having money or having group superiority contributed to plagiarizing. "If you can afford to buy a paper and have constant access on your smart phone or iPad to the Internet, why not use it to get your work done faster and easier than everyone else?" "If you are in an upper class you have to maintain a certain image of being smarter—so you may have to plagiarize for it."

A *leisure* dimension was mentioned in 14.2 percent of responses, with one student even justifying plagiarism because Sunday is a religious day. . . . Several pointed to elements of leisure such as football or partying: "Our culture emphasizes that having a good time in college is more important than learning—especially at our school where football and partying is the main focus."

Table 3 American Cultural Values That Contribute to or Deter Plagiarism

VALUE	CONTRIBUTE *n* (%)	DETER *n* (%)
Activity/work	7 (2.9%)	59 (24.6%)
Democracy	2 (0.8%)	54 (22.5%)
Efficiency/practicality	26 (10.8%)	6 (2.5%)
Equal opportunity	20 (8.3%)	21 (8.8%)
Freedom	42 (17.5%)	117 (48.8%)
Individualism	79 (32.9%)	73 (30.4%)
Leisure	34 (14.2%)	20 (8.3%)
Material comfort	14 (5.8%)	2 (0.8%)
Progress	N/A	12 (5.0%)
Racism/group superiority	39 (16.3%)	9 (3.8%)
Science	44 (18.3%)	6 (2.5%)
None	25 (10.4%)	7 (2.9%)

Responses in Table 3 with at least 30 percent agreement were examined in multiple response tables considering endorsement of contributing values to plagiarism. . . .

Deterring Values

Table 3 also reports on American cultural values that may deter plagiarism. Very clearly, the most common response (48.8 percent) was students expressed a *Freedom* theme, i.e., making a morally responsible choice to "do the right thing." Sentiment was that *not* plagiarizing is a moral choice, that plagiarizing amounted to a "group project," and that the moral high ground was not simply following others' bad example. *Individualism* as a deterrent value was next most commonly mentioned (30.4 percent), with students evidencing the importance of individual merit. . . . "We are a competitive country and our achievements are based on personal merit—if you cheat through college you will fail at your job."

The value of hard work (*activity/work*) as a deterrent was identified in 24.6 percent of the responses. "We are taught that hard work will make you achieve more." *Democracy* (or values students discerned under the term) appeared in 22.5 percent of the answers. This theme was evidenced in a variety of ways, including viewing stealing as violating others' rights by taking someone's words and using them as one's own. An *equal opportunity* or fairness value was evident in 8.8 percent of the responses. "Everyone deserves an equal and fair opportunity; it isn't equal opportunity for everyone if some are just cheating."

. . .

Discussion

Students at this large southern university were unanimous in their responses about being able to define plagiarism. All indicated that they knew what it was and were able to discern the difference between traditional and Internet plagiarism. Other researchers have not found this degree of knowledge and consensus (Devlin and Gray 2007; Park 2003). . . . But the fact that *all* students in the survey were able to define accurately the term plagiarism, whether Internet or non-Internet, indicates that a poor understanding of what constitutes plagiarism (Dee and Jacob 2010), is not the case on this campus. . . .

Most students surveyed for this research (84 percent) believed that plagiarism is widespread on all college campuses and indicated that they know who is doing it on their campus. . . . Almost three-fourths of the respondents thought that the practice is part of their campus culture. . . . students were divided over whether it is part of the popular culture (30 percent), subculture (25 percent), or dominant culture (9 percent). When discussing culture in this context, other studies have either discussed the phenomenon of academic dishonesty as a conflict between youth culture and the norms of the educational system (Colnerud and Rosander 2009) or they have declared college campuses as having a "culture of cheating" (Callahan 2004, p. 197). Students in the present study were in an introductory sociology course and had read a chapter dealing with culture several weeks prior to the survey. Therefore, responses can be interpreted at least in part due to their comprehension of the material. . . .

Students in this survey were in agreement on the ethical implications of plagiarism; the vast majority indicated that the practice was wrong, whether through the Internet or not. Interestingly, however, a small group of students perceived Internet plagiarism to be slightly less serious than conventional plagiarism. This minority is consistent with previous research that suggests today's students . . . felt that this behavior did not constitute plagiarism (Baker et al. 2008). . . . Recently, when students were asked if the practice was wrong, nearly all respondents believed that it was, but almost half of them felt that it is socially acceptable (Bernardi et al. 2008).

Justifications for Plagiarism: Implications for Higher Education

Some justifications for plagiarism are revealing in their implications for reducing it. Of particular significance was that close to half of the students believed that the faculty played a significant role in some way in generating a permissive atmosphere for plagiarism. In short, they perceive that faculty often do not care, are too busy to monitor what they are doing, or do not have the technical expertise to detect it. They reported as being much less likely to plagiarize if the faculty indicated early on and often the serious nature of the offense and that they would be caught and punished. . . .

Thus, one can infer that an institutional shift in emphasis will have to occur. Higher education administration, to ensure the academic integrity of the teaching enterprise, should place much more emphasis than in the past on the role of the faculty in not only sensitizing students to the seriousness of plagiarism, but that they will be vigilant and competent in its detection, and that students will be held accountable for the behavior. . . .

There is another dimension to the faculty responsibility issue. It can be argued that students recently out of the high school experience have a tendency to attribute any outside-of-the-classroom assignments as "busy work." Thus, since the very legitimacy of such assignments can be in question, some will rationalize plagiarism as a justified practice (Yardley et al. 2009). This points to the importance of faculty diligence in explaining the purpose of homework assignments and their linkage to course objectives. . . . It is imperative professors make it obvious how assignments link to course objectives and what the students will get out of them. Punishment and reward are both operative here.

Other insights into the prevalence of plagiarism coalesce around the usual challenges of being a student. Problems of time management (40.3 percent) topped the list of reasons. Many students are not prepared academically or emotionally for the challenges of university-level work, or they are not focused on academic accomplishment as central to their university experience. . . . These are students mostly at the beginning of their college experience (61 percent of those who participated in the survey were freshman). They may not yet know how to manage their time demands or yet know how much studying is required or expected of them to be successful. Therefore, it would behoove administration to include during freshman orientation a segment on time management skills. Plagiarism as a means to an end is revealing of instrumental values of this generation of college students. Simply put, the emphasis is on getting a good grade for minimal work. . . .

Rationalizations for the practice included the fact that the Internet is, after all, a public source of information. Although students defined Internet plagiarism accurately, and the vast majority stated it carries the same ethical implications as conventional plagiarism, some still feel justified in copying from the Internet rather than from conventional written works. Students often stated that ideas on the Internet were not copyrighted and therefore were for everyone to use at will. Thus, one can infer that the faculty's challenge is to reassert the concept of intellectual property, specifically in regard to information on the Internet. This also poses a challenge to institutions, as educating faculty on Internet copyright and intellectual laws may also be necessary.

The Influence of Cultural Values on Plagiarism: Implications for Higher Education

When students were asked if any American cultural values contributed to plagiarism, a third of the respondents stated that individual achievement and personal success contribute to the practice of plagiarism, as it helps them get good grades and graduate. Hofstede concluded that . . . "as the level of individualism for a country increased, students perceived unethical actions as being more acceptable" (Bernardi et al. 2008, p. 375). America's emphasis on science to improve one's life was given in reference to using the Internet to plagiarize. The body of evidence indicates that digital or Internet plagiarism has surpassed conventional forms (Stephens et al. 2007). Individual freedom to do as one wants, and the need for leisure time were also indicative of the sample's newfound independence. Group superiority was directly related to the students seeing plagiarism as occurring within certain social groups and not in others.

Students felt overwhelmingly that American cultural values deter plagiarism rather than contribute to it. Personal freedom to do what is right topped this list of values. Respondents felt that plagiarism would not improve their personal success and thus concluded that individual achievement and success deters them from its use. Along those same lines, people in the United States tend to value action over reflection and taking control of events over passively accepting them, activity and work. Interestingly, respondents stated that democracy and free enterprise deterred them from plagiarizing, since stealing someone's ideas takes away their freedom of speech.

First, a case can be made that leaders in higher education need to reduce the emphasis on competition and grades. By de-emphasizing competition and protecting students' privacy in terms of achievement levels, the process of learning becomes the desired outcome, instead of empirical measures and public acknowledgement. Students themselves acknowledge that learning isn't the goal but good grades are. Secondly, administrators need to encourage faculty to embrace teaching along with other academic pursuits. Priority should be given to achieving a better balance between educating students and the research function with its emphasis on grants and publication. Students currently perceive faculty to care more about their career than teaching. Lastly, a social norms campaign should be devised that directly addresses student misperceptions of the incidences of academic misconduct. . . . [T]he effectiveness of an anti-plagiarism campaign depends on providing students with accurate information about their peers' behaviors, which allows them to adjust their perceptions.

. . .

References

Baker, R. K., Berry, P., and Thornton, B. (2008). "Student Attitudes on Academic Integrity Violations." *Journal of College Teaching & Learning* 5 (1), 9.

Bernardi, R. A., Baca, A. V., Landers, K. S., and Witek, M. B. (2008). "Methods of Cheating and Deterrents to Classroom Cheating: An International Study." *Ethics and Behavior* 18 (4), 373–91.

Callahan, D. (2004). *The Cheating Culture: Why More Americans Are Doing Wrong to Get Ahead* (1st ed.). Orlando: Harcourt.

Colnerud, G., and Rosander, M. (2009). "Academic Dishonesty, Ethical Norms and Learning." *Assessment and Evaluation in Higher Education* 34 (5), 505–517.

Macionis, J. J. (2008). *Society: The Basics* (10th ed.). Boston: Pearson.

Selwyn, N. (2008). "Not Necessarily a Bad Thing: A Study of Online Plagiarism Amongst Undergraduate Students." *Assessment & Evaluation in Higher Education* 33 (5), 465–79. doi:10.1080/02602930701563104.

Stephens, J. M., Young, M. F., and Calabrese, T. (2007). "Does Moral Judgment Go Offline When Students Are Online? A Comparative Analysis of Undergraduates' Beliefs and Behaviors Related to Conventional and Digital Cheating." *Ethics & Behavior* 17 (3), 233–54. doi:10.1080/10508420701519197.

Williams, R. (1970). *American Society.* Third edition. New York: Knopf.

Yardley, J., Rodriguez, M. D., Bates, S. C., and Nelson, J. (2009). "True Confessions?: Alumni's Retrospective Reports on Undergraduate Cheating Behaviors." *Ethics & Behavior* 19 (1), 1–14. doi:10.1080/10508420802487096.

Comprehension Questions

1. What do Heckler and Forde want to learn through their study, and what use do they think that information will have?
2. How did Heckler and Forde conduct their study, and what are its most interesting ethical aspects?
3. What interesting information did the study uncover about students' understanding of what plagiarism is?
4. What reasons did students give for plagiarizing?
5. Which cultural values considered in the study were cited by students as supporting plagiarism, and which as opposing plagiarism?
6. Based on the reasons students gave for plagiarizing, what changes to higher education do Heckler and Forde recommend?
7. What do the cultural values students proposed in favor of and against plagiarizing tell us about how universities and colleges can best respond to the problem?

Discussion Questions

1. Why do you think people plagiarize? Do Heckler and Forde cover all the reasons, or are there others?

2. Recall the possible reasons students cited in favor of plagiarizing. Which of these reasons and values do you think count as genuinely moral, rather than just expressing personal preference? Do any of them strike you as plausible justifications for plagiarism?

3. The students surveyed for this study pointed to cultural values both in support of and in opposition to the practice of plagiarism. They also agreed that plagiarism is unethical. Why do you think the cultural values opposing plagiarism trump those supporting it, especially since students' behavior doesn't always match their professed values?

4. A surprising number of students surveyed in this study suggested that instructors may be the reason that many students plagiarize. Do you think instructors are in some sense morally responsible for plagiarism? Does that lessen the wrongness of plagiarizing? Explain your view.

Cases

Consider this argument:

> It's unfair that we judge people based on whether they're good writers. Lots of smart people can speak clearly about an issue, or complete whatever practical task needs completing, but still have trouble articulating their thoughts on paper. It isn't that they don't understand or have the relevant real-world skills; instead, it's that they struggle to get words on paper in the right sort of way. Unfortunately, this can have big consequences for them, since you've got to be able to write to get through school. People who are like this ought to plagiarize to make up for the unfairness of how we judge them. It isn't their fault that we focus so much on writing and so little on what's spoken or done.

Is this a good defense of plagiarism? Would you blame someone who plagiarized and offered this argument in her defense? Why or why not?

50

=== ſ ===

A Moral Case Against Certain Uses of Plagiarism Detection Services

J. Caleb Clanton

One strategy for dealing with the prevalence of plagiarism is to use online plagiarism detection services (PDSs). PDSs, such as Turnitin, generate reports estimating the likelihood of plagiarism in each paper. The use of PDSs, of course, has its advocates and critics. Some endorse it as a deterrent to plagiarism, while others express concern over its legality and the ostensibly unfair burden of proof it places on students. J. Caleb Clanton grants that if an instructor has good reason to suspect plagiarism of a particular student, requiring submission via a PDS is sensible. On the other hand, he contends that requiring all students to do so without provocation and as a default measure for written assignments isn't so sensible. Clanton argues that the latter isn't justified by familiar appeals to deterrence. He claims, moreover, that even if it curbs plagiarism, it encourages the wrong sorts of motivations, a result that is ultimately detrimental to the aim of higher education to inspire civic virtue in students.

Clanton, J. Caleb. 2001. "A Moral Case Against Certain Uses of Plagiarism Detection Services." *International Journal of Applied Philosophy* 23(1): 17–26. doi: 10.5840/ijap20092312

...

The statistics on academic dishonesty are staggering. In a survey published in *U.S. News and World Report*, 75 percent of the college students who were asked admitted to some form of cheating.[1] In another survey, which involved students from nine state universities, 70 percent confessed that they had cheated on exams, 84 percent admitted to cheating on written assignments, and 52 percent said they had lifted lines from a website without giving due credit. A survey conducted by Don McCabe of over 4,500 high school students indicated that 72 percent had cheated on written assignments, 15 percent of students had submitted papers that were mostly not their own work, and 52 percent had directly cut and pasted sentences from websites without providing proper citation. And, the Center for Academic Integrity at Duke University reported that, of the 18,000 private and public high school students surveyed, more than 60 percent admitted to some form of plagiarism.[2]

There seems to be a serious problem. No wonder, then, that many school systems, colleges, and universities have started using plagiarism detection services (PDSs) such as Turnitin, a web-based service that crosschecks student papers against the web, a massive archive of journals and periodicals, and a database of over 22 million student papers that have been collected.[3] After a student's work has been scanned, Turnitin provides instructors with an "originality report," which more-or-less estimates the likelihood that the paper has been plagiarized and by what means. Students are told upfront when their written works are to be vetted by a PDS; in fact, it is legally problematic to use a PDS without notifying students and gaining their consent to have their papers scanned and added to the database.[4] But often nowadays, students are *required* to submit their papers via PDSs. And again, that may seem understandable.

Nonetheless, the use of PDSs remains a controversial issue for a variety of reasons, and I have my own doubts about whether using PDSs is appropriate, though my concerns are a bit different from the typical worries. Some critics point out that PDS technology is imperfect enough that it can produce false positives. While this might be true, it should be noted that PDSs merely offer an originality report—albeit based on probabilities—to be used at the discretion of the instructor; in itself, the originality report does not constitute an accusation of plagiarism, but rather a tool to be used by the instructor in making a decision about whether to pursue further action. Besides, the fact that technological improvement may be in order does not alone entail that the technology should be altogether abandoned, only improved. Perhaps more important, other critics raise legal concerns asking whether a PDS such as Turnitin violates students' intellectual property rights: iParadigms, the company that markets Turnitin, is a for-profit business, and when Turnitin scans students' papers it adds them to the database that it uses in checking for plagiarism. However, a recent memorandum opinion written by US District Court Judge Claude M. Hinton has argued that Turnitin's use of student papers does not constitute copyright infringement because it falls within the legal domain of fair use.[5] Some critics claim that instructors *requiring* students to consent to the terms of a PDS's user agreement is tantamount to consent under duress. Yet, Judge Hinton has argued that third party duress (on the part of the school system or instructor) does not invalidate the contract entered into between the student and the PDS.[6] Still, other critics claim that there is an issue about whether the use of PDSs somehow violates the *privacy* rights that students are guaranteed by the Family Educational and Privacy Act. But, of course, if the user agreement between students and PDSs is indeed a legitimately binding contract, then this concern seems less than forceful.

While I recognize the importance of these sorts of issues, focusing exclusively on the legal issues involved in this matter may distract us from the important moral issues afloat. Rather than focusing on the legal concerns, I mean to argue here that unless we can reasonably suspect a student of academic dishonesty, it is *morally* problematic for instructors and school systems to require her to run her paper through a PDS. This sort of point has already received some preliminary attention by a number of critics, most notably by the Caucus on Intellectual Property and Composition/Communication Studies (CCCP-IP):

> The use of PDSs places students in a position of being "guilty until proven innocent" which casts them as in need of being policed, rather than as trustworthy learners who are motivated to pursue their educational goals with integrity. Not only is this unfair to the majority of students who do not plagiarize, but it conflicts with best practices for fostering student engagement and learning.[7]

While I think the CCCP-IP is largely on target, I do not think the Caucus goes far enough in addressing this point. Thus, I will argue here that, even if we insist that the benefits of PDS use are worth the costs of saddling students with an undeserved burden of proof, *blanket* PDS use—that is, using PDSs across the board and without reasonable suspicion—is problematic because it conflicts with one of the central aims of educational institutions: to cultivate the moral character of students. Although blanket PDS use may in fact deter plagiarism, it does not create an environment conducive to the formation of honor, *and it may even be a hindrance.*

I.

The most prominent argument for using PDSs is that it helps deter plagiarism. It is easy enough to imagine how the argument goes: When teachers use PDSs, plagiarizing is riskier for students than it would have been otherwise, and they no doubt realize this—so when they know their papers will go through a PDS, they are less likely to plagiarize. Notably, the deterrence argument is the main argument that iParadigms gives in marketing Turnitin. For example, the company's website says: "Turnitin's plagiarism prevention is often so successful that institutions using our system on a large scale see measurable rates of plagiarism drop to almost zero."[8] The marketers at iParadigms also could take the argument farther, if they wanted to. If they are connoisseurs of Aristotle, they might add that deterring plagiarism reinforces good behavior in students, getting them in the habit of writing their own papers, and thereby it aids their moral development by instilling such habits. For that matter, the claim might also be that when honest students get low grades while we let their peers rake in the perks of cheating, we effectively *encourage* cheating. Some 90 percent of students who were asked already think that cheaters never get caught or receive appropriate punishment, and 85 percent of students think cheating is needed to "get ahead."[9] Honest students are likely to feel like they are losing out in much the same way that one who pays the subway fee might feel like a sucker when he sees someone else jump the turnstiles.

Another sort of argument for using PDSs is related to that last point, though it is less consequentialist than the first argument is. This second sort of argument says that PDSs help teachers give students what they *deserve*—the honest students, as well as the cheaters. There are at least two variations on this argument. One of them let's call the *desert-identifier version*; it says that PDSs are an effective means by which to charge guilty students and exonerate innocent students who are wrongly accused— that is, to identify *who* deserves *what*. The other version is what we can call the *desert-fairness version*; it claims that educators owe it to honest students to use some sort of effective mechanism of catching cheaters.

There is some sense in that claim, of course. It might be unjust if, for example, honest students earn high grades, while their peers cheat their way to even higher grades. This could result in medical schools, for instance, accepting the cheaters and denying admission to the honest students.[10] . . .

. . .

In spite of this desert argument, though, there still may be problems with requiring *all* students to submit their papers through a PDS—such a blanket requirement does not follow from the desert argument above. Admittedly, perhaps the desert argument shows that the use of a PDS is appropriate in certain cases—namely, cases in which a teacher can reasonably suspect that a particular student has plagiarized, and the teacher runs *just that* student's paper through a PDS. And maybe educators should use an *effective* means of ensuring fairness—maybe they owe that to honest students. But it is not clear that PDSs are a means of that sort. Perhaps all we need are teachers who are savvy enough to catch cheaters and who are good enough at what they should do. As the CCCP-IP correctly notes:

> The use of plagiarism detection services can have the effect of transferring responsibility for identifying and interpreting instances of plagiarism from the instructor to computer software. *The use of technology is not a substitute for good teaching.* Instructors have an obligation to their students to be clear about the roles and mutual responsibilities inherent in college writing. Teaching with integrity means that discussions about academic honesty should be a central part of the learning process, *a role that technology can never fulfill.*[11]
>
> So, if the desert argument is going to justify the blanket use of PDSs, it will need to be coupled with some form of the first sort of argument I mentioned above, namely, the argument about deterrence and habit-formation. So let me now consider *that* argument.

II.

While the deterrence argument has intuitive appeal, it is not without its drawbacks. One of them is that it runs roughshod over an important point—namely, that the blanket use of PDSs saddles students with an undue burden of proof. When an instructor requires all students to submit written work via a PDS as a matter of blanket routine, students have to clear a certain hurdle before the instructor will read their papers.[12] Of course, that might seem insignificant, if it is true that an honest student has nothing to fear from a PDS. But when an instructor has no clear reason to suspect that any particular student in his class has cheated, he has no reason to saddle his students with a burden of proof—doing so would be uncalled for.

To illustrate this point with an analogy: Think of how morally problematic it seems to dole out group punishment—for example, to punish a whole class of students until the guilty member of the class admits to wrongdoing or until the whole class is scared away from future misbehavior. We tend to think this kind of punishment is unjust—unjust for the same sort of reasons for which a deontologist would oppose a strictly instrumentalist/consequentialist view on punishment.[13] On a strictly instrumentalist view, punitive practices would be justified insofar as they are instrumental in achieving desirable consequences and nothing else. Thus, group punishment can be justified if it deters wrongdoing or outs the guilty party. But, a view of that sort rubs against the grain of our better moral intuitions concerning justice. We generally think we should not punish people unless they *deserve* it. For example, if Jane did not break the law, we would think it is unfair to punish her as a scapegoat for someone else's criminal behavior—even if doing so would help bring about certain benefits like, for instance, quelling a riot or quieting a lynch mob. And what I mean to say is that it is similarly unfair to put a burden of proof on every student in class just because some student somewhere might be a cheater—even if doling out such a burden of proof would help bring about certain benefits like, for instance, deterring plagiarism.[14]

Of course, my analogy above might seem off base. "It's not just that some undergraduate somewhere *might* be a cheater," one could object. "In light of the surveys in which student after student *admits* to cheating, we have plenty of reason to suspect *all* students of cheating." But that objection overlooks an important distinction between collective guilt and individual guilt. Though surveys suggest that more than half of all students have cheated at some point, these surveys tell an instructor nothing about *which* students in *her* class are cheaters. In this sense, if the surveys are what lead us to use PDSs, our use of PDSs is no more defensible than racial profiling. And racial profiling can seem highly problematic: it seems strange to think that when the Los Angeles police department stops a particular African-American man for speeding, they can *reasonably* suspect him of having drugs or a weapon simply because the statistical tables of the U.S. Department of Justice indicates that 44 percent of all drug offense defendants and 54 percent of all weapons offense defendants in the 75 largest counties were black non-Hispanic.[15] It seems strange to us precisely because what is true of a group is not necessarily true of a particular member of the group. By the same token, it is one thing to say that students *on the whole* are dishonest, and it is another to say that a *certain* student is. . . .

III.

Now, we might insist that the benefits of deterring plagiarism and promoting moral development as well as academic fairness are worth the costs of putting the burden of proof on students. But even if they *are* worth it, the blanket PDS use is problematic not only because it cannot avoid the tension between the goal of keeping students honest and treating them with dignity—that is, treating them as though they are not suspects—but because it conflicts with one of the main purposes of educational institutions: to cultivate citizens.[16] This consideration does not get much attention within the two philosophical frameworks that the arguments for PDSs spring from, a framework that favors utilitarianism and a framework that centers on desert. And while those frameworks might be appropriate for thinking about the liberal democratic state, they are not always appropriate for thinking about the policies that educators and educational institutions should adopt. Unlike governments, educational institutions should be concerned about something more than simply maximizing liberty to pursue one's own good in one's own way or ensuring fair procedures for students. Educational institutions should be concerned with students' motives and with the project of cultivating students' characters, especially cultivating honor. For, the project of sculpting moral character is central to the task of cultivating citizens. But to carry out that project, we have to take certain risks, namely the risk that cheaters might in fact get away with cheating.

Here's what I mean. Suppose it is true that the blanket use of PDSs deters a lot of plagiarism and promotes good behavior among students. Even then, the good behavior is most likely driven by the wrong motivations: the fear of getting caught and being punished. Clearly, PDSs are not concerned with *why* a student is not cheating—that is, whether the student is acting out of integrity or is just afraid of getting caught. Consequently, PDSs at best only dis-incentivize bad academic behavior; they do not instill honor. In fact, perhaps the opposite is true: blanket PDS use might even encourage students to think that the chief reason to not cheat is that they will get caught and punished if they do. And that is a far cry from cultivating honor in students. . . .

The point worth taking away here is that there is an important difference between doing the right thing for egoistic reasons and doing the right thing because one is motivated to do the right thing—and this is a difference *that should make a difference*, so to speak, for those concerned about moral education and character formation. For, students do eventually graduate to the larger workforce and society, and screening devices like PDSs are likely nowhere to be found. And, it is the job of educational institutions to cultivate citizens to be poised to do more than simply doing what will help them avoid punishment—especially when no one will catch them if they do less. Accordingly, there is an important difference between a student who avoids plagiarism in order to avoid the punishment for himself and a student who avoids plagiarism for the sake of being honorable, trustworthy, and decent. The problem, though, is that widespread, blanket use of PDSs could have the unfortunate effect of structurally reinforcing the cultivation of the former and not the latter.

. . .

IV.

I submit that trust, rather than suspicion, should be the default posture that teachers take toward students: Unless we can reasonably suspect that particular students are cheating, we should trust them. Why? Various arguments come to mind, perhaps the strongest of which would be an epistemic argument of sorts. But instead of arguing for trust in that manner here, I will simply point out that distrust is surely unacceptable.

Suppose that we (educators) make distrust our default posture toward students, that is, we treat everything that is submitted to us by students as though we were suspicious of its authorship. Accordingly, we remain suspicious of students' papers, exams, etc. until they pass the test of a PDS or some such. If that seems appropriate, then one should ask: Why stop *there*, given why distrust seems appropriate in the first place? Why not as a matter of policy (aimed at deterring dishonesty and ensuring academic fairness) require every student to pass a polygraph test prior to registering for a course or even enrolling in school? Of course, most of us would think that using polygraphs is going too far, even if it were logistically feasible. But, there is no *principled* distinction between using lie detectors and the policy of requiring students to submit their work via a PDS when there are no grounds for reasonable suspicion. And, like polygraph requirements, blanket PDS use seems to send the wrong message to students—"we don't trust you because you can't be trusted; instead we're here to police you." . . .

Now, a proponent of PDS use might wish to object here. The objection is that blanket PDS use, rather than sending a message of distrust, actually conveys a concern on behalf of the educators for honest students who might lose out if cheaters reap the rewards of easy cheating while honest students do not. In fact, an objector might add that, even if PDSs are ineffective at catching cheaters, their blanket use helps convey the right kind of message to the students (a concern for fairness and desert), and it is that *message* that counts. But, it is not clear why blanket PDS use is needed for conveying this sort of message. In fact, if an instructor properly uses the PDS—in cases where there are grounds for reasonable suspicion—then the concern for fairness is adequately conveyed. But, even if that is not the case, the problem with this kind of objection is that it assumes that the purpose of the school, like the state, is to ensure fair procedures. But, this misses the point about the proper aim of educational institutions: to create conditions under which honor and character formation can emerge.

No doubt many PDS proponents will persist in thinking that blanket PDS use is simply analogous to security screening at the airport. And, presumably, the inconvenience, privacy encroachment, and the burden of proof imposed on passengers are all justified to the extent that they are necessary to protect against the risk of terrorism or some other grave danger.[17] Hence, airport security screening is consistent with Mill's harm principle.[18] But, one should note the dissimilarity between airport screening and blanket PDS use. Whereas airport screening imposes a burden of proof on passengers with the aim of protecting against public harm, the burden of proof imposed by blanket PDS use provides no clear protection against public harm in a way that would justify abandoning the default posture of trust that should otherwise govern teacher-student relationships. At best, it could be argued that the burden of proof imposed by PDSs helps prevent "harm" to the honest students in the sense of putting them at an unfair disadvantage to cheaters in applying, say, to medical school. But, at the very least, it is not clear that being put at such an unfair disadvantage is equivalent to being harmed in the relevant sense. Or, the objector might wish to claim that the public good secured by blanket PDS use is that it keeps the educational institution—and, in turn, the diplomas and degrees it grants—from being tarnished. But, note that this sort of objection relies upon a tacit acknowledgement of the purpose of the institution—to graduate *virtuous* citizens—in which case this objection fails on its own terms. For failing to cultivate honor in students sullies the institution far more than letting cheaters slip by, because when we have failed in cultivating honor we have shirked one of the central tasks of the institution.

. . .

Comprehension Questions

1. What are some common concerns raised over the use of PDSs?
2. What are the two main arguments that Clanton discusses for using PDSs?
3. Why does Clanton think that a blanket requirement to submit via PDSs is unfair to students?
4. How, according to Clanton, does indiscriminate use of PDSs conflict with the goals of educational institutions?
5. Why should trust, and not suspicion, be the default attitude of instructors toward students?

Discussion Questions

1. Clanton compares regularly requiring all students to submit their work via PDSs to racial profiling. Do you agree with that comparison? Are there any morally significant differences? Explain your view.
2. A key reason Clanton gives for rejecting the blanket use of PDSs is that it is detrimental to students' virtue. Do you agree with his assumption that educational institutions should seek to influence students' character, or do you think doing so is overly paternalistic? Explain your view.
3. Whether blanket use of PDSs inhibits virtuous character traits depends partially on the message their use sends to students. Clanton says that it's a message of distrust, but mentions the possible view that it's rather one of concern. In your experience, is one of these closer to the truth than the other?

Case

> At the University of Waterloo, if professors want to use a plagiarism detection service, they are required to put this clause in their syllabuses:
>
> > Plagiarism detection software (Turnitin) will be used to screen assignments in this course. This is being done to verify that use of all materials and sources in assignments is documented. Students will be given an option if they do not want to have their assignment screened by Turnitin. In the first week of the term, details will be provided about arrangements and alternatives for the use of Turnitin in this course.[19]
>
> Is this a good requirement? Should students have the right to opt out? Does this place an unreasonable burden on faculty, or is it an important way of respecting students?

Notes

1. *US News & World Report*, November 22, 1999.
2. [Editor's Note: At one point, the references for these statistics appeared at www.plagiarism.org, though they no longer do. Similar numbers appear on the current version of the site.]
3. Nearly 100,000 scanned student documents are added to Turnitin's database every day. Some 7,000 educational institutions have contracted with Turnitin. See Judge Claude Hilton, *Memorandum Opinion*, United States District Court for the Eastern District of Virginia, Alexandria Division, March 11, 2008.
4. To avoid legal problems, Turnitin requires students to create a profile on their website prior to submission. In this process, students must consent (by clicking "I agree") to the user agreement that spells out the terms and conditions of the use of their work.
5. Judge Claude Hilton, *Memorandum Opinion*, United States District Court for the Eastern District of Virginia, Alexandria Division, March 11, 2008, 12–19.
6. Judge Hilton argues: "Though Plaintiffs plead duress, there is no evidence that anyone was coerced in any fashion by Turnitin or iParadigms. Insofar as Plaintiffs' duress defense is asserted against Plaintiffs' respective school, rather than Defendant iParadigms, there is no support for the proposition that a contract can be invalidated on the basis of third party duress. . . . Nevertheless, even if there was evidence of coercion by iParadigms, or even if a claim of third party duress by the school systems was viable, such coercion would not rise to the level of an 'unlawful or wrongful act.' Schools have a right to decide how to monitor and address plagiarism in their school and may employ companies like iParadigms to help do so. As the Supreme Court has recognized in

the constitutional contact, 'the rights of students in public schools are not automatically coextensive with the rights of adults in other settings' and the 'rights of students must be applied in light of the special characteristic of the school environment'" (10–11). Judge Claude Hilton, *Memorandum Opinion*, United States District Court for the Eastern District of Virginia, Alexandria Division, March 11, 2008.

7. CCCC-IP, "Caucus Recommendations Regarding Academic Integrity and the Use of Plagiarism Detection Services," 2. Available online at http://www.immagic .com/eLibrary/ARCHIVES/GENERAL/NCTE_US/CCCC-IPpositionstatement Draft%209%2016%2006.pdf

8. [Editor's Note: This was indeed part of Turnitin's marketing strategy at one point—see, e.g., http://www.immagic.com/eLibrary/ARCHIVES/GENERAL/ GRANTCUS/I050728P.pdf—though it seems not to appear on the current version of the company's site.]

9. [Editor's Note: see Note #2.]

10. In court and elsewhere, people have claimed that it *is* unjust for medical schools to give admission to those who haven't earned high enough grades. See, for instance, *Regents of the University of California v. Bakke*, 438 U.S. 265 (1978)—although, it should be noted that this case deals with this issue relative to affirmative action.

11. CCCC-IP, "Caucus Recommendations Regarding Academic Integrity and the Use of Plagiarism Detection Services," 2, emphasis added. Available online at http://www.immagic.com/eLibrary/ARCHIVES/GENERAL/NCTE_US/ CCCC-IPpositionstatementDraft%209%2016%2006.pdf

12. In the complaint filed against Fairfax County Public Schools system and the Tucson Unified School District, students were required to submit their work via Turnitin. Accordingly, if a student refused to submit via Turnitin, they received a zero. See Judge Claude Hilton, *Memorandum Opinion*, United States District Court for the Eastern District of Virginia, Alexandria Division, March 11, 2008, 3–4.

13. See, e.g., James Rachels's discussion of this point in his *Elements of Morality* (New York: MacGraw-Hill, 2007), 133–40. See also Joel Feinberg, *Doing and Deserving* (Princeton: Princeton University Press, 1970); and Immanuel Kant, *The Metaphysical Elements of Justice*, trans. John Ladd (Indianapolis: Bobbs-Merrill, 1965), 99–107.

14. We avoid this problem if we use PDSs only when we can reasonably suspect a particular student of plagiarizing. But note that if a PDS isn't being used as a mandatory blanket screen, but merely as an investigative tool on the basis of special suspicion, then the PDS use no longer has the same sort of deterrent effect! And that means, that the strongest argument in support of blanket PDS use—that they act as plagiarism deterrents—is significantly diminished. For, PDSs mostly act as a plagiarism deterrent to the extent that they are used as a required screen for all papers. An analogy here might be something like this:

Chopping off the heads of smokers may have a desired effect of getting smokers to quit—but only if killing is used unfairly, i.e., to kill people who do not really deserve to die. If we killed a death-row inmate "for smoking," it is not clear that this would actually deter anyone from smoking given that many people think he deserves to die anyway. But, if we killed little old grandmothers and teenage pop-stars for smoking, then *that* would likely catch the attention of smokers and have a deterring effect. But, it would clearly be undeserved killing as well, even if it had the desired deterring effect.

15. According to the 2004 statistical tables of the US Department of Justice's Bureau of Justice Statistics, 44 percent of all drug offense defendants and 54 percent of all weapons offense defendants in the 75 largest counties were black non-Hispanic. The U.S. Census Bureau data for 2004 indicates that the overall population of these 75 counties was 16 percent black non-Hispanic.

16. What follows draws upon the structure of Michael Sandel's argument against the use of advertisements in schools. See his essay, "Commercials in the Classroom" in *Public Philosophy* (Harvard University Press, 2005), 73–6.

17. Presumably, mandatory drug testing for student athletes is justified on similar grounds: Even though drug testing encroaches on a student's private life, it helps protect the tested student and other students from injury while playing sports. Clearly, this argument is less forceful than the argument in support of airport screening because of the greater degree of harm at stake.

18. John Stuart Mill. *On Liberty* (London: Longmans, Green, Reader, and Dyer, 1869), 21–2.

19. https://uwaterloo.ca/learn-help/instructors/turnitin

═══ 🐌 ═══

51

Seven Arguments Against Extra Credit

Christopher A. Pynes

....

From the student's point of view, it may seem that whether an instructor gives opportunities for extra credit just depends on whether they're caring, generous, sympathetic (but perhaps also ingratiating) people. In any event, it probably doesn't seem like a matter of principle whether or not it is given. And maybe instructors take the same attitude too. Christopher Pynes argues otherwise—in fact, he contends that there is no good reason for it to ever be offered. He considers some arguments in favor of giving extra credit and attempts to explain where they go wrong. Pynes also provides a laundry list of arguments highlighting a variety of problematic aspects of extra credit for students and instructors alike. The cumulative force of these arguments amounts to a formidable challenge to anyone desiring to take a principled stand in favor of extra credit opportunities.

....

Pynes, Christopher A. 2014. "Seven Arguments Against Extra Credit" *Teaching Philosophy* 37(2): 191–214. doi: 10.5840/teachphil20144414

. . .

Introduction

There is a clear tension between the purpose of grading student work and a student's desire to obtain a higher grade, especially when the higher grade is the result of "extra credit" assignments. I explore this tension, and ultimately, argue for an anti–extra credit thesis: extra credit is pedagogically unjustified and should not be used. Another way to express the claim is: there are no good arguments for the use of extra credit assignments in the college classroom. . . .

The three best arguments for justifying the offering of extra credit are what I name the "Relevance" argument, and two "Academic Virtues" arguments: "Research Virtues" and the "Mission Virtues." I then present seven anti–extra credit arguments, the two most cogent of which are the "Equity" argument and the "Addition Paradox." . . .

Any discussion of extra credit has to be done within the confines of a discussion of grading in general. . . . The following definitions of grading and extra credit are presented as both uncontroversial and commonly understood. . . .

1. Grading is, ideally, used to measure learning or to measure the quality of work done on a given academic task—for example, papers, quizzes, group projects, exams, or speeches.[1]
2. An extra credit assignment's purpose is to provide an opportunity for a student to increase a grade by performing additional work.[2]

. . . I will . . . defend (1) against two common objections presented below as pro–extra credit arguments.

Additionally, I shall argue that (2) is incoherent as a grading concept given the truth of (1).

. . .

Three Pro–Extra Credit Arguments

The "Relevance" Argument for Extra Credit

Proponents of extra credit offer the following argument in its defense.[3] When a guest speaker is going to give a lecture in town, or some other academically worthy out-of-class event is being held, the professor should offer extra credit to students who attend the event. If merely attending the event isn't enough to justify offering extra credit, then proponents often suggest requiring a short paper to rigor up the requirement. On its face, this seems to be a legitimate pedagogical method of trying to get students engaged in the real world on subjects and topics that are relevant to their studies at the university. I name this the "Relevance" argument because it is an attempt, even if a weak one, to help students make relevant connections between their classes and the real world.[4]

Notably, there are often cross-purposes at work when there are guest speakers visiting a department or university. The host department or university wants the guest speaker to be greeted by a respectably-sized audience that includes both students and faculty. So there is a genuine desire to get warm bodies in the seats. Extra credit is, therefore, used as a way to incentivize (or motivate) students to attend the "relevant" event. . . . But one might be tempted to ask why this is a good pedagogical reason to assign extra credit. Can mere bodies in seats with a tempting offer of extra credit constitute a legitimate grading method? Typically the extra credit in these instances is an all-or-nothing affair, although it need not be. Students attend the event, write the required number of relevant pages, and thus earn the extra credit—say, ten points. This satisfies the definition of extra credit, (2) from above, but it is not grading in the sense expressed in (1).[5] . . .

The "Academic Virtues" Arguments for Extra Credit

There are two versions of the "Academic Virtues" arguments. . . . The first is the "Academic Research Virtues" argument, and the second is the "Academic Mission Virtues" argument. It should also be clear that these arguments are an attempt to put pressure on the definition of the purpose of grading—claim (1) from above—as much as they are a defense of extra credit. These arguments attempt to use extra credit grading as a way of fostering other ideals; thus, they go beyond mere grading and are serious threats to standard models of grading as expressed in (1) and defended by authors like Close (2009).

Let's begin with the "Academic Research Virtues" argument. Psychology researchers need to have access to large groups of volunteers in order to conduct certain kinds of research studies. The usual way psychology faculty incentivize (or motivate) participation in research studies is by offering extra credit to students who participate in them.[6] . . .

. . .

We should ask: how does the psychology researcher's need for research subjects benefit students and student learning when students participate as the research subjects? The answer is that there isn't a clear benefit. One possibility, however, is that students who voluntarily participate in research studies for extra credit will benefit academically from the experience. In "Extra Credit as Incentive for Voluntary Research Participation," Padilla-Walker and colleagues state, "Because the educational value of research participation (e.g., learning about the research process) is essential to satisfying the ethical requirements of student research participation . . ., a number of studies have examined the potential education benefits of participation in research, and the results have been mixed" (Padilla-Walker et al. 2005: 150). In the conclusion of their study, they write:

> Although good students commonly obtained extra credit, the greatest percentage of students who participated in research for extra credit were those who already had an A in the class. . . . [I]t is clear that the majority of students did not take advantage of this educational opportunity, which raises questions regarding the education utility of such practices. Indeed, students who would seemingly benefit the most from this opportunity were the least likely to voluntarily participate. (Padilla-Walker et al. 2005: 152)

. . .

The "Academic Mission Virtues" argument focuses on the mission of the class over and above teaching just course material.[7] This is to say that there are some virtues an instructor attempts to instill in students that go beyond graded material in the class. These are activities that are good for the student (e.g., attending class and participating in discussions), good for the department (e.g., participating as a research volunteer), and good for the community (e.g., volunteer work). These academic virtues, the argument goes, are often best fostered via extra credit. In essence, this argument is an attempt to put pressure on the purpose of grading, or the original purpose of grading, claim (1).[8]

This is an important and interesting argument, and a simple reply without giving a full defense of (1) is possible while maintaining that these are virtues our classes should foster in addition to grading for course content and performance. First, it should be noted that not every required aspect of a class is graded. We frequently ask students to do things, like attend class or read material, on which they will not be tested. Let us take class attendance as an academic virtue that faculty want to foster and explore graded versus non-graded use as it relates to ungraded mission fostering.

When it comes to class attendance, there are three schools of thought. First, no credit of any kind (positive or negative) should be given for class attendance. I subscribe to this view. Second, attendance should be a factor of one's grade in a positive manner. For example, some faculty members I know make upwards of 40 percent of the course grade based on attendance alone. Third, there are those who only give negative grades for not attending class. In other words, after a set number of absences, a student's grade is negatively affected. The second and third versions of attendance grading are pedagogically unacceptable for different reasons.

In the second case, students who show up get credit for something they should be doing anyway. This seems to put the evaluation or graded reward in the wrong place, and it doesn't account for learning or engagement at all. By attending class students get the added benefit of the class experience and lecture, so they are rewarded twice. Likewise, the third example punishes students twice. Students lose out by not getting the classroom experience and lecture material, and their grades are negatively affected by losing attendance grades. So in both cases, there is either too much benefit, as in the second case, or too much harm, as in the third. . . . Thus, graded attendance is not a legitimate grading process. . . . Even though there are lots of academic mission virtues we would like to foster in our students, like class attendance, we can't use the grade book to foster them all. . . .

At this point, we might ask: What then should the situation look like in terms of needing to foster academic virtues as an additional element of a class? There are obvious, legitimate pedagogical solutions to things like motivation that do not include using the grade book and extra credit. For example, faculty could make certain features of the class mandatory but not graded. Faculty members already do this often without realizing it, by requiring students to read material that isn't going to be discussed in class or even tested on. We could require students to attend two outside philosophy events but not provide a grade for attendance. Attendance at the event will be a requirement for earning a course grade, but it will not be a weighted factor of the course grade. English faculty members do this when they have students do ungraded "writing to learn" assignments, like requiring a rough draft.[9] How this works is that students write and get feedback, but the rough draft isn't graded, only the final paper. This allows for evaluating skills at the end of a process rather than grading the process of learning the skills. . . . Thus virtues can be fostered without the "reward" of counting the virtue fostering as graded course work.[10] . . .

But even more important empirical issues arise. Do these extra credit assignments actually foster the academic virtues (like reading and attendance) in question, and do students take advantage of such opportunities? Does it actually motivate students? Several studies in the psychology literature say the answer is no to both questions. Henley and Savage's 1993 paper answered the first question. They found that the video games and survey participation didn't foster academic virtues. But what if an extra credit assignment does try to foster academic virtues? Will students participate then?

Randy Moore's 2005 paper aptly demonstrates how extra credit expectations don't fit behavior. His three-year study with 1,216 undergraduates in introductory biology classes for non-science majors showed that, of two possible extra credit assignments, only 15 percent did the first assignment, 21 percent did the second, and 12 percent did both. Only 24 percent of the students did even one extra credit assignment, but when we contrast this with the survey data from the start of the class where 81 percent said they would submit an extra credit assignment, we see that this isn't so.[11] What is more interesting in this case is which students did the extra credit. Moore writes, "Approximately 40 percent of all students who earned an A did at least one extra-credit assignment, 20 percent who earned a B did at least one, 18 percent who earned a D did at least one, and 5 percent who earned an F did at least one extra credit assignment" (Moore 2005: 13). So we learn that effort level required to complete the extra credit assignment seems to correlate with grades, and that the extra credit offer doesn't actually motivate students who aren't already motivated. Likely, part of the reason this particular version of extra credit wasn't done to the extent that students claimed is because it is very similar in rigor to the actual assignments in the class. For some reason extra credit has gotten to a point where it is seen as something that should be easier than the original course work, and in Moore's case, it was not.

. . .

The Seven Arguments Against Extra Credit

There are at least seven cogent arguments in defense of the anti–extra credit thesis. Let's begin with the "Equity" argument, which is offered to undercut the strength of the pro–extra credit, "Relevance" argument. The four arguments following the "Equity" argument are not supposed to be definitive arguments against using extra credit. The final two arguments, however, are each sufficient as defenses of the anti–extra credit thesis. All seven arguments combined, make any attempt to justify using extra credit assignments impossible. . . .

The "Equity" Argument

The "Equity" argument undercuts the justification of the "Relevance" argument. It is given that every student in a class should have an equal opportunity to earn the same grades as every other student; they all take the same exams, write the same number of papers, and so on.[12] So any assignment or extra credit that one student has the opportunity to complete must be made available to all the other students in the class. Both required work and extra credit work should be assigned or provided on an equal basis. The "Equity" argument is defended minimally with the use of course syllabi and other equity-making strategies.[13]

The "Equity" argument simply recognizes that not all students are able to attend an event occurring outside of scheduled class time, as the pro–extra credit "Relevance" argument requires. Students can, and often do, have any number of justified conflicts to attending an out-of-class event, such as other scheduled classes, jobs, volunteer activities, family obligations, sporting events, university obligations, or studying. If this is the case, then going to a philosophy lecture or other outside event would present an undue burden on students and prevent them from having equal access to the extra credit opportunity and final grade. The basic issue is equity or fairness. . . . So even though an extra credit event is relevant and promotes virtues, it does so at the cost of fairness. . . .

. . .

The "Unnecessary Burden" Argument

The "Unnecessary Burden" argument is based on the simple fact that extra credit assignments mean extra work for the faculty member. If a faculty member has between three and four classes a semester with anywhere from thirty to fifty students in each class, then it can become quite a bookkeeping task to keep track of regular grades earned, much less the additional extra credit assignments. Moreover, if the extra credit assignment is graded in a meaningful way[14] (that is, not the all-or-nothing . . . style assessment), then there is an even greater grading burden over and above the strictly administrative task of keeping track of which students attended an event. And if we take equity seriously, then there is the added burden of providing additional, relevant extra credit opportunities for everyone. Put another way, if the syllabus requires a certain amount of graded work and the professor has agreed to grade the work and the students have agreed to do the work, then any additional work is just that: additional. It is by definition extra work, and thus an unnecessary burden on both the professor and the student. And if we take the "Equity" argument seriously and give every student the same opportunity to do extra credit work, then the amount of total work will rapidly increase. Even though the "Unnecessary Burden" argument isn't definitive to undercut all justifications for extra credit, it is, for many faculty members, a cogent reason or sufficient condition not to provide extra credit assignments at the individual level, especially if the course includes sufficient graded material to justify assigning a grade in the first place.

The "Moral Hazard" Argument

Mark Wilson puts forth the "Moral Hazard" argument when he writes: "The existence, or the hope, of extra credit may induce students to prepare less carefully for exams and papers with the expectation that additional points can be earned on future assignments" (Wilson 2002, 97). Essentially, a moral hazard situation occurs when people in an economic-type situation change their behavior relative to loss prevention when they can be protected from the risk. Extra credit does just this. . . .

. . .

What is worrisome in these cases is that students who believe extra credit will save them in the end don't do some of the work required for the class. If they continue to neglect their work, the moral hazard escalates until the student's grade is beyond recovery. At that point, they fail to even attempt the extra credit since it will be of no use. It would seem that to rectify low grades, the professor, in offering extra credit opportunities, is not only fostering moral hazard, but essentially has dirty hands in trying to create the good of higher grades without a corresponding increase in learning. . . .

The "Grade Inflation" Argument

Everyone should be aware that there is a grade inflation epidemic at every level of education.[15] In fact, the sole purpose of extra credit is to increase the student's grade through additional work, which is why extra credit rarely causes a student's grade to be lowered—the asymmetry of extra credit. So by eliminating extra credit, we remove one cause of grade inflation. Here is how extra credit typically contributes to grade inflation. To make the example easy, let's look at a class that uses an absolute method for assigning grades. If you get a certain number of points in the class, you get a particular grade. For example, in a class with 1,000 total possible points, 900 points or higher would earn an A. So if a student could add points to her total and increase her grade, then this is ipso facto grade inflation. What has occurred in these types of cases is that grading as a measure of learning is undercut and the grade is unjustly inflated. This is to claim that extra credit by its very nature goes against the general claim of (1).

. . .

The "Failure in Conception" Argument (Bonus Points on Exams)

This particular argument is aimed at extra credit possibilities on exams—like "bonus questions"—but it applies to entire class grades as well. In other words, the "bonus problem" problem is really an instance of the general extra credit problem.

Professors sometimes include a bonus question on an exam in an effort to give students an opportunity to earn a higher score or just to show off. This is a form of extra credit, and it falls prey to a special kind of objection. To understand this, we must first look at how these types of bonus questions are constructed. When it comes to the failure in conception argument for bonus questions on exams, there are two extremes: easy and hard. For example, if the bonus question is so easy that the vast majority of the students will get the answer right and earn the bonus points, then it is just like scaling an exam score set upward depending on how much the bonus question is worth. So, for example, a five-point bonus question that is so easy that most students will get it right will increase their score by five points or about half a letter grade. . . .

A high tide raises all ships in the same way that an easy bonus question raises (nearly) all grades. Without a principled way to justify the easy version of the bonus questions, what occurs is grade inflation. Nearly all the grades are raised for no good reason except for the point of giving a bonus question.

In the case of hard bonus questions, only the A students are able to earn the extra credit points. But these students don't "need" the points to raise their grades; they are already as high as they can go. So it would actually fail as an instance of extra credit because it doesn't satisfy the criterion set forth in (2) to increase the student's grade.[16] And if the bonus questions are structured so students could guess the answer, then there is an element of luck involved in the grading process, and this is clearly not a fair method of judging work and a clear violation of the purpose of grading defined in (1).

. . .

The "Assigned Work Paradox"

Typically a student . . . asks to do some extra work to get extra "points" or replace a missed assignment to increase her grade. My typical reply to this type of request is the same as what most parents tell their children when they ask for a new pet: Why should I get you another pet (dog, cat, snake, etc.) when you can't take care of the one you have? . . .

The point is, why would a professor want to give extra credit work to a student who has failed to demonstrate an ability to do the originally assigned work? Many students seem to think that another assignment to replace a missed one or make up for poor performance makes perfect sense. It would be interesting to survey students to determine if they thought a person who skips a day of work should be allowed to make it up at another time and get a raise. . . .

The "Addition Paradox"

The "Addition Paradox" is the best anti–extra credit argument of all. . . . Yes, grades are assigned given the quality of a certain quantity of work: a B (say 85) for 30 percent of the class. Clearly more work of a certain quality should not entitle a person to a higher, qualitative grade with extra credit work of a similar quality to the original grade. Basically, this is the difference between being a Benthamite and a Millian about extra credit and grades. Some professors are Millians when it comes to grading. No increase in quantity will increase the quality; all more D work does is keeps the grade at a D. Most students and parents, however, are Benthamites when it comes to grades: They believe that more completed work means more points, which means a higher grade. . . . Students feel they need to get to a point level any way they can, and the easiest way to "earn" more points is via extra credit. The problem is you can't just pile up a bunch of D-quality work and expect to earn an A. But this is the kind of thing that happens when faculty allow students to gain extra points to increase their grades.

. . .

Conclusion

Well-meaning professors who want to motivate students, foster learning, and promote academic virtues have tried to use extra credit as a way to achieve those goals. The evidence showing that using extra credit supports those goals is inconclusive at best and negative at worst. The best efforts to justify the use of extra credit run into multiple objections ranging from fairness to conceptual incoherence. Moreover, any attempt to justify the use of extra credit will have to properly reply to the seven anti-extra credit arguments I've presented, which cannot be done.

My conclusion is simple: Don't offer extra credit opportunities. . . . There are no good arguments justifying the use of extra credit. It fosters moral hazards, promotes a system of grade inflation, makes professors (and other graders) work more than necessary, and creates paradoxes. Just say "no" to extra credit.[17]

References

Carkenord, David M. (1994). "Motivating Students to Read Journal Articles." *Teaching of Psychology* 21 (3) (October), 162–64.

Close, Daryl. (2009). "Fair Grades." *Teaching Philosophy* 32 (4) (December), 361–98.

Corsum, David L. (2000). "Extra Credit ≠ Extra Learning." *Journal of Hospitality & Tourism Education* 12 (3), 4–7. http://dx.doi.org/10.1080/10963758.2000.106 85285

Druger, Marvin. 2000. "A Perspective on Exams and Grading." *Journal of College Science Teaching* 30 (3) (November), 210–12.

Grove, James L. (2000). "Students' Perceptions of Extra Credit." *Journal of Hospitality & Tourism Education* 12 (1), 27–30. http://dx.doi.org/10.1080/10963758.2 000.10685265

Grove, James L. (2003). "Perceptions of Extra Credit by Hospitality and Tourism Faculty." *Journal of Hospitality & Tourism Education* 14 (3), 38–43. http://dx.doi.org/10.1080/10963758.2003.10697026

Hassel, Holly, and Jessica Lourey. (2005). "The Dea(r)th of Student Responsibility." *College Teaching* 53 (1), 2–13. http://dx.doi.org/10.3200/CTCH.53.1.2-13

Henley, Tracey B., and Indy L. Savage. (1993). "Who Earns Extra Credit These Days?" *The Journal of Psychology* 128 (3), 311–14. http://dx.doi.org/10.1080/002 23980.1994.9712734

Hill, G. William IV, Joseph J. Palladino, and James A. Eison. (1993). "Blood, Sweat, and Trivia: Faculty Ratings of Extra-Credit Opportunities." *Teaching of Psychology* 20 (4) (December), 209–13.

Immerwahr, John. (2011). "The Case for Motivational Grading." *Teaching Philosophy* 34 (4) (December), 335–46.

Johnson, Valen E. (2003). *Grade Inflation: A Crisis in College Education*. New York: Springer-Verlag.

La Lopa, Joseph M. (2000). "Shuffling Deck Chairs on the Titanic: A Rebuttal to the Article on Extra Credit ≠ Extra Learning." *Journal of Hospitality & Tourism Education* 12:3: 8–9. http://dx.doi.org/10.1080/10963758.2000.10685286

Moore, Randy. (2005). "Who Does Extra-Credit Work in Introductory Science Courses?" *Journal of College Science Teaching* 34 (7) (July–August), 12–16.

Norcross, John C., Heather S. Dooley, and John F. Stevenson. (1993). "Faculty Use and Justification of Extra Credit: No Middle Ground?" *Teaching of Psychology* 20 (4) (December), 240–42.

Norcross, John C., Linda J. Horrocks, and John F. Stevenson. (1989). "Of Barfights and Gadflies: Attitudes and Practices concerning Extra Credit in College Courses." *Teaching of Psychology* 16 (4) (December), 199–203.

Oley, Nancy. (1992). "Extra Credit and Peer Tutoring: Impact on the Quality of Writing in Introductory Psychology in an Open Admissions College." *Teaching of Psychology* 19 (2) (April), 78–81.

Padilla-Walker, Laura M., Ross A. Thompson, Byron L. Zamboanga, and Larissa A. Schmersal. (2005). "Extra Credit As Incentive for Voluntary Research Participation." *Teaching Psychology* 32 (3), 150–53. http://dx.doi.org/10.1207/s15328023top3203_2

Rojstaczer, Stuart. (2003). "Where All Grades Are Above Average." *Washington Post* (January 28).

Thorne, B. Michael. (2000). "Extra Credit Exercise: A Painless Pop Quiz." *Teaching of Psychology* 27 (3), 204–5. http://dx.doi.org/10.1207/S15328023TOP2703_09

Wickline, Virginia B., and Valeriya G. Spektor. (2011). "Practice (Rather than Graded) Quizzes, with Answers, May Increase Introductory Psychology Exam Performance." *Teaching of Psychology* 38 (2), 98–101. http://dx.doi.org/10.1177/0098628311401580

Wilson, Mark L. (2002). "Evidence that Extra Credit Assignments Induce Moral Hazard." *Atlantic Economic Journal* 30 (1) (March), 97.

Comprehension Questions

1. According to Pynes, what are the purposes of grading and of extra credit assignments, respectively?

2. Why do some say that the relevance of an extra credit assignment is what justifies offering it? What problems does that view face?

3. How are extra credit assignments supposed to encourage research and other academic virtues, and what considerations undermine that idea?

4. How is assigning extra credit assignments unfair in some circumstances?

5. What negative consequences do extra credit assignments have for instructors who offer them?
6. How can having available extra credit opportunities lead to a moral hazard situation for students?
7. What is grade inflation, and why does Pynes think extra credit assignments contribute to it?
8. What's wrong with offering extra credit for bonus questions on an exam?
9. If a student consistently produces low-quality work, how is that reason to deny offering that student extra credit?

Discussion Questions

1. Have you ever thought that a professor *ought* to make an extra credit opportunity available? Why?
2. Which of the arguments against offering extra credit do you think is the strongest? What's so compelling about it? What plausible objections might someone make to that argument, and how would you respond?
3. Instead of graded extra credit assignments, Pynes thinks instructors could offer ungraded requirements (like attending guest lectures) to encourage students' academic virtues. What do you think about this proposal? Would it be effective? Explain your view.
4. Imagine you are a well-meaning instructor and you want your students all to do well. But you are convinced by Pynes's arguments that extra credit is not a legitimate means to give students a boost. What else can you do for them? Will it be as effective as extra credit?

Case

Consider the following:

> Matthew Guterl, a professor of Africana and American studies at Brown University, says that he does not, as a rule or as an exception, offer extra credit. He does make individual exceptions in a couple of different ways, though. "My [anti-]extra-credit policy doesn't extend to students who are in a legitimate and serious personal crisis, or who've been struck by some serious bad luck. And sometimes I schedule events at night, and students who work can't make those, generally," Guterl says. "I try hard to individuate my responses for students who have a real

need for help, or flexibility, or just a second chance, while also holding the line against those who were just inattentive to the syllabus or just have priorities that don't include the work for my class."[18]

Is Pynes's view compatible with what Guterl does? If so, how? If not, then how might Pynes criticize Guterl's approach?

Notes

1. My claim is consistent with Close's "Model 3," that "grading is an information process concerning mastery of course content" (Close 2009: 368). The "measuring" I refer to in my principle is what gives rise to the information that Close is proposing in his model.

2. This point is really brought home by the fact that extra credit opportunities are rarely presented in such a way that the student's grade could be negatively affected by completing the extra credit assignment. Some claim there are other purposes for extra credit, and I address those purposes in the pro–extra credit section.

3. I haven't found any articles providing prolonged defense of the use of extra credit. Norcross, Dooley, and Stevenson (1993) do provide a list of the justifications provided by faculty using extra credit in their study, and those justifications are a variety of those I present. But if there are other pro–extra credit arguments, they will have to successfully reply to all the anti–extra credit arguments as well.

4. This could be called the motivation argument, but I prefer at this point to call it the relevance argument. I address the other types of motivation arguments later in the paper. See Immerwahr (2011) for more on student motivation arguments.

5. If one were tracking the principles from Close's paper, this kind of extra credit grading would violate principles 1.2, 1.6, 2, and 2.1.

6. Because most universities offer psychology as a general education requirement, there seems to be an unlimited supply of willing volunteers for research participation.

7. I owe this general view of extra credit, but not the name, to an anonymous reviewer at *Teaching Philosophy*.

8. Close makes similar claims when defending his principle 2.2 that "grades and grading practices generally should not be based on instrumental grounds" (Close 2009: 338).

9. This kind of "writing to learn" assignment was used at the University of Tennessee, Knoxville, to help satisfy word requirements set by the state legislature. Students had to write 5,000 words in certain classes, but that didn't mean that every writing assignment had to be graded. It would be nearly impossible

for some of the faculty to grade that many words in a semester given 4/4 course loads, which is upwards of 200 students a semester.

10. Wickline and Spektor (2011) found that ungraded, practice quizzes with feedback increased students' exam scores more than graded quizzes. This is just one study, but it supports the idea that fostering virtues with required, ungraded work can create better outcomes than grading all required work.

11. The extra credit assignment was to submit written answers to missed questions on the exam. This seems to be as relevant an extra credit assignment as one could provide—especially since the final exam was cumulative. So doing the extra credit was a way to motivate and prepare for the final exam. Motivation, virtues, and relevance were all present, but the students didn't take advantage of the extra credit opportunity.

12. I have in mind here Close's Principle 1, "grading should be impartial and consistent;" 1.1, "grade components should have determinate weights expressible as fractions of the final grade;" 1.2, "grade components and their weights should be published at the beginning of the term;" and 1.3: "'forced' grouping of a set of scores into As, Bs, Cs, Ds, and Fs is an inherently unfair method of grading."

13. For a full defense of equity, see Close (2009). He believes that all of his grading principles promote fairness, but principle 1.5—"every student must receive a mark for every grade component in the course" (Close 2009: 374)—is particularly powerful in this regard.

14. I have Close's principle 2—"Grading should be based on the student's competence in the academic content of the course"—and principle 2.1—"Grades should be assigned on the basis of an expert evaluation of student work" (Close 2009: 381–88).

15. Loyola Law School in Los Angeles recently increased the GPAs of every student retroactively, by one-third of a point to help students be more competitive in the job market. See the *Chronicle of Higher Education*, 1 April 2010. http://chronicle.com/article/A-California-Law-School-Will/64949/.

16. It might if the total course grade is affected by the problem.

17. I would add we should just say no to the point system as well. I don't use it, but I certainly understand that it makes life easier for professors who don't want to explain how to take two papers at 10 percent each, ten quizzes at 20 percent combined, and a midterm and final at 30 percent each and come up with a final grade. To be honest, that's a job for Excel, but adding points is easier for both students and faculty—and that's why people do it.

18. https://chroniclevitae.com/news/989-dear-student-are-you-sure-you-want-extra-credit

PART XI

The Aims of Education

52

Should Students Have to Borrow?

Autonomy, Well-Being, and Student Debt

Christopher Martin

There are relatively few who think that society should make no provisions in order to make higher education broadly accessible to the public. Yet it remains contentious whether it ought to be made accessible to everyone—not just the poor. It's Christopher Martin's view that society should in fact provide higher education freely to all. He reviews some purported differences between higher education and other goods that are commonly held to merit free provision for all, arguing that these are only apparent differences. Martin claims that democratic societies have an interest in their citizens' personal autonomy, and that guaranteeing their autonomy requires not only freely provided childhood education, but also freely provided higher education. Taking on debt for higher education, he believes, can limit individual self-realization, and removing that burden would benefit recipients of free higher education as well as society more broadly.

Martin, Christopher. Forthcoming. "Should Students Have to Borrow? Autonomy, Wellbeing, and Student Debt." *Journal of Philosophy of Education*. Reprinted with permission of John Wiley & Sons.

. . .

Governments across the world are citing increased global competitiveness and a slow economy as reasons for reducing funding to higher education. In the context of a stressed health care system and under-resourced public schools, state funding of higher education seems like a relative luxury.[1] Why should the public pay for something that benefits relatively few? It should be no surprise, then, that the orthodox view on higher education financing is that students should bear an increasing proportion of the costs of provision and, where necessary, meet that cost through debt financing. Is this view justified? To be sure, recent attention to this question has been driven by some new economic realities. For many students, private debt is the only means of accessing post-secondary education. The cost of tuition has consistently outpaced inflation and the financial crisis has led to a significant decrease in the employment prospects for the same generation who have to borrow the most in order to attend (see Green and Zhu, 2010; Tal and Enenajor, 2013). . . .

Higher education appears trapped in a broken model of provision. . . . In order to fix a broken system we need to rethink the *value* of higher education provision in a post-expansion era. In this article I defend the idea that higher education has the same moral importance as welfare goods such as health care and basic schooling and should therefore be free in principle. . . .

I. Choice, Welfare and Basic Goods

. . . One might be tempted to assume that higher education has the same prevalence and importance as established welfare goods like health care and basic schooling. From here it would simply be a matter of extending the kinds of arguments one might employ in defending free access to these goods to the higher education context. However, this plainly isn't the case. It was not until the post-WW2 boom that higher education seriously expanded beyond traditional elites to include a large and diverse segment of the population. One can also observe, along with expansion, a corresponding diversification of the *kind* of education one could receive: In addition to the liberal arts, vocational, specialist and other kinds of programming all came on offer as choices for students.[2] Furthermore, expansion and diversification was the product of one important, perhaps even signature, difference between higher education and goods such as health and schooling. Namely, choice has much greater normative significance in the allocation of higher education goods than basic goods. This is an important consideration because, in the kind of society we live today, the idea of "choice" has developed a close conceptual link to *consumer* choice (see Elster, 1986; Lewinsohn-Zamir, 1998; Le Grand, 1991, 2011; Glennerster, 1991). . . . The widespread belief that adults seeking to enter the higher education system are making a consumer choice . . . has a strong influence on the idea that higher education provision is a privilege and not a basic good.

Why does choice have greater normative significance for both the allocation and value of higher education provision? First, consumption of higher education goods is entirely voluntary. The student freely chooses to consume it and so they accept responsibility for allocation of that good in terms of time, effort *and* payment for service. Second, the consumption of higher education goods is mundane, satisfying but one preference along a continuum. An adult can choose not to consume higher education goods in order to satisfy other preferences and, while we might question the wisdom of that choice, it wouldn't generate the same moral concern as someone refusing urgent medical care or dropping out of school. Third, even in those cases where large numbers of the population choose to consume higher education goods and services the particular preference being satisfied differs depending on the individual. . . . No singular human need is being served by the provision of higher education. Finally, consumption is self-serving because (in economic terms) consumption by definition satisfies the preferences of the individual consumer. The reason I am consuming that good is because I believe that it will make *my* life better in some way.

This sets higher education apart when placed alongside basic welfare goods. Basic social goods are in a sense morally special—they are goods that have such singular place and importance in our lives that their allocation should not be determined by an ability to pay (Segal, 2007, p. 343). For example, we value the public health care system because health care helps people get back to a relatively normal state of function when they get sick (Daniels, 2001). Further, . . . we generally accept the idea that health care has at least as much payoff for the community as the person seeking care, for example in the treatment of communal disease. . . . Higher education understood as a voluntary choice undertaken by a consumer, however, doesn't have that same moral importance. Therefore, the state has no principled reason to cover the cost of its provision.[3]

II. Higher Education and Equality of Opportunity

. . . Some defenders of fee-for-access have argued that tuition fees are a fair means of financing the system so long as students don't have to pay up front. Loans enable students to attend who otherwise could not afford to do so. . . . In fact, this is just the line that some liberal egalitarians take. Harry Brighouse, for example, . . . argues, quite convincingly, that the fact that the well-off have more supplementary resources to fall back on makes them more likely to take the "risk" of an investment in higher education, and we should remove these barriers to that investment for the poor where possible (2004).

Yet, Brighouse argues that while students shouldn't be put off from attending because of their financial situation it would be unfair for students to attend higher education for free. . . .

> Because the person undergoing higher education is the primary beneficiary, and because it is reasonable to hold him accountable for his behavior, it is unreasonable to ask others to pay for it, especially if those others are not getting a benefit. (2004, p. 3, emphasis mine)

I think Brighouse's conclusion is the very one we should arrive at when we undertake an egalitarian analysis of HE provision as it is conventionally understood—as a socioeconomic privilege. But I maintain that a conventional analysis isn't enough of a fix. . . . Fairness cannot entirely make up for scarcity of personal resources. . . . if one can formulate some general reasons why the experience of costless higher education importantly contributes to human flourishing, one could set out some initial terms under which the provision of higher education holds value for all citizens, not simply for those jockeying for socioeconomic privilege. This is the line of thinking I'd like to develop in the remainder of this article.

III. Well-Being and the Demands of Personal Autonomy

Liberal respect for autonomy makes the case for higher education as a morally special good on par with health care and basic schooling a difficult one to make. However, this problem only remains compelling if we leave unchallenged the premise that educational provision for autonomy ends at childhood. . . .

. . . [John] White sees general education as an initiation into the conditions necessary for the free pursuit of a good life. In the early years especially, these conditions involve the acquisition of the *general* dispositions and capacities required for anyone to effectively carry out that pursuit. However, the role of philosophy in setting out the terms of that initiation is gradually lessened as the student moves closer and closer to the autonomous state, to the point at which they move out of the compulsory stage and the burden falls entirely on the individual to build up a unique picture of the kind of person they want to be and how they want to flourish. This picture can include, but not require, a higher education. Philosophy has very little to offer to the justification of higher education because the HE system will differ depending on the different political and economic decisions made by particular societies and their (consumer) clientele. Normative claims about the aims of education, about what people *ought* to learn, only apply to the compulsory level.

I think that this conclusion arises from a misconceived comparison. White argues that childhood is categorically different from higher education and so grounding educational aims in an account of higher education is mistaken. But if White's argument is about the justification of educational entitlements at different levels of society, the comparatives in question are administrative structures (school systems with universities) and stages of life (childhood with adulthood). Therefore, if the analysis is to be logically consistent White should not be comparing childhood to higher education. This conflates a stage of life with an administrative category. Rather, he should be comparing the educational needs of children with the educational needs of *adults*.

. . . [T]he latter comparison, between the needs of children and the interests of adults, is more revealing. Now it is clear that we cannot legitimately impose educational aims on autonomous adults in the same way that we impose aims on children.[4] "Needs" here should not be construed in a paternalistic way. At the adult stage autonomy and choice figure prominently in one's flourishing. This is an important difference. However, this difference only requires a shift in emphasis, from the role of education in *promoting* a self-directed life to the role of education *in* a self-directed life. We should be concerned less with trying to fashion values and aims of higher education deemed good for everyone regardless of what they may actually want . . ., and focus instead on the relationship between the autonomous pursuit of educational interests and living a good life. This relationship is connected to a number of philosophically relevant questions, including the extent and limits of our freedom to engage in self-development, the social, moral and political responsibilities we have with respect to that development, as well as the role of the state in supporting those freedoms and responsibilities. . . . To claim that such questions can be sufficiently answered through consumer choice glosses them just as badly, and in much the same way, as claiming that what children need can be answered by reference to the contingent standards of child-rearing currently popular with parents.

In fact, White's own account of personal autonomy offers resources for addressing such questions. For White, personal autonomy is defined as "self-directedness in the conduct of one's life" (1991, p. 93). He specifies one important feature of personal autonomy that justifies it as an educational ideal, namely, that such autonomy is well suited for the promotion of human flourishing in the kind of society that we live in today.... However, personal autonomy is not only good for, but also *necessary* to, flourishing. Our basic institutions are run on the assumption that people will live broadly autonomous lives (White, 1991, p. 99). Prevailing norms around marriage and choice of occupation, for example, operate on the expectation that we independently arrive at decisions within these spheres.

It is for this reason that societies like ours are morally responsible to prepare all children for a life of personal autonomy.... However, the *demands* that personal autonomy place on our decision-making capacities have a direct implication for the *kind* of educational provision to which children are entitled. White is therefore concerned that on one reading our institutions actually make few demands of citizens. As he puts it,

> [P]eople in our kind of society are not directed by convention or authority in the selection of marriage partners, occupation or place of residence . . . but the institutions concerned with marriage, work, consumer-choice etc. within which we flourish, themselves embody conventions. It would be quite easy for people in our kind of society to make choices within these areas, yet never to reflect on the conventional structure itself. (White, 1991, pp. 99–100)

Why is this a problem? Were it to be the case that the freedom to choose within conventional structures was all that we need in order to live a good life in a society like ours, educational provision would be rightly limited to a *choice-supporting* education with no questioning of that conventional structure (the norms, values and assumptions) defining that range of choice....

White is able to resist such thin educational provision by making a distinction between "weak" and "strong" personal autonomy. When we are weakly autonomous, we really do choose "for ourselves"—making choices that best satisfy our individual preferences. Autonomy in the strong sense, on the other hand, involves critical reflectiveness about our basic social structures, including a concern for the extent to which, and ways in which, those social structures work to promote the well-being of *others*. In the latter, "we are working with a conception of personal well-being that embraces concern for others, at both intimate and less intimate levels: It is now part of my own flourishing that I promote the flourishing of my friends and of others" (p. 102)....

This is all well and good, but ... we have to ask: which view of personal autonomy do we *really* need in order to flourish, "in a society like ours"? The case largely turns on the kind of autonomy that our institutions demand of us....

...

Autonomy-supporting institutions like ours, unlike merely "choice-supporting ones," operate with a conception of well-being in play that is logically connected to ideals of democratic life. Democratically informed concern for the well-being of others should lead to an interest in addressing those obstacles, broadly conceived, that undermine the flourishing of fellow citizens: political obstacles, such as underrepresentation in government, or economic obstacles, in terms of the harmful effects of growing inequality. In fact, even those who would treat our basic institutions as merely "choice-supporting," seeing them only as a means to their own ends, are unavoidably led back to wider social and political concerns because it is in their interest to do so (p. 103). Securing my economic well-being, for example, cannot but lead to wider considerations of economic policy, debt and changing labor conditions, considerations that impact on the whole of society. Having an interest in the wider society is in each person's own individual interest.

Now, it is because I accept White's argument that personal autonomy is instrumentally necessary for living a good life in our kind of society, and that our institutions (ideally) ought to support autonomy in accordance with a democratic social vision, that I argue higher education institutions should play a more fundamental role in democratic life than the current model of provision implies. We can justify this belief by first understanding higher education, not as an arbitrary administrative category or socioeconomic privilege, but as an institution with a role continuous with the autonomy-supporting project that begins in the school system.

Why suppose such continuity? ... it seems inconsistent to argue for an educational institution aimed at providing children with a *foundation* for a life of personal autonomy and not see it as at least plausible that there should be an educational institution designed to *support* this autonomy at an adult stage of life. By White's own admission, citizens can stray from the wider conception of well-being for which they have been educated and come to value autonomy only in the weaker sense (p. 100). . . . Strong autonomy has to be supported over a lifetime. It is simply unreasonable to expect that students receiving a compulsory education, even if they are relatively successful in achieving the aims set out by that form of education, ought be entirely self-sufficient in living and choosing in accordance with that strong conception.

. . .

IV. Freedom and Student Debt

Post-compulsory autonomy-support provides a basis for thinking about the value of higher education as a morally special good on the order of schooling or health care while fully acknowledging one of its distinctive features: freedom of choice. Higher education provision should be allocated as a free, basic social good for the reason that it is essential for the support of one's personal autonomy in the adult stage of life—a capacity fundamental for well-being in a society like ours. However, the support of personal autonomy at the post-compulsory stage requires the freedom to undertake a *reflective and comprehensive* assessment of the various possibilities that knowledge and understanding can play in life without formal or material coercion. Accordingly, post-compulsory institutions have the responsibility of ensuring that students are not unduly constrained in ways that would undermine this freedom.

. . . Making access to provision conditional on willingness to borrow erodes the practical freedom necessary for such provision to have autonomy-supporting value in the first place. In order to pay for higher education, students increasingly need to leverage what they borrow in the present against their (hoped for) future ability to pay. This greatly constrains their latitude for sufficiently reflective educational choice. . . . While in a debt-financed model of allocation students are free to choose in theory, in practice they are increasingly compelled to choose programs primarily based on improved economic prospects/survival (i.e., future earnings and employment) lest they place a significant burden on themselves . . . for a good portion of their lives. . . .

Debt financing of higher education does more than cut into the earning potential of students. It places an *unreasonable* demand on personal autonomy because the student who needs to borrow in order to attend will risk significant hardship if they exercise this autonomy in a strong, widely

reflective way. In other words, debt compels the student to pursue their well-being in a weakly autonomous manner. We can see this by contrasting a scenario in which allocation is a basic entitlement with one in which it isn't. In the former, choosing a course of study that may be less financially rewarding places some financial burden on the chooser, but this burden is autonomously chosen as part of a more comprehensive consideration of one's own self-development and well-being. If I choose to learn how to be a science-fiction writer I may not make much money, but high remuneration is not part of my conception of the good (or else I would choose otherwise).
. . .

However, in the debt-financed scenario the student has to pay for their self-development, and for the borrowing student debt is necessary for accessing such development. The borrowing student risks significant hardship because of the debt that will accrue. This hardship . . . is the price they pay for the continued exercise of their personal autonomy. But this is in fact a kind of trap because debt actually *precludes* a reflective choice. The borrowing student must be mindful of their debt obligation and so a strongly autonomous choice is not in the cards. "What I want to learn" is a relatively luxurious consideration. This introduces a qualitative shift in the choice situation: from a decision about "how I want to flourish," of which anticipated future income is one consideration among many, to "what do I have to choose in order to flourish at all," of which income and debt repayment is critical. There are obvious equity implications to consider here. Being part of a larger social vision in accordance with a wide conception of well-being now becomes a relative luxury for those who can afford it and highly risky for those who can't. In a liberal democracy personal autonomy should not depend on how well or worse off one is. Yet this is exactly what debt financing of higher education does.

This last consideration has implications that extend beyond the individual to the well-being of the larger liberal democratic community. . . . When the community acknowledges my claim and provides me with an opportunity to develop myself, I am both recognized and respected as a full member of society. When I understand myself as a member of society, I am more likely to be moved by the idea that, having received such support, I have an obligation to use this support in a way that contributes.

However, debt financing dramatically changes both the scope of my obligation and the relationship between my self-development and the larger society. The debt financing of social goods is both de-socializing and de-democratizing. By requiring the individual to make a demand on his (future) self in order to supply a basic good as opposed to making a claim on society (Gourevitch, 2012, p. 135), that individual rightly sees his obligation as extending no further than what he can pay back monetarily, usually to a private lender. In turn, the democratic community has no morally legitimate claim on citizens to share their developed talents in the spirit of a larger social vision of society. The student is, in a sense, liberated from the demand to pursue an other-regarding, strongly autonomous life. . . .

. . .

References

Barnett, R. (1990). *The Idea of Higher Education*. Buckingham, Society for Research into Higher Education and Open University Press.

Bokor, J. (2012). *University of the Future: A Thousand Year Old Industry on the Cusp of Profound Change*. Ernst and Young.

Bou-Habib, P. (2010). "Who Should Pay for Higher Education?" *Journal of Philosophy of Education*, 44(4), 479–95.

Brighouse, H. (2004). "Paying for Higher Education: Are Top-Up Fees Fair?" *Éthique et économique* 2(1).

Brighouse, H. and McAvoy, P. (2010). "Privilege, Well-being, and Participation in Higher Education." In Y. Raley and G. Preyer (eds.), *Philosophy of Education in the Era of Globalization*. New York, Routledge.

Clayton, M. (1993). "White on Autonomy, Neutrality and Well-Being." *Journal of Philosophy of Education* 27, 101–13.

Daniels, N. (2001). "Justice, Health and Healthcare." *The American Journal of Bioethics* 1 (2), 2–16.

Elster, J. (1986). "The Market and the Forum." In J. Elster and A. Aanund (eds.), *The Foundations of Social Choice Theory*. Cambridge, Cambridge University Press, 103–32.

Epprecht, M. (2004). "Work-Study Abroad Courses in International Development Studies: Some Ethical and Pedagogical Issues." *Canadian Journal of Development Studies* 25 (4), 687–706.

Glennerster, H. (1991). "Quasi-Markets for Education?" *The Economic Journal* 101, 1268–76.

Gourevitch, A. (2012). "Debt, Freedom, and Inequality." *Philosophical Topics* 40, 135–51.

Green, F. and Zhu, Y. (2010). "Overqualification, Job Dissatisfaction, and Increasing Dispersion in the Returns to Graduate Education." *Oxford Economic Papers* 62 (4), 740–63.

Kitcher, P. (2009). "Education, Democracy, and Capitalism." In H. Siegel (ed.), *The Oxford Handbook of Philosophy of Education*. Oxford, Oxford University Press, 300–18.

Kotzee, B. and Martin, C. (2013). "Who Should Go to University? Justice in University Admissions." *Journal of Philosophy of Education* 47 (4), 623–41.

Layard, P. R. and Layard, R. (2011). *Happiness: Lessons from a New Science*. Harmondsworth, Penguin.

Le Grand, J. (1991). "Quasi-Markets and Social Policy." *The Economic Journal* 101, 1256–67.

Le Grand, J. (2011). "Quasi-Market versus State Provision of Public Services: Some Ethical Considerations." *Public Reason* 3 (2), 80–89.

Lewinsohn-Zamir, D. (1998). "Consumer Preferences, Citizen Preferences, and the Provision of Public Goods." *Yale Law Journal* 108 (2), 377–406.

McCowan, T. (2012). "Is There a Universal Right to Higher Education?" *British Journal of Educational Studies* 60 (2), 111–128.

Peterson, S. A. (1984). "Privatism and Politics: A Research Note." *The Western Political Quarterly* 37 (3), 483–89.

Rothstein, J. and Rouse, C. E. (2011). "Constrained After College: Student Loans and Early-Career Occupational Choices." *Journal of Public Economics* 95, 149–63.

Segall, S. (2007). "Is Health Care (Still) Special?" *Journal of Philosophy* 15 (3), 342–61.

Tal, B. and Enenajor, E. (2013). *Degrees of Success: The Payoff to Higher Education in Canada*. New York: CIBC World Markets.

Trow, M. (2006). "Reflections on the Transition from Elite to Mass to Universal Access: Forms and Phases of Higher Education in Modern Societies Since WWII." In J. J. F. Forest and P. G. Altbach (eds.), *International Handbook of Higher Education: Part One: Global Themes and Contemporary Challenges; Part Two: Regions and Countries*. Dordrecht, Springer.

UK Government (2011). *Supporting Analysis for the Higher Education White Paper*. BIS Economics Paper No. 14. London, Department for Business, Innovation and Skills.

White, J. (1991). *Education and the Good Life: Autonomy, Altruism, and the National Curriculum*. Advances in Contemporary Educational Thought, vol. 7. New York: Teachers College Press.

White, J. (1997). "Philosophy and the Aims of Higher Education." *Studies in Higher Education* 22, 7–17.

White, J. (2013). "Philosophy, Philosophy of Education, and Economic Realities." *Theory and Research in Education* 11 (3), 294–303.

Comprehension Questions

1. What is unique about the current situation facing students who are considering taking on debt to attend college?
2. What is a basic good, and what reasons are there for denying that a college education counts as a basic good?

3. Why do some people think higher education should be partially financed without debt for the poor, even though they deny it is a basic good?
4. What reason does Martin give for thinking the rationale for free provision of education for children extends also to support the free provision of college education?
5. What's the difference between the weak and strong forms of personal autonomy?
6. Why does Martin think that student debt is inconsistent with personal autonomy?
7. How, according to Martin, is free provision of college education supposed to contribute to society?

Discussion Questions

1. How are you financing your studies? If you're taking out loans, are you concerned about being able to pay them back?
2. Martin thinks that college education ought to be free in order to ensure everyone's full autonomy. Do you agree with Martin that this is a likely consequence of making college free?
3. Suppose that Martin is right: Free provision of education is in fact connected to people being fully autonomous. Do you think that's the only or best way to get this result?
4. Besides supporting individual autonomy, Martin thinks that free provision of higher education would also be beneficial to society. If you received a free education, do you suppose you would be more likely to find ways to return that favor to society?

Case

Matt Bruenig, a political commentator, wrote this in 2015:

> [T]he typical line you hear about free college is that it should be a right of students because they have worked hard and done everything right. The implicit suggestion of such rhetoric is that students are really owed free college as the reward for not being like those less virtuous high school graduates who refuse to do what it takes to better themselves through education. Needless to say, such thinking is extremely damaging to a broader egalitarian project, even more so in some ways than its goal of setting aside a part of our national income for the inegalitarian aim of making college free.

If we are actually going to push a free college agenda, it should not be under a restrictive students' rights banner, but instead under a general pro-welfare banner. The goal of free college should not be to help students per se, but instead to bind them to a broader welfare benefit system. By presenting their tuition subsidies and living grants as indistinguishable from benefits for the disabled, the poor, the elderly, and so on, it may be possible to encourage wealthier students to support the welfare state and to undermine students' future claims of entitlement to the high incomes that college graduates so often receive. After all, the college income premium would only be possible through the welfare benefits to which the rest of society—including those who never went to college—has contributed.[5]

What is Bruenig saying in the first paragraph? Does it apply to Martin's proposal? Why or why not? Moreover, what is Bruenig saying in the second paragraph? On his view, what should the goal of free college be? How might free college accomplish that goal? And how does *that* fit with Martin's proposal?

Notes

1. See Kitcher, 2009, and White, 2013, on ongoing tensions between economic competition and democratic education.
2. See Trow's Weberian analysis of the diversification and expansion of higher education (Trow, 2006).
3. I say "principled" here because some governments justify public subsidy for tuition on the grounds that such subsidy is necessary for generating positive externalities—aggregate social benefits unintended by the individual consumer such as reduced crime and increased voter participation. Note the conditional nature of the policy: If enough students enrolled in higher education without a subsidy, those subsidies would no longer be justified. For an excellent example of such a policy, see the UK government's BIS Economics Paper No. 14 (2011).
4. I say "same way" because, having chosen a course of study, it is entirely appropriate to impose aims internal to that programming on the student. The student chooses to study a profession but the criteria and aims internal to that professional are not up to the student. Further, certain institutions such as universities have an explicit allegiance to general values such as the pursuit of truth, and so any student seeking to attend a university can be expected to abide by those values (see Kotzee and Martin, 2013).
5. https://newrepublic.com/article/123022/case-against-free-college

53

From Knowledge to Wisdom
The Need for an Academic Revolution
Nicholas Maxwell

"The main goal of higher education is learning, imparting knowledge to students. It's a secondary issue whether this ends up benefitting students and society more broadly." Nicholas Maxwell rejects this seemingly commonsense outlook. He argues that it has things backward. The main thing, in higher education, should be pursuing what's good for society, and all teaching and research should be designed to advance that goal. Those active in higher education—students, instructors, and so on—are, in Maxwell's view, civil servants of a sort. He argues that there is something deeply irrational about our current academic institutions and practices. They have enabled us to accumulate considerable knowledge and to act on a greater scale, with previously unimaginable global consequences. But they suffer, Maxwell claims, from a lack of wisdom. We have achieved a great deal, but without reflecting on what is worth achieving in the first place, an approach he thinks is responsible for many problems we now face on a global scale. What's needed, then, is a wisdom-based approach, where reflections on value lead the way and shape how we acquire knowledge and put it into practice.

Maxwell, Nicholas. 2007. "From Knowledge to Wisdom: The Need for an Academic Revolution." *London Review of Education* 5: 97–115.

From Knowledge to Wisdom

. . .

We need to bring about a wholesale, structural revolution in the aims and methods, the entire intellectual and institutional character of academic inquiry. At present academic inquiry is devoted to acquiring *knowledge*. The idea is to acquire knowledge, and then apply it to help solve social problems. This needs to change, so that the basic aim becomes to seek and promote *wisdom*—wisdom being understood to be the capacity to realize what is of value in life for oneself and others. . . . Instead of devoting itself primarily to solving problems of knowledge, academic inquiry needs to give intellectual priority to the task of discovering possible solutions to problems of living.

The social sciences need to become social philosophy, or social methodology, devoted to promoting more cooperatively rational solving of conflicts and problems of living in the world. Social inquiry, so pursued, would be intellectually more fundamental than natural science. The natural sciences need to recognize three domains of discussion: evidence, theories, and aims. Problems concerning research aims need to be discussed by both scientists and non-scientists alike, involving as they do questions concerning social priorities and values. . . . Education needs to change so that problems of living become more fundamental than problems of knowledge, the basic aim of education being to learn how to acquire wisdom in life. Academic inquiry as a whole needs to become somewhat like a people's civil service, having just sufficient power to retain its independence and integrity, doing for people, openly, what civil services are supposed to do, in secret, for governments. These and many other changes, affecting every branch and aspect of academic inquiry, all result from replacing the aim to acquire knowledge by the aim to promote wisdom by cooperatively rational means (see Maxwell, 1976, 1984, 2004).

The Crisis of Science without Wisdom

. . . I . . . suggest that changing the aims and methods of academic inquiry would help us tackle . . . global problems. It is . . . of decisive importance to appreciate that . . . global problems have arisen because of a massive increase in scientific knowledge and technology without a concomitant increase in global wisdom. Degradation of the environment due to industrialization and modern agriculture, global warming, the horrific number of people killed in war, the arms trade and the stockpiling of modern armaments, the immense differences in the wealth of populations across the globe, rapid population growth: All these have been made possible by the rapid growth of science and technology since the birth of modern science in the seventeenth century. Modern science and technology are even implicated in the rapid spread of AIDS in the last few decades. It is possible that, in Africa, AIDS has been spread in part by contaminated needles used in inoculation programs; and globally, AIDS has spread so rapidly because of travel made possible by modern technology. And the more intangible global problems indicated above may also have come about, in part, as a result of the rapid growth of modern science and technology.

That the rapid growth of scientific knowledge and technological know-how should have these kinds of consequences is all but inevitable. Scientific and technological progress massively increase our power to act: in the absence of wisdom, this will have beneficial consequences, but will also have harmful ones. . . . As long as we lacked modern science, lack of wisdom did not matter too much: our power to wreak havoc on the planet and each other was limited. Now that our power to act has been so massively enhanced by modern science and technology, global wisdom has become, not a luxury, but a necessity.

. . .

The Damaging Irrationality of Knowledge-Inquiry

. . .

. . . Scientific rationality, so-called, is actually a species of damaging *irrationality* masquerading as rationality.

Academic inquiry as it mostly exists at present, devoted to the growth of knowledge and technological know-how—*knowledge-inquiry* I shall call it (Maxwell, 1984, chapters 2 and 6)—is actually profoundly irrational when judged from the standpoint of contributing to human welfare. Judged from this all-important standpoint, knowledge-inquiry violates three of the four most elementary, uncontroversial rules of reason that one can conceive of (to be indicated in a moment). And that knowledge-inquiry is grossly irrational in this way has everything to do with its tendency to generate the kind of global problems considered above. . . .

Knowledge-inquiry demands that a sharp split be made between the social or humanitarian aims of inquiry and the *intellectual* aim. The intellectual aim is to acquire knowledge of truth, nothing being presupposed about the truth. Only those considerations may enter into the intellectual domain of inquiry relevant to the determination of truth—claims to knowledge, results of observation and experiment, arguments designed to establish truth or falsity. Feelings and desires, values, ideals, political and religious views, expressions of hopes and fears, cries of pain, articulation of problems of living: All these must be ruthlessly excluded from the intellectual domain of inquiry as having no relevance to the pursuit of knowledge—although of course inquiry can seek to develop factual knowledge about these things, within psychology, sociology or anthropology. Within natural science, an even more severe censorship system operates: an idea, in order to enter into the intellectual domain of science, must be an empirically testable claim to factual knowledge.

The basic idea of knowledge-inquiry, then, is this. First, knowledge is to be acquired; then it can be applied to help solve social problems. For this to work, authentic objective knowledge must be acquired. Almost paradoxically, human values and aspirations must be excluded from the intellectual domain of inquiry so that genuine factual knowledge is acquired and inquiry can be of genuine human value, and can be capable of helping us realize our human aspirations.[1]

This is the conception of inquiry which, I claim, violates reason in a wholesale, structural and damaging manner.

But what do I mean by "reason"? As I use the term here, rationality appeals to the idea that there are general methods, rules or strategies which, if put into practice, give us our best chance, other things being equal, of solving our problems, realizing our aims. Rationality is an aid to success, but does not guarantee success, and does not determine what needs to be done.

Four elementary rules of reason, alluded to above, are:

1. Articulate and seek to improve the articulation of the basic problem(s) to be solved.
2. Propose and critically assess alternative possible solutions.
3. When necessary, break up the basic problem to be solved into a number of *specialized* problems—preliminary, simpler, analogous, subordinate problems—(to be tackled in accordance with rules [1] and [2]), in an attempt to work gradually toward a solution to the basic problem to be solved.
4. Inter-connect attempts to solve the basic problem and specialized problems, so that basic problem solving may guide, and be guided by, specialized problem solving.

No enterprise which persistently violates (1) to (4) can be judged rational. If academic inquiry is to contribute to the aim of promoting human welfare, the quality of human life, by intellectual means, in a rational way, in a way that gives the best chances of success, then (1) to (4) must be built into the whole institutional/intellectual structure of academic inquiry.

. . .

. . . [G]ranted that academic inquiry has, as its fundamental aim, to help promote human welfare by intellectual and educational means,[2] then the *problems* that inquiry fundamentally ought to try to help solve are problems of living, problems of action.

From the standpoint of achieving what is of value in life, it is what we *do*, or refrain from doing, that ultimately matters. Even where new knowledge and technological know-how are relevant to the achievement of what is of value—as it is in medicine or agriculture, for example—it is always what this new knowledge or technological know-how enables us to *do* that matters. All the global problems discussed above require, for their resolution, not merely new knowledge, but rather new policies, new institutions, new ways of living. Scientific knowledge, and associated technological know-how have, if anything, as we have seen, contributed to the creation of these problems in the first place. Thus problems of living—problems of poverty, ill-health, injustice, deprivation—are solved by what we do, or refrain from doing; they are not solved by the mere provision of some item of knowledge (except when a problem of living *is* a problem of knowledge).

. . . [I]n order to achieve what is of value in life more successfully than we do at present, we need to discover how to resolve conflicts and problems of living in more *cooperatively rational* ways than we do at present. There is a spectrum of ways in which conflicts can be resolved, from murder or all out war at the violent end of the spectrum, via enslavement, threat of murder or war, threats of a less extreme kind, manipulation, bargaining, voting, to cooperative rationality at the other end of the spectrum, those involved seeking, by rational means, to arrive at that course of action which does the best justice to the interests of all those involved. A basic task for a kind of academic inquiry that seeks to help promote human welfare must be to discover how conflict resolution can be moved away from the violent end of the spectrum towards the cooperatively rational end.

Granted all this, and granted that the above four rules of reason are put into practice, then at the most fundamental level, academic inquiry needs to:

1. Articulate, and seek to improve the articulation of, personal, social and global problems of living that need to be solved if the quality of human life is to be enhanced (including those indicated above).
2. Propose and critically assess alternative possible solutions— alternative possible *actions, policies, political programs, legislative proposals, ideologies, philosophies of life.*

In addition, of course, academic inquiry must:

3. Break up the basic problems of living into subordinate, specialized problems—in particular, specialized problems of knowledge and technology.
4. Inter-connect basic and specialized problem solving.

Academic inquiry as it mostly exists at present can be regarded as putting (3) into practice to splendid effect. The intricate maze of specialized disciplines devoted to improving knowledge and technological know-how that go to make up current academic inquiry is the result. But, disastrously, what we have at present, academic inquiry devoted primarily to improving knowledge, fails to put (1), (2) and (4) into practice. In pursuing knowledge, academic inquiry may articulate problems of knowledge, and propose and critically assess possible solutions, possible claims to knowledge—factual theses, observational and experimental results, theories. But, as we have seen, problems of *knowledge* are not (in general) problems of *living*; and solutions to problems of *knowledge* are not (in general) solutions to problems of *living*. Insofar as academia does at present put (1) and (2) into practice, in departments of social science and policy studies, it does so only at the periphery, and not as its central, fundamental intellectual task.

. . .

. . . In devoting itself to acquiring knowledge in a way that is unrelated to sustained concern about what humanity's most urgent problems are, as a result of failing to put (1) and (2) into practice, and thus failing to put (4) into practice as well, the danger is that scientific and technological research will respond to the interests of the powerful and the wealthy, rather than to the interests of the poor, of those most in need. Scientists, officially seeking knowledge of truth *per se*, have no official grounds for objecting if those who fund research—governments and industry— decide that the truth to be sought will reflect their interests, rather than the interests of the world's poor. And priorities of scientific research, globally, do indeed reflect the interests of the First World, rather than those of the Third World.[3]

. . .

Wisdom-Inquiry

Inquiry devoted primarily to the pursuit of knowledge is, then, grossly and damagingly irrational when judged from the standpoint of contributing to human welfare by intellectual means. At once the question arises: What would a kind of inquiry be like that is devoted, in a genuinely rational way, to promoting human welfare by intellectual means? I shall call such a hypothetical kind of inquiry *wisdom-inquiry*, to stand in contrast to knowledge-inquiry.

. . .

The primary change that needs to be made is to ensure that academic inquiry implements rules (1) and (2). It becomes the fundamental task of social inquiry and the humanities (1) to articulate, and seek to improve the articulation of, our problems of living, and (2) to propose and critically assess possible solutions, from the standpoint of their practicality and desirability. In particular, social inquiry has the task of discovering how conflicts may be resolved in less violent, more cooperatively rational ways. It also has the task of promoting such tackling of problems of living in the social world beyond academe. Social inquiry is, thus, not primarily social *science*, nor, primarily, concerned to acquire knowledge of the social world; its primary task is to promote more cooperatively rational tackling of problems of living in the social world. Pursued in this way, social inquiry is intellectually more fundamental than the natural and technological sciences, which tackle subordinate problems of knowledge, understanding and technology, in accordance with rule (3). . . .

. . .

The natural and technological sciences need to recognize three domains of discussion: evidence, theory, and aims. Discussion of aims seeks to identify that highly problematic region of overlap between that which is discoverable, and that which it is of value to discover. Discussion of what it is of value to discover interacts with social inquiry, in accordance with rule (4).

. . .

Cultural Implications of Wisdom-Inquiry

Wisdom-inquiry does not just do better justice to the social or practical dimension of inquiry than knowledge-inquiry; it does better justice to the "intellectual" or "cultural" aspects as well.

From the standpoint of the intellectual or cultural aspect of inquiry, what really matters is the desire that people have to see, to know, to understand, the passionate curiosity that individuals have about aspects of the world, and the knowledge and understanding that people acquire and share as a result of actively following up their curiosity. An important task for academic thought in universities is to encourage nonprofessional thought to flourish outside universities. . . .

Knowledge-inquiry . . . all too often fails to nourish "the holy curiosity of inquiry" (Einstein, 1949, p. 17), and may even crush it out altogether. Knowledge-inquiry gives no rational role to emotion and desire; passionate curiosity, a sense of mystery, of wonder, have no place, officially, within the rational pursuit of knowledge. The intellectual domain becomes impersonal and split off from personal feelings and desires; it is difficult for "holy curiosity" to flourish in such circumstances. Knowledge-inquiry hardly encourages the view that inquiry at its most fundamental is the thinking that goes on as a part of life; on the contrary, it upholds the idea that fundamental research is highly esoteric, conducted by physicists in contexts remote from ordinary life. Even though the aim of inquiry may, officially, be *human* knowledge, the personal and social dimension of this is all too easily lost sight of, and progress in knowledge is conceived of in impersonal terms, stored lifelessly in books and journals. Rare is it for popular books on science to take seriously the task of exploring the fundamental problems of a science in as accessible, non-technical and intellectually responsible a way as possible.[4] Such work is not highly regarded by knowledge-inquiry, as it does not contribute to "expert knowledge."

The failure of knowledge-inquiry to take seriously the highly problematic nature of the aims of inquiry leads to insensitivity as to what aims are being pursued, to a kind of institutional hypocrisy. Officially, knowledge is being sought "for its own sake," but actually the goal may be immortality, fame, the flourishing of one's career or research group, as the existence of bitter priority disputes in science indicates. Education suffers. Science students are taught a mass of established scientific knowledge, but may not be informed of the *problems* which gave rise to this knowledge, the problems which scientists grappled with in creating the knowledge. Even more rarely are students encouraged themselves to grapple with such problems. And rare, too, is it for students to be encouraged to articulate their own problems of understanding that must, inevitably arise in absorbing all this information, or to articulate their instinctive criticisms of the received body of knowledge. All this tends to reduce education to a kind of intellectual indoctrination, and serves to kill "holy curiosity."[5] Officially, courses in universities divide up into those that are vocational, like engineering, medicine and law, and those that are purely educational, like physics, philosophy or history. What is not noticed, again through insensitivity to problematic aims, is that the supposedly purely educational are actually vocational as well: the student is being trained to be an academic physicist, philosopher or historian, even though only a minute percentage of the students will go on to become academics. Real education, which must be open-ended, and without any pre-determined goal, rarely exists in universities, and yet few notice. . . .

In order to enhance our understanding of persons as beings of value, potentially and actually, we need to understand them empathetically, by putting ourselves imaginatively into their shoes, and experiencing, in imagination, what they feel, think, desire, fear, plan, see, love and hate. For wisdom-inquiry, this kind of empathic understanding is rational and intellectually fundamental. Articulating problems of living, and proposing and assessing possible solutions is, we have seen, the fundamental intellectual activity of wisdom-inquiry. But it is just this that we need to do to acquire empathic understanding. Social inquiry, in tackling problems of living, is also promoting empathic understanding of people. Empathic understanding is essential to wisdom. . . .

. . .

References

Appleyard, B. (1992). *Understanding the Present: Science and the Soul of Modern Man*. London: Picador.

Aron, R. (1968). *Main Currents in Sociological Thought*, vol. 1 1968; vol. 2, 1970. Harmondsworth: Penguin.

Berlin, I. (1980). *Against the Current*. London: Hogarth Press.

Berman, B. (1981). *The Reenchantment of the World*. Cornell University Press, Ithaca.

Einstein, A. (1949). "Autobiographical Notes." In P. A. Schilpp, ed. *Albert Einstein: Philosopher-Scientist*. Illinois: Open Court, 3–94.

Einstein, A. (1973). *Ideas and Opinions*. London: Souvenir Press.

Farganis, J. (ed.). (1993). *Readings in Social Theory: The Classic Tradition to Post-Modernism*. New York: McGraw-Hill.

Feyerabend, P. (1978). *Against Method*. London: Verso.

Feyerabend, P. (1987). *Farewell to Reason*. London: Verso.

Gay, P. (1973). *The Enlightenment: An Interpretation*. London: Wildwood House.

Hayek, F. A. (1979). *The Counter-Revolution of Science*. 1979, Indianapolis: LibertyPress.

Laing, R. D. (1965). *The Divided Self*. Harmondsworth: Penguin,.

Langley, C. (2005). *Soldiers in the Laboratory*. Folkstone: Scientists for Global Responsibility.

Marcuse, H. (1964). *One-Dimensional Man*. Boston: Beacon Press.

Maxwell, N. (1974). "The Rationality of Scientific Discovery," *Philosophy of Science* 41, 123–53 and 247–95.

Maxwell, N. (1976). *What's Wrong With Science?* Frome, England: Bran's Head Books.

Maxwell, N. (1980). "Science, Reason, Knowledge and Wisdom: A Critique of Specialism." *Inquiry* 23, 19–81.

Maxwell, N. (1984). *From Knowledge to Wisdom*. Blackwell, Oxford (2nd edition, enlarged, London: Earthscan, 2007).

Maxwell, N. (1998). *The Comprehensibility of the Universe*. Oxford: Oxford University Press.

Maxwell, N. (2001). *The Human World in the Physical Universe*. Lanham, MD: Rowman and Littlefield.

Maxwell, N. (2004). *Is Science Neurotic?* London: Imperial College Press.

Maxwell, N. (2005). "Popper, Kuhn, Lakatos and Aim-Oriented Empiricism." *Philosophia* 32, 181–239.

Nowotny, H., Scott, P. and Gibbons, M. (2001). *Re-Thinking Science*. Cambridge: Polity Press.

Penrose, R. (2004). *The Road to Reality*. London: Jonathan Cape.

Popper, K. R. (1959). *The Logic of Scientific Discovery*. London: Hutchinson.

Popper, K. R. (1961). *The Poverty of Historicism*. London: Routledge and Kegan Paul.

Popper, K. R. (1962). *The Open Society and Its Enemies*. London: Routledge and Kegan Paul.

Popper, K. R. (1963). *Conjectures and Refutations*. London: Routledge and Kegan Paul.

Roszak, T. (1973). *Where the Wasteland Ends*. London: Faber and Faber.

Schwartz, B. (1987). *The Battle for Human Nature*. New York: W. W. Norton

Smith, D. (2003). *The Atlas of War and Peace*. London: Earthscan.

Snow, C. P. (1986). *The Two Cultures: And a Second Look*. Cambridge, UK: Cambridge University Press.

Comprehension Questions

1. What, roughly, is the difference between knowledge and wisdom?
2. What is the overall effect of science's lack of wisdom?
3. How does Maxwell think of reason, and in what way is knowledge-inquiry irrational on that understanding of reason?
4. What changes are in order for academic inquiry to become rational in Maxwell's sense?
5. Why does Maxwell say inquiry into the social world is more important than inquiry into the natural world?
6. What is the importance of curiosity for Maxwell, and what problems does it face currently?

Discussion Questions

1. Are you attracted to the idea that education should be about cultivating wisdom? Why or why not? Can you imagine any downsides to that idea?
2. Maxwell's view is that some major global problems, like climate change and global poverty, are results of or continue to persist because of the lack of wisdom in academic inquiry. Do you think that is right? Why or why not?
3. Is it generally true, as Maxwell claims, that the pursuit of academic inquiry is value-neutral? What values, if any, do you see at work in academia as you know it?
4. On Maxwell's view, getting a college education should be a sort of public service. You likely don't think of yourself—as a student—in quite that way. Should you alter your attitude? Why or why not?

Case

Consider this recent story from *The Guardian*:

> Scientists in Britain are ready to genetically modify human embryos for the first time as part of a research effort to shed light on the root causes of recurrent miscarriages. Researchers at the Francis Crick Institute in London could receive approval for the controversial work as early as

Thursday when the government's fertility watchdog meets to consider the proposal. If the regulator grants a research licence, the UK team stands to become only the second in the world to modify genes in human embryos. All of the embryos used in the work will be donated with consent by couples who have a surplus after IVF treatment.

Kathy Niakan and her team want to use a powerful new procedure called gene editing to disable certain genes in early stage human embryos. The scientists will then observe how the embryos grow until they are a week old, before destroying them. The experiments should help unravel the complex genetic instructions that turn a freshly-fertilized egg into a healthy embryo. "The research could lead to improvements in fertility treatment and to a better understanding of the first stages of life," Niakan told reporters at a briefing in London. Under British law, the embryos cannot be transferred to women to achieve a pregnancy.[6]

These scientists are using a new genetic-editing technology called "Crispr-Cas9." This technology promises to revolutionize biological research, since it allows for precise modifications of individual genes. Would Maxwell call this *knowledge-inquiry*? Or is this precisely the sort of research that Maxwell is calling for? If you aren't sure, what would you need to know (about the technology or the contexts in which it's being deployed) in order to answer these questions?

Notes

1. For a much more detailed exposition of knowledge-inquiry, or "the philosophy of knowledge," see Maxwell (1984, chapter 2). For evidence that knowledge-inquiry prevails in academia, see Maxwell (1984, chapter 6; 2000; 2007, chapter 6). I do not claim that everything in academia accords with the edicts of knowledge-inquiry. My claim is, rather, that this is the only candidate for rational inquiry in the public arena; it is the dominant view, exercising an all-pervasive influence over academe. Work that does not conform to its edicts has to struggle to survive.

2. This assumption may be challenged. Does not academic inquiry seek knowledge for its own sake—it may be asked—whether it helps promote human welfare or not? Later on, I will argue that the conception of inquiry I am arguing for, wisdom-inquiry, does better justice than knowledge-inquiry to *both* aspects of inquiry, pure and applied. The basic aim of inquiry, according to wisdom-inquiry, is to help us realize what is of value in life, "realize" meaning both "apprehend" and "make real." "Realize" thus accommodates both aspects of inquiry, "pure" research or "knowledge pursued for its own sake" on the one hand, and technological or "mission-oriented" research on the other—both, ideally, seeking to contribute to what is of value in human life. Wisdom-inquiry, like sight, is there to help us find our way around. And like sight, wisdom-inquiry

is of value to us in two ways: for its intrinsic value, and for practical purposes. The first is almost more precious than the second.

3. Funds devoted, in the United States, UK, and some other wealthy countries, to military research are especially disturbing: see Langley (2005) and Smith (2003).

4. A recent, remarkable exception is Penrose (2004).

5. I might add that the hierarchical conception of science indicated here does better justice to the scientific quest for understanding than does orthodox standard empiricist views: See Maxwell (1998, chapters 4 and 8; 2004, chapter 2).

6. http://www.theguardian.com/science/2016/jan/13/uk-scientists-ready-to-genetically-modify-human-embryos

Education for Citizenship in an Era of Global Connection

Martha Nussbaum

···

According to Martha Nussbaum, the debate about how to incorporate diversity into college education isn't just a political squabble; it
concerns the very purpose of college education. She points back to
ancient Greece and Rome to argue that the value of a college education is its ability to aide us in realizing ourselves as humans and citizens. She claims, moreover, that given the ongoing and continued
collapse of barriers between all sorts of social groups (national, ethnic,
religious, etc.) across the globe, it is imperative that we embrace diversity. We must do so to the extent that it makes us into the sort of
people who possess the right skills for getting along in such a world.
Nussbaum discusses three capacities college education ought to foster
in students to that end, illustrating along the way what she takes to be
appropriate means of achieving this goal in the classroom.

···

· · ·

    In 424 BC, the great ancient Greek comic playwright Aristophanes
produced his comedy *Clouds*, about the dangers of Socrates and the

Nussbaum, Martha. 2002. "Education for Citizenship in an Era of Global Connection." *Studies in Philosophy and Education* 21: 289–303. Copyright © 2002, Springer. Reprinted with
permission.

"new education." A young man, eager for the new learning, goes to a "Think-Academy" near his home, run by that strange notorious figure Socrates. A debate is staged for him, contrasting the merits of traditional education with those of the new discipline of Socratic argument. The spokesman for the old education is a tough old soldier. He favors a highly disciplined patriotic regimen, with lots of memorization and not much room for questioning. He loves to recall a time that may never have existed—a time when young people obeyed their parents and wanted nothing more than to die for their country, a time when teachers would teach that grand old song, "Athena, glorious sacker of cities"—not the strange new songs of the present day. Study with me, he booms, and you will look like a real man.

   . . .

His opponent is an arguer, a seductive man of words—Socrates seen through the distorting lens of Aristophanic conservatism. He promises the youth that he will learn to think critically about the social origins of apparently timeless moral norms, the distinction between convention and nature. He will learn to construct arguments on his own, heedless of authority. He won't do much marching. Study with me, he concludes, and you will look like an intellectual . . . The message? The new education will subvert manly self-control, turn young people into sex-obsessed rebels, and destroy the city. The son soon goes home and produces a relativist argument for the conclusion that he should beat his father. The same angry father then takes a torch and burns down the Think-Academy. . . . Twenty-five years later, Socrates, on trial for corrupting the young, cites Aristophanes' play as a major source of prejudice against him.

Should a liberal education be an acculturation into the time-honored values of one's own culture? Or should it follow Socrates, arguing that "the examined life" is the best preparation for citizenship? Almost five hundred years later, in the very different culture of the Roman Empire of the first century AD, the Stoic philosopher Seneca reflected on this same contrast, creating, in the process, our modern concept of liberal education.

Seneca begins his letter by describing the traditional style of education, noting that it is called "liberal" (*liberalis*, "connected to freedom"), because it is understood to be an education for well-brought-up young gentlemen, who were called the *liberales*, the "free-born." He himself, he now announces, would use the term "liberal" in a very different way. In his view, an education is truly "liberal" only if it is one that "liberates" the student's mind, encouraging him or her to take charge of his or her own thinking, leading the Socratic examined life and becoming a reflective critic of traditional practices. . . . Seneca goes on to argue that only this sort of education will develop each person's capacity to be fully human, by which he means self-aware, self-governing, and capable of recognizing and respecting the humanity of all our fellow human beings, no matter where they are born, no matter what social class they inhabit, no matter what their gender or ethnic origin. "Soon we shall breathe our last," he concludes in his related treatise *On Anger.* "Meanwhile, while we live, while we are among human beings, let us cultivate our humanity."

In the contemporary United States and Europe, as in ancient Athens and Rome, higher education is changing. New topics have entered the curricula of colleges and universities: the history and culture of non-Western peoples and of ethnic and racial minorities within the US, the experiences and achievements of women, the history and concerns of lesbians and gay men. These changes have frequently been presented in popular journalism as highly threatening, both to traditional standards of academic excellence and to traditional norms of citizenship. . . .

But we can defend many of the changes in traditional models of liberal education. . . . In fact, by and large, the changes that we witness are attempts to follow Seneca's advice to cultivate our humanity. Seneca's ideas of cultivated humanity and world citizenship have had a large influence on modern democratic thought. . . . And these ideas have long been at the root of our aspirations, as we construct a higher education that is not simply pre-professional, but a general enrichment of and a cultivation of reasonable, deliberative democratic citizenship.

Today's universities are shaping future citizens in an age of cultural diversity and increasing internationalization. All modern democracies are inescapably plural. . . . If our institutions of higher education do not build a richer network of human connections it is likely that our dealings with one another will be mediated by the defective norms of market exchange. A rich network of human connections, however, will not arise magically out of our good intentions: we need to think about how our educational institutions contribute to that goal.

The new emphasis on "diversity" in college and university curricula is above all, I would argue, a way of grappling with the altered requirements of citizenship in an era of global connection, an attempt to produce adults who can function as citizens not just of some local region or group but also, and more importantly, as citizens of a complex interlocking world and function with a richness of human understanding and aspiration that cannot be supplied by economic connections alone. In this attempt, the humanities . . . play a central role.

. . .

In *Cultivating Humanity*, I have argued that three capacities, above all, are essential to the cultivation of humanity in today's interlocking world. First is the capacity for critical examination of oneself and one's traditions—for living what, following Socrates, we may call "the examined life." This means a life that accepts no belief as authoritative simply because it has been handed down by tradition or become familiar through habit, a life that questions all beliefs and accepts only those that survive reason's demand for consistency and for justification. Training this capacity requires developing the capacity to reason logically, to test what one reads or says for consistency of reasoning, correctness of fact, and accuracy of judgment.

Testing of this sort frequently produces challenges to tradition, as Socrates knew well when he defended himself against the charge of "corrupting the young." But he defended his activity on the grounds that democracy needs citizens who can think for themselves rather than simply deferring to authority. . . .

This norm of deliberative democracy has not been fully realized in our modern democracies, any more than it was in ancient Athens. . . .

. . . Political deliberation can proceed well in a pluralistic society—if citizens have sufficient respect for their own reasoning and really care about the substance of ideas and the structure of arguments. The responsibility for instilling these values lies with our institutions of higher education.

I believe that for this reason instruction in philosophy is an indispensable part of higher education. . . . What is crucial is plenty of opportunity for interchange between faculty and students, and many writing assignments, carefully evaluated with ample comments. . . .

Many American universities and colleges, however, have been able to construct curricula that require all students to take one or two courses in philosophy. . . . Let me mention just one example of the effects of such required courses, a student named Billy Tucker at a business college named Bentley College in Waltham Massachusetts. Tucker went to Bentley because he planned to focus on marketing and did not want a more general academic education. . . . Tucker encountered a very gifted teacher, originally from India, named Krishna Mallick. Mallick began with the trial and death of Socrates. . . . She also showed a film about Socrates, and the combination really grabbed the imagination of this young man. . . . He thought it was so odd that Socrates did not escape from prison when he had the chance, but died for the activity of arguing. This example stung his imagination, and he got more and more interested in the course, which continued by presenting the basics of formal logic, so that students could then discover examples of valid and invalid reasoning in newspaper editorials and political speeches. Tucker did really well on this, and was amazed to discover that he actually had a good mind—he had thought he was not that kind of person. . . .

Tucker told me that this experience gave him an entirely new attitude to political debate: He had never understood that you can argue on behalf of a position that you do not hold yourself. Now he is more likely to see political argument as a process of searching for good answers, rather than just a way of making boasts and establishing your status. Now he knows how to ask what assumptions both sides share, where their differences really lie, and what the structure of each argument is. . . . I believe that such abilities can be cultivated in many different types of classes, but that philosophy does the best job of educating the mind in this way. . . .

But now to the second part of my proposal. Citizens who cultivate their humanity need, further, an ability to see themselves as not simply citizens of some local region or group but also, and above all, as human beings bound to all other human beings by ties of recognition and concern. . . . the world around us is inescapably international. Issues from business to agriculture, from human rights to the relief of famine, call our imaginations to venture beyond narrow group loyalties and to consider the reality of distant lives. . . . we very easily think of ourselves in group terms—as Americans first and foremost, as human beings second—or, even more narrowly, as Italian-Americans, or heterosexuals, or African-Americans first, Americans second, and human beings third if at all. We neglect needs and capacities that link us to fellow citizens who live at a distance, or who look different from ourselves. This means that we are unaware of many prospects of communication and fellowship with them, and also of responsibilities we may have to them. . . . Cultivating our humanity in a complex interlocking world involves understanding the ways in which common needs and aims are differently realized in different circumstances. This requires a great deal of knowledge that American college and university students rarely got in previous eras, knowledge of non-Western cultures, of minorities within their own, of differences of gender and sexuality.

. . .

Education for world citizenship has two dimensions: the construction of basic required courses that all students take (part of the "liberal education" or "general education" component of a U.S. university education) and the infusion of world-citizenship perspectives in more advanced courses in the different disciplines. Let me give one example at each level, making my description concrete enough to give you an idea of the actual classroom experience.

At Scripps College, in Pomona California, . . . the freshman class, consisting of 250 women, crowds the lecture hall, with eager energy and expectation. Their freshman core course is about to meet, to discuss feminist criticisms of the international human rights movement as a false Western type of universalism, and responses that other feminists have made to those criticisms, defending the human rights movement against the charge of Westernizing and colonizing. . . . called "Culture, Values, and Representation," this course . . . studies the central ideas of the European enlightenment—in political thought, history, philosophy, literature, and religion. . . . The study of the Enlightenment is then followed by critical responses to it: by formerly colonized populations, by non-Western philosophy and religion, by Western postmodernist thought, including feminist thought. The course then turns to responses that can be made to those criticisms.

. . . Its clear focus, its emphasis on cross-cultural debate and reasoning, rather than simply on a collection of facts, and its introduction of non-Western materials through a structured focus on a single set of issues, all make it a valuable introduction to further questioning on these issues. Above all, the course has merit because it plunges students right into some of the most urgent questions they will need to ask today as world citizens: questions about the universal validity or lack of validity of the language of rights, the appropriate way to respond to the legitimate claims of the oppressed. . . .

. . .

Another important aspect of the course's success that needs comment is its interdisciplinary character. Faculty from many different departments are brought together and given financial support to work on the course during the summer, exchanging ideas and getting one another's disciplinary perspectives. Such financial support for development of new ideas in a deliberative interdisciplinary framework is crucial to making the course as rich as it is.

Now let me turn to a program that aims to affect more advanced course in each of the disciplines. . . .

At St. Lawrence University, a small liberal arts college in upstate New York, . . . a group of young faculty, gathering despite the vacation, talk with excitement about their month-long visit to Kenya to study African village life. Having shared the daily lives of ordinary men and women, having joined in local debates about nutrition, polygamy, AIDS, and much else, they are now incorporating the experience into their teaching—in courses in art history, philosophy, religion, women's studies. Planning eagerly for the following summer's trip to India, they are already meeting each week for an evening seminar on Indian culture and history. Group leaders Grant Cornwell from Philosophy and Eve Stoddard from English talk about how they teach students to think critically about cultural relativism, using careful philosophical questioning in the Socratic tradition to criticize the easy but ultimately (they argue) incoherent idea that toleration requires us not to criticize anyone else's way of life. Their students submit closely reasoned papers analyzing arguments for and against outsiders' taking a stand on the practice of female circumcision in Africa.

Again, notice that the success of this program requires interdisciplinary discussion. . . . What is indispensable is the time to sit together and read and work together, learning how the problems of a region of the world look from historical, economic, religious, and other perspectives. Each faculty member will ultimately go on to incorporate this knowledge into the standard course offerings in his or her field. Thus, Economics now offers a course on "African Economies." Art History offers a course focused on representation of the female body in African art. Philosophy offers a course in cultural relativism and the critique of relativism. Biology offers a course in AIDS and the African experience. . . .

These same two levels need to be considered when we consider what students should learn about minorities and previously excluded groups in their own nation. Once again, the basic courses that all students take should contain a new emphasis on the diversity of the nation's own population. Thus in many American universities discussions of U.S. history and constitutional traditions now contain a focus on race, the changing situation of women, and the role of immigration and ethnic politics, that would have been previously unknown. . . . Literature courses increasingly focus on works by women and expressing the experience of excluded racial minorities; economics, art history, biology, religious studies—all these can find ways of confronting students with the reality of a multi-ethnic and multicultural society. . . .

. . .

This brings me, in fact, to the third part of my proposal. Citizens cannot think well on the basis of factual knowledge alone. The third ability of the citizen, closely related to the first two, can be called the narrative imagination. This means the ability to think what it might be like to be in the shoes of a person different from oneself, to be an intelligent reader of that person's story, and to understand the emotions and wishes and desires that someone so placed might have. The narrative imagination is not uncritical: for we always bring ourselves and our own judgments to the encounter with another, and when we identify with a character in a novel, or a distant person whose life story we imagine, we inevitably will not merely identify, we will also judge that story in the light of our own goals and aspirations. But the first step of understanding the world from the point of view of the other is essential to any responsible act of judgment, since we do not know what we are judging until we see the meaning of an action as the person intends it, the meaning of a speech as it expresses something of importance in the context of that person's history and social world. . . .

This ability is cultivated, above all, in courses in literature and the arts. Preparing citizens to understand one another is not the only function of the arts in a college curriculum, of course, but it is one extremely important function, and there are many ways in which such courses may focus on the requirements of citizenship.

. . . The moral imagination can often become lazy, according sympathy to the near and the familiar, but refusing it to people who look different. Enlisting students' sympathy for distant lives is thus a way of training, so to speak, the muscles of the imagination.

This point was vividly put by Ralph Ellison, one of America's great novelists, in his novel *Invisible Man*. In an introduction to a reissue of the novel in 1981, Ellison explicitly links the novelist's art to the possibility of American democracy. By representing both visibility and its evasions, both equality and its refusal, a novel, he wrote, "could be fashioned as a raft of hope, perception and entertainment that might help keep us afloat as we tried to negotiate the snags and whirlpools that mark our nation's vacillating course toward and away from the democratic idea." . . . [A] democracy requires not only institutions and procedures, it also requires a particular quality of vision, in order "to defeat this national tendency to deny the common humanity shared by my character and those who might happen to read of his experience" (xxvi).

Let me show you a bit of how Ellison's novel does this, by commenting on its opening paragraph.

A voice speaks to us, from out of a hole in the ground. We don't know where this hole is—somewhere in New York, it appears. It is a warm hole, and full of light. . . . The voice tells us that he loves light, and he can't find much of it in the outside world. Light confirms his reality. Without light, and that is to say virtually always in the world above, he is invisible, formless, deprived of a sense of his own form and his "vital aliveness."

> I am an invisible man. No, I am not a spook like those who haunted Edgar Allan Poe; nor am I one of your Hollywood-movie ectoplasms. I am a man of substance, of flesh and bone, fiber and liquids—and I might even be said to possess a mind. I am invisible, understand, simply because people refuse to see me. Like the bodiless heads you see sometimes in circus sideshows, it is as though I have been surrounded by mirrors of hard, distorting glass. When they approach me they see only my surroundings, themselves, or figments of their imagination—indeed, everything and anything except me.

> . . .

Ellison's novel concerns a refusal of acknowledgment, a humanity that has been effaced. . . . The refusal to see the Invisible Man is portrayed as a moral and social defect, but also, more deeply, as a defect of imagination, of the inner eyes with which we look out, through our physical eyes, on the world. The people around the Invisible Man see only various fantastic projections of their own inner world, and they never come into contact with the human reality of his life. *Invisible Man* explores and savagely excoriates these refusals to see, while at the same time inviting its readers to know and see more than the unseeing characters. . . . In this way, it works upon the inner eyes of the very readers whose moral failures it castigates, although it refuses the easy notion that mutual visibility can be achieved in one heartfelt leap of brotherhood.

. . .

. . . Defeating these refusals of vision requires not only a general literary education, but also one that focuses on groups with which our citizens' eyes have particular difficulty.

. . . I think that here the "liberal education" part of the US system has a special strength, enabling all students to get a common imaginative awakening through confrontation with carefully chosen literary works. It is very difficult to see how students bound for careers in business and industry, for example, will get such a training from courses in those disciplines alone.

Our campuses educate our citizens. This means learning a lot of facts, and mastering techniques of reasoning. But it means something more. It means learning how to be a human being capable of love and imagination.

... It is all too easy for the moral imagination to become narrow. ... Think of Charles Dickens's image of bad citizenship in his novel *A Christmas Carol*, in his portrait of the Ghost of Jacob Marley, who visits Scrooge to warn him of the dangers of a blunted imagination. Marley's Ghost drags through all eternity a chain made of cash boxes, because in life his imagination never ventured outside the walls of his successful business to imagine the lives of the men and women around him, men and women of different social class and background. Scrooge is astonished at the spectacle of his old friend wearing this immense chain. "I wear the chain I forged in life," he tells Scrooge. "I made it link by link and yard by yard. I girded it on of my own free will, and of my own free will I wore it." Trying to deny what he is hearing, Scrooge, terrified, blurts out, "You were always a good man of business, Jacob." "Business," the Ghost dolefully intones. "Mankind was my business. Charity, mercy, benevolence were all my business." (Here in Dickens's own Christian way he is directly alluding to Seneca's ideas of cultivated humanity, and to related ideas of mercy and benevolence.) Then, turning to Scrooge, the Ghost asks, "Don't you feel the weight of the chain you bear yourself?" "My chains!" Scrooge exclaims. "No no." And then, in a smaller voice, "I am afraid."

Scrooge got another chance to learn what the world around him contained . . ., traveling to homes rich and poor, to a lighthouse on the sea, to the poverty of his own clerk's home only a mile or so away in Camden town in North London, but a very long mile indeed, the mile that divides rich from poor. We need to produce citizens who have this education while they are still young, before their imaginations are shackled by the weight of daily duties and self-interested plans. We produce all too many citizens who do drag cash boxes around with them, whose imaginations never step out of the counting house. But we have the opportunity to do better, producing Socratic citizens who are capable of thinking for themselves, arguing with tradition, and understanding with sympathy the conditions of lives different from their own. Now we are beginning to seize that opportunity. That is not "political correctness," that is the cultivation of humanity.

References

Aristophanes, *Clouds.*
Dickens, C. (1843/1984). *A Christmas Carol.* Harmondsworth: Penguin.

Ellison, R. (1992). *Invisible Man*. New York: Random House.

Nussbaum, M. C. (1997). *Cultivating Humanity: A Classical Defense of Reform in Liberal Education*. Cambridge, MA: Harvard University Press.

Plato, *Apology.*

Seneca, *On Anger.*

Plato, "Crito."

Comprehension Questions

1. What was at stake in the debate about education in ancient Greece?
2. According to Seneca, what is a "liberal" education?
3. What's the link between Seneca's views of education and present-day calls for diversity in college education?
4. What moral value is there in being able to critically examine oneself and one's traditions?
5. What goes into being a "world-citizen," as Nussbaum sees it?
6. How can taking interdisciplinary courses enrich your college education?
7. Why does Nussbaum think we are better off by cultivating our narrative imagination, and what does doing so involve?
8. How does Dickens's *A Christmas Carol* illustrate the dangers of a lack in narrative imagination?

Discussion Questions

1. Do you want your school to prepare you to be a world citizen? Why or why not?
2. Nussbaum recommends developing certain abilities in order to thrive as morally responsible people in a globalized world. What abilities that she doesn't discuss could also help in that project?
3. Nussbaum begins by describing the controversy between conservative and progressive views of the aims of education. What current controversies in college education further illustrate these different perspectives? Is Nussbaum's analysis useful for making sense of them?
4. As she canvases some of the virtues that college education should be instilling in students, Nussbaum describes some courses that, on her view, do this well. Have you taken any courses like the ones she describes? In your experience, did they have the positive moral impact she attributes to them?

Case

> Suppose that Nussbaum is right: Students ought to take courses that culti-
> vate "an ability to see themselves as not simply citizens of some local
> region or group but also, and above all, as human beings bound to all other
> human beings by ties of recognition and concern." But suppose your col-
> lege doesn't offer courses that cultivate this ability. What should you do?
> Here's what some students at Emerson College did in the spring of 2015:
>
> > Hundreds of students from Emerson College marched into a faculty
> > meeting on Tuesday and called for more diversity training for profes-
> > sors and classes for students at the school... [The] goal of the protest
> > was to ask the administration for more cultural sensitivity training for
> > faculty members, and to require students to enroll in more "culturally
> > enlightening" classes. Emerson President Lee Pelton estimated about
> > two hundred students, outnumbering faculty by two to one, came to
> > the meeting. Willie Burnley Jr., twenty-one, a junior who was part of
> > the demonstration, said the protest urged students to walk out of class
> > and announce to faculty the changes that they want. More than three
> > hundred students walked through almost every building on campus,
> > chanting slogans such as "education not discrimination," he said.[1]
>
> What do you think of this strategy? What might make it the right choice?
> What might make it the *wrong* choice? Can you think of other ways to en-
> courage your school to cultivate the abilities that Nussbaum discusses?

Note

1. http://www.bostonglobe.com/metro/2015/04/28/emerson-students-call-for
   -faculty-training-classes-racial-insensitivity/Kf61MQrbC5prY0z7NMYkpN/
   story.html

Claiming an Education

Adrienne Rich

What are you getting yourself into when you sign up for a college education? Obviously, you want to learn. And you probably want your degree to advance your career prospects. Is that it? Adrienne Rich thinks that there's much more to it. She suggests that you should think of your education as entering into a contract. It is a choice that imposes important responsibilities on you. On the one hand, Rich maintains, it involves taking responsibility for yourself, not settling into what is easy and comfortable, but facing all of life's challenges to attain your aspirations. (Rich's comments are directed in particular to women, as this was originally a commencement speech at a women's college, but also because she sees women as being particularly pressured to conform to stereotype and tradition rather than defining themselves.) On the other hand, the choice to educate yourself also requires you to make sure that others—like instructors—recognize your aims and potential. In short, claiming an education should be neither passive nor one-sided. Your education, she thinks, depends significantly on what you make of it and on your having the respect of your professors and peers.

For this convocation, I planned to separate my remarks into two parts: some thoughts about you, the women students here, and some thoughts about us who teach in a women's college. But ultimately those two parts are indivisible. If university education means anything beyond the processing of human beings into expected roles, through credit hours, tests, and grades (and I believe that in a women's college especially it might mean much more), it implies an ethical and intellectual contract between teacher and student. This contract must remain intuitive, dynamic, unwritten; but we must turn to it again and again if learning is to be reclaimed from the depersonalizing and cheapening pressures of the present-day academic scene.

The first thing I want to say to you who are students, is that you cannot afford to think of being here to receive an education: you will do much better to think of being here to claim one. One of the dictionary definitions of the verb "to claim" is: to take as the rightful owner; to assert in the face of possible contradiction. "To receive" is to come into possession of; to act as receptacle or container for; to accept as authoritative or true. The difference is that between acting and being acted upon, and for women it can literally mean the difference between life and death.

One of the devastating weaknesses of university learning, of the store of knowledge and opinion that has been handed down through academic training, has been its almost total erasure of women's experience and thought from the curriculum, and its exclusion of women as members of the academic community. Today, with increasing numbers of women students in nearly every branch of higher learning, we still see very few women in the upper levels of faculty and administration in most institutions. Douglass College itself is a women's college in a university administered overwhelmingly by men, who in turn are answerable to the state legislature, again composed predominantly of men. But the most significant fact for you is that what you learn here, the very texts you read, the lectures you hear, the way your studies are divided into categories and fragmented one from the other—all this reflects, to a very large degree, neither objective reality, nor an accurate picture of the past, nor a group of rigorously tested observations about human behavior. What you can learn here (and I mean not only at Douglass but any college in any university) is how men have perceived and organized their experience, their history, their ideas of social relationships, good and evil, sickness and health, etc. When you read or hear about "great issues," "major texts," "the mainstream of Western thought," you are hearing about what men, above all white men, in their male subjectivity, have decided is important.

Black and other minority peoples have for some time recognized that their racial and ethnic experience was not accounted for in the studies broadly labeled human, and that even the sciences can be racist. For many reasons, it has been more difficult for women to comprehend our exclusion, and to realize that even the sciences can be sexist. For one thing, it is only within the last hundred years that higher education has grudgingly been opened up to women at all, even to white, middle-class women. And many of us have found ourselves poring eagerly over books with titles like: *The Descent of Man, Man and His Symbols, Irrational Man, The Phenomenon of Man, The Future of Man, Man and the Machine, From Man to Man, May Man Prevail?, Man, Science and Society,* or *One Dimensional Man*—books pretending to describe a "human" reality that does not include over one-half the human species.

Less than a decade ago, with the rebirth of a feminist movement in this country, women students and teachers in a number of universities began to demand and set up women's studies courses—to claim a women-directed education. And, despite the inevitable accusations of "unscholarly," "group therapy," "faddism," etc., despite backlash and budget cuts, women's studies are still growing, offering to more and more women a new intellectual grasp on their lives, new understanding of our history, a fresh vision of the human experience, and also a critical basis for evaluating what they hear and read in other courses, and in the society at large.

But my talk is not really about women's studies, much as I believe in their scholarly, scientific, and human necessity. While I think that any Douglass student has everything to gain by investigating and enrolling in women's studies courses, I want to suggest that there is a more essential experience that you owe yourselves, one which courses in women's studies can greatly enrich, but which finally depends on you in all your interactions with yourself and your world. This is the experience of taking responsibility toward yourselves. Our upbringing as women has so often told us that this should come second to our relationships and responsibilities to other people. We have been offered ethical models of the self-denying wife and mother; intellectual models of the brilliant but slapdash dilettante who never commits herself to anything the whole way; or the intelligent woman who denies her intelligence in order to seem more "feminine," or who sits in passive silence even when she disagrees inwardly with everything that is being said around her.

Responsibility to yourself means refusing to let others do your thinking, talking, and naming for you; it means learning to respect and use your own brains and instincts; hence, grappling with hard work. It means that you do not treat your body as a commodity with which to purchase superficial intimacy or economic security; for our bodies to be treated as objects, our minds are in mortal danger. It means insisting that those to whom you give your friendship and love are able to respect your mind. It means being able to say, with Charlotte Bronte's Jane Eyre: "I have an inward treasure born with me, which can keep me alive if all the extraneous delights should be withheld or offered only at a price I cannot afford to give."

Responsibility to yourself means that you don't fall for shallow and easy solutions—predigested books and ideas, weekend encounters guaranteed to change your life, taking "gut" courses instead of ones you know will challenge you, bluffing at school and life instead of doing solid work, marrying early as an escape from real decisions, getting pregnant as an evasion of already existing problems. It means that you refuse to sell your talents and aspirations short, simply to avoid conflict and confrontation. And this, in turn, means resisting the forces in society which say that women should be nice, play safe, have low professional expectations, drown in love and forget about work, live through others, and stay in the places assigned to us. It means that we insist on a life of meaningful work, insist that work be as meaningful as love and friendship in our lives. It means, therefore, the courage to be "different"; not to be continuously available to others when we need time for ourselves and our work; to be able to demand of others— parents, friends, roommates, teachers, lovers, husbands, children—that they respect our sense of purpose and our integrity as persons. Women everywhere are finding the courage to do this, more and more, and we are finding that courage both in our study of women in the past who possessed it, and in each other as we look to other women for comradeship, community, and challenge. The difference between a life lived actively, and a life of passive drifting and dispersal of energies, is an immense difference. Once we begin to feel committed to our lives, responsible to ourselves, we can never again be satisfied with the old, passive way.

Now comes the second part of the contract. I believe that in a women's college you have the right to expect your faculty to take you seriously. The education of women has been a matter of debate for centuries, and old, negative attitudes about women's role, women's ability to think and take leadership, are still rife both in and outside the university. Many male professors (and I don't mean only at Douglass) still feel that teaching in a women's college is a second-rate career. Many tend to eroticize their women students—to treat them as sexual objects—instead of demanding the best of their minds. (At Yale a legal suit [*Alexander v. Yale*] has been brought against the university by a group of women students demanding a stated policy against sexual advances toward female students by male professors.) Many teachers, both men and women, trained in the male-centered tradition, are still handing the ideas and texts of that tradition on to students without teaching them to criticize its anti-woman attitudes, its omission of women as part of the species. Too often, all of us fail to teach the most important thing, which is that clear thinking, active discussion, and excellent writing are all necessary for intellectual freedom, and that these require hard work. Sometimes, perhaps in discouragement with a culture which is both anti-intellectual and anti-woman, we may resign ourselves to low expectations for our students before we have given them half a chance to become more thoughtful, expressive human beings. We need to take to heart the words of Elizabeth Barrett Browning, a poet, a thinking woman, and a feminist, who wrote in 1845 of her impatience with studies which cultivate a "passive recipiency" in the mind, and asserted that "women want to be made to think actively: their apprehension is quicker than that of men, but their defect lies for the most part in the logical faculty and in the higher mental activities." Note that she implies a defect which can be remedied by intellectual training; not an inborn lack of ability.

I have said that the contract on the student's part involves that you demand to be taken seriously so that you can also go on taking yourself seriously. This means seeking out criticism, recognizing that the most affirming thing anyone can do for you is demand that you push yourself further, show you the range of what you can do. It means rejecting attitudes of "take-it-easy," "why-be-so-serious," "why-worry-you'll-probably-get-married-anyway." It means assuming your share of responsibility for what happens in the classroom, because that affects the quality of your daily life here. It means that the student sees herself engaged with her teachers in active, ongoing struggle for a real education. But for her to do this, her teachers must be committed to the belief that women's minds and experience are intrinsically valuable and indispensable to any civilization worthy the name: that there is no more exhilarating and intellectually fertile place in the academic world today than a women's college—if both students and teachers in large enough numbers are trying to fulfill this contract. The contract is really a pledge of mutual seriousness about women, about language, ideas, method, and values. It is our shared commitment toward a world in which the inborn potentialities of so many women's minds will no longer be wasted, raveled away, paralyzed, or denied.

Comprehension Questions

1. In what sense is there a contract involved in college education, and what's wrong with the idea of receiving an education?
2. What challenges do women face in their pursuit of a college education that men tend not to face?
3. What does it mean to take responsibility for yourself in college education?
4. What does the unwritten contract of college education demand of instructors?
5. How can it be a sign of respect that you receive criticism from others?

Discussion Questions

1. Why did you come to college? Did you come to "claim an education"? Why or why not?
2. Rich prepared these remarks in the late 1970s, and she is especially concerned with encouraging women to succeed in higher education and professionally despite social and cultural obstacles standing in their way. Are her recommendations still apt for women today? Why or why not?
3. Part of Rich's unwritten contract places burdens on instructors to recognize students. She explains why this is especially important for women. In what ways do you think it applies to all students?
4. The unwritten contract Rich describes has two parts to it. Can you think of additional responsibilities you take on when you choose to get a college education? What are they?

Case

Consider this:

> Money troubles interfere with the academic performance of about one-third of all college students, and a similar number of students regularly skip buying required academic materials because of the costs, according to a survey released [in 2012] ... About three-fifths of students surveyed reported that they often worry about having enough money to cover ordinary costs, and students who spend the most hours at paying jobs are, not surprisingly, those feeling the most financial stress. Among those who work more than 20 hours a week, about three-fifths said that their jobs got in the way of school work....

The survey findings parallel [other studies] which show that as a drain on students' mental health, finances rank second only to academics, and ahead of intimate relationships, lack of sleep and family problems. About one-third of students in those surveys say that in the prior year, financial concerns have been "traumatic or very difficult to handle."[1]

How do the financial burdens on students affect their ability to follow Rich's advice? What does it look like to follow Rich's advice when you're also working twenty hours per week? If economic challenges are getting in the way of "claiming" an education, then what does that imply about the students who face those challenges? Are they not getting a real education? Should they not be in college? Do we—as a society—owe them something? Or is there another implication entirely?

Note

1. http://www.nytimes.com/2012/11/15/education/money-troubles-add-to
   -students-burden-before-graduation-study-finds.html